MAIMONIDES AND CONTEMPORARY TORT THEORY

Maimonides lived in Spain and Egypt in the twelfth century and is perhaps the most widely studied figure in Jewish history from medieval times until the present day. This book presents, for the first time, Maimonides' complete tort theory and how it compares with other tort theories both in the Jewish world and beyond. Drawing on sources old and new as well as religious and secular, *Maimonides and Contemporary Tort Theory* offers fresh interdisciplinary perspectives on important moral, consequentialist, economic, and religious issues that will be of interest to both religious and secular scholars. The authors mention several surprising points of similarity between certain elements of theories recently formulated by North American scholars and the Maimonidean theory. Alongside these similarities significant differences are also highlighted, some of them deriving from conceptual-jurisprudential differences and some from the difference between religious law and secular-liberal law.

YUVAL SINAI is a professor at Netanya College Law School, and the president of Orot Israel College. He served as a visiting professor at Yale University, McGill University, Hebrew University, and Bar-Ilan University. He has received grants from the Israel Science Foundation and Schusterman Foundation, and has received the Riklis Prize for studies in Jewish law.

BENJAMIN SHMUELI is Associate Professor at Bar-Ilan University Law School, Israel. He has served as a senior research scholar at Yale Law School and a visiting professor at Duke Law School. He has received grants from the Israel Science Foundation, The Memorial Foundation for Jewish Culture, the Schusterman Foundation, and the Israel Institute Research Grant. He has also received the Riklis Prize for studies in Jewish law.

CAMBRIDGE STUDIES IN LAW AND JUDAISM
Series Editor – Mark Goldfeder

Editorial Board
Ira Bedzow (NY Medical College),
Noa Ben-Asher (Pace)
Saul Berman (Columbia)
David Blumenthal (Emory)
Erwin Chemerinsky (UC Irvine)
Adam Chodorow (Arizona State)
Dena Davis (Lehigh)
Elliot Dorff (American Jewish University)
Lenn E. Goodman (Vanderbilt)
David Flatto (Hebrew University)
Steven Friedell (Rutgers)
Moshe Halbertal (NYU/Hebrew U)
Michael Helfand (Pepperdine)
Samuel J. Levine (Touro)
Brigit Klein (Hochschule für Jüdische Studien Heidelberg)
Suzanne Last Stone (Cardozo)
Fred Lawrence (Brandeis)
Sanford Levinson (University of Texas)
Phil Lieberman (Vanderbilt),
Timothy Lytton (Albany)
Benny Porat (Hebrew University)
Ronen Reichman (Hochschule für Jüdische Studien Heidelberg)
Mark Rosen (Chicago-Kent)
Jeffrey Roth (Fordham)
Chaim Saiman (Villanova)
Lena Salaymeh (Tel Aviv)
Eliezer Segal (Calgary)
Keith Sharfman (St. John's)
Stephan Wendehorst (Geissen)
George Wilkes (Edinburgh)
John Witte, Jr. (Emory)

The law and religion movement is a growing field dedicated to studying the religious dimensions of law, the legal dimensions of religion, and the interaction of legal and religious ideas, institutions, norms and practices. *Cambridge Studies in Law and Judaism* cultivates scholarship on Jewish topics in law and religion including translations, historical accounts of the foundations of the Jewish legal system, and innovative comparative studies. Its mission is to break new ground in studying what Jewish law has, can, and should offer to public, private, penal, and procedural law and legal theory.

Maimonides and Contemporary Tort Theory

LAW, RELIGION, ECONOMICS, AND MORALITY

YUVAL SINAI
Netanya College Law School & Orot Israel College

BENJAMIN SHMUELI
Bar-Ilan University

WITH THE HON. GUIDO CALABRESI
Yale Law School

CAMBRIDGE
UNIVERSITY PRESS

University Printing House, Cambridge CB2 8BS, United Kingdom

One Liberty Plaza, 20th Floor, New York, NY 10006, USA

477 Williamstown Road, Port Melbourne, VIC 3207, Australia

314–321, 3rd Floor, Plot 3, Splendor Forum, Jasola District Centre, New Delhi - 110025, India

103 Penang Road, #05-06/07, Visioncrest Commercial, Singapore 238467

Cambridge University Press is part of the University of Cambridge.

It furthers the University's mission by disseminating knowledge in the pursuit of education, learning and research at the highest international levels of excellence.

www.cambridge.org
Information on this title: www.cambridge.org/9781316631249
DOI: 10.1017/9781316832042

© Yuval Sinai and Benjamin Shmueli 2020

This publication is in copyright. Subject to statutory exception and to the provisions of relevant collective licensing agreements, no reproduction of any part may take place without the written permission of Cambridge University Press.

First published 2020
First paperback edition 2022

A catalogue record for this publication is available from the British Library

Library of Congress Cataloging in Publication data
NAMES: Sinai, Yuval, 1971– author. | Shmueli, Benjamin, 1971– author. | Calabresi, Guido, 1932– contributor.
TITLE: Maimonides and contemporary tort theory : law, religion, economics, and morality / Yuval Sinai, Netanya College Law School & Orot Israel College; Benjamin Shmueli, Bar-Ilan University,
Israel ; with Guido Calabresi, Yale Law School
DESCRIPTION: New York : Cambridge University Press, 2019. | Series: Cambridge studies in law and Judaism | Includes bibliographical references and index.
IDENTIFIERS: LCCN 2019037776 (print) | LCCN 2019037777 (ebook) | ISBN 9781107179295 (hardback) | ISBN 9781316631249 (paperback) | ISBN 9781316832042 (ebook)
SUBJECTS: LCSH: Torts (Jewish law) | Torts–Philosophy. | Maimonides, Moses, 1135-1204.
CLASSIFICATION: LCC KBM834 .S56 2019 (print) | LCC KBM834 (ebook) | DDC 346.0301–DC23
LC record available at https://lccn.loc.gov/2019037776
LC ebook record available at https://lccn.loc.gov/2019037777

ISBN 978-1-107-17929-5 Hardback
ISBN 978-1-316-63124-9 Paperback

Cambridge University Press has no responsibility for the persistence or accuracy of URLs for external or third-party internet websites referred to in this publication, and does not guarantee that any content on such websites is, or will remain, accurate or appropriate.

Contents

List of Figures		*page* xi
	Introduction	1
1	**Initial Presentation**	5
	A. Jewish Law of Torts in General and in Maimonides' Writings	5
	B. Why Maimonides?	16
	C. Contemporary Tort Theories: A General Perspective	18
	D. Abstract	28
	E. The Method	31
2	**Tort Liability in Maimonides' *Code*: The Downside of the Common Interpretation**	39
	A. Introduction: The Modern Study of Jewish Tort Theory as a Story of "Self-Mirroring"	39
	B. The Ownership and Strict Liability Theory vs. the Fault-Based Theory (*Peshiah*)	42
	1 The Difficulties of the Concept of *Peshiah*	42
	2 The Common Interpretation of the *Code*: The "Ownership and Strict Liability Theory"	43
	C. Exegetical and Conceptual Difficulties of the Common Interpretation of Maimonides	46
	1 Maimonides Did Not Impose Comprehensive Strict Liability on the Tortfeasor	46
	2 Maimonides' Use of the Term *Peshiah* in Different Places	50
	3 The Theory of Ownership Contradicts Various Rulings in the *Code*	53
	4 The Problem with Finding a Convincing Rationale for the Ownership Theory	56

	D. Difficulties in Understanding Some Elements of Tort Liability Mentioned in the Code	62
	1 Rulings That Are Difficult to Interpret According to Either Ownership or Fault-Based Theories	62
	2 Providing a Rationale for the Exemption in Tort in Exceptional Cases	65
	3 Standard of Care in Damages Caused by a Person to the Property of Another: Absolute/Strict Liability or Negligence?	68
	4 Deterrence of Risk-Causing Behavior	70
	E. Re-examining the Opening Chapter of the Book of Torts in the *Code*: Control as a Central Element of Liability in Tort	72
	F. Conclusion	78
3	**The Foundations of the Maimonidean Theory: Different Goals for Different Categories of Damage**	80
	A. Introduction	80
	B. The Scope of Tort Law: *Nezikin* as a Middle Ground between Civil and Criminal Law	82
	1 The Legal Classification of the Book of Torts	82
	2 Relations between Torts, Criminal Law and Contract Law in Contemporary Jurisprudence	87
	3 Penal Characteristics of Tort Law in Maimonides' Theory	93
	C. Conceptualization of Distinct Categories of Damage: A Differential Perception	96
	1 Introduction	96
	2 Internal Distinctions in the Laws of Property Damages	98
	3 Between Laws of Property Damages and Laws of Wounding and Damaging	108
	4 Between Laws of Wounding and Laws of Damaging	111
	5 Between Laws of Theft and Laws of Robbery and the Return of Lost Property	118
	6 Between Laws of Damages to Neighbors and Standard Laws of Torts	124
	D. The Goals of Tort Law: A Pluralistic Perception	131
	1 The Major Goals of the Book of Torts: Removal of Wrong and the Prevention of Damage	132
	2 Distributive Justice – Book of Acquisition	134
	3 Maimonides as a Pluralistic-Differential Scholar	136
4	**The Deontological and Religious Elements of Maimonides' Tort Theory**	138
	A. Deontological Elements of Maimonides' Tort Theory	138
	1 The Philosophical Elements: "The Welfare of the Body"	138

      2 "The Welfare of the Soul" and the Idea of the Sanctity of Human Life   141
      3 The Social-Pedagogic Effect of Tort Law: Acquisition of Good Qualities   143
  B. The Religious Elements of Maimonides' Tort Theory   159
      1 The Religious Dimension in Jewish Law in General and in Tort Law in Particular   159
      2 The Prohibition Against Causing Harm   160
      3 The Religious and Theological Aspects   171
      4 The Duty to Rescue: A Religious or a Moral Obligation?   173
      5 Visual Trespass   185
  C. Imposing Liability for Risk-Creating Behavior: Deontological and Utilitarian Considerations   187
  D. A Comparative Look: Between Maimonides and Contemporary Tort Theory   192
      1 Theories of Corrective Justice: From Aristotle to Contemporary Scholars   192
      2 Between Maimonides and Theories of Corrective Justice   202
        (a) Between Maimonides and Weinrib   203
        (b) Between Maimonides and Other Approaches of Corrective Justice   211
      3 Various Considerations alongside Considerations of Efficiency in Calabresi's Theory as Opposed to Maimonides' Theory   213
        (a) Deontological Considerations and Rules of Inalienability   213
        (b) Between Maimonides and Calabresi   217
  E. Conclusion   220

5 **Consequentialist Considerations in the *Guide for the Perplexed***   222
  A. Consequentialism, Law and Economics, and Maimonides   222
  B. The Starting Point: Consequentialist Considerations in Maimonides' Texts   227
      1 Prevention of Acts Causing Damage and the Effective Ability to Control Test (EAC)   227
        (a) The General Rule of Liability   229
        (b) Exceptions: Cases of Exemption from Liability   232
        (c) Splitting the Liability between the Tortfeasor and the Injured Party (The Case of the Goring Ox)   235
      2 Maimonides' Consequentialist Analysis of Criminal Sanctions and Punitive Damages   238
        (a) Deterrence as the Major Goal of Punitive Damages   238
        (b) A Test Case: Payments of a Thief as Opposed to a Robber   241
        (c) Four- and Five-Fold Payments for the Theft of Sheep and Cattle   246

C. A Comparative Look: Similarities and Differences Between the
    Guide and Contemporary Law and Economics Scholarship — 251
    1 Calabresi, Posner, and Maimonides' Test for Tort Liability — 251
        (a) Calabresi's Cheapest Cost Avoider and the EAC Test — 252
        (b) Posner's Hand Formula, Contributory Negligence, and
             Maimonides — 260
    2 The Multiplier Approach, the Societal Redress
       Extra-Compensatory Damages Approach, and Maimonides'
       Test for Punitive Damages — 268
        (a) Maimonides and Possible Parallels in Contemporary
             Criminal Law — 269
        (b) Maimonides' Approach to the Difference between a Thief
             and a Robber: Between the Multiplier and the Societal
             Redress Extra-Compensatory Approaches — 270
        (c) The Uniqueness of Maimonides' Approach in Incentivizing
             the Injured Party to Take Precautions as a Precondition for
             High Punitive Damages — 277
D. Conclusion — 280
Appendix: The Rules of Liability and Contributory Negligence
         According to Maimonides in the *Guide* 3:40 Compared
         with Calabresi and Posner — 282

6 **Revisiting the Problematic Texts of the *Code* in Light of the
   Guide and Contemporary Scholarship** — 284
   A. Using a Consequentialist Rationalization in Various Places in
       the *Code* — 284
   B. The EAC Test as the Basis for Tort Liability — 289
   C. Best Decision Maker in Maimonidean Texts — 291
   D. Imposing Liability on the Injured Party — 292
   E. Splitting the Liability Between the Parties (the *Tam* Ox) — 301
   F. Incentive for Preventing Damages: Imposing Liability for
       Risk-Causing Behavior — 305
   G. Conclusion — 308

7 **Maimonides' Standard of Care: A Differential Liability Model** — 310
   A. Presenting Maimonides' Differential Liability Regime — 310
       1 Damage Caused by a Person to the Property of Another: Strict
          Liability and Exemption Only in Cases of Force Majeure — 312
       2 Injury Caused by a Person to the Body of Another: Three
          Different Standards of Care — 316
       3 Property Damage: Negligence — 321
       4 Murder: Fault — 323

B. Differential Liability: Scheme, Rationale, and Historical
   Background   328
   1 Scheme   328
   2 Rationale   328
   3 Historical Background, Circumstances, and Nature of the
     Tortfeasors: Between Maimonides' Time and the Modern Era   333
   4 Conclusion   336

8 **Maimonides as a Pluralistic-Differential Scholar and Contemporary
   Tort Law Theories: A Dialogue and Lessons**   338
   A. From Contemporary Tort Law to Maimonides: Characterizing
      Maimonides as a Pluralistic-Differential Scholar   338
   B. Dialogue Between Maimonides and Current Pluralistic Approaches 340
      1 Introduction   340
      2 Current Mixed-Pluralistic Approaches: An Overview   341
         (a) Izhak Englard: "Complementarity" – An Attempt to Reach
             Harmony between Corrective and Distributive Justice   342
         (b) Gary Schwartz: Optimal Deterrence as the Dominant Goal
             and Its Constraint by Corrective Justice Considerations 343
         (c) Mark Geistfeld: Out of a Number of Possible Efficient
             Outcomes, the Most Moral Will Be Chosen   346
         (d) Fleming James Jr. and Christopher J. Robinette: A Casuistic
             Approach   347
      3 Placing Maimonides on the Pluralistic Approaches Scale   349
   C. From Maimonides to Contemporary Law   353
      1 Possible Lessons for Contemporary Tort Law Theories   353
         (a) Creating a Pluralistic-Differential Framework in Modern
             Tort Law   353
         (b) Possible Dissociation between the Element of Control
             and Strict Liability   354
         (c) Distinction between Harms Caused by a Person and Harms
             Caused by Property   355
         (d) Possible Distinction between the Tort of Robbery and
             the Tort of Theft   359
         (e) Caution when Learning Lessons from Religious Law
             for Modern Secular Law   360
      2 Bridging between Seemingly Dissimilar Approaches   367
         (a) Between Economics and Morality   367
         (b) Blurring the Distinction between Civil and Criminal   368
         (c) Possible Bridge between Economic Approaches Based
             on Fault and Economic Approaches Based on Strict
             Liability   370

		(d) Bridging between an Economic Approach and a Social Approach with Respect to Punitive Damages	371
	D.	Conclusion	371

9	**Reflections on Maimonides' Tort Theory (Guido Calabresi)**	373
	A. "We Imagine the Past to Remember the Future" – Between Law, Economics, and Justice in Our Era and according to Maimonides	373
	1 Preface	373
	2 Empirical Differences in Time and Their Implications	374
	3 Are there Differences between the Differential Liability and the Cheapest Cost Avoider/Best Decision Maker Doctrines?	375
	4 On Justice and Deontological Considerations	377
	B. A Combination of Goals in Punitive Damages: Maimonides, the Common Law, and the U.S. Supreme and State Court Rulings	379
	1 Maimonides' Emphasis on Consequentialist Considerations	379
	2 Maimonides as Pluralist	383
	3 Action in Trespass and Action in Case: Two Approaches Pushing Each Other in the Common Law	384
	4 Tort Law as a Middle Ground between Civil and Criminal Law	385
	5 Punitive Damages: The Economic Multiplier Approach vs. the Punitive Approach, Supreme and State Court Rulings	386
	6 The Combination of Goals in Relation to the Issue of Punitive Damages	388
	7 Putting Incentives on the Victim to Take Precautions and the Possibility of Reducing Punitive Damages	393
	C. Conclusion	395

Index	397

Figures

5.1	Placing Maimonides' approach to the difference between a thief and a robber between the modern approaches	*page* 276
7.1	A person causing damage to the property of another: almost strict liability	315
7.2	Injury caused by a person to the body of another: three different standards of care	321
7.3	Property damage: negligence	323
7.4	Offense of murder: degrees according to Maimonides	325
7.5	The complete scheme of differential liability	329

Introduction

Maimonides – Rabbi Moses ben Maimon – was born in Spain at 1135 and died in Egypt in 1204. He was known in the Jewish tradition as the "Great Eagle" due to his eminence in so many fields: as a jurist, philosopher, scholar, physician and theologian. Maimonides is perhaps the best-known and most widely studied figure in Jewish history from medieval times until the present day.

Much research has been devoted to different aspects of Maimonides' work, including the period and the place in which he operated, the connection between his work and Geonic literature, his philosophy, the tension between Maimonides as halakhic decisor and Maimonides as philosopher, his various essays and the relationship between them, contradictions in his approach, and his views on medicine, religion, and science. Despite the abundance of research on Maimonides, very little has been written about Maimonides as a jurist in general, and about his tort theory in particular. Apart from some research on narrowly focused examinations of his stance on a few individual tort-related issues, Maimonides' comprehensive tort theory is in fact understudied. No research has yet been published that presents a systematic study of Maimonides' tort theory in full, in and of itself, as reflected in the entire array of his halakhic and philosophical corpus. Needless to say, Maimonides' tort theory has not been studied as compared with other tort theories in his time, before his time or in our time.

This book presents, for the first time, Maimonides' complete tort theory both in and of itself, and as compared with other tort theories both in the Jewish world and beyond it, in Maimonides' times and prior thereto, and as compared with modern Western theories. It provides a comprehensive and accessible description of his innovative theory. Not only will the book present the details of the rulings relating to tort, but it will also seek to establish a rational, systematic legal theory that allows for a full description and overview of Maimonides' comprehensive conception of tort law, its objectives and its foundations.

The book also offers a new perspective on the understanding of Jewish legal and philosophical tradition, and more generally on the place of traditionalism and religious values in medieval Middle Eastern, Judeo-Islamic life and thought, as opposed to modern Western-liberal life and thought. The proposed perspective is brought into relief by comparing the Maimonidean theory to contemporary tort theories. The book therefore presents Maimonides' complete tort theory as an important Jewish source that engages, for the first time, in a legal and philosophical dialogue with the leading theoretical tort texts of Western scholarship. The book illuminates points of continuity and contrast between these systems. The Maimonidean medieval-religious sources and contemporary scholarship speak in very different idioms, but they address many of the same themes. Drawing on sources old and new, pre-modern-Jewish and modern-liberal-secular, the book offers fresh interdisciplinary perspectives on important moral, consequentialist, economic, and religious issues that will be of interest to both religious and secular scholars.

The Maimonidean theory of tort is revealed in light of all of his works – halakhic as well as philosophical. This book recounts a story that has been neglected by the scholars and the commentators on Maimonides: a story about the rationalization of tort laws that was told by Maimonides in the *Guide of the Perplexed* [hereinafter: *The Guide*], his well-known philosophical work, from which it emerges that tort law has two meta-objectives. The more predictable objective is the deontological aim of removing wrong – a type of corrective justice, and the second, which is surprising in view of the period in which it was first conceived, is the social-consequentialist objective of preventing damages, which has some similarity to basic approaches of the economic analysis of the law. Alongside the deontological and social-consequentialist aspects of tort law, there is also a religious dimension, which Maimonides emphasizes less, and this includes the prohibition against causing harm, and a blurring of the boundaries between the criminal law and tort law.

The basic structure of Maimonides' tort theory relies on a special criterion of tort liability which we call "the effective ability to control test" (EAC), a test that is substantively different from all the tests that have been suggested to date in the common interpretation of Maimonides and the Talmud. Once Maimonides has determined who is the effective avoider of damage, he applies a special model, which we call the differential-pluralistic model. According to this model, for each of three categories in tort – damage caused by property; a person injuring his fellow; a person damaging the property of another – Maimonides sets a different standard of care on the scale between negligence and strict liability. Maimonides' model of differential-pluralistic liability, which represents more than one objective of tort law, with some objectives being more dominant than others in relation to different types of tort laws, may engage in a cautious dialogue with various modern tort theories. The inception of such a dialogue is to be found in volume 26(1) of the *Yale Journal of Law & the Humanities* (2014), which was devoted in large part to a conversation between the authors of the present book and one of the pioneers of the field of economic analysis of law, Guido Calabresi,[1] who graciously agreed to write Chapter 9 of this book. Whereas the conversation focuses on the comparison between Maimonides and Calabresi, the book goes further and broadens the comparison to include a comparison between Maimonides and other prominent modern scholars, among them Ernest Weinrib, the prominent corrective justice scholar, who commented on the main arguments of this book.[2] We will mention several surprising points of similarity between certain elements of the theories that were formulated by the cream of the scholars from leading North American universities and between significant elements of the Maimonidean theory that was conceived some eight hundred years ago in Egypt. Alongside the similarity between the theories, we will also highlight significant differences, some of them deriving from conceptual-jurisprudential differences, some from the difference between religious law and secular-liberal law, and some from the differences in the historical, cultural, and socioeconomic backgrounds.

EDITIONS USED

Quotations from the *Mishneh Torah* – the *Code* – and its traditional commentaries are cited from the Frankel edition. We have used the Yale Judaica Series English translation of *The Code of Maimonides*: Hyman Klein's translation of The Book of Torts (New Haven, CT: Yale University Press, 1954), and Isaac Klein's translation of The Book of Acquisition (New Haven, CT: Yale University Press, 1951).

Quotations from *The Guide of the Perplexed* (written originally in Arabic) are generally cited from the English translation of *The Guide of the Perplexed* by Shlomo Pines (Chicago, IL: University of Chicago Press, 1963). In some places, where indicated, the English translation is either the authors' own translation of the Michael Schwartz Hebrew translation (Jerusalem: Tel Aviv University Press, 2002),

---

[1] Senior Judge, United States Court of Appeals for the Second Circuit; Sterling Professor Emeritus of Law and Professorial Lecturer in Law, Yale Law School. See Yuval Sinai & Benjamin Shmueli, *Calabresi's and Maimonides's Tort Law Theories – A Comparative Analysis and A Preliminary Sketch of a Modern Model of Differential Pluralistic Tort Liability based on the Two Theories*, 26 YALE J. L. & HUMAN. 59 (2014), and the comment: Guido Calabresi, *We Imagine the Past to Remember the Future – Between Law, Economics, and Justice in Our Era and according to Maimonides* 26 YALE J. L. & HUMAN. 135 (2014). See also Guido Calabresi, in a response to Benjamin Shmueli & Yuval Sinai, *A Contemporary View on the Maimonidean Tort Theory: A Consequentialist Analysis of Punitive Damages as a Test Case*, following a lecture at a panel on *A Contemporary View of the Maimonidean Tort Theory – Law, Religion, Economics and Morality*, Wolff Lecture 2016, Institute on Religion, Law & Lawyer's Work, Fordham Law, January 26, 2016.

[2] See Ernest J. Weinrib, Cecil A. Wright Professor of Law at the University of Toronto Faculty of Law, a comment to Yuval Sinai & Benjamin Shmueli at a panel on *Aristotelian, Greco-Arab and Islamic Moral Theories: A Comparative Study of Jewish Medieval Tort Theory* in THEOLOGIANS IN A JURIST'S ROBE: RELATIONS BETWEEN THEOLOGY AND LAW IN THE JUDAEO-ISLAMIC MILIEU, The Freidberg Jewish Manuscript Society in collaboration with Anne Tanenbaum Centre for Jewish Studies, University of Toronto, March 20, 2017.

or the English translation by Moses Friedlander (2nd edition, New York, NY: Dover Publications, 1956).

Our heartfelt gratitude is extended to Guido Calabresi for his friendship, for his gracious, generous investment of time in our joint study of the similarities and differences between Maimonides and modern theories, and for agreeing to write a chapter for this book. Our thanks to Yale University, where most of this book was written during the time we spent there on our sabbatical in 2013–2015, Yuval Sinai as the Schusterman Visiting Professor of Law and both Yuval Sinai and Benjamin Shmueli as Senior Research Scholars and later on as Senior Research Scholars during 2015–2016. We wish to thank the former Dean, Prof. Robert Post, the current Dean, Prof. Heather Gerken, and Georganne Rogers, the Executive Assistant to the Dean, for making this period possible and so pleasant for us. Special thanks go to Christine Hays and Steven Fraade for their assistance and the hospitality shown to Prof. Sinai while at Yale University. Also, special thanks to Shahar Lifshitz and Ariel Bendor for enabling Prof. Shmueli to take the sabbatical leave at Yale and to Prof. Sinai Deutch for enabling Prof. Sinai to take the sabbatical leave at Yale.

We are grateful to the Israel Science Foundation and to the Bar-Ilan and Netanya College Law Schools for their support in the publication of this book. We are indebted to Deborah Sinclair for her professional and meticulous efforts in the linguistic editing and translation of this work. Many thanks to all those who read and commented on various sections of the book: Phillip Ackerman-Lieberman, Hanoch Dagan, Izhak Englard, Noah Feldman, Steven Fraade, Ehud Guttel, Christine Hayes, Bernard Jackson, Yishai Kiel, Gideon Parchomovsky, Ariel Porat, Benjamin (Benny) Porat, Christopher Robinette, Daniel Sinclair, Alex Stein, Ernest Weinrib and Eyal Zamir, and to our research assistants: Uli Bedel, Eliya Chisdai, Michael Goral, Alex Greenberg, Omer Greenman, Shmuel Marom, Elad Morgenstern, Alex Porat, Amir Rafeld, Shmuel Dov Sussman and Danny Weisberg. I would like to thank the content manager, Becky Jackaman, and the commissioning editor, John Berger, at Cambridge University Press; the senior project manager at SPi Global, Divya Arjunan; and everyone else who was involved in the publication of this book at Cambridge University Press and SPi Global, for their tremendous help in completing this project and producing a polished final product. We wish to thank Matteo Godi, Judge Calabresi's law clerk during the 2018–2019 term, for his edits and comments on Chapter 9. Special thanks to Ofir Shmueli for constant and intensive technical support. Finally, Yuval Sinai wishes to thank his dear wife Ruhama and his dear children and family, and Benjamin Shmueli wishes to thank his dear children, brothers and sister, mother and family for their great patience and their unfailing support.

1

Initial Presentation

A. JEWISH LAW OF TORTS IN GENERAL AND IN MAIMONIDES' WRITINGS

Maimonides' theory of torts was developed when the "Great Eagle" lived in Egypt, and it is based on his reading of the biblical and talmudic literature on torts. Yet his theory also provides a groundbreaking, independent, and conceptual analysis of the biblical and talmudic rules in this area of law.

Moshe Halbertal argued that Maimonides himself did not consider the *Mishneh Torah* (*Code of Maimonides*, hereinafter: *the Code*), his main halakhic work, to be merely a "summary of the *halakhah*," despite his own description of it as such in several places; rather, his approach was that "the *Mishneh Torah* is *halakhah* itself."[1] According to this approach, which likewise emerges from a close examination of Maimonides' words, "*Mishneh Torah* does not merely summarize the earlier halakhic literature; it actually replaces it."[2] Even those who find it difficult on principle to accept the radical reading proposed by Halbertal, and who generally tend towards the moderate reading, will be convinced after having read the present work – so we hope – that the Book of Torts (*Sefer Nezikin*), the 11th of the 14 books of the *Code*, at least, should not be regarded merely as a simple summary of the talmudic *halakhah*, but as much more than that. True, in many cases Maimonides was faithful to the talmudic *halakhah*; nevertheless, we aim to elucidate a systematic Maimonidean tort theory, fairly substantial parts of which not only do not stem directly from the Talmud and sometimes even seem to contradict it, but which to a great extent constitutes a refashioning of Jewish tort law.

---

[1] MOSHE HALBERTAL, MAIMONIDES: LIFE AND THOUGHT 96–181 (Princeton, NJ: Princeton University Press, 2014).
[2] *Ibid.* at 185.

Before we discuss the principal features of the Maimonidean theory of tort, we will review briefly the general features of the Jewish law of torts. This will enable us to examine the extent to which the Maimonidean theory is novel vis-à-vis the talmudic and posttalmudic theories of tort. In general, it is correct to say that Jewish tort law has not been widely researched. Several studies of Jewish tort law do exist, some of which are mentioned in the following chapters, but mostly they are concerned with the details of the various laws and not with the principles.[3] Indeed, several scholars have offered modern descriptions of Jewish tort law. Most have viewed Jewish tort law as part of Jewish civil law and laws of obligations.[4] They have characterized the majority of compensation in tort that the tortfeasor pays to the victim as payments intended as restitution for the damage caused rather than as a punishment or a fine.[5] Scholars of Jewish law, too, have not usually distinguished

---

[3] See ILAN SELA, PAYMENTS FOR INFLICTING PERSONAL INJURIES IN JEWISH LAW: BETWEEN CRIMINAL LAW AND CIVIL LAW 15 (Doctoral Dissertation, Bar-Ilan University, Ramat Gan, 2008) (Heb.).

[4] See primarily ASHER GULAK, PRINCIPLES OF JEWISH LAW, Book II, 14 (Berlin: Dvir, 1922) (Heb.), who writes that similar to Roman jurisprudence, in Jewish law, too, obligations in respect of damages belong to the laws of obligations, which are divided into two: "One source from which many obligations were imported is a negotiated transaction that was concluded between the negotiating parties, a legal transaction, by which they take upon themselves various obligations; *a second source of obligations is the damages* that a person brings about or causes to the property of another, and that imposes upon the damager or the cause an obligation of payment." *Ibid*. Gulak writes that "indeed our law already from the time of the Talmud distinguished between obligations that are entailed by the damage and obligations that are entailed by a business transaction." However, even Gulak himself comments (*ibid*. n. 2) that the *braita* of R. Oshaya and R. Hiyya, *Bava Kamma* 4b, includes among the heads of damage the obligation of the four watchmen, and this constitutes a difficulty for Gulak's position, since it is clear that leasing, borrowing and depositing for no charge or for payment fall within the category of business transactions. Indeed, he comments on Maimonides' approach in Laws of Rentals 2:3, whereby a person who was negligent in his watch is a damager, and therefore the obligations of watching are the same as the obligations for damage. See *ibid*. that Gulak himself relies on the opinion of the majority of the commentators who disagree with Maimonides, and who hold that the obligations of the watchmen arise from the legal contract, and are not due to damage. For our purposes, however, Maimonides' position is of particular importance, as elucidated later in the chapter.

[5] See, e.g., SHALOM ALBECK, GENERAL PRINCIPLES of the Law of Tort in the Talmud 40 (2nd ed., 1990) (Heb.) ("The obligation of the damager, whether he caused damage with his body or with his property, is to make up for the damage of the injured party, and not a punishment for the damager so that he should transgress no more"). See also YA'AKOV S. ZURI, TREATISE OF HEBREW LAW – TORT OF NEGLIGENCE 10–11 (London: Urim 1937) (Heb.), who emphasizes that "the Sages of the Talmud understood the difference between payment for damage, which is repairing the losses in relation to the injured party, and between a fine which is a penalty intended to have a beneficial effect in the future," and also, "the payments are not a fine, but are intended only to repair that which is crooked and to restore the former situation, insofar as possible." And *see also* GULAK, *supra* note 4, at 202, who writes that "obligation for the damage which comes as a payment for the economic loss due to the victim (monetary obligation) is always estimated in accordance with the actual loss and with the loss of property incurred in relation to the victim's property. The law governing this obligation is like other monetary obligations that are imposed upon a person and upon his heirs after him." Together with this,

between the different types of damages, and many of them have in fact stressed the common factors between the different types of damages that are caused by a person's property, i.e., the heads of damage,[6] and between physical injury or property damage to another caused by the person himself.[7] The rationales presented by most of the Jewish law scholars as the basis for tortious liability are very similar to the popular modern conceptions, particularly amongst the proponents of corrective justice, with the emphasis on the regime of fault/negligence.[8] Thus, for example, many scholars have explained that liability in torts is based on the single element of *peshiah* (negligence or fault).[9] Other scholars, however, were of the opinion that tort liability is not based solely on *peshiah*. One scholar stressed, alongside the element of *peshiah*, the prohibition against causing injury.[10] Another stressed mainly the "system of ownership and absolute liability" that exists, in his opinion, alongside

    he does in fact note that there are a number of obligations in respect of damages that are considered as a fine and a penalty, but he specifies there are exceptional damages such as the double payment imposed upon the thief, and other fines.

[6] See, e.g., ALBECK, *supra* note 5, at 19–20 ("Examination of the details of the Talmudic laws of damages leads to the conclusion that there are no single heads of damage without fundamental rules. Moreover, the heads of damage in the Talmud have only one single rule whereby a person is liable for the damages he caused, and that is *peshiah*" (negligence/fault)).

[7] See, e.g., ALBECK, *supra* note 5, at 173 ("In several places, the Talmud differentiates between injury to his body and economic damage, i.e., between a person who injures another physically and a person who damages his property. However, both are subject to the same laws, and there is only one difference between them"). This also emerges from the words of Zerah Warhaftig, *The Basis for Liability for Damages in Jewish Law*, STUDIES IN JEWISH LAW 211 (1985) (Heb.). Warhaftig was of the opinion that two approaches (that of *peshiah* and that of ownership) lie at the base both of liability for the economic damage suffered by a person (p. 220) and of his liability for damage that the person himself caused (p. 222).

[8] See, e.g., ZURI, *supra* note 5, at 11, who writes that "a person is not liable for his damages unless his actions involve some fault, whether to a large or a small degree." And "fault" is interpreted by him mainly as "negligence" (*peshiah*).

[9] Warhaftig correctly wrote (*supra* note 7, at 212) that "scholars of Jewish law are certain of their conclusion that Jewish law recognizes only the system of *peshiah*." Indeed, as Warhaftig says, this was the opinion of prominent veteran scholars such as CHAIM TCHERNOWITZ, SHI'URIM BETALMUD, "DAMAGES" 97:4. GULAK, *supra* note 4, at 210, emphasizes that *peshiah* is the basis for the obligation for monetary damages ("The main obligation of a person for damage caused by his property is due to his negligence in watching over the objects that caused the damage"), as well as the basis for the obligation for damage caused by a person's body (*see also ibid.* at 202: "A person is liable for the damages because he is responsible for them having taken place, i.e., because there was some fault on his part that led to them"). Particularly notable in this context is ALBECK, *supra* note 5, who sought to base all the details of tort law on the element of *peshiah* (*see, e.g., ibid.* at 26: "In actual fact, there is only one head of damage for all of torts, and that is *peshiah*").

[10] ZURI, *supra* note 5, at 9, defining "damage" as dependent upon three factors: the first, "the fault or negligence in relation to the person doing the damage"; the second, "an act of wrongdoing to the body of another, his dignity or his property, an act that is prohibited under the law"; and the third is "the loss caused to another by the act of damaging."

the "system of *peshiah*."¹¹ It will be emphasized that these views are not necessarily a matter only of modern scholarly proclivities. Some early talmudic commentators viewed tort law as part of civil law,¹² whereas many of the later commentators – and even some of the earlier commentators and decisors – emphasized the prohibition against causing injury as the main element of liability in tort law.¹³ What is common to all the scholars is the focus on one main aim of tort law, for the most part deontological: the absence of a principled, substantive distinction between different types of damagers and victims;¹⁴ insufficient attention to the clear connection between tort law and criminal law; and ignoring the unique religious dimension of Jewish tort law.

Against this background, Maimonides' unique theory, which differs significantly in most of the above areas, stands out. This theory emerges from a parallel analysis of all Maimonides' writings, and particularly from a comparative examination of what he wrote on torts in the *Code* and the *Guide*.

What is the nature of the systematic theory that Maimonides expounds, according to our contention, in the field of tort law?

The following principal aspects will be discussed at length in the book:

(a) The scope of tort law in Maimonides' theory is much wider than what is common in modern law, and it includes not only purely civil law (from the field of the law of obligations) but also laws which have a significant connection to criminal law. According to Maimonides, tort law is an intermediate field between civil law and criminal law, and some types of tortious compensation have a punitive dimension.

(b) A fundamental division into different types of tortious events in accordance with the nature and type of the damage, and with the identity of the tortfeasor and the victim (what we call a "differential" approach)

---

[11] Warhaftig, *supra* note 7, at 213.
[12] See, e.g., R. MENAHEM HAMEIRI, at the beginning of BEIT HABEHIRAH ON BAVA KAMMA 1, who noted the common denominator in all three tractates, *Bava Kamma, Bava Metzia* and *Bava Batra*, namely that all three are monetary claims (*tviot mamoniot*) "in what has no criminal law aspect at all."
[13] See, e.g., Tur, who wrote at the beginning of Laws of Tort, *Hoshen Mishpat* 378:1: "Just as it is prohibited to commit theft and robbery of the property of another, so it is prohibited to cause damage to his property"; R. YAAKOV KANIEVSKY, KEHILLOT YAAKOV ON BAVA KAMMA, chapter 1 ("On the Prohibition against Harming Another") (Bnai Brak 5748)(Heb.). For an extensive discussion of the elements of the prohibition *see infra* Chapter 4.
[14] This is true not only for those who attribute no significance at all to the distinction between the types of damages, such as ALBECK (*supra* note 5) and Warhaftig (*supra* note 7), but even a scholar such as GULAK (*supra* note 4, at 23–24) distinguishes between injury caused by a person to the body of another and damages caused to the property of another. However, this distinction is not substantive, and he did not even think it necessary to discuss the different damages in different chapters as he did in separating injury to a person's own body (pp. 213–25) and damage to his own property (pp. 227–37).

emerges from the classification of the Book of Torts in the *Code*. Central to this classification is a fundamental distinction between damage caused by a person's property (Laws of Property Damages) and damage caused by the person himself (Laws of Wounding and Damaging); the distinction between the damage that is caused by a person's property (damages caused by animals) and between the damage caused by a person's action (pit and fire); a distinction between a person causing physical injury to another person (Laws of Wounding) and a person causing damage to the property of another (Laws of Damaging); a distinction between standard tort law (which is included in the Book of Torts in the *Code*), and nuisance and damage caused by neighbors (which is included in the Book of Acquisition in the *Code*).

(c) Tort law does not have one single objective;[15] rather, Maimonides presents the various aims of tort law that he discussed in his various writings, and principally in the *Guide*. There are two central contentions with regard to the objectives: (1) In Maimonides' theory, the various objectives work together and are not necessarily regarded as contradictory; (2) Some objectives are more dominant than others in relation to different types of tort laws. Thus, for example, in relation to classical torts that are civil in nature, such as monetary damage, caused either by a person or by his property, Maimonides in the *Guide* emphasizes the removal of the wrong, i.e., corrective justice, which is deontological in nature, as well as prevention of damage, which is a consequentialist objective. In relation to damage that involves a criminal law element, however, such as damage caused by wounding, theft and robbery, Maimonides presents a penal, deterrent rationale, which too is consequentialist in nature. In the *Guide*,[16] Maimonides emphasizes distributive justice in his description of the goals of the Book of Acquisition and the Book of Judgments in the *Code*, including the laws of nuisance and the liability of watchmen. The *Code*, too, adverts to the religious-prohibitive aspect, in the prohibition against causing damage.

Maimonides' tort theory may be read in more than one way. In the present book, two alternative readings – both of them modern – will be presented and juxtaposed with one another. The first reading, which we call the *yeshivah* reading, is based on the common interpretation of Maimonides' works on the part of many of the heads

---

[15] For a discussion on the different aims of tort law *see*: Glanville L. Williams, *The Aims of the Law of Tort*, 4 Current Leg. Prob. 137, 138 (1951), *reprinted in* Mark Lunney & Ken Oliphant, Tort Law: Text & Materials 18 (3rd ed., 2008); W. Page Keeton et al., Prosser and Keeton on Torts 20–26 (5th ed., 1984); Benjamin Shmueli, *Legal Pluralism in Tort Law Theory: Balancing Instrumental Theories and Corrective Justice*, 48 U. Mich. J.L. Reform 745 (2015).

[16] 3:42.

of the Lithuanian *yeshivot* (talmudic academies) in recent generations. The *yeshivah* reading, which was adopted to various extents by several scholars in the wake of the research of Zerah Warhaftig,[17] concentrates exclusively on the reading of a number of texts from the Book of Torts in the *Code*, on the basis of which they attribute to Maimonides what Warhaftig defined as the "ownership and strict liability theory." We believe that the *yeshivah* reading of the Maimonidean approach to torts is mistaken, and that it does not reflect Maimonides' view. Our argument is that the ownership and strict liability theory is not an accurate expression of Maimonides' position. In our opinion, that theory raises serious difficulties, both conceptual-principled and exegetical, and it is inconsistent with several of Maimonides' rulings in the *Code*, which appear to contradict it. The words of the illustrious scholar of the *Code*, Isidore Twersky, are well known: "[t]o a great extent the study of Maimonides is a story of 'self-mirroring'."[18] To a great extent, so we shall argue, the *yeshivah* reading of the Maimonidean approach to torts is a case of "self-mirroring" on the part of the proponents of the said interpretation: the rabbis of the Lithuanian *yeshivot* interpreted Maimonides' words in keeping with the new methodology of *yeshivah* study that was developed in their days.

The focus of our study is a different reading, which we propose for the first time in this book. This alternative reading seeks to provide an appropriate response to the said difficulties, in its presentation of Maimonides' full tort theory in light of what he wrote in other works apart from the *Code*, particularly in his great philosophical work, the *Guide*, as well as through the prism of modern theories of tort law.

Indeed a substantial part of the second, new reading that we propose focuses on a careful analysis of several Maimonidean texts in the *Guide* that have been completely overlooked, not only by the rabbis advocating the *yeshivah* reading but also by some modern scholars who discussed, even if only partially, Maimonides' tort and penal theories. This is only natural, for the *Guide* preoccupies mainly philosophers, whereas scholars of Jewish law and the sages of the *yeshivah* world are concerned primarily with studying the *Code* and comparing it to the talmudic passages. However, one of the far-reaching changes to Judaism wrought by Maimonides is his fascinating and challenging integration of *halakhah* with philosophy, or if you will, of the *Code* with the *Guide*. And indeed, our book is intended as a presentation of the halakhic-philosophical theory of tort law according to Maimonides, as it emerges from a close reading of his writing both in the *Code* and the *Guide*, as well as in his other works. The contribution of the present book is primarily in exposing that neglected story of the goals and rationales of tort law as told by Maimonides in the *Guide*. In substantial sections of the present book we will attempt to elucidate what is written in the *Guide*, comparing it closely to what

---

[17] Warhaftig, *supra* note 7.
[18] ISADORE TWERSKY, INTRODUCTION TO THE CODE OF MAIMONIDES (*MISHNEH TORAH*) 358 (New Haven, CT: Yale University Press, 1980).

Maimonides wrote in the *Code* (although the latter work, too, is discussed at length in substantial parts of our book).

The rationalization of tort law found in the *Guide* is surprising in its innovation and creativity, and it is particularly remarkable when compared to pre-modern tort theories in general, and to the halakhic mainstream in particular. What Maimonides wrote in the *Guide* provides wide scope – so we will argue – for drawing comparisons with modern tort theories, including deontological theories such as corrective justice and the basic theories of the founding fathers of the economic analysis of (tort) law.

From the aspect of the theory of tort law it might be assumed, in view of the substantial differences that exist between the main principles of economic analysis of the law and the accepted approaches towards tort law in Jewish law, that the proponents of economic analysis of the law in our day would present very different positions from those of Maimonides with respect to the elements of tortious liability. Indeed, at first glance it is very difficult to identify points of contact between the approaches. On one side stands the approach of the economic analysis of the law, which refers to consequentialist conceptions of tort law and seeks to increase the cumulative welfare, considering cost versus benefit and pointing to those with deep pockets and efficient distributors of damage.[19] This instrumentalist approach understands tort law as an instrument for promoting economic and social goals.[20] On the other side are positioned the common approaches of the Jewish tort laws with their religious rhetoric of a prohibition against causing harm,[21] which are similar to a large extent to those deontological, moral, and social conceptions designed to compensate the victim and right the wrong (by the damager himself), even if this is not necessarily efficient.[22] These approaches base the attribution of tort liability on the element of *peshiah*,[23] i.e., negligence/fault of the damager. *Peshiah* is somewhat similar, at least *prima facie*, to the approach of fault that is the underlying purpose of

---

[19] On deep pockets and distribution of the damage, *see, e.g.*, GUIDO CALABRESI, THE COSTS OF ACCIDENTS: A LEGAL AND ECONOMIC ANALYSIS 40–41 (New Haven, CT: Yale University Press, 1970).

[20] On instrumentalist goals as opposed to goals that concentrate on the parties to the tort themselves, *see* Shmueli, *supra* note 15, and the references there.

[21] *See, e.g.*, the beginning of TUR on Tort Law, Hoshen Mishpat 378: "Just as it is forbidden to steal one's fellow's property, so it is prohibited to damage his property, even if he does not benefit, because a person who causes damage whether deliberately or inadvertently is obligated to pay."

[22] Although, one can also find, amongst the authorities of Jewish law, use of utilitarian considerations, as posed by certain scholars. *See, e.g.*, (on tort law): Yehoshua Liberman, *Economic Efficiency and Making of the Law*, 15 J. LEG. STUD. 387 (1986). And *see* (on economic considerations in Jewish law in general): Roman A. Ohrenstein, *Economic Thought in Talmudic Literature in Light of Modern Economics*, 26 AMER. J. ECON. & SOCIOLOGY 185 (1968); AARON LEVINE, FREE ENTERPRISE AND JEWISH LAW: ASPECTS OF JEWISH BUSINESS ETHICS (1980); Yehoshua Liberman, *The Economics of the Halakhah: The Beginning of a New Field of Research?* 12 DINE ISRAEL 7 (1986-5745).

[23] This element was especially stressed by ALBECK, *supra* note 5.

corrective justice, unlike the approach that regards a person's ownership of his property as the basis for his liability for damage caused by that property, such as the damages caused by the ox, the pit, and fire.[24] The question therefore arises as to whether it is indeed possible to conduct a dialogue between those who apparently do not speak the same legal language, and who, on the contrary, display differences both in the terminology and in the methods of analysis that they use. Various texts in the *Code* that deal with the actual tortious liability are formulated in a manner that resembles the approach of corrective justice, and the adherents of corrective justice could certainly interpret certain parts of Maimonides' tort theory and the distinctions that he makes, for example between a fine (*knas*) and monetary obligation (*mammon*), or between the person causing bodily injury and the damager, in accordance with their approach. Thus, Maimonides surely seems closer to the approach of corrective justice, and he does not make wide use of economic analysis of the law;[25] he certainly does not invoke the modern utilitarian terms employed by those engaging in an economic analysis of the law. The converse is also true: those engaging in an economic analysis of the law do not incorporate prohibitions and religious norms into their theories, as Maimonides does in the *Code*, and only naturally, they do not share identical outlooks in relation to morality and justice. With all that, we will try to show that it is definitely possible to conduct a conversation between the approaches of the two sides, and the outcomes of that conversation may be truly surprising.

Maimonides' innovation finds expression in several aspects, first and foremost in his very aspiration towards a rational, conceptual and relatively abstract presentation of uniform principles that underlie the laws of torts. This innovation was real and substantive. It must be recalled that legal thought in antiquity and in the Middle Ages was very different from the modern approach, which began in the period of the Enlightenment and was influenced on the European Continent by Kantian philosophy. Abstract conceptualization of legal principles and the quest for uniformity is a modern phenomenon. Both classical Roman law and the major Jewish halakhic texts are primarily casuistic, and the level of abstraction is generally very low. As mentioned, there have been attempts to base tort liability in the talmudic legal tradition on a uniform principle of *peshiah*, but these attempts encountered difficulties and were the subject of criticism by scholars.[26]

In this context, it should be emphasized that the Talmud is not an abstract code of laws, but a collection of descriptions of cases considered by the *halakhah*. This fact not only says something about the historical circumstances in which the Talmud

---

[24] See Warhaftig, *supra* note 9 (discussing at length the dispute of the Jewish sages over the years on the question of the basis for tort liability).

[25] Although these considerations are liable to underlie Maimonides' various rulings and positions, as we shall *see* infra in Chapters 5 and 6.

[26] Izhak Englard, *Research of Jewish Law – Its Nature and Function*, in MODERN RESEARCH IN JEWISH LAW 21, 57–64 (Bernard S. Jackson ed., Leiden, 1980); Steven F. Friedell, *Some Observations on the Talmudic Law of Torts*, 13–14 DINE ISRAEL 65 (1986–88).

was created, but it also impacts on the nature of the *halakhah* that takes shape in the Talmud, for the halakhic rulings do not apply to abstract principles that preceded these cases, but to the concrete cases that have a role to play in the shaping of the casuistic *halakhah*.

As such, the talmudic legal tradition, in that it was based on exegesis of the laws of the Torah which themselves were essentially casuistic, has not striven to identify a uniform, abstract principle governing all cases of liability in torts. Abstraction and generalization are the products of a later enterprise undertaken by Maimonides.

Maimonides' work, according to our contention, definitely displays an aspiration to identify meta-principles in tort, as evident in the two main objectives of tort law that he specified. In the *Guide*, Maimonides explains the reasons for tort law – as explicated in the Book of Torts in the *Code* – and according to him, "they are all concerned with the removal of wrong (or as translated by Pines: "with putting an end to acts of injustice") and with the prevention of acts causing damage."[27] It should be noted that here, Maimonides refers explicitly to two main objectives (which are of course accompanied by secondary, more marginal objectives, such as the religious objective). The first is not surprising: it is in keeping with traditional, deontological legal thinking – "the removal of wrong" – and looks backwards, i.e., after the damage has already been done. It comes to correct the wrong and thus constitutes a type of Aristotelian corrective justice that has parallels in Jewish law. The second objective presented by Maimonides in the *Guide* is innovative against the backdrop of the period in which it was formulated. This objective looks to the future, and its nature is preventive – "the prevention of acts causing damage." This objective is extremely similar to the consequentialist approach typical of many of the proponents of the economic analysis of law.

In the *Guide* (3:40) Maimonides viewed the prevention of causing harm as only one – albeit central – consideration in determining tort liability. However, Maimonides posited this idea alongside numerous and varied other considerations, especially deontological and religious ones, in addition to some distributive considerations.[28]

One notable example of Maimonides' assignation of great importance to consequentialist considerations in the sense of creating incentives for future behavior is found in the following chapter of the *Guide* (3:41), where he explains that the purpose of the criminal sanctions and punitive damages (in torts) is to deter the tortfeasor. Indeed, this text in the *Guide* appears to express, possibly better than any other Maimonidean text or any other classical halakhic text, the use of consequentialist theory and the emphasis on preventive measures in medieval rabbinic sources. Unlike other cases in which some basic (as opposed to modern) economic analysis

---

[27] GUIDE 3:40 (Pines, 355). We preferred "removal of wrong" as translated by Friedlander, 342.
[28] *Ibid.* at 3:42, regarding the issue of the liability of watchmen.

of law can be identified in Jewish medieval texts, in relation to the issue of punitive damages it seems that Maimonides indeed presented, more than 800 years ago, an original and relatively highly developed economic analysis. In doing so, he sought to solve one of the most difficult and fascinating puzzles that had challenged the Jewish sages for generations, i.e., to provide a comprehensive rational explanation, based on consequentialism and considerations of deterrence, for the penal laws and laws of tort in *halakhah*.

Maimonides' tort theory, especially in relation to property damages, is constructed, in our view, on three different levels. At the first level are the objectives of tort law mentioned earlier. These objectives, presented by Maimonides in the *Guide*, constitute the foundation-stone of his tort theory. At the second level stands the Maimonidean test of liability in torts, especially in property damages, which we will define later as the "effective ability to control test" (EAC test). At the third level is what we call the Maimonidean differential model. Before discussing the details of the second and third levels, we will once again stress that this three-tiered Maimonidean structure is the inevitable outcome of that second, new reading proposed in this book, which is significantly different from the *yeshivah* reading, that attributed to Maimonides a theory of ownership and strict liability. There are two separate elements in this theory – "ownership" and "strict liability" – although they are, of course, related (as Warhaftig claims, the person causing the damage has strict liability by virtue of his ownership of the object that caused the damage[29]). According to the common interpretation, the element of ownership determines tort liability – a person must pay compensation for damages caused by his ox, because the ox is his property, whereas strict liability expresses the standard of care that is required of the owner – who is always liable for damage caused by his property, even if he was not negligent. We disagree with both components of the theory of ownership and strict liability; that is to say, we believe that Maimonides did not adopt the ownership theory as the criterion for determining tort liability, nor did he advocate a comprehensive standard of care at the level of strict liability for all cases of damage.

The Maimonidean test for tort liability – the second level of the theory – that we propose is based on a reading of the *Guide*. In the *Guide*, Maimonides departed from the line of interpretation accepted by many halakhic scholars who based tort liability on *peshiah* on the part of the defendant; rather, he sought to base liability for damages caused by a person's property on another, unique basis – the EAC. According to the Maimonidean EAC test, we argue, liability is imposed on the effective damage avoider.

Let us now move on to the third and final level of Maimonides' tort theory – the standard of care (or liability regime) that is required of the effective damage avoider in order to hold him liable. We suggest that Maimonides accepted a complex

---

[29] Warhaftig, *supra* note 7, at 216.

liability regime, which we call a differential model. A careful examination of Maimonides' conceptualizations in the Book of Torts in the *Code* reveals that he favored different liability regimes for different categories of damage. This differentiation means that he does not consistently apply one liability regime to all types of tort cases. Maimonides' tort theory, we argue, is based upon a fundamental distinction between two questions: (a) on whom to impose tort liability; and (b) what is the standard of care that should be imposed in each case, on the scale ranging from negligence to strict liability.

Maimonides answered the first question by applying the aforementioned EAC test, i.e., the test that determines who should be held liable. However, determination of the *identity* of the effective damage avoider does not necessarily mean that the answer to the second question is that strict liability is imposed on the avoider, as Warhaftig[30] and Haut,[31] as well as some contemporary law and economics scholars,[32] argued. This is because the standard of care is topic dependent, according to Maimonides. Liability often gravitates toward a level that is higher than negligence but lower than strict liability.

Naturally, Maimonides' comprehensive approach must be examined against the backdrop of the medieval Middle Eastern Judeo-Islamic world in which he operated. We have undertaken such an examination in the book. In fact, some of the elements of the Maimonidean theory have parallels in the Greco-Arab and Muslim (*shari'a*) philosophical and legal literature, and perhaps Maimonides, who certainly was aware of much of this literature, was inspired by some of the ideas expressed therein.[33] However, in addition to any similarities we may find between these theories and that of Maimonides, there are certainly differences. For example, Aristotle is mentioned in contemporary tort scholarship in relation to two forms of justice in particular – corrective and distributive – whereas Maimonides presented a broader theory of justice.

After having offered a full exposition of Maimonides' approach to tort law in the first part of the book, we will proceed to the presentation of a more surprising, and possibly less predictable, comparison, i.e., we will draw, very cautiously, some lessons and concepts from the contemporary analysis of torts for Maimonides' tort theory, and vice versa. We will demonstrate how each of these theories may help create a better understanding of the other.

---

[30] *Ibid.*
[31] Irwin H. Haut, *Some Aspects of Absolute Liability under Jewish Law and Particularly, Under the View of Maimonides*, 15 DINE ISRAEL (1989–90).
[32] *See, e.g.*, Guido Calabresi & Jon T. Hirschoff, *Toward a Test of Strict Liability in Torts*, 81 YALE L.J. 1055 (1972).
[33] *See, e.g.* Gideon Libson, *Parallels between Maimonides and Islamic Law*, in THE THOUGHT OF MAIMONIDES: PHILOSOPHICAL AND LEGAL STUDIES 209–48 (Ira Robinson et al. eds., Lewinston, NY, 1980); MARK R. COHEN, MAIMONIDES AND THE MERCHANTS: JEWISH LAW AND SOCIETY IN THE MEDIEVAL ISLAMIC WORLD (Princeton, NJ: Princeton University Press, 2017).

B. WHY MAIMONIDES?

Why have we chosen Maimonides' tort theory as the subject of our research?

The choice of Maimonides, being such a great and central scholar in Jewish culture, should be understood as only natural. Nevertheless, it requires some explanation in view of the existence of no less-natural alternatives, such as the Talmud or the *Shulhan Arukh*. In all his writings, and not only in the *Code*, Maimonides emerges as one of the greatest sages after the completion of the Talmud – if not the greatest – as the popular saying goes: "From Moses (son of Amram – the biblical Moses) to Moses (son of Maimon – Maimonides) there has been none like Moses," which expresses the enormous admiration of the Jews for the man and his work. The greatness of Maimonides is evident in his commentaries on talmudic issues, juxtaposing them with one another, revealing their halakhic meaning and determining the *halakhah*. The greatness of Maimonides derives also from the fact that in his *Code*, which is the greatest and most original book of rulings on Jewish law in existence,[34] Maimonides introduced a substantive change in methods of codification of the *halakhah*, in the concentrated material from the Scripture up to his time and its organization by subject matter. In this context, some unique characteristics of Maimonides's work should be noted in particular: his classification of halakhic material, determining the subjects and the decision as to which subjects should be grouped together and which separated in the framework of the exposition. These characteristics are also, and particularly, evident in tort law in relation to which, as we shall see later in the chapter, Maimonides in the Book of Torts in the *Code* drew major distinctions between different types of damages, such as the fundamental distinction between damage caused by a person to the body of another and damage caused to his property. Maimonides also aspired to identify a basic leading principle underlying the details of the laws.

The choice to study Maimonides also derives from the fact that there is no other prominent halakhist who has presented a comprehensive, detailed, methodical-doctrinaire and rational theory of Jewish tort law. It is true that most of the laws cited by Maimonides in the *Code* are not his innovations but rather, have their source in the Talmud; therefore, one may ask why we do not choose to present the talmudic tort theory, similar to several studies published on this subject. The answer is that the attempts to identify a unified, coherent halakhic talmudic theory in relation to tort law are extremely problematic. This is due to the multiplicity of conflicting approaches and stances of the Tannaim and Amoraim, the internal contradictions between the different discussions, and the preference for casuistic analysis rather than analytical-doctrinaire analysis of the bases of tort law.[35]

---

[34] MENACHEM ELON, JEWISH LAW 977 (5748) (Heb.).
[35] On the methodological difficulties involved in analyzing talmudic texts (and on the importance of using scientific tools of critical Talmudic research), *see* YUVAL SINAI, THE JUDGE AND THE JUDICIAL PROCESS IN JEWISH LAW, Introduction 21 (2010) (Heb.).

Similarly, it is extremely difficult to identify the rational jurisprudential considerations underlying the talmudic law of torts, to such an extent that recently, one scholar has questioned whether such considerations indeed exist, writing that the contents of the talmudic *halakhah* in relation to various tort issues (cases of exemption in tort) are based on the reliance on a creative exegetical exposition of Scripture, and he says that the halakhic system of tort law in the Talmud "is completely detached from other considerations that are relevant to other laws of tort. To be blunt, this is not an internal legal theory, but a theory which is primarily a neutralization of the legal dimension in this branch of the *halakhah*."[36] In his critique of this approach, another scholar posed the following incisive question: "If the principle of tortious liability does not underlie the exceptional laws (cases of exemption in tort) ... what is their legal logic?"[37] He issues a call to "try to explain the meaning of the exceptional laws through recourse to various rationales, such as considerations of economic efficiency, social-constitutional considerations, ethical considerations, religious objectives and others."[38] A discussion of the difficulties involved in finding jurisprudential rationales that underlie the talmudic laws of tort is beyond the scope of our research,[39] but the existence of these difficulties provides additional significant support for our decision to present as a representative Jewish model the tort theory of Maimonides (and not that of the Talmud), for Maimonides' proclivity for rational-philosophical-conceptual thinking is famous: as he himself attests, "My intention ... is to bring the laws closer to reason."[40]

Indeed, as we shall attempt to show, Maimonides' theory of torts – the underlying rationale of which, both in relation to the laws of liability in tort and in relation to the exceptional laws which exempt damagers from payment of full compensation for various reasons, was thoroughly explained in the *Guide*[41] – is suited in unparalleled manner (and certainly more so than the Talmud, but also more so than other

---

[36] Avishalom Westreich, *Tort Law – Between Religion and Law: Interpretative and Legal Processes in the Law of Torts in the Talmud*, 26 SHENATON HAMISHPAT HA'IVRI 203, 209 (5769–71) (Heb.).

[37] Benjamin Porat, *What Is a Scientific Explanation in Jewish Law? Meditations Following Avishalom Westreich's Article*, 26 SHENATON HAMISHPAT HA'IVRI 237, 238 (5769–71) (Heb.). By virtue of the above question, Porat claims that "on this point, the argument in the article focuses, problematically, the discussion on the question of the desirable nature of the scientific explanation in Jewish law research." And *see also* Westreich's article in response: *A Few Words on Research in Jewish Law*, 26 SHENATON HAMISHPAT HA'IVRI 245 (5769–71).

[38] Porat, *supra* note 37.

[39] We, as stated, do not presume to present the talmudic theory of tort, nor do we wish to express our view in this framework on the actual disagreement between Westreich and Porat in relation to talmudic tort law in particular, and in relation to the interesting question of what is a scientific explanation in Jewish law, in general. On our view concerning the ideal method in Jewish law, *see* the introduction to Sinai's essay, *supra* note 35, at 20–23.

[40] RESP. RAMBAM, Blau ed. 252.

[41] GUIDE 3:40–41.

halakhic works) to serve as a rational, coherent model of tort law in general (and not only of the exceptions) through use of those considerations mentioned above: "considerations of economic efficiency, social-constitutional considerations, ethical considerations, religious objectives and others."

There are, it is true, major halakhic works other than those of Maimonides, such as the *Tur* and the *Shulhan Arukh*; however, unlike Maimonides' writings, these codes of *halakhah* do not provide a full, comprehensive picture of the entire body of tort law. These codes are intended to cite only those laws which have practical, actual significance in the days of those authors. Consequently, they omit significant subjects that are discussed in the Book of Torts of the *Code*.[42]

Accordingly, it was absolutely necessary to opt for Maimonides' theory of tort as the basis for a comparison with contemporary tort theories.

C. CONTEMPORARY TORT THEORIES: A GENERAL PERSPECTIVE

And now for a number of the fundamental elements of contemporary tort law, which will provide a basis for the following chapters for the purpose of comparing the different approaches. We do not presume to cover all the bases of tort liability in modern law in general; our focus is too narrow for that. We will concentrate on those fundamental elements that are required for the basic comparison between Maimonides' theory and the contemporary law: the purpose of tort law, standards of care in tort law and the question of the proximity of tort law to criminal law. All these issues, as well as others, will be discussed in depth in the following chapters. But we will already point out that engaging these questions vis-à-vis contemporary law will be useful not only for the comparison itself; dealing with the modern terms and contemporary theories will shed light on Maimonides' theory. They will help

---

[42] Thus, for example, the authors of *TUR* and *SHULHAN ARUKH* did not include in their words the Laws of Murderers that are cited at the end of Maimonides' Book of Torts (*see* Rema's Introduction to *SHULHAN ARUKH*, Hoshen Mishpat 425, that "[in relation to] all those who are liable to death at the hands of the court in these days, we do not have the power to lash them or exile them or execute them." Accordingly, these laws were not regulated in detail in the *SHULHAN ARUKH*). Neither did these authors include the laws of the "*mu'ad*" ox [the ox who became habituated to goring] and the ox who killed a person, which are regulated in detail by Maimonides the Laws of Property Damages, chapters 6–7, 10–11. (*TUR* explained this in Hoshen Mishpat 389:2: "For he is not judged now, since a panel of 23 judges is required".) In addition, in these books the rationales underlying the laws were not presented, whereas Maimonides in the GUIDE did discuss the rationales, and what he wrote explain the particulars of the laws that he enumerated in the *Code*. Furthermore, due to the judicial methodology employed by R. Joseph Karo in the *SHULHAN ARUKH* (to decide according to the majority amongst three eminent authorities: Rif, Maimonides and Rosh), coherence is not always maintained in the rulings that he cites in this book of laws, and he not infrequently rules on a particular subject in accordance with a certain approach, whereas on another subject he will adopt a different, contrary approach. Similarly, R. Joseph Karo sometimes cites two views of the law without deciding between them. As opposed to this, Maimonides' work displays coherence, and his halakhic rulings general display uniformity and clarity.

reveal Maimonides' tort theory and present it in a full and organized way. Finally, we will also endeavor to reverse the process and offer certain cautious proposals from Maimonides' approach to contemporary law.

First, to the goals of tort law. We will present monism in tort law theory, that is, approaches that adhere to one single goal of tort law as the sole explanation for the theory of tort law, as opposed to pluralism in tort law theory, that is, identifying more than one goal underlying the theory of tort law.

To this day, legal scholars have spent relatively little time discussing the goals of tort law in a comprehensive fashion and prioritizing them in the event of a clash. Instead, scholars usually focus on efforts to examine, develop, or critique a particular aim – usually corrective justice, distributive justice, or optimal deterrence – for a specific purpose, a process which has been variably termed "unified," "monistic," or "integrated."[43]

Unlike these approaches, "mixed" or "pluralistic" theories of tort law attempt to integrate several of the considerations underlying the different goals to balance between various goals of tort law.[44] The existing pluralistic approaches differ from each other in different aspects. Therefore, this part will present and analyze the central goals of tort law and the monistic approaches that exist in the world of theory

---

[43] *Cf.* Steven J. Burton, *Normative Legal Theories: The Case for Pluralism and Balancing*, 98 IOWA L. REV. 535, 537 (2013) ("Robust pluralist theories take all relevant values into account and balance them when they compete.") There are different pluralistic possibilities. See *ibid.* at 544 and n. 20; John C.P. Goldberg, *Ten Half-Truths about Tort Law*, 42 VAL. U. L. REV. 1221, 1246–48 (2008). Goldberg defines pluralism in torts differently than is common. See *ibid.* at 1249 ("As I have just noted, the standard way to be pluralistic about tort law is to assign tort law various different 'purposes,' such as deterrence and compensation. The journey to this sort of position typically works backward from remedy to theory. The remedy most closely associated with tort law is, of course, the damages payment. The question then asked is: What agendas can government advance by ordering this sort of payment? Here we are led to the ideas of deterrence, compensation, and restoration"). Goldberg and Benjamin Zipursky present a different approach – civil recourse. See *ibid.* at 1252 ("The civil recourse account of tort is simultaneously limiting and capacious. It is limiting in insisting that tort law is something, not nothing or everything. The basic idea is that tort has certain central features – private rights of action, substantive requirements (*e.g.*, proof of injury and breach of a duty owed to the victim), characteristic procedures (court-supervised resolution), etc. – that, taken together, reveal a consistent concern to enable persons who have been victimized in certain ways to respond to that victimization by obtaining a certain kind of satisfaction, through law, as against the wrongdoer... Yet at the same time it is capacious. Because it frames the enterprise in terms of defining wrongs and empowering victims to respond to wrongs, rather than as an enterprise that seeks to achieve a collective goal such as deterrence or loss-spreading, it is not embarrassed by features that other theories are forced to regard as facially dysfunctional."). *See also* John C.P. Goldberg & Benjamin C. Zipursky, *Torts as Wrongs*, 88 TEX. L. REV. 917 (2010); John C.P. Goldberg & Benjamin C. Zipursky, *Tort Law and Moral Luck*, 92 CORNELL L. REV. 1123 (2007).

[44] *Cf.* Burton, *supra* note 43, at 537 ("A monist theory takes one and only one value into account and, consequently, hopes to avoid balancing competing values." Burton also notes that "[o]ver the last four decades, monist theories have proliferated, notably those based on efficiency").

of tort law. In the following chapters we shall see that Maimonides' theory of tort law cannot possibly be regarded as a monistic approach.

Steven J. Burton writes: "An intelligent approach to the study of law must take account of its purpose, and must be prepared to test the law critically in the light of its purpose."[45] Indeed, various factors concerning the nature of tort law stand in the way of a general consensus concerning the goals of tort law.[46] Some scholars even argue that tort law developed without any clear aim, or that underlying tort law is a mixture of goals, not all of which apply suitably in every given case.[47] Others assert that the lack of consensus on the goals of tort law is due to the common law roots of this law, which resulted in its *ad hoc* development in every jurisdiction.[48] Accordingly, scholars also claim that until the nineteenth century, tort law was never considered an independent branch of the law in the common law countries or, at least, not as a comprehensive branch equivalent to contracts or criminal law.[49]

Even now, no general consensus exists concerning the goals of tort law.[50] However, based on the literature's entire body of theories, identifying some primary, independent goals of tort law, drawn in part from civil and criminal law,[51] is possible.

Distributive justice and deterrence are goals that deal primarily with steering the behavior of actual or possible future tortfeasors, as part of an instrumentalist theory, which perceives the law as a device for promoting social goals. These can possibly be classified as goals with an instrumentalist rationale that does not necessarily focus on the actual parties. Compensation and corrective justice, however, belong to another category, which focuses on the concrete parties to the tort (corrective justice on the concrete tortfeasor and injured party, and compensation mainly on the concrete injured party) rather than on principles and elements extraneous to the concrete parties.

Corrective justice focuses on correcting the wrong a particular tortfeasor committed against a particular victim. The examination is limited solely to the relations between the two parties.[52] According to most corrective justice

---

[45] Williams, *supra* note 15, at 157.
[46] See Prosser & Keeton on Torts, *supra* note 15, at 1–7; KENNETH S. ABRAHAM, THE FORMS AND FUNCTIONS OF TORT LAW 14 (3rd ed., 2007); W.V.H. ROGERS, WINFIELD & JOLOWICZ ON TORTS 1 (16th ed., 2002).
[47] See, e.g., Williams, *supra* note 15, at 152; ABRAHAM, *supra* note 46, at 14; WINFIELD & JOLOWICZ, *supra* note 46, at 1.
[48] ABRAHAM *supra* note 46, at 14; Christopher J. Robinette, *Can There Be a Unified Theory of Torts? A Pluralist Suggestion from History and Doctrine*, 43 BRANDEIS L.J. 369, 390–98 (2005).
[49] E.g. Robinette, *supra* note 48, at 393.
[50] See, e.g., Prosser & Keeton on Torts, *supra* note 15, at 1–7; Williams, *supra* note 15, at 138; Abraham, *supra* note 46, at 14; WINFIELD & JOLOWICZ, *supra* note 47, at 1.
[51] Robinette, *supra* note 48, at 398.
[52] Ernest J. Weinrib, *Corrective Justice*, 77 IOWA L. REV. 403, 410 (1992) ("In Aristotle's account of corrective justice, quantitative equality pairs one party with another. Corrective justice treats the defendant's unjust gain as correlative to the plaintiff's unjust loss. The disturbance of the

approaches, this goal is reached mostly through reliance on culpability (in negligence) and causation between the action of the tortfeasor and the damage to the injured party. If the tortfeasor has breached her duty of care, she must pay the injured party.

Different theories of corrective justice exist.[53] The most prominent contemporary theoretician in the area of corrective justice is Ernest J. Weinrib, who asserts that corrective justice is conclusive. Weinrib espouses limiting the examination solely to the relations between the two concrete parties – the tortfeasor and the injured party – and disregarding any consideration extraneous to the parties.[54] It seems that he perceives corrective justice, which relies on culpability and causation, as the sole legitimate goal of tort law.[55] The principle of correlativity is primary in Weinrib's theory – only the tortfeasor must pay the whole sum of damages to only the injured party: no less and no more.[56]

---

equality connects two, and only two, persons. The injustice that corrective justice corrects is essentially bipolar").

[53] *See, e.g.*, George P. Fletcher, *Fairness and Utility in Tort Theory*, 85 HARV. L. REV. 537 (1972) (stating that the use of the tort law system in order to attain social aims creates an inappropriate mixture between corrective justice and distributive justice). Fletcher himself takes corrective justice as a derivative of examining the risk that every party may cause to the other party. In his opinion, in every liability regime (negligence, strict liability, and intentional torts) one should examine the reciprocal risks that the parties create. If the risks are reciprocal or relatively equal, then the defendant should not be held liable if he caused the damage. But if the wrongdoer put the plaintiff at risk in a nonreciprocal and unilateral way, and the plaintiff was harmed, then the defendant should be held liable. Reciprocal risk exists where from the outset, the defendant's activity puts the plaintiff at risk more than the opposite activity, or when from the outset the risks are nonreciprocal, but become reciprocal due to the negligence of the defendant. *See* also JULES L. COLEMAN, RISKS AND WRONGS (1992) (arguing that the parties have a duty to correct the harms their torts have created as a moral basis for liability, and therefore for compensation); RICHARD A. EPSTEIN, A THEORY OF STRICT LIABILITY (1980) (offering a theory of strict liability based not on culpability but on causality).

[54] WEINRIB, CORRECTIVE JUSTICE, *supra* note 52; ERNEST J. WEINRIB, THE IDEA OF PRIVATE LAW 5, 56–83 (1995); Ernest J. Weinrib, *The Gains and Losses of Corrective Justice*, 44 DUKE L. J. 277 (1995).

[55] *See* WEINRIB, CORRECTIVE JUSTICE 72–75 (2012) (explaining that the law should choose one avenue of justice, because corrective and distributive justice cannot be integrated. Only corrective justice accomplishes justice aims); Ernest J. Weinrib, *Tort Law: Correlativity, Personality, and the Emerging Consensus on Corrective Justice*, 2 THEORETICAL INQ. L. 107, 108 (2001) (addressing the centrality of corrective justice).

[56] *See, e.g.*, Weinrib, *Correlativity, Personality, and the Emerging Consensus on Corrective Justice, supra* note 55. For a critique on Weinrib *see* Stephen R. Perry, *The Moral Foundations of Tort Law*, 77 IOWA L. REV. 449 (1992) (presenting a different approach to corrective justice); Bruce Chapman, *Pluralism in Tort and Accident Law, Philosophy and the Law of Torts* 250 *passim* in PHILOSOPHY AND THE LAW OF TORTS (Gerald J. Postema ed., 2001) (rejecting monism and demonstrating intensively from Weinrib's approach and summarizing that "just as the compensation theorist could not purge the system of compensation completely of deterrence-like concerns under a strategy of criterial separation, so the corrective justice theorists cannot, even in his own terms, hold onto the purity of corrective justice within tort law").

Others see compensation, or restoring the *status quo ante*,[57] as an independent and even predominant goal.[58] Some perceive it as an important secondary principle that other goals aim to achieve.[59] If the tortfeasor cannot provide compensation for his tortious act, it is of social importance to find others who can provide compensation, such as a deep pocket close to the tortfeasor. The question of who pays is sometimes considerably less salient according to this goal.[60] Therefore, even if the direct tortfeasor is not the source of compensation, anyone else, like an insurer or employer, or the state or a public fund could provide compensation.[61] In this manner, compensation differs from corrective justice. Also, compensation is provided based on not only the tortfeasor's culpability or fault but also on other grounds, which varies from the fault-based emphasis of corrective justice.[62]

Distributive justice is concerned with allocating "slices of the cake" that make up the aggregate welfare of society. This view ascribes to law the role of allocating the costs of accidents fairly according to some measure of merit and redistributing benefits from the stronger and wealthier segments of society to those who

---

[57] *See, e.g.,* ABRAHAM, *supra* note 46, at 14; Christopher H. Schroeder, *Corrective Justice and Liability for Increasing Risks*, 37 UCLA L. REV. 439, 466–67 (1990); WALTER J. BLUM & HARRY KALVEN JR., PUBLIC LAW PERSPECTIVES ON A PRIVATE LAW PROBLEM: AUTO COMPENSATION PLANS 13 (1965); Stephen Sugarman, *Doing Away with Tort Law*, 73 CAL. L. REV. 555, 591 (1985).

[58] DAN B. DOBBS, THE LAW OF TORTS, §10, 17 (2000) ("Compensation of injured persons is one of the generally accepted aims of tort law. Payment of compensation to injured persons is desirable. If a person has been wronged by a defendant, it is just that the defendant make compensation. Compensation is also socially desirable, for otherwise the uncompensated injured persons will represent further costs and problems for society" (reference omitted)).

[59] Williams, *supra* note 15, at 137, 172–73; Prosser & Keeton on Torts, *supra* note 15, at 5–6 ("There remains a body of law which is directed toward the compensation of individuals, rather than the public, for losses which they have suffered within the scope of their legally recognized interests generally, rather than one interest only, where the law considers that compensation is required. This is the law of torts." *ibid.* at 5–6 (references omitted). The authors refer also to Cecil A. Wright, *Introduction to the Law of Torts*, 8 CAMB. L. J. 238 (1944): "The purpose of the law of torts is to adjust these losses, and to afford compensation for injuries sustained by one person as the result of the conduct of another." *Ibid.* at 6). *See also* Ariel Porat, *Offsetting Risks*, 106 MICH. L. REV. 243, 256 (2007) (examining compensation as an independent goal, though awarding more space to optimal deterrence).

[60] Williams, *supra* note 15, at 137, 151–53, 173.

[61] *See* IZHAK ENGLAND, THE PHILOSOPHY OF TORT LAW 13, 18, 220–23 (1993) (discussing mass torts and market share liability as suitable examples for compensation funds which replace the traditional tort system, and which are not compatible with traditional corrective justice).

[62] *See* DOBBS, *supra* note 58, at 15 (discussing the differences between compensation and corrective justice, and arguing that "[A] corrective justice system of tort law will compensate only those who are injured by some conduct that can be called a wrong. A tort system based solely on social policy might conceivably seek to exact compensation from defendants who have caused harms by accident but not by wrongdoing or, alternatively, might provide a social system of insurance for everyone."); Chapman, *supra* note 56, at 302–03 (discussing Weinrib's approach and differentiating between corrective justice and compensation by an outside institution).

are in need.[63] It is therefore an instrumental goal. It binds all potential parties to the distribution of wealth and other resources. It benefits society for the purpose of promoting social goals, and it does not focus solely on the two specific parties to a tort.[64]

Some regard loss distribution as an independent goal, while others see it as a part of distributive justice[65] or a part of the goal of compensation.[66] Loss distribution means that society's losses must be distributed among the social strata that use the service or product that caused the damage. Accordingly, liability is imposed on whoever can spread and distribute the loss to a large number of participants in an activity (e.g., drivers or consumers) so that each of them will bear a small share of the cost of righting the wrong or fixing the tort at the lowest cost.[67] For example, providers of services can offset risk by raising the cost of their product slightly, thereby spreading the loss to the consumer public. This is a form of self-insurance that uses the very public that comprises the community of potential injured parties. Another method of redistribution is to impose the burden of loss on the wealthy ("deep pockets") rather than on all members of the relevant group, since the wealthy are able to absorb the loss without prejudicing their social and economic status.[68] These individuals are also able to self-insure, as insurance companies naturally distribute loss on the basis of insurance arrangements that are created in accordance with market forces.[69] Even though independent rationales justify distributing loss, it is *not* an independent goal of tort law in our opinion. Rather, it is a technique for implementing a goal, because liability for the deep pocket entails transferring wealth from the stronger to the weaker party.

---

[63] See, e.g., Guido Calabresi, *Some Thoughts on Risk Distribution and the Law of Torts*, 70 YALE L. J. 499 (1961); Gregory Keating, *The Idea of Fairness in the Law of Enterprise Liability*, 95 MICH. L. REV. 1266 (1997).

[64] DOBBS, *supra* note 58, at § 9, 13–14 (2000).

[65] ENGLARD, *supra* note 61, at 55; Izhak Englard, *The System Builders: A Critical Appraisal of Modern American Tort Law*, 9 J. LEGAL STUD. 27 (1980).

[66] See ABRAHAM, *supra* note 46, at 17–18. In any event, loss distribution is not a part of corrective justice, since its rationale is to spread the loss even among participants of the relevant activity who have no fault in causing that loss.

[67] CALABRESI, *supra* note 19, at 50–54; *see also*, generally, Calabresi, *Some Thoughts on Risk Distribution*, *supra* note 63 (discussing of the various meanings of "distributing the losses." Calabresi argues that loss distribution may have three different meanings: (1) spreading the losses, both interpersonally and intertemporally; (2) those who are most able to pay will bear the burden of losses; (3) the enterprises which give rise to a loss should bear the burden, "whether or not this accomplishes the prior two aims." *Ibid.* at 499. In order to decide when and how to distribute losses, one must examine the theoretical justifications for each of these three meanings and presume that these three are not always consistent with each other.) *Ibid.*

[68] FOWLER V. HARPER & FLEMING JAMES, JR., THE LAW OF TORTS (1956) at 759, 762–64 (arguing that "the best and most efficient way to deal with accident loss [is] to distribute the losses involved over society as a whole or some very large segment of it"); CALABRESI, *supra* note 19, at 40–41.

[69] CALABRESI *supra* note 19, at 39–42, 46–48 (presenting a few methods of loss distribution, including social and private insurance as systems of distributing losses).

While distributive justice focuses on distributing aggregate welfare, optimal deterrence – another instrumental goal, derived from law and economics – seeks to increase aggregate welfare and maximize the wealth in society.[70] Optimal deterrence seeks to maximize wealth and increase efficiency by avoiding imposing liability on a tortfeasor at a rate that is lower than the cost of the loss the tortfeasor has caused.[71] This provides an incentive for the potential tortfeasor to avoid a tort, commensurate with the cost of the loss caused by that tort. Optimal deterrence also seeks to avoid over-deterrence, or overcautious behavior that the imposition of an excessive amount of liability may cause.[72] Optimal deterrence aspires to limit the loss of welfare caused when two activities clash by attempting to introduce changes into the nature or scope of those activities. It seeks to prevent losses from risky activities when the expected benefits of those activities are less than the expected costs.[73] In this way, optimal deterrence becomes an effective means of changing the nature and scope of the parties' activities and an efficient means of increasing the aggregate welfare ensuing from conflicting activities.[74]

Ronald H. Coase,[75] Guido Calabresi,[76] and Richard A. Posner[77] were the principal leaders of the (tort) law and economics revolution.[78] According to Coase, when two actions clash, as long as the transaction costs is low, the optimal outcome will be

---

[70] See, e.g., Richard A. Posner, *The Value of Wealth: A Comment on Dworkin and Kronman*, 9 LEG. STUD. 243, 244 (1980) (arguing that maximizing the aggregate welfare, i.e., wealth maximization, is nothing but the principle of compensation); Ronald H. Coase, *The Problem of Social Cost*, 3 J. L. & ECON. 1, 29 (1960) (discussing the aim of promoting the economic welfare according to Pigou); ENGLARD, *supra* note 61, at 227 (criticizing law and economics, which insists on absolute economic efficiency, and trying to reach the objective of achieving aggregate social welfare for disregarding the bilateral relationship between the concrete litigants).

[71] Posner, *supra* note 70, at 244.

[72] See, generally, Robert Cooter, *Prices and Sanctions*, 84 COLUM. L. REV. 1523 (1984) (presenting how legal rules advance deterrence); CALABRESI, *supra* note 19, at 69 (explaining that the objective of tort law is to prevent the costs resulting from a tort event, or at least to reduce them as much as possible as part of a theory postulating a need to reach optimal deterrence, based on the understanding that it is not possible and not desirable to try to prevent all accidents because the cost would be infinitely high).

[73] Richard A. Posner, *A Theory of Negligence*, 1 J. LEGAL STUD. 29, at 40–41 (1972) (explaining that liability is based upon risks caused by the acts of the tortfeasor and not upon actual harms); Jerry Green, *On the Optimal Structure of Liability Laws*, 7 BELL J. ECON. 553, 554 (1976).

[74] Posner, *supra* note 73, at 48.

[75] Coase, *supra* note 70.

[76] Guido Calabresi, *First Party, Third Party, and Product Liability Systems: Can Economic Analysis of Law Tell Us Anything About Them?* 69 IOWA L. REV. 833 (1984); Calabresi & Hirschoff, *supra* note 32.

[77] RICHARD A. POSNER, ECONOMIC ANALYSIS OF LAW (7th ed., 2007); Posner, *A Theory of Negligence*, *supra* note 73; Richard A. Posner, *The Economic Approach to Law*, 53 TEX. L. REV. (1975) 757.

[78] Mataja's analysis, in the late 19th century, is a strong sign of this revolution. See Izhak Englard, *Victor Mataja's Liability for Damages from an Economic Viewpoint: A Centennial to an Ignored Economic Analysis of Tort*, 10 INT'L REV. L. & ECON. 173 (1990).

obtained by the parties themselves, and not through judicial intervention that determines who owns the right (regarding nuisance, for example, intervention that determines who must desist from causing a nuisance and harming the other party).[79] Calabresi constructed his strict liability theory by examining the cheapest cost avoider or as later formulated, the best decision maker, for allocating the costs associated with the loss in a tort.[80] Posner relied on the fault-based Learned Hand formula, which compares the costs of prevention to the expected cost of the harm in order to determine culpability.[81]

Underlying this instrumentalist theory is an economic calculation of the cost of precautions, i.e., of taking measures against risks to prevent the loss (this cost is not solely financial but also a matter of convenience, time, etc.), while emphasizing the importance of economic efficiency in preventing future accidents or reducing their number and costs. This concept may be contrary to corrective justice, which requires the tortfeasor to remunerate the injured, regardless of cost-benefit analyses.[82]

Scholars have rarely discussed the entire set of tort law goals and their proper balance in order to achieve a pluralist solution in the event of a clash between them. Instead, most scholarship focuses on a single unified-monistic theory.

It seems that optimal deterrence and corrective justice are now considered tort law's two primary unified-monistic goals. Scholars who seek optimal deterrence and corrective justice do not necessarily try to reconcile or harmonize conflicting confronting goals but instead examine a single goal in a sectorial, self-interested

---

[79] Coase, *supra* note 70, at 15 (explaining that most of the time it is unrealistic to assume that there are no costs at all in carrying out market transactions).

[80] CALABRESI, *supra* note 19, at 26–31 (developing the test known as the cheapest cost avoider, whose objective is to reach an optimal point of deterrence where the total costs of the accident and the costs of preventing the accident will be smallest. In this way, tort law will achieve optimal deterrence at the lowest cost, avoid accidents, and increase the aggregate welfare. According to the cheapest cost avoider, strict liability is imposed on the person who can prevent the damage in the cheapest way. The objective is a reduction in the number of accidents and of the costs of those that occur. In light of problems with the cheapest cost avoider test, Calabresi, together with Hirschoff, improved this test and devised the similar-but-different test of the "best decision maker." *See* Calabresi & Hirschoff, *supra* note 32, at 1060–61. According to this doctrine, liability is imposed on the entity that belongs to the group that is in the best position to reach "[A] decision as to which of the parties to the accidents is in the best position to make the cost-benefit analysis between accident costs and accidents avoidance costs and to act on that decision once it is made. The question for the court reduces to a search for the cheapest cost avoider ... The issue becomes not whether avoidance is worth it, but which of the parties is relatively more likely to find out whether avoidance is worth it.").

[81] POSNER, *supra* note 77, at 167–71; ROBERT COOTER & THOMAS ULEN, LAW AND ECONOMICS at 349–53 (5th ed. 2007). For critics on the Hand formula *see* Goldberg, *supra* note 44, at 1248 and the references in footnote 59. According to Weinrib, the English and Commonwealth approach differs from the Hand formula and thus is closer to corrective justice, because it disregards the cost of precautions – an integral part of the Hand formula. See Weinrib, *supra* note 55, at 148; Chapman, *supra* note 56, at 311–12 (discussing Weinrib's approach).

[82] DOBBS, *supra* note 58, at 14, 19.

manner. Some of these unified-monistic theories focus on social-economic principles (for example, law and economics as optimal deterrence, corrective justice, feminism, or human rights approaches as distributive justice). These theories are instrumental in nature. Accordingly, they divert the focus away from the specific parties to the tort, contrary to the strictness of corrective justice.

By contrast, pluralistic theories, which have been neglected to some extent, are unwilling to focus on a sole goal of tort law, however important that goal may be.[83] However, all pluralistic theories rely in this way or another on monistic theories, in trying to balance them.[84]

The book will deal with the goals of tort law in an intensive manner, and with a comparison, in this respect, between the goals presented by Maimonides and between the objectives in contemporary law and the different approaches with respect to each objective. As already mentioned, we will argue that Maimonides strongly emphasizes two objectives, one of which is similar to corrective justice, and the other, to a consequentialist approach that is similar to one of the understandings of efficient deterrence – nor does he neglect other considerations, both religious and distributive. We will therefore see that Maimonides is not a monist but a pluralist, and we will attempt to examine his pluralistic approach, against the background of his times, as opposed to contemporary pluralistic theories that are different both methodologically and substantively.

The book will not only deal with the objectives of tort law, but also with the subsection of standard of care. We shall see that Maimonides presents an approach that

---

[83] Cf. Burton, *supra* note 43, at 535 ("The monists' call for meta-principles is a red herring. Sweeping it aside clears the path to a thorough analysis of pluralism, balancing, and monism."). "Monist legal theories suffer from a telling normative deficiency. Due to their monism, such theories are not capable of satisfying the finality and inclusiveness conditions for normativity. Therefore, they cannot reach the normative goal by justifying final recommendations about what the law should be, all things considered ... To be capable of success, a theory must satisfy two necessary conditions for normativity – finality and inclusiveness, among others. Pluralist theories can satisfy both. The monism of monist theories, however, precludes them from satisfying either. Because no other kinds of theories are relevant, it follows logically that all normative legal theories should be pluralist." *Ibid.* at 562, 575. Burton demonstrates his thesis from contract law. Also, Burton argues that the law is fundamentally pluralist. *Ibid.* See Duncan Kennedy, *Form and Substance in Private Law Adjudication*, 89 HARV. L. REV. 1685, at 1723–24 (1976) (posing a similar argument).

[84] Cf. Burton, *supra* note 43, at 574–75 (emphasizing, despite his opposition to monism and support for pluralism, that "[m]onist arguments can, and often should, be components in pluralist theories. Thus, a monist efficiency argument could support a preliminary and tentative conclusion about what the law should be. A monist fairness argument could do the same. If both arguments are sound and concur in their conclusions, the theory should recommend that conclusion, all else being equal. If the arguments come apart, the law should balance and reflect both values in an accommodation or compromise or, if necessary, the stronger argument should control."). Burton also discusses possible claims of monism against pluralism, *e.g.*, pluralism being less predictable than monism (a parameter that is not necessary or sufficient, in Burton's opinion, for a success of an approach). See *ibid.* at 561–62, 571–73. *See also ibid.* at 568–74 (for more possible critics of monism on pluralism).

is not only pluralistic but also differentialist. It in fact applies a different standard of care for each category of cases, in accordance with the rationale relevant to that category. In this aspect, too, a conversation will be possible with modern approaches that examine different standards. It is the norm in modern law to identify two standards that are different from each other and that are located at opposite ends of the standard-of-care scale – absolute liability and negligence, with intermediate standards separating them. Absolute liability means the imposition of tort liability on the defendant, usually the damager, irrespective of the question of whether he was negligent or acted inappropriately. The harmful act per se creates the liability. This standard has advantages and disadvantages, as we will see. The representative of this standard is primarily Calabresi, although his is a special approach of absolute or strict liability, which is sometimes prepared in practice to impose liability on the victim as well, or on third parties and not necessarily on the damager. In some categories of cases, this approach appears to be close to that of Maimonides. At the other end of the scale is the approach of negligence based on culpability. The damager will pay only if his deeds are in fact culpable, i.e., if he did something that he ought not to have done according to the standard of reasonableness, or if he did not do something that he ought to have done according to that standard. This standard, too, has advantages and disadvantages, as we shall see, and the main proponent of this standard is Posner, who presents an economic approach to negligence, based on Hand's formula. Here, too, we shall see that in some of the categories, this approach is close to that of Maimonides. In other categories, Maimonides applies intermediate approaches between negligence and absolute liability. Indeed, in contemporary law too we find different standards of care applied in different categories. For example, in most states, the dominant standard in the majority of the tort categories is that of negligence based on fault; in some states, however, absolute or strict liability is also recognized, for example, in relation to compensation for bodily harm in road accidents or in cases of products liability, and intermediate arrangements are also recognized, i.e., of liability that is not absolute but has some elements of fault.[85] These arrangements, too, can be found in Maimonides' work, in other categories of cases.

The mission here is three-fold: first, to map out, for the first time, and to present the categorization of tort liability in Maimonides' work, i.e., to identify the various categories of tortious occurrences and to present the standard of care that Maimonides selected for each such category; secondly, to compare for this purpose the classic

---

[85] See DOBBS, *supra* note 58, at 2–3 (discussing fault, negligence, expanding and limiting liability for fault and strict liability). For negligence as standard or conduct *see*: *ibid.* at 257–352; Prosser & Keeton, *supra* note 15, at 160–234. For limited duties *see ibid.* at 356–85. For imputed negligence, such as vicarious liability, servants, independent contractors, and more, *see ibid.* at 499–533. For strict liability *see ibid.* at 534–83; DOBBS, *ibid.* at 941–68. For principles of negligence vs. strict liability and more in products liability, *see ibid.* at 969–1045; Prosser & Keeton, *ibid.* at 677–724. For full and partial immunities *see ibid.* at 1032–75.

approaches of negligence and of absolute or strict liability; third, to try to explain, largely by use of contemporary tools, with due caution due to the differences in the times and the material, why Maimonides chose a different standard in each category of cases, which made of him not only a pluralist but also a differentialist.

Understanding the theory of Maimonides in its entirety enables us to pinpoint exactly where to place Maimonides on the scale among the different monistic and pluralistic scholars. Also, Maimonides regards justice as one of the elements of the consequentialist way of thinking. In doing so, Maimonides indeed takes into account consequentialist considerations, but he definitely subjugates himself to deontological constraints. This method may provide unexpected support for contemporary law and economics scholars who argue that being efficient does not necessarily mean being immoral.

Finally, in the course of the discussion, an important comment regarding the connection between tort law and criminal law will be made.

The fields of contemporary tort law and contemporary criminal law are completely different both in their nature and in the modes of proof that they employ. Indeed, the two areas meet at some points, such as the issue of punitive damages (which will be discussed in Chapter 5), or compensation for the victim of a crime in the framework of a criminal process. Overall, however, the two areas remain distinct in modern law. In ancient law in general, and Jewish law in particular, however, the fields of criminal law and civil law have encroached on each other, and in many civil areas – particularly in tort law – matters are framed in terms of criminal punishment. In various chapters of the book we will see that the conversation between criminal law and tort law is in fact more significant in Jewish law in general, and in Maimonides' theory in particular, and this will have implications for the discussion of the overall approach of Maimonides to tort law, both in terms of goals and of standards of care, as well as implications for specific issues such as punitive damages. Despite a certain distance with regard to this matter between Maimonides' theory and contemporary law, we will also find interesting points of contact between the theories on this matter.

We are aware, however, of the danger of reading ancient texts and ancient scholars in modern ways, and we have tried to avoid anachronisms.

D. ABSTRACT

The book contains three main parts: (a) Questions; (b) Answers; and (c) Dialogue. Chapter 2 presents the questions to be dealt with in the book. Chapters 3–7 supply answers, and Chapters 8–9 offer a dialogue between Maimonides and various contemporary tort theories.

In Chapter 2 we will present the difficulties facing those who seek to understand Maimonides' tort theory as it appears in the *Code* alone, and according to the common interpretation (the "*yeshivah* reading"). Several contemporary scholars, as well as rabbis from the Lithuanian *yeshivot*, identified a different element as an alternative to the element of *peshiah*, i.e., the element of ownership, and some say ownership and strict liability, by virtue of which liability is imposed for damage caused by a person's property. We will examine this approach critically and conclude that it does not accurately reflect Maimonides' position, for it raises serious difficulties, both conceptual-principled and exegetical. We will point to a trend of new explanations of the Jewish sources through the speculum of the common tort theories in the twentieth century in the world of Jewish law. Chapter 2 will leave us with many open questions, which will be answered in the subsequent chapters.

Chapter 3 introduces the foundations of the Maimonidean theory: the scope of tort law, its connection to criminal law, the classification of the different categories of tort law (different goals for different categories of damage) and the various objectives underlying each of these categories. We argue that understanding Maimonides's tort theory and providing a complete view of his theory requires three things. The first is an awareness that Maimonides' theory incorporates various goals and considerations that operate in concert. The second is the understanding that Maimonides introduced different goals for different categories of damage. In each category of damage one goal (or more) is (or are) more dominant than the others. The third is to focus both on what Maimonides wrote in his *Code* and in the *Guide*, as well as in his other works such as *Commentary to the Mishnah* and Maimonides' Responsa.[86]

In Chapter 3 we will also discuss the fact that the scope of tort law in Maimonides' theory is much broader than in modern law, and it includes not only purely civil laws (from the area of the laws of obligations) but also laws which have a significant connection to criminal law. According to Maimonides, the law of torts is an area midway between civil law and criminal law. A fundamental division into different types of torts – which we call the "differential conception" – emerges from the classification of the Book of Torts in the *Code*, at the center of which are the following important distinctions: (a) the basic distinction between damages that are caused by a person's property (Laws of Property Damages) and damages that are caused by the person himself (Laws of Wounding and Damaging); (b) the distinction between damages that are caused by a person's possessions (Laws of Damages Caused by Animals) and damages caused by a person's actions (pit and fire); (c) the distinction between a person who causes physical injury to another (Laws of Wounding) and a person who damages the property of another (Laws of Damaging); and (d) the distinction between regular damage and between nuisance and damages to neighbors and more. There is no one single purpose to the law of torts: in his

---

[86] While retaining an awareness of the differences between the Responsa and the MISHNEH TORAH, as pointed out by Hanina Ben-Menahem, *Maimonides on Equity: Reconsidering the Guide for the Perplexed III:34*, 17 J. L. & RELIG. 19 (2002).

various works, and particularly in the *Guide*, Maimonides presents various objectives in this branch of law.

Chapter 4 introduces the deontological and religious elements of Maimonides' tort theory and discusses the meta-halakhic-philosophical basis for this theory. We will examine the deontological, religious, and criminal elements in the Maimonidean theory vis-à-vis the major elements of prominent modern (as well as ancient Aristotelian and Greco-Arab) corrective justice theories, such as those presented by Weinrib.

Chapter 5 will examine consequentialist elements in Maimonides' tort theory, based primarily on what he wrote in the *Guide*. We will see that although Maimonides' theory is not consequentialist in the full sense of this term, several significant elements of consequentialism are to be found in his theory, notwithstanding the concurrent presence of other important elements. In the matter of punitive damages and criminal sanctions, this element is strongly emphasized – more so than in other cases. After a discussion of this important aspect of Maimonides' tort theory, we will proceed to a comparative examination of the similarities and the differences between this theory and the modern theories of law and economics regarding torts, including the theories of some of the fathers of the economic analysis of law in general and of tort law in particular. After raising questions regarding the problematic texts in the *Code* in Chapter 2, and presenting consequentialist – and not only deontological – objectives of Maimonides' tort theory as the two main objectives of tort law, as seen in Chapters 3–5, Chapter 6 revisits some of the problematic texts in the *Code*. Chapter 6 attempts to cast light on those problematic texts in view of the consequentialist objective of tort law elucidated in the *Guide*, thereby resolving some of the difficulties that were raised in Chapter 2 in light of the analysis undertaken in Chapters 3–5. Revisiting some problematic texts will serve as leverage for further understanding the Maimonidean theory in the next chapter.

Chapter 7 attempts to define accurately the standard of care adopted by Maimonides in his *Code*, based on his interpretation of the talmudic texts, with respect to four categories of damage: (a) damage caused by a person to the property of another; (b) damage caused by a person who injures another; (c) damage caused by property, and (d) murder. In relation to each of these four categories, Maimonides proposed a standard of care that lies on the scale between fault, negligence and strict liability. We present a scheme that illustrates Maimonides' differential model and explains its rationale with respect to the hierarchy in the different standards of care applied in different cases. We also describe the historical background, circumstances, and nature of the tortfeasors in Maimonides' time and in the contemporary era. This is essential for an understanding of the differential liability model in itself and as compared to contemporary models.

Chapter 8 draws some cautious lessons from a contemporary analysis of torts for Maimonides' theory of torts and vice versa. The first part of the chapter offers a full conceptual description of the Maimonidean theory, based on the previous chapters, and also characterizes Maimonides as a pluralistic-differential scholar. We show that as opposed to contemporary approaches to torts, which emphasize law and economics and corrective justice, Maimonides' approach should be characterized as pluralistic and not monistic. After showing how contemporary approaches shed light on Maimonides' approach, we can move, in the other part of the chapter, in the opposite direction; that is, we can draw some careful – but important – lessons from the Maimonidean theory for contemporary tort law. We suggest one possible way of learning lessons from Maimonides' theory for contemporary law which may help enrich the current tort law discourse. The argument that Maimonides is a true pluralist enables us to draw a careful comparison between Maimonidean and contemporary pluralistic approaches to tort law, such as those of Glanville Williams, Fleming James Jr., Izhak Englard, Gary Schwartz, Mark Geistfeld, Christopher Robinette, Steven Burton, John Goldberg, and Benjamin Zipursky. This comparison reveals differences among the approaches, as well as advantages and disadvantages of each approach.

Chapter 9 includes some insights and observations of the Hon. Prof. Calabresi on the major elements of the Maimonidean theory, especially those that are similar – more or less – to contemporary tort law and economics. Calabresi discusses law, economics, and justice in our era and in Maimonides' theory of torts. Among other things, Calabresi considers the question of whether there are differences between the differential liability model presented by Maimonides, and contemporary theories of the economic analysis of tort law. Calabresi deals specifically with the issue of punitive damages and discusses the innovative analysis of Maimonides compared to the multiplier approach, distributive justice as presented by Maimonides, and his optimal deterrence model.

E. THE METHOD

We note that on our journey through different episodes of the Maimonidean story, we travel in two directions: from bottom to top and from top to bottom. From bottom to top means telling the story in chronological order: *Bible → Talmud → Code → Guide → Contemporary*. From top to bottom means telling the story by revisiting both Maimonides' writings in his *Code* in light of his later writings in his *Guide*, and by revisiting the Maimonidean texts in the *Guide* and the *Code*, in light of contemporary methods, that is: *Contemporary → Guide → Code*.

The interdisciplinary character of the book requires invoking various methodologies, such as those utilized in the study of comparative law, legal history, law and religion, Judaic studies, legal theory, and economic analysis of law.

We will examine six books that are relevant to the subjects discussed in the present work. We will look at the similarities and the differences between our work and these books, and in the course of so doing we will discuss some methodological perspectives that are developed in our own book.

Many books written by eminent scholars have dealt with different aspects of Maimonides' multifaceted personality. Most of these books do not deal at length with Maimonides' halakhic approach but rather, with his philosophical approach only; a few of them, however, do touch on Maimonides' halakhic approach and its relationship to his philosophical approach. Two books are particularly notable in this context. The first, considered to be the classic academic work on the *Code of Maimonides*, is Isadore Twersky's *Introduction to the Code of Maimonides (Mishneh Torah)* (New Haven, CT: Yale University Press, 1980). In recent years, the great interest in Maimonides has grown even more, and eminent scholars have lately published books on Maimonides' works in the most prestigious university presses. A very recent example is the second book that we will mention: Moshe Halbertal, *Maimonides: Life and Thought* (Princeton, NJ: Princeton University Press, 2014).

Twersky's book deals with a variety of topics that impact on our subject, including the structure, formulation, method, and classification used by Maimonides in the *Code*. It also deals extensively with the connection between *halakhah* and philosophy, and with the similarities and the differences between the *Code* and the *Guide*. Owing to the fact that Twersky's book is an introduction to the *Code*, its discussion is framed in very general terms and it does not engage in detailed and comprehensive analyses of the various issues. There is also little reference to Maimonides as a jurist, and the book lacks an analysis of Maimonides' basic jurisprudence, and comparisons between this and other jurisprudential approaches. It is clear that in these aspects, our project differs from that of Twersky, in that our discussion is devoted primarily to the fairly extensive jurisprudential aspects of Maimonidean thought in relation to tort law and criminal law, and we compare Maimonides' tort theory to other pre-modern and modern tort theories. As we have said, no work has done this to date, and in this lies the major innovation of our present study. Of course, in many senses our book references Twersky's findings and examines whether these findings are consistent with the Book of Torts – one of the fourteen books of the *Code* – to which extensive discussion is devoted in our book. Thus, for example, Twersky brought to our attention Maimonides' special system of classification and the level of sophistication of his wording, which according to Twersky approach perfection. Naturally, Twersky does not go into very much detail, but we aim to do so. We will examine with great care Maimonides' sophisticated classification in the Book of Torts and discuss his sources, the considerations that guided him and the conceptual-jurisprudential insights which this work affords; but we will also discuss the problems involved in that classification. Maimonides' wording in his rulings will also occupy us.[87] In his book, Twersky dwells on the difference between the line of

---

[87] Although unlike Twersky, who praised Maimonides' formulations and thought they were just about perfect, in Chapter 2 we will discuss at length a not-so-successfully worded ruling at the beginning of the Book of Torts, which led many to adopt a mistaken interpretation of his theory.

thinking in the *Code* and that in the *Guide*. He demonstrates that the tendency in the *Guide* was to point out the social utility of the laws of the Torah, unlike the *Code*. He also discusses the contradictions and differences between the two works. In our book, we will discuss at length the similarities and differences between the *Code* and the *Guide*, examining them in a very concrete context: a detailed, painstaking comparison between certain chapters in part 3 of the *Guide* that deal with rationalization of the various areas of law and between the Book of Torts in the *Code*.

Similar to Twersky's book, Halbertal's book on Maimonides is also of a general nature, and as such it is not designed to deal with the specific issue of tort law, as is our book. Halbertal deals with a wide range of aspects relating to Maimonides' multifaceted image, and he does not focus on a comprehensive examination of the economic and legal aspects of Maimonides' thought or on drawing a comparison between these aspects and other jurisprudential theories. Indeed, Halbertal, who teaches Jewish law at New York University School of Law, occasionally presents illuminating comparisons in his book between Maimonides' thought and modern theories of jurisprudence, but as we have said, this is only one aspect amongst many that are discussed by Halbertal. Our book avails itself of important insights offered by Halbertal and applies them to tort law. A first example of our recourse to Halbertal's book is mentioned earlier with respect to his instructive discussion of the two possible readings of the objective of the *Code* and its relationship to the Talmud, and the implications of this discussion for an examination of the relationship between the Book of Torts and the Talmud that are discussed in our book (and which largely support Halbertal's proposal). A second example relates to Halbertal's contention, with which we agree, that Maimonides' halakhic thought and his philosophical thought complement each other and are integrated in the *Code*. Our book is openly supportive of the possibility of integration between the *Code* and the *Guide*, even though we are also aware of the differences between the two works. Here we must look briefly at the position adopted in our book concerning the relationship between the *Code* and the *Guide*.

We are fully aware that the *Guide* speaks in a different idiom to that of the *Code*. Many scholars and commentators have addressed the differences between the *Guide* and the *Code*. Some scholars even refer to "two different Maimonides": the traditional halakhist of the *Code*, and the controversial and innovative philosopher of the *Guide*.[88]

We also point out the difference between the two works in relation to torts. The focus in the *Guide* is on a general overview of the consequentialist and "policy" considerations: all this is absent from the *Code*. We note that the classical *yeshivah* curriculum, reflected in the writings of Lithuanian scholars in the last two centuries

---

[88] JACOB S. LEVINGER, MAIMONIDES AS PHILOSOPHER AND CODIFIER (Jerusalem: Bialik Institute, 1989) (Heb.).

does not usually refer to the *Guide* as a source that can enlighten the ways of the *Code*.[89] But in fact, many researchers have been able to find a link between the *Guide* and the *Code* in various areas, and we intend to follow this path with due caution. We are convinced that it is not possible to present the complete tort theory of Maimonides based on the *Code* alone, with its contradictions and premature statements, without the statements about the incentives for preventing damage and the EAC test that appear in the *Guide*. These statements in the *Guide* represent a crystallized, clear, and more mature overview of the foundations of tort liability, which was probably developed fully at a later stage of Maimonides's life. Indeed, we argue that at least regarding tort law, the two books are in many ways complementary. As such, one can revisit the earlier texts of the *Code* and find that many of the views expressed there may best be rationalized in a comprehensive manner in light of the later *Guide*'s overview, notwithstanding that in the *Code*, Maimonides used a formulation that is closer to that of the talmudic and biblical texts. This formulation does not consistently fit, both literally and conceptually, with the terms and concepts he used in the *Guide*.

We will now move on to the third and fourth books, which are part of the relatively new trend to publish research dealing with the relationship between Judaism and common contemporary views. There are even those who believe that this is part of the process of developing a new field of research which has aroused great interest, i.e., Judaism and economics. We will mention two prominent scholars in this area: Aaron Levine and Yehoshua Liebermann.[90] In this context we will discuss jointly two books: AARON LEVINE, *ECONOMIC, MORALITY AND JEWISH LAW* (New York: Oxford University Press 2012), and *THE OXFORD HANDBOOK OF JUDAISM AND ECONOMICS* (AARON LEVINE ed., New York: Oxford University Press 2010).

Economic Morality and Jewish Law compares the way in which welfare economics and Jewish law determine the propriety of the economic action. Exposing what philosophers would call a consequentialist ethical system, welfare economics evaluates the worthiness of an economic action based on whether the action would increase the wealth of society in the long run. In sharp contrast, the author argues, Jewish law espouses a deontological system of ethics. Despite the very different approaches that welfare economics and Jewish law take in evaluating the worthiness of an economic action, the author reveals a remarkable symmetry between the two systems in their ultimate prescriptions for certain economic issues. The second book

---

[89] We discuss their interpretation of Maimonides' CODE *infra* in Chapter 2.
[90] Liebermann, too, published important studies in these areas, including some which have ramifications for tort law and for our research. *See, e.g.,* Yehoshua Liebermann, *The Coase Theorem in Jewish Law*, 10 J. LEG. STUD. 293 (1981); Yehoshua Liebermann, *Economic Efficiency and Making of the Law: The Case of Transaction Costs in Jewish Law*, 15 J. LEG. STUD. 387 (1986).

edited by Levine also contains many studies, and even though each was written from a different perspective and by a different author, they still all adopt a similar line.

Our book continues the dialogue between economics and Jewish law, and several of Levine's insights and conclusions are acceptable to us, such as the difference between deontology, which receives greater emphasis in Judaism, and consequentialism, which features more in modern economics. The conclusions of our research are, of course, compatible with Levine's argument that alongside the differences, there are also many parallels between Judaism and economics. However, there are some significant differences between the works. The first concerns the object of the comparison – economics or law. Whereas Levine and most authors in this field of "Judaism and economics" are mainly from the field of economics, and they therefore compare Judaism primarily with the research conducted by modern economists, we, the authors of the present book, are legal scholars. As such, our book focuses primarily on a comparison between Jewish *law* (rather than "Judaism" in its entirety) and modern jurisprudential theories, including those of the founding fathers of the economic analysis of law, Calabresi and Posner, who are federal judges and prominent legal scholars (as well as scholars in the field of law and economics). Another difference relates to the area of research of our book – tort law – and to the particular personality who is its subject – Maimonides. In the two abovementioned books, there is no particular focus on Maimonides' unique legal-philosophical thought and his unique theory in the area of tort law, which in our view integrates, in a fascinating manner, deontological, economic and religious considerations. Levine's work focuses even less on the methodological problems involved in the comparison between Jewish sources from the pre-modern period and contemporary economic theories. In our book, however, the subject of the problems of comparing Maimonides' times (the Middle Ages) to the modern period receives a good deal of emphasis.

As noted, in our opinion there is room for a dialogue between Maimonides' theory and contemporary theories, but it is important to examine the substance of the dialogue carefully. Not every encounter between the two theories is feasible methodologically. For example, it is not acceptable to conduct an intensive dialogue that gives the impression that premodern Jewish law and modern methods are on the same wave-length and converse in the same language. What, then, is the appropriate meeting point between contemporary and ancient legal theories? From the perspective of Jewish law, and specifically from the Maimonidean point of view, it makes sense to examine various phenomena in the area of torts using the tools of modern methods, including those of law and economics. It is obvious that halakhic sages, including Maimonides, had no knowledge of modern economics and of the method of law and economics. They did not utilize the categories of this method in their thinking, and they did not formulate their views to fit its principles and details. Nevertheless, it is possible that in certain cases the halakhic sages intuitively adopted a position that would be explained well by modern scholarship. In our opinion, this is particularly evident in the case of Maimonides' tort theory.

In the same way, pre-eminent modern scholars have argued that the insights of law and economics have been present *de facto* in the judgments of the common law. In their opinion, judges of the common law made intuitive use of such insights, without being aware of the later existence of the methods of law and economics. A closer comparison to the field of Jewish law is found in the explanation provided by Nobel Laureate in Economics, Prof. Robert Aumann, to tractate *Ketubbot*, *mishnah* 10:3.[91] This *mishnah* presents an apparently incomprehensible method for dividing the estate of a deceased person between several of his widows in several different situations. Many commentators had difficulty explaining the rationale of this *mishnah* and made various suggestions. Aumann developed a special algorithm that explained the different outcomes presented in the *mishnah*. Clearly, the sages of the *Mishnah*, as well as its classical commentators, did not use this algorithm. Nor did Aumann claim that this use of the algorithms applies to all areas of the *halakhah* or even to a particular group of cases. He simply showed that there is a difficult text in the *Mishnah* and the specific algorithm which he developed solves the difficulty. This method seems to us the proper way to use modern methods, especially of law and economics, in the area of Jewish law. This is what we tried to accomplish in this book, bearing in mind the earlier-mentioned reservation about reading ancient texts and ancient scholars in modern ways.

Indeed, the difficulties involved in drawing comparisons between the ancient period and the Middle Ages on the one hand, and the modern era on the other, is a subject that is strongly emphasized in our book. We are very aware of it, *inter alia*, in light of the fifth book that we will mention in this section: IZHAK ENGLARD, CORRECTIVE AND DISTRIBUTIVE JUSTICE: FROM ARISTOTLE TO MODERN TIMES (Oxford: Oxford University Press, 2009). In this book, Englard recounts the intricate history of the distinction between corrective and distributive justice. This distinction is elaborated in the fifth book of ARISTOTLE'S NICOMACHEAN ETHICS. Englard offers readers a historical perspective that is vital for a deep understanding of the distinction between ancient and modern concerns.

There are many points of similarity between Englard's book and our own, for they both conduct an intergenerational dialogue between legal theories that were presented by thinkers – Aristotle and Maimonides – who lived many centuries ago, and later legal theories from the Middle Ages until the present day. Englard's book also includes an interesting chapter on the way in which Aristotle's distinction between corrective justice and distributive justice was accepted by Jewish rabbis and scholars. In this context, it is our intention to reveal (in Chapters 3–4) for the first time the possible existence of a real link between what Maimonides wrote in part 3 of the

---

[91] Robert J. Aumann & Michael Maschler, *Game-Theoretic Analysis of a Bankruptcy Problem from the Talmud*, 36 J. ECONOMIC THEORY 195 (1985).

Guide and Aristotle's said distinction – a possibility not discussed by Englard. Admittedly, Maimonides did not make explicit, direct use of Aristotle's distinction between corrective justice and distributive justice, nor did he even mention it. However, we believe that in the *Guide* it is possible to find expressions that are very reminiscent of – though not identical to – those two types of justice discussed by Aristotle. We assume that Maimonides "corresponded" with the two types of Aristotelian justice and interpreted them in his own unique way, which is certainly not identical to that of Aristotle. We addressed Englard's book on another important point as well. Englard draws a comparison between modern jurisprudential thought and jurisprudential thought in antiquity and in the Middle Ages, and points out that such a comparison involves extremely complex methodological problems. This is true, in our opinion, not only in relation to the comparison drawn by Englard between Aristotle's words as originally formulated and the way in which they were understood in later periods, but also in relation to the comparisons we make between Maimonides and modern theories.

The awareness of the differences in ways of thinking between the modern era and the Middle Ages is important to all who wish to examine what Maimonides says in the light of modern legal theory. Above, we already touched upon the subject of the abstract conceptualization of legal principles and the quest for uniformity according to Maimonides as compared to ancient times. We shall now examine another point: Maimonides' starting point in the *Guide* was that every precept and every law has a rational reason. In other words, he himself did not fashion the laws according to a certain principle but sought to examine the law that exists – in Scripture and in the Oral law – on the basis that there is an analytical logic to them and they are not purely arbitrary. Maimonides claims that a rational reason can be found for every precept and law. In this there is a fundamental difference between the contemporary theories and that of Maimonides: today, the intellectual effort is directed at molding tort law according to a principle or principles – i.e., a normative approach – whereas in the Middle Ages, the effort was directed at explaining the existing law. Englard discussed this in the abovementioned book. Consequently, in Maimonides' eyes – as we will see in Chapter 3 – there is no problem in explaining a particular law according to different principles, as long as they are rational. He has no difficulty in basing a particular law on several reasons. On the contrary: the more rational reasons there are, the better. He can therefore base a certain law on the idea of recompense, on the idea of general deterrence, on the idea of individual deterrence or on the perfection of attributes (overcoming the evil inclination) and on various and varied religious reasons. We are of course aware of the substantive differences between the trend of the contemporary approach – which is normative – and the Maimonidean trend, which is primarily "explanatory," attempting to provide a rational analytical basis for the existing law in accordance with a philosophical-religious conception. Against this background, the monism and pluralism that we encounter in Maimonides' work has a meaning that is not absolutely identical to the meaning assigned to these terms by some scholars in our generation. Nevertheless, we will attempt to prove that in certain cases Maimonides appears to be a pluralist in a sense that is closer to the modern meaning; he did not settle for merely explaining the existing law, but also sought to set up a type of normative and conceptual legal model by means of which to formulate guiding principles in the legal area under discussion. A prominent example of this is the incisive model of punishment, which includes four elements that affect the level of punishment, presented by Maimonides in the *Guide*. He proposes a conceptual-normative and relatively abstract analysis of an ideal model of punishment comprising four main components and which includes, as we shall argue in Chapter 5, various elements of efficient deterrence.

And now for the last book. Eyal Zamir and Barak Medina address the required balance between consequentialist and deontological considerations in *Law, Economics, and Morality* (Oxford: Oxford University Press, 2010). They examine the possibility of combining economic methodology and deontological morality through the explicit and direct incorporation of moral constraints into economic models. In addition, they argue that the normative flaws of economic analysis can be rectified without relinquishing its methodological advantages. Zamir and Medina illustrate the implementation of their proposed balanced approach in several legal fields. An analysis of tort law is not presented by Zamir and Medina, even though it may be valuable in this discourse, especially given the fact that, as mentioned above, the founding fathers of the economic analysis of law – Coase, Calabresi, and Posner – and the preeminent scholar in the field of corrective justice in private law – Weinrib – all focus on the analysis of tort law. Our book analyses this combination in tort law as well by suggesting that the Maimonidean way of incorporation of moral considerations into consequentialist-social models, which is adopted in the present book, can be valuable in this discourse.

2

Tort Liability in Maimonides' *Code*:

The Downside of the Common Interpretation

A. INTRODUCTION: THE MODERN STUDY OF JEWISH TORT THEORY
AS A STORY OF "SELF-MIRRORING"

Isadore Twersky showed us that "[t]o a great extent the study of Maimonides is a story of 'self-mirroring',"[1] and that the answers given by modern and medieval scholars and rabbis to some questions on the concepts of Maimonides "were as different as their evaluations of Maimonides, tempered of course by their own ideological convictions and/or related contingencies."[2]

Much of the response to Maimonides' opening passages of the Book of Torts (*Sefer Nezikin*) in the *Code* (*Mishneh Torah*) can also be described as a story of "self-mirroring." His words have stimulated a great deal of interest over the last 150 years, both among the rabbis who were active in this period, particularly the heads of the Lithuanian talmudic academies (*yeshivot*) and among some scholars of Jewish law. All of them regarded Maimonides' words, which we shall examine in this chapter, as the major source of a theory that explains the basis for tort liability for property damages that is substantively different from the fault-based liability theory, which is accepted by the mainstream of commentators and scholars as the common talmudic theory. In this chapter we describe the tort theory attributed by some of the rabbis and scholars to Maimonides, i.e., the "ownership and strict liability theory" (OSL), and examine critically the sources on which they relied. This chapter will present the difficulties in explaining Maimonides' tort theory according to the *Code* alone, as is common in what we call the *yeshivah* reading – that of some Lithuanian rabbis and some scholars. In contrast the following chapters will introduce a full resolution of these difficulties by reference to Maimonides' other works too, and in particular

---

[1] ISADORE TWERSKY, INTRODUCTION TO THE CODE OF MAIMONIDES (*MISHNEH TORAH*) 358 (New Haven, CT: Yale University Press, 1980).
[2] *Ibid*. Twersky made this statement in the context of the relationship between *halakhah* and philosophy in Maimonides' thought, but it is equally applicable to our topic.

the *Guide of the Perplexed* (hereinafter, the *Guide*), and not just the *Code*, and in view of modern theories of tort law. An understanding of what Maimonides wrote in his various works and a comparison of his writing with other tort theories will help enlighten us on his theory; only thereafter will we be able to take a fresh look at what he wrote in the *Code*, and to offer a reading that addresses the serious difficulties discussed in this chapter.

Our central argument in this chapter is that the OSL does not accurately reflect Maimonides' position, for it presents serious difficulties – both conceptual-principled and exegetical – and it does not comport with certain of Maimonides' rulings in the *Code*, which appear to contradict this theory.

As we discussed in Chapter 1, jurisprudential thought in ancient times was much less abstract in nature than in modern times. Attempts were indeed made to base tort liability in *halakhah* on a uniform principle of *peshiah* (negligence/fault), but in what follows we will see that these attempts encountered difficulties and drew criticism from many scholars. The talmudic legal tradition, in that it is based on the interpretation of the biblical laws which themselves are casuistic in nature, did not seek a single, abstract principle for all cases of tort liability.[3] Hence, the Talmud was untroubled by the fact that there were different reasons and justifications in relation to the specific cases of liability. Awareness of the differences in thinking between the modern and pre-modern periods, we argue, is important for examining Maimonides in light of modern jurisprudential theory, without falling into the trap of "self-mirroring".

An examination of modern twentieth-century Jewish law scholars who sought to define the basis for liability for damages under Jewish law will reveal that they often presented the Jewish law tort theory in a fashion somewhat similar to the prevalent tort theories in the Western world. To a large extent it may be said that these scholars look at Jewish law tort theory and define it through the prism of the common tort theories in their time in modern Western jurisprudence (the Common law, Roman law, and European Continental law). This phenomenon manifests itself clearly in the emphatic position of most scholars of Jewish law, particularly those who were active a century ago, when scientific research of Jewish law was becoming established, but also more modern scholars, who claimed that Jewish law recognizes a *peshiah* fault-based theory only.[4] Identification of Jewish

---

[3] See AVISHALOM WESTREICH, HERMENEUTICS AND DEVELOPMENTS IN THE TALMUDIC THEORY OF TORTS AS REFLECTED IN EXTRAORDINARY CASES OF EXEMPTION (PhD thesis, Ramat Gan; Bar-Ilan University, 2006) (Heb).

[4] Cf. the statement of ZERAH WARHAFTIG, THE BASIS FOR LIABILITY FOR DAMAGES IN JEWISH LAW, STUDIES IN JEWISH LAW 211, 212 (Ramat Gan: Bar Ilan University, 1985) (Heb.): "Scholars of Jewish law are adamant in their conclusion that Jewish law recognizes only the system of *peshiah*." Indeed, as Warhaftig says, this was the opinion of prominent veteran scholars such as CHAIM TCHERNOWITZ, SHI'URIM BETALMUD, "DAMAGES", 97:4; ASHER GULAK, FOUNDATIONS OF JEWISH LAW, vol. 2, 202–03, 210 (Heb.); YA'ACOV SHMUEL ZURI, TALMUDIC LAW, vol. 6, 11–24, 61 (Heb.). This was also the opinion of a contemporary scholar of Jewish law, Shalom Albeck, whose well-known work on tort law is based entirely on the development of the

law tort theory with the doctrine of *peshiah* rendered it extremely close to the traditional legal view (in both Roman and Common law), according to which liability was based on the fault of the person who caused the damage – fault-based tort theory. Indeed, some scholars were even explicit in their use of the tort-related expression from the Common law – *negligence*,[5] by virtue of which the liability of the person who caused the damage lies in the fact that he had a duty to guard, or a duty of care, and to the extent that a breach of this duty of care caused the damage, liability is that of the tortfeasor. An example of this is provided by a scholar of Jewish law active in the first half of the last century, Yaakov Shmuel Zuri, who drew a parallel between the talmudic principle of *peshiah* and the tort of negligence in English law.[6] Zuri also emphasized the similarities between the different degrees of *peshiah* under Jewish law and the different meanings attributed to the term "culpability" (*culpa*) in Roman law[7] – which was discussed by Asher Gulak,[8] one of the pioneers of scientific research of Jewish law in the renascent settlement in the Land of Israel.[9] Establishing *peshiah* as the supreme principle of tort law in Jewish law received significant support following publication of the well-known book by Shalom Albeck (1965),[10] one of the leading contemporary scholars of Jewish law. Albeck attempted to show that the concepts of negligence and foreseeability underlie all the rules of Jewish tort law.[11]

---

  principle of *peshiah*: SHALOM ALBECK, GENERAL PRINCIPLES OF THE LAW OF TORT IN THE TALMUD (2nd ed., Tel-Aviv: Dvir, 1990) (Heb.).

[5] See, e.g., Shalom Albeck, *Torts*, in MENACHEM ELON ed., THE PRINCIPLES OF JEWISH LAW 319–20 (Jerusalem: Encyclopedia Judaica, Keter Publishing House, 1975) ("The basis of liability – negligence. The Talmud states that a man could be held liable only for damage caused by his negligence *(peshi'ah)*").

[6] ZURI, *supra* note 4, at 13–14. See also ibid. at 11.

[7] *Ibid.* at 15–16.

[8] See GULAK, *supra* note 4, at 202–03, who in distinguishing between the different parameters of *peshiah* invoked the parallel terms in Roman Law: "A person's maliciousness in damages, that is his doing something deliberately, which under normal circumstances can lead to injury *(dolus)*; within the parameters of *peshiah* is included inadvertent lack of caution or negligence with respect to something, which under normal circumstances can lead to injury *(culpa lata, culpa levis)*."

[9] We agree with Steven F. Friedell, *The Role of Jewish Law in a Secular State*, 24 JEWISH L. ASSOC. STUDIES 100, 104 (2013) (hereinafter Friedell 2013), who argued that "it is likely that Gulak was himself trying to interpret Jewish law so that it would be in accord with the then-accepted view in Western legal systems that liability for unintentional injuries should be based on fault." A different view was presented by Judge Moshe Drori of the Jerusalem District Court in CC (Jer.) 5380/03 *Estate of R. v. Tz.* (2009) Tel Aviv DC 2009(1) 8, 208, at 299 (Isr.), who favors the view of Asher Gulak, whose work on Jewish law was written before the establishment of the State of Israel and was therefore not influenced by a desire to make Jewish law compatible with the law of the State. We think that while it is true that Gulak's work predated the State, undoubtedly one of the objectives of his work was to establish Jewish law as the national law of the renewed Zionist settlement in the Land of Israel, and Friedell was therefore correct.

[10] ALBECK, *supra* note 4. The first edition was published in 1965, but later we refer to the page numbers in the second, 1990 edition.

[11] See Albeck, *Torts*, *supra* note 5, at 320, arguing that *peshiah* is negligence, and that "[n]egligence is defined as conduct which the tortfeasor should have foreseen would cause damage." See also ALBECK, *supra* note 4, at 20: "Peshiah is conduct which a person must

The views of these modern scholars who sought to base the element of tort liability in Jewish law on the element of *peshiah* alone drew criticism both from several learned modern rabbis, including R. Yehiel Yaacov Weinberg[12] and R. Nachum Rabinovitch,[13] and from other scholars of Jewish law, mentioned later, who took issue mainly with the approach of Shalom Albeck. In light of the rabbinic views of the preceding one hundred and fifty years (the *yeshivah* reading), several of these scholars – Weinberg and Warhaftig in particular – identified a different element as an alternative to the element of *peshiah*, i.e., the element of ownership, and some say ownership and strict liability, by virtue of which liability is imposed for damages caused by a person's property. In the next section, we will first briefly discuss the theory of *peshiah* versus the alternative theory – the theory of ownership – on the basis of which the common interpretation of Maimonides' rulings in the *Code* was formulated, as presented by the rabbis of the Lithuanian *yeshivot* and some modern scholars. We will then discuss the conceptual-exegetical difficulties of the theory of ownership.

B. THE OWNERSHIP AND STRICT LIABILITY THEORY VS. THE FAULT-BASED THEORY (*PESHIAH*)

1 *The Difficulties of the Concept of* Peshiah

Although Albeck's book, GENERAL PRINCIPLES OF LAW OF TORT IN THE TALMUD, is considered the most comprehensive scholarship to date analyzing most of the talmudic rules, it was strongly criticized by scholars such as Izhak Englard,[14] Steven Friedell,[15] Benzion Schereschewsky,[16] Zerah Warhaftig,[17] and Irwin Haut.[18] These scholars agreed that although the concept of *peshiah* (based on the elements of negligence and foreseeability) is emphasized in some talmudic texts or by some commentators, and although this concept is indeed a major

---

realize will entail damage, because it is something that happens frequently and as a matter of course" (foreseeability), "and a person who caused damage under one of the heads of damage is liable if he was at fault" (negligence).

[12] See R. YEHIEL YAACOV WEINBERG, RESP. SERIDEI ESH vol. 4, 125 (Jerusalem, 1979).
[13] Nachum L. Rabinovitch, *Liability for Property that Caused Damage*, in Zvi Haber ed., 25 MA'ALIOT – MAIMONIDES' 800 YEARS COMMEMORATIVE VOLUME 71–72 (Ma'aleh Adumim, 2005) (Heb.).
[14] See Izhak Englard, *Research of Jewish Law – Its Nature and Function*, in Bernard S. Jackson (ed.), MODERN RESEARCH IN JEWISH LAW 21, 57–64 (Leiden, 1980) (criticizing Albeck's method in general), and esp. 60–63 (criticizing his book on Torts).
[15] Steven F. Friedell, *Some Observations on Talmudic Law of Torts*, 13–14 DINE ISRAEL (1986–1988) 65–110 (originally published in 15 RUTGERS L.J. 897 (1984), hereinafter Friedell 1986); idem, *Liability Problems in* Nezikin: *A Reply to Professor Albeck*, 15 DINE ISRAEL 97–105 (1989–90) (hereinafter Friedell 1986).
[16] In a book review: See Book Review, 1 MISHPATIM 275 (1968–69) (Heb.).
[17] WARHAFTIG, *supra* note 4.
[18] Irwin H. Haut, *Some Aspects of Absolute Liability under Jewish Law and Particularly, Under the View of Maimonides*, 15 DINE ISRAEL 7 (1989–90).

principle that explains some of the talmudic rules, nevertheless the concepts of *peshiah*, negligence, and foreseeability do not explain *all* the talmudic rules. We agree with the criticism levelled by England and Friedell, who argued that *peshiah* should not be viewed as all-encompassing; it is certainly very likely that a different principle of liability exists. But what is this principle? In the next section we shall present the common description of the alternative basis, which many attribute to Maimonides, and discuss the problems it involves.

2 The Common Interpretation of the Code: The "Ownership and Strict Liability Theory"

In the first *halakhah* of Laws of Property Damages which opens the Book of Torts in the *Code*, Maimonides writes: "If any living creature under human control causes damage, its owner must pay compensation for it was his property that caused the damage."[19]

Here Maimonides introduces the rationale for tort liability for damages caused by a person's property, without reference to the element of *peshiah*. Instead, Maimonides states that it is the element of ownership of the property causing the damage which created the liability, i.e., the fact that the damage was caused by a person's property. This surprising disregard by Maimonides of the element (of *peshiah*) considered to be the predominant element in creating tort liability under the common interpretations of the Talmud, and his emphasis, instead, on the element of ownership fired the imagination of many, including those who authored or adopted the *yeshivah* reading. Their conclusion is that the end of Maimonides' sentence – "for it was his property that caused the damage" – implies that the basis for tort liability is that the damage was caused by *his property* whether he was negligent (*peshiah*) in caring for the property or not. This is the common explanation of Maimonides' tort liability theory, which we call the *yeshivah* reading.[20]

Following the conceptual methodology they pioneered, these rabbinic scholars asked about the theoretical and practical differences between the two theories – *peshiah* and ownership.[21]

---

[19] *Code*, Laws of Property Damages 1:1. The translation is based on a combination of the translation by Hyman Klein, The Code of Maimonides – The Book of Torts (New Haven: Yale University Press, 1954) and the translation by Eliyahu Touger, Mishneh Torah (Chabad, Moznaim).

[20] See, e.g., R. Isser Zalman Meltzer, Even Ha'azel, Hilkhot Nizkei Mamon 1:1, para. 14; Commentary of R. Haim Halevi (Soloveitchik) on Maimonides, Hilkhot Nizkei Mamon 4:11; Weinberg, *supra* note 12, vol. 4, at 125–32; Shi'urei R. Aharon Lichtenstein, Bava Metzia 38–41 (Alon Shvut, 2013).

[21] See, e.g., Even Ha'azel, ibid.; R. Shimon Shkop, Commentaries of R. Shimon Yehuda Hacohen Shkop, Bava Kamma, sec. 1; Novella Hagranat, Bava Kamma, sec. 1; Commentaries of R. Chaim Telz, Bava Kamma, sec. 1; Commentaries of R. Shmuel Rozovsky, Bava Kamma, sec. 1; Weinberg, *supra* note 12; R. Y.H. Sarna, *Foundations of Liability in Tort Law*, in Memorial Book for R. Chaim Shmuelevitz 582–97 (Jerusalem, 1986).

In modern Jewish law scholarship, a typical example of analysis of these two approaches to tort liability emphasizing Maimonides' unique tort theory may be found in Zerah Warhaftig's well-known article,[22] frequently quoted in the last three decades by researchers and jurists.[23] Warhaftig takes a firm stand against the mainstream fault-based theory accepted by most Jewish law scholars. He claims:

> Another look at the sources will prove to us that the fault-based theory is not the exclusive theory, and the sources also support a theory of strict liability i.e., the "method of causation of the damage" whereby the person who caused the damage is responsible for damage caused by his property, and obviously for damage caused by himself (his body) even when there is no fault on his part, as long as the actions of the victim himself did not cause the damage.[24]

Maimonides' rulings in the *Code* served as a major anchor for grounding the OSL theory according to Warhaftig. What Maimonides wrote also served as a central source for another scholar, Irwin H. Haut. Haut argued that there are aspects of absolute/strict liability in Jewish law, and he compares these aspects to the existing approaches in modern Anglo-American law.[25]

Warhaftig explains Maimonides' approach according to the *yeshivah* reading as a theory of OSL. He infers from the earlier-cited text of the *Code* that "it is the property connection that serves as the basis for their liability for the damage."[26] Warhaftig and others[27] contend that according to Maimonides, the basis for tort liability for damages caused by one's property is –

> the relationship of ownership: as if the liability is imposed on the harmful object, and because an object cannot pay, liability is imposed on the owner of the object, whether he is at fault or not. One's property is not only for one's pleasure and use, but it also imposes liability and obligations on one.[28]

---

[22] WARHAFTIG, *supra* note 4, at 218–21.

[23] This was also the subject of discussion in the framework of a judgment of an Israeli District Court: CC (Jer) 5380/03, *supra* note 9. Judge Drori surveys at length the various possibilities of deriving an approach from Jewish law that imposes strict liability on different tortfeasors, referring extensively to Warhaftig's said article. At the Court's request, a group of scholars at the Center for Practical Application of Jewish Law at Netanya Academic College ("YISHMA") submitted its opinion, *Ahrayut Nizkit shel Hevrat Shemirah B'gin Nezek Shegaram Shomer* ("Liability in Tort of a Security Company for Damage Caused by a Guard") (Jan. 13, 2005), ("YISHMA"). The opinion was written by Moshe Be'ari & Yuval Sinai. In response, Michael Wygoda, Director of the Jewish Law Department of Israel's Ministry of Justice, expressed his view in *Ahrayut Benezikin begin Retzah Beneshek Mufkad* ("Liability in Tort for Murder with a Deposited Weapon") (May 16, 2005), available at www.daat.ac.il/mishpat-ivri/havat/46-2.htm (hereinafter: Wygoda). For a summary of the different views and for a renewed proposal for a solution, see Friedell 2013, *supra* note 9.

[24] WARHAFTIG, *supra* note 4, at 213. Some rabbis also attribute to Maimonides an OSL theory. See, e.g., SOLOVEITCHIK, *supra* note 20, and LICHTENSTEIN, *supra* note 20.

[25] Haut, *supra* note 18.

[26] WARHAFTIG, *supra* note 4, at 220.

[27] See the references in *supra* notes 20–21.

[28] WARHAFTIG, *supra* note 4, at 216.

Modern scholars such as Warhaftig and Haut differ from the *yeshivah* reading in their approaches. The differences relate to the details of the theory attributed to Maimonides, the extent to which it differs from the common *peshiah* theory and whether Maimonides favored the theory of strict liability for the person whose property caused damage. Nonetheless, all agree that Maimonides ascribed great significance to *ownership per se* of the property in torts.

Warhaftig interprets Maimonides radically as departing from the theory of *peshiah*, arguing that not only does Maimonides recognize ownership as a basis for liability for the damages caused by a person's property, but that this theory involving ownership, which Warhaftig attributes to Maimonides, leads us logically to a theory of strict liability.[29]

Even in relation to damages that are caused by the person himself, Warhaftig explains that these two theories – *peshiah* and OSL – are related to the element of liability in tort.[30] According to OSL, the tortfeasor is not liable for the damages only in the event that the contributory negligence of the injured person amounted to 100 percent, for in that case, the latter bears the liability, and he cannot sue another to remedy the situation. In his attempt to base the theory of strict liability as an exclusive regime that applies to all types of tortfeasors, Warhaftig relies on Maimonides' rulings,[31] from which it emerges, in his opinion, that Maimonides adopted the approach of strict liability when the damage was caused by a person's property (*nizkei mamon*), and also when the damage was caused by the person himself, who caused damage to others (*adam ha'mazik*).[32]

We agree with the substance of Warhaftig's argument that Maimonides did not adopt the theory of *peshiah* as an exclusive theory, but we do not agree that Maimonides advocated strict liability in a comprehensive and exclusive manner for all types of tortfeasors.[33] As we shall see later, Maimonides' conception of the element of *peshiah* is more complex, and he does not reject the theory outright, as Warhaftig would claim, but rather refines it and incorporates it as an important, although not exclusive, component in his tort theory. In our view, therefore, Maimonides' approach to tort liability should not be categorized as based on *peshiah* on the one hand, nor on strict liability on the other, even though it contains elements of both.

---

[29] *Ibid.*
[30] *Ibid.* at 222.
[31] *Ibid.* at 224.
[32] WARHAFTIG, *ibid.* mentions two rules from Laws of Wounding and Damaging: 6:1 (a person's liability for damage caused to the property of another), and 1:12 (a person's liability for injury he caused to the body of another). Attribution of the theory of strict liability to Maimonides, at least with respect to damage caused by a person's body, appears in Haut's article, *supra* note 18.
[33] In Chapter 7 we will show that indeed, strict or almost strict liability should be imposed upon a person who causes damage to the property of another. But this is not the case, in our view, when a person injured another, or when the damage was caused by the person's property, for then, as we shall prove, Maimonides adopted a standard of care lower than strict liability (closer to negligence).

It should be mentioned that many of the later authorities (*Aharonim*) who headed the Lithuanian *yeshivot* did not argue that those two theories of tort liability were as radically opposed as Warhaftig claimed. Admittedly, according to some rabbis associated with the *yeshivah* reading, there are two conditions for obligating a person to pay that are accepted by all the commentators and authorities as being cumulative. In order for a person to be liable for damage caused by property, the property that caused the damage had to have belonged to him, and there also had to have been *peshiah* in his guarding of the property. These two cumulative conditions lead the *yeshiva* reading to ask whether it is the failure to guard that engenders the obligation to pay, since the obligation to guard is a function of ownership; or does the obligation to pay stem from the fact that it is the property of the defendant that caused the damage, but if he guarded the property as required he is exempt, and one cannot, therefore, speak of strict liability according to Maimonides, as Warhaftig claims. In other words, this question focuses on which of the two conditions for liability for the damage caused by the defendant's property is the *principal* condition.[34]

C. EXEGETICAL AND CONCEPTUAL DIFFICULTIES OF THE COMMON INTERPRETATION OF MAIMONIDES

1 *Maimonides Did Not Impose Comprehensive Strict Liability on the Tortfeasor*

As noted, in his attempted advocacy of the theory of OSL, Warhaftig relied heavily on Maimonides' choice of words.[35] Warhaftig's conclusion that in Maimonides' view, a person bears strict liability for damage caused by his property is based on an ostensibly surprising ruling by Maimonides. Maimonides rules that placing an animal with a watchman also transfers to the watchman the tort liability in the event that the animal causes damage. Even though watchmen are not the formal owners of the animal, "these individuals assume the owner's responsibilities."[36] However, further in the same ruling Maimonides distinguishes between different cases in which the animal caused damage, and the question is whether the watchmen are indeed always liable, and whether the owner can be held liable when the watchmen are exempt: "When does the above apply? When he did not guard the animal at all. If, however, he guarded the animal in an excellent manner, as

---

[34] See *EVEN HA'AZEL*, *supra* note 20; R. SHIMON SHKOP, *supra* note 21; R. SHMUEL ROZOVSKY *supra* note 21. Later we will attempt to show that like Warhaftig's explanation, this interesting explanation offered by the later authorities cannot withstand criticism.

[35] WARHAFTIG, *supra* note 4, at 218 (indicating that "the best proof of the theory of ownership and the principle of strict liability together can be seen in the following words of Maimonides").

[36] Laws of Property Damages 4:4. The translation is from ELIYAHU TOUGER, *MISHNEH TORAH* (Chabad, Moznaim).

he should, and it got loose and caused damage, the watchman is not liable, and the owners are liable, even if the animal kills a human being."[37]

Many of the commentators on Maimonides were surprised by Maimonides' ruling,[38] which raises an obvious difficulty: if the watchmen guarded the animal in an excellent manner, why is the owner liable? Warhaftig concludes from this ruling that Maimonides adopted the OSL.[39] Accordingly, an owner is liable for damages caused by his animal even if there is no fault on his part: the animal was handed over to the watchmen to be guarded, the watchmen guarded it in an excellent manner, and nevertheless the owner is liable. This outcome, according to Warhaftig, is incomprehensible if *peshiah* is the basis for tort liability, since once the animal was placed with the watchmen, the watchmen assumed the owner's place with respect to the duty to guard and with respect to tort liability. However, adds Warhaftig, this ruling is consistent with the theory of OSL, for according to this theory, the owner of the animal remains its owner even though he has given it to the watchmen, and therefore remains obligated to pay compensation for damage done by his animal due to his ownership *per se*. This was also the explanation given by some later authorities who held that the basis for liability according to Maimonides is ownership.[40]

However, it appears that this explanation is based on an incorrect text of the ruling quoted earlier in this chapter, as printed in the common editions of the *Code*. On the basis of the correct wording of the ruling, as amended by Maimonides himself, not only is there no proof that Maimonides advocated a theory of OSL, but it is very difficult to explain the corrected version according to this theory.

Maimonides himself was asked about the logic of this ruling by the Sages of Lunel (Provence),[41] and he answered that a scribal error had occurred in the copying of the rulings, in that the words "and the owners are liable", which Maimonides attests that he himself inserted as an addendum to his book, were inserted by the copyists in the incorrect place.[42] Following, therefore, is the accurate version of Maimonides' ruling, as corrected by Maimonides himself:

> When a person entrusts his animal to an unpaid watchman or to a paid watchman or to a renter or a borrower, he assumes the position of the owner and if the animal causes damage – the watchman is held liable. When does the above apply? When he did not guard the animal at all. If, however, he guarded the animal in an excellent manner, as he should, and it got loose and caused damage – the watchman is not liable [and the owners, too, are exempt]. And if he guarded the animal in an inferior manner if he is an unpaid watchman – he is exempt, and

---

[37] Ibid.
[38] See, e.g., RA'ABAD, KESSEF MISHNEH, LEHEM MISHNEH on Laws of Property Damages 4:4.
[39] WARHAFTIG, *supra* note 4, at 219.
[40] See e.g., SOLOVEITCHIK, *supra* note 20; WEINBERG, *supra* note 12, 126:3.
[41] See RESP. RAMBAM (Blau edition), no. 433 p. 713.
[42] In his responsum, *ibid.*, Maimonides states that there was a scribal error and that the text should be corrected as indicated earlier.

the owners are liable, even if the animal kills a person; and if he is a paid watchman or a renter or a borrower – he is liable.[43]

The amended version of the ruling makes it clear that if the owner gave his animal to a watchman who guarded it in an excellent manner, as he should, and the animal got loose and caused damage, the watchman is exempt, and neither is the owner liable in this case to pay for the damage caused by his animal. It is therefore clear that this amended version removes the basis for a Maimonidean OSL theory. Nevertheless, it is interesting that many of the earlier and the later authorities posed abundant questions and devised many explanations on the basis of the incorrect version that had been preserved in the manuscripts and made its way into the printed editions of the *Code*. Warhaftig surpassed them all, and surprisingly insisted on perpetuating the incorrect version,[44] from which he sought to adduce strong proof for the ownership theory. But Warhaftig's explanation (and the *yeshivah* reading commentators who commented on the incorrect version) is very problematic in view of Maimonides' express words in his response to the Sages of Lunel[45] stating that the version in circulation was incorrect and should be amended as quoted earlier.[46] According to the amended version of the ruling, a distinction must be drawn between two cases: (1) the owner gave his animal to a paid watchman who "guarded the animal in an excellent manner as he should and it got loose and caused damage – the watchman is not liable", and the owner is not liable in such a case to make compensation for the damage caused by his animal; and (2) The owner gave his animal to an unpaid watchman who guarded it in an inferior manner – the owner

---

[43] The earlier-amended version is according to Maimonides' responsum, as worded in the MISHNEH TORAH, "YAD PESHUTA" edition, NACHUM L. RABINOVITCH ed. (Jerusalem: Maaliyot Press, 2006), at 120, and not the erroneous wording quoted in other printed editions.

[44] Warhaftig mentions Maimonides' response to the Sages of Lunel in which he says that the text in the printed editions is incorrect. Nevertheless, he relied on the interpretation of R. NAHUM ASCH (author of TZIONEI MAHARAN), that the text in the printed editions should not be erased, despite Maimonides' explicit statements, "because in relation to some matters Maimonides in his old age did not remember the source for his words, and those who succeeded him 'found and pointed out the source', but you should still take the original version of Maimonides' text." RABINOVITCH, *supra* note 13, at 72 note 4, very correctly commented: "How far do we go?!," and indeed, Warhaftig's position is very problematic.

[45] See *supra* note 41. Indeed, in MIRKEVET HAMISHNEH (a commentary on Maimonides' *Code*) *ad loc.*, R. Shlomo Mahalma expresses doubts about the authenticity of this responsum by Maimonides, but See R. Prof. Sh. Z. Havlin, *The Attitude to "Questions of Text" in Rabbinic Literature*, BEIT HAVA'AD 5763–2003, who wrote that there is no basis for doubting the authenticity of the responsum.

[46] This emendation was accepted by some of the commentators on Maimonides *ad loc.*: *Kessef Mishneh* (R. Joseph Karo, author of SHULHAN ARUKH), *Lehem Mishneh*, and by some of the commentators on SHULHAN ARUKH: BI'UR HAGRA, HOSHEN MISHPAT 396:18; R. JOSHUA FALK KATZ, SEFER ME'IRAT EINAYIM (a commentary to SHULHAN ARUKH) *ad loc.*, 18. Nevertheless, it should be noted that there are some authorities who stand by the text found in the versions of Maimonides in our hands (and not the corrected text). See, e.g., *Maggid Mishneh, ad loc*. And see additional commentaries in the COLLECTION OF TEXTUAL VARIATIONS, S. Frankel edition (Jerusalem: Yeshivat Ohel Yosef, 1982).

is liable for the damages. But what is the difference between the cases, and what is the basis for tort liability in light of which the ruling in its amended version can be explained? Not only can this ruling not be explained by OSL, but it is even difficult to explain it by the theory of *peshiah*, for in both cases the owner gave the animal to the watchman and it was the latter who guarded the animal in one way or another. From the owner's perspective it is hard to find a difference between the two cases that can lead to him being exempt from payment in the first case, whereas in the second case he will be considered at fault and will be liable for payment.[47] The basis for liability is clearly not ownership *per se*, as Warhaftig argues, for were this so, the owners would have to pay whenever the watchman was exempt from payment, i.e., strict liability.

Indeed, with all due respect, Warhaftig's statement that Maimonides adopted, in principle and comprehensively, an approach that held the tortfeasor to strict liability seems unacceptable. We have seen that many of the leading rabbis of the Lithuanian *yeshivot*, too, did not believe that Maimonides held such a radical view, even though they admitted that he adopted an approach that attributed great importance to the fact of ownership of the property that caused damage. Many talmudic sources point out that Jewish law does not impose strict liability on the owner of property for every tortious event that is caused by the object. As an example we will cite the famous *mishnah*: "If a man brought his flock into an enclosure and shut it in properly and it nevertheless came out and caused damage, he is not liable."[48] Maimonides, too, did not refrain from citing this *mishnah* as law: "If one brings sheep into an enclosure and secures them with a gate able to withstand a normal wind and a sheep gets out and does damage, the owner is exempt."[49]

If Warhaftig's claim that the owner of the property bears strict liability for damages it caused is correct, why is the owner not held liable when his sheep caused damage, even when he is guarding his property himself?![50]

A similar picture emerges from other rulings that exempt the owners of objects from damages caused by those objects. Thus, for example, in the following ruling: "If one's jar [full of water] is broken in the public domain and a person [the injured person] slips on the spilt water or is injured by the shards of the jar, the owner [of the jar – the tortfeasor] is legally exempt because he is the victim of circumstances beyond his control."[51] Here too, one may ask why strict liability is not imposed on the owner of the jar that caused the damage?

---

[47] The basis of liability lies in another element to be discussed *infra* in Chapter 5. It is based on a special criterion of tort liability which we call "the effective ability to control test" (EAC), a test that is substantively different from all the tests that have been suggested to date in the common interpretation of Maimonides and the Talmud.
[48] M *Bava Kamma* 6:1.
[49] *See* Laws of Property Damages 4:1.
[50] As Wygoda, *supra* note 23, asked in relation to Warhaftig's theory.
[51] Laws of Property Damages 13:7.

Warhaftig and Haut's[52] argument that Maimonides tended to the theory of strict liability in relation to damages caused by the person himself does not hold up.[53]

Similar to what was said at the beginning of this chapter regarding the proclivity of many modern scholars to explain the basis for tort liability in Jewish law (*peshiah* or negligence) in keeping with the common legal approaches in their times, particularly in the nineteenth and the beginning of the twentieth centuries, it is definitely conceivable that the attempt – unsuccessful, in our opinion – of Warhaftig and Haut to attribute to Maimonides a theory of strict liability is connected to the time, the context and the purpose in relation to which these two studies were conducted.[54]

2 Maimonides' Use of the Term Peshiah in Different Places

Even if we assume that the theory of ownership is rational and coherent (and we do not believe it is), it is very difficult to accept the position that the basis of tort liability

---

[52] Haut discusses several of Maimonides' rulings in *Some Aspects of Absolute Liability*, supra note 18, from which he draws conclusions about the existence of absolute/strict liability in Maimonides' approach; however, the author presents only those rulings dealing with the liability of a person who himself caused damage to another, and not rulings that deal with damages caused by property or with a person who causes bodily injury to another.

[53] As we will see at length in Chapter 7, which presents additional relevant sources, a careful analysis of Maimonides' writings reveals that Maimonides in no way advocated a comprehensive unitary standard of care, namely, strict liability, as Warhaftig claims, in relation to all kinds of damages; rather, he supported a differential standard of care whereby the level of liability depends on the kind of damage caused, on who caused the damage, and to whom the damage was caused. Additional relevant sources that contradict Warhaftig's theory will be presented *infra*, section 3.

[54] The work was done in the second half of the twentieth century, and what these two scholars had in mind were, of course, the modern tort theories that developed in the twentieth century imposing strict liability on the person causing the damage, for which the authors attempt to find parallels in Jewish law. Moreover, one of the objectives of Warhaftig's research was the absorption of ideas from Jewish law into the modern positive law of the State of Israel. Zerah Warhaftig (1906–2002) was a jurist and a Religious-Zionist political leader in Israel, one of the signatories to the Declaration of Independence and an important legislator who sought to integrate the principles of Jewish law into the secular Israeli law. It is important to understand the context in which Warhaftig's study on the basis of tort liability was first published in 1976. This study, like much of Warhaftig's research, was conducted in the course of his work in the field of legislation in the State of Israel. And indeed, at the beginning of his study of the basis for liability for damages in Jewish law, Warhaftig describes the tendency of modern tort law was to move over to a theory of strict liability. In this context Warhaftig refers to the Compensation for the Victims of Road Accidents Law that was enacted in Israel in 1975, according to which the liability of the person causing the accident due to use of a motorized vehicle will be strict and complete, and it is irrelevant if there was or was not fault on the part of the injuring party and if there was or was not fault or contributory fault on the part of others. Against this background, in Warhaftig's attempt in his research to prove that in Jewish law too, and in particular, in Maimonides' approach, there are echoes of a tort approach that imposes strict liability on the person causing harm irrespective of fault, which he calls the theory of OSL. Haut's attempt in his article of 1989 to identify various aspects of absolute/strict liability in Jewish law, particularly in Maimonides' writing, must also be understood in light of the fact that he was an American scholar who wished to find a parallel between Jewish law and the American Common law.

according to Maimonides is explained purely by means of that theory of ownership, unconnected in any way to the question of whether the owner of the property was at fault or was negligent in guarding the property that caused damage. This is because in various places in the Book of Torts of the *Code*, Maimonides does use the talmudic term *peshiah*.[55] In several places Maimonides even explains that imposing or not imposing tort liability is connected to the existence or absence of the element of fault and negligence in the conduct of the person causing the damage, and he uses the express term *peshiah*.[56]

Indeed, there is no doubt that according to the *yeshivah* reading of many of the earlier-mentioned later authorities,[57] and as opposed to Warhaftig's explanation, Maimonides, too, integrates the element of *peshiah* into his theory, at least as a marginal condition, alongside the element of ownership. However, the method of the later authorities, too, appears to have several very problematic aspects. Regarding the rationale: it is simpler to explain that it is negligence (*peshiah*) in guarding that engenders the liability for compensation, for in that case it seems reasonable to impose tort liability on the person who was at fault, due to his fault. However, if the lack of guarding is only a marginal condition of the liability, as the later authorities argue, and the imposition of liability arises due to the very fact that it was the owner's property that caused the damage, what justification is there for this imposition of liability?

From a conceptual point of view, it is easier to understand Warhaftig's explanation, according to which the gap between the theories of *peshiah* and ownership is clear and significant, particularly in view of the obvious connection that he makes – and which to him is coherent – between the ownership theory and the theory of strict liability. Nevertheless, it is clear that Warhaftig's explanation, insofar as it touches upon Maimonides' writings, does not accurately and completely reflect Maimonides' theory. On the other hand, according to the said *yeshivah* reading of the later authorities the two theories appear to resemble each other very closely, to the extent that it is difficult to find a practical difference between them. The conceptual-analytical difficulties of the approach of the later authorities arise even in the absence of a satisfactory explanation for the way in which the two said parameters – ownership of the property and negligence (*peshiah*) in guarding – are supposed to integrate into Maimonides' theory.

Admittedly, some of the later authorities were aware of this problem. There were those who suggested that the two theories are differentiated by some halakhic

---

[55] On use of the term "*peshiah*" see, e.g., Laws of Property Damages 2:15; 3:11. Additional rules will be mentioned later.
[56] In the singular, *pash'a* – was at fault, and in the plural, *pash'u* – were at fault. See esp. Laws of Property Damages 4:7; 12:7; Laws of Wounding and Damaging 1:11. Other rules in which the term "*peshiah*" appears in the context of torts: Laws of Wounding and Damaging 7:18; Laws of Leasing and Hiring 2:3.
[57] *Supra*, end of section B.

ramifications. Thus, for example, some held that the two theories differ in relation to the question of who bears the burden of proof in the case of a doubt: must the injured party bring proof that the owner of the property that injured him did not guard his property properly, or must the owner of the property bring proof that he guarded the property as required and therefore he should be exempt?[58] If the basis for liability is the fact that his property caused the damage, and the element of lack of fault (*peshiah*) is only a marginal condition and a reservation to the obligation, i.e., where the owner of the property was not at fault in his guarding of the property he must be exempted, then in order to be exempt, the owner must bring proof that he guarded the property as required. If, however, it is the element of *peshiah* itself that is the basis for the liability to pay compensation, then the injured party must prove that the owner was at fault in his guarding in order that he be obligated to pay. However, this difference appears to be only procedural, and we are looking for a more substantive explanation.

It would seem that the inclination of later authorities to present two possible different explanations for liability for property damage is the result of the classic *yeshivah* method developed primarily by the leading rabbis of the Lithuanian *yeshivot* in the nineteenth century, especially members of the Brisker,[59] or Soloveitchik, school (related to the founder of the Brisker school, R. Hayyim Soloveitchik, 1853–1918). Let us take a brief look at the main features of the Lithuanian *yeshivah* method, with an emphasis on the Brisker school, and see how this method finds expression in the Lithuanian rabbis' *yeshivah* reading of Maimonides' position regarding the basis for the tort obligation.

Many of the works of the Briskers are structured as a commentary on the *Code*, and the Briskers set out to "defend" the Maimonidean approach by introducing a distinction – often structured as a two-sided query – that refines the traditional understanding of the legal rule under review.[60] The query often demonstrates that there are two ways to understand the mechanism through which the legal rule is said to work. The Briskers then show how Maimonides and his critics disagree over the precise construction of the legal mechanism, often through a discussion of how the various sub-rules interact in a given case.[61] The name given to this

---

[58] See SHMUEL ROZOVSKY, *supra* note 21, who cited a dispute on this matter between the books *PNEI YEHOSHUA* and *HAZON ISH*.

[59] The Brisker method was described by NORMAN SOLOMON, THE ANALYTIC MOVEMENT – HAYYIM SOLOVEITCHIK AND HIS CIRCLE (Atlanta: Scholars Press, 1993). Solomon, at 86–89, describes the "analytical positivism and the Soloveitchik school" and argues that Hart's five characteristics of positivist analytic jurisprudence (H.L.A. Hart, *Legal Positivism and the Separation of Law and Morals*, 71 HARV. L. REV. 593, 601–02 note 25 (1958) display similarities to the Brisker/ Soloveitchik school. Chaim Saiman showed that in the closing decades of the nineteenth century the Brisker school, especially R. Hayyim, "offered a conceptual and 'scientific' vision of *halakhah*" that is a "form of nineteenth-century legal scientism." See Chaim Saiman, *Legal Theology: The Turn to Conceptualism in Nineteenth-Century Jewish Law*, 20 J. OF L. & RELIGION 39, 40 (2006).

[60] Saiman, *ibid.* at 50.

[61] *Ibid.* at 51.

two-sided query is *hakira* [literally: "investigation"], and while the Briskers were not the first rabbinic writers to use this term, they popularized it and made it a central feature of their analysis.[62]

Indeed, one of the main tools of analytical study in the *yeshivah* is the *hakira*. In *yeshivah* terms, a *hakira* assumes that there are two possible explanations of a specific rule, and we must examine which of the two is consistent with the details. A basic assumption that underlies a *hakira* of this type is that only one of the two explanations is correct. In modern terms, this is a monistic, dichotomous approach. The *hakira* of the *yeshivah* reading of Maimonides – most of the exponents of which were schooled in the Brisker method[63] – regarding the two possible ways of explaining the basis for tort liability ("*peshiah*" or "his property that caused damage"), and Maimonides' identification with only one of the possibilities, constitutes a clear expression of the dichotomous *yeshivah* method in the style of Brisk. But this method is not problem-free,[64] and the *yeshivah* reading of Maimonides' approach is not the only possible one. It should therefore come as no surprise that we have not found even one classical commentator on Maimonides from earlier periods (twelfth through eighteenth centuries) who attributed to him the theory of ownership specifically, as opposed to the theory of *peshiah*. In our view, this is because this common interpretation of the rabbis of the Lithuanian *yeshivot* is the necessary outcome of their method, which led them to adopt a monistic approach that favors one of these two – *peshiah* or ownership – over the other. But it does not necessarily reflect the position of Maimonides himself, as we will argue in the next section, whose approach was definitely not monistic, but rather, combined different elements without ranking one above the other.

3 The Theory of Ownership Contradicts Various Rulings in the Code

Another thorny problem facing those who attribute the ownership theory (Warhaftig) or the theory of property that caused damage (the *yeshivah* reading) to

---

[62] Ibid.

[63] See their writings, *supra* notes 20–21.

[64] One contemporary scholar has criticized the dichotomous *yeshivah* methodology with respect to the foundation for liability in property damages. Michael Avraham, *On the Nature of the Analytical "Hakirot"*, 3 MEISHARIM 61 (2004) (Heb.), can be viewed at www.yhy.co.il/content/view/413/168/lang,he. According to Avraham's view, there are not two explanations of which only one is correct; rather, there is a third explanation – the correct one – and it is constructed from a logical amalgamation of the first two explanations. In other words, the *peshiah* theory and the ownership theory should not be viewed as two separate theories, but as two theories that come together and complement each other. This exegetical approach seems to us to be more reasonable than the common dichotomous approach expounded by the later authorities, but it too is flawed, for it does not explain exactly the role of each component – *peshiah*/negligence and ownership of the property – and the manner in which the two components complement each other within the normative halakhic tort framework in general, and in the tort theory of Maimonides in particular.

Maimonides as the basis for liability for damage to property is the fact that these theories are inconsistent with various rulings in the *Code*. In the *Code*, Maimonides exempts the owner from liability for damages caused by his property or holds a person who cannot be considered the formal owner of the property that caused the damage liable. We will cite several typical examples. The first is the "slave example."

Maimonides rules, following the Talmud, that in the event that a slave caused damage, his master cannot be held liable for this damage. The explanation for this ruling is noteworthy:

> [F]or one is not liable for damage done by his slaves, although they are his chattels [and a man is liable for damage caused by his property], seeing that they have minds of their own and he is unable to keep watch over them. Moreover, should he be annoyed at his master, a slave might go and set fire to a wheat stack worth a thousand dinar or do similar damage.[65]

Several of the later halakhic authorities struggled to explain Maimonides' ruling, and claimed that it is inconsistent with the *yeshivah* reading of his words at the beginning of the Book of Torts from which, as noted, later authorities and other scholars derived that the basis for liability according to Maimonides is that the defendant is the owner of the property that caused the damage. If, some asked, it was indeed the case that liability was imposed on the owner for the damage caused by his property due to the fact of his ownership of that property, as those later authorities and scholars argue, is there justification for not holding the owner liable for damage caused by his slaves?[66] From Maimonides' words, however, the law is clearly that the master is exempt from liability, even though the slave is his property, for the master is not able to watch over him.

We now proceed to examples of cases in which the ownership theory attributed to Maimonides does not accommodate various types of tortfeasors who are liable for the damages caused by different objects, even though they are not the owners of those objects.

According to Jewish law there are different types of property damages for which liability is incurred. Clearly the liability for damage caused by animals, with which Maimonides deals in the ruling at the beginning of Laws of Property Damages, can usually be properly explained by the ownership theory – the owner of the animal is liable for the damages caused by the animal.[67] According to the *halakhah*, however, a person is liable for the damage caused by objects that are not necessarily owned by

---

[65] Laws of Theft 1:9.
[66] See, e.g., EVEN HA'AZEL on *Hilkhot Nizkei Mamon* 1:1, no. 15; WEINBERG, *supra* note 12, at 128 note 7.
[67] And indeed, in relation to damages caused by animals as well, there are cases in which even a person who is not the formal owner is held liable. An example of this is Maimonides' earlier-mentioned ruling (Laws of Property Damages 4:4), whereby "the watchman takes the place of the owner." However, it would appear that this does not constitute a significant difficulty for those who attribute the ownership theory to Maimonides, for they can say that watchmen

him. Thus, for example, if a person makes an opening in a fence to allow the animal of another to pass through, he must pay for the damage caused by the animal,[68] even though he is not the owner of the animal. Similarly, a person must pay for the damage caused by a pit that he dug, and Maimonides rules that liability to pay compensation falls upon the digger of the pit, even though the pit is not situated on private property but rather, in the public domain.[69] Note that he is held liable not only when he dug the pit himself but also when the pit appeared by itself, or when it was dug by an animal but the person did not cover it; then the person who did not cover the pit is liable for the damage it causes.[70] The same applies to a person who lights a fire and the fire spreads and causes damage, whether the person lit the fire in the field of another[71] or whether he lit it on his own property but did not keep it away from neighboring property as he ought to have done, and it spread and caused damage.[72] Not only is the person who lights the fire liable for the damage it caused, but Maimonides also rules as follows:

> If one's courtyard catches fire, and a fence falls down independently of the fire and it spreads into the next courtyard, the rule is that the owner is liable if he could have restored the fallen fence but failed to do so. This is analogous to one's ox getting out and causing damage, in which case the owner is liable, for he ought to have taken care of it but failed to do so.[73]

The analogy drawn by Maimonides between the liability of a person whose courtyard caught fire and the fire spread and caused damage in another courtyard, and that of the owner of an ox which went out and gored is not clear under the theory of ownership. True, the ox has an owner who should be held liable, but does the fire that caused damage have an owner? In cases of damage caused by a pit or by fire, it is difficult to speak of "ownership"; why therefore is the person who sets the fire or the person who digs the pit or who did not cover the pit liable for the damage caused by these things?

Several of the rabbis of the Lithuanian *yeshivot* strove hard to answer these questions. R. Shimon Shkop introduces an interesting, original innovation in defining ownership in tort as inhering in the person who created the damage,[74] and he compares this to the laws of patents and intellectual property that have developed in Western legal systems, particularly over the last two hundred years, which confer ownership of a new creation or invention on the creator or inventor.

---

become quasi-owners due to the contractual connection that they have to the object of their watch. And cf. *Even Ha'azel, Ibid.* at 14.
[68] Laws of Property Damages 4:2.
[69] *Ibid.* 12:1.
[70] *Ibid.* 12:3.
[71] *Ibid.* 14:1.
[72] *Ibid.* 14:2.
[73] *Ibid.* 14:4.
[74] Commentary of R. Shimon Yehuda Hacohen Shkop, *Bava Kamma* 1.

In a similar fashion, says R. Shkop, the person who created the obstacle and the pit and who lit the fire is the owner for the purpose of torts. This is an innovation which greatly extends the concept of ownership beyond the simple, common meaning in the Jewish sources,[75] and it is therefore not surprising that R. Shkop referred to the modern, Western "laws of the nations." Undoubtedly this innovation is beset by legal and analytical difficulties in relation to the problematic analogy from the laws of (intellectual) property to tort law. Indeed it appears to us that R. Shkop was pushed to propose an innovative – and problematic – interpretation (that reaches the distant realms of "the laws of the nations") due to the conceptual-legal difficulty involved in explaining the laws of the pit and of fire according to the common theory of property ownership.[76] But his explanation does not have any basis in either the talmudic or the Maimonidean tort theory. The idea of ownership of the person who created the damage just does not seem to fit to the major patterns and concepts of Jewish private law.

4 The Problem with Finding a Convincing Rationale for the Ownership Theory

In our view, the most serious problem with the ownership theory, according to which the basis for holding a person liable for damage caused by his property is his very ownership of that property, lies in the fact that it is difficult to establish its rationale, as opposed to the logical and comprehensible theory of *peshiah*. According to the theory of *peshiah*, the basis for tort liability lies in the culpable conduct of the person causing the damage, whose guarding was faulty and consequently damage which he ought to have foreseen was caused; this – as most scholars argue – is very clearly comparable to the common rationale for the model of negligence in the common law systems. But what is the rationale underlying the ownership theory? Most of the later authorities did not even bother to explain this, going no further than simply to present the fact of a person's property having caused the damage as the basis for obligating him, as the owner of the damaging object, to pay compensation. This is a formalistic, axiomatic determination, the underlying

---

[75] We did find that in the context of damages caused by a pit, the scriptural wording was: "[t]he owner of the pit shall make it good; he shall give money unto the owner of them," (Exodus 21:34) and Rashi comments there: "This means the one who occasioned the damage. Although the pit was not his – for he dug it in the public thoroughfare – Scripture regards him as its 'owner' insofar as he becomes responsible for the damage caused by it" (Rashi based himself on Bava Kamma 29b). However, this would not seem to mean true ownership of the pit; rather, the person is liable in respect of the pit as if he were its owner, as implied by the Talmud (*ibid.*), that a pit that is not in a person's possession but Scripture treated it as if it were in his possession. This is the reason that R. Shimon Shkop drew an analogy from the laws of intellectual property. However, one may argue that *ba'al* in the biblical Hebrew source was not in fact restricted to – if it at all meant – "owner" in the modern sense.

[76] This theory was accepted by R. Shkop himself, *supra* note 74.

logic of which is difficult to fathom. One must really ask why ownership *per se* should justify imposing tort liability in the absence of fault on the part of the owner? Why is it sufficient that an object belonging to the defendant caused damage in order to obligate him to pay compensation?

The *yeshivah* reading of Maimonides' approach to the basis for tort liability posed many problems, and later authorities struggled to find its rationale;[77] several of them were not prepared to accept a rationale based on ownership theory.[78] The difficulty in finding a convincing rationale for the tort liability being due to ownership is so serious that it led one authority to reject outright the famous *hakira* of the later authorities, owing to the lack of logic on the ownership side of the *hakira*. This authority is of the opinion that there is only one plausible explanation of the basis for tort liability (*peshiah*), i.e., the person was at fault in guarding the objects for which he is responsible.[79] The difficulty in understanding the rationale underlying the ownership theory as compared to the simple rationale of the theory of *peshiah* increases in light of the narrow manner in which some later authorities explained the difference between these two systems. As will be recalled, they explained that even according to the approach whereby the basis of tort obligation is the fact that it was the owner's property that caused damage, the absence of *peshiah* in guarding is a marginal condition of the obligation. But if the element of *peshiah* is a necessary and obvious component of the tort liability, is there also a need for the element of ownership? What is there in the element of ownership that is not present in the element of *peshiah*, and what is its role in establishing the basis for liability?

It is difficult to find a clear, uniform answer to these questions, but several later authorities and contemporary scholars have made various, interesting proposals, some of them extremely creative.

We have already discussed R. Shimon Shkop's innovative proposal whereby he defines ownership in tort as inhering in the person who created the damage. Moreover, R. Shkop's definition of ownership constitutes a departure from the common definition of this term in the halakhic sources, and there is no support for it in Maimonides' writings either.[80] It also raises the conceptual and analytical difficulties entailed by the problematic comparison that he draws between Jewish tort law and modern intellectual property law. However, even if we accept the proposal whereby the person who created the damage is its owner, the major

---

[77] See e.g., EVEN HA'AZEL, *supra* note 21; SHMUEL ROZOVSKY, *supra* note 21.
[78] See e.g. R. ELIEZER MENACHEM SHACH, AVI HA'EZRI, HILKHOT NIZKEI MAMON 1:1, who explained that according to Maimonides' approach too, the basis of the liability was the theory of *peshiah* and not the theory of ownership.
[79] R. YEKUTIEL YEHUDAH HALBERSTAM, DIVREI YATZIV, HOSHEN MISHPAT 71–72 (Jerusalem: Sefah Haim ed., 2001). R. Halberstam was the rabbi of Sanz.
[80] And indeed R. Shkop himself, in his Commentary (*supra* note 74), did not cite any ruling from the *Code* to support what he said.

question remains: R. Shkop's proposal explains, at most, why the person creating the obstacle is considered the owner, but it does not explain why, as the owner, he should be held liable for the damage resulting from that obstacle.

There are other explanations for the ownership theory.

According to Warhaftig's approach, "the right of ownership brings with it the duty concerning the risks associated with ownership. The owner of the property enjoys it, but must also bear the burden of losses that his property causes to others,"[81] or in the words of R. Weinberg, "at the basis of this responsibility is the view that a person's property is not only for his pleasure and use, but it also imposes obligations on him, and in this case, an obligation to pay for damages."[82]

Even though Warhaftig and R. Weinberg's explanation seems preferable to that of R. Shkop, it still does not explain the jurisprudential theory that underlies their axiomatic assumption that the right of ownership also imposes various obligations on the owner, including the obligation to pay for damage caused by his property.

Warhaftig[83] compares this jurisprudential theory to the business risk theory that developed in France at the beginning of the twentieth century, whereby the owner of the business, factory or plant must factor into his business expenses the cost of damage caused by his business to others through no fault on his part. Calculation of the costs of running a business must be based on the fact that every growth in business activity increases the risk of causing harm to others, and liability for compensating the injured party must figure in the anticipated costs of that activity. In modern terms, we would call this risk management – a business that wishes to make a profit and which also has the potential to cause damage must calculate income as against anticipated costs in order to calculate the anticipated profits and *inter alia* to determine, accordingly, the cost of the product (obviously, taking into account other parameters such as competition, market conditions and so forth). Those anticipated costs include the compensation that a potential causer of damage will be required to pay as a result of the damage he causes. In the modern age, the cost of insurance covers the cost of damages in most businesses, and the risk management undertaken by modern sophisticated concerns conduct must examine anticipated costs, including the cost of damages. This includes damage caused by workers of the potential tortfeasor, when the damage is caused in the framework of the employment of that worker and there has been no deviation from the authority granted to him by the employer. One utilitarian rationale that can be presented for holding a person liable for damages that his worker caused to others, or even to himself, is that the worker can be regarded as the instrument through which the employer profits, and the business is therefore dependent on the worker. Hence, the employer must also pay for the damages that the worker causes, and not simply enjoy

---

[81] WARHAFTIG, *supra* note 4, at 216.
[82] WEINBERG, *supra* note 12.
[83] WARHAFTIG, *supra* note 4.

the benefits and profits from his work. This is quite similar to the rationale presented by Warhaftig and Weinberg.[84]

The business risk theory is applicable and certainly suited to the economic thinking of the twentieth century, in the wake of the industrial and consumer revolutions that saw the construction of huge plants for mass production, the operation of which necessarily caused great damage to the environment. It is difficult, however, to attribute a similar theory to the talmudic sages who were active two thousand years ago, or to Maimonides, who wrote his works eight hundred years ago in a commercial and economic reality that was much more primitive, in which those causing the damage were usually the farmer, the blacksmith, the wagoner, or an individual craftsman, rather than the huge factories that exist today.

It will be stressed that we are certainly not opposed to comparing the tort theory of Maimonides to contemporary economic theories, and we do so throughout this book. Indeed, we, too, will attempt *infra* to explain Maimonides' approach according to modern theories of scholars in the field of law and economics. To do so it will be necessary to show that the lines of thought and the rationales are similar. This was not done by Warhaftig, who simply mentioned the modern theory ("theory of business risk"), without showing that its elements also existed in the writings of Maimonides and other halakhic authorities.

The great difficulty in finding a satisfactory explanation for the *yeshivah* reading led one contemporary scholar, Michael Avraham, to despair of finding the basis on the purely jurisprudential level.[85] He therefore proposed that we examine this position on meta-halakhic, and possibly even metaphysical, planes. He proposed two directions for explaining the ownership theory as the basis of tort liability: one is that in fact, the ox itself that caused the damage has an "obligation" to pay, and when the ox has an owner, that obligation is assigned to the owner. The other explanation is that there is a metaphysical (and not purely legal) relationship between a person and his property: the property is part, or is in the peripheral circle, of the person himself, and it does not simply "belong" to him on the legal plane. For this reason, a person is liable to pay for the damage caused by his property, just as he is liable to pay for damage caused by his body.

Support for the assumption on which the first explanation is based, i.e. that the *halakhah*, in principle, imposes tort liability on the offending animal itself, can certainly be found in various scriptural,[86] talmudic and post-talmudic sources. Some

---

[84] WARHAFTIG, *ibid.*; WEINBERG, *supra* note 12. And *cf.* Tony Honoré, *The Morality of Tort Law*, in PHILOSOPHICAL FOUNDATIONS OF TORT LAW 73, 94 (David G. Owen ed., 1995) ("We are responsible for the outcome of our conduct (outcome-responsibility) ... a just distribution of risks requires us to make good the harm our conduct causes to others in return to the benefit and credit that accrues to us").

[85] Michael Avraham, *On Liability for Compensation for Property that Caused Damage*, MIS-HPETEI YISRAEL – DINE NEZIKIN (Shlomo Grintz ed., 2003) (Heb.).

[86] For a scholarly summary of the subject of the liability of the owners of animals in biblical and Jewish sources as compared to other historical sources (Christian, Roman and others),

early authorities gave this as the reason for stoning the ox that killed a person,[87] and this approach is backed by various talmudic[88] and possibly even scriptural[89] sources. Indeed, even though imposing tort liability on animals seems strange and unacceptable in the world of modern rational Western jurisprudence, such an approach is not strange to positions that may be discerned in various sources of Jewish law (and other ancient legal systems),[90] and it may even explain certain talmudic passages. Nevertheless, because our concern is to explain Maimonides' tort theory, we must always bear in mind what Maimonides wrote in the chapter explaining the reasons for tort law in the *Guide*,[91] and in this context it is sufficient to quote his well-known statement opposing the approach whereby the ox that killed a person is stoned as a punishment to the ox itself: "The killing of an animal that has killed a human being is not a punishment to the animal, as the dissenters[92] insinuate against us, but it is a fine imposed on the owner of that animal."[93]

In view of Maimonides' clear rejection of the criminal liability of the ox for the damage it has caused, Avraham's explanation of the *yeshivah* reading imposing liability on a person for damage caused by his property as a possible explanation of Maimonides' stance must be dismissed, even if it is capable of rebutting the position of other authorities.

The second explanation proposed by Abraham assumes that there is a metaphysical, and not solely legal, relationship between the person and his property, and the person is liable for all damage that his immediate environment – that which is considered part of him – does to another. Avraham suggests that the closest circle around a person is his body, and he is therefore liable, even in situations of unavoidable mishap (*ones*). The second closest circle surrounding a person is his property, and therefore if his property caused damage, he is liable to pay; here, however, he is not liable in cases of unavoidable mishap, and if he kept proper watch over his property he is exempt, for this periphery is more remote than his own person. Even though this explanation is interesting and original, and support for it may possibly be found in extra-halakhic, non-rational sources such as

---

See: Bernard S. Jackson, *Liability for Animals: An Historico-Structural Comparison*, 24(3) INT. J. FOR THE SEMIOTICS OF L. 259 (2011) (hereinafter: Jackson 2011).

[87] See Nahmanides' *Commentary to Genesis* 9:5; SEFER HAHINUKH Precept 52; *Hagahot Harashash* on Bava Kamma 45:1, s.v. *afilu*.

[88] See ALBECK's proofs, *supra* note 4, at 128–130.

[89] In Genesis 9:5, it is written: "And surely your blood of your lives will I require; at the hand of every beast will I require it…" Nahmanides' commentary on this verse is well known: he remarks that according to the literal scriptural meaning it would appear that the animal is responsible for spilling the person's blood and it is therefore punished.

[90] Jackson 2011, *supra* note 86.

[91] *Guide* 3:40. Extensive analysis of this chapter of the *Guide* will appear in Chapters 3–5.

[92] The Schwartz edition, *ibid.* note 12, cites Munk and Pines, according to whom the reference was to the Karaites. The Karaitic proclivity for interpreting Scripture according to its literal meaning, namely, that the ox that kills is punished, is well known.

[93] *Ibid.* p. 575, Schwartz edition.

the Kabbalah and Hassidism, it is very distant from the normal patterns of halakhic thought. In any case, it is difficult to believe that Maimonides would have accepted this explanation as the basis for tort liability for damage to property, since Maimonides is known as the absolute rationalist, who strove "to bring the laws close to the intellect,"[94] and he does not hesitate to vehemently reject halakhic stances that are not rational, nor to erase them from his books or replace them with other approaches.[95]

In our view, none of the earlier-mentioned explanations of Maimonides' approach – some of which are rather contrived – provide solid and convincing theoretical insights that clarify what exactly is the basis of liability for damages in general and for property damages in particular, and why Maimonides departed from the common theory of *peshiah* that was dominant in talmudic and post-talmudic sources. Most of these explanations encounter great difficulty in justifying the various rulings in the *Code* (in which Maimonides enunciates rules without explanation) that appear to contradict the substantiated explanations of the ownership theory; hence the great confusion in explaining Maimonides' method.[96]

Most importantly, although the explanations offered by Warhaftig and by rabbis of recent generations are intriguing, they do not reflect Maimonides' approach in light of his explicit statement in the *Guide*,[97] which these scholars and rabbis appear to have ignored.

If we wish to find a convincing rationale for Maimonides' approach, it will be necessary to analyze more deeply and more carefully his general theory of torts, as emerges from all of his various works – assuming, as we do, that Maimonides indeed did not adopt the theory of *peshiah* (as an exclusive basis), but rather, sought to base tort liability on an alternative rationale. But this alternative rationale is not one of the rationales of the ownership theory attributed to him – wrongly, in our opinion – by later authorities and scholars. So what is this alternative rationale? A first step towards its exposition will be taken near the end of this chapter by means of a new, careful examination of the first ruling in the Laws of Property Damages.

---

[94] Resp. Rambam, *supra* note 41, no. 222.
[95] Twersky already pointed out that Maimonides includes among the objectives of his *magnum opus*, the *Code*, the education the masses and eradication of superstitious beliefs from amongst the vulgar people, for they too are forbidden to hold such beliefs: See Twersky, *supra* note 1, at 77–79. Yaakov Levinger argued that Maimonides omitted or changed the reasoning for rules cited in the Talmud insofar as they were incompatible with his rational-scientific-philosophical approach. See Yaakov Levinger, Maimonides as Philosopher and Decisor 100–111 (Jerusalem: Mossad Bialik, 1989) (Heb.). For a broader discussion of this topic, see Yaakov Levinger, Oral Law in Maimonides' Thought 92–155 (Jerusalem: Magnes Press, 1965) (Heb.) (hereinafter: Levinger 1965).
[96] To illustrate this see *Even Ha'azel*, *supra* note 21. Even though the author, R. Meltzer, is of the opinion that in principle, the basis of liability according to Maimonides is "his property caused damage" (the ownership theory), he struggles to explain, in light of this theory, several of Maimonides' rulings that appear to contradict this rationale.
[97] 3:40.

D. DIFFICULTIES IN UNDERSTANDING SOME ELEMENTS
OF TORT LIABILITY MENTIONED IN THE CODE

The Book of Torts in the *Code* contains many rulings, most of which are based on the Talmud but some of which were refashioned by Maimonides and reflect his particular approach to torts. Quite a few of these rulings refer to additional important elements that impact on tort liability (over and above the elements mentioned earlier). Several rulings aroused great interest amongst the Maimonidean commentators and scholars, who sought an explanation for rulings which seem, at least at first glance, to require explaining either because they are difficult to understand according to both of the common theories – *peshiah* and ownership – or because they deviate to some extent from what appears in the talmudic sources. We will briefly discuss some examples of these questionable rulings. In order to resolve the difficulties, a deep understanding of Maimonides' theory of torts, in all its aspects, is necessary, and we attempt to acquire this understanding in the following chapters.

1 *Rulings that Are Difficult to Interpret According to Either Ownership or Fault-Based Theories*

In Section C.3, we dealt with rulings in the *Code* that are difficult to explain under the ownership theory, but simple under the theory of *peshiah*. However, there are quite a few rulings in the *Code* that are difficult to explain under either theory. In this section we will discuss two typical examples, and further examples will be mentioned in later sections.

The first example is the primacy of place accorded by Maimonides to a person's *intention* to cause damage as the basis for liability for damages caused due to a person breaching a fence that prevented his neighbor's animal from getting loose, and as a result the animal strayed and caused damage to others. Maimonides distinguishes between two situations in relation to this matter: "If one breaks down a fence enclosing his neighbor's animal so that it gets out and causes damage, the rule is as follows: If the fence is strong and firm he is liable."[98]

Maimonides ruled that a person who breaches the fence of his neighbor must pay for the damage caused by the animal (belonging to the neighbor, not to the person who broke down the fence) that got out, if it got out by itself. However, this was not how he ruled in the case of brigands who breached the fence: in that case, the law is that the brigands are not liable for the damages caused by the animal that got out, unless the brigands led the animal out themselves – only then will they be liable.[99] Many of the classical Maimonidean commentators struggled to explain the difference between the two situations, in which the actions of the persons causing the

---

[98] Laws of Property Damages 4:2.
[99] *Ibid.* 4:1.

damage were identical: they broke open the fence, following which the animal went out by itself and caused damage: why is the regular person who breached the fence liable in this case, but the brigand who did so is exempt?[100]

This question was posed by Maimonides himself. In his responsum, Maimonides resolves the difficulty by means of a distinction between a person who intends to steal and one who intends to cause damage:

> There is a great difference between brigands who breached the enclosure and a person who breached his neighbor's fence enclosing his animal. For in the case of the brigands, it was *their intention to steal* the animal, and therefore as long as they did not take it out of the owner's domain, they are not liable and [the damage] was not done within their own domain, but if they led it out it is done within their own domain and they are liable for the damages; but if they left it there they did not cause the damage *that they intended to cause*, which is the theft, and they are therefore exempt. But one who breaches a fence enclosing his neighbor's animal – *his intention is not to steal* – and what he intended only was that the animal should go out and cause damage, and that the owner will be held liable for the damage, and therefore he [the one who breaches a fence] is liable for that damage like any other tortfeasor. And this is the difference between a brigand and a person breaching the fence of his neighbor, and all of this is correct, and is based on the fundamental principles of law.[101]

Maimonides' responsum in the matter of the brigands will be analyzed in depth in the following chapters; for our purposes here, we will simply mention that not only is the basis for liability that Maimonides emphasizes, i.e., the *intention* of the person causing the damage, incompatible with the ownership theory – according to which the person breaching the fence ought to have been exempt since he is not the owner of the animal – but it is also incompatible with the theory of *peshiah*, for according to that theory, emphasizes Albeck, "[p]ayment of compensation is not dependent on the culpability and the intentions of the tortfeasor."[102]

---

[100] See commentaries of Ra'abad, *Bi'urei Hamaggid Mishneh* and *Migdal Oz ad loc.* Following them were many others who discussed this topic.

[101] RESP. RAMBAM, (Fraiman edition), no. 339.

[102] ALBECK, *supra* note 4, at 40. *See also ibid.* at 32. In fact, the modern common law approach too is that the tort of negligence is not included in the intentional torts, but in the unintentional torts, that are based on recklessness and negligence. Although not in all the jurisdictions. In Israel, for example, which is a Common law state, this distinction is blurred, and the case law of the Supreme Court, which constitutes binding precedent, states explicitly that the tort of negligence may also include intentional acts. See CA 2034/98 *Amin v. Amin* (1999) IsrSC 53(5) 69, para. 13, per Justice Englard (Isr.). An English translation of the ruling is available at http://elyon1.court.gov.il/files_eng/98/340/020/q07/98020340.q07.htm. The Israeli Civil Wrongs Ordinance (New Version) 5732–1972, 2 LSI 12 (1972), § 35 (Isr.) contains a number of torts that include a mental element (of intention, calumny and so forth) but these torts are not normally invoked, because plaintiffs usually prefer basing claims on other torts which do not contain these requirements. The element of calumny may be relevant for determining punitive damages, for example.

Therefore, for an understanding of the basis for tort liability according to Maimonides, one will not necessarily look solely to the element of *peshiah* nor to the element of ownership (nor both together); an additional element will also be considered, namely, the *intention* of the tortfeasor. This is a new, unique element that is emphasized in Maimonides' responsum, and it must be considered, together with other elements, in any attempt to explain Maimonides' tort theory.

Let us now move on to another example of a ruling that accords neither with the theory of ownership nor with that of *peshiah*. Following the Talmud, Maimonides rules on the liability for injury caused by a dog when a person who was not the owner incited the dog, causing it to bite a third person or the inciter himself.[103] Maimonides writes as follows on this case:

> If one incites another's dog against a third person he is legally exempt but morally liable.[104] But the owner of the dog is liable for half of the damage[105] caused because, since he knows that his dog bites when incited, he ought not to have left it loose. If, however, one incites another's dog against himself, the owner of the dog is exempt, because whenever anyone who has acted abnormally first (is injured by) another who is acting abnormally, the latter is exempt.[106]

What is the basis for differentiating between a situation where one person incited the dog of another (the dog-owner) against a third person, in which case the dog-owner is liable, and a situation where that same person incited the same dog against himself (and the dog bit the inciter), in which case the dog-owner is exempt? This appears to be problematic according to both the ownership theory and the theory of *peshiah*. According to the ownership theory, the law ought to have been that just as in the first case, the dog-owner is liable for damages caused to a third person by his dog, so too the dog-owner ought to have been held liable for the damages caused to the inciter himself in the second case. From the point of view of ownership of the dog, there is no difference between the two cases, and why, therefore, should the rulings differ?

Indeed, it would appear from Maimonides' formulation that the basis for the liability of the dog-owner is not the ownership *per se*, for he justifies the liability of the dog-owner by his fault in knowing that if someone incites his dog to cause harm, the dog bites: he was therefore at fault in allowing the person to incite the dog. However, according to the fault-based (*peshiah*) theory as well, the basis for distinguishing the two cases is difficult to understand. If fault is based on the principle of

---

[103] *Bava Kamma* 24b.
[104] A person who incites an animal is exempt under human law, because he himself did not perpetrate a damaging act but was only the indirect cause of the damage; from a moral point of view, however, he bears responsibility and must pay, but the court cannot force him to do so.
[105] Here we are not discussing the question of distribution of liability between the causes of the damage; our aim is primarily to discuss the question of the liability in principle of the owner of the dog and of the inciter. As for the question of distribution, *See* Ra'abad's question on Maimonides' ruling, and also *see Maggid Mishneh ad loc.*
[106] Laws of Property Damages 2:19.

foreseeability, and the dog-owner ought to have foreseen that the dog would bite as a result of the incitement, and he was at fault in allowing a person to incite his dog, why is he exempt when the inciter himself, rather than a third party, is injured? From the point of view of the conduct of the dog-owner, there is no difference between the two cases: in both cases it must be said that he was at fault in allowing another to incite the dog. Albeck proposes an explanation for the law governing the inciter in keeping with his approach (supporting the theory of *peshiah*).[107] He explains that the inciter himself changed the *status quo*, and he ought to have known that it is normal for a dog to attack the inciter, but this would usually not occur when he incites it against a third person. Therefore, suggests Albeck, the inciter introduced a change (by inciting the dog against himself), and the dog acted normally and therefore its owner is exempt. However, this explanation is difficult to accept: is it in fact a norm of animal behavior that a dog will turn on a person inciting it, but not on a third person against whom it is incited? And why should the dog-owner and not the inciter be liable in the first case? Should not the inciter have foreseen the damages that would result from his incitement, and therefore ought he not to have been liable for the injury caused to a third person when he incited the dog? If one wishes to say that the dog-owner was at fault in that he did not guard his dog, which was likely to attack another person, why should he be exempt from liability when the inciter incited the dog against himself?

Undoubtedly the rule regarding the inciter requires a more convincing explanation, one that is not based on the normal rhetoric of *peshiah* or the ownership theory.

2 Providing a Rationale for the Exemption in Tort in Exceptional Cases

The exceptional cases in which the owner of the property that caused damage is exempted from liability for the damage aroused lively interest both on the part of the rabbis and of the scholars,[108] for there is nothing like an exception to teach us about the rule in general. There were many, therefore, who sought to cast light on the exceptional cases, each person according to his approach and to his preferred tort theory. At the same time, so it seems to us, the cases of exemption in tort are difficult to understand according to both the ownership theory and that of *peshiah*. The exceptional cases mentioned in the Talmud are also discussed in the rulings in the *Code*, and many of them require explanation.

One of the striking features of talmudic tort law is its extremely limited scope of liability (compared to contemporary tort law liability).[109] Consider, for example, the limited scope of liability of the owner for the damage done by his animal. This kind

---

[107] ALBECK, *supra* note 4, at 127.
[108] See, e.g., WESTREICH, *supra* note 3.
[109] Friedell 1986, *supra* note 15, at 75.

of tortfeasor is subdivided by the Talmud (following Scripture) into three distinct categories. The first category is tooth (*shen*), which refers to damage done by an animal through a normal act of *eating*. The second category is foot (*regel*), which refers to damage done by an animal with its foot in the course of its normal walking. The third category is horn (*keren*), which refers to damage done by the animal with its horn – i.e., by goring. The general principle of liability in the first two categories is that one pays full damages for the damage done by his animal as a result of walking or eating something that belongs to another only when the animal is on the property of the damaged party without permission. However, there is no liability for damage done by the animal when walking or eating in the public domain. The general principle of liability in the third category (*keren*) is significantly different from the principles of the two first categories. Unlike liability for tooth and foot, liability for horn applies both on the injured party's premises and in the public domain. However, the *halakhah* limits liability for horn to half damages, which are payable only from the body of the damaging animal itself.[110] The said payments for horn apply only to an animal that is *tam* [literally: innocent], meaning that its destructive act can be considered an aberration, since it has not become a habitual offender. However, if the animal repeats a particular destructive act three times and its owner is duly warned about each incident, then the animal becomes a *mu'ad* [literally: warned]. The owner is put on notice that his animal has this destructive tendency, and if it causes any subsequent damage through that act, the owner must use any and all assets to pay full damages for that subsequent damage. These basic rules that derive from the Talmud and the Bible are all accepted by Maimonides.

The sources of the rulings in the *Code* are talmudic, and the rulings are not exegetical innovations of Maimonides, but Maimonides not infrequently brought these laws into line with his approach and his tort theory. A good example of this is to be found in Bernard Jackson's insightful research on Maimonides' definitions of *tam* and *mu'ad*.[111] According to Jackson, Maimonides' definitions of *tam* and *mu'ad*, which receive so much emphasis in the first chapter of Laws of Property Damages, contain revision and reorganization of the talmudic materials.[112]

In examining the reasons for the exceptional rulings, the following questions arise: what is the difference between damages caused by tooth and foot on the one hand and damage from horn on the other, and how does this difference explain the differences in the respective laws? Why are the owners of animals that caused damage in the public domain by eating or walking exempt, and why are they liable for the damage caused as a result of their animals goring, even when the damage occurred in the public domain?

---

[110] See Laws of Property Damages 1:2.
[111] Bernard S. Jackson, *Maimonides' Definitions of* Tam *and* Mu'ad, 1 JEWISH L. ANNUAL 168–76 (1978) (hereinafter Jackson 1978).
[112] *Ibid.* at 169.

The exceptional law of the *tam* ox is particularly hard to explain. Why is the law applicable to it different from the other laws applying to damage caused by animals? What is the reason for the fact that only in relation to horn damage is there a difference between *tam* and *mu'ad* oxen? Why are only half damages paid in the case of a *tam* ox and not full damages?

It is especially difficult to answer these questions according to the ownership theory. If the basis for tort liability is that it was the person's property that caused the damage, what justification is there for exempting the owners from damage caused by their animal eating or walking in the public domain? And why is the owner of a *tam* animal that gored liable for only half damages?

Recourse to the theory of *peshiah* to explain the differences in the law between the different categories of damage caused by an animal is not problem-free either. Albeck, true to his approach, explains that when the law states that the tortfeasor is exempt from liability, such as in the case of damage from tooth and foot in the public domain, the reason is that damage occurs frequently there, and the victim should have foreseen that he could be injured, and should have taken care; he was at fault in not doing so.[113] But such explanations – which peg everything on foreseeability – seem problematic, and Friedell wrote, rightly in our opinion: "But these explanations are inherently weak because the concept of foreseeability is sufficiently plastic to permit almost any case to be termed foreseeable or unforeseeable."[114]

Albeck's assertion that damages from tooth and foot are common in the public domain, too, contradicts Maimonides' explicit statement that "[T]ooth and foot in the public domain are exempt, because this is something that we cannot guard against, *and they rarely cause damage there.*"[115]

As Friedell wrote, the law governing the *tam* ox is especially difficult to understand according to the theory of *peshiah*.[116] Even the possible interpretation whereby the law of the *tam* ox is an exception that deviates from the regular rules cannot be reconciled with Maimonides' approach which, as Jackson showed,[117] viewed the

---

[113] ALBECK, *supra* note 4, at 103–09.
[114] Friedell 1989, *supra* note 15, at 98.
[115] *Guide* 3:40. We will deal at length with Maimonides' statement in Chapter 5; for our purposes here suffice it to say that damages of tooth and foot in the public domain are not common.
[116] Friedell 1986, *supra* note 15, at 85–88. ALBECK, *supra* note 4, at 115–16, explains the tendency to be lenient in the matter of a *tam* ox in that goring is not frequent and it is difficult to foresee, and according to his approach, as will be recalled, liability in tort depends on foreseeability. But as Friedell correctly wrote, *ibid.* at 85:

> Albeck's approach does not explain the Talmudic rule on liability of ox owners: the owner is liable for gorings even though he has used reasonable care. According to the Talmud, the ox owner is liable for gorings even if he tied up his ox with reasonable precaution. The owner is excused from liability only if he exercised substantially more than reasonable care. This liability rule contradicts Albeck's theory that one is not liable when damage is unforeseeable.

[117] Jackson 1978, *supra* note 111.

distinction between *tam* and *mu'ad* as a fundamental, principled distinction in the rules of liability, and not merely as an aberration.

3 Standard of Care in Damages Caused by a Person to the Property of Another: Absolute/Strict Liability or Negligence?

With respect to a person who causes damage to the property of another, we learn from the *Mishnah* that a person is liable for all damages he caused,[118] and the Talmud comments that the tortfeasor must pay, whether the damage occurred unintentionally, by unavoidable mishap (*ones*) or intentionally.[119] Commentators are divided as to the degree of unintentionality or unavoidability of the *ones* that the tortfeasor must demonstrate. Some maintain that he is liable if the *ones* was not total, but in the case of an absolutely unavoidable *ones* (for example, if a man is blown off the roof by an abnormal wind and causes damage)[120] he is exempt.[121] However, some interpreted Maimonides' opinion as meaning that a person who injures must be held liable even in a case of an absolutely unavoidable *ones*,[122] i.e., Maimonides' ruling regarding the tortfeasor was based on a regime of strict liability. As Maimonides writes:

> If one damages another's property, he must pay full compensation; for whether one acts inadvertently or accidentally, he is regarded as one who acted deliberately. Thus, if one falls from a roof and breaks articles, or if one stumbles while walking and falls on an article and breaks it, he must pay full compensation.[123]

The sources presented thus far indicate that Maimonides advocated a regime of strict liability. It is therefore no surprise that Warhaftig relied on these rulings, as we have seen, in stating that Maimonides' theory was that of OSL and not *peshiah*,[124] according to which the tortfeasor would be exempt in cases of total *ones*.

It seems, however, that Maimonides imposed the lower degree of strict – rather than absolute – liability, as he holds that even a person who causes damage to

---

[118] M Bava Kamma 2:6.
[119] Sanhedrin 72b.
[120] As in the ruling in Tur, *Hoshen Mishpat* 378:1–2 (exempting from liability a person who fell in an uncommon wind and harmed another person's body or property).
[121] See, e.g., *Tosafot Bava Kamma* 27b, s.v. *veshmuel* (distinguishing between *ones* that is a type of theft, in which case liability is imposed, and duress that is a type of loss, in which case liability is not imposed); Rosh, *Bava Kamma* 3:1; Rema, *Hoshen Mishpat* 378:1.
[122] See, e.g., *Maggid Mishneh* on Maimonides' Laws of Wounding and Damaging 6:1; Schach, *Hoshen Mishpat* 378:1 (explaining that in the opinion of Maimonides and of SHULHAN ARUKH he is liable in a case of an absolutely unavoidable mishap as well). Nahmanides also rules according to this opinion in his commentary to *Bava Metzia* 82b, s.v. *ve'ata* (explaining that when the sages held liable a man who caused damage in a case of an unavoidable mishap, they did so even in when the mishap was absolutely unavoidable, such as falling off the roof in a strong storm, and even when it is entirely uncommon, as the windstorm in which Elijah ascended to heaven, and they similarly held liable the person who had a stone in his lap without realizing it, and the stone fell and caused damage – even though there is no greater *ones* than this).
[123] Laws of Wounding and Damaging 6:1.
[124] See WARHAFTIG, *supra* note 4, at 224.

another's property is exempt from payment in cases that he defines as a "strike from heaven", as per his ruling in the ladder example:

> If one is climbing a ladder and a rung slips from under him and it falls and causes damage, the rule is as follows: If the rung was not strong and firmly fixed, he is liable. But if it was strong and firmly fixed and yet it slipped, or if it was rotted (eaten by worms), he is exempt, for this damage is a strike from heaven. The same rule applies in all similar cases.[125]

Commentators on Maimonides had a hard time explaining this ruling. Ra'abad[126] wondered how it is possible to define the breaking of a rung or the fact that it has been eaten by worms as an act of heaven. It is true that it can be considered an unavoidable mishap (*ones*), but Maimonides had already ruled at the beginning of the same section (quoted earlier) that the tortfeasor is liable even in the case of an unavoidable mishap. What is the difference between these tortfeasors who have caused an unavoidable mishap and the person who climbs a ladder and a rung breaks under him?

Modern scholars of Jewish law who espoused OSL[127] as well as those who adopted the theory of *peshiah*[128] struggled with the answer to this question. This is not surprising: the explanation is patently inconsistent with both of these theories, for it is clear that in Maimonides' opinion, the standard of care in relation to a person who causes damage is higher than *peshiah* or negligence and lower than absolute liability.

The great difficulty involved in the attempt to explain all the talmudic laws – including the laws relating to the standard of care, according to the theory of *peshiah*, understood by some scholars to be identical to negligence or foreseeability[129] – is illustrated by what Friedell wrote:[130]

> Moreover it is difficult to explain all of the Jewish tort rules as based on either a concept of negligence or foreseeability. Consider the case of a man who climbs onto a roof carrying a knapsack. He puts the knapsack down and lies down. An unusual wind blows him and his knapsack off the roof, causing injury below. The ruling in this hypothetical case is that he is liable for the injury caused by his body but not for the injury caused by his property.[131]

---

[125] Laws of Wounding and Damaging 6:4. *See also* Laws of Property Damages 14:2 (providing an additional example of a strike from Heaven).

[126] Laws of Wounding and Damaging 6:4.

[127] *See* WARHAFTIG, *supra* note 4, at 224–27; Haut, *supra* note 18, at 41–46.

[128] *See* Shalom Albeck, *A Person Causing Damage under Duress in the Laws of the Talmud*, 16–17 BAR ILAN 86–87, end of note 1 (1979) (Heb).

[129] *See supra* note 4.

[130] Steven F. Friedell, *The Role of Jewish Law in a Secular State*, 24 JEWISH L. ASSOC. STUDIES 100, 104 (2013).

[131] This became the binding halakhic decision: SHULHAN ARUKH, Hoshen Mishpat 378:2; 411:2, and it would appear that Maimonides, too, accepted this. *See* Laws of Damaging and Wounding 1:12; 6:1.

However, writes Friedell:

> This conclusion is hard to justify on the basis that he was negligent with respect to one of these injuries but not the other, or that one of the injuries was foreseeable but not the other.[132] Similarly, when he is blown off the roof, it is hard to understand why damage for *nezek* [physical damage] is foreseeable but that damage for pain and medical expense is only foreseeable if the wind was of normal strength.[133] Some principle other than foreseeability seems to be operating.

These rulings that impose different standards of care in accordance with the nature of the entity causing the damage (a person or his property) are therefore difficult to explain according to the theory of *peshiah*; needless to say they are incomprehensible according to OSL.[134]

4 Deterrence of Risk-Causing Behavior

Maimonides suggests a far-reaching approach that promotes deterrence of risk-causing behavior even if it did not cause actual damage, as shown in his ruling in the *Code*:

> If an animal at pasture strays into fields and vineyards, the owner should be warned three times even if it has done no damage. If [then] the owner of the animal does not take care of it and prevent it from pasturing there, the owner of the field has the right to slaughter the animal in a ritually valid matter and then say to its owner, "Come and sell your meat." For one is forbidden to cause damage willfully with the intention of paying for the damage he causes. Even to bring about damage indirectly with this intention is forbidden.[135]

Maimonides' rule is far-reaching, as it entitles the person who *may* sustain damage caused by the animal, even if the animal did not yet cause damage, to seek relief on his own and slaughter the animal. It is for this reason that this ruling was opposed by some of the great halakhic authorities, foremost among them Ra'abad. In his criticism of Maimonides' ruling, Ra'abad writes that not only "have such things not been written in the Talmud" and they are Maimonides' innovations, but even in principle one must object to them, because "someone who has a herd of animals, his entire herd is not slaughtered, but if he causes damage to the world, he will pay without any warning." Ra'abad is saying that there is no permit to slaughter an animal that trespassed onto the field of another, for it has not yet caused damage.

---

[132] But see ALBECK, *supra* note 4, at 177.
[133] But see Albeck, "Torts", *supra* note 5, at 320–22 (suggesting that more specific damage is foreseeable when the defendant is grossly negligent).
[134] For it is not clear why strict liability is imposed on a person who causes damage, and his liability is set at a lower standard of care if it is his property that causes damage, for these are things which he owns.
[135] Laws of Property Damages 5:1.

Even if the animal has caused damage, it must not be slaughtered; at most, its owner can be made to pay compensation for the damage it has caused (even if he was not forewarned that his animal is trespassing). This seems to be a conceptual controversy between Ra'abad, who focuses on correcting the wrong caused to the victim by the tortfeasor (a corrective justice type of approach), and as long as no harm was caused to the injured nothing should be done to the tortfeasor – only "if he causes damage to the world, he will pay" – and Maimonides, who focuses on *preventing* damage. According to Maimonides, even if the animal has not yet actually caused damage, it is possible to prevent the tortfeasor, who in this case is the owner of an animal, from persisting in the activity that may cause damage to another, if it transpires that this owner is a "serial negligent," one who did not take serious supervisory measures and precautions, despite having previously been warned three times.[136]

In fact, the ruling in this case does not necessarily contradict the theory of *peshiah*, for it can be argued that the owner of the animal was at fault in his guarding of it, if he did not take serious supervisory measures and precautions, even though he had been warned repeatedly to guard it properly, and therefore it was right to punish him. In the subsequent ruling, however, Maimonides adds:

> Because of this [that the animal are not properly watched and they therefore stray into the fields of others and cause damage],[137] the Sages forbade the rearing of small cattle or small wild animals in the Land of Israel in regions containing fields or vineyards but allowed it only in the wooded and desert regions of the Land of Israel.[138]

On this ruling, Albeck, who supports the theory of *peshiah*, asks:

> Why were they more severe, making a ruling in relation to all small animals, and fining the person who was not at fault in the same way as a person who was at fault (*pasha*) in watching his animals? Why did they not fine only the person whose animals strayed into the fields of another, for example, the owner of the field would be permitted to slaughter the animal that was grazing in his field [in accordance with Maimonides' first ruling]?[139]

In other words: why did Maimonides adopt different legal solutions in the two consecutive rulings quoted earlier – in the first ruling, he penalized only the person who was at fault in watching over the animal, and in the second ruling he totally forbade the rearing of the animals[140] – when Maimonides himself bound the two rulings together (in beginning the second ruling with the words "Because of this"),

---

[136] Note the three warnings are based on the traditional definition of *muʿad*, though extended from warnings of actual attacks (if indeed it was always earlier restricted in that way).
[137] See Maimonides' wording in his COMMENTARY TO THE MISHNAH, *Bava Kamma* 7:7: "It is forbidden to rear small animals in the Land of Israel because they spread over the fields."
[138] Laws of Property Damages 5:2.
[139] Albeck, *supra* note 4, at 112.
[140] The ruling is found already in the Mishnah (as per note 137).

hinting that there is a single legal policy common to both? What is this policy, and on what is it based? The answer to Albeck's question must be sought in jurisprudential realms, to be visited in the following chapters, which go beyond the theories of ownership and *peshiah* that have been discussed till now. Nevertheless, we can already say that the sources that have been presented up to this point in this chapter point to a different major element underlying Maimonides' tort theory: this element is neither *peshiah* nor ownership, but rather, involves control. This will be discussed in the following section of this chapter.

E. RE-EXAMINING THE OPENING CHAPTER OF THE BOOK OF TORTS IN THE *CODE*: CONTROL AS A CENTRAL ELEMENT OF LIABILITY IN TORT

Having seen the serious conceptual-theoretical and exegetical difficulties facing those who attribute the ownership theory to Maimonides, we ought to reexamine the ruling that opens the Book of Torts, from which the *yeshivah* reading deduced that Maimonides was of the opinion that the basis for tort liability is that "it was his property that caused the damage," and not failure to guard and *peshiah*. In the course of examining the first ruling and the first chapter of the Book of Torts, we will also encounter the process by which Maimonides fashioned the Book of Torts and some of the principles that guided him in the task of arranging and classifying the materials relevant to the laws of tort.[141]

Prior to the time of the Lithuanian rabbis with their *yeshivah* reading of Maimonides, we do not find that any connection was made between the ruling opening the *Code* and the question of the basis for tort liability (whether due to a person's property having caused the damage or due to *peshiah*). However hard we looked, we could not find a similar connection in the classical commentaries to the *Code* or in the works of the prominent authorities who flourished in the Middle Ages and later, in the period preceding the era of the Lithuanian rabbis.[142] This phenomenon poses a question: why did the classical authorities and the commentators who were very familiar with Maimonides' style and form of expression not mention that the first ruling implies that he regarded ownership of the property as the basis for liability?

---

[141] Extensive discussion of these questions is beyond the scope of our study. And *See* Twersky, *supra* note 1, at 238–323.

[142] Even in the index to halakhic literature in the *Collection of Textual Variations*, S. Frankel edition (Jerusalem: Yeshivat Ohel Yosef, 1982), *supra* note 46, relating to the said ruling, there was no reference to the work of classical commentators and authorities in relation to Maimonides' famous inference that the main basis of the obligation is fact of the person's property having caused damage, with the exception of one single head of a Lithuanian *yeshivah* (who lived in the twentieth century), R. Isser Zalman Meltzer, in his work *Even Ha'azel*, *supra* note 20. And as we shall see *infra* note 154-157. From the words of *Maggid Mishneh* and the Gaon of Vilna, it transpires that they were aware of Maimonides' use of the formulation, "for it was his property that caused damage," but they do not appear to have seen this as some kind of fundamental conceptual determination with respect to the basis for tort liability.

We believe that this is because this *yeshivah*-reading interpretation, which is so common among the Lithuanian rabbis, reflects the orientation towards abstract, analytical and conceptual thinking.[143] However, the *yeshivah* reading of Maimonides' first ruling is not the only possible understanding, and a different, simpler interpretation is certainly conceivable.

We would like to propose another interpretation, whereby Maimonides' use of the expression "for it was his property that caused the damage" in the first ruling of Laws of Property Damages does not necessarily mean that this is the basis of the owner's liability for damages caused by his property, as assumed by those later authorities. Maimonides only wished to emphasize that in the Laws of Property Damages he is concerned purely with damages caused by a person's property, and not with other types of damage, which he discussed in the Book of Torts in other, separate groups of rulings, i.e., Laws of Wounding and Damaging, dealing with injury caused by a person himself to the body of another (wounding) or to his property (damaging). It was a type of methodological comment, we argue, aimed at clarifying the contents of Laws of Property Damages and nothing more.

In this context it is important to pay attention to the legal classification used by Maimonides in the Book of Torts in the *Code*. This is a detailed and sophisticated classification that has profound implications for the various objectives of tort law.[144] The classification that Maimonides uses in the Book of Torts demonstrates extensive use of certain parameters, on the basis of which he differentiates between various rulings: (a) How was the damage caused? Was it caused by an animal owned by the person or did it result from a wrong that the person caused by his actions? (b) Who suffered the damage? Was it an animal, property, or a person? In light of these parameters, the tort laws are ordered from the least to the most serious. They begin primarily with rulings concerning damage caused to property by property owned by the tortfeasor (Laws of Property Damages), and with damage caused by a person who robs or steals the property of another (Laws of Theft and Laws of Robbery and Lost Property). They then move on to bodily injury (Laws of Wounding and Damaging) and finally to homicide (Laws of Murder and Preservation of Life). These parameters are also the context for the basic distinction made by Maimonides between damage caused by a person's property *(nizkei mamon)* and damage caused by the person himself *(hovel u'mazik)*.

Strong support for the proposed interpretation[145] can be adduced from the draft of the *Code* written in Maimonides' own hand, found in the Cairo Genizah, which

---

[143] For a description of the methodology of the heads of the Lithuanian *yeshivot*, see text near note 59.

[144] The following chapter consists of a detailed analysis of some of the main characteristics of the classification, and later we present only the major structure of the Book of Torts which is relevant to our discussion.

[145] According to which the statement "for it was his property that caused the damage" in the opening ruling of the Book of Torts was made by Maimonides in order to create and emphasize the distinction between Laws of Property Damages and Laws of Wounding and Damaging.

was located close to Maimonides' place of residence in Fostat (on the outskirts of Cairo).[146] Quite a number of folios written in Maimonides' own hand were discovered in the Genizah, mostly single folios from first versions (drafts) of his works. Particularly prominent amongst these drafts were the drafts of the *Code*, including the first page of the Laws of Property Damages. From this draft, as well as from other drafts of the rulings in the *Code*, it is possible to enter the Maimonidean workroom and witness the process of formation of the *Code* in general, and of the Book of Torts in particular. As is known, Maimonides quite often corrected and amended what he wrote in the *Commentary to the Mishnah* and in the *Code*.[147] It has been pointed out that in the format of the *Code* initially planned by Maimonides, the Book of Civil Law (*Sefer Mishpatim*) apparently contained the Books of Torts, Acquisition and Civil Law.[148] The first folio, which has already been published, contains the beginning of Laws of Property Damages, and according to the caption heading the page, it is the first page of the Book of Civil Law in the first version.[149] From an examination of this draft folio it transpires that Maimonides made two significant changes, apparently simultaneously, to the wording of the title of the first rulings in the Book, and in the wording of the first ruling in the first chapter. The first change relates to the name of the rulings in the Book. From the draft it emerges that these rulings were initially entitled "Laws of Torts" (*Hilkhot Nezikim*), and then Maimonides changed the title of the book to the Book of Torts (*Sefer Nezikim*) and the title of the first group of rulings of to "Laws of Property Damages" (by erasing the word "Torts" and writing "Property Damages" – *nizkei mammon* – over it). This possibly indicates that the initial intention was to include the laws of property damages and the laws of wounding and damaging together in Laws of Torts,[150] which includes all types of damages; only at a later stage did Maimonides decide

---

[146] For a facsimile of the draft and an analysis of the text See Nachum L. Rabinovitch & Itzhak Sheilat, *A New Autograph Fragment of* Mishneh Torah in Zvi Haber ed., 25 MA'ALIOT – MAIMONIDES' 800 YEARS COMMEMORATIVE VOLUME (Ma'aleh Adumim, 2005) (Heb.), at 11–21.

[147] Maimonides himself, on different occasions, remarked that there are some matters about which he changed his mind over the years, and the opinion cited in the *Code* is the main one, and that he retracted what he had written in the *Commentary to the Mishnah*: see IGGEROT HARAMBAM (Bennett), Letter 6, p. 58; RESP. RAMBAM (Blau edition) no. 217, at 383. The possibility that Maimonides changed his mind is taken into account also in order to resolve internal contradictions in the body of the *Code*. For Maimonides' own evidence about changes he made while re-editing, See RESP. RAMBAM *ibid.* no. 345, p. 618.

[148] Eliezer Horowitz, 38 *Hadarom* 32 (Tishrei, 5734–1974), at 4.

[149] Rabinovitch & Sheilat, *supra* note 146, at 11.

[150] So, presume Rabinovitch & Sheilat, *ibid.* at 15. They further suggest (at 13) that from the caption on the page of the draft it would appear that in its original format, there were only twelve books comprising the *Code*. The eleventh book was a book of law, and it included the Book of Torts, of Acquisition and of Civil Law, thus bringing the final number to fifteen, one more than originally planned (at the final stage the laws of tort were split into two: Laws of Property Damage and Laws of Wounding and Damaging). Later, Maimonides decided to divide the book into three books – Torts, Civil Law and Acquisition.

upon a more detailed classification and on the sub-division that he made in the final version of the Book of Torts between Laws of Property Damages and Laws of Wounding and Damaging as totally separate rulings that deal with different types of damage. In the same draft, Maimonides changed the wording of the ruling that opened Laws of Torts (which later became Laws of Property Damages). Initially, Maimonides wrote only that "[i]f any living creature under human control causes damage, its owner must pay compensation, whether a domestic animal or a wild animal or a bird." Only at the second stage, at which he amended the title of the rulings to Laws of Property Damages, did he also delete the end of the first ruling, replacing it with the words "for it was his property that caused damage," to obtain the final version that is found in the texts that we have before us: "If any living creature under human control causes damage, its owner must pay compensation, for it was his property that caused the damage." Hence, it is clear from this draft written by Maimonides himself that not only did the phrase, "for it was his property that caused the damage" not appear in the first version of the ruling, but it was added only at the same time as the change in the title of the rulings and the transition to Laws of Property Damages. It would certainly appear that there is a direct connection between the change of the title to Laws of Property Damages and the addition of the phrase, "for it was his property that caused the damage" in the opening ruling.

One Maimonidean scholar, Yaacov Levinger, noted that often, the rulings opening the books of the *Code* or a particular group of rulings (such as Laws of Property Damages or Laws of Wounding and Damaging) use different expressions which are merely linguistic variations of the titles of groups of rulings in the *Code*, and it would appear that the various differences in formulation between the titles of the books and their opening rulings are only semantic.[151] Twersky, too, wrote that because Maimonides crafted an innovative method of classification in the *Code*, he sometimes hints at the nature of the various rulings and the mode of classification in the opening paragraphs of the various groupings.[152] Hence, it would seem perfectly reasonable that in adding the words "for it was his property that caused the damage" to the opening ruling, Maimonides in no way intended to imply a substantive, unitary legal-conceptual basis (ownership theory) underlying tort liability. Indeed, even though the element of ownership of the damaging property appears in various places in halakhic literature, as well as in Maimonides' work, as one of the necessary conditions of liability,[153] nowhere have we found that Maimonides attempts to see in

---

[151] LEVINGER 1965, *supra* note 95, at 18–20.
[152] TWERSKY, *supra* note 1, at 282.
[153] *See, e.g., Commentary of Maimonides* to M Bava Kamma 1:2, where he says that the *mishnah* enumerated "five conditions and said that a person would not be liable to pay for the damages that were caused by his property if one of the conditions was lacking," including the third condition mentioned in the *mishnah*, i.e., "special property," the meaning of which, according to Maimonides, is as follows: "The property from which the damage comes must be specific and its owner must be specific." Ownership of the property is one of the preconditions for tort obligation, but this should not be viewed as the actual basis of tort liability.

ownership the essential principal legal element on which all of tort law is based (as an alternative to *peshiah*). It may be assumed, we suggest, that Maimonides used this addition only to connect the opening rule to the subject-matter of the group of rulings that it opens, and he does this by invoking the term "property that caused damage" in a sense identical to "property damages" (*nizkei mamon*) – the general title of this group of rulings – both of them semantic terms which were not invented by Maimonides but which are based on similar terms that appear in talmudic literature.[154] Maimonides therefore points out at the end of the first ruling that the damages that are caused by a living creature (discussed in the first chapter of the Laws of Property Damages) fall within the wider category of "property that caused damage,"[155] i.e., Laws of Property Damages include all the damage that is caused not by the act of a person himself, but by various objects.[156] Further support for the proposed interpretation can be adduced from an examination of Maimonides' interpretation of the first *mishnah* in *Bava Kamma*, where he writes: "The four heads of damage (mentioned in the *mishnah*) are *damages that are caused by a person's property*." From Maimonides' words it appears that he is simply noting a common characteristic of the types of damages mentioned in the *mishnah* (damages that are caused by animals, a pit and fire), i.e., the damages that are caused by the person's property but not those caused by the person himself, and it is hard to imagine that he is referring to more than that. This language used by the young Maimonides in his *Commentary to the Mishnah* would appear to parallel the language he used at a later stage in the *Code*, in the opening ruling of Laws of Property Damages. Thus it may be assumed that in the *Code* as well, the expression, "for it was his property that caused damage" must be understood in the same sense (as in the *Commentary to the Mishnah*) that is concerned only with the technical nature of the property damages and not with the basis for theoretical-jurisprudential tort liability. Maimonides sought thereby to stress the difference between Laws of Property Damages that open the Book of Torts and Laws of Wounding and

---

[154] This is apparently what the Vilna Gaon meant in saying that the source of the expression, "for his property caused damage" used by Maimonides is in the words of Talmud, *Bava Kamma* 3a, "There is gratification [derived by the animal] from its damage, and [the animal] is your [the owner's] property, and [the obligation of] watching it is on you." (Similar expressions appear in *Bava Kamma* 6a). Note that the Vilna Gaon did not write that Maimonides has any fundamental legal basis (that is, that the basis for the tort liability is ownership). The expression "property damage", too, is not a new coinage of Maimonides, but it comes from the Talmud. See, e.g., *Bava Kamma* 6b, where the distinction is made between "property damages" (*nizkei mammon*) and "bodily harm" (*nizkei gufo*).

[155] Similar to what was said by one of the classical commentators on Maimonides, the author of *Maggid Mishneh*, at the beginning of the Book of Torts, says that "the rules of property damages and their concern is that the person's property and its owner must pay."

[156] Maimonides adopts a similar method in relation to most of the rulings that open a group of rulings: he usually makes use of a term that connects the subject matter of the first ruling with the subject matter of the entire group.

Damaging and the other rules in the Book of Torts that deal with damage caused as a result of the actions of the person himself.[157]

Careful examination of the draft of the first ruling in the Laws of Property Damages is likely to bring out another point that was ignored by most of the later authorities dealing with this ruling. It appears that the main expression in this ruling, to which attention must be paid, consists of the words, "under human control". This expression has appeared in the various formulations of this ruling beginning with the first draft, up to the finished formulation (unlike the expression "for it was his property that caused damage", which was added only at a later stage), in all of which the basic form of the ruling is preserved: "If any living creature *under human control* causes damage, its owners must pay compensation." This expression, which highlights the element of a person's control of the object that caused the damage rather than its ownership, reveals the central element underlying a person's liability for property damages according to Maimonides.[158] Conclusive proof of this can be found in Maimonides' ruling in the example of the slave. This ruling – exemption of the master from damages caused by his slave – poses a thorny problem for those who attribute to Maimonides the ownership theory, for it is not clear why the master is exempt from liability for damages caused by his slave: the master is the owner of the slave, and what is the difference between a slave and other living creatures? Maimonides makes it clear, however, that the basic law is that a master is not to be held liable for damages caused by his servants, even though they are his property for "they [the slaves] have minds of their own and he is *unable to keep watch over them.*"[159] What this means is that the important element for the purpose of tort liability is the practical possibility of maintaining effective control on the part of the master over the actions of the slave (which does not exist here, as slaves have minds of their own), and not the fact of his formal-legal ownership of the slave, which is insufficient to create liability, as emphasized by Maimonides.

Now, having identified the element that determines tort liability for property damages according to Maimonides, i.e., a person's *effective control* over the

---

[157] *Maggid Mishneh* wrote, *ad loc.*, concerning the order of the rulings in the Book of Torts, that "initially the damages caused by the property were clarified, and then the damage done by a person was explained," or in a slightly different version, in his introduction to the Laws of Property Damages, he asserted that Maimonides placed the rulings on property damages first "because these are the damages that do not involve the actions of a person, since it was his property that caused the damage, and all the other rules deal with human activity." It appears that *Maggid Mishneh* regarded the term "property damages" as a substantive term that indicates the subject of the said rulings, as opposed to the matters discussed in Laws of Wounding and Damaging, as well as the other rulings in the Book of Torts (Laws of Theft, Laws of Robbery and Laws of Murderers).

[158] And cf. R. Shimon Shkop, *supra* note 21, no. 1, s.v. *ukhmo khen* – a second explanation of a person's liability for his property (according to this explanation, control of the object, and not necessarily the proprietary right of ownership, is what defines the object as a person's property for the purpose of liability in torts).

[159] Laws of Theft 1:9.

damaging object, and not his ownership of that object, several of the exegetical difficulties mentioned earlier that confronted those who attributed the ownership theory to Maimonides disappear. In various places the *Code* refers to different types of tortfeasors who are liable for damage caused by different objects, even though they are not the formal-legal *owners* of those objects, e.g., the person who breaches his neighbor's fence enclosing his animal must pay for the damages caused by the animal, even though he is not the owner, and a person is liable for damages caused by a pit and fire even though he can hardly be called the owner from a proprietary-legal point of view. These examples are difficult to explain according to those who understand ownership as the basis of liability. However, if we say, as suggested, that practical *effective control*, not ownership, is the decisive element for the purpose of tort liability, we see that this element indeed exists in relation to the person who breaches the fence allowing the animal to stray and cause damage, for although he is not the formal owner, in practice it was he who had control over the animal's movements outside its enclosure from the moment that he decided to allow it to get out by breaching the fence. The element of effective control is also present in relation to a person for whom it is practically possible to cover the pit or douse the fire and he does not do so – he is then liable for the damages caused by the pit and the fire even though we would not call him the formal owner of these things.

F. CONCLUSION

In this chapter we saw that Maimonides' approach to tort liability cannot be described as fault-based (*peshiah*) only or based solely on strict liability. There are also serious problems facing those who hold that the basis for liability in tort according to Maimonides is the element of ownership of the property that caused the damage. Indeed, this theory does not correctly reflect Maimonides' opinion. We also discussed the centrality of the element of control in Maimonides' theory. It is surely not to be assumed that Maimonides operated on the same assumptions as those adopted by some modern tort theoreticians and practitioners, who tend to see torts as a unified whole dominated by negligence, all expressive of a single principle.

However, exposure of the element of control, which – as opposed to ownership or fault – is the major, though not exclusive element underlying a person's liability for damage caused by objects under his control, as emerges from our analysis of the ruling at the beginning of the *Code*, constitutes only a first step towards understanding Maimonides' tort theory. Most of the problems raised earlier still require resolution, for we must still investigate the rationale for Maimonides' approach. Why should a person who controls an object that caused damage be liable in torts? What is the jurisprudential theory underlying this liability? How does the theory explain the various rulings mentioned earlier which are difficult to understand both under the ownership theory and the theory of *peshiah*? How does the element of *peshiah* mentioned by Maimonides in certain places in the *Code* fit in with the element of control? What is the rationale underlying the central distinction between the Laws of Property Damages (*nizkei mamon*) and the Laws of Wounding and Damaging (*hovel umazik*)? What is the required standard of care according to Maimonides in relation to different types of damages and why? What are the aims of tort law according to Maimonides, and how do they impact on the different laws?

These questions and others have no clear answer in the rulings in the *Code* that have been discussed till now. The puzzle therefore remains largely unsolved: a complete solution to the puzzle will be available only after we obtain a more complete picture of Maimonides' position in his other works, as discussed in the following chapters.

3

The Foundations of the Maimonidean Theory:

Different Goals for Different Categories of Damage

A. INTRODUCTION

An understanding of Maimonides' tort theory and the provision of a *complete* view of his theory (which will be presented in detail in the following chapters) require three things. The first is an awareness that Maimonides' theory incorporates various goals and considerations that operate in concert. The second is the understanding that Maimonides introduced different goals for different categories of damage. In each category of damage one goal (or more) is (or are) more dominant than the others. The third is to focus both on what Maimonides wrote in his *Code* and in the *Guide*, as well as in his other works such as *Commentary to the Mishnah* and *Maimonides' Responsa*.[1]

A detailed analysis of the deontological and religious aspects of Maimonides' theory will be undertaken in Chapter 4, and of the consequentialist aspects in Chapter 5. In this chapter, we will address the following elements of the Maimonidean theory: the scope of tort law, its connection to the criminal law, the classification of different categories of tort law and the various aims that underlie each of the categories of tort law.

The following three principle aspects will be discussed at length in this chapter:

1. The scope of tort law in Maimonides' theory is much wider than what is common in modern law, and it includes not only purely civil-private law (from the field of the law of obligations) but also laws which have a significant connection to criminal law. According to Maimonides, tort law is an intermediate field between civil-private law and criminal law, and some types of tortious compensation have a punitive dimension.

---

[1] While retaining an awareness of the differences, as pointed out by Hanina Ben-Menahem, between the Responsa and the Code. See Hanina Ben-Menahem, *Maimonides on Equity: Reconsidering* The Guide for the Perplexed III:34, 17 J. L. & Relig. 19 (2002).

The Book of Torts in the *Code* includes not only the classical laws of tort (in the eyes of the modern jurist), such as the laws pertaining to damages that were caused by a person and by his property, but also areas which in modern law are included in the criminal law, such as the laws pertaining to murderers, to theft and to robbery. In fact, the Book of Torts can be regarded as a civil-criminal mix. Maimonides also included other areas that have a connection with tort law in other Books of the *Code*, such as the laws pertaining to nuisance (included in the Laws of Neighbors) which he included in the Book of Acquisition (*Sefer Kinyan*), the laws pertaining to watchmen or bailees, included in the Book of Civil Laws (*Sefer Mishpatim*), and other laws in additional places in the *Code*.

2. A fundamental division into different types of tortious events in accordance with the nature and type of the damage, and with the identity of the tortfeasor and the victim (what we call a differential approach) emerges from the classification of the Book of Torts in the *Code*, central to which is a fundamental distinction between damage caused by a person's property (Laws of Property Damages) and damage caused by the person himself (Laws of Wounding and Damaging); the distinction between the damage that is caused by a person's property (damages caused by animals) and between the damage caused by a person's action (pit and fire); a distinction between a person causing physical injury to another person (Laws of Wounding) and a person causing damage to the property of another (Laws of Damaging); a distinction between regular damage and nuisance and damage caused by neighbors. These distinctions between the different types of tort law have ramifications, as will be explained in Section B of this chapter.

3. Tort law does not have one single goal; rather, Maimonides presents the various goals of tort law that he discussed in his various writings, and principally in the *Guide*. There are two central contentions with regard to the goals: (1) in Maimonides' theory, the various goals work together and are not necessarily regarded as contradictory; (2) some goals are more dominant than others in relation to different types of tort laws. Thus, for example, in relation to classical torts that are civil in nature (such as monetary damage, where a person is the tortfeasor), Maimonides in the *Guide* (3:40) emphasizes the removal of the wrong (which in fact constitutes what is presently called corrective justice) and prevention of acts causing damage (a consequentialist dimension). In relation to damage that involves a criminal law element, however, such as damage caused by wounding, theft and robbery, Maimonides in the *Guide* (3:41) presents a penal, deterrent rationale (which is also consequentialist). In the *Guide* (3:42), Maimonides emphasized distributive justice in his description of the goals of the Book of Acquisition and the

Book of Civil Laws in the *Code*, including the laws of nuisance and the liability of watchmen. The *Code*, too, adverts to the religious-prohibitive aspect, in the prohibition against causing damage.

B. THE SCOPE OF TORT LAW: *NEZIKIN* AS A MIDDLE GROUND BETWEEN CIVIL AND CRIMINAL LAW

Maimonides' theory of torts is based on his reading of the talmudic literature on torts. Yet his theory also provides a groundbreaking, independent, and conceptual analysis of the biblical and talmudic rules of torts.

We will analyze two central aspects of the Maimonidean theory of tort as emerges from the Book of Torts (*Sefer Nezikim*) in the *Code*, in which Maimonides fashions tort law in his own special way, which is not identical to the way in which these laws were fashioned in the main sources of talmudic tort literature.[2] The first aspect, which is the main focus of our discussion in this section, relates to the fashioning of tort law as an intermediate field between civil-private law and criminal law. A second aspect, with which we will deal in the next section, relates to the refashioning of the elements of liability in tort for damages caused by a person's property and by the person himself.

1 The Legal Classification of the Book of Torts

Tractate *Bava Kamma* is the main source of talmudic literature dealing with tort law.

The opening *mishnah* in *Bava Kamma* indicates that there are only four primary damagers or *avot*:[3] the ox, the pit, the tooth, and fire. Each primary damager represents a head of damage with its own unique defining characteristics, and all other cases of damage not specifically addressed by the Bible can be classified as belonging to one of these four primary heads of damage.

Nevertheless, as explicated in the Talmud (*Bava Kamma* 4b–5a), different sages compile different lists of damagers. The most extensive of these lists is that of R. Hiyya, who lists twenty-four damagers, including the negligent custodian, the thief, the robber, the rapist, the seducer, and others.[4]

However, in defining the topics that are included in the Book of Torts in the *Code*, Maimonides deviated from the formulations appearing in the talmudic

---

[2] Our argument is that what Maimonides says does not always express the talmudic mainstream. Nevertheless, and as we shall see in this chapter, here and there it is possible to find hints in specific talmudic sources for Maimonides' approach.

[3] Literally: father damager – the Mishnah's term for any damager specifically mentioned in the Bible. See Rashi's interpretation to this *mishnah*, s.v. *arba'a*.

[4] R. Oshaya, T *Bava Kamma* 9a, chose a more restricted list than that of R. Hiyya, which includes thirteen heads of damage, including damage caused by a person's property (the four heads of damage mentioned in the Mishnah), with the addition of injuries caused by a person to another, and damages caused by the various watchment.

literature in certain aspects.⁵ In the Book of Torts, Maimonides included more topics than were mentioned in the limited formulation in the *mishnah* that includes only four categories of damagers. However, in his *Code* Maimonides did not include all the topics mentioned in the broader formulation of R. Hiyya; rather, he formulated his own revised version, which included many of the topics in R. Hiyya's extended formulation, but also additional topics that are not mentioned there.

In the Book of Torts, Maimonides included the following topics: Laws of Property Damages, which include the four heads of damage that are caused by a person's chattels, i.e., damage by animals, by a pit and by fire; Laws of Theft, in which he discusses the laws of the thief and the payments he must make; Laws of Robbery and Lost Property; Laws of Wounding and Damaging, in which Maimonides deals with the laws applying to a person who causes injury to another or who damages his property; and Laws of Murderers and Preservation of Life, in which Maimonides deals with the punishment for a person who commits murder or manslaughter, as well as the laws pertaining to preservation of a person's body. Maimonides included in the Book of Torts topics that are not included in R. Hiyya's extended list, such as Laws of Murderers and Preservation of Life and Laws of Restoration of Lost Property. On the other hand, several tort topics that are mentioned in R. Hiyya's list were discussed by Maimonides in other books of the *Code*, but not in the Book of Torts. For example: laws relating to damage caused by watchmen were included in the Book of Civil Laws (*Sefer Mishpatim*);⁶ laws of damages caused by plotting witnesses are included in the Book of Judges (*Sefer Shoftim*);⁷ and laws of damages caused by rape, seduction and slander were included in the Book of Women (*Sefer Nashim*).⁸ The laws relating to damage caused by neighbors and nuisance were also regulated by Maimonides in the framework of the Laws of Neighbors in the Book of Acquisition (*Sefer Kinyan*)⁹ and not in the Book of Torts.

The legal classification employed by Maimonides in the Book of Torts in the *Code* is noteworthy. This is a detailed and sophisticated classification that has

---

5 Indeed, as Shamma Friedman showed in *Mishneh Torah – Hahibbur Hagadol*, BIRKAT MOSHE JUBILEE VOLUME 353–68 (Ma'aleh Adumim, 2012) (Heb.), the structure of the MISHNEH TORAH as well as the manner in which it is arranged is influenced to a great extent by the order in the Mishnah in general, and the same applies with respect to the arrangement of the Book of Torts, which is based, so Friedman argues, "almost entirely according to the *mishnah* in Bava Kamma" (at 364). However, it would seem that this does not contradict our following proposal, whereby there is a jurisprudential logic to the structure and organization of the Book of Torts. Friedman too admits that the order of the MISHNEH TORAH "is similar in certain places to the order of the Mishnah, but it is also different from it, due to improvements made by Maimonides" (*ibid*. at 367), and in relation to the order of the Book of Torts, too Friedman admits that although it is "almost entirely according to the *mishnah* in Bava Kamma," Maimonides finessed this and added "improvements" (*Ibid*. at 364).
6 Laws of Rentals and Laws of Borrowing and Entrusted Objects in the Book of Civil Laws.
7 Laws of Witnesses, Chapter 18, in the Book of Judges.
8 Laws of Virgin Maidens, Book of Women.
9 Laws of Neighbors, chaps. 9–11.

far-reaching consequences with regard to the various objectives of tort law. The following are some of its main characteristics.

First, regarding the *Code*. In general, Maimonides does not appear to consider the Book of Torts to be an integral part of classical private-civil law, which he included in the Book of Civil Laws and the Book of Acquisition, but rather as situated somewhere between civil-private and criminal law. Maimonides includes in the Book of Torts not only topics which modern eyes would clearly regard as relating to torts, such as laws of damage by chattels, and the laws pertaining to a person who causes damage to the property of another, but also topics that modern eyes would regard as clearly criminal, such as the laws of the murderer, the thief, and the robber. We can also identify a gradual transition from rulings of a more civil character, included in the first part of the Book, such as those relating to property damage and loss, to rulings of a more punitive nature that are included in the last part of the Book, such as those concerning bodily injury (Laws of Wounding) and murder. This in fact means that the Book moves from dealing more with civil-private law to dealing more with criminal law, by including the following categories: laws of property damages, laws of theft, laws of robbery and lost property, laws of wounding and damaging, and laws of murderers and preservation of life.

Secondly, the classification that Maimonides employs in the Book of Torts makes extensive use of certain parameters, on the basis of which he differentiates between various rules: (a) How was the damage caused? Was it caused by an animal owned by the person or as a result of a wrong that the person caused by his actions? (b) Who suffered the damage? Was it an animal, property, or a person? (c) What damage was caused? Was it property damage only or was it bodily injury? In light of these parameters, the tort laws are ordered from least to most serious. They begin primarily with rulings concerning damage caused to property by property owned by the damager (Laws of Property Damages), and concerning damage caused by a person who robs or steals the property of another (Laws of Theft and Laws of Robbery). They then move on to bodily injury (Laws of Wounding) and finally to manslaughter (Laws of Murderers).

In light of these parameters, Maimonides draws a basic distinction between the laws of damage caused by one's property – property damages[10] – and the laws of damage caused by the person himself – the causer of bodily injury or damage to property. Among the laws applying to those causing bodily injury and damage he clearly distinguishes between a person who damaged another's property (Laws of Damaging) and one who physically injured another (Laws of Wounding).

Special attention must be paid to the fifth and last unit of laws in the Book of Torts, which deals with the greatest possible injury possible and its prevention: Laws of

---

[10] Within these rules there are secondary distinctions, such as those between rules of property damage, damage caused by beasts belonging to a person (ox damages), and damage caused by persons (pit and fire). Moreover, he distinguishes between an ox that gores another ox and one that gores a person.

Murderers and Preservation of Life. True, these laws, too, deal with damages, but as opposed to all other tort laws, in which the damager or the thief pays compensation, in relation to murder Maimonides states: "The court is warned against accepting ransom from a murderer, even if he offers all the money in the world and even if the avenger of blood agrees to let him go free."[11] The reason for this, says Maimonides, is because "… the life of the murdered person is not the property of the avenger of blood but the property of God …. There is no offense about which the law is so strict as it is about bloodshed"[12] and "… although there are worse crimes than bloodshed, none causes such destruction to civilized society as bloodshed."[13]

At the end of the Laws of Murderers and Preservation of Life – which conclude the Book of Torts – Maimonides deals with a person's obligation to preserve his own life, such as the obligation to build a rail around the roof.[14] This is simply an example of much wider obligations: in relation to anything that is liable to entail danger, there is a duty to set it at a distance and to guard against it and to ensure that it is in good repair;[15] this also includes the prohibition against eating food that is dangerous to one's health.[16] This attaching of the laws of self – preservation to the laws of murderers is intended to show that the prohibition against murder is anchored in the sanctity of life, which necessitates not only restrictions on violence but also active preservation of life. The flip side of the prohibition against spilling blood is the commandment to save life, "for if one destroys the life of a single Israelite, it is regarded as though he destroyed the whole world, and if one preserves the life of a single Israelite, it is regarded as though he preserved the whole world."[17] The reason for this, as Maimonides wrote in the *Guide*, is that "one who is able to save an individual from perishing and refrains from saving him may be said to have killed him."[18] Maimonides greatly extended the scope of the duty to rescue. According to Maimonides, not only does anyone who is able to save another from death and does not do so violate the prohibition, "You shall not stand idly by the blood of your neighbor (Leviticus 19:16)," but this is also the law with respect to a person who is able to prevent damage or loss to his fellow, whether with his body or with his property.[19]

According to Maimonides, tort law is part of the whole range of laws that are intended to ensure decency in the person and in society, as will be analyzed at length in the following chapter dealing with Maimonides' jurisprudence. In that

---

[11] Laws of Murderers and Preservation of Life 1:4.
[12] *Ibid.*
[13] *Ibid.* 4:9.
[14] Laws of Murderers and Preservation of Life 11:1–4.
[15] *Ibid.* 11:4.
[16] *Ibid.* 11:5–12; 12:1–6.
[17] *Ibid.* 1:16.
[18] GUIDE 3:10 (Pines, 439).
[19] *See* his formulation in Laws of Murderers and Preservation of Life 1:14; *See infra* Chapter 4, Section B.4.

context, Maimonides posits in the *Guide* that the jurisprudence of the Torah is based on three levels, which are included in three groups of precepts:

> The precepts which relate to the prevention of wrong and violence; they are included in our book in the section *Torts*;... precepts respecting fines, e.g., the laws of theft and robbery [which are also included in the Book of Torts in the Code – Y.S. & B.S.] ... [and] those laws which regulate the business transactions of men with each other [that are contained in the Book of Acquisition and the Book of Civil Laws].[20]

From Maimonides' words it is evident that tort law and criminal law complement each other, and as stated, both are included in the Book of Torts, for without punishment of the damager, "injury would not be prevented at all, and persons scheming evil would not become rarer."[21] He also emphasizes there that "[t]hey are wrong who suppose that it would be an act of mercy to abandon the laws of compensation for injuries; on the contrary, it would be perfect cruelty and injury to the social state of the country. It is an act of mercy that God commanded, 'judges and officers thou shalt appoint to thee in all thy gates' (Deuteronomy 16:18)."[22]

This is the appropriate point at which to address that earlier-mentioned principal characteristic of Maimonides' tort theory, namely, the blurring of the boundaries between the laws of tort and criminal law.[23]

Now, Maimonides also drew distinctions in the various rulings in the Book of Torts between criminal and monetary aspects.[24] Maimonides also ruled, following the Talmud, that when an act has been performed which is subject to a severe penal sanction, such as the death penalty, the offender is not liable, in addition, to pay tortious compensation. He is sanctioned only in criminal law and not in tort law.[25]

At the same time, it is certainly possible to say in general that Maimonides' Book of Torts contains monetary rulings and penal rulings side by side, and the boundaries between the two types of rulings are not infrequently blurred.

In modern law, tort law and criminal law are two completely different fields of law in their nature and in their modes of proof. It is true that in modern law too, there are some points of contact between the two areas, such as punitive damages (which

---

[20] GUIDE 3:35, according to Friedlander's translation, at 329-30. And *see* the discussion of R. NAHUM RABINOVITCH in STUDIES IN MAIMONIDES' THEORY 61 (2nd expanded ed., 5770) (Heb.) on orders, obligations and objectives in Maimonides' theory.
[21] GUIDE 3:35 (Friedlander, 330).
[22] Ibid.
[23] This blurring of boundaries also occurs in other sources in the talmudic and post-talmudic literature. See R. ISRAEL ZEV GUSTMANN, KUNTRAS SHI'URIM, BAVA KAMMA, lecture 2 (Jerusalem 5756), who summarizes the positions on the question of whether tort laws are part of the laws of property or of criminal law.
[24] Maimonides sometimes even treated the different aspects of a particular matter separately, such as the law of the pursuer, the monetary aspects of which he dealt with in Laws of Wounding and Damaging 8:13-16, whereas the criminal aspects were dealt with in Laws of Murderers 1:6-13.
[25] *See* Laws of Wounding and Damaging 4:3-5; Laws of Murderers 1:4.

will be discussed in Chapter 5), or compensation for the victim of a crime in the framework of a criminal process, but overall, modern law retains the distinction between the two areas. As opposed to this, in ancient law in general, and in Jewish law in particular, there has been a mixing of the fields of criminal law and civil-private law, such that in many civil areas – particularly in tort law – we find matters framed in terms of criminal punishment. A clear expression of the fact that tort law has a strong connection to criminal law can be seen from Maimonides' differentiation in the *Code* between the books that deal with clearly financial matters – Book of Civil Laws and Book of Acquisition – and between the Book of Torts, which includes different laws: laws of property damages, laws of theft, laws of robbery and lost property, laws of wounding and damaging, laws of murderers and preservation of life. This is a unique system of classification, in that it includes laws that are usually classified as civil-private (such as the laws of property damages, lost property and wounding and damaging) alongside laws which are normally classified as criminal (such as theft, robbery and murder). One would be hard-pressed to find a codex of tort law similar to that of Maimonides in modern Western systems of law.

2 Relations between Torts, Criminal Law and Contract Law in Contemporary Jurisprudence

Some scholars regarded tort law in the common law and in general as laws which came from a different legal field, for it is quite clear that they were not part of the law from time immemorial. Thus, there were those who thought that tort law in fact developed from the criminal law, and in fact, until today there are provisions for cases in which the same facts constitute both a criminal offense and a tort.[26] In the past, the relief in such cases was awarded by the same court, but with time this changed.[27] Nevertheless, even though there are two different tracks today, there is still a strong connection between the criminal law and tort law.[28] The law of torts

---

[26] PROSSER & KEETON, ON TORTS 8 (5th ed., 1984) [hereinafter PROSSER & KEETON] (adding that obviously, not every criminal offense today is also a tort, and not every tort is an offense: *ibid.* at 9); WILLIAM SEARLE HOLDSWORTH, A HISTORY OF ENGLISH LAW vol. III, 317–18 (London, 3rd ed., 1923), vol. VIII, 301 ff. (1923) (expanding on crime and tort in general); FREDERICK POLLOCK & PHILIP AISLABIE LANDON, POLLOCK'S LAW OF TORTS 455 (14th ed., 1939) (discussing criminal and tort law with respect to trespass). In the past, the rule that "trespass is merged in a felony" pertained in English law, and by virtue of this rule, the right to bring an action in tort did not exist if the facts also constituted a felony. *See*: JOHN WILLIAM SALMOND & R. F. V. HEUSTON, SALMOND ON THE LAW OF TORTS 778 (14th ed., London, 1965) [hereinafter: SALMOND].

[27] PROSSER & KEETON, *supra* note 26, at 8; DAN B. DOBBS, THE LAW OF TORTS 4 (2000) ("In the development of English law, tort law arose out of criminal law. Judges who imposed punishment upon lawbreakers at one time also occasionally imposed civil liability. Judges and lawyers gradually perceived that criminal punishment and civil liability had related but distinct purposes. Tort law developed into a separate field in itself, aimed at providing distinctly civil remedies.").

[28] PROSSER & KEETON, *supra* note 26, at 9; Izhak Englard, *The Different Types of Damages*, THE LAWS OF TORT 165 (Gad Tedeschi ed., 1st. ed., 1969) (Heb.) (arguing that in ancient times in

entered into the place where there the law wished to relate to the victim of the crime as well and to compensate him, and since then, it has developed independently.[29] At the same time, clear traces of the criminal source remain, including the goal of deterrence, which according to certain scholars contains a punitive element,[30] and matters such as punitive damages,[31] compensation for victims in the criminal process,[32] and others.[33] Scholars emphasize that tort law sometimes serves – or should serve – as a type of criminal law for the purpose of imposing quasi-criminal sanctions, when the law is not interested in prohibiting the activity completely but

general, the distinction between liability in torts and criminal liability was not at all accepted, and in any case it was not absolute. After tort law was assigned a specific role of repairing the damage, there were those who felt conceptually uncomfortable with awarding monetary compensation for noneconomic damages, for this appeared to be punitive.) And *see* Christopher J. Robinette, *Can There Be a Unified Theory of Torts? A Pluralist Suggestion from History and Doctrine*, 43 BRANDEIS L.J. 369, 372–82 (2005) (providing an historical overview. Robinette explains that several theories exist that attempt to establish whether there is a unified theory of tort law, and he reviews mainly the approach of Holmes and his separation between intentional and unintentional torts, discussing at length the question of whether underlying tort law in general, or in cases in which strict liability is applied in particular, is in fact a substantive penal theory. Robinette proceeds to examine various theories and the extent to which they are based on criminal law). *See ibid.* at 396–90.

[29] Cf. PROSSER & KEETON, *supra* note 26, at 8 ("Although restitution is sometimes a stated condition of probation of a convicted offender, a criminal prosecution is not concerned directly with compensation of the injured individual against whom the crime is committed, and the victim's only part in it is that of an accuser and a witness for the state. So far as the criminal law is concerned, the victim will leave the courtroom empty-handed. The civil action for a tort, on the other hand, is commenced and maintained by the injured person, and its primary purpose is to compensate for the damage suffered, at the expense of the wrongdoer. […] The state never can sue in tort in its political or governmental capacity […]." They explain that some of the behaviors – offenses and torts – bear the same names and terminology, also for the same reason, i.e., that in the common law, torts and offenses were adjudicated in the same process. *Ibid.* at 8. But they add that "tort and criminal law have developed along different lines, with different ends in view […]." *Ibid.* at 8).

[30] Glanville L. Williams, *The Aims of the Law of Tort*, 4 CURRENT LEG. PROBLEMS 137 (1951), reprinted in MARK LUNNEY & KEN OLIPHANT, TORT LAW: TEXT & MATERIALS 18 (3rd ed., 2008) (arguing that the aim of deterrence in tort law originates in the aim of criminal deterrence, but also regards justice as one of the aims of tort law); JOHN AUSTIN, LECTURES ON JURISPRUDENCE OR THE PHILOSOPHY OF POSITIVE LAW, vol. 1 504 (5th ed.) (seeing punishment of the wrongdoer as a goal of tort law); see also Clarence Morris, *Rough Justice and Some Utopian Ideas*, 24 ILL. L. REV. 730 (1930); DOBBS, *supra* note 29, at 4 ("The purpose of criminal punishment is primarily to vindicate the state's interests in deterring crime and imposing justice. The purpose of tort liability is in no way inconsistent, but its emphasis is different. It is primarily to vindicate the individual victim and victim's rights and secondarily to confirm and reinforce public standards of behavior."). *See also* Englard, *supra* note 27, at 165 (citing various scholars, according to whom it is actually the compensation for non-economic damages that is characterized by punishment of the wrongdoer).

[31] PROSSER & KEETON, *supra* note 26, at 9–15; Percy H. Winfield, *The Province of the Law of Tort* 200 ff. (TAGORE LAW LECTURES DELIVERED IN 1930) (1931) (who distinguished between punitive damages and punishment). This matter will be discussed infra Chapter 5.

[32] Winfield, *ibid.* at 202 ff.; SALMOND, *supra* note 26, at 9, note 2.

[33] Such as: conduct that is both criminal and tortious. *See* DOBBS, *supra* note 27, at 4.

wishes to introduce a strong deterrent to its execution, and thus, tort law serves *de facto* as a type of criminal law.[34]

There are those who explain that in ancient law, tort law served as a type of vengeance, albeit symbolic. Compensation payments serve as a substitute for revenge and forcibly taking the law into one's own hands. Today, in most cases nothing remains of this except for the psychological element, for in most bases it is the spreader of the loss with deep pockets – the insurance – that pays.[35] As opposed to this, Calabresi explains that in fact, the criminal law served as a deterrent reason for compensation, and with the passage of time this function was transferred to tort law, even if in some cases.[36] If the torts had still been subject to criminal punishment, people would not refrain from doing not only things which were quite dangerous, but from any act that might entail danger.[37] The punishment was too severe, and because in early societies of the common law, they did not really want to punish severely (by hanging, or lashes and suchlike) for theft, negligence or negligence on the part of a worker, they looked for ways in which to deter other than by criminal punishment, and thus they came to tort law.[38] According to Calabresi, tort law has an important connection with both contract law and criminal law, positioned in the space between them.[39] With respect to the connection between tort law and criminal law, it appears that deterrence too serves as a common aim, and according to Calabresi, the two systems work alongside each other.[40] However, on this point there is apparently a difference between Calabresi and Maimonides. Earlier we saw that for Maimonides, the element of quasi-criminal moral culpability was clearly present in the different parts of tort law, and particularly with regard to wounding.

---

[34] *See, e.g.*, GUIDO CALABRESI, THE FUTURE OF LAW AND ECONOMICS: ESSAYS IN REFORM AND RECOLLECTION 129 (Yale University Press, 2016) (presenting an example from family law and referring to Benjamin Shmueli, *Post Judgment Bargaining with a Conversation with the Honorable Judge Prof. Guido Calabresi*, 50 WAKE FOREST L. REV. 1181 (2016)); Dan M. Kahan & Eric A. Posner, *Shaming White-Collar Criminals: A Proposal for Reform of the Federal Sentencing Guidelines*, 42 J. L. ECON. 365 (1999) (calling to use shaming and apologies as a substitute to criminal sanctions).

[35] *See* Albert A. Ehrenzweig, *A Psychoanalysis of Negligence*, 47 N.W.U. L. REV. 855 (1953).

[36] *See* Guido Calabresi, *Toward a Unified Theory of Torts*, 1:3 JTL – Journal of Tort Law, article 1, at 6–7 (2007).

[37] *Ibid.* at 9.

[38] *Ibid.* at 4–5. At the same time, there are those who are of the opinion that within deterrence – not only optimal but also of the classical kind – there lies an aspect of justice. *See* Israel Gilad, *On the Complementarity Approach to the Goals of Tort Law*, IZHAK ENGLARD BOOK 57, 71–72 (Daphne Barak Erez & Gideon Sapir eds., 2010) (Heb.).

[39] Guido Calabresi, *Torts – The Law of the Mixed Society*, 56 TEXAS L. REV. 519 (1978); Calabresi, "Toward a Unified Theory of Torts," *supra* note 36, at 1–2.

[40] Calabresi, "Torts – The Law of the Mixed Society," *supra* note 39, et passim. On rejection of the approach whereby the existence of a contractual system alone or of a penal system alone is sufficient, *see ibid*. at 527; CALABRESI, THE FUTURE OF LAW AND ECONOMICS, *supra* note 34, at 118–19 (comparing prevention in torts to prevention in criminal law, in a discussion of limitation as opposed to prevention in the framework of specific deterrence).

Nevertheless, there are clearly many differences between tort law and criminal law. These include the criminal law requirement of intent for the purpose of the *mens rea*, whereas in tort law, negligence usually suffices;[41] as well as the existence of criminal sanction for harming the security of society even if no harm is caused.[42] There are also many procedural differences, primarily the criminal prosecution by the state, as against a private action in torts by the injured party,[43] due to harm to the public.[44] Of course, there is also a difference in the burden of proof: beyond reasonable doubt in criminal law, as opposed to the balance of probability – preponderance of the evidence – in tort law.[45]

One might also have concluded that tort law arose from contract law, or from a lacuna that became evident in the use of contract law, even though it is now clear that contract and tort are two different areas of law. This is because the two have much in common (first and foremost, that they are both branches of the law of obligations), to the extent that it is sometimes difficult to distinguish between these two areas of law.[46] Moreover, both contract law and tort law may sometimes be applied to the same behavior.[47] Let us first address the difference between them, which derives primarily from the way in which the obligation arises.

Dobbs writes:

[C]ontract duties are created by the promises of the parties, while tort duties are created by the courts and imposed as rules of law. On this view, the province of torts is wrongs and the province of contract is agreements or promises. Another conventional view […] asserts that contracts are largely about economic matters such as buying and selling; many torts typically involve physical harms.[48]

He adds and explains that contract law in fact reflects an arrangement or a regime of strict liability, whereas tort law relies mainly on fault,[49] and that contract law focusses on negotiation and the preparation of drafts of contracts, whereas tort law is largely occupied with litigation.[50]

In addition, the principal relief in contract law is enforcement; compensation constitutes secondary relief. In all events, a basic condition for the application of contract law is the existence of prior relations between the parties (or at least negotiations towards such relations). When damage is caused in the framework of

---

[41] DOBBS, *supra* note 29, at 5.
[42] DOBBS, *supra* note 29, at 5.
[43] DOBBS, *supra* note 29, at 5; PROSSER & KEETON, *supra* note 26, at 7; JEROME HALL, GENERAL PRINCIPLES OF CRIMINAL LAW 240–46 (2nd ed., 1960); Winfield, *supra* note 31, at chapter 8.
[44] PROSSER & KEETON, *supra* note 26, at 7.
[45] DOBBS, *supra* note 29, at 5.
[46] PROSSER & KEETON, *supra* note 26, at 655; Warren A. Seavey, *Book Review*, 45 HARV. L. REV. 209 (1931); Robinette, *supra* note 28, at 407–09 (explaining that matters of medical negligence and informed consent lie at the border between tort law and contractual law).
[47] PROSSER & KEETON, *supra* note 26, at 656.
[48] DOBBS, *supra* note 29, at 5. See also PROSSER & KEETON, *supra* note 26, at 655–56.
[49] DOBBS, *supra* note 29, at 5.
[50] Ibid.

contractual relations, the contract serves as a strong basis to explain why the damager must compensate the victim: he has various obligations towards him by virtue of the agreement between them.[51] However, when the damager causes damage and there is no existing contract between him and the victim, e.g., in cases of road accidents, the question arises as to the source of liability of the damager, and why he must compensate the victim. In many cases even today, the answer in torts is that a contract exists between the parties, such as in the case of a doctor who treats a patient or a manufacturer whose faulty product harms the consumer. But tort law applies even where there is no prior contract between the parties, and they are complete strangers, such as in cases of accidents and many others.[52]

The answer to the question of whether tort law developed from criminal law or from contract law may not be unequivocal. It may be that tort law grew both from the need to recognize the rights of the victim of the crime which were not

---

[51] *Ibid.* at 6 ("[I]t is usually true that rules of law govern tort cases, while the parties' agreement determines contract liabilities; but the parties' agreement controls their rights only because courts accept a rule of law that says so. For this reason, a rule of law ultimately lies behind both tort and contract. […] [C]ontractual promises sometimes create or at least underlie tort duties, so that what begins as contract ends as tort if one of the parties is injured. […] A third area of overlap occurs when tort law is invoked to protect contract rights." And *see* there additional matters which according to Dobbs connect contractual law with tort law. Dobbs also mentioned, *ibid.* an approach which he calls radical, suggesting that there is no substantive difference between the systems of law, and the differences are primarily manipulative, connected to whether the courts wish to punish or not, or to emphasize public policy: *ibid.* at 6. As opposed to this, he also presents a more moderate approach, according to which the differences between the systems of laws are more a matter of degree than of kind, and that contract law involves promises, whereas tort law involves foreseeability on the part of the parties, and not usually specific promises, and the existence of tort law between strangers proves this. See *ibid.* at 6–7. Another nexus between tort law and contract law is in the context of the tort – recognized in some legal systems – of causing breach of contract. Another nexus is the matter of participation – indemnification – between tortfeasors, which is a type of contract, as well as the issue of subrogation. We will not expand on these here. For the effects of contract law on tort law with respect to autonomy, *see* Robinette, *supra* note 28, at 395–96.)

[52] DOBBS, *supra* note 27, at 7 ("Numerous tort cases are characteristically disputes between strangers, that is, people who have no special relationship marked by contract. Such cases cannot be thought of as involving any contract law or any overlap with the field of contracts."). And *see* the famous case of Donoghue v. Stevenson [1932] A.C. 562 (dealing with the question of how liability may be imposed on a manufacturer in a case in which the person who was harmed by the product did not purchase the product, and therefore no contractual relations had formed between the parties. The Court imposed a tortious obligation by virtue of the need to love one's fellow, as mandated by the religious precept "You shall love your fellow as yourself." For a discussion of this and on reaching the conclusion that an obligation in torts is negative, by way of the duty to refrain from harming another, and not by way of the positive commandment to love one's fellow, *see*: HCJ 164/97 Conterm Ltd. V. Finance Ministry, Customs and VAT Division [Feb. 4, 1998], Cheshin J., available at https://supreme.court.gov.il/Pages/SearchJudgments.aspx?&OpenYearDate=1997&CaseNumber=164&DateType=1&SearchPeriod=8&COpenDate=null&CEndDate=null&freeText=null&Importance=null and also http://versa.cardozo.yu.edu/opinions/conterm-ltd-v-finance-ministry. See *also* CA 2034/98 Amin v. Amin [October 4, 1999], Englard J., available at https://supremedecisions.court.gov.il/Home/Download?path=English Verdicts\98\340\020\Q07&fileName=9802034o.Q07.txt&type=4 and at http://versa.cardozo.yu.edu/opinions/amin-v-amin).

recognized in the criminal law, and in the framework of which there was no room to conduct a detailed discussion of their realization, as well as from cases of damages that were incurred outside of any contractual framework. Indeed, Christopher Robinette argues that

> Tort law developed on an ad hoc basis as new fact situations presented themselves, to be resolved as best suited the needs of the communities in which they arose. Furthermore, the "rules" that were created in this process were not conceived to be related to one another; what has become torts was essentially the residual category or "catch-all" of the common law. As such, it was constantly intermingled with concepts from the more "pure" areas of law, such as criminal law, contracts and property. [...] As White noted, tort and criminal law often overlapped. However, criminal law was not the only area of law to intermingle with torts; contracts and property did so as well. The existence of criminal, contract and property concepts within tort doctrines makes it even less likely that torts has an integrating principle. [...] [I]t was the common law's residual area of civil liability; not conceived to be a coherent subject matter. Perhaps as a result, there has been a significant influence on tort doctrines of concepts from other areas of law. These concepts from criminal law, contracts and property are based on goals foreign to, and not necessarily consistent with, the tort goals.[53]

In modern legal literature, and particularly in the path-breaking article of Kenneth Mann on civil-criminal sanctions,[54] the argument was raised that legal changes that occurred in the modern period led to the development of an intermediate field – civil law that has a penal goal (to avenge and to deter), which led to a new type of sanction: the punitive-civil sanction.[55]

Maimonides, as we have seen, surely agreed that tort law and criminal law were intermeshed, but he placed far less accent on the connection between tort law and contract law, as we shall see in the following part. However, this does not necessarily rule out the possibility that according to Maimonides too, contract law had some effect on tort law, particularly in relation to laws concerning the liability of watchmen for damages they caused, in which the contractual basis is dominant.

---

[53] Robinette, *supra* note 28, at 390, 394, 412 (and *see ibid*. at 393, citing G. EDWARD WHITE, TORT LAW IN AMERICA: AN INTELLECTUAL HISTORY 3, 293 (2003) ("Although William Blackstone and his eighteenth-century contemporaries, in their efforts to classify law, identified a residual category of noncriminal wrongs not arising out of contract, torts was not considered a discrete branch of law until the late nineteenth century. [...] From its origins the field of torts has been defined by its residual status. It has been conceived as a field of civil actions, but not encompassing those arising out of contract; a field separate from criminal law, but often overlapping it").

[54] *See* Kenneth Mann, *Punitive Civil Sanctions: The Middleground Between Criminal and Civil Law*, 101 YALE L.J. 1795 (1992). Mann pointed out the problems that arise from blurring these boundaries and suggested a novel, challenging solution to these problems: the fashioning of a new theory of law for an intermediate area, a theory that will combine, in a novel way, elements both from the civil paradigm and the criminal paradigm.

[55] These sanctions are characterized by the fact that it is not possible to categorize them as civil or criminal, because they have characteristics from both areas, and they are liable to be activated both by individuals – e.g., punitive damages – and by the state – e.g., civil fines.

3 Penal Characteristics of Tort Law in Maimonides' Theory

We have seen that in the field of Jewish law too, as presented in Chapter 1 of this book, many scholars have offered modern descriptions of Jewish tort law. Most viewed Jewish tort law as part of Jewish civil-private law and laws of obligations. However, Maimonides had a different view. In Maimonides' classificatory system in the Book of Torts, he refrained from classifying tort law unequivocally as an area that is included clearly and exclusively in the framework of either civil-private law or criminal law.[56] Indeed, many of the laws that are cited in Maimonides' Book of Torts include aspects that are not only civil, for some of the payments – even though they are paid to the injured person-victim and not to the community or the state – are imposed not only as compensation, but also have a clear punitive aspect. Thus, for example, two-fold, four-fold, and five-fold payments for theft constitute not only compensation and restitution for the victim, but also a type of punitive damages that reflect an interesting policy of penal considerations, as Maimonides writes in the *Guide*.[57] At the same time, two-fold, four-fold and five-fold payments do not constitute a regular penal fine, for these payments are not made to the state but to the victim, and therefore they should be likened to the punitive damages that exist in modern law.[58] This is also the case in relation to payments for wounding, which[59] have a clear penal dimension alongside the civil one.[60] Nevertheless, as we will see later in the chapter, Maimonides distinguishes between the types of damage that are more closely related to the criminal law (a person who wounds and injures) and those that are more civil in nature (monetary damages). A more stark and clear distinction between the criminal law and tort law emerges from the *Guide*, in which Maimonides distinguishes between tort law – in which he includes only monetary damage and damage that a person causes to the property of another – and laws of restoration of lost property, on the one hand,[61] and criminal law, in which he includes the laws of a person who wounds another, laws of murderers, laws of theft and robbery, and more, on the other.[62] This distinction is more similar – though not identical – to the modern distinction between classic tort law and criminal law. However, in the *Code*, as opposed to the *Guide*, Maimonides includes all these laws in the Book of Torts.

---

[56] For as we know, the obligation to classify within the various frameworks the various laws or their provisions often leads to a type of dead end for various branches of law. Indeed, it might not be right to classify them in one particular framework or another, but rather, within a type of interim framework that has various civil-criminal aspects, such as in the proposal of Kenneth Mann, *supra* note 54.

[57] GUIDE 3:41.

[58] As will be argued and developed *infra* Chapter 5.

[59] As will be seen in Section C.4.

[60] For a precise analysis of the criminal and the civil components of the payments for the injury caused by a person who wounds another, see ILAN SELA, PAYMENTS FOR INFLICTING PERSONAL INJURIES IN JEWISH LAW: BETWEEN CRIMINAL LAW AND CIVIL LAW (PhD Thesis, Bar Ilan University, Ramat Gan, 2008) (Heb.), which is devoted to this subject.

[61] Which he dealt with in the GUIDE 3:40.

[62] *Ibid.* 3:41.

To complete the discussion of the penal characteristics of tort law in Maimonides' theory, we will mention an additional central distinction that Maimonides draws between damage caused by a person to the body of another, and damage caused by a person to a property of another. An expression of this important distinction lies in the fact that in the Book of Torts in the *Code*, we find Laws of Wounding and Damaging, to teach us that there is a difference between "wounding" (a person's body) and "damaging" (property). Maimonides' main innovation does not lie in the mere fact of the distinction between "wounding" and "damaging," for this technical-conceptual distinction between a person who injures another person and a person who damages the property of another has a basis both in the Bible[63] and in the Talmud.[64] Rather, it lies in the fact that according to Maimonides, there is a fundamental-substantive-legal difference between "laws of wounding" and "laws of damaging,"[65] and not merely a technical-conceptual one. As we will see in the following section, the laws of a person who injures another are more closely connected to criminal law than are the laws of a person who damages the property of another.[66] Ilan Sela correctly wrote that Maimonides' view that compensating bodily injury is considered to be a punishment (fine) has various legal ramifications, and it is the rules of criminal law, or at least some of them, that govern the laws of wounding, and not the regular civil-private law.[67] The detailed ramifications of the distinction between the laws of wounding and those of damaging will be elucidated at length in the following section. However, it should be pointed out here briefly that in relation to the person causing damage to property, too, there are some laws which are punitive in nature. An example of this is damages that is defined as not discernible, i.e., there has been no physical change in the form of the thing that has been damaged.[68] It will be emphasized that this is not a matter lying on the periphery of tort law, for many of the cases of damages are defined according to

---

[63] Two separate scriptural verses teach liability for damages caused by man, one dealing with a person who injures another person, and the other dealing with a person who damages property. The verse that speaks of a person who damages property is Leviticus 24:21: "One who strikes an animal shall pay for it," and the verse that speaks of damage caused by one person to another is Exodus 21:24: "An eye for an eye," which is explained by the Talmud (*Bava Kamma* 84a) and by Maimonides (Laws of Wounding and Damaging 1:5) as referring to monetary compensation.

[64] See, e.g., *Bava Kamma* 4b. R. Oshaya distinguishes between two types of injury caused by a person: injury of another person, and injury of an ox (i.e., property).

[65] As emphasized in the Book of Torts, Laws of Wounding and Damaging 5:11: "There is another difference between personal injury and damage to property."

[66] Rabbis from the Brisk school have already discussed the question of whether the payments for damage and wounding should be seen as criminal or civil. And see, e.g., the notes on the lectures of R. J. B. Soloveitchik on Tractate *Bava Kamma*, 4–6, 182–83, 188, 192, 217, 491–93 (New York 5764). For a similar discussion on the part of other later authorities, see KUNTRESEI SHIURIM, BAVA KAMMA, 21.

[67] SELA, *supra* note 60, at 20–21.

[68] According to the definition in the ENCYCLOPAEDIA TALMUDIT vol 8, 702, s.v. *hezek she'eino nikkar*.

the *halakhah* as damage that is not discernible.[69] If one causes damage that is not discernible to another's property, states Maimonides:

> he is exempt from paying compensation according to scriptural law, seeing that the property has not been altered and its form has not been adversely affected. But the Sages, on the authority of the Scribes, declared him liable inasmuch as he has reduced the value of the property, and he must pay the amount by which he has reduced its value.[70]

However, the basis of the obligation in relation to damage that is not discernible is punitive and not civil; in other words, it is a fine (even though it is paid to the victim), as Maimonides explains: "This payment is a penalty imposed by the Sages on the offender to prevent mischievous persons from defiling another's ritually clean food and saying, 'I am exempt.'"[71] Therefore, patently criminal law reservations apply to this payment:

(a) the obligation is personal only (and for example, there is no liability of an heir);
(b) the obligation depends on the *mens rea* of the wrongdoer who bears liability.

Accordingly, Maimonides rules:

> Consequently, if one who has caused damage that is not discernible dies, the compensation may not be collected from his estate. For the Sages penalized only the person who transgressed and caused the damage, but they did not penalize the heir, who committed no such act. Similarly, if one inadvertently or accidentally causes damage that is not discernible, he is exempt, because the Sages penalized only that person who knowingly intended to inflict damage.[72]

Moreover, it is not only in the Laws of Wounding and Damaging, but also in the Laws of Property Damages that Maimonides cites a number of laws that are clearly penal in nature. One outstanding example of this is the stoning of an animal that killed a

---

[69] For a comprehensive definition of damage that is not discernible, *see* the lecture of R. AHARON LICHTENSTEIN, DINA DEGARMEI 75 (Alon Shvut, 5769): "Discernible damage is physical damage to the object. Nondiscernible damage is damage that is not physical, but related to Jewish law. For example, imposition of the status of impurity on a pure object (for example, a ritual pouring of the wine of another which nullifies its kosher status, even though this cannot be seen physically in the wine itself. It is also a matter of tainting that which is holy, even if this does not render it impure, such as puncturing the ear of an animal in a way that cannot be seen but which renders the animal unfit for sacrificial purposes – the authors). The examples cited in the *gemara* deal with a change of halakhic status – even though on its face, a change in legal status that causes damage (for example, decreasing the legal value of currency) will be considered damage that is not discernible."
[70] Laws of Wounding and Damaging 7:1.
[71] Ibid. 7:3.
[72] Laws of Wounding and Damaging 7:3. R. LICHTENSTEIN, *supra* note 69, at 92, concluded from this ruling (the source of which is in *Gittin* 44b) regarding the nature of nondiscernible damage, that is not considered damage by virtue of rabbinical law either, i.e., that even at the level of rabbinical law there is no inbuilt halakhic basis for obligating the damager in respect of damage that is not discernible; rather, this is purely a fine, which is intended to prevent an undesirable social phenomenon.

person, which according to Maimonides in the *Guide*, "is a punishment for its [the animal's] owner."[73] Even the "atonement fine" (*kofer*) paid by the owner of an animal (when the owner has already been warned that the animal is dangerous)[74] that kills a person is not a regular civil payment, but is clearly punitive. As Maimonides says in the *Code*, the Oral Tradition interprets the biblical statement (Exodus 21:29), "And its owner shall also be put to death," as implying death by the hand of God, but if the owner pays an atonement fine for the person killed, he is pardoned.[75] In Maimonides' opinion, the purpose of the atonement fines, which are paid to the victim, are atonement for the owner of the animal, and a substitute for the death penalty.[76]

C. CONCEPTUALIZATION OF DISTINCT CATEGORIES OF DAMAGE: A DIFFERENTIAL PERCEPTION

1 Introduction

Maimonides did not view all types of damage as being of one piece; rather, he drew a fundamental distinction between different types of damages, each of which had a particular objective that was not necessarily relevant to another type of damage. The basic division into different types of damages, which we call the differential perception, arises from the conceptual system of classification of the Book of Torts in the *Code*. Central to this system are the fundamental distinction between damages that are caused by a person's property (Laws of Property Damages) and damages that are caused by the person himself (Laws of Wounding and Damaging); an internal distinction within the laws of property damage between animals who cause damage (including the basic distinction between an animal whose owner has been warned

---

[73] GUIDE 3:40 (Pines, 556).
[74] Only in the case of a *mu'ad* ox that killed is the owner liable to pay an atonement fine. *See* Laws of Property Damages 10:2.
[75] *Ibid.* 10:4.
[76] He therefore rules that "if an ox belonging to two partners kills, each [of the partners] must pay the full ransom, for each needs complete atonement" (Laws of Property Damages, 10:5). The obligation to pay atonement fines depends on the fault of the owner of the animal, and therefore he pays the fine only if the beast that killed was *mu'ad*, as Maimonides explains: "For since the owner has been warned that he has an ox in his herd which has killed three times, it is his duty to keep guard over all his animals, and since he does not keep guard, he must therefore pay ransom [the atonement fine]." (Laws of Property Damages 10:3). For the said reason, in the case of an animal that was stoned that belongs to young orphans, deaf people and the mentally incompetent, "guardians need not pay ransom [atonement fine]. This is because ransom is a form of atonement, and minors, deaf mutes and imbeciles are not legally culpable and do not require atonement" (Laws of Property Damages 10:6). In this ruling, clear expression is given to the difference between regular tort compensation and payment of atonement fines, for it may be asked: given that the Sages ordered that a guardian be appointed to watch over the animals of minors and deaf mutes and mental incompetents, and he is even obligated to pay for the damages that the animal caused (Laws of Property Damages 6:3–4), why should he not also pay an atonement fine? The answer is that the atonement fine has a personal-penal-religious nature (atonement), and therefore it is not imposed on the guardian, even though he must pay regular compensation for damages that the animal in his charge caused.

due to previous incidents of injury, and an animal who has not injured previously) and the laws of the pit and of fire; the distinction between a person who injures another with his body (Laws of Wounding) and a person who causes damage to the property of another (Laws of Damaging); a distinction between the laws of theft, and the laws of robbery and lost property; a distinction between regular damages mentioned in the Book of Torts and between nuisance and damage to neighbors (which are regulated in the Book of Acquisition and not in the Book of Torts) and more. These distinctions between different types of tort laws have practical ramifications. For example, different regimes of liability (or standards of care) apply with respect to the different types of damages;[77] the distinction between a person who causes damage (to the property of another) and a person who wounds (bodily injury) impacts upon the possibility that the victim will allow the damager to cause him damage (valid condition-making) or injury (invalid condition-making) and upon a request for forgiveness (which is required in relation to physical injury); the distinction between a person's property that caused damage and damage that was caused by the person himself has ramifications for liability in tort in cases of unclear causation, and more.

Here it should be noted that Maimonides' distinction between different types of damage, on the basis of which his differential model is constructed, is also liable to be affected by the distribution of the different types of damages mentioned in the Book of Exodus.[78] Bernard Jackson's comprehensive study of the biblical law expounded in the *Misphatim* portion of the Book of Exodus[79] includes extensive discussion of the tort laws and criminal laws included therein, as well as a detailed analysis of the differences between the various categories mentioned in the verses, including assault,[80] the goring ox,[81] theft,[82] pit,[83] and fire.[84] We have no intention of deciding between the different interpretations of the scriptural verses that have been offered. It would appear, however, that many parallels may be found between Maimonides' formulations in the *Code*, and his distinctions between different types of tortfeasors and between the verses in the *Mishpatim* portion. The similarity between Maimonides' formulation and the scriptural verses is also evident in several of the prominent characteristics of the various categories, such as the required standard of care in each,[85] as well as the connection of the various

---

[77] Which will be explained at length in Chapter 7.
[78] Exodus 21:1–22:16
[79] BERNARD JACKSON, WISDOM-LAWS: A STUDY OF THE *MISHPATIM* OF EXODUS 21:1–22:16 (Oxford: Oxford University Press, 2006).
[80] Exodus 21:18-19; JACKSON, *ibid.* at 172–208.
[81] Exodus 21:28-36; JACKSON, *ibid.* at 255–89.
[82] Exodus 21:37-22:3; JACKSON, *ibid.* at 291–312.
[83] Exodus 21:33-34; JACKSON, *ibid.* at 313–21.
[84] Exodus 22:4-5; JACKSON, *ibid.* at 321–30.
[85] *See, e.g.*, the verses that deal with injury in the Torah (Exodus 21:18–19), according to Jackson's interpretation (*ibid.* at 173): "deal with assault which occurs in the course of a quarrel – a case of intentional but unpremeditated injury." And *see also ibid.* at 180. A similar requirement of intention also arises from Maimonides' formulations in the rulings in Laws of Wounding and Damaging.

payments to the criminal law.[86] These findings support what we said in the previous chapter,[87] i.e., that Maimonides' formulations in the Book of Torts and in the *Guide* at times appear to have been strongly influenced by the scriptural formulations.

2 Internal Distinctions in the Laws of Property Damages

We shall begin with a discussion of the distinctions drawn by Maimonides in Laws of Property Damages, with which he began his Book of Torts. In Laws of Property Damages itself, Maimonides drew many distinctions, most of which were based on the Talmud, between different types of damages. However, here too Maimonides chose to adopt a system of organization which was innovative as compared to the Talmud.

One of the prominent characteristics of a legal system is its system of organization. It is common to distinguish between two such systems: the casuistic system of law, which comprises a collection of discrete cases, and codification, which incorporates the particular cases into rules and principles.[88] An outstanding example of this can be found in the area of tort law. In a casuistic system, tort law is a collection of particular torts (norms that describe occurrences of damage); in a codificatory system, tort law is based on a general, comprehensive tort, a type of mega-tort, that determines the liability of the tortfeasor.[89] The organization and the structure of the biblical, talmudic and post-biblical tort laws are a clear example of the distinction between codification and casuistry.

Tort law in the Bible is organized primarily according to cases, in keeping with the common legal system in the Bible, which is casuistic.[90] In these cases, four types of damage are distinguished: the goring ox, the pit, fields (or orchards) being eaten or trampled by animals, and fire. In an interesting article, Itzhak Brand examined the organizing methods of tort law in the tannaitic literature.[91] Brand suggests that the

---

[86] See, e.g., Jackson's discussion, *ibid.* at 133–38, of the essence of the biblical ransom (*kofer*) which replaces the punishment (death). A similar approach emerges from what Maimonides writes in the CODE and in the GUIDE.

[87] Following Bernard S. Jackson, *Maimonides' Definitions of* Tam and Mu'ad, 1 JEWISH L. ANNUAL 168 (1978).

[88] Black's Law Dictionary, "Code," 8th ed. 2004, pp. 274–73.

[89] A. TUNC (ED.), INTERNATIONAL ENCYCLOPEDIA OF COMPARATIVE LAW, XI (I), s.v. *Torts*, Tübingen-Boston-2, London 1983, chs. 2, 5, 10.

[90] C. HAUFTMAN, HISTORICAL COMMENTARY ON THE OLD TESTAMENT, EXODUS, 86–89; WILLIAM H. C. PROPP, EXODUS 19–40: A NEW TRANSLATION WITH INTRODUCTION AND COMMENTARY (Anchor Bible) 185–86 (New York 2006); Dale A. Patrick, *Casuistic Law Governing Primary Rights and Duties*, 92:2 J. BIBLICAL LITERATURE 180–84 (1973); Bernard S. Jackson, *Exodus 21:18–19 and the Origins of the Casuistic Form*, 33:4 ISRAEL L. REV. 816–20 (1999).

[91] Itzhak Brand, *Heads of Damage – Legal Systems in the* Midrashim *of* Tannaim, 46 MAD'EI HAYAHADUT 17–40 (5767) (Heb.).

midreshei hamekhiltot scriptural exegeses from the schools of R. Ishmael and R. Akiva are divided on the question of whether it is possible to establish a uniform meta-principle for obligations in tort. Each has its own rules. Nevertheless, the opening *mishnah* in *Bava Kamma* connects the two processes in the two *mekhiltot*.

The *mishnah* first presents the four heads of damage: "There are four primary damagers: the ox, the pit, the *mave'h* (damage caused by an animal grazing or trampling) and the fire."

The *mishnah* then contrasts the various damagers with one another. By doing so, the *mishnah* intends to answer the question of why it was necessary for the Torah to mention liability for each of the four damagers separately:[92]

> The ox is not like the *mav'eh*, and the *mav'eh* is not like the ox. And neither this nor this (the ox and the *mav'eh*), which are living things, are like the fire, which is not a living thing. And neither this nor this (the ox, the *mav'eh* and the fire), whose ways is not to go forth and damage, are like the pit, whose way is not to go forth and damage.

The *mishnah* answers that each of the damagers possesses a unique prominent stringent feature, the presence of which could have been thought to be essential for liability.[93] It concludes: "The characteristic common to all of them is that their way is to damage, and the obligation for watching them is upon you, the owner."

The *mishnah* means that from the fact that each of these four damagers possesses different characteristics, it is evident that no single one of these characteristics is critical for liability. Rather, it is the characteristics common to *all* of them to which the owner's liability may be traced. These characteristics are: (a) the fact that these objects tend to cause damage from time to time if not watched, and (b) the fact that it is the owner who is responsible for watching them.

The difficulty in this type of eclectic editing lies in the fact that the two parts of the *mishnah* – the beginning and the end – contradict each other, and at very least render each other superfluous: if the framework of the damages can be defined by means of a uniform common denominator, as is done at the end of the *mishnah*, then there is no need for the heads of damage mentioned at the beginning. Alternatively, if the framework is based on the heads of damage that differ from each other, this contradicts what they have in common.

What path did Maimonides take? We will see that he clearly chose the path of generality and sought the broad common denominator.

A noteworthy phenomenon is the fact that Maimonides chose not to emphasize the central distinction made in tractate *Bava Kamma* in the Mishnah and in the

---

[92] Seemingly, the Torah could have mentioned only one or some of these damagers, and liability for the others could have been derived from those mentioned.

[93] Thus, had the Torah prescribed liability for only one of the damagers, it would not have been known that the owner is liable for the other damagers as well, which do not possess this salient feature.

Talmud, which is the distinction between the aforementioned four heads of damage. Instead, Maimonides chose to band together all the types of damage that are caused by an animal. As he wrote in the first ruling of Laws of Property Damages which opens the Book of Torts in the *Code*:

> If any living creature under human control causes damage, its owners must pay compensation for it is their property that caused the damage. When Scripture says, *if one man's ox hurt another's* (Exodus 21:35), the term ox includes any other domestic animal as well as wild animals and birds. Scripture speaks of damage by an ox merely because it is a common occurrence.[94]

Hence, according to Maimonides, the three heads of damage that involve the ox – damage from tooth, foot, and horn – should not be regarded as separate heads of damage, but as part of one general head of damage that includes all types of damages caused by animals.[95] In fact, only as the chapter proceeds does Maimonides note separately the three mishnaic categories of the general head of damage of "ox": "Three principal classes of injury may be caused by an ox: injuries by the horn, by the tooth and by the foot."[96]

The separation between the three mishnaic categories is required due to the differences between them with respect to the extent of liability. For example, in the public domain, damages by horn incur liability, but damages by tooth and foot are exempt. However, despite these differences between the mishnaic categories, Maimonides' opinion is that from the conceptual-principled point of view they have a basic common denominator, i.e., they are injuries caused by animals, which differentiates them from other types of damage.

We have seen, therefore, that the main distinction in the Mishnah and the Talmud between the four types of damage is not the main distinction in light of which Maimonides formulated the laws of property damages. Instead of distinguishing between the four heads of damage, Maimonides offered two different central distinctions within the laws of property damages – distinctions that are not really emphasized as general fundamental distinctions in the talmudic literature, even though they are mentioned in the *Talmud*. To a considerable extent these

---

[94] Laws of Property Damages 1:1.
[95] This was discussed by R. GUSTMANN, *supra* note 23, at chap. 1, sec. 11, p. 7. A similar conclusion as to Maimonides' ruling was arrived at by R. YITZHAK ZEEV HALEVI SOLOVEITCHIK, HIDDUSHEI MARAN RI"Z HALEVI, LAWS OF PROPERTY DAMAGES 66, 72–73 (Jerusalem 5379). A similar approach resonates in the words of Shmuel in *Bava Kamma* 3b, whereby the term "ox" in the Mishnah includes all kinds of damages that are caused by the ox, i.e., tooth, foot and horn. However, in his commentary to M Bava Kamma 1:1, Maimonides adopted Rav's interpretation of the *mishnah*, whereby "mav'eh" is damage caused by the tooth, and ox is the horn. Hence, one learns that Maimonides' position in the CODE whereby all damages caused by animals come under the one head of damage does not stem from his commentary on the Mishnah.
[96] Laws of Property Damages 1:10.

distinctions were developed and formulated by Maimonides as meta-distinctions, with far greater weight than was attributed to them in the talmudic literature.

In a ground-breaking study, Bernard Jackson[97] identified an important innovation introduced by Maimonides, who deliberately chose not to open the first rulings in the first chapter of his Book of Torts with the famous enumeration of tort principles, *arba'ah avot nezikin* – the traditional categories of damage caused by animals mentioned in the beginning of *Bava Kamma* in the Mishnah and the Talmud. Rather than invoking the obvious classification of "four heads of damage," Maimonides chose, later in the chapter, to emphasize the difference between an ox that is *tam* and one that is *mu'ad*:

> The one which did an act which it is its way to do always, in accordance with the custom of its species – that is the one (traditionally) called *mu'ad*; and the one which changes and does an act which all its kind so do always, for example the ox which gores or bites – that is the one (traditionally) called *tam*.[98]

Maimonides adopted the distinction between *tam* and *mu'ad* not as a marginal one relating only to the exceptional law of the ox that gored, but as a major classification, affecting all damages caused by animals,[99] by virtue of which a distinction is to be made between cases in which full compensation must be paid and those in which only half compensation is due:[100]

> How much compensation must the owner pay? If the animal caused damage by doing things which are natural and normal to it – for example, if one's animal eats another's straw or hay or does damage with its foot while walking – the owner must pay compensation for the whole of the damage from the best of his property .... If,

---

[97] *Supra* note 87.

[98] Laws of Property Damages 1:4, as translated by Jackson, *ibid.* at 168.

[99] *See* Laws of Property Damages 1:5: "There are five actions with respect to which an animal is regarded as innocuous (*tam*) and which are such that if an animal makes a habit of any of them, it becomes forewarned (*mu'ad*) with respect to that action, to wit: an animal is not forewarned with respect to (1) goring, (2) jostling, (3) biting, (4) squatting upon large articles, or (5) kicking. If, however, it makes a habit of any one of these acts, it becomes forewarned with respect to it. The tooth, on the other hand, is forewarned from the outset with respect to eating what is suitable for the animal; the foot is forewarned from the outset with respect to breaking things as it walks along; and any animal is forewarned from the outset with respect to squatting upon small pottery jars, or similar objects, and crushing them." These rules refer to regular animals. There are, however, five species of animals, which are deemed forewarned from their earliest existence (the wolf, the lion, the bear, the panther, and the leopard). *See ibid.* 1:6. An echo of Maimonides' distinction between an animal that is *mu'ad* and one that is *tam* can be found in *Bava Kamma* 4a. There, however, this was said incidentally relating to the particular case and not as a major distinction that was fundamental to property damages, as formulated by Maimonides.

[100] Jackson, *supra* note 87, at 169. Jackson further argued that Maimonides took an independent view of the biblical scheme, and did not simply adopt the mishnaic/talmudic conceptualizations of the material. According to Jackson, Maimonides came up with his own innovative conceptualizations; these are not necessarily driven by the legal and economic issues, but sometimes by broader philosophical issues (as demonstrated in Jackson's article).

however, it acts in an unusual way and causes damage by doing things which are not habitual to it – for example, if an ox gores or bites – the owner must pay for half of the damage.[101]

If this is the case, the need to understand the reason for the distinction between *tam* and *mu'ad* becomes more pressing, and we will deal further with this issue at a later stage.[102]

Another central internal distinction that Maimonides draws in the Laws of Property Damages is the distinction between damages caused by animals owned by a person, and damages caused by the actions of a human being – that of the pit and the fire. Here, too, Maimonides departed from the order of the *mishnah* that opens tractate *Bava Kamma*, which analyzes the heads of damage in this order: the ox (which gored with its horns), the pit, the tooth (damages caused by the tooth or the foot of an animal), and fire. In the Laws of Property Damages, however, Maimonides arranged the precepts,[103] and the subjects accordingly, in a slightly different order: he began with all the damages caused by animals, dealing with them in the first eleven chapters of the Laws of Property Damages, and only thereafter did he proceed to deal with damages caused by the pit and fire, in the last three chapters of Laws of Property Damages.[104] The basis for the said distinction is explained by Maimonides in the *Guide*, where he states that the purpose of tort law is "the prevention of acts causing damage." According to Maimonides:

> To provide great incentive to prevent damage, a man is held liable for all damage caused by his property or as a result of his actions, so that the man will pay attention and guard it lest it causes damage. Therefore we are held liable for the damage that our beasts cause, so that we may guard them. The same is true for fire and pit, which are the product of human action, and he can make sure to guard them so that they cause no damage.[105]

Maimonides distinguishes between damages caused by a person's property and damages resulting from his actions: this is the distinction between damages caused by an animal and those of fire and pit, which are the "product of human action." It will be noted that the structure of this statement in the *Guide* reflects and explains the structure of the laws of damages in the *Code*.[106] In the *Guide*, Maimonides placed

---

[101] Laws of Property Damages 1:2.
[102] *Infra* Chapter 5.
[103] *See* Maimonides' introduction to the Laws of Property Damages, indicating that these laws contain four positive commandments: (1) the laws regarding damage caused by [the goring of] an ox; (2) the laws regarding damage caused by the grazing [of an animal]; (3) the laws regarding damage caused by a pit; (4) the laws regarding damage caused by fire.
[104] A similar classification is evident in his Introduction to the COMMENTARY ON THE MISHNAH, p. 47, Shilat ed., where he mentioned the "laws of ox and pit and fire."
[105] GUIDE 3:40, 574 (the authors' translation of the Shwartz edition).
[106] Nahum Rabinovitch addressed this in *Liability for Property that Caused Damage*, 25 MA'A-LIYOT 79–80 (5765) (Heb.).

"all damage caused by a person's property" before damage "caused by his actions," and he did the same with respect to the order of the chapters in the Laws of Property Damages. The explanation for this phenomenon is that in this way, the objective of providing a "great incentive to prevent damage" is realized. In other words,

> that a person will be liable for the damage caused by his actions – that is hardly new. Needless to say, he is liable for a damaging action done by him personally, for this is required of a person even if he is not warned ... but even if he sat and did nothing to prevent the damage when he had the ability to do so, in respect of this, too, it is not so surprising that he should be required to pay. However, for damage done by his property, of which he was unaware and did not will it, surely if the Torah should obligate him in respect of this, it attests to the importance of the insistence upon avoiding damage.[107]

Accordingly, Maimonides opened the Book of Torts with the Laws of Property Damage, and not with the laws concerning a person who causes damage in which, as stated, not much was new. In the Laws of Property Damages he opened with those damages which incur liability because it was the person's property that caused the damage: these are the most innovative with respect to the actual liability in torts. Only later did Maimonides address the laws of damages caused by a person's actions – pit and fire damage – in which there is less innovation.

It will be noted that Maimonides' distinction in the *Guide* between damages caused by a person's property and damages caused as a result of his actions is not identical to the talmudic distinction between "damages caused by property" and "damages inflicted by a person."[108] The difference is this: according to the Talmud, damage caused by fire and pit are included in "damages caused by property," and only damages caused directly by a person himself are included in the category of damages inflicted by a person; this distinction was actually adopted by Maimonides in the *Code*.[109] In the *Guide*, on the other hand, Maimonides departed from the talmudic classification that he had adopted in the *Code*, and instead he included fire and pit in the damages that are caused by a person's actions. From where did Maimonides derive the said distinction? It would appear that Maimonides based his distinction on the scriptural verses. We have already mentioned Jackson's claim that at the beginning of the Book of Torts in the *Code*, Maimonides sometimes followed the formulations in the scriptural verses rather than those in the Talmud.[110] It appears that here too, in the *Guide*, Maimonides adopted the biblical distinction between a person's liability for the damages caused by animals that belong to him, in

---

[107] Rabinovitch, *ibid*.
[108] *See, e.g., Bava Kamma* 4a.
[109] In his distinction in the Book of Torts between Laws of Property Damages (which include damage caused by animals as well as pit and fire damages) and Laws of Wounding and Damaging (which include damage caused directly by a person himself).
[110] *See supra* Chapter 2.

respect of which the Bible states in the book of Exodus that the perpetrator of the damage is "an ox"[111] or "a man's ox"[112] and the person liable for the damage is "the owner of the ox"[113] or "its owner,"[114] and damages caused by a pit and a fire, in respect of which the Bible states that the perpetrator of the damage is the person who dug the pit or lit the fire: "And if a man shall dig a pit"[115] and "He that kindled the fire shall surely make restitution."[116] This is consistent with Maimonides' proclivity in part 3 of the *Guide* to explain laws as they appear in the Bible (and not necessarily in accordance with their talmudic interpretation) – a phenomenon that recurs often in the two chapters of the *Guide* that we have discussed in the present chapter (infra Section D).

The distinction between damage that is caused by a person's property and damage caused by his actions find expression in the difference between these two categories with respect to the definition of the element of tortious liability and to the scope of the compensation that is paid. Some of the later commentators sought to distinguish between damages caused by the property of the damager, such as damages caused by animals, and those that are defined as "hazardous," which are the pit and the fire.[117] The pit and the fire are distinct from damage caused by the property of the damager in that by their very nature they are considered "hazardous," liable to cause damage. We will first discuss the different talmudic definitions of pit and fire, and then look at the legal rationale of the distinction between the two, and the implications of the distinction for Maimonides' theory.

Let us begin with the talmudic parameters of the *pit*. A person must refrain from creating a public hazard, and if he does create such a hazard and it causes injury to a person or animal, he is liable to pay for the damage. The biblical prototype for this hazard is a *pit* that one digs and fails to cover properly, exposing the public to injury.[118] The essential characteristics of *pit* are that it constitutes an immediate danger and that it is stationary (i.e., the injured party is the one who approaches it). The Talmud categorizes *pit* thus: "[f]rom its very inception a *pit* is prone to damage [literally: the pit's initial creation was for damage], and it is your [i.e. the digger's] property, and the obligation of watching it is on you."[119] A pit in the public domain

---

[111] Exodus 21:28–32.
[112] Ibid. 21:35–36.
[113] Ibid. 21:28.
[114] Ibid. 21:36.
[115] Ibid. 21:33.
[116] Ibid. 22:5. Some Bible scholars (such as Finkelstein and Otto) argued that the Bible in the *Mishpatim* portion suggests a different distinction, i.e., between the "law of things" and the "law of persons." However, Jackson has shown that the biblical verses do not support this distinction. See JACKSON, *supra* note 79, at 266–70.
[117] R. GUSTMANN, *supra* note 23, sec. 13:4. Other later authorities wrote in a similar vein in relation to the pit, in which the obligation is due to having created the problematic thing. See, *e.g.*, R. ELIEZER SHACH, AVI EZRI: LAWS OF PROPERTY DAMAGES 12:3.
[118] See Exodus 21:33–34.
[119] Bava Kamma 3b.

is capable of causing damage from the moment it is dug; no further action on the part of the pit is necessary to cause the damage. By contrast, an ox and a fire are not damaging forces upon their very creation (or even at the point at which the owner is negligent in watching them); they must go forth and cause damage through independent action.

Let us now examine the parameters of the talmudic obligation of a person in relation to damages caused by *fire*. A person is liable for the damage done by the fire he sets or owns (e.g., a glowing coal) and fails to prevent from spreading.[120] The essential characteristic of fire is that it tends to travel to what it destroys through the agency of other natural forces (viz. normal winds and breezes). There is a question in the *Talmud* as to whether a person's fire is deemed "his property" (just like his animal), or whether it is also deemed "his arrows" (i.e., his own, ongoing force).[121]

We dealt with the technical difference between damage caused by a *pit* and that caused by *fire*. Let us now proceed to the legal distinction between a pit and fire. One possible distinction, as proposed by one commentator, stems from the language of the Bible, which distinguishes between a *pit* and *fire* in three aspects: (a) with respect to a pit, it is written, "the owner of the pit" whereas in relation to fire, "the owner of the fire" is not mentioned; (b) in relation to fire, it says, "the one who ignited the fire" shall surely pay, whereas in relation to the pit it does not say that the person who opened or dug the pit shall pay; (c) in relation to the pit, it is written, "who opens" or "who digs," i.e., who opens or digs with his hands, whereas in relation to fire it says, if a fire "goes forth," which means, even by itself.[122] By virtue of these distinctions, concludes that commentator, one must

> distinguish in relation to the actual obligation between pit and fire, for in a pit the obligation is not due to the act of digging and opening, but due to the ownership of the pit, and the digging and opening make the person the owner of the pit, which is not the case in relation to fire, where the obligation is not due to being the owner of the fire, but because of the act of igniting, as it says, "the one who ignites" the fire".[123]

A similar distinction between the "owner of the pit" and the "one who ignites" arises, in our opinion, from Maimonides' language in Laws of Property Damages, in his definition of damages from a pit as opposed to those from fire, and in his reference to the biblical verses. He defines *pit* damages as follows: "If one digs a pit in a public domain and an ox or a donkey falls into it and dies, the owner of the pit must pay for the whole damage caused ... For Scripture says, '*the owner of the pit shall make it good*' (Exod. 21:34)."[124]

---

[120] This is mentioned in Exodus 22:5.
[121] See *Bava Kamma* 22a–23a. The practical differences are discussed by the Talmud there.
[122] R. GUSTMANN, *supra* note 23, 13:4.
[123] *Ibid.* sec. 18.
[124] Laws of Property Damages 12:1.

Maimonides emphasizes that a person who digs the pit is defined as the "owner of the pit," referring to the scriptural definition, which for him constitutes not only a technical characteristic but also the legal basis for the obligation to pay compensation. In other words, the very fact that a person created the hazard of the pit makes him the "owner of the pit" and obligates him to pay compensation, even if he does not possess formal ownership of the pit. According to another of Maimonides' rulings, this means that a person is considered the owner of the pit not only if he actually dug it, but also if the pit was formed without his intervention. As he says:

> Whether one digs a pit deliberately or whether it has been formed of itself or by a domestic or a wild animal, the owner is liable for the damage it causes, since it is his duty to fill it up or cover it and he did not do so. It makes no difference whether one digs a pit or purchases it or is given it as a present, for when Scripture says, 'The owner of the pit shall make it good' ... it means every case in which the pit has an owner.[125]

The liability of a person in relation to a pit which has opened spontaneously or been dug up by an animal is far-reaching relative to the limited scope of tortious liability of a person for damages caused by his property,[126] who in similar cases is exempt from payment,[127] and we agree with the view that the difference in the scope of liability stems from the difference between the legal basis of liability of the pit, which entails liability for the fact of creating the hazard of which he is the owner, as opposed to that of the property of the damager.[128]

In defining the obligation to compensate for damages caused by *fire*, too, Maimonides adopted the scriptural definition which emphasizes the "one who kindles" the fire:

> If one kindles a fire in another's field and the fire spreads and causes damage, he must pay for the damage, for Scripture says, *If fire break out and catch in thorns so that shocks of corn or the standing corn ... are consumed, he that ignites the fire shall surely make restitution* (Exod. 22:5).[129]

In our view, Maimonides' emphasis on "he that kindles the fire" in accordance with the biblical text also expresses the legal basis for the obligation of the one who ignites the fire, as well as the proximity between the obligation of the one who ignites the

---

[125] *Ibid.* 12:3.
[126] Indeed, one of the earlier authorities' view payment in relation to the pit as a penalty and not as a monetary obligation, due to its exceptional nature and its gravity. See Rashba, *Bava Kamma* 2b, according to the explanation of Rabbi Gustmann, *supra* note 23, second chapter, sec. 3, p. 13. However, it does not seem that Maimonides defined pit as a penalty, but he certainly agreed that the scope of the obligation of a person for pit-related damages is greater than his obligation for damages caused by his property.
[127] Cf., *e.g.*, Laws of Property Damages 4:1.
[128] *See* AVI EZRI, *supra* note 117.
[129] Laws of Property Damages 14:1.

fire and that of a person for the damages that he himself caused to the property or person of another, in accordance with the rulings in Laws of Wounding and Damaging. This proximity also finds expression in the scope of the payments that the one who ignites the fire must pay in cases in which another person is injured as a result of the fire, which is wider than what is paid by a person for damages caused by his property.

From Maimonides' rulings, which are based on the talmudic sources,[130] we see that there are cases in which damage that is caused by fire is attributed to the person himself, being defined as damage caused by a person (rather than in the category of property that causes damage), with all the ramifications, such as liability for payment of greater compensation in the event that a person is injured as a result of the fire, and even to the imposition of capital punishment for killing a person, as he says:

> If a fire spreads and harms a person by burning him, the one who has kindled it is liable for the injury of that person, for his enforced idleness, his medical treatment, his pain, and the humiliation he suffers, just as if he had injured him with his own hand.[131] For although the fire is the kindler's chattel, he is regarded as one who has caused injury with a missile. If, however, one's animal or pit injures a person, he is liable only for the damage suffered, as we have explained.[132]

From this ruling it emerges that there is a difference between the outcome of the damage caused by fire, which is similar in certain circumstances to the damage caused by a person who injured another,[133] and the outcome of damage caused by an animal or by a pit,[134] which is deemed property damage for which payment is exacted only for the injuries suffered by another person, and there is no capital liability for killing him.

---

[130] See *Bava Kamma* 22a–23a.

[131] See Laws of Wounding and Damaging 1:1.

[132] Laws of Property Damages 14:15. *See also ibid.* 11:6 (liability of ox only for damage), 13:2 (liability of pit only for damage).

[133] Indeed, according to Maimonides's approach, a distinction must be made between the above-cited case, *ibid.* 14:15, in which the person who kindled the fire is defined as the damager, and the cases in which it is defined as the property of the damager, for which he must pay only for the damages, as he says there, at 14:4: "If one's courtyard catches fire, and a fence falls down independently of the fire and it spreads into the next courtyard, the rule is that the owner is liable if he could have restored the fallen fence but failed to do so. This is analogous to one's ox getting out and causing damage, in which case the owner is liable, for he ought to have taken care of it but failed to do so." The explanation is that because there was always a fence, and the fire could not spread, then kindling a fire is not similar to shooting an arrow, and when the fence later fell unrelated to the fire, this is a new event. Therefore, the obligation of the person who kindled the fire is when he did not erect a fence to protect his property, which later spread and caused damage.

[134] R. GUSTMANN, *supra* note 23, chap. 13, sec. 10, p. 202, already noted that there are many halakhic differences between a pit and fire, even though the liability in relation to them both is due to the problem they create.

3 Between Laws of Property Damages and Laws of Wounding and Damaging

One of the main distinctions that Maimonides draws in the Book of Torts is between damage that is caused by a person's property (Laws of Property Damages) and damage caused by a person's body (Laws of Wounding and Damaging).[135] This distinction, too, has a basis in the Bible and the Talmud,[136] but Maimonides expanded it and used it as one of the major legal axes of his tort theory. It has many ramifications: the principal one relates to the extent of the compensation imposed upon a person who wounds another (bodily injury), which is extremely broad compared to the compensation he must pay for property damage, from the aspect of the scope of heads of damage. Maimonides ruled that "[i]f one wounds another, he must pay to him for five effects [heads] of injury, namely, damages, pain, medical treatment, loss of employment, and humiliation,"[137] i.e., the one who inflicts a wound on his fellow can be liable for five aspects of injury: he must pay for the physical damage he caused the victim, he must pay for the pain suffered by the victim, he must pay the expenses of healing the wound, he must pay for the victim's inability to work as a result of the wound, and he is also liable for the humiliation he caused his victim. For property damage (caused by a person's animal or his property or by the person himself), however, the damager pays only for the major effect of injury (*nezek*), and he is exempt from paying for the other four effects of injury. The tendency to be more strict with respect to the person causing bodily injury as opposed to a person who damages another's property or a person whose property caused damage stems both from the fact that the damage that was caused to the body of the injured person is considered to be more serious (and of a punitive nature) than simple monetary damage caused to his property, and from the fact that a damager who wounded another is sane, and has a high-grade duty of care with respect to the consequences of his action. For this he must pay compensation for all the effects of injury caused to the victim, and this is not so when his property, and not he himself, caused the damage. The main difference between the Laws of Property Damage and the Laws of Wounding relates to the position of these laws on

---

[135] This distinction emerges not only from the division between the Laws of Property Damages and Laws of Wounding and Damaging in the Book of Torts in the CODE. In the GUIDE, too, Maimonides divides the biblical commandments into different groups, and includes laws of wounding in the sixth group, which includes the commandments relating to criminal activity (GUIDE 3:41), and not in the fifth group that contains the commandments found in the Book of Torts (3:40).

[136] See, e.g., the distinction between property damages and physical injuries in *Bava Kamma* 4a. ALBECK, in his INTRODUCTION TO MISHNAH BAVA KAMMA 10-15, already discussed the order and the contents of the *mishnayot* in that tractate, emphasizing the clear distinction between the first part of the tractate that deal with damages that are caused by a person's property (chapters 1–6) and the second part of the tractate (chapters 7–10) that deals with damages caused by a person by way of theft, wounding and robbery.

[137] Laws of Wounding and Damaging 1:1.

the scale between criminal law and civil-private law. Whereas the laws of wounding have a close connection to criminal law, the laws of property damage are much closer to regular civil-private law. This is evident, for example, in Maimonides' definition of the payments made by a person for damages caused by his property: "Whenever full compensation is payable, the payment is a monetary obligation that the damager must pay just as one who borrows from another must pay a loan."[138] According to Maimonides, the obligation to pay for the damage appears to be a monetary obligation in all respects, similar to the payment of a debt created by a loan.[139]

This difference finds expression, as stated, in the nature of the compensation paid, which derives from applying the effects of injury to a totally different extent for damages caused by a person's property and for those caused by wounding another. Some later authorities already concluded from what Maimonides wrote that whereas the payments that are made as compensation for regular monetary damage are intended to make restitution to the injured party for the monetary loss he suffered, and to restore the former situation insofar as possible, the payments for wounding are not intended to make restitution for the monetary loss.[140] Some understood this from Maimonides' ruling,[141] from which they deduced that "the human body is deemed a person's property"[142] and therefore injury that is caused to the body is not considered to be compensable monetary damage. Indeed, we see that in the framework of payments for wounding, there is an obligation to pay for humiliation suffered, despite the fact that this is not considered monetary damage. In addition, payment must be made for loss of employment, i.e., for prevention of profit, rather than for monetary damage. With respect to medical expenses, these would not seem to constitute a monetary obligation that can be assessed on a one-time basis, but a personal obligation to heal the wounded person totally even when the payment of damages that is made for the wounds is not sufficient to make up for all the wounded person's losses. From this it emerges that payment of the five effects of injury is not intended to make up for the wounded person's losses.[143]

Another important ramification of the distinction between damages caused by property and those caused by a person relates to the regime of liability (standard of care) required for each type of tort. As we will see later in the chapter,[144] fault is required at the level of negligence in order to obligate a person to pay compensation for damage caused by his property, as opposed to the regime of liability that is

---

[138] Laws of Property Damages 2:7.
[139] What R. Gustmann writes, *supra* note 23, chapter 1, sec. 5 p. 5, is therefore surprising.
[140] HIDDUSHE RABBENU HAIM HALEVI SOLOVEITCHIK, HILKHOT TO'EN VENIT'AN 5:3, s.v. *ela*; R. GUSTMANN, *supra* note 23, chapter 21, sec 2, p. 194.
[141] Laws of Property Damages 10:14.
[142] R. GUSTMANN, *supra* note 23.
[143] This is also the reason, as R. Haim Halevi Soloveitchik writes, that Maimonides deduced these five effects from the scriptural verses and not from reasoning. See Laws of Wounding 1:1-9.
[144] *Infra* Chapter 7.

required to obligate a person who has caused damage to the property of another (almost absolute liability).

This distinction, too, is related to the extra caution that is required of a person not to damage the property of another, due to his ability to control his actions, as opposed to the difficulty in controlling the actions of his animal. Nevertheless,[145] due to the unique penal nature of the laws of wounding, even the liability regime in that context requires (for some payments) a minimal *mens rea* (at the level exceeding negligence).

The said distinction between damage caused by a person's property and damage that a person causes to the property of another also finds expression in relation to awarding damages in cases of uncertain causation – an issue that we have discussed extensively elsewhere.[146] Here we will focus on Maimonides' unique theory on this matter.

In talmudic sources we find two central approaches to the possibility of awarding partial compensation in situations of uncertain causation. The approach of the majority of the Sages is that of the first model, "all or nothing" ("he who takes from his friend bears the burden of proof").[147] But the Sages' approach is not the only one. Another opinion that appears in the *Talmud* is that of Symmachus, who disagrees with the Sages and allows the award of partial compensation (i.e., 50 percent each) in cases of uncertain causation ("they must divide equally").[148] Halakhic authorities and decisors were divided on the question of whose view – that of the Sages or of Symmachus – was normative under Jewish law. The majority view was that of the Sages (i.e., he who takes from his friend bears the burden of proof).[149] The minority view was that money of undecided ownership (arising from factual uncertainty) must be divided according to Symmachus's position.[150] As shown elsewhere,[151] even according to the majority of Jewish legal authorities – first among them Maimonides – which in principle adopted the Sages' approach, there were cases in which considerations of judicial policy required an award of 50–50 compensation (i.e., "they must divide equally"), thus following Symmachus. According to Maimonides, the

---

[145] *Infra* Chapter 7.
[146] Yuval Sinai & Benjamin Shmueli, *Liability under Uncertain Causation? Four Talmudic Answers to a Contemporary Tort Dilemma*, 30 BOSTON U. INT. L. J. 449 (2012).
[147] M Bava Kamma 3:11. In that *mishnah*, there are additional cases that articulate the rule that "he who takes from his friend bears the burden of proof." For an expanded discussion on this topic, *see* Yuval Sinai, *The Doctrine of Affirmative Defenses in Civil Cases – Between Common Law and Jewish Law*, 34 N.C. J. INT'L L. & COM. REG. 111, 142–50 (2008).
[148] Symmachus enunciated the principle that "Money, the ownership of which cannot be decided, has to be equally divided," using the Hebrew term *yachloku*, which literally means "they must divide equally." *See, e.g.*, Bava Kamma 46a.
[149] *See, e.g.*, Tosafot on Bava Kamma 46a, s.v. *hamotzi*; R. Isaac Alfasi on Bava Kamma, ch. 5; Rabbenu Asher on Bava Kamma, ch. 5; CODE, Laws of Property Damages 9:2; TUR & SHULHAN ARUKH, Hoshen Mishpat 223:1.
[150] *See* M Bava Kamma 46a.
[151] Sinai & Shmueli, *supra* note 146.

distinction between damage caused by a person and damage caused by a person's property places an alternative limitation on the possibility of awarding partial compensation in cases of uncertain causation. In other words, although the outcome ought to be "all or nothing," a certain fine of partial compensation is imposed if the damage was caused by a human being.

If we were to apply this limitation to contemporary tort law, we would impose a "fine" of partial compensation in cases of uncertain causation that involve one person causing harm to another (e.g., medical malpractice), but not when the harm was caused by a person's property (e.g., harm caused by animals, or by a manufactured product such as a car or a machine). In other words, if contemporary law were to adopt the Maimonidean model in cases of uncertain causation, the law applying to a victim suing for increased risk caused by a doctor who was negligent in his treatment would be different from the law applying to a victim suing for increased risk as a result of a dog bite or defect product.

After having addressed the distinction between property damages and a person who wounds and damages, let us proceed to a discussion of the internal distinction within the laws of wounding and damaging, i.e., the distinction between the one who wounds and the one who damages.

4 Between Laws of Wounding and Laws of Damaging

What is the difference between the laws governing wounding, and those governing damaging (causing damage to the property of another)? The unique features of the laws of wounding relate not only to the amount of compensation, but also to the nature of the compensation and their purpose, which is different not only from that of damage caused by one's property but also from the laws governing a person who damages the property of another. According to Maimonides' approach – and of course, the source of this approach lies in the biblical verses and the talmudic literature[152]– the compensation for damages caused to another by a person who wounded him are not considered part of civil-private law (as compensation for damages caused to the property of another by a person or by his property)[153] but as part of criminal law, or at very least, as part of an intermediate framework that is

---

[152] Which devoted a special chapter in *Bava Kamma* – Chapter 8 – to the laws of wounding, while the laws of property damages and those of the person who causes injury are dealt with in Chapters 1–6.

[153] And cf. Maimonides's formulation in Laws of Property Damages 2:7: "Whenever a person must pay full damages, the payment is considered to be a monetary obligation that he is liable to pay, as if he had borrowed money from another." R. GUSTMANN, *supra* note 23, chapter 2, sec. 3, p. 24, concluded from this formulation that Maimonides' approach is that compensation is not paid for damages as a punishment but rather in the framework of civil-private law "as if he had borrowed money from another." However, this would seem to be correct only with respect to the Laws of Property Damages or the laws pertaining to a person who damaged the property of another, but not with respect to a person who inflicted injury on another, which is deemed to be penal.

situated between civil-private and criminal law.[154] In other words, even though compensation for bodily injury caused by the injurer is capable of restoring the situation of the injured person to its prior state, this is not its only objective. It has a punitive dimension, which involves the application of criminal law to a certain extent also within the framework of laws of wounding.[155]

An important expression of the penal nature of the laws of wounding concerns the nature of the payment that the injurer makes to the injured party. The Bible states, "An eye for an eye,"[156] but as is known, the Sages interpreted this to mean that one does not injure the limbs of the one causing the wounds, but imposes upon him monetary compensation: "An eye for an eye – money."[157] But is the objective of the payment made by the injurer indeed civil compensation, or a penal fine? From what Maimonides writes it emerges that the biblical injunction of "An eye for an eye" must not be ignored, and even though it is not practical, it is extremely significant in relation to the way in which the act of wounding and its legal ramifications must be regarded.

In the opening to the Laws of Wounding and Damaging in the *Code*, Maimonides indeed wrote that a person who wounds another must pay him for five effects, and stresses that these are payments that are made to the victim and not the imposition of the penalty of injuring the limb of the injurer.[158] From Maimonides' rulings in the *Code*[159] and from what he writes in the *Guide*,[160] (even though there are differences between them), it is evident that the payments imposed upon the injurer must be regarded as a criminal penalty that comes in place of the physical punishment – injuring a limb – which by virtue of the biblical law should have been imposed on the injurer. Indeed, it appears that this is not purely symbolic; rather, it is very significant in terms of values.[161] Moreover, in the Book of Commandments, Maimonides defines the compensation paid by a person who wounds another as "Laws of Fines".[162] In the *Code*, too, Maimonides rules that some of the five effects of injury, which are the payments paid by the injurer to another (damages, pain,

---

[154] As SELA showed, *supra* note 60.
[155] For extensive discussion of the scope of application of criminal law, See SELA, *ibid*.; GUSTMANN, *supra* note 23, chapter 21.
[156] Exodus 21:23.
[157] See e.g. Bava Kamma 83b and 84a.
[158] Laws of Wounding and Damaging 1:3.
[159] Laws of Wounding and Damaging 1:1–4.
[160] GUIDE 3:41.
[161] What is the meaning of the biblical injunction, "An eye for an eye" in view of the commentary of the Jewish sages (which was adopted by Maimonides) who did not interpret the verses literally and ruled that this was referring to monetary payment (a fine) and not corporal punishment? This was explained clearly by the well-known philosopher, EMMANUEL LEVINAS, DIFFICULT FREEDOM – ESSAYS ON JUDAISM 146–47 (The Johns Hopkins University Press, trans. Sean Hand, 1990). Also see infra Chapter 4, Section A.3.
[162] Book of Commandments, positive commandment 236. This emerges from the commentary on M Bava Kamma 8:1.

medical treatment, loss of employment and humiliation) are not defined only as compensation in tort, the objective of which is to compensate the injured party, but also – although some disagree with him – that the monies are also paid as a fine (punitive compensation), aimed at punishing the person who wounds another.[163]

Sela mentioned the ethical dimension underlying the definition of wounding according to Maimonides' approach:

> In classifying the laws of wounding within the framework of "criminal law" or at least not in the framework of "civil law" like all other tort law, there is an important moral statement, whereby one cannot, or more precisely, one ought not to relate to a person's body in purely economic terms. The attempt to assess the value of a person's hand to its owner in economic terms in loss of capacity to work, apart from the fact that in many cases this is a fiction which has no connection to reality, has the capacity to introduce a value dimension to a person's body in economic terms.[164]

Another practical ramification of the distinction that Maimonides draws between Laws of Wounding and the Laws of Damaging concerns the need for forgiveness on the part of the victim:

> If one inflicts a personal injury on another, he may not be compared to one who damages another's property. For if one damages another's property, atonement is effected for him as soon as he pays whatever is required. But if one wounds another, atonement is not effected for him even if he has paid for all the five effects, or even if he has sacrificed all the rams of Nebaioth, for his sin is not forgiven until he begs forgiveness of the injured person and is pardoned.[165]

An examination of Maimonides' rulings on this matter indicates that the request for forgiveness from the injured person is an inseparable part of the legal treatment of the injurer, and it joins the payment of compensation to complete the "atonement" of the injurer; this, as opposed to a general-religious request for atonement, which is required also from the person who damages the property of another as a moral obligation in the framework of the laws of repentance,[166] but it is not part of the

---

[163] Laws of Wounding and Damaging 5:6–7. Indeed Ra'abad, in his critical scholia to Laws of Wounding and Damaging 5:6 and Laws Pertaining to Disputes between Plaintiffs and Defendants 1:16, disagrees with Maimonides and holds that all the payments are monetary. And there are commentators who are divided on the nature of the payments for injury. According to Maimonides, the basis for the law governing the person who injures another does not belong in the category of criminal law, but the Bible prescribed that instead of administering corporal punishment, a fine is exacted from him, whereas Ra'abad disagrees with Maimonides and views causing injury to another as a matter of tort law. See AVRAHAM ALTER FEINTUCH, SEFER HAMITZVOT LERAMBAM IM PERUSH PIKKUDEI YESHARIM vol. 1, 526 (Jerusalem 5760). On the distinction between payment for damages as a fine and payment of damages as compensation for loss see also HIDDUSHEI RABBENU HAIM HALEVY, HIL. TO'EN VENIT'AN 5:3.
[164] SELA, supra note 60, at 340.
[165] Laws of Wounding and Damaging 5:9.
[166] See Maimonides' ruling in Laws of Repentance 2:9.

legal obligation of the damager, of which he disposes upon making payment to the victim.[167] In terms of the modern theory of criminal law, the request for atonement as required by Maimonides can be regarded as a type of restorative justice.[168] The use of forgiveness as a tool has been widely used in the restorative justice programs. Victims take an active role in the process. Meanwhile, offenders are encouraged to take responsibility for their actions, "to repair the harm they've done – by apologizing, returning stolen money, or community service."[169] However, there is also a significant difference between Maimonides' approach and the modern approach of restorative justice. Whereas according to Maimonides, asking for forgiveness comes *together* with the obligation to pay compensation for the injury and not in its place, modern approaches of restorative justice commonly talk mainly about seeking forgiveness and appeasement that *replace* the accepted punishment, without providing a satisfactory response to the actual violation of rights. Indeed, there has been criticism of the movement for restorative justice.[170] However, it seems that the criticism does not apply to Maimonides' approach, which is superior to that of restorative justice in that Maimonides does not forgo the need for payment of compensation for the injury to the victim's body, but rather, adds the obligation to seek forgiveness.

It should be mentioned that in modern law, a request for forgiveness is usually irrelevant, except for two central cases: in criminal law, at the stage of sentencing, and in libel cases, for the purpose of reducing the compensation or the sentence in the case of a criminal process. There have been suggestions to enact, for certain cases, a statutory requirement to express regret and apologize as a general – not religious – form of legal relief, in tortious actions as well.[171]

In certain states in the United States, these suggestions have indeed been adopted in the context of medical malpractice, whereby there is a place for an immediate apology

---

[167] According to the convincing explanation of SELA, *supra* note 6060, at 317–18.
[168] Restorative justice is an approach to justice that focuses on the needs of the victims and the offenders, as well as the community involved. This contrasts with more punitive approaches where the main aim is to punish the offender or satisfy abstract legal principles.
[169] *A New Kind of Criminal Justice*, PARADE 6 (October 25, 2009).
[170] According to Allison Morris, *Critiquing the Critics: A Brief Response to Critics of Restorative Justice*, 42 BRITISH J. OF CRIMINOLOGY: INT. REV. OF CRIME & SOCIETY 596 (2002), the following are some of the most common criticisms that are used against the practicality or realism of restorative justice: "restorative justice erodes legal rights; restorative justice results in net-widening; restorative justice trivializes crime (particularly men's violence against women); restorative justice fails to 'restore' victims and offenders; restorative justice fails to effect real change and to prevent recidivism; restorative justice results in discriminatory outcomes; restorative justice extends police powers; restorative justice leaves power imbalances untouched; restorative justice leads to vigilantism; restorative justice lacks legitimacy; and restorative justice fails to provide 'justice'."
[171] *See, e.g.*, Benjamin Shmueli, *Tort Litigation between Spouses: Let's Meet Somewhere in the Middle*, 15 HARV. NEGOT. L. REV. 201 (2010) (demonstrating from intrafamilial tort actions against spouses); Benjamin Shmueli, *Love and the Law: Or, What's Love Got to Do With It?* 17 DUKE J. OF GENDER L. & POLICY 131 (2010) (demonstrating from intrafamilial tort actions against parents).

to the victim of medical negligence and his family, and the arrival at a quick (and cheap) settlement.[172] However, this process has come under criticism, due to the fact that such laws of apology constitute in fact a reform of tort law via the back door, and they express a victory for the insurance lobby which is interested in reducing dramatically the compensation awards for medical malpractice, and for this purpose it exploits the victims and their families in their difficult moments.[173] If this is so, a sweeping requirement for mandatory apology, such as that posited by Maimonides in relation to bodily injury, does not exist as a comprehensive, inclusive requirement in today's common law. This is an innovation of Maimonides and Jewish law.

According to Maimonides, another difference between injury to a person's body and damage to his property which has its basis in the Talmud relates to the question of whether the consent of the victim to the harm being done to him exempts the damager from paying compensation. Maimonides believed that there are cases in which the law acts in a paternalistic fashion, *inter alia* due to the moral aspect, and does not accept the assumption that a person knows how best to take care of his affairs.[174] An example of this approach emerges from Maimonides' ruling that requires a damager to pay for injuries he caused the victim, even if he did so with the explicit consent of the victim. Maimonides rules as follows:

> There is another difference between personal injury and damage to property. If one says to another, "Blind my eye, or cut off my hand, with the understanding that you are to be exempt," he is nevertheless liable for the five aspects since it is quite certain that a person does not really consent to such treatment. But if one says to another, "Tear my coat, or break my jar, with the understanding that you are to be exempt," he is exempt.[175]

---

[172] See, e.g., Kahan & Posner, *supra* note 34; Chandler Farmer, *Striking a Balance: A Proposed Amendment to the Federal Rules of Evidence Excluding Partial Apologies*, 2 BELMONT L. REV. 243 (2015); Lauren Gailey, *"I'm Sorry" as Evidence? Why the Federal Rules of Evidence Should Include a New Specialized Relevance Rule to Protect Physicians*, 82 DEF. COUNS. J. 172 (2015); Michael B. Runnels, *Apologies All Around: Advocating Federal Protection for the Full Apology in Civil Cases*, 46 SAN DIEGO L. REV. 137 (2009).

[173] Yonathan A. Arbel & Yotam Kaplan, *Tort Reform through the Back Door: A Critique of Law and Apologies*, 90 S. CAL. L. REV. 1199 (2017) ("We argue that the widely-endorsed 'apology law' reform – a change in the national legal landscape that privileged apologies – is, in fact, a mechanism of tort reform, used to limit victims' recovery and shield injurers from liability. While legal scholars overlooked this effect, commercial interests seized the opportunity and are in the process of transforming state and federal law with the unwitting support of the public." *Ibid.* at 1199).

[174] A similar approach was adopted by Guido Calabresi & A. Douglas Melamed, *Property Rules, Liability Rules, and Inalienability: One View of the Cathedral*, 85 HARV. L. REV. 1089 (1972). They adopt a paternalistic approach of inalienability, by virtue of which, for example, they rule out the possibility of a person selling his organs for the purpose of implantation in another. Over the years, the literature on inalienability extended it also to the creation of restrictions on transferring rights, and not only prohibitions and permissions. *See, e.g.*, Susan Rose-Ackerman, *Inalienability and the Theory of Property Rights*, 85 COLUM. L. REV. 931 (1985).

[175] Laws of Wounding and Damaging 5:11.

Characterization of the damages that a person causes to property as monetary-civil in nature and the injuries caused by a person to the body of another (wounding) as criminal, is connected to the fact that forgiveness on the part of the injured party does not exempt the injurer from compensation, whereas it does exempt the person causing property damage from payment, on the other. Indeed, the common approach in modern law is that the criminal law deals with the violation of protected interests of society, and therefore when a person commits a crime he causes damage to society and not only to the person injured by the criminal act. For this reason, the consent of the individual to the injury being done to him is irrelevant, and it therefore does not exempt the perpetrator since it does not diminish the violation of the social interest that it is protecting.[176] An interesting expression of this approach, which does not regard the consent of the individual as outweighing all else, emerges from Maimonides' ruling quoted from the Laws of Wounding and Damaging 5:11, whereby the injurer is required to pay for the injuries he caused the victim even if the victim gave his explicit consent to being injured. According to Maimonides, the prohibition against causing bodily harm, and particularly injuries which entail permanent physical disability, to the extent of losing a limb, is a peremptory norm (*jus cogens*). As such, even if the victim had drawn up an explicit agreement with the injurer which clearly stated that the injurer will be exempt from the payment of damages, this provision cannot exempt the injurer from the payment of the tortious compensation, for a paternalistic assumption exists that "it is certain that the person does not really consent."[177] Presumably, this means that this is not the person's *true* will that his limb be amputated,[178] even if there was apparently no particular coercion and he consented of his own free will. All this, adds Maimonides, as opposed to property damage, in respect of which the damaged party has the power to exempt the damager from tortious payments and to exempt him from criminal liability.[179]

---

[176] See SELA, *supra* note 60, at 308–09.

[177] SHULHAN ARUKH, Hoshen Mishpat 421:12 interpreted Maimonides' words as being of wide application, i.e., even if the injured party said specifically "on condition that you are exempt," the wounder must pay (and *see* Maggid Mishneh on Laws of Wounding 5:11, who stressed that according to Maimonides, it is never possible to negotiate in relation to irreparable injury to limbs). This outcome is not in accordance with the decisors who hold that if a person says in no uncertain terms that it his intention to exempt the person who injures him, the injurer is exempt from paying (See Rema on SHULHAN ARUKH, Hoshen Mishpat 421:21–22).

[178] This conception is very much in keeping with that of Maimonides in view of his well-known rulings in Laws of Divorce 2:20, concerning cases in which the husband is lawfully compelled to divorce his wife, and "he is beaten until he consents." Maimonides asks, "Why is this *get* not void, for he is being compelled?" His answer is most incisive: there is no coercion in this case, but rather, revelation of the *true* will, to follow in the way of the Torah. The same can also be said here, that the person's true desire is not to transgress against the prohibition against injuring one's body.

[179] Laws of Wounding and Damaging 5:11.

One of the differences between civil-private law and criminal law is connected with the requirement that there be a *mens rea* as a basis for a criminal obligation, for a criminal cannot be convicted absent fault, and absolute liability should not be imposed upon him. From the rulings of Maimonides, too, it emerges that minimal *mens rea* is required in order to obligate a person to make restitution payments for the injuries,[180] and as we will see,[181] the regime of liability that is required in order to obligate a person who wounds another is at a higher level (for some payments) – more than negligence – as compared with the regime of liability that is required to obligate a person for the damage that was caused by his property (negligence).

The punitive dimension of the laws of the injurer also expresses itself in the fact that intention is required as a precondition for full payment of all the five effects of injury, as Maimonides says: "If one *intentionally* injures another, he is liable for the five effects wherever the injury occurs."[182] The element of intention to cause harm is required particularly in order to obligate a person with payments for embarrassment or humiliation, according to Maimonides, and therefore a person who acts without intent is exempt from paying compensation for the humiliation.[183]

Another aspect related to the elements of the obligation to pay compensation for wounding was presented by Maimonides in his definition of the prohibition against wounding another: "One is forbidden to wound either himself or another. Not only one who wounds another but even one who strikes a law-observing Israelite in the course of a quarrel, whether an adult or a minor, whether a man or a woman, transgresses a negative commandment,"[184]

This condition, whereby the offense of wounding must take the form of striking "in the course of a quarrel" (*derekh nitzaion*) indicates that a person does not transgress the prohibition against striking unless the striking occurred in the course of a quarrel. Maimonides presumably derives this condition from the scriptural verses that deal with wounding and in which the element of *nitzaion* is mentioned.[185] The condition for the perpetration of the offense of striking – that it be "in the course of a quarrel" – may be significant in two ways: (1) It may be interpreted such that the words "in the course of a quarrel" describe the *mens rea* of the injurer, i.e., a person transgresses against the prohibition of wounding only if he knowingly wounded the other person and if he had criminal intent to physically harm the other person; (2) The expression "in the course of a quarrel" could be understood as a circumstance that is in fact part of the factual elements (*actus reus*) of the transgression. According to the second interpretation, which is preferable, as

---

[180] For an extensive analysis of Maimonides' position on the *mens rea* required of a person who inflicts injury, see SELA, *supra* note 60, at 196–209.
[181] *Infra* Chapter 7.
[182] Laws of Wounding and Damaging 1:16.
[183] *Ibid.* 1:12. See also *ibid.* 1:10.
[184] *Ibid.* 5:1.
[185] See Exodus 21:22: "If people are fighting [*ki yinatzu*]."

Ilan Sela proved[186] – correctly, in our opinion – the words "in the course of a quarrel" indicate that in order for the circumstances that constitute the transgression of wounding to pertain, the striking and the wounding must be done with the aim of injuring and destroying the body of the other person. It is true that normally, intention is included in the framework of the *mens rea* of the offense, but sometimes, the role of intention changes, and there are offenses in which intention does not fulfill its normal role as an element of the criminal intent that determines the degree of guilt of the offender, but rather, it constitutes part of the factual elements of the offense.[187] Sela suggests that these cases should also include the condition of "in the course of a quarrel," the meaning of this condition being that the striking had to be done with the intention of injuring, or more precisely, not for the purpose of reproof.[188] He summarizes the "punitive aspect" that emerges from Maimonides' theory on our subject:

> Particularly remarkable in this matter is Maimonides' approach, which mentioned this condition of "in the course of a quarrel" in the actual definition of the prohibition. In addition to the fact that striking that is not "in the course of a quarrel" is exempt from payment for wounding, such as in the case of a father who chastises his son and the rabbi who chastises his pupil,[189] one can also consider the punitive aspect of payment for wounding, and the fact that these payments serve not as compensation for the injured person (or not only as compensation for the injured person) but as a punishment for the wounder for the transgression of wounding.[190]

5 Between Laws of Theft and Laws of Robbery and the Return of Lost Property

Particular attention has been devoted in the research literature to the following question: why did Maimonides separate the Laws of Theft (*genevah*) from the Laws of Robbery (*gezelah*)? Are these not two quite similar property offenses?

---

[186] What we say later in the chapter reflects the thorough and convincing analysis of SELA, *supra* note 60, at 294–304, who deals at length with the bounds of "in the course of a quarrel" according to Maimonides.

[187] For examples of this in Israeli law and Jewish law, *see* Yaacov Habba, *Intention as a Component of the Definition of the Offense in Jewish Law and Israeli Law*, 20 MEHKEREI MISHPAT 177, 180 ff. (5763) (Heb.).

[188] SELA, *supra* note 60, at 299. For this reason, SELA proves, beating that is administered as a reaction to the past, whether as a punishment or for another purpose, is beating that is done "in the course of a quarrel," and as opposed to this, beating whose purpose is to improve the future conduct of the person who is beaten is not "in the course of a quarrel." Therefore, the exemption given to a father who chastises his son and a teacher who chastises his pupil is clear: they are acting to correct and improve the ways of the son or the pupil in the future, and therefore their beating does not occur "in the course of a quarrel."

[189] CODE, Laws of Murderers 5:6.

[190] SELA, *supra* note 60, at 305.

The answer to this question lies in the fact that according to the Maimonidean tort theory, the legal parameters of theft are significantly different from those of robbery. True, the actual distinction between the action of the thief (*ganav*), who attempts to conceal his deeds, and that of the robber (*gazlan*), who is not afraid and acts in a way that can be observed, lies in the Talmud,[191] and is not Maimonides' innovation. However, Maimonides refashioned and added depth to the said distinction. Whereas some talmudic commentators and decisors believed that the distinction between the actions of the thief and those of the robber is technical and not substantive, and that these are two variations of a single general prohibition against theft or robbery,[192] according to Maimonides the distinction between the thief and the robber is much more than a matter of the mere technical difference in the actions. The Maimonidean theory created a deep, fundamental distinction between two separate legal areas – laws of theft and laws of robbery.[193] In separating, in the *Code*, the laws of theft and the laws of robbery into two distinct legal fields (and combining the laws of robbery with the laws pertaining to lost property), despite the large number of common properties and common laws of theft and robbery, Maimonides determined that the thief and the robber are different in their essence. This is not confined only to the special laws applying to each of them, such as double, four-fold or five-fold payments made by the thief (and not the robber!), or the distinction in the actual technical actions of the thief and the robber. According to Maimonides – and this is his main innovation – the legal parameters of the laws of theft are substantively different from those of the laws of robbery, and this manifests itself in many ways. Following Maimonides, many later commentators tried to address the question of the basis for the principled distinction between the laws of theft and the laws of robbery; this is not the place to discuss their suggestions.[194] Our objective is to examine carefully the implications of what Maimonides himself writes. In the Laws of Theft, Maimonides defines the difference between the thief and the robber thus:

> A thief is one who takes another's property away secretly without the owner's knowledge, as when he puts his hand into another's pocket and takes money out without the owner's awareness, or commits a similar act. If, however, one takes something openly and in public by force, he is not a thief but a robber.[195]

---

[191] Bava Kamma 79b.
[192] According to some opinions, the prohibition against robbery also includes a prohibition against theft, i.e., robbery is theft, but it is done in such a way that the owner is unaware of it. See ENCYLOPAEDIA TALMUDIT 6, s.v. genevah, 205.
[193] The MISHNAH, too, in M Bava Kamma, deals with the laws of theft in Chapter 7 and the laws of robbery in Chapter 9, but this does not necessarily mean that two separate areas of law are being discussed.
[194] See ABRAHAM WEINROTH, THEFT AND ROBBERY – FUNDAMENTAL ISSUES (Mossad Harav Kook, Jerusalem, 2002) (Heb.) (containing a broad analytical summary of the proposals of the later commentators and decisors).
[195] Laws of Theft 1:3.

Whereas in the Talmud, the principal distinction between the thief and the robber is connected to the concealed as opposed to the open action,[196] Maimonides draws the distinction between them somewhat differently. The distinction between the thief and the robber lies in the owner's knowledge of their activity. The thief, in order to succeed in carrying out his plot, tries to avoid confrontation with the victim of the theft, and conceals himself from any element that can expose him. The victim discovers what has happened to him only after the event, and even then, he is still confused and in doubt about what happened to his property. The main characteristic of the thief, which Maimonides repeats in Laws of Theft 1:3, is that he takes the property of another "without the owner's knowledge/awareness." The robber, on the other hand, does not shrink from confrontation with the victim, nor with others. He acts openly vis-à-vis the victim and others. This mode of action requires him to act "by force," for if he would not employ force and violence, he would not obtain that which he seeks. In other words, the main weapon of the thief is concealment, whereas that of the robber is strength. The thief flees from confrontation with the victim, as opposed to the robber who comes with the intention of confronting and leaving, the confrontation having achieved the upper hand. The thief takes "secretly," for his proclivity is primarily to hide from the victim and from others, for if they were to see him they would warn the victim or they would seize him, and his plan would be foiled. This is not the case with the robber, in respect of whom Maimonides provides a fuller definition in the Laws of Robbery:

> Who is deemed a robber? One who takes another's property by force. Thus if one snatches an object from another's hand, or enters another's premises without his permission and takes articles, or if one seizes another's slave or his animal and makes use of them, or if one enters another's field and eats its produce, or commits any similar act, he is deemed a robber, as we find it exemplified in the scriptural verse: *And he plucked the spear out of the Egyptian's hand* (II Samuel 23:21).[197]

The crux of the definition of the robber is that he acts with "force" against the victim.[198] The presence or absence of other people at the scene of the incident is irrelevant to the robber. He trusts in his own strength and in the fear that he will instill in all those around him. But we will see that the difference between the thief and the robber has an even more basic manifestation. Maimonides begins the Laws of Theft by defining the prohibition issued by the Bible:

---

[196] *Bava Kamma* 79b.
[197] Laws of Robbery and Lost Property 1:3.
[198] A similar definition is evident in what Maimonides writes in the Book of Commandments, negative commandment 247: "Theft refers to taking someone else's property through scheming and in secret. Robbery refers to taking someone else's property against his will and with open force, as highway robbers do." And cf. his formulation *ibid.* negative commandment 244: "We are forbidden to steal money" as opposed to no. 245: "We are forbidden to commit robbery, i.e., taking something which is not ours by open force and violence."

> Whenever a person steals property that is worth a *pe'rutah* or more, he transgresses a negative commandment, as Exodus 20:13 states: "Do not steal."
>
> Lashes are not administered for the violation of this commandment, for one is obligated to give compensation. For the Torah requires a thief to compensate the party from whom he stole.[199]

Let us compare this to the opening of the Laws of Robbery:

> Whoever robs an object worth a *pe'rutah* from a colleague transgresses a negative commandment, as Leviticus 19:13 states: "Do not rob."
>
> Violation of this negative commandment is not punished by lashes, because it can be corrected by the fulfillment of a positive commandment. For if a person robs, he is obligated to return what he obtained by robbery, as *ibid*. 5:23 states: "And he shall return the article he obtained by robbery." This is a positive commandment.[200]

In the prohibition against theft, the emphasis is on money and the payments (fines), because the act of theft does not express a relationship between the thief and the victim: the thief is not usually acquainted with the victim. The action of the robber, on the other hand, certainly expresses the relationship of the robber vis-à-vis the victim. Therefore the Bible formulates the obligation borne by the robber not as a punishment in the form of an obligation to pay, as is the case with the thief, but as a positive commandment of restitution of the stolen property, the object of which is not merely to restore the property to the victim, but also to rebuild correct relations between them.[201] The comment that the prohibition, "Thou shalt not commit theft [*lo tignovu*]" is in fact directed at the act of theft itself, which cannot always be corrected by merely restoring the stolen property and requires additional punishment, is very incisive.[202] The law of the thief is not a commandment to the thief to correct the transgression, but rather an order to the court to punish the transgressor. This is as opposed to the prohibition "Thou shalt not commit robbery [*lo tigzolu*]," which can be set right by means of performance of the positive commandment, "and he shall restore that which he took by robbery": the robber himself will put to right the wrong that he committed.[203] For the prohibition against robbery, the Bible did not fix a

---

[199] Laws of Theft 1:1 (as translated in the Chabad edition).

[200] Laws of Robbery and Lost Property 1:1 (as translated by the Chabad edition).

[201] In accordance with the reasonable suggestion of FEINTUCH, *supra* note 163, vol. 2, at 866. According to this principle, he sought to explain what Maimonides wrote in Laws of Theft 1:3: "Accordingly, if an armed brigand commits theft, he is not deemed a robber but a thief, even though the owner is aware of his action at the time he is stealing. Feintuch writes as follows (p. 867): The owner's awareness at the time of the act is not the main factor in robbery, but that the act is done openly and in public *against his fellow*. The law applying to armed brigands does not belong in this category.

[202] NACHUM RABINOVITCH, *YAD PESHUTAH LESEFER NEZIKIN*, Laws of Theft, Introduction, at 6.

[203] *Ibid*. And cf. WEINROTH, *supra* note 194, at 121, who explained that robbery relates to the prohibition against unlawfully holding another's money. Restitution constitutes putting this possession to rights. As opposed to this, theft goes beyond the bounds of the civil-private law of

penalty, but it ordered the robber himself to right the wrong. The transgression of the prohibition against theft, on the other hand, entails punishment, which finds expression in fines (double, four-old and five-fold payment) that the Bible imposed on the thief.[204] This fundamental distinction drawn by Maimonides has various ramifications, which will not be elucidated at present.[205]

An important question concerns the liability regime and/or the *mens rea* that is required for the purpose of obligation as a thief or a robber. The question is whether in relation to both theft and robbery, as opposed to regular tort law, the thief or the robber must have taken the article with the intention of depriving its owner of it, or is intention to thieve or to rob unnecessary in order for the wrong of theft or robbery to be constituted?

Maimonides' position in response to this question is not absolutely clear. The commentators and decisors were divided on this question.[206] There were those who understood Maimonides as saying that there is a duty of restoration as the result of an action with respect to property which is not intended to deny the ownership of another, even in a case of absolute coercion; consequently, in his view the act can be defined as theft even in the absence of intention to acquire ownership of the property.[207] However, the proof that was brought for this view is indirect and founded on various assumptions that are not necessarily valid.[208] In our view, clear proof can be adduced for the fact that according to Maimonides, *mens rea* and intention to commit theft are required for the purpose of liability for theft from Maimonides' famous responsum[209] concerning the difference between armed brigands and another person who broke into an enclosure and as a result, the animal escaped and caused damage, as elucidated in the previous chapter. As will be recalled, in that responsum Maimonides distinguished between the thief and the damager with respect to intention: whereas the damager does not require special intention to cause damage in order to incur liability for the damage he caused,

---

unlawfully holding the money of another, and it also has a punitive aspect that derives from the prohibited act of taking that was committed. This act of taking the property of another is not corrected by restitution, for the criminal act that was committed cannot be "restituted," and only its monetary consequences can be repaired.

[204] In certain circumstances the Bible even allowed the victim of the theft to kill that thief, as specified in Laws of Theft Chap. 9.

[205] And *see* NACHUM RABINOVITCH, *YAD PESHUTAH LESEFER NEZIKIN*, Laws of Theft 1:1; *Ibid.* 1:3; WEINROTH, *supra* note 194, at 118–22.

[206] *See* WEINROTH, *ibid.* at 74–99; *ENCYCLOPAEDIA TALMUDIT*, vol. 5, 461 s.v. *gezel* (on obligating an inadvertent robber).

[207] WEINROTH, *ibid.* at 93–95, deduced this from the CODE, Laws of Theft 2:16.

[208] Thus, for example, Weinroth attempts to resolve the difficulty raised by Ra'abad on the CODE, *ibid.*, by recourse to the explanation of the author of *MAHANEH EPHRAIM*, Hil. *Gezelah*, sec. 7, according to which this is a case in which the watchman does not know that the property is stolen. However, other commentators suggested other solutions to Ra'abad's question, and *see* *HAMAFTEAH LERAMBAM*, Frankel edition, Laws of Theft 2:16. In all events, Weinroth's conclusion is not the only possible one.

[209] RESP. RAMBAM (Fraiman edition), no. 339.

intention to commit theft is necessary in order to be liable for the theft. Intention as a necessary condition of liability for theft is clearly explained in light of the fundamental approach of Maimonides to the effect that the payments imposed upon the thief constitute a penalty. As stated, one of the main differences between the criminal law and private-civil law, from ancient times until today, lies in the fact that penal law requires a *mens rea* in order for a person to be liable to punishment. A similar distinction would appear to underlie the distinction made by Maimonides between the damager and the thief in his responsum.

Why does the Bible fine and punish the thief for his actions, but not the robber? Maimonides answer thus in the *Guide*:

> A robber is not ordered to pay anything as fine (Leviticus 5:24); the additional fifth part (of the value of the robbed goods) is only an atonement-offering for his perjury. The reason for this rule is to be found in the rare occurrence of robbery: theft is committed more frequently than robbery, for theft can be committed everywhere; robbery is not possible in towns, except with difficulty; besides, the thief takes things exposed as well as things hidden away; robbery applies only to things exposed; against robbery we can guard and defend ourselves; we cannot do so against theft; again, the robber is known, can be sought, and forced to return that which he has robbed, whilst the thief is not known. On account of all these circumstances the law fines the thief and not the robber.[210]

Maimonides' explanation of the difference between a robber and a thief is different from the theological explanation in the Talmud,[211] and he deals with this issue[212] in light of his fundamental consequentialist approach, whereby criminal sanctions are imposed in view of the ultimate goal, which is to achieve deterrence.

After understanding the difference between laws of theft and the laws of robbery, we may address another question which concerned many scholars: Why did Maimonides attach the laws pertaining to lost property to the laws of robbery? The Laws of Lost Property, which discusses the conditions under which a person acquires for himself objects that have been found, would apparently be better integrated into the Book of Acquisition.[213] It has been suggested that this stems from the arrangement of the Book of Torts in accordance with the mishnaic *Bava Kamma*, with

---

[210] GUIDE 3:41 (Friedlander 579–80).
[211] See *Bava Kamma* 79b.
[212] *Infra* Chapter 5.
[213] See e.g. Haym Soloveitchik, *Reflections on Maimonides' Classification of Mishneh Torah: Real Problems and Imaginary Problems*, 4 MAIMONIDEAN STUDIES 109–10 (2000) (Heb.); MOSHE HALBERTAL, MAIMONIDES: LIFE AND THOUGHT 202 (Princeton NJ: Princeton University Press, 2014); Friedman, *supra* note 5, at 362-65. And indeed, such an arrangement is evident in other halakhic codifications in Jewish law. In the *TUR* and the *SHULHAN ARUKH*, the laws of theft and the laws of robbery were connected and discussed one after another, whereas the laws of lost property were placed separately elsewhere. In R. Shneur Zalman of Liadi. *SHULHAN ARUKH HARAV* (Jerusalem 5753), the laws of theft and of robbery appeared together.

improvements.[214] However, a better suggestion is that the attachment of the laws pertaining to lost property to those of robbery lies in the centrality of the prohibition against robbery within the obligation to restore lost property.[215] As we have seen, the Bible did not fix a penalty for the prohibition against robbery, but it ordered the robber himself to right the wrong, as emphasized by Maimonides in the opening of the Laws of Robbery: "For if a person robs, he is obligated to return what he obtained by robbery." Now, a person who does not return a lost item in his possession is considered a robber, since the item still belongs to the owner who lost it. Support for this suggestion can be found in what Maimonides himself wrote, that a person who transgresses the commandment of restoring lost property by taking the lost property without returning it to its owner transgresses, *inter alia*, the prohibition against robbery.[216]

6 Between Laws of Damages to Neighbors and Standard Laws of Torts

Another area of law that is connected with tort laws is that of the laws of damages to neighbors. This subject is discussed in the talmudic literature.

The second chapter of *Bava Batra* deals with the limitations imposed upon a person's use of his property because of the damage that his activities may cause to a neighbor's property or enterprise. The extent of these limitations is the subject of a fundamental dispute between Tannaim, which runs through the entire chapter.[217]

Maimonides did not include the laws of damages to neighbors in his Book of Torts; rather, he addressed these laws in the Book of Acquisition as part of the Laws of Neighbors.[218] This phenomenon requires an explanation. Laws governing damages to neighbors should be regarded as part of the laws of nuisance that in most modern legal systems are included in tort law. Why did Maimonides not include these laws in the Book of Torts?

It would seem that according to Maimonides, there is a fundamental difference between the regular laws of torts and the laws of damages to neighbors, which he

---

[214] Friedman, *supra* note 5, at 364.
[215] See, e.g., NACHUM RABINOVITCH, YAD PESHUTAH LESEFER NEZIKIN, MAVO LEHILKHOT GEZE-LAH VE-AVEDAH, vol. 2, 243(2006); HALBERTAL, *supra* note 213. On the problems with this explanation see Haym Soloveitchik, *supra* note 213; Friedman, *ibid.*
[216] Laws of Robbery and Lost Property 11:2.
[217] The Sages hold that, generally speaking, the responsibility for preventing damage rests upon the one who is causing the damage. R. Yossi, however, holds that a person is generally entitled to use his own property as he pleases, and it is up to the threatened party to ensure that his property is not damaged. However, where damage to a neighbor results directly from an activity performed within a person's property Rabbi Yossi agrees that it is the responsibility of the one engaging in such activity to prevent damage from occurring. The technical term for this type of activity is *giri dilei* – "his arrows" (*Bava Batra* 22b). The analogy is to a person standing on his property and shooting arrows into the courtyard of his neighbor, which he is obviously forbidden to do. See Maimonides, Laws of Neighbors 10:5.
[218] Laws of Neighbors, Chapters 9–11.

viewed as part of the laws of acquisition. But what is the legal basis for this fundamental difference between the laws of damages to neighbors and the laws governing property damages, wounding and damaging etc.? This subject occupied various commentators and decisors, who asked the following question: there are many types of damages in respect of which, in the framework of talmudic discussions of removal of harm in the second chapter of *Bava Batra*, the Talmud presents fundamental disputes between the Sages as to whether the potential damager must distance harm from his neighbor, or whether the potential victim must distance himself from the harm. Hence the question arises: these damages are apparently included in the four heads of damage mentioned in *Bava Kamma*, by virtue of which a person must pay for the damages he causes to another person; why, therefore, did the Talmud have doubts about whether the one who caused the damage was obliged to distance the harm from his neighbor? There are those who answered that the damages discussed in the second chapter of *Bava Batra* are caused by the person's regular practices; therefore, if liability for their prevention is borne by the damager, his ability to make use of his property would be affected.[219] According to this conception, the principles of rule-making must be changed with respect to laws of neighbors. The desire to allow for a reasonable life-style and proper neighborly relations, and to prevent a contraction of the normal scope of usage of the neighbor, motivates the *halakhah* to exempt from liability to pay in cases in which liability would be imposed if the matter did not fall within a system of laws of neighbors.[220] Others emphasized the fact that the damages discussed in the second chapter of *Bava Batra* are damages that occur within the domain of the damager, and as such they are not subject to standard tort law, which does not apply other than to a person who caused damage in the public domain or within the domain of another person.[221]

What Shalom Albeck wrote is instructive in explaining the nature of damages to neighbors as compared to the regular tort laws:

> The laws of easements that cause damage to neighbors, like all the other laws of acquisition, indicate the rights that a person has in his land, whereas the laws of the heads of damages [standard laws of tort – Y.S & B.S.] teach us when a person is liable to pay if he caused damage to those rights. In other words: laws of acquisition, including laws of damages of neighbors, tell us what rights a person has that another person is forbidden to violate, and the laws of tort teach us about the laws applying to a damager who violates to those rights. The laws of damages to neighbors determine the rights that a person has in the land, and no other person in the world is permitted to stop him from invoking those rights, in the same way as the laws of ownership or of leasing determine the rights of a person in the land; the laws

---

[219] NETIVOT HAMISHPAT 155:18.
[220] This is how the approach of NETIVOT HAMISHPAT, ibid. was explained by R. Aharon Lichtenstein, *Dina deGarmi* 190-91(Alon Shvut 5768) (Heb.).
[221] BIRKHAT SHMUEL, Bava Batra no. 13-13 (in the name of R. Haym Soloveitchik).

of the heads of damages, however, do not determine rights in land or in other property, but they establish rights vis-à-vis the damager, who must pay for the damage, like the right of a lender vis-à-vis a borrower who must repay his debt.[222]

We find therefore, as Albeck concludes, that

> the laws of acquisition, and the laws of damages to neighbors in general, deal with a person's rights until he incurs damage, whereas the laws of tort deal with his rights after he incurs damage. As has been explained, the former rights are in the property and the latter rights are in the damagers, who must pay.[223]

In our view, this fundamental distinction proposed by Albeck in the context of talmudic civil law is probably what lies behind Maimonides' decision to include the laws of damages to neighbors in the Book of Acquisition and not in the Book of Torts. There are several legal ramifications of the distinction between the laws of damages to neighbors and the standard laws of tort.

The first ramification of this distinction between damages to neighbors and standard tort law (the four heads of damage) is that with respect to the laws of damages to neighbors, the victim can take out a surety against the neighbor causing him harm, and force him to set the dangerous object at a distance, whereas in regular tort law the victim cannot force the damager, prior to the damage being caused, to remove the dangerous object and to ensure that it does not cause damage: rather, if it causes damage, he must pay for that damage.[224] Indeed, it is obvious that virtually all of the remedies that are mentioned in the context of the laws of damages to neighbors in the Book of Acquisition are injunctions and concern the removal of harm and not payment of compensation,[225] whereas in the Book of Torts all the remedies that are mentioned by Maimonides are the payment of compensation and not injunctions.[226] The reason for this is clear, in our view. The laws of damages to neighbors are part of the Book of Acquisition, and as such, property rule operates in relation to them (according to the concepts of Calabresi and Melamed);[227] as such, the orders that can be obtained in relation

---

[222] SHALOM ALBECK, CIVIL LAW IN THE TALMUD 447 (Jerusalem-Tel-Aviv, 1976) (Heb.).
[223] Ibid.
[224] Ibid. at 448.
[225] The position accepted by most commentators and decisors, including Maimonides, is that even if the neighbor did not remove the damage and caused damage, he is exempt from payment in most cases with certain exceptions. See ENCYCLOPAEDIA TALMUDIT, vol. 10, 586–89, s.v. harhakat nezikin.
[226] An exception is the ruling of Maimonides in Laws of Property Damages 5:1 regarding the prohibition against causing damage. It will, however, be borne in mind that there, too, Maimonides is referring to the *religious prohibition* against causing damage, and to the ability of the victim to take matters into his own hands. Maimonides is in no way setting down a property rule by means of which the victim can take out an injunction against the damager in the rabbinical court.
[227] In their famous article of 1972 on the four rules, Calabresi and Melamed (*supra* note 174) discussed several means through which the law protects rights, enabling their realization and

to them are injunctions to remove the harm. In standard tort law, as opposed to this, the liability rules that impose upon the damager an obligation to pay compensation for damages that were caused are operative.

The differences between injunctions and the removal of harm that are issued in the framework of the laws of neighbors and between the orders to pay compensation for damages that are issued in the framework of tort law finds effective expression in the following ruling of Maimonides: "If a house and an upper chamber are owned by two people respectively, then the owner of the house should not make an oven within his house unless there is a space of four cubits above it."[228]

Up to this point, Maimonides is dealing with a law from the area of laws pertaining to neighbors, by virtue of which it is at most possible to issue orders for removal of the harm. But what will happen if nevertheless, and despite the fact that the owner of the ground floor placed the oven at a proper distance, a fire broke out and caused damage to the owner of the second floor? Maimonides answers as follows: "Even if he has left the prescribed space, should a fire break out and cause damage, he must pay for the damage, as will be explained in the proper place."[229]

Why, if he left the prescribed space, should he pay if a fire broke out? Some explain Maimonides' position by saying that the reason that a minimum distance was set between the stove and the ceiling of the ground story, which was the floor of the second story, was purely as a security measure, i.e., in order to lessen the risk of the damage occurring.[230] Therefore, if the owner of the ground story left the prescribed space, he fulfilled his obligation of removing the harm and therefore is not regarded as a person who causes damage. Nevertheless, even if he removed the harm by the minimum amount, "it may happen" that the fire breaks out and spreads and causes damage,[231] and because the fire causes the damage, he will be obligated to pay compensation by virtue of the head of damage of "*fire*".[232]

> enforcement: (a) inalienability, by virtue of which a right cannot be transferred, in order to protect it, for example, in the case of delegitimazation of the sale of organs or of babies; (b) property rules, which protect rights in a strong manner, even if not at the level of inalienability, *e.g.*, by being able to maintain a nuisance as part of the realization of a property right or taking out injunctions to remove a nuisance; (c) a weaker protection than the two previous ones – liability rules, by virtue of which a victim receives compensation for violation of his right, but the damaging behavior can continue if it is more efficient to cause harm on the one hand and pay the victim on the other.

[228] Laws of Neighbors 9:11.
[229] *Ibid*. Maimonides' statement "as will be explained in the proper place" refers to the Book of Torts, Laws of Property Damages 14:2.
[230] KETZOT HAHOSHEN 155:1, and the author wrote there that if the owner placed the stove less than the required distance away, this is considered "certain damage, and he is not permitted to cause damage in order to pay, and therefore he must set it at a distance at which it will not cause direct damage in order to pay."
[231] KETZOT HAHOSHEN, ibid.
[232] With respect to which Maimonides ruled, in Laws of Property Damages 14:2, that if he did not remove it appropriately and the fire spread and caused damage, he has an obligation to pay.

In the modern terms of Calabresi and Melamed it could be said that Maimonides undoubtedly draws an interesting distinction between a property rule and a liability rule: the owner of the stove must place it at a distance, hence, this is use of a property rule for the benefit of the victim. Apparently, if the owner of the stove did not place it at a distance, the victim would be able to act against him and take out an order that would obligate him to do so. However, as an exception to the situation described in footnote 225 of this chapter, whereby a person will not pay compensation even if he did not respect his neighbor's property right not to incur damage, here in the case of the stove he will pay compensation, even if he placed the stove appropriately according to the property rule. If so, we have here an interesting combination between a property rule and a rule of liability, or a partial property rule: the damager is not required to remove the hazard – the stove – totally. He need only place it at a distance. However, placing it at a distance does not prevent the damage as would removing the hazard completely. It only reduces the risk that damage will ensue. From a property point of view, therefore, the victim is required to reduce the risk, and society does not require him to remove it completely. Why? In our view, this stems from that same rationale as described in the beginning of this section, i.e., the desire to allow a certain minimal level of communal life between neighbors. If that neighbor chose to use his stove, he indeed had reduced the risk, but did not prevent it. His benefit from the stove, which still endangers the neighbor, obligates him to pay for damage that he caused.

A second ramification of the distinction between damages to neighbors and standard tort law relates to the possibility of acquiring the right to cause damage to the neighbor under the laws of damage of neighbors, as opposed to the absence of any possibility of causing damage to the body of the other person or to his property.[233] Since according to Maimonides, the laws of damages to neighbors are part of the Book of Acquisition, it may therefore be said that just as a person can acquire the movable or immovable property of another person, so too he may purchase the easement that causes damage to a neighbor from that neighbor/victim, to the extent that the latter forgives him, as Maimonides rules:

> With respect to any of the prescribed distances mentioned in the proceeding chapters, if one does not keep the proper distance and the other sees it and is silent the latter thereby waives his right to challenge the first and cannot thereafter change his mind and compel him to withdraw to the proper distance. This obtains if it is apparent that he has waived his right, as when he helps the first at the time or tells him to do it or sees the other doing it alongside his property without leaving the required distance and is silent and does not protest, because whoever holds unchallenged an easement that damages the neighbor's property acquires title to that easement.[234]

---

[233] ALBECK, *supra* note 222, at 447–48.
[234] Laws of Neighbors 11:4.

In tort law, as opposed to this, the victim cannot transfer any property right to the damager. Therefore, not only can the damager not acquire permission to injure the body of the other person, as in the above (Laws of Wounding 5:11) ruling of Maimonides specifying that one cannot negotiate in relation to bodily harm, but also with respect to permission to cause damage to the property of another, where we saw that Maimonides's position, following that of the Mishnah, is that a person can negotiate with his fellow – "Tear my coat and be exempt from payment" – the one who tears has no property right in the coat itself. The owner of the coat has merely promised that he would forgive him for the damage. As such, if he has not yet torn the coat, or if he has begun but not finished tearing it, the injured party may change his mind and protest to the person tearing that he should not continue, and if he nevertheless continued and tore the coat, he will pay for the damage. This is different from damage to neighbors, in relation to which Maimonides ruled that if the victim forgave him and did not protest to his neighbor that he had not left the required distance, he can no longer change his mind, since he has granted him a property right relating to land, and as such it can be transferred, as opposed to a contractual right that cannot be transferred.[235]

It seems that here, the distinction made by Calabresi and Melamed between types of protections of entitlements can be invoked. When the victim consents to the damager tearing his garment, this is in fact a type of contract between them, which still leaves the property in the hands of the owner of the garment. He does not transfer ownership of the garment to the damager who subsequently does with it as he wishes. The garment still belongs to the victim. He only allows the damager to tear it, and even asks him to do so. Therefore, the victim, who is still the owner of the garment, can still change his mind, and then, if the damager nevertheless tears the garment, he will have to pay, as in every other case of causing damage.[236] In the case of land, the law is different. Here, damage to the land of the victim was done after the victim had in fact transferred to the damager the property right to use his land himself for the purpose that damaged the land. This is a property right, and it does not allow the victim to change his mind, unlike the case of the garment.

Regarding bodily injury, the situation is even clearer. Maimonides, as we have said, ruled that one cannot negotiate in relation to bodily harm. The modern parallel, in Calabresi and Melamed's terms, is inalienability. There are rights which cannot be transferred, even if a person wishes to transfer them, and even for payment.[237] Bodily harm – such as selling a kidney – is a good example of this.

---

[235] See KETZOT HAHOSHEN, 155:16, which is explained by means of the fundamental distinction between the laws of property and the laws of tort.
[236] In fact, as derived from the property principle for the benefit of the victim, but when the property is destroyed, then there is no choice and the practical outcome of the property rule is a payment.
[237] Over the years, the literature on inalienability extended this also to the creation of a limitation on the transfer of rights, and not only prohibitions or permissions.

A third ramification of the distinction between damages to neighbors and standard tort law relates to the fact that for the purpose of the laws pertaining to damages to neighbors, a person can prevent his neighbor from performing actions that cause purely psychological damage and that do not entail real monetary damage[238] and which therefore are not defined as damage in standard tort law; it is also clear that according to Maimonides the damager will not be required to pay for the damage. For example, let us examine the following rulings of Maimonides in the Laws of Neighbors:

(1) Carcasses, graves, and tanneries must be kept fifty cubits from the town.[239]
(2) He who constructs on his property … a privy … must, in order that it do no harm to his neighbor, do so at a distance where the … smell of the privy … will not reach his neighbor.[240]
(3) If one is accustomed to work in his place with blood or with carrion, and the like, and ravens and similar birds come for the blood and eat it and annoy his neighbor with their noise and shrieking or with the blood on their feet, with which they soil the fruit while they perch on the trees, then if his neighbor is a sensitive man or a sick man who is harmed by this shrieking, or if his neighbor's fruits become damaged by the blood, the former must desist from that work or do it at a distance that will not cause any damage, because this is comparable to the damage resulting from the smell of a privy and the like, where unchallenged practice does not constitute a right.[241]

These rulings of Maimonides deal with the obligation to remove the damages from smell, filth and noise to which a person must not expose his neighbor in order not to cause him psychological damage, and they are part of the Laws of Neighbors, the purpose of which is to allow for reasonable neighborly relations. Needless to say, it may be inferred from what Maimonides writes that there is no payment for these types of damages,[242] and in the Book of Torts Maimonides did not count these sorts of damages amongst the types of damages that are included in the heads of damages of standard tort law.

A fourth ramification of the distinction between damages to neighbors and standard tort law relates to the question of the regime of liability that applies. With respect to standard tort law, as we will see,[243] Maimonides rules that the owner of

---

[238] ALBECK *supra* note 222.
[239] Laws of Neighbors 10:3.
[240] *Ibid.* 11:1.
[241] *Ibid.* 11:5.
[242] For a discussion of the approaches of the decisors to the question of whether with respect to each of these removals, there is an obligation to pay when the damage was caused because the danger was not removed, see AVRAHAM SHEINFELD, TORTS 194–95 (Jerusalem: The Jewish Legal Heritage Society, 1991) (Heb.).
[243] *Infra* Chapter 7.

property that caused damage must pay only to the extent that he was negligent, but if he was compelled, then absolute liability is not imposed upon him. The obligation to prevent damages to neighbors, on the other hand, does not in any way depend on the question of whether the owner of the nuisance was negligent or not, but on the property question of the laws of neighbors: does an obligation exist to remove the potentially damaging objects to a distance?[244]

D. THE GOALS OF TORT LAW: A PLURALISTIC PERCEPTION

In this section we will argue that according to the Maimonidean theory, tort law does not have one single goal, but rather several goals which he presented in his various works. In the *Guide*, Maimonides presented two meta-goals in relation to pure torts (property damage, and damage caused by a person): removal of wrong and injustice (corrective justice) and prevention of damage (consequentialist). With respect to the damages from wounding, theft, robbery and murder he presented a criminal rationale; and with respect to the Book of Acquisition, including the laws of nuisance and the liability of guards, Maimonides present a rationale that contains elements of distributive justice. In the *Code*, there is also room for the religious-prohibitive aspect: the prohibition on causing harm. We will deal with each goal separately in the following chapters and draw some cautious lessons from a contemporary analysis of torts for Maimonides's theory of torts and vice versa.

This section contains a brief initial presentation of these goals. As explained in Chapter 1, comprehensive discussion of the goals of tort law and prioritization of these laws in the event of a clash between them has been scarce in the legal literature to date. The focus has usually been on the examination, development or critique of one particular goal – usually corrective justice, distributive justice, or optimal deterrence – for a specific purpose. This process has been variously termed "unified," "monistic," or "integrated."[245] The existing pluralistic approaches, which attempt to integrate several of the considerations underlying the different goals to balance between various goals of tort law, differ from each other in different aspects.[246] The objectives of tort law and the principal monistic approaches which exist in the modern world of the theory of tort law were presented in the beginning of this book.[247]

We argue that Maimonides' approach is not monistic. There are two central contentions with respect to the goals of tort law according to Maimonides' theory: (a) Different goals operate alongside each other and are not regarded as

---
[244] ALBECK, *supra* note 222.
[245] *Supra* Chapter 1, Section C.
[246] *Infra* Chapter 8.
[247] *Supra* Chapter 1, Section C.

contradictory; (b) The dominance of different goals varies according to the particular type of tort law (e.g., criminal with respect to wounding, distributive justice with respect to nuisance, consequentialist with respect to property damage).

1 The Major Goals of the Book of Torts: Removal of Wrong and the Prevention of Damage

In the *Guide*, Maimonides explains the reasons for the laws of tort – laws that are set out in the Book of Torts in the *Code* – and he says that they are all concerned with "the removal of wrong and with the prevention of injury,"[248] or, according to Shlomo Pines' translation, "All of them are concerned with putting an end to acts of injustice and the prevention of acts causing damage." Note that Maimonides explicitly mentions two goals: the first goal – "the removal of wrong" – looks backward, for once the damage has already occurred, it seeks to right the injustice that has been done, which is a type of corrective justice; the second goal – "the prevention of damages" – looks forward, and its nature is preventive. This is more similar, as we shall see,[249] to the consequentialist conception that is typical of the proponents of the economic analysis of law. It will be stressed that the preventive goal, on which Maimonides focusses primarily in the *Guide*, constitutes a significant component of the array of considerations of tort liability, to such an extent that in the opening to his explanation of the details of the tort laws, Maimonides accords this goal the attribute of "considerations of justice".[250] Today we might define this as "preventive justice," i.e. that the consequentialist objective of finding the effective way of preventing the damage can be considered as no less justified than the corrective objective of compensating for wrongs after they have occurred.[251]

In enumerating the objectives of tort law in the *Guide*, Maimonides emphasized primarily the consequentialist element of preventing damage, without detracting from other elements mentioned in the *Guide* and in his other works. We would stress that we are not claiming that all the details of tort law can be explained by consequentialist rationalization, as proposed by Maimonides in the *Guide* for the rules pertaining to tort law. Maimonides' statement in the *Guide* that the reasons for the commandments have in view the utility of a given commandment in a general

---

[248] GUIDE 3:40, 574 (according to Friedlander's translation).
[249] *Infra* Chapter 5.
[250] GUIDE 3:40, 574 ("These laws contain considerations of justice to which I will draw attention." A detailed discussion of all Maimonides' considerations of justice (corrective, distributive and preventive) as compared to modern scholars will be undertaken in Chapters 4–8).
[251] *Cf.* Gary T. Schwartz, *Mixed Theories of Tort Law: Affirming Both Deterrence and Corrective Justice*, 75 TEX. L. REV. 1801, 1832–33 (1997) (seeing optimal deterrence in tort law as "more just" than corrective justice, which he calls "protective justice". In his view, deterrence involves not only economic-utilitarian but also ethical and moral principles. We expand on Schwartz's approach *infra* in Chapter 8).

way, not an examination of its particulars,[252] is well known. Of course, there are other major elements that determine liability in torts which are mentioned in the *Code* but not in the *Guide*. In the *Guide* Maimonides placed the concept of preventing damage alongside corrective justice and various other considerations – some of them mentioned in the *Code* – especially deontological and religious, as well as some distributive ones, as we shall see in the next chapter.[253] What is emphasized in the *Guide*, however, are the consequentialist elements on the basis of which Maimonides seeks to impose tort liability.[254]

Halbertal states that a correct understanding of Maimonides' work begins with familiarity with his personality (which he refers to as "Moses the Man") and the historical context in which he operated ("Moses of his generation"), as well as, *inter alia*, his attitude towards the Jewish and non-Jewish sages of his generation, and the Mediterranean basin in which he flourished (Spain – the Maghreb – Egypt).

Regarding this theory, we suggest that there is a possible connection between Maimonides' emphasis on prevention of damage as a meta-goal and his profession as a doctor[255] who strongly advocated what is known today as preventive medicine.

We also suggest that Maimonides' views (and particularly his emphasis on *preventing damages*) were partly inspired by his experience as a prominent physician in twelfth century Egypt. As well as being one of the most influential religious figures of the Middle Ages, Maimonides was also a pioneer in a wide variety of medical practices. He was initially appointed court physician to the Regent of Egypt while the Sultan (Saladin the Great) was fighting the Crusades; later Maimonides was appointed physician to the Sultan's son and heir to the throne.

Maimonides' occupation as the chief physician in the Egyptian royal household led him to examine priorities and to carry out cost-benefit analyses. His particular medical prowess lay in the fact that he specialized in means of preventing disease, through correct nutrition, physical exercise, performance of difference activities at different times of the day and more. Is there a connection between Maimonides' proclivity for preventive medicine[256] and his emphasis on the goal of tort law as preventing damage? We have no clear proof of this, but it is conceivable that the two are connected.

---

[252] Guide 3:26.
[253] *See, e.g.,* Guide 3:42, 591, regarding the issue of liability of watchmen.
[254] These elements will be analyzed *infra* Chapter 5.
[255] *See* Daniel Sinclair, *Maimonides' Rational and Empirical Epistemology and its Influence on Bio-Medical Halakhah*, in Moses Maimonides & His Practice of Medicine (Kenneth Collins et al. eds., Haifa: Maimonides Research Institute, 2013).
[256] He was "a great figure of medical history who emphasised that the important aspects of medicine included preventative medicine," as indicated by Dan Magrill & Prabhu Sekaran, *Maimonides: An Early but Accurate View on the Treatment of Haemorrhoids,* 83 Postgrad Med. J. 352, 354 (2007). *See also* Fred Rosner, *Moses Maimonides and Preventive Medicine,* 51 J. History of Medicine & Allied Sciences 313 (1996).

2 Distributive Justice – Book of Acquisition

Izhak Englard recounts the intricate history of the distinction between corrective and distributive justice,[257] a distinction which is elaborated in the fifth book of Aristotle's *Nicomachean Ethics*. Englard offers readers a historical perspective that is vital for a deep understanding of the distinction between ancient and modern concerns.

There are many points of similarity between Englard's book and our own, for they both conduct an intergenerational dialogue between legal theories that were presented by thinkers – Aristotle and Maimonides – who lived many centuries ago, and between later legal theories from the Middle Ages until the present day. Englard's book also includes an interesting chapter on the way in which Aristotle's distinction between corrective justice and distributive justice was accepted by Jewish rabbis and scholars. In this context we point out, for the first time, the possible existence of a real link between what Maimonides wrote in part three of the *Guide* and between Aristotle's said distinction (a possibility not discussed by Englard). Admittedly, Maimonides made no explicit, direct use of Aristotle's distinction between corrective justice and distributive justice, nor did he even mention it. However, we believe that in the *Guide* it is possible to find expressions that are very reminiscent of – although not identical to – those two types of justice discussed by Aristotle. We assume that Maimonides "corresponded" with the two types of Aristotelian justice and interpreted them in his own unique way, which is certainly not identical to that of Aristotle.

In our opinion, Maimonides alludes to corrective justice in the *Guide* 3:40, when he refers to "removal of wrongs," or according to another translation, "putting an end to acts of injustice" as one of the two meta-objectives of tort law.[258] Distributive justice, or at least the Maimonidean version of distributive justice, is indicated by Maimonides in chapter 42 of the *Guide*, when he explains that the laws of property that are included in the Book of Laws and in part of the Book of Acquisition in the *Code* are based on the following rationale:

> All of them have an evident reason. For they consist in an estimation of the laws of justice with regard to transactions that of necessity occur between people and see to it that these do not deviate from the course of mutual help useful for both parties, lest one of them should aim at increasing his share in the whole and at being the gainer in all respects.[259]

Maimonides' words indicate an approach that combines utilitarian considerations with distributive ones. Maimonides is indeed in favor of increasing aggregate

---

[257] Izhak Englard, Corrective and Distributive Justice: From Aristotle to Modern Times (Oxford: Oxford University Press, 2009).
[258] We will discuss the bounds of corrective justice extensively in the following chapter.
[259] Guide 3:42, according to Pines' translation.

welfare. But he qualifies this by saying that increasing aggregate welfare must not disregard distributive considerations, and a situation in which one person alone "aim[s] at increasing his share in the whole and at being the gainer in all respects" cannot be permitted.

Maimonides invokes this principle in explaining the limitation placed on profits made by sellers. There is a halakhic prohibition against misleading a buyer or a seller regarding the nature of a product or its price.[260] There is also a *halakhah* regulating repayment of the difference or cancellation of the transaction in the event that the price that has been paid for an item (whether deliberately or inadvertently) is too high or too low by a margin of at least one sixth (16.666 percent) as compared to its real value.[261] In the *Guide*, Maimonides explains this *halakhah* in accordance with his fundamental approach to limitations that should be placed on profits: "First and foremost there should be no swindling in buying and selling, and only the usual and habitually recognized profits should be sought. Conditions have been laid down under which the contract becomes valid."[262]

The laws of the four watchmen or bailees, and their liability for damages cause to objects for which they were responsible, are also explained on the basis of a combination between utilitarian and distributive considerations. As Maimonides states:

> the law of the four kinds of bailees: the fairness of the law is evident. If one keeps the property of his neighbor for nothing, without deriving therefrom any benefit for himself, and is only obliging his neighbor, he is free from all responsibility. And if any injury is done to the property, the owner alone must bear the loss. He who borrows a thing keeps it only for his own advantage, while the owner lends it to him to oblige him; he is therefore responsible for everything; any loss in the property must be borne by the borrower. If one takes wages for keeping the property or pays for using it, he as well as the owner profit thereby; the losses must therefore be divided between them. It is done in this manner; the bailee pays for any loss caused through want of care, namely, when the property is stolen or lost; for this happens only when the bailee does not take sufficient precaution. The owner, on the other hand, bears such losses as cannot be prevented; namely, if by accident the animal falls and breaks its limbs, or is carried away by armed men as booty, or if it dies.[263]

Even though Maimonides in the *Guide* does not specifically discuss damages to neighbors, it seems to us that they too are explained on the basis of the fundamental distributive rationale which according to Maimonides underlies property laws in general. As we have seen, the laws of nuisance and the laws of neighbors are, according to Maimonides, classified as part of the Book of Acquisition and in the

---

[260] *See* Laws of Sales, chapter 12.
[261] *Ibid.* 12:2:3
[262] GUIDE 3:42 (according to Pines' translation).
[263] GUIDE 3:42 (according to Friedlander's translation).

framework of property laws. Therefore, in our opinion, it is clear that on the one hand, an owner is entitled to realize his ownership of his own place, but on the other hand, he must do so without causing too much damage. As we will see in the following chapter, it is true that in relation to standard tort law, too, Maimonides combined considerations of distributive justice in different contexts, particularly in his discussion of assessing the damage that the damager must pay. But in the laws of nuisance and of neighbors, the distributive considerations assume a far more important position.

3 Maimonides as a Pluralistic-Differential Scholar

We saw that according to Maimonides, there are several goals. In the *Guide* Maimonides strongly emphasized the goal of removal of the wrong, which is an objective parallel to corrective justice. However, he also strongly emphasized consequentialist considerations, and in doing so he actualized and demonstrated the second central goal that he presented in the *Guide*, which is that of avoidance of damage – an objective that is parallel to the present-day optimal avoidance. Alongside these goals, Maimonides' writings also contain considerations that are moral-deontological and religious at base, which of course correspond less with the modern theoretical approaches, as well as clear markers of distributive justice. This is a pluralistic approach, and in no way is it monistic like the approaches that were presented in Chapter 1.[264]

We are naturally aware of the substantive differences between the trend of the contemporary approach – which is normative – and that of Maimonides, which is primarily *explanatory*, in an effort to base the existing law on a rational conceptual foundation in accordance with a philosophical-religious conception. Against this background, as argued *infra* Chapter 8, monism and pluralism as these are used in relation to Maimonides have a meaning that is not absolutely identical to the meaning attributed to these terms by some scholars in our generation. Nevertheless, in certain cases, as shown in Chapter 8, Maimonides appears to be a pluralist in a sense that is closer to the modern sense.

The understanding that today there exist monistic doctrines as opposed to pluralistic ones allows us to understand that Maimonides is not monistic. This constitutes one step in the direction of learning from contemporary theories about Maimonides' theory and placing it on the pluralistic, rather than the monistic scale, if we are to use those modern terms.

But this is not enough. In the next chapters we will examine the nature of the Maimonidean pluralistic approach as opposed to contemporary pluralistic approaches. What is special about a pluralistic approach is not only that several

---

[264] *Supra* Chapter 1, Section C.

objectives are considered, or that one objective is emphasized. The question is how these objectives are combined in a given situation or cluster of situations, and what happens when these objectives clash. In other words, in order to be a true pluralist, it is not enough to simply not be a monist. One must show that one is combining the different objects logically, or prioritizing them in general or in particular cases in a logical way.

4

The Deontological and Religious Elements of Maimonides' Tort Theory

As we saw in Chapter 3, Maimonides regards efficient prevention of damage as only one – albeit a very central – consideration in determining liability in torts, amongst many other considerations, which will be addressed in this chapter.

In the first half of this chapter we shall discuss the philosophical, deontological, pedagogical, and religious elements of the Maimonidean tort theory. We shall then compare Maimonides' approach with modern approaches to tort law, including corrective justice approaches, considering the similarities and the differences between them.

A. DEONTOLOGICAL ELEMENTS OF MAIMONIDES' TORT THEORY

1 The Philosophical Elements: "The Welfare of the Body"

First, we will discuss briefly the meta-halakhic, philosophical basis of Maimonides' tort theory, which is substantially different from the mode of thinking of modern theorists of secular-general law in general, and the economic approach to tort law in particular. This basis will help us to elucidate Maimonides' tort theory, including his combination of the deontological considerations of morality – removal of the wrong (corrective justice) – with considerations of prevention of harm, which, as we shall see in the following chapter, are mainly utilitarian considerations. In our view, these two main objectives of tort law comport with the subject of the welfare of the body, which Maimonides discusses at length in the *Guide*.

The purpose of the biblical commandments is to achieve the welfare of the person and to bring him to a state of perfection. According to Maimonides, there are two levels to the perfection of the person, and the biblical commandments are designed to achieve them both together, according to his well-known statement in the *Guide*: "The Law as a whole aims at two things: the welfare of the soul and the welfare of the body."[1] Although the aim of the welfare of the soul is indubitably greater in nobility, as Maimonides says,[2] the second aim – the welfare of the body – "is prior in nature and time." It "consists in the governance of the city and the welfare of the states of all its people according to their capacity,"[3] in light of the fact that an isolated individual cannot achieve perfection, for "an individual can only attain all this through a political association, it being already known that man is political by nature."[4] For the welfare of the body, an organized social-political structure is necessary, whereas the welfare of the soul is of a personal nature.[5] What is included in the welfare of the soul? Maimonides explains: "Welfare of the soul consists in the multitude's acquiring correct opinions corresponding to their respective capacity."

Maimonides proceeds to explain what is included in the welfare of the body:

> Welfare of the body comes about by the improvement of their ways of living one with another. This is achieved through two things. One of them is the abolition of their wronging each other. This is tantamount to every individual among the people not being permitted to act according to his will and up to the limits of his power, but being forced to do that which is useful to the whole. The second thing consists in the acquisition by every human individual of moral qualities that are useful for life in society so that the affairs of the city may be ordered.[6]

Maimonides subsequently provides a brief description of welfare of the body:

> The welfare of the states of people in their relations with one another through the abolition of reciprocal wrongdoing and through the acquisition of a noble and excellent character. In this way the preservation of the population of the country and their permanent existence in the same order become possible.[7]

Maimonides' description of welfare of the body, as presented by some scholars, has some similarities to the Greco-Arab formulations of Ibn Rushd (often Latinized as Averroes, a medieval (1126–1198) Andalusian polymath, who wrote on Aristotelian and Islamic philosophy) and Al-Farabi (a philosopher and jurist who wrote on political philosophy, Damascus 872–950)[8] and others.[9]

---

[1] GUIDE 3:27 (translated by Pines). "Soul" to Maimonides refers to a person's intellectual world, and "body" refers primarily to the political and psychological world of a person (and not only to his physical body).

[2] GUIDE 3:27.

[3] Ibid. Therefore, "[t]his second aim is the more certain one, and it is the one regarding which every effort has been made precisely to expound it and all its particulars."

[4] Ibid. See also GUIDE 2:40.

[5] And see R. NAHUM ELIEZER RABINOVITCH, THE WAY OF TORAH – CHAPTERS IN THE PHILOSOPHY OF HALAKHAH AND CONTEMPORARY ISSUES 51–52 (5759–1999) (Heb.).

[6] GUIDE 3:27.

[7] Ibid.

[8] Compare Maimonides' statement that man is political by nature to R. WALZER, AL-FARABI ON THE PERFECT STATE chapter 15 (Oxford 1985).

[9] See Steven Harvey, A New Islamic Source of the Guide of the Perplexed, MAIMONIDEAN STUDIES vol. 2, at 31–59, 34 (Arthur Hyman ed., New York, 1991); Steven Harvey, On Ibn Rashid, Maimonides and the Perfect State, Studies of Philosophical Issues: PRESENTATION AT AN

Tort law, is intended to order the relations between people (injurers and injured persons), and is designed to prevent people from harming one another, and therefore it belongs to those areas of the *halakhah* that are directed primarily at the welfare of the body; tort law must act to enhance the welfare of society and shape a person's qualities, bringing him to internal balance and perfection. It is to these two types of "welfare of the body" that Maimonides appears to be referring in the chapter in the *Guide* explaining the reason for the Book of Torts.[10] There Maimonides mentions two aims of tort law, i.e., "they are all concerned with putting an end to acts of injustice (or removal of wrong) and with the prevention of acts causing damage."[11] Indeed, in that same chapter in the *Guide*, Maimonides explains several of the rulings included in the Book of Torts in accordance with these two aims.

Thus, for example, Maimonides writes that the laws pertaining to the return of a lost object realize both purposes of welfare of the body – social utility and the acquisition of excellent qualities:

> The situation with regard to the commandment to return a lost thing is clear, for while this is an excellent moral quality from the point of view of good relations, it is also useful because there is reciprocity. For if you do not return a thing lost by somebody else, the thing lost by you will not be returned, just as your son will not honor you if you do not honor your father. There are many other examples of this.[12]

We see that Maimonides combines a clear utilitarian rationale ("reciprocity") with a clear social-educational rationale – the acquisition of moral qualities.[13]

The rationale of the welfare of the body, the removal of wrong, the prevention of harm and the establishment of an orderly society is invoked by Maimonides to explain several *halakhot* not only in relation to the laws of lost property, but also in tort law. Thus, for example, Maimonides explains the law under which the injured person is paid compensation from the best of the tortfeasor's property[14] in terms of the rationale of prevention of damage, and as he writes in his *Commentary to the Mishnah*: "So that damage and wresting control [of another's property] should not

---

EVENING IN HONOR OF SHLOMO PINES ON HIS 80TH BIRTHDAY, JERUSALEM 5752 (PAPERS OF THE ISRAEL ACADEMY OF SCIENCES/DIVISION FOR HUMANITIES) 19–31, at 23, note 113 (Heb.); ELIEZER ZE'EV BERMAN, IBN BAJA AND MAIMONIDES, CHAPTER IN THE HISTORY OF POLITICAL PHILOSOPHY 99, 102–04 (Jerusalem 1959, PhD thesis, Hebrew University, Tzilum Tel Aviv Press, 1977).

[10] GUIDE 3:40.
[11] *Ibid.* (Pines' translation).
[12] *Ibid.*
[13] Accordingly, Maimonides (in the GUIDE, *ibid.*) explains several of the laws included in the Book of Torts according to one or both of the aims of the welfare of the body. Thus, for example, he explains the laws of robbery as directed at improving [moral] qualities ("It is already known that coveting is prohibited because it leads to desire and desire is prohibited because it leads to robbery"), and the laws of the broken-necked calf as having a utilitarian-practical goal (discovery of the murderer).
[14] Laws of Property Damages 1:2.

increase amongst people."[15] In the *Code*, too, Maimonides mentions several laws that rely on the same rationale of the prevention of harm.[16] Thus, for example, he writes in Laws of Property Damages that it is forbidden for a person to allow his animals to wander in the fields, due to a concern that they will cause damage.[17] Furthermore, he writes that the reason that a Gentile whose oxen gored the ox of an Israelite is fined for the entire value of the damage is because

> this is a fine imposed upon the Gentile (*goy*) because, being heedless of the scriptural commandments, he does not remove sources of damages. Accordingly, should he not be held liable for damage caused by his animals, he would not take care of them, and thus would inflict loss on other people's property.[18]

Up to this point we have dealt with the expressions of "welfare of the body" in tort law. Can expressions of the "welfare of the soul" also be found in this area of law?

2 "The Welfare of the Soul" and the Idea of the Sanctity of Human Life

In terms of tort theory, we have emphasized the existence of several competing rationales in the *Guide* and the *Code*, all of which fall within the limits of Maimonides' notion of the welfare of the body. The psychological considerations function in two complementary ways: on the one hand, they effect a change in the individual, regardless of the benefit to the broader society. On the other hand, they also contribute to the welfare of human society, in the sense that the transformative effect on the human psyche is conducive to a more perfect society.

What seems, however, to be missing from the taxonomy of torts (as presented in the *Guide* 3:40) is the first and – according to Maimonides as stated in the *Guide* – the most important and noble rationale for the Torah's precepts, namely the welfare of the soul and the human intellect. While Maimonides did not mention the objective of the welfare of the soul in the context of his tort theory described in the *Guide* 3:40, he did express this objective in the Book of Torts in the *Code*. We posit that the idea of the sanctity of human life, emphasized in the Laws of Murderers and the Preservation of Life in the Book of Torts in the *Code*, is an expression of the welfare of the soul (תיקון הנפש), as emerges clearly from the title of the section (הלכות רוצח ושמירת נפש) – the second part is clearly directed at the welfare of the soul (תיקון הנפש). Consider, for example, the following assertion:

---

[15] COMMENTARY TO THE MISHNAH, *Gittin* 5:1. And *see* the edition of Dror Fixler (Ma'aleh Adumim, 2016) of the COMMENTARY *ibid.* at 255–56.
[16] For a detailed analysis of these laws, *see infra*, Chapter 6.
[17] Laws of Property Damages 5:1. We will deal with this source later.
[18] *Ibid.* 8:5. Note that Maimonides' explanation of this law was sociological-rational, unlike that of the Talmud, which derived this from biblical verses. See *Bava Kamma* 38a. YA'AKOV LEVINGER pointed this out in MAIMONIDES' HALAKHIC PHILOSOPHY 103 (Jerusalem, 1965) (Heb.). This is only one example, amongst others, in which the Talmud bases a law on scriptural verses, whereas Maimonides allows himself to base them on reason.

The court is warned against accepting ransom from a murderer [to save him from execution], even if he offers all the money in the world and even if the avenger of blood agrees to let him go free. For the life of the murdered person is not the property of the avenger of blood but the property of God, and Scripture says, "Moreover ye shall take no ransom for the life of a murderer" (Numbers 35:31). There is no offense about which the law is so strict as it is about bloodshed, as it is said: "So shall ye not pollute the land wherein ye are; for blood, it pollute the land" (Numbers 25:33).[19]

In the same chapter, *halakhah* 16, with regard to the saving of human life, Maimonides asserts: "For if one destroys the life of a single Israelite, it is regarded as though he destroyed the entire world, and if one preserves the life of a single Israelite, it is regarded as though he preserved the entire world."

From the last citation it emerges that the idea of the sanctity of human life expresses not only a physical aspect of the body, but also a spiritual, psychological aspect of man: that he is of great significance to the entire world.

The idea of the sanctity of human life is rooted in Maimonides' biblical and Talmudic heritage.[20] Scholars have long noted the distinctiveness of the Bible's disposition towards human life[21] (when compared against other ancient Near Eastern cultures) as reflected, for example, in the biblical distinction between the shedding of innocent blood and crimes against property, a distinction echoed by Maimonides.[22]

Maimonides did not simply rehearse these ideas, entrenched in the biblical and rabbinic heritage. He made them into the cornerstone of his Book of Torts.[23] The very structure of the book of torts as a whole, beginning with property damages, moving on to theft and robbery, then to bodily injuries, and culminating in the laws of the murderer and the preservation of life, the greatest damage possible, tells us something about the *telos* of the Book of Torts, about the purpose of the Torah's precepts pertaining to tort law. It is in this context that the philosophical-theological rationale concerning the sanctity of human life illuminates Maimonides' overall system of tort

---

[19] Laws of Murderers and the Preservation of Life 1:4. *See also* GUIDE 3:41. We are grateful to Yishai Kiel for enlightening us in his response to a lecture we delivered at the University of Toronto (March 20, 2017) on aspects concerning welfare of the soul, as emerge from the Laws of Murderers in the CODE.

[20] *See, e.g., Ketubot* 37b; *T Yevamot* 8:7; *M Sanhedrin* 4:5.

[21] *See, e.g.,* YAIR LORBERBAUM, IN GOD'S IMAGE – MYTH, THEOLOGY AND LAW IN CLASSICAL JUDAISM, esp. chap. 6, at 218–23 (Cambridge University Press, 2015).

[22] Unlike other ancient Near Eastern religions and cultures, the ideology of the Bible generally maintains that humanity (and not only the king) was made in God's image and therefore, human life is unquantifiable, and the shedding of innocent blood cannot be rectified through monetary compensation. These dimensions of biblical ideology, particularly the emphasis placed on the sanctity of human life, were carried into the talmudic discussions. For a broader discussion, *see* LORBERBAUM, *ibid.*

[23] On the distinctiveness of Maimonides' approach vis-à-vis the approaches of the Sages regarding the crime of murder, *see* Yair Lorberbaum, *Maimonides on the Image of God: Philosophy and Halakhah – the Crime of Murder, the Criminal Process and the Death Penalty*, 68 TARBIZ 533 (5759–2009) (Heb.).

theory, in the sense that many laws contained in the Book of Torts, especially the Laws of Wounding and the Laws of Murderers, are intended to facilitate knowledge of, and respect for, the sanctity of human life created in image of God.

Indeed, it appears that in Maimonides' view, the shedding of blood is detrimental not only to the image of God and the welfare of the soul, but it is also harmful to the welfare of the body, destroying social order and the world. He writes: "For although there are worse crimes than bloodshed, none causes such destruction to civilized society as bloodshed. Not even idolatry, nor immorality nor desecration of the Sabbath, is equal of bloodshed."[24]

In light of Maimonides' acute awareness of the importance of the idolatrous backdrop to the Torah's precepts, it is conceivable that he viewed the idea of the sanctity of human life as a direct contrast to the surrounding ancient Near Eastern cultures, for which human life was dispensable and quantifiable. Whether or not Maimonides actually made such a claim with regard to the ancient Near Eastern cultures (as he did with regard to the ritual and sacrificial laws of the Torah),[25] he definitely knew about the practice of blood money that heavily influenced Islamic law. He may therefore have regarded the sanctity and unquantifiability of human life as a philosophical-theological truth requiring indoctrination via an elaborate tort system.

We must recall that from what Maimonides wrote in the *Guide*, as quoted at the beginning of the previous paragraph, it emerges that the principal goals of tort law are directed at the welfare of the body, namely, removal of wrongdoing and prevention of harm, and the goal of welfare of the soul receives no mention in the context of tort law. The goal of welfare of the soul finds more emphasis in the Book of Torts in the *Code*, particularly in Laws of Murderers and in Laws of Wounding, which deal with the integrity of the soul and the body; however, it is not emphasized in the Laws of Property Damages and the Laws of Theft, Robbery, and the Restoration of Lost Property, which are property-related torts by nature.

In sum: according to Maimonides' conception, tort law as a whole is designed to realize two aims in particular. In the following chapter we will expand on the first aim: the prevention of damage from the aspect of the utilitarian rationale that is emphasized in the *Guide*. In this Chapter, however, we shall discuss the other aim, which is emphasized by Maimonides in his discussion of tort law in various contexts in various of his works: this is the social-pedagogic aim: the acquisition of excellent qualities.

3 *The Social-Pedagogic Effect of Tort Law: Acquisition of Good Qualities*

A typical example of the great importance that Maimonides attributes to the acquisition of good qualities, as demonstrated in Section 1 (regarding welfare of the body) can be seen in the Book of Commandments, in relation to the prohibition

---

[24] Laws of Murderers and the Preservation of Life 4:9.
[25] GUIDE 3:29–30, 32, 37, 46–47.

against cursing another person.[26] Maimonides regards the restrictions that the Torah imposed on cursing another person as intended to shape the moral character of the perpetrator and to prevent him from acquiring bad qualities such as vengeance and anger that cause him to hurt others. Why did the Torah formulate the prohibition in terms of "Thou shalt not curse the deaf"? What is special about the deaf person? Maimonides answers thus:

> We might think that the Torah prohibits cursing a Jew only when he will hear it, because of the shame and pain he feels, but there is nothing wrong with cursing a deaf person, since he doesn't hear it and doesn't feel any pain as a result. The Torah therefore told us that this too is forbidden, because it is concerned not only with the one who is being cursed, but with the one who is uttering the curse. A person is prohibited from gearing himself for revenge and becoming accustomed to getting angry.[27]

Maimonides' approach is that educating a person towards good qualities is an important aim in itself, and it should be pursued even where no harm has actually been done, such as in the case of the deaf person who does not hear the curse and is in fact not harmed; nevertheless, it is prohibited to curse him. The author of *Sefer Hahinukh* (The Book of Education) noted:

> Maimonides, of blessed memory, said of the reason for this commandment, that it should not drive the person who curses to vengeance and not accustom him to becoming angry ... and it seems to me from his words that he is not concerned about harm to the person who is the target of the curse, but that the Torah is steering the curser away from vengeance and that he should not become accustomed to angering.[28]

Indeed, Maimonides' reason is not the only possible one for prohibiting such cursing, and more likely reasons are conceivable.[29] But precisely for this reason, Maimonides' unique approach, which he presents clearly and at length in the Book of Commandments,[30] is remarkable, in that he views the cursing of the deaf person as a paradigm for the general proclivity of the Torah in the laws of tort to be "concerned not only with the one who is being cursed, but with the one who is uttering the curse."

---

[26] Book of Commandments, negative commandment 317.
[27] Ibid.
[28] SEFER HAHINUKH, negative commandment 239, at 317 in the Chavel edition (Jerusalem: Mossad Harav Kook 1990).
[29] And indeed, the author of SEFER HAHINUKH himself (*ibid.*) suggests two reasons for the prohibition against cursing, which in his opinion are sounder than the reason proposed by Maimonides. The first reason is that "in this vein our Sages said that a covenant is sealed with the lips, i.e., a person's words have power." In other words, the deaf person may indeed not have heard the curse, but the curse nevertheless had an effect and harmed him. (Maimonides, as a rationalist, would surely have disagreed with this kind of reason.) The second reason is utilitarian: "To terminate disagreement between people."
[30] Which is not at all characteristic of the Book of Commandments, in which Maimonides normally expresses himself with great brevity.

At this point, the novelty of Maimonides' approach as opposed to that which is accepted in modern jurisprudence should be emphasized. One of the important distinctions between the different types of behaviors which can legitimately – or not – be regulated in legislation was developed by the renowned British philosopher John Stuart Mill (1806–1873) in his work, *On Liberty*.[31] In this work, he established the basis for the liberal conception whereby the state must respect the liberty of the individual to act as he wishes, and restricting that liberty in legislation is not permitted other than in cases in which the individual seeks to act in a way that causes harm to the other or to society as a whole. This principle is sometimes called the "harm principle", and by virtue of this principle Mill objected to religious legislation, because he assumed that behavior contrary to religious dictates, even if they are binding, does not cause harm to society, and therefore society is not permitted to impose them upon the individual. In keeping with this way of thinking, he objected on principle to paternalistic legislation aimed at prohibiting behavior that caused harm to those effecting the behavior. Such legislation, which according to Mill was not intended to protect the interests of society or the interests of those to whom the law was addressed, was regarded by him as unjustified legislation (with certain exception), since he believed that every person is entitled to decide upon his own fate as he wishes.[32] Clearly, in our view, Mill would not have permitted the law to restrict the right of a person to curse a deaf person, for no harm was caused to the deaf person. But it is precisely this approach to which Maimonides objects, in his emphasis of the harm done to the curser himself.

Indeed, consideration of the immoral conduct of the damager and not only the situation of the victim is one of the outstanding characteristics of Maimonides' tort theory, and it manifests itself in many contexts, some of which we will mention later in this section.

In Laws of Theft in the *Code*, for example, Maimonides writes that not only is it "prohibited to steal an object of however small a value," but "it is also forbidden to steal in jest, or to steal an object with the intention of returning it, or with the intention of paying for it."[33] In the Book of Commandments, Maimonides adds that it is forbidden to steal even if the thief intends to return the stolen property to the victim, and his intention was solely to "anger and confuse the victim and afterward to return it to him."[34]

From a formal point of view, the crime of theft was not committed; why, therefore, does Maimonides prohibit such acts? His answer is that "[a]ll these acts are forbidden, lest one become accustomed to practicing them."[35]

Maimonides explains that underlying the said prohibitions is the concern that a person will become accustomed to steal, i.e., an educational basis for the acquisition

---

[31] JOHN STUART MILL, ON LIBERTY (2nd ed., London, 1959).
[32] *Ibid.* at 21–30, 179–98.
[33] Laws of Theft 1:2.
[34] Book of Commandments, negative commandment 244.
[35] Laws of Theft 1:2.

of good qualities by each person in order that he not descend to becoming a professional thief and criminal. In other words, it is not the loss of the stolen object on the part of the individual victim or society as a whole that underpins these prohibitions, but the damage that it does to the soul of the thief himself, who becomes accustomed to acts of fraud, deception and falsehood.[36]

According to Maimonides, it is also proper "for the court to impose corporal punishment upon minors for theft, the punishment being administered in proportion to their strength, in order that they not become accustomed to stealing. The same procedure should be followed if they do other damage."[37] Note that the reason that Maimonides gives for punishing minors who steal or cause other damages is educational: "[I]n order that they should not become accustomed to stealing." In other words, because this is not a specific prohibition – since minors are not bound by the commandments – it concerns the acquisition of bad habits and bad traits. Maimonides therefore permits punishing the minors, because when they become adults it will be difficult to correct these faults that were formed when they were young.[38]

The concern that a person will descend into a life of crime is the basis for other rulings in Laws of Theft and Laws of Robbery. Thus, for example, Maimonides writes that not only are theft and robbery prohibited, but "[i]t is prohibited to buy from a thief any property he has stolen, such buying being a great sin, since it encourages criminals and causes the thief to steal other property. For if a thief finds no buyer, he will not steal."[39] From that quote it emerges that whosoever buys from a thief commits a twofold crime: (a) By buying the stolen goods he helps the thief reap the fruits of his crime; (b) He encourages the thief to continue to steal in the future, for if he had no one to sell to, he would not steal.[40] Without customers, the thief would at most steal for his own private purposes. But when he finds buyers, there is a serious concern that he will be tempted to steal again, until theft eventually becomes his principal occupation. Again, we see that Maimonides is concerned about actions that will encourage a thief to steal again and become a professional, serial thief. He also broadens the prohibition against encouraging robbery in any way, whether directly (by means of buying) or indirectly (by helping in or by benefitting from the robbery).[41]

---

[36] This is based on *Sifra Kedoshim* (2:5).
[37] Laws of Theft 1:10.
[38] A similar conception, whereby minors must be prevented from causing damage, also emerges from Maimonides' Commentary to M Bava Kamma 8:4, which exempted minor children from liability for wounds that they inflicted on others; nevertheless, in his commentary to this *mishnah* Maimonides ruled that "The Dayan must administer a hard blow to prevent damage to other people." Here we see the idea even more clearly – the Dayan, and not the parents, must beat them to educate them; neither is the payment of compensation to the person injured by those minors required.
[39] Laws of Theft 5:1.
[40] And cf. *Gittin* 45a: "It is not the mouse that steals, but the hole that steals."
[41] See also Laws of Robbery and Lost Property 5:1–2: "It is forbidden to buy from a robber property obtained by robbery, and it is also forbidden to assist him in making alterations to enable him to acquire title to it. For if one does this or anything similar to it, he encourages transgressors and

In other places, too, Maimonides ruled that the person who was known to be a serial robber could be fined and punished.[42]

In Laws of Robbery in the *Code*, Maimonides rules that not only is robbery prohibited, but acting in certain ways that do not amount to robbery, such as the coveting and desiring, are also prohibited. As Maimonides writes:

> If one covets the male slave or the female slave or the house or goods of another, or anything that it is possible for him to acquire from the other, and he subjects the other to vexation and pesters him until he is allowed to buy from him, then he transgresses the negative commandment, Thou shalt not covet (Exodus 20:14), even if he pays him a high price for it[43]

This is a far-reaching ruling, for a person who covets has not physically committed the crime of robbery, and the prohibition applies to the illegitimate thought itself. Maimonides defines the prohibition as being against "occupying our thoughts with schemes of how to acquire the property of others from amongst us."[44] The crime lies in the very fact of occupying one's thoughts with schemes of how to acquire the property, and the act itself does not belong to the substance of the prohibition.[45] Maimonides extended the prohibition even further, beyond the thought which ends in acquiring the object, to the actual coveting in a person's heart, even when it has not been actualized by acquiring the coveted object. As he writes: "If one desires another's house or his wife or his goods or any similar thing that he might buy from him, he transgresses a negative commandment as soon as he thinks in his heart how he is to acquire the desired object and allows his mind to be seduced by it."[46]

Why is it forbidden to covet and to desire? Maimonides answers thus:

> Desire leads to coveting, and coveting to robbery. For if the owner does not wish to sell, even when he is offered a high price and is greatly importuned, it will lead the coveter to rob him ... Moreover, if the owner should stand up to him to protect his property, this may lead to bloodshed.[47]

---

himself transgresses ... It is forbidden to derive any benefit from property obtained by robbery even after hope of recovery has been abandoned."

[42] See, e.g., Laws of Robbery and Lost property 3:6: "if this person is known to rob, or to withhold money illegally, or to do these things time after time, we may impose fine on him"; *ibid.* 4:1: "The Sages have penalized robbers by allowing the person robbed to confirm his claim by taking an oath that the object in question is his and then recover it from the robber, provided that there is a presumption supported by two witnesses that the defendant has robbed him."; *ibid.* 5:9: "When persons are presumably robbers and all their property is presumably obtained by robbery, because they are robbers by occupation, such as tax collectors and bandits, it is forbidden to benefit from them, since the presumption is that their occupation involves robbery."

[43] *Ibid.* 1:9.

[44] Book of Commandments, negative commandment 265.

[45] And *see* Ra'avad's critical scholia to Maimonides, Laws of Robbery and Lost Property 1:9, according to which the prohibition is dependent upon an *action*, but *Maggid Mishneh, ad loc.* is correct in saying that according to Maimonides, the main prohibition is dependent on the *thought*, as we wrote earlier in the chapter.

[46] Laws of Robbery and Lost Property 1:10.

[47] *Ibid.* 1:11.

We again see that what concerns Maimonides is not necessarily the question of whether the damager perpetrated a wrongful act that actually damaged the property of another; rather, Maimonides is concerned about the person forming bad qualities, even if these qualities have not entailed actual harm to another. Maimonides looks to the future and is particularly interested in the process that the person undergoes, and he also prohibits those acts that affect a person's soul, such as desire, covetousness, cursing the deaf, to the extent that these actions corrupt a person's soul and set him on a slope on which he is liable to descend into a world of crime, theft, robbery, or violence.[48] Maimonides' aim is also to prevent that person from doing the specific act to another whose property he covets, for example, as well as to prevent him from doing such things to others in the future, but this is achieved through the acquisition of good qualities.

Another expression of the importance attributed by Maimonides to the acquisition of good qualities in the framework of the laws of robbery is to be found in his approach to robbing a Gentile. The halakhic authorities were in disagreement on the question of whether there is a prohibition against stealing from a Gentile, and, if such a prohibition does exist, what is the scope of this prohibition.[49] Maimonides' position on this matter, however, was clear and unequivocal: "On the authority of Scripture, it is forbidden to take by robbery anything whatever, even a Gentile must not be robbed nor may money due him be withheld. And if one does rob him or withhold money due him, he must make restitution."[50]

Several of the commentators on Maimonides struggled to find a source for the ruling cited here from Laws of Robbery and Lost Property 1:2, since the Talmud cites situations in which it is not prohibited to steal from the Gentile, and even according to those who hold that there is a prohibition, it is not scriptural.[51] However, these

---

[48] Cf. Book of Commandments, negative commandment 266: "The prohibition is that we are forbidden to occupy our thoughts with our desire for someone else's property and to develop a craving for it, and dwell upon it, since this will lead us to scheme to acquire it. The expression used for this prohibition is the Divine statement, 'Do not desire *[lo titaveh]* your neighbor's house.' These two prohibitions *[lo tah'mod* and *lo titaveh]* do not have the same goal. The first prohibition, *lo tah'mod,* forbids buying someone else's belongings, whereas the second, *lo titaveh,* prohibits even having the feeling of desire and envy... The explanation of this passage is as follows: If one sees a fine object that belongs to his brother, and allows his thoughts to gain control over him, and develops a desire for it, he transgresses the Divine statement, 'Do not desire' *[lo titaveh].* Then his love for the object will become stronger and he will carry out a plan to acquire it – coaxing him and pushing him to sell it or to trade it for something better and more expensive. Should he reach his goal, when he acquires it, he also transgresses the prohibition, 'Do not be envious,' since by pushing and scheming he acquired his friend's object even though he had no intention of selling it. At this point, he has transgressed two prohibitions, as we have explained. If, however, the owner, because of his love for the object, refuses to sell or trade it, then his great desire for it will cause him to take it by force and violence. At that point he also transgresses the prohibition, 'Do not commit robbery.'"

[49] For a summary of the views, *see* ENCYCLOPAEDIA TALMUDIT 5, s.v. *gezel hagoi,* 487–95.

[50] Laws of Robbery and Lost Property 1:2.

[51] *See, e.g., Kessef Mishneh* on Maimonides, *ibid.* who questioned Maimonides and argued that even according to Maimonides's approach, "this prohibition is not scriptural." And *see* SEFER HA-MAFTE'AH, Frankel edition, on Maimonides, which mentioned the copious literature from

commentators did not read Maimonides' unequivocal words in the *Commentary to the Mishnah*,[52] in which he came out strongly against the mistaken conception that permits misleading or stealing from the Gentile, "because the fact that many people, or even a few, think that such misleading is permitted in relation to Gentiles is incorrect, and it is an incorrect view." Maimonides does not sit back after citing proof that stealing from a Gentile is scripturally forbidden, but he presses on and stresses the moral, religious and educational aspects of the prohibition:

> And deceitful practices and schemes and all types of usury and forgeries and crookedness with the Gentiles are not permitted. The Sages said: It is forbidden to create a misleading impression, even vis-à-vis a Gentile. And even more so if this is the cause of desecration of the Divine Name, for then the sin will be greater, and people will acquire evil qualities due to all these evil acts in relation to which God Himself says that He abhors them in themselves, no matter to whom they were done, as it is said: "For all that do such things, even all that do unrighteously, are an abomination unto the Lord thy God."[53]

We again see the extent to which Maimonides was concerned that "people will acquire evil qualities due to all these evil acts" in the context of the laws governing robbery.[54]

Now we turn to another example of a law that is designed to instill good qualities. In the Laws of Murderers and the Preservation of Life, Maimonides, following the Talmud,[55] rules in relation to the *mitzvah* to help another person load up his animal or unload it:

> If one encounters two animals, one crouching under its burden and the other unburdened because the owner cannot find anyone to help him load, he is obligated to unload first to relieve the animal's suffering, and then to load the other. This rule applies only if the owners of the animals are both friends or both enemies (of the person who comes upon them). But if one is an enemy and the other a friend, he is obligated to load the enemy first, in order to subdue his evil impulse.[56]

Why is the person obligated to load the enemy's animal first? Did not Maimonides rule at the beginning of this *halakhah* that unloading an animal takes precedence over loading it up, due to the importance of the principle of preventing the animal from suffering. If so, why did Maimonides rule at the end of the *halakhah* that if the

---

commentators and authorities who discussed the question of the prohibition of stealing from a gentile.

[52] COMMENTARY TO THE MISHNAH, Kelim 12:7. As opposed to most commentators, R. Rabinovitch relied on what appeared in the COMMENTARY TO THE MISHNAH, in the explanation of Maimonides's ruling in the CODE, see: YAD PESHUTA LESEFER NEZIKIN, LAWS OF ROBBERY AND LOST PROPERTY 1, 2, 253–55.

[53] COMMENTARY TO THE MISHNAH, ibid.

[54] See also Laws of Robbery and Lost Property 11:3–5 (regarding the return of lost property).

[55] Bava Matzia 32b.

[56] Laws of Murderers and the Preservation of Life 13:13.

owner of the animal is an enemy, he must first be helped to load up the animal, even though the other animal is in the meanwhile crouching under its burden and is suffering? Maimonides answers that this is "in order to subdue his evil impulse." In other words, both owners of the animals require help equally. However, when the person in need is one's enemy, the scales are loaded not only with helping the other, but also with the challenge of overcoming alienation, distance, discomfort. Therefore, this case takes precedence.[57]

One may ask why the "evil impulse" is a factor here. There are cases in which not only is it permitted to hate a person, but it is even a *mitzvah* (commandment) to do so, as Maimonides himself wrote in the following *halakhah*: "The Sages decreed that if one all alone sees another committing a crime and warns him against it and does not desist, one is obligated to hate him until he repents and leaves his evil ways."[58] It seems that when Maimonides wrote that it is a *mitzvah* for a person to help the enemy – even an enemy whom one is commanded to hate – "in order to subdue his evil impulse", the intention was to instill a habit of control over feelings of hatred and anger,[59] similar to his writing elsewhere that many *mitzvoth*

> all habituate the mental powers. Just as revenge and blood libel were prohibited, when He said, "Thou shalt not take vengeance, nor bear any grudge," so "Thou shalt surely release it with him" (=the *mitzvah* to help unloading the animal of an enemy), "Thou shalt surely help him to lift it up" (=the *mitzvah* to help loading up the animal of an enemy) etc., in order to weaken the power of jealousy and anger.[60]

Indeed, Maimonides dealt at length, in several places, with the importance of control over feelings of anger and the desire for vengeance,[61] and what he said is well-known:

> Anger is also an exceptionally bad quality. It is fitting and proper that one move away from it and adopt the opposite extreme. He should school himself not to become angry even when it is fitting to be angry.... Therefore, they have directed that one distance himself from anger and accustom himself not to feel any reaction, even to things which provoke anger. This is the good path.[62]

---

[57] Jonathan Sacks, Covenant and Conversation 2009, *Mishpatim* – Helping an Enemy, available at http://rabbisacks.org/covenant-conversation-5769-mishpatim-helping-an-enemy/.
[58] Laws of Murderers and the Preservation of Life 13:14.
[59] R. Nahum Rabinovitch, *Yad Peshutah Lesefer Nezikin*, Laws of Murderers and the Preservation of Life 13:13.
[60] The Introduction to the Commentary to the Mishnah, *Avot* 4, Yitzhak Shilat edition, 239.
[61] Laws of Human Dispositions 2:3. In this context, what Maimonides wrote in his Introduction to the Commentary to the Mishnah, *Avot*, Yitzhak Shilat edition, Maimonides' Introductions to the Mishnah, 239–40, is well known: he explained that the famous sin of Moses our Teacher – the sin of the Waters of *Meribah* [=dispute] is merely a one-time deviation from the path of good qualities in the direction of anger. On criticism of the quality of anger, and on overcoming anger, *see* also Guide 3:8.
[62] Laws of Human Dispositions 2:3.

The importance of overcoming feelings of hatred and vengeance is stressed by Maimonides in his explanation of the prohibition on bearing a grudge:

> [H]e should wipe the matter from his heart and never bring it to mind. As long as he brings the matter to mind and remembers it, there is the possibility that he will seek revenge. Therefore, the Torah condemned holding a grudge, [requiring] one to wipe the wrong from his heart entirely, without remembering it at all.[63]

This is a good quality which permits a stable environment, trade and commerce to be established among people. Maimonides explains in similar fashion the commandment to help one's enemy in loading up his animal.[64] Special emphasis on the deontological-educational aspects is evident from the way in which Maimonides relates to the precepts concerning weights and measures in Laws of Theft. These precepts impose an obligation on a person who uses inaccurate weights, or measures land in a manner that is not accurate and thus steals from the person to whom he is selling by giving him less than what he undertook to sell. Maimonides does not settle for merely citing the details of the relevant rulings, as he normally does in the *Code*; rather, in a special *halakhah* he points out the enormous moral gravity involved in not being meticulous about weights and measures. He writes: "The punishment for unjust measures is more severe than the punishment for immorality, for the latter is a sin against God only, the former against one's fellow man."[65]

Elsewhere, Maimonides mentions in a more general way the greater religious gravity of sins against one's fellow man vis-à-vis sins against God, with the emphasis on all the violations enumerated in the Book of Torts in the *Code*, such as wounding, robbery etc. (and not just weights and measures).[66] In his *Commentary to the Mishnah* Maimonides further explains that not only is the punishment more severe with respect to the commandments between a person and his fellow than those between man and God, but the ramifications of observing the commandments

---

[63] Laws of Human Dispositions 7:8.
[64] Laws of Murderers and the Preservation of Life 13:13. Might Maimonides in this ruling have followed the Sages' translations into Aramaic of the biblical verse in Exodus 23.5? The Aramaic translations impart an emotional dimension to the commandment, "Thou shalt surely release it with him." Onkelos writes: "Release what is in your heart against him, and release it with him." Jonathan Sacks expressed this well (SACKS, *supra* note 57), writing that there is something special in the Torah's approach to hatred and haters: "In speaking about enemies, the Torah is realistic rather than utopian. It does not say: 'Love your enemies.' Saints apart, we cannot love our enemies, and if we try to, we will eventually pay a high psychological price: we will eventually hate those who ought to be our friends. What the Torah says instead is: when your enemy is in trouble, come to his assistance. That way, part of the hatred will be dissipated. Who knows whether help given may not turn hostility to gratitude and from there to friendship." One may assume that Maimonides would have agreed wholeheartedly!
[65] Laws of Theft 7:12.
[66] *See* Laws of Repentance 2:9.

of the first type for the moral conduct of people towards each other and for the social utility of observing them are greater.[67]

It is noteworthy that at the end of the passage (from the *Commentary to the Mishnah*), Maimonides, in keeping with the above-quoted passage of the *Guide*,[68] mentions the utility of observing commandments that are related to the "welfare of the body," which is the acquisition of good qualities, and in all events also contributes to the creation of a society with a higher moral level, for the ultimate benefit both of the person who observes the commandments and of society in general.

The education of the injurer also involves the fact that he must feel what the victim feels, and not only make do with the payment of compensation. This may be inferred from what Maimonides writes about obligating a person who wounded another to make monetary payment, and not imposing corporal punishment, as is liable to be implied by the literal text, "an eye for an eye." Maimonides writes as follows:

> If one wounds another, he must pay compensation to him for five effects of injury ... for when Scripture says, *An eye for an eye* (Exodus. 21:24; Leviticus 24:20), it is known from tradition that the word translated *"for"* signifies payment of monetary compensation.
>
> When Scripture says, *As he hath maimed a man so shall it be rendered unto him* (Leviticus, *ibid.*) it does not mean that the injurer himself is to be wounded in the manner he wounded the other, but only that the injurer deserves to be deprived of a limb or to be wounded to the same extent, and consequently that he need only pay for the injury he inflicted.[69]

Ultimately, the injurer is not subjected to corporal punishment and he makes a monetary payment. So why did Maimonides stress that a person who wounded another and caused him physical damage was deserving of being punished by having the same physical injury inflicted on him?[70]

---

[67] COMMENTARY TO THE MISHNAH, *Peah* 1:1: "All the commandments are first divided into two, one part the special commandments between the individual person and God, such as *tzitzit*, *tefillin*, the Sabbath and idolatry, and the other part the commandments that relate to the proper conduct of relations between people, such as the warning against theft, and deception, and hatred, and grudge-bearing, and the commandment to love each other, and that we should not cheat each other, and that one person will not stand by in the face of harm to another ... is a type of Equity, which is not, whereby which concerns the relationship between law and morality. If a person observes the special commandments that are for him in what is between him and his Maker, he will be rewarded by God in the World to Come ... and if he observed the commandments relating to the proper conduct of relations between people, he will be rewarded in the World to Come for observing the commandment, and he will benefit in this world for his good conduct with people, for if he acts in this way and his fellow acts in this way, he will also gain that benefit".

[68] See text *supra* near note 6.

[69] Laws of Wounding and Damaging 1:1–3.

[70] In the GUIDE 3:41, he went even further, stating the "If he has injured the latter's body, he shall be injured in his body," following the literal sense of the text, and despite the accepted commentary of the Sages whereby he pays money and is not punished corporally.

We can understand from this that the payments serve as a type of atonement fine for the wounder who by virtue of the basic law ought to have been subjected to bodily harm, but instead of this the victim exacts an atonement payment from him.[71] However, something else can be learnt from this. It appears that Maimonides wishes to shape the awareness of the person who injures his fellow, that he should understand that it is not enough to pay him compensation but that he must feel, even if not physically, the pain felt by the victim who suffered bodily injury.

The renowned philosopher Emmanuel Levinas explained this clearly:

> Violence calls up violence, but we must put a stop to this chain reaction. That is the nature of justice. Such is at least its mission once the evil has been committed. Humanity is born in man to the extent that he manages to reduce a mortal offence to the level of a civil lawsuit, to the extent that punishing becomes a question of putting right what can be put right and re-educating the wicked. Justice without passion is not the only thing man must possess. He must also have justice without killing[72]

However, adds Levinas, there is a great risk in this system that settles for compensation only for personal injury:

> But here the drama hots up. This horror of blood, this justice based on peace and kindness, is necessary and henceforth is the only possible form of justice, but does it preserve the man it wishes to save? For it leaves the way open for the rich! They can easily pay for the broken teeth, the gouged-out eyes and the fractured limbs left around them. Outrage and fracture take on a market value and are given a price, and this contradiction does not stem only from the law that substitutes a fine for suffering for everything we pay with a light heart and a healthy body comes down to a fine, and a financial fracture is not a mortal one. The world remains a comfortable place for the strong, provided that they keep their nerve. The evolution of justice cannot move towards this rebuttal of all justice... We must save the spirit of our codes by modifying their letter ... The Bible speeds up the movement that brings us a world without violence, but if money or excuses could repair everything and leave us with a free conscience, the movement would be given a misinterpretation. Yes, eye for eye. Neither all eternity, nor all the money in the world, can heal the outrage done to man. It is a disfigurement or wound that bleeds for all time, as though it required a parallel suffering to staunch this eternal haemorrhage.[73]

---

[71] Laws of Wounding and Damaging 1:1–3. Some *Aharonim* drew an inference from Maimonides' above statement whereby the primary obligation in relation to injuries is to deprive the injurer of a limb, whereas payment of compensation is merely blood money. See HAZON YEHEZKEL on T Bava Kamma 9:10 and Shevu'ot 3:10; AVI EZRI, Hilkhot Hovel u-Mezik 5:6 s.v. *ve-asher*. A similar inference can be made from the GUIDE 3:41, where Maimonides wrote that to a murderer alone, no indulgence shall be shown and no blood money (or "atonement fine" – *kofer*) accepted and he must be killed: this would imply that for injuries, money may be exacted.
[72] EMMANUEL LEVINAS, DIFFICULT FREEDOM – ESSAYS ON JUDAISM, 146–47 (The Johns Hopkins University Press, trans. Sean Hand, 1990) (Heb.).
[73] *Ibid.*

This is also the reason that when a person inflicts physical injury on another, it is insufficient in Maimonides' view for him to compensate the victim monetarily, and he must ask the victim to forgive him.[74]

The *mitzvah* of returning lost property, too, as Maimonides wrote in the *Guide*,[75] is intended to educate a person towards the acquisition of good personal qualities. Examination of the Laws of Lost Property in the Book of Torts is likely to reveal the emphasis the Maimonides placed on establishing rules of moral behavior for the finder of lost property. Thus, for example, Maimonides ruled that even in a case in which the Talmud exempts the finder of lost property from returning the item to its owner, the finder must, from a moral-educational point of view, nevertheless make an effort to do that which is upright and good and return the object. There are several examples of this in Maimonides' writings. The first example is Maimonides' ruling, pursuant to the talmudic law[76] that

> [if one finds lost property] in a public highway or a large square, or in assembly halls or lecture halls … or in any other place frequented by the general public, whatever he finds belongs to him, even if an Israelite comes along and identifies it. For the owner will abandon hope of its recovery as soon as he loses the property.[77]

Up to this point Maimonides' ruling is in total accord with the talmudic law, but he proceeds with a moral directive: "Yet even though it belongs to the finder, if he wishes to follow the good and upright path and do more than the strict law requires, he must return the property to an Israelite who identifies it."[78]

Now to the second example. Maimonides ruled, in accordance with talmudic law: "If one finds a sack or a basket, the rule is as follows: If he is a scholar or a respected elder who is not accustomed to taking such things in his hand, he need not concern himself with them."[79] Indeed, the *halakhah* exempts elders and dignitaries from returning lost property.[80] But what is the law if that same elder or learned dignitary nevertheless wishes to return the object to its owner, even though he is legally exempt from doing so? The Talmud has no clear answer to this question,[81] and the medieval sages disagreed as to the law in such a case. According

---

[74] Laws of Wounding and Damaging 5:9. We dealt with this issue in Chapter 3.
[75] GUIDE 3:40.
[76] *Bava Metzia* 24:a–b.
[77] Laws of Robbery and Lost Property 11:7.
[78] *Ibid.*
[79] *Ibid.* 11:13.
[80] *Bava Metzia* 30a.
[81] In *Bava Metzia* 30b, the Talmud indeed cites the example of R. Ishmael, who despite being old and exempt from the commandment of loading and unloading, acted beyond the letter of the law and bought the logs from the person who needed help in uploading. However, this example cannot be used as explicit proof in our case, as Rosh wrote in the reference in note 82 *infra*, for from this example we can learn only that the elder was permitted to act beyond the letter of the law only by way of forgoing his property, as R. Ishmael did, but he is not permitted to demean himself and to help with the unloading and loading, or with returning lost property if it is not in his way.

to one view, that elder or dignitary is forbidden to return the object.[82] Maimonides, however, chose a different approach. In his view, "If one follows the good and upright path and does more than the strict law requires, he will return lost property in all cases, even if it is not keeping with his dignity."[83]

A further expression of Maimonides' principled position, whereby despite the fact that the *halakhah* exempts the elder and the dignitary from fulfilling the *mitzvah* of returning lost property, he should nevertheless fulfill the *mitzvah* beyond the letter of the law, emerges from his ruling in relation to the *mitzvah* of helping in the loading and unloading of his fellow's beast of burden. In Maimonides' view, this *mitzvah* is closely linked to the *mitzvah* of returning lost property, for they both are directed at a person's obligation to prevent his fellow incurring a loss of property.[84] On the one hand, similar to the *mitzvah* of returning lost property, Maimonides ruled that "If one is an elder unaccustomed to loading or unloading, he is exempt, seeing that the act is not keeping with his dignity."[85] Even though this is the fundamental scriptural law, here too Maimonides ruled in similar vein to his ruling in relation to returning lost property, that it is befitting that the elder and the dignitary should not invoke their exemption from fulfilling the *mitzvah*:

> The general rule is as follows: In every case where if the animal were his own he would load or unload it, he must load and unload another's, but if one is pious and does more than the letter of the law demands, even if he is a prince of the highest rank, still if he sees another's animal crouching under its burden of straw or sticks or the like, he should help unload and reload.[86]

In relation to this ruling, too, as in relation to Maimonides' ruling regarding the return of lost property, there was an authority who disagreed and held that it is forbidden for the elder and the dignitary to demean themselves and to load and unload beasts of burden.[87] *Prima facie*, the reason behind the dissenting view is clear,[88] whereas Maimonides' approach is hard to understand, for if the Torah

---

[82] PISKEI HA-ROSH, Bava Metzia 2:21: "The reason is clearly explained there: For because the Torah exempted the elder, who must not demean himself, it is forbidden for that elder to return lost property, which would demean the dignity of the Torah in a situation in which he is exempt."

[83] Laws of Robbery and Lost Property 11:17.

[84] On the close connection in Maimonides' theory between the commandment to return lost property and the commandment to help a fellow unloading and loading a beast of burden, see R. NAHUM RABINOVITCH, YAD PESHUTAH LESEFER NEZIKIM, Laws of Murderers, Introduction to Chapter 13.

[85] Laws of Murderers and the Preservation of Life 13:3.

[86] Ibid. 13:4.

[87] See PISKEI HA-ROSH, *supra* note 82; TUR, Hoshen Mishpat 272.

[88] And indeed, there are those who ruled in accordance with Rosh's approach. *See, e.g.*, TUR, *ibid.*, who, after citing Maimonides on the matter of unloading and loading then cited Rosh. It appears that he agrees with Rosh, and therefore, in Laws of Lost Property, Hoshen Mishpat 263, TUR did not cite Maimonides regarding action beyond the letter of the law; this is how this omission is explained in *Beit Yosef* 263. Rema ruled likewise in his glosses on SHULHAN ARUKH,

exempted a person from the *mitzvah* of returning lost property, and it exempted the elder from the *mitzvah* of loading and unloading due to the assault on his honor, on what basis does Maimonides say that it is appropriate that the elder forego his dignity and return the lost object?[89] In line with Maimonides, Rabbi Yosef Karo wrote that if an elder returns a lost item, this is not regarded as demeaning the Torah. On the contrary, he enhances the dignity of Heaven in that he takes care of his fellow, even though he is exempt.[90] In these cases, the elder waived the privilege afforded to him as an "elder for whom it is not dignified," and beyond the letter of the law[91] he returned the lost property and loaded up the animal.

Thus, in Maimonides' view, there is nothing wrong if a person who is exempt from returning lost property or loading a beast of burden returns the property or loads up the beast beyond the letter of the law; quite the contrary – this is befitting,

---

Hoshen Mishpat 263:3: "Some disagree and prohibit returning [the property] for it is not dignified, unless he wishes to go beyond the letter of the law – then he shall pay from his own money"; *Ibid.* 272:3.

[89] And indeed, some of the commentators on Maimonides referred to the talmudic passage concerning R. Ishmael (*Bava Metzia* 30b) as a source for his ruling. See, e.g., MAGGID MISHNEH and KESSEF MISHNEH on Laws of Robbery and Lost Property 11:17; HAGAHOT MAIMUNIOT, *Hil. Rozeah* 13:2. However, as we noted, *supra* note 81, this provides no clear proof of Maimonides' approach, as Rosh writes.

[90] BEIT YOSEF, Hoshen Mishpat 263:2. In its determination of the law in practice in SHULHAN ARUKH, *Hoshen Mishpat* 263:2, the ruling was like that of Maimonides; *ibid.* 272:3.

[91] On the norms of conduct "beyond the letter of the law" mentioned by Maimonides, much has been written in the Jewish law research literature dealing with the difference between the different types of moral and legal norms. See MENACHEM ELON, JEWISH LAW – HISTORY, SOURCES, PRINCIPLES vol. 1, 141–89 (trans. Bernard Auerback & Melvin J. Sykes, 1994); MOSHE SILBERG, THE WAY OF THE TALMUD 97–139 (Heb.). This is not the place to dwell on this complicated issue concerning the relationship between law and morality. For our purposes, Silberg's incisive definition, *ibid.* at 132, whereby "beyond the letter of the law" is a type of Equity, which is not forced upon a person (this is the opinion of some authorities, including Maimonides. Indeed, there are those who hold that "beyond the letter of the law" is enforced. See the summaries in ELON, *ibid.* 156–57), and its identifying mark is that the person who volunteers to act beyond the letter of the law waives the exceptional exemption, and returns to the primary law which obligates him. What happens in relation to "beyond the letter of the law," according to SILBERG, *ibid.* is "bending the letter of the law inwards, bringing it closer to the central kernel." Indeed it would appear that this description aptly describes Maimonides' approach described above. See, e.g., R. Zvi Yehuda b. Yaakov, *Beyond the Letter of the Law* sec. 3 at www.psakim.org/Psakim/File/853. Now, from what Maimonides writes in Chapter 4 of his Introduction to the COMMENTARY TO THE MISHNAH, *Avot* it would seem *prima facie* that there is a negative side to acting beyond that which the Torah commanded. However, R. YITZHAK SHILAT, MAIMONIDES' INTRODUCTIONS TO THE MISHNAH, 286–88 (Heb.) writes convincingly that this does not contradict the positive aspect of conducting oneself beyond the letter of the law, in the cases mentioned in the above texts from Laws of Robbery and Lost Property, and as he wrote in his summary, *ibid.* at 288: "The laws of the Torah are indeed 'the letter of the law,' but we identify in them a trend of education towards piety, and therefore we are called upon to act in a way that is 'beyond the letter of the law' wherever this is clearly an ethical matter – excluding superfluous extremism of the type 'What the Torah prohibited is not enough for you' – and this is considered to be conduct 'on the path of the good and the straight' (see Laws of Robbery and Lost Property 11:7, 17)."

for he then is taking the path of the upright and the good, and acquiring for himself good qualities, and thus the rationale of "welfare of the body" is fulfilled.

A final example of the emphasis placed by Maimonides on the educational process for the injurer relates to the manner in which one must treat a robber who wishes to repent and return the stolen property. The general law is that the robber must return the stolen property, as Maimonides rules: "If one commits robbery, he must return the very object he robbed ... Thus, even if one takes a rafter by robbery and builds it into a structure, by the law of Scripture he must pull down the whole building and give back the rafter to its owner..."[92]

However, even though this is the basic talmudic law, the "laws relating to rehabilitation of penitents"[93] are mentioned in the very specific context of a stolen rafter, and in keeping with the Talmud, Maimonides wrote: "The Sages, however, have made a rule for the benefit of penitents, that the robber may repay its value and need not demolish the building."[94] However, Maimonides derived a broader principle from the talmudic law relating to the stolen rafter and as he wrote in the *Commentary to the Mishnah*:

> And every object that the robber stole and subsequently did something with it for which reason he is unable to return the stolen object itself without incurring some loss, he must pay the value of that stolen object at the time of the robbery, And this was instituted on account of rehabilitation of penitents, in order that their penitence not be made too difficult.[95]

Indeed, in light of the fact that the main obligation involved in the Laws of Robbery is to "return the stolen object", and this also involves – as we saw in the previous Chapter – restoring the former situation and rehabilitation of the relationship with the victim of the robbery, then Maimonides' insistence on the process of repentance that the robber must undergo is clear. As he writes in expressed in Laws of Repentance:

> Neither repentance nor the Day of Atonement atone for any save for sins committed between Man and God, for instance, one who ate forbidden food, or had forbidden coition and the like; but sins between man and man, for instance, one injures his neighbor or curses his neighbor or plunders him, or offends him in like matters us ever not absolved unless he makes restitution of what he owes and begs the forgiveness of his neighbor. And, although he make restitution of the monetary debt, he is obliged to pacify him and to beg his forgiveness.[96]

---

[92] Laws of Robbery and Lost Property 1:5.
[93] *Bava Kamma* 94b.
[94] Laws of Robbery and Lost Property 1:5.
[95] COMMENTARY TO THE MISHNAH, *Eduyot* 7:9. And *cf.* what he wrote in COMMENTARY TO THE MISHNAH, *Gittin* 5:5.
[96] Laws of Repentance 2:9. Note that Maimonides mentioned the robber but not the thief. According to our discussion in the preceding chapter, this is understandable, for robbery is truly an offence between one person and another, in that the robber inflicts personal harm on

Maimonides attributed great importance to enabling the robber to repent by means of creating a process which would help the sinner to return to the path of righteousness with the help of two components which complement each other. One is the creation of awareness on the part of the robber of the gravity of his deed. The second is by introducing leniencies into the rigid laws of robbery. In fact, these two components do have a talmudic source, but the Talmud did not connect the two, and they were the subjects of two separate discussions.[97] Maimonides, however, regarded these two components as parts of a whole educational-awareness process, which create an entire program of rehabilitation of the robber. Maimonides writes:

> If one robs another of property worth a *perutah* [the smallest denomination of currency], it is regarded as if he took his life... Nevertheless, if property taken by robbery no longer exists, and the robber wishes to repent and comes of his own accord to return the value of the robbed property, the Sages have ruled that this should not be accepted from him. Instead, he should be helped and forgiven, so as to encourage penitents in the right path. And if one accepts the value of robbed property, he does not act in the spirit of the Sages.[98]

Here it should be mentioned that although Maimonides' ruling is based on a precedent mentioned in the Talmud,[99] many of the medieval authorities did not rule in accordance with the talmudic precedent, saying that it contradicts other talmudic discussions from which it emerges that "it is a routine matter to recover from the robbers that which they stole and to prosecute them if they did not return the objects."[100] And indeed, one can understand the position of those authorities who did not rule in accordance with the enactments of the Sages whereby one does not accept the object from the robbers, for this is an extreme enactment that is likely to harm those who were robbed and to be too easy on the robbers. However, from Maimonides' words it emerges that the enactment of the Sages was precisely for that robber who on his own initiative "wishes to repent and comes on his own accord to return the value of the property he obtained by robbery."[101] Only with respect to a robber who is in the process of repenting[102] is it appropriate to help him return to the path of goodness by means of waiving return of the value of the stole property. However, it is clear that Maimonides, too, is of the opinion that a robber who has not initiated an encounter with the person he robbed, and it is necessary to sue him

---

his victim in taking the object away from him. Theft, on the other hand, is a property offence only and has no personal dimension. In light of this, it is clear why only in relation to the robber is a process of repentance and rehabilitation necessary.
[97] *Bava Kamma* 119a (the first element), and *Bava Kamma* 94b–95a (the second element).
[98] Laws of Robbery and Lost Property 1:13.
[99] *Bava Kamma* 94b–95a.
[100] In the words of Rabbenu Tam, *Tosafot Bava Kamma* 94b s.v. *biyemei rabbi*. See also HAGAHOT MAIMUNIOT, *Hil. Gezelah ve-Avedah* 1:13.
[101] Laws of Robbery and Lost Property 1:13.
[102] So MAGGID MISHNEH inferred from Maimonides, *ibid.*

in court, will not benefit from the enactment, and the value of the property that was stolen will be collected from him.

We now arrive at the religious dimension and to the basis for the prohibition against causing harm.

B. THE RELIGIOUS ELEMENTS OF MAIMONIDES' TORT THEORY

1 *The Religious Dimension in Jewish Law in General and in Tort Law in Particular*

The question we would like to raise in this section is whether, despite the diverging emphases placed by Maimonides on different objectives relating to different types of tort law, as presented in the previous chapter, there is a common denominator that unifies the different legal types included in his discussion. One could argue that the scarlet thread that runs throughout the Book of Torts in the *Code*, although perhaps not in the equivalent discussion in the *Guide*, is the *religious* component in Maimonides' tort theory. The claim that Jewish law is a religious legal system has long been, and continues to be, put forward by both traditional scholars of Jewish law and contemporary academic researchers.[103]

It must be stressed that the religious-moral prohibition is the outstanding feature of the system of Jewish law, in which the conversation is primarily that of duties of conduct and not of rights (as in most modern-day Western legal systems).[104] Religious duties and prohibitions are addressed to people and instruct them how to conduct themselves, as in the well-known statement of Moshe Silberg:

> Jewish jurisprudence – if I may say so – is a jurisprudence which does not depend on judges. The function of the law is not to prescribe for the judge – how to decide; it prescribes for the person how to conduct his life. Even the paying of a debt – the basic foundation of all civil law – is a divine commandment, and the right of the claimant is only a reflection of the religious obligation which rests on the debtor.[105]

This is expressed in the myriad religious precepts (prohibitions and positive commandments) that are part of the Jewish law system. As Silberg says:

---

[103] *See, e.g.,* CHRISTINE HAYES, WHAT'S DIVINE ABOUT DIVINE LAW? EARLY PERSPECTIVES (Princeton; Oxford: Princeton University Press, 2015); Yuval Sinai, *The Religious Perspective of the Judge's Role in Talmudic Law*, 25 J. L. & RELIGION 357 (2009–10): Haim Shapira, *"For the Judgement is God's" – Human Judgment and Divine Justice*, 27 J. L. & RELIGION 273 (2012). For a different view see Hanina Ben Menachem, *Is Talmudic Law a Religious Legal System? A Provisional Analysis*, 24 J. L. & RELIGION 379 (2008–09).
[104] On the advantages of the regime of obligations in Jewish law, and the manner in which it advances the social order, *see* Robert M. Cover, *Obligation: A Jewish Jurisprudence of the Social Order*, 5 J. L. & RELIGION 65 (1987).
[105] MOSHE SILBERG, TALMUDIC LAW AND THE MODERN STATE 48 (Ben Zion Bokser trans., Marvin S. Winer ed., 1973).

We see the deep impression registered by the religious commandment in the field of law ... not alone the specific area of religious or ritual law. Even the code of civil law, *Hoshen Mishpat* [one of the parts of the *Shulhan Arukh* that deals with private law], is in practice a way of life, *Orah Hayyim* ["way of life" – another part of the *Shulhan Arukh* dealing with daily religious obligations], which defines man's behavior.[106]

Therefore, in the eyes of Jewish law, the judge does not decide between two litigants, and he is not obliged to apply sanctions in order for the litigants to comply with what he says,[107] but rather, the judge

[N]otifies the defendant who lost how much he must pay, and he notifies the claimant who won how much he is permitted to accept. Herein is the total competence of the judge and herein is his sole authority. For the two litigants themselves are obligated by the Torah – they are obligated even prior to the rendering of the judgment not to transgress the commandments "Thou shalt not rob" or "Thou shalt not oppress."[108]

The religious dimension of tort law roughly includes the notion of a prohibition against causing damage to another's property,[109] body[110] or life;[111] the obligation to preserve the property,[112] body, and life of one's fellow humans;[113] the idea that any infringement and transgression of these obligations and prohibitions results in a state of religious sin that requires atonement[114] and, in some cases, also the procuring of forgiveness from the offended party.[115] In this context, one may argue, the notion of monetary payment functions not merely on the level of civil restitution, nor simply as a form of punitive payment in the more criminally-oriented contexts of physical injuries, theft and robbery, but also, and no less importantly, as a form of religious atonement.

2 *The Prohibition Against Causing Harm*

Several halakhic authorities emphasized the religious dimension that constitutes a significant source of tort law, in that it establishes a prohibition against causing harm. Thus, for example, R. Ya'akov ben Asher, the renowned fourteenth century (Spain) authority and author of *Arba'a Turim*, opened the Laws of Torts, which follow the Laws of Theft and the Laws of Robbery, by emphasizing the prohibitive-religious

---

[106] *Ibid.* at 51.
[107] *Cf.* ELON, JEWISH LAW, *supra* note 91, at 144.
[108] SILBERG, *supra* note 105, at 49.
[109] Laws of Property Damages 5:1.
[110] Laws of Wounding and Damaging 5:1.
[111] Laws of Murderers and the Preservation of Life 1:1.
[112] Laws of Robbery and Lost Property 11:20.
[113] Laws of Murder and Preservation of Life 1:14.
[114] Laws of Repentance 1:1.
[115] Laws of Wounding and Damaging 5:9; Laws of Repentance 2:9.

aspect common to all these laws, writing: "Just as there is a prohibition against theft and robbing one's fellow of his property, so too it is prohibited to cause harm to his property, even if one does not benefit therefrom, for one who causes harm, whether willfully or inadvertently, must pay."[116] The commentators on the *Arba'a Turim* learned from this that just as in relation to theft and robbery, there is a prohibition against the actual taking of the property of one's fellow unlawfully, so too in tort law there exists an independent prohibitive dimension that exists alongside the obligation to pay compensation; in all events, even if the person causing the harm paid for the harm, this does not exempt him from the prohibition involved in causing harm to another.[117] The author of *Sefer Arba'a Turim* wrote in a similar vein in his introduction to the Laws of Property Damages, saying as follows: "Just as a person is forbidden to injure his fellow, and if he caused him injury he must pay, so too must he take care not to damage the property of his fellow, and if he did cause damage he must pay";[118] and he also opened the Laws of Wounding by stressing the prohibitive aspect: "A person is forbidden to strike his fellow, and if he struck him, he is in violation of a negative commandment."[119] Recognition of the prohibitive dimension of tort law can also be seen in the words of several *Geonim*,[120] and several *Rishonim*,[121] but it was the subject of particular interest in the writings of the *Aharonim*, who discussed extensively the questions connected with the nature of the prohibition against causing harm, and its scriptural source.[122] The words of a number of *Aharonim* indicate that the very obligation to take care with respect to the property of a person in order not to cause him harm has its basis in the prohibition against causing harm.[123] There were those who wished to claim that the prohibition against causing harm existed in places in which the person causing the injury was exempt from paying compensation for the harm he caused.[124]

Maimonides also regarded the religious-moral prohibition against causing harm as a very significant element of his tort theory, alongside the utilitarian

---

[116] TUR, Hoshen Mishpat 378:1.
[117] See BAYIT HADASH and PERISHAH on TUR, ibid.
[118] TUR, Hoshen Mishpat 389:1.
[119] Ibid. 420:1.
[120] See, e.g., R. Ahai Gaon, who formulated the prohibition against damaging the property of one's fellow in two places in SEFER HA'SHE'ILTOT (Parshat Mishpatim 61; Parshat Emor 111).
[121] See, e.g., Hiddushei ha-Rashba to Bava Kamma 2b, relating to tort law as laws of prohibitions.
[122] See, e.g., R. YAAKOV KANIEFSKY, KEHILLOT YAAKOV, Bava Kamma 1; R. BARUKH BER LEIBOWITZ, BIRKHAT SHMUEL, Bava Kamma 2; R. ISRAEL ZEV GUSTMANN, KUNTRAS SHI'URIM, BAVA KAMMA, 1:18. For an extensive discussion of the different possibilities, see LESSONS OF AHARON LICHTENSTEIN ON BAVA KAMMA (DINA DE-GARMI) 169–80 (Alon Shvut 5773) (Heb.).
[123] See, e.g., R. YITZHAK MEIR KNOBLIVITCH, COMMENTARY ON TRACTATE BAVA KAMMA 4 (Sha'arei Zion Institute, Jerusalem, 5762) (Heb.) who deduced from what was said by Hatam Sofer, R. Haim Soloveitchik and his student, the author of BIRKHAT SHMUEL, that "the obligation of guarding another's property so as not to cause financial damage to the other is not due to an obligation to provide compensation but a prohibition against damaging."
[124] See BIRKHAT SHMUEL, Bava Kamma 2.

objective of preventing harm and others. Maimonides stresses, at the beginning of the fifth chapter of Laws of Property Damages in the *Code*, that "it is forbidden for a person to cause damage and then to pay for the damage he caused. Even being an [indirect] cause of damage is forbidden." Nevertheless, he explains that for various reasons, it is sometimes permitted to cause damage, but only sometimes, and only in order to attain important objectives. Even then, the damager must pay for the damages. Thus, for example, there are cases in which it is permissible to create a situation which has the potential for causing damage, when the activity as a whole is desirable from an economic point of view; however, in the event that damage is caused, the damager must pay because he is the prime beneficiary of the activity.[125]

From a comparative point of view, using contemporary terms, it could be said that rule 3 of Calabresi and Melamed's rules of liability – the liability rule in favor of the harm-doer, which means that subject to the rules of inalienability, there are cases in which it is permitted for a person to cause harm and to pay for the damage he has caused[126] – is somewhat reminiscent of the rule that Maimonides presents here. Obviously, Maimonides would emphasize the unusual nature of those cases,[127] and clearly the secular law does not recognize a religious moral (Divine) obligation, but the principle is somewhat the same.

The prohibitive dimension in Maimonides' tort theory is also emphasized in relation to a number of tortious acts in respect of which it is taught that "although one is not held liable according to human law, one is indeed held liable according to the laws of God."[128] The prohibition against causing damage to another's property stands in correlation to the more obvious prohibitions pertaining to the

---

[125] E.g., "Those who open their gutters and rake out their cesspools have no right to pour the water onto a public domain in the summer but have the right to do so in the winter. Nevertheless, if a person or an animal is hurt by the water, they must pay full compensation" (Laws of Property Damages 13:13). In a similar vein he ruled: "Anyone has a right to place his manure and animal droppings in a public domain during the season for putting out manure and to heap it there for thirty days in order that it should be crushed by the feet of men and beasts. Yet, if it causes harm, the owner is liable" (Laws of Property Damages 13:15). As such, it was permissible to put out manure in certain seasons so that it would be "crushed by the feet of men," for this allowed for the development of the agrarian economy, and the Sages therefore held that the benefit to society as a whole outweighed the danger of harm to individuals. However, precisely because of the fact that the owner [of the animal] derives benefit from this permission he must take responsibility for the property of others, and it another was injured, he must pay. Another example: a person who is in danger and saves himself by causing damage to the property of another must pay (Laws of Wounding and Damaging 8:2), even though it is certainly permitted to save oneself (despite the fact that it involves causing damage to another), since nothing outweighs the saving of life (see: BERUR HALAKHAH, in Talmud Bavli with *Halakhah Berurah* and: BERUR HALAKHAH, *Bava Kamma* 60b, 148, explaining Maimonides' approach).
[126] Guido Calabresi & A. Douglas Melamed, *Property Rules, Liability Rules, and Inalienability: One View of the Cathedral*, 85 HARV. L. REV. 1089, 1116, 1119 (1972).
[127] However, in some cases Maimonides did apply rule 3. See, e.g., *supra* note 125.
[128] See Laws of Property Damages 4:2; *ibid.*, 14:14; Laws of Evidence (*Hilkhot Edut*) 17:7.

criminally-oriented acts of inflicting bodily injuries, theft, robbery, and murder, which are likewise included in the Book of Torts.[129]

Beyond the prohibition against causing damage to another's property, Maimonides stresses that there is also a positive obligation to save another's property from damage or loss, an obligation which is tantamount to the obligation to save the body and life of others.[130]

Asher Gulak wrote as follows regarding the nature of religious obligation according to Jewish law:

> There are obligations in which all the main elements of compulsion are missing, and they arise only by virtue of the good will of the debtor. According to human law, there is no liability here, because a direct consequence of human laws is that they are enforced, but that is totally missing here; this obligation exists only as a moral or religious obligation imposed upon the debtor.[131]

This approach of Jewish law, which in our context manifests itself in the form of the prohibition against causing harm found in Maimonides' theory[132] with no sanction being applicable to a person who violates the prohibition, is very different from that of some of the great Western jurists, and particularly the exponents of legal positivism such as John Austin and Hans Kelsen, both of whom considered the sanction to constitute a central element in the definition of law.[133] According to Austin, there can be no law without a sanction,[134] and the role of the sanction is two-fold: first, it is designed to identify an order issued by the sovereign as a binding order; second, its purpose is to create motivation for the subject to obey the order for fear of punishment.[135] In Kelsen's theory, too, there is a necessary connection between

---

[129] See the following section.

[130] Thus, in the Laws of Robbery and Lost Property 11:20 Maimonides writes: "If one sees water flooding and threatening to destroy another's building or field, one must place a barrier in the water's path and prevent it, for Scripture says, 'And you shall do the same with anything else that your neighbor loses' (Deuteronomy 22:3) – including the loss of his land."

[131] ASHER GULAK, THE FOUNDATIONS OF JEWISH LAW II, 18 (1922) (Heb.). On the obligation in Divine law, see in detail ENCYCLOPEDIA TALMUDIT vol. 7, 382–96 (s.v. *dine shamayim*); ELON, *supra* note 91, at 145–47.

[132] Laws of Property Damages 5:1.

[133] For a description of the place of these sanctions in the jurisprudence of Austin and Kelsen, see OMER SHAPIRA, JURISPRUDENCE 43–50, 121–24 (2007) (Heb.). It is noteworthy that not all the positivists were of the view that there is no law without a sanction. Hart claimed that the law comprised not only orders or rules that imposed obligations, but also rules that granted power and authority which are not based on sanctions. For a description of Hart's position and arguments against Austin, see SHAPIRA, *ibid.* 44–50, 71–73. There are those who believe that the distance between Hart, Austin and Kelsen regarding the element of sanction in the law is not so great. See, e.g., Leo Kanowitz, *The Place of Sanctions in Professor H.L.A. Hart's Conception of Law*, 5 DUQ. U.L.R. 1 (1996).

[134] JOHN AUSTIN, THE PROVINCE OF JURISPRUDENCE 13–14 (David Campbell & Philip Thomas eds., 1998): "… It is only by the chance of incurring evil, that I am bound or obliged to compliance. It is only by conditional evil, that duties are sanctioned or enforced".

[135] Colin Tapper, *Austin on Sanctions*, CAMBRIDGE L.J. 271, 281 (1965).

the legal obligation and the sanction. According to Kelsen, a legal system is based on its ability to exercise power and to compel, by means of sanctions, the execution of the legal norms (coercive order),[136] and the order becomes a legal obligation by virtue of the fact that the law creates a connection between the performance or failure to perform a certain action, and punishment of the individual to whom the order is addressed.[137]

It will, however, be noted that insofar as the quotation from Laws of Property Damages 5:1 of Maimonides refers to the actual prohibition against causing damage, it does not refer to a purely religious prohibition: it sometimes has real legal consequences. Indeed, let us recall that by virtue of the prohibition against causing damage, Maimonides permits the owner of a field to slaughter an animal that had entered his field several times, even though it had not yet caused damage, as a preventive-deterrent action against the owner of the animal, who did not take care to watch it properly.[138] Moreover, Maimonides bases the general prohibition – a type of injunction issued by the Sages against raising domestic animals (such as goats or sheep) in the Land of Israel where there are fields and vineyards – on the actual prohibition against causing damage, for such animals habitually enter fields and vineyards and cause damage, and as stated, it is prohibited for a person to damage or to be the cause of damage, even if he intends to pay. Therefore, according to Maimonides, it was permitted to raise domestic animals only in places where they would not cause damage, i.e., in fields and desert areas.[139] Later,[140] we will further argue that in Maimonides' opinion, the prohibition against causing harm also serves as a social instrument for promoting behavior that is socially efficient, i.e., the ramifications of the prohibition against causing harm do not affect only the religious-deontological dimension but also the utilitarian one. Of course, this may also contribute to increased social solidarity, to the creation of civil responsibility and concern for the other and for the promotion of communality – an important aim in itself, characteristic of Jewish law in general, and of Maimonides' philosophy in particular.

The prohibition against causing harm does indeed constitute an important element that is mentioned by Maimonides; however, the weight of this prohibitive-moral element in Maimonides' tort theory should not be overstated. What

---

[136] HANS KELSEN, PURE THEORY OF LAW (1967) 33.
[137] Ibid. at 115: "If the law is conceived as a coercive order, then a behavior can be looked upon as objectively legally commanded (and therefore as the content of a legal obligation) only if a legal norm attaches a coercive act as a sanction to the opposite behavior".
[138] Laws of Property Damages 5:1. Maimonides also ruled that a person who does not remove the object causing the damage should be ostracized: "He who keeps in his premises something which may cause damages, such as a bad dog, or a broken step ladder, is ostracized until he will remove the damaging article" (Laws of Torah Study 6:14). One should not underestimate social punishments, which in certain periods were extremely effective.
[139] Laws of Property Damages 5:2.
[140] Chapter 6.

Maimonides writes, similar to the talmudic sources, does not provide a basis for a conception whereby the payments for monetary damage as a whole should be regarded as a punishment relating to the prohibition against causing harm.

Maimonides' words clearly indicate that the basis for the obligation to pay for property damages is civil and not criminal or religious, and he therefore compared this obligation to the obligation of the debtor to repay his loan. As he said: "Whenever full compensation is payable, the payment is a monetary obligation that the defendant must pay just as one who borrows from another must repay a loan."[141] He then emphasizes that "[t]he general rule is as follows: Whenever the compensation payable is for the actual damage caused, the obligation is deemed a monetary one."[142] Indeed, as we shall see in Section D, this shows that the basic element of the obligation in payments for damages is similar to corrective justice.

Thus, Maimonides' conception would appear to be that the prohibition against causing property damages is an important element – although not necessarily the most important element (as other halakhic scholars possibly thought)[143] – that exists alongside no less important elements, such as the prevention of harm, optimal deterrence, emphasis on the moral conduct of the damager and others.

Upon examination of Maimonides' placement of the prohibition against causing harm in his tort theory, the following question arises: why did Maimonides not begin his Laws of Property Damages, too, with mention of the scriptural prohibition that is the source of liability for these damages? Why did he not deal with these laws as he dealt with all other types of harm included in the Book of Torts, all of which opened with the biblical source of the prohibition as the basis for legal liability? R. Nachum Rabinovitch suggests – correctly, in our view – that the great innovation in Laws of Property Damages is that they often deal with a person's liability for damage caused by his property in the absence of any personal culpability whatsoever, in that the person is held liable for damages that were not caused directly by himself. As such, it is clearly not possible to formulate either positive or negative commandments that are directed at the individual and require him to do or refrain from doing certain acts.[144] The four commandments that Maimonides enumerated

---

[141] Laws of Property Damages 2:7.
[142] Ibid. 2:8.
[143] See supra in the beginning of this section.
[144] R. NACHUM RABINOVITCH, YAD PESHUTAH, supra note 52, Introduction to the Laws of Property Damages 13. He was preceded by the MAGGID MISHNEH, in his introduction to the Book of Torts, who explained that Maimonides in his Book of Torts placed the laws of property damages at the beginning, "because these damages are not done by a person, for it is the property that causes the damage, and the other laws are concerned with human actions. The laws concerning that in relation to which a person has not been warned should precede that in relation to which a person is warned...," from which it emerges that there is no prohibition (caution) imposed on a person whose property causes damage, as opposed to a person who caused damage himself through his actions, in relation to which a prohibition exists. This distinction is also evident from Maimonides' formulation in the GUIDE 3:40, which distinguishes clearly between damages caused by a person's property and those caused by human

at the beginning of Laws of Property Damages are a special type of commandment that he defines as *dinim* – laws.[145] These commandments are not addressed to each individual as a personal order to do or refrain from doing something, but rather, they establish laws by which society as a whole must conduct itself.[146] It is the *judges* on whom the task falls to execute the scriptural commandments classified as *dinim*. From the application of these commandments arise both the obligations and the rights of various individuals in the different situations, for these commandments create a binding halakhic reality; the main addressees for the fulfilment of these commandments, however, are those in whose hands the legal system lies.

Another possible answer to the question of why Maimonides did not open the Laws of Property Damages with the biblical prohibition against causing harm – one which does not necessarily contradict the first answer and to a large extent complements it – relies on a well-known conceptual jurisprudential distinction that originates in the approach of R. Shimon Shkop (1859–1939), one of the most original and influential thinkers in the Lithuanian yeshiva world.[147] R. Shkop developed a famous distinction between two separate areas of *halakhah*: the area of commandments – *mitzvot* – which lays down prohibitions and imposes obligations, and the area of private-monetary norms – which R. Shkop terms *"Torat ha-Mishpatim"* ("Theory of Civil Law") – which regulates the private civil law field in the *halakhah*, such as property law, tort law, the law of obligations etc.[148] This is not the place for an extensive discussion of the said distinction between commandments and prohibitions (the religious norm) on the one hand, and the theory of civil law on the other.[149] For our purposes we will invoke the theory proposed by Shai Wozner, whereby "the distinction made by R. Shimon Shkop between the area of commandments and the area of civil law is in fact an attempt to understand the different nature of behavioral obligations and financial obligations."[150] R. Shkop's rules of

---

actions. For further discussion see Chapter 3. For a discussion of the question of why Maimonides did not formulate the first ruling in Laws of Wounding and Damaging in the normal manner of mentioning the prohibition and then the obligation to pay, see R. Rabinovitch's convincing explanation, *ibid*. Introduction to the first Chapter of Laws of Wounding and Damaging 6.

[145] The *din* of the ox, the *din* of the tooth, the *din* of the pit and the *din* of the fire. In the short list of positive commandments, the wording is: "(237) laws regarding the damages [caused by] an animal"; "(240) laws regarding the damages [caused by] the grazer"; "(238) to discuss the damages [caused by] a pit"; "(241) laws regarding the damages [caused by] fire."

[146] On the distinction between *"dinin"* and other commandments, see Maimonides, Book of Commandments, positive commandment 95: "And you should keep this principle in mind whenever a *din* is enumerated – it does not necessarily mean that we are commanded to perform a certain action but rather that a certain case [whenever it comes up] must be judged according to certain laws."

[147] See Shai Wozner, Legal Thinking in the Lituanian Yeshivoth – The Heritage and Works of Rabbi Shimon Shkop (Hebrew U. Press: Jerusalem, 2016) (Heb.).

[148] See R. Shimon Shkop, *Sha'arei Yosher* 5:1.

[149] For extensive discussion, *see* Wozner, *supra* note 146, at 220–84.

[150] *Ibid*. at 232.

"civil law" are not behavioral norms that impose an obligation relating to behavior, but rather, rules of definition, i.e., rules that define legal situations. Shai Wozner describes this as follows:

> The monetary obligation is therefore a type of status, a state of legal affairs of the debtor, which has various normative ramifications stemming from other rules, which are rules of power (that relate to the owner of the right) or rules of obligation (that are imposed on the debtor himself or on the beth din).[151]

Wozner proceeds to illustrate R. Shkop's distinction between obligations of behavior and financial-monetary obligations:

> Thus, for example, the obligation to give the money to the lender does not stem from the financial debt per se, but from a combination of the financial debt with a rule of obligation ("repaying a creditor is a *mitzvah*") that instructs the debtor to fulfil the financial duty that he bears. If we think of the various examples of financial-monetary obligations, such as the obligation of the injurer to pay for the damage he caused, the obligation of the robber to return the stolen object (...), the obligation of an employer to pay his workers a wage and so forth, we can therefore distinguish between two stages in each of them: at the first stage, the injurer, the robber and the employer are subject to monetary obligations by virtue of civil law: the injurer owes money to the victim, the robber owes money to the person robbed and the employer owes money to the worker, At this stage, the monetary obligations are in fact states of affairs which in themselves do not obligate the debtor to take any action. Only at the second stage is there a *mitzvah* (which is an obligatory rule) to fulfil their monetary obligations and to pay the owners of the right that which is owed to them.[152]

Use of the said distinction between monetary obligations (civil law), and behavioral obligations which find expression in the religious commandments and prohibitions in the context of torts, may shed light on the Maimonidean distinction discussed in this section until now between the obligation to pay in torts and the prohibition against harming, which are mentioned as separate, distinct elements in the Book of Torts in Maimonides' *Code*. According to this suggestion, Maimonides' approach in his Laws of Property Damages is similar to the approach of R. Shkop, as we shall elucidate now. At the first stage, at the beginning of the Laws of Property Damages, he defined the criterion for liability in tort, the criterion of effective control, by virtue of which he imposed tort liability upon the effective damage preventer (the EAC test).[153] The result of tort liability – the obligation of the defendant to pay for the damage – is also defined at the beginning of Laws of Property Damages as a monetary obligations and a legal status, and not as a religious behavioral obligation as Maimonides says: "Whenever full compensation is payable,

---

[151] *Ibid.* at 233.
[152] *Ibid.* at 233–34.
[153] Which he mentioned in the GUIDE 3:40, as explained at length in the following chapter.

the payment is a monetary obligation that the defendant must pay just as one who borrows from another must repay a loan."[154] Maimonides compared two monetary obligations – the obligation to pay for damage and the obligation to repay a loan, both of which are obligations of the "civil law" type according to R. Shkop's terminology; they are matters of monetary obligations and legal status, and do not include a behavioral obligation. This is the first stage.

Only in the fifth chapter of Laws of Property Damages does Maimonides proceed to the second stage, namely, imposing a behavioral obligation pursuant to the religious prohibition not to harm. By virtue of this prohibition, Maimonides prohibits causing damage, and this prohibition also applies where the person paid for the damage he caused: "For one is forbidden to cause damage willfully, with the intention of paying for the damage he causes."[155] According to Maimonides, the prohibition against causing harm imposes a behavioral obligation as he then says: "Because of this [prohibition against causing damage], the Sages forbade the rearing of small cattle or small wild animals in the Land of Israel in regions containing fields or vineyards, but allowed it only in the wooded and desert regions of the Land of Israel."[156]

According to our proposal, Maimonides presented a completely different theory from that mentioned at the beginning of this section in relation to the placement of the prohibition against harming. According to the latter theory, the religious prohibition against harming is the source and the foundation for a person's obligation to guard his property in order that it not cause damage, and the result of a breach of this obligation is the obligation to pay for the damage caused. According to the Maimonidean theory – so we argue – the order is reversed: the monetary obligation to pay for the damage is not the outcome of the religious obligation; rather, it precedes it in that it is a legal status that resembles the obligation to repay a loan, and it is determined by the Maimonidean criterion of tortious liability (the EAC test). The monetary obligation does not impose a behavioral obligation: the behavioral obligation is imposed only at the second stage, at which the religious prohibition against harming is determined. Thus, according to Maimonides, the religious element (the prohibition against harming) is important in that it imposes a behavioral norm in a certain form, but this religious element is not the foundation nor the main element of the obligation in torts as others thought. Rather, it is an element of secondary importance according to Maimonides. This conclusion derives, *inter alia*, from the difficulty in identifying the biblical source for the prohibition against property damage, for Maimonides does not mention any such source.

The fact that Maimonides, contrary to his usual practice, did not mention a scriptural source for the prohibition against causing damage to the property of

---

[154] Laws of Property Damages 2:7.
[155] *Ibid.* 5:1.
[156] *Ibid.* 5:2.

another has surprised many.[157] R. Nachum Rabinovitch would seem to be correct in suggesting that this is connected to Maimonides' fundamental approach, whereby the purpose and the objective of the commandments serve as a general, inclusive framework by virtue of which the individual precepts are created, even if these precepts do not appear explicitly in the Bible.[158] According to this approach, it appears that Maimonides regards the prohibition against causing harm as stemming from the very fact that the Bible punishes the harm-doer and imposes upon him an obligation to prevent harm.[159] In light of this, Maimonides deduces that where the Sages thought that the possibility of causing harm was high, they ordered that the activity that was liable to cause the harm be prevented, even though the harm had not yet eventuated, for in this way they were promoting the objective of the Torah in preventing harm. Maimonides consequently went on to write in the Book of Torts: "Because of this" – i.e., because "one is forbidden to cause damage" – "the Sages forbade the rearing of small cattle or small wild animals in the Land of Israel in regions containing fields or vineyards."[160] It was on this basis that the Sages enacted certain bans on activities that could potentially cause damage to neighbors.[161]

As we have said, Maimonides does not specify the scriptural verse on which the prohibition against harming is based, causing many to wonder;[162] some authorities, however, looked to general sources from which such a prohibition might possibly be derived. One Spanish *Rishon* suggested, as a basis for this prohibition, the following sources: "Do not put a stumbling block before the blind," and "You shall love your fellow as yourself."[163] Another Spanish *Rishon* implies that the prohibition against harming is included in the verse, "Do not… rob your neighbor."[164] Some *Aharonim* proposed the commandment to restore lost property as a possible source for the prohibition against causing harm.[165] The commandment to restore lost property includes not only the returning of the lost object, but also prevention of a situation of monetary loss. The Talmud mentions an obligation to barricade a stream of water

---

[157] And indeed, some were of the opinion that the prohibition against causing damage is rabbinical only, rather than scriptural. See MISHNEH LE-MELEKH, *Hilkhot Rozeah* 2:2. MINHAT HINUKH 53:5 disagreed.

[158] See R. NACHUM L. RABINOVITCH, STUDIES IN MAIMONIDES (Maaliyot Press: Jerusalem 1998), pp. 77–92 (Heb.).

[159] RABINOVITCH, *ibid.* at 82 (referring to Maimonides' emphasis on prevention of damages in the GUIDE 3:40).

[160] Laws of Property Damages 5:2.

[161] See Laws of Neighbors, Chapter 9.

[162] See *supra* notes 157 and 122.

[163] *Yad Rama, Bava Batra* 26a, no.107.

[164] Leviticus 19:13. See Rabbenu Yona in his *Commentary to Mishnah Avot* 1:1; R. GUSTMANN, *supra* note 122. From the above words of *Tur*, *supra* near note 116, too, a connection between the commandment not to commit robbery and the prohibition against causing damage emerges.

[165] See *Kehillot Yaakov* and *Kuntresei Shiurim*, *supra* note 122. See also LICHTENSTEIN, *supra* note 122, at 178–79; *Hagahot ve-Hiddushei Rashash, Ketubot* 18b.

that threatens to destroy a neighbor's field.[166] Indeed, even though Maimonides did not specifically mention the obligation to prevent financial loss as the basis for the prohibition against causing harm, he emphasized and extended the application of this obligation in the Book of Torts.

A person's duty to prevent damage that is likely to be caused to the another's property is proposed by Maimonides in the framework of the Laws of Lost Property, in his ruling: "If one sees water flooding and threatening to destroy another's building or land, he must place a barrier in its way to stop it, for Scripture says, *With every lost thing of thy brother's* (Deuteronomy 22:3), including also loss of his land."[167] This ruling contains a novel element in the extension of the obligation to restore lost property on two levels:

(a) Application of the duty to restore lost property not only to chattels but also to real property, when water is about to cause it damage;
(b) Extension of the obligation to prevent damage that is preventable. In modern theories of tort law it is difficult to find a similar conception imposing a duty upon a person to prevent damage to another person's property to the extent that he is able to do so.

From Maimonides' words (Laws of Robbery and Lost Property 11:20), several *Aharonim* understood by way of an *a fortiori* argument that this law of the loss of land is the source for the prohibition against harming: if the preventative action of removing the cause of the harm is included in the commandment to restore lost property, how much more so is it prohibited for a person to physically cause another person to incur a financial loss.[168] However, to regard the law applying to loss of land as a source for the prohibition against causing harm is problematic in our view, for Maimonides placed no special emphasis on this law, nor did he discuss it in the context of the prohibition against causing harm. It is also difficult to assume that such a fundamental law – the prohibition against causing harm – has its source in an *a fortiori* deduction from another marginal law.

It should also be mentioned that according to Maimonides' approach, there is also a specific prohibition on causing the destruction of property, even if no particular person is harmed thereby.[169]

We will conclude with the opinion of one of the *Aharonim* who argued that the prohibition, "Do not stand by your neighbor's blood" underlies the prohibition against causing harm.[170] Now, Maimonides did not state explicitly that that verse was the source of the said prohibition, and as we said, in our view Maimonides apparently did not base the prohibition on a particular verse. Undoubtedly, however,

---

[166] *Bava Metzia* 31a.
[167] Laws of Robbery and Lost Property 11:20.
[168] LICHTENSTEIN, *supra* note 122, at 129.
[169] CODE, Laws of Kings 6:10.
[170] HIDDUSHEI HATAM SOFER, *Bava Kamma* 2b.

the prohibition, "Do not stand by your neighbor's blood" was emphasized by Maimonides, and he discussed the parameters of this prohibition in the context of the duty to save lives, as elucidated in Section 4.

3 The Religious and Theological Aspects

Despite the difficulty involved in determining the scriptural source for the prohibition against causing damage to another's property, and the fact that Maimonides waited, as it were, until the fifth chapter of the Laws of Property Damages to inform us that "it is forbidden for a person to cause damage," we posit nonetheless that the ubiquity of the religious-prohibitive dimension in the Book of Torts and the sense of equivalence that exists between the prohibitions and obligations pertaining to property damages, bodily injuries, theft, robbery and murder underscore the internal continuity between the various sections included in Book.

Thus, for example, in the opening ruling in Laws of Theft, Maimonides points to the commandment "Ye shall not steal" (Leviticus 19:11) as a source for the prohibition against stealing, and in the opening ruling in Laws of Robbery, he identifies the commandment, "Thou shalt not … rob [thy neighbor]" (Leviticus 19:13) as the source for the prohibition against robbery; at the beginning of the laws pertaining to the return of lost property, Maimonides cites the positive and negative commandments relevant to situations involving the return of lost property;[171] in the opening ruling of the laws pertaining to bodily harm caused by a person who wounds, Maimonides cites the source for the prohibition against a person wounding, whether himself or another person;[172] in the ruling opening Laws of Murderers, Maimonides cites the Sixth Commandment, "Thou shalt not murder," as a source for the prohibition against murder.[173]

It should be stressed that the attempt to isolate and abstract the civil and criminal rationales reflected in Maimonides tort theory is important mainly insofar as the discussion in the *Guide* is concerned, but it is perhaps somewhat problematic when applied to the *Code*. In the context of the latter, it is the overarching theology of sin and atonement[174] that ultimately links the different sections of the Book of Torts and creates a conceptual continuum between the laws of property damage, the laws of theft and robbery, the laws of bodily injuries, and the Laws of Murderers and the Preservation of Life. This is not to say that there are no significant differences between the various civil and criminal rationales operating in each section. However, it would seem that the structure of the Book of Torts as a whole, and the inherent interconnectedness of its various sections, are

[171] Laws of Robbery and Lost Property 11:1–2.
[172] Laws of Wounding and Damaging 5:1.
[173] Exodus 19:13.
[174] We are grateful to Yishai Kiel for enlightening us in his response, *supra* note 19, on aspects concerning the theological aspects found in the CODE.

underwritten by a common adherence to a theological paradigm governed by the system of sin and atonement.

While we have seen that monetary payments due for property damages should not, as a whole, be regarded as a punitive measure for transgressing the prohibition against causing damage to another's property, it should be stressed that the interpretation of these payments solely in terms of civil restitution, devoid of religious and theological significance, misses a major point in Maimonides' conception of tort law. Consider, for example, the laws of bodily injuries:

> If one inflicts a personal injury on another, he may not be compared to one who damages another's property. For if one damages another's property, atonement is effected for him as soon as he pays whatever is required. But if one wounds another, atonement is not effected for him even if he has paid for all the five effects, or even if he has sacrificed all the rams of Nebaioth, for his sin is not forgiven until he begs forgiveness of the injured person and is pardoned.[175]

On the overt level, Maimonides seems to stress here the difference between the laws governing damages caused by people to property and those governing bodily injuries, insofar as the former requires only monetary compensation, while the latter requires both monetary payment (be it punitive or compensatory) and the procuring of the injured party's forgiveness. That said, Maimonides uses the term "atonement" (*kapparah*) for both property damages and bodily injuries, rather than the civil notions of compensation or restitution, thus triggering the theological arena of penitence. Unlike physical injuries which necessitate the procuring of verbal forgiveness from the offended party alongside monetary payments in order to meet the religious requirement of atonement, the payments due for property damages are sufficient to meet this end. Since both physical injuries and property damages constitute a transgression of a religious prohibition, both require atonement. The difference lies in the fact that, unlike bodily injuries, property damages do not offend another's person and therefore do not require verbal forgiveness beyond monetary restitution.

The passage from Laws of Wounding and Damaging 5:9 should be read intertextually in light of Maimonides' assertion in the Laws of Repentance 2:9, in which he discusses the relationship between religious atonement, monetary compensation, and procuring verbal forgiveness from the offended party:

> Repentance and the Day of Atonement atone only for sins pertaining to the relations between a person and God, for example, a person who ate forbidden foods or engaged in forbidden sexual relations, or the like. However, sins pertaining to the relations between a person and his fellow humans; for example, someone who injured another, curses another, robs him, or the like – such a sinner will never be forgiven until he pays the offended party what he owes and appeases this person. Even if he paid the money he owes, he must appease his fellow human and ask for forgiveness.

[175] Laws of Wounding and Damaging 5:9.

Once again, the reason property damages do not require appeasing and procuring verbal forgiveness from the offended party beyond monetary compensation is because they do not involve injury to another's person. This difference, however, hardly excludes tortious acts in the narrow sense from the overarching religious paradigm of sin and atonement that governs Maimonides' Code. It is tempting to read Maimonides' claim regarding the need to appease the offended party and procure forgiveness in cases of bodily injuries in the light of contemporary attempts to introduce apology laws into the tort system. It must be stressed, however, that for Maimonides, both the monetary payment and the psychological-emotional dimension of forgiveness are intended not merely to restore the offended party to his or her prior state, but also, and perhaps more importantly, to atone for his sins.

Since monetary payments due for tortious acts are intended to achieve not only civil restitution but also religious atonement, it should come as no surprise that Maimonides took great pains to decide on the question of whether one can procure atonement even when, for some reason, monetary restitution cannot be made in full, as in the case of a stolen object that can no longer be returned. The question, to be sure, is essential and pertains not only to the criminal act of theft but also to property damages.[176] The idea that compensatory payments due for tortious acts, not unlike punitive payments due for bodily injuries, function in the religious sphere – not so much in terms of a criminal sanction as in terms of a means for procuring atonement, forgiveness, and religious rectification – highlights the overlapping roles of Maimonides as theologian and jurist.

4 The Duty to Rescue: A Religious or a Moral Obligation?

Maimonides greatly extended the scope of the duty to rescue. According to Maimonides, not only does anyone who is able to save another from death and does not do so violate the prohibition, "You shall not stand idly by the blood of your neighbor,"[177] but this is also the law with respect to a person who is able to prevent damage or loss to his fellow, whether with his body or his property, but does not do so.[178]

Maimonides writes:

> If one person is able to save another and does not save him, he transgresses the commandment, *neither shalt thou stand idly by the blood of thy neighbor* (Leviticus 19:16). Similarly, if one person sees another drowning in the sea, or being attacked by bandits, or being attacked by wild animals, and although able to rescue him

---

[176] In this context we should mention the "atonement fine" (*kofer*) paid by the owner of an animal (when the owner has already been warned that the animal is dangerous) that kills a person, which is not a regular civil payment.
[177] Leviticus 19:16.
[178] See his wording in Laws of Murderers and the Preservation of Life 1:14.

either alone or by hiring others, does not rescue him; or if one hears Gentiles or informers plotting evil against another or laying a trap for him and he does not call it to the other's attention and let him know; or if one knows that a Gentile of violent person is going to attack another and although able to appease him on behalf of the other and make him change his mind, he does not do so; or if one acts in any similar way – he transgresses in each case the injunction, *Neither shalt thou stand idly by the blood of thy neighbor* (ibid.).[179]

In Maimonides' view, therefore, the duty to rescue is broad, applying to rescuing both a person's life as well as his property, as he writes: "We have been abjured not to be negligent in saving even one life in Israel when we see him in danger of his life or facing loss" (i.e., monetary loss),[180] and therefore he wrote, "A person who suppresses testimony – this too shall be included in the warning ["Neither shalt thou stand idly by the blood of thy neighbor"] because he sees the property of his fellow about to be lost and he could restore it to him by telling the truth."[181] The broad application also manifests itself in the measures that the rescuer must adopt (Laws of Murderers and Preservation of Life 1:14), in relation to the injunction, "Neither shalt thou stand idly by the blood of thy neighbor": not only if he is able to rescue him himself is he obliged to do so, but even if he can hire others to rescue him, he must do so. The general obligation to save life was applied by Maimonides as a specific duty of the doctor

> who is commanded to heal the ill of Israel, and this is included in the explanation of that which is written "And thou shalt restore it to him" (Deuteronomy 22:2), including his life,[182] for if he sees that it is in danger and he can save him, he must do so by physical intervention, or with his money, or through his knowledge.[183]

The ramifications of the duty to rescue, according to Maimonides, touch upon the law of the pursuer, although that law is broader and includes additional elements apart from the duty to rescue. As is known, talmudic law states that when a person is pursuing another with the intention of killing him, the person being pursued, and others as well, may harm the pursuer in order to save the pursued from the former's murderous scheme.[184] The post-talmudic halakhic sages discussed the meaning of the talmudic law, asking whether the *halakhah* permitting the pursued person to kill the pursuer was designed to punish the pursuer, or whether it was intended to save the pursued?[185] The first explanation was adopted by Rashi and the

---

[179] Laws of Murderers and the Preservation of Life 1:14.
[180] Book of Commandments, negative commandment 297. What appears in parenthesis is according to the commentary PIKUDEI YESHARIM.
[181] Ibid.
[182] See Bava Kamma 81b; Sanhedrin 73a.
[183] COMMENTARY TO THE MISHNAH, Nedarim 4:4.
[184] See Sanhedrin 73a.
[185] For an extended discussion of this question see AHARON ENKER, FUNDAMENTALS OF JEWISH CRIMINAL LAW 316–33 (Bar Ilan University Press: Ramat Gan, 2007) (Heb.).

Tosafists, who were of the opinion that the basis of the law was to stop the pursuer from committing the crime, even at the cost of killing him[186] – a possibility that is liable to sound strange to the modern jurist. Maimonides, however, adopted the second interpretation, which seems much more reasonable, whereby the major and deciding consideration in allowing the pursuer's life to be taken is to save the life of the pursued, which is in danger.[187] The matter of saving the pursuer himself from sinning, which was emphasized by Rashi and the Tosafists, receives no mention from Maimonides.[188] However, despite the relatively broad application of the duty to rescue according to Maimonides, following the Talmud[189] Maimonides refrained from extending this duty even further, as opposed to other authorities, as illustrated later in the end of this section.

Is the duty to rescue regarded as a legal obligation? This subject has been treated by several contemporary scholars, who were primarily concerned with the differences on this issue between Jewish law and the common law.[190] The main difficulty confronting them was defining the difference between a legal obligation and a moral duty, in light of the unique approach of Jewish law, which is significantly different from that which is accepted in modern law. In modern law, there are two main criteria for distinguishing between a moral and a legal obligation: the normative criterion – has the obligation been codified? – and the enforcement

---

[186] See Rashi's commentary on the *mishnah* in *Sanhedrin* 73a, s.v. *ve'elu*; *Tosafot ad loc.*, s.v. *lehatzilo benafsho*.

[187] As he writes in his COMMENTARY TO THE MISHNAH, *Sanhedrin* 8:7: "And this matter of saving is that we are commanded to rescue this person being pursued from the pursuer who wishes to kill him or to inflict a criminal act on him." The same emerges from what he writes in the Book of Commandments, positive commandment 247: "We are commanded to save the pursued person from the one who is pursuing him in order to kill him, even at the cost of the life of the pursuer." This can also be seen in his ruling in Laws of Murderers 1:6: "When a person is pursuing a fellow with the intention of killing him – even if the pursuer is a minor – every Jewish person is commanded to attempt to save the person being pursued, even if it is necessary to kill the pursuer."

[188] From the fact that one must [attempt to] save the life of the person being pursued, even if it means killing a minor pursuer, according to Maimonides (Laws of Murderers 1:6), it emerges that this is not a matter of punishing the pursuer, for a minor is not subject to punishment. The inference that ENKER, *supra* note 185, at 325, drew *inter alia* from the ruling concerning the minor pursuer, whereby according to Maimonides: "There is no condition in the law of the pursuer that the pursuer himself must commit a crime in order that it be permissible to kill him in order to save the pursued person" makes sense. And *cf.* on this matter R. Haym Soloveitchik in his novella on Laws of Murderers 1:9, who infers from Maimonides' ruling on the matter of the fetus who is considered "as a pursuer" that "the basis of the law of killing the pursuer lies in the law of saving the pursued."

[189] *Sanhedrin* 73a.

[190] For a comprehensive summary *see*: Eliezer Ben-Shlomo, *The Duty to Rescue Lives*, 39 HAPRAKLIT 414, 429–30 (1990) (Heb.) [hereinafter: Ben-Shlomo 1990]; Eliezer Ben-Shlomo, *The Duty to Rescue the Life of a Jew*, 14 REFUAH U-MISHPAT 4 (1996) (Heb.) [hereinafter: Ben-Shlomo 1996]; Aaron Kirschenbaum, *The Bystander's Duty to Rescue in Jewish Law*, 8 J. OF RELIGIOUS ETHICS 204 (1980); Ernest Weinrib, RESCUE AND RESTITUTION, in Martin P. Golding (ed.), JEWISH LAW AND LEGAL THEORY 539 (New York, 1993).

criterion – is it possible to enforce the obligation and impose a sanction on the violator? Before examining the position of Jewish law, we will briefly review the different positions adopted by modern legal systems.

The various legal systems are extremely cautious about imposing liability in cases of pure omission or inaction, both in the area of tort law and in the area of criminal law.[191] Anglo-American common law does not normally impose a duty to rescue, whereas most European legal systems impose a limited duty to rescue in extreme situations of "easy" rescue, i.e., rescue that does not involve endangerment on the part of the rescuer and does not require the investment of significant resources on his part.[192] Thus, for example, as opposed to the Anglo-American approach, the Russian Criminal Code of 1960 forbids a person to refrain from offering help to one whose life is in danger, when the help was required immediately, and could have been given without serious risk to the person offering help or anyone else.[193] In Germany, too, the duty to rescue is anchored in the German Criminal Code: the law there is that a person who does not render assistance in the course of accidents or a common danger or emergency, although help is necessary and could be expected of him under the circumstances (particularly if it is feasible without substantial danger to himself and without violating other important duties), is liable to imprisonment not exceeding one year or a fine.[194] The French Criminal Code devotes a special section to failure to rescue a person in danger, in relation to three types of omissions.[195] In all three the punishment is identical: between three months' and five years' imprisonment and/or a fine.[196] The courts have dealt mainly with the interpretation of three elements in the law: (1) the existence of a "danger to a person's body" and the requirement that the danger be real, present, permanent and immediate; (2) the element of intention, and willful blindness as satisfying the requirement of intention; and (3) the "ability to rescue," which is examined at the time of the event and not according to subsequent developments.[197] Even though this is a penal law, its main aim is to encourage acts of rescue.[198] Similar provisions exist in Holland, Belgium, Hungary, Czech Republic, Poland, Italy and in several Swiss cantons.[199]

---

[191] ARIEL PORAT, TORTS I 185 (2013) (Heb.).
[192] Ibid. at 135.
[193] Section 127 of the Russian Criminal Code, as cited by Ben-Shlomo 1990, supra note 190, at 416.
[194] Section 323c of the German Criminal Code. See https://ec.europa.eu/anti-trafficking/sites/antitrafficking/files/criminal_code_germany_en_1.pdf.
[195] P.A. PAGEAUD, Actualité Juridique vol. 5, 13–25 (1973); Ben-Shlomo 1990, supra note 190, at 415.
[196] PAGEAUD, ibid.; Ben-Shlomo 1990, ibid. at 415–18; Neal Hendel, The "You Shall Not Stand Idly by Your Brother's Blood Law, 5758–1998" – Inspiration and Reality, 29 MEHKEREI MISHPAT 229, 270 (2001) (Heb.).
[197] Ben-Shlomo 1990, supra note 190, at 415; PAGEAUD, ibid.
[198] Ben-Shlomo, ibid. at 418.
[199] Ibid. at 416.

English law, on the other hand, contains no basis for imposing a duty to rescue.[200] It imposes no obligation on a stranger — neither in tort law nor in criminal law — to rescue another person.[201] Reluctance to impose a duty to rescue is found in the legal systems of states that follow the common law.[202] Of course, in the absence of a source for the duty to rescue, no sanction is imposed on a stranger who chooses to refrain from rendering assistance, even if it would be very easy to help, such as notifying the rescue services that someone is drowning.[203] In the famous case in the matter of *Donoghue*, which served as a basis for imposing a duty of care under English law, the Court explained that the common law does not lay down a duty in tort for not performing a rescue,[204] and this was also the ruling in later judgments of the House of Lords, in the seventies and eighties, in the cases of Home Office and Smith.[205] In the *Donoghue* case, the Court said that the religious obligation, "You shall love your fellow as yourself," is translated in the world of law as a duty not to do harm,[206] but in the Home Office and Smith judgments it was explained that this duty does not relate to the conduct of the Good Samaritan, and had the Good Samaritan chosen not to rescue, he would not have been under any obligation whatsoever under English law.[207] Similarly, the general principles of tort law in England exempt a person from liability for damage that stems from a pure omission.[208] Consequently, a stranger does not bear a duty to rescue.[209] Scholars explain that in fact a person who rescues without an obligation in English law is regarded as a volunteer, and therefore

> The general principle adopted by English law is that a person who does a kindness to his fellow without being asked to do so, and who acts without mistake, coercion or fraud, is not entitled to indemnification ... duties are not imposed on people behind their backs, just as they are not granted a benefit against their will.[210]

Now, over time the judgments of the English courts have increasingly recognized a financial obligation vis-à-vis the rescuer, based on the principle of unjust enrichment, but the transition to this recognition is neither sharp nor consensual,

---

[200] Hendel, *supra* note 196, at 231.
[201] *Ibid.*
[202] *Ibid.*
[203] *Ibid.*
[204] Donoghue v. Stevenson [1932] A.C. 562 (H.L.) (U.K.). For discussion, *see* Hendel, *supra* note 196, at 232.
[205] Smith v. Littlewoods Organisation Ltd [1987] 2 A.C. 247; Home Office V. Dorset Yacht Co. Ltd [1970] 2 A.C. 1060. For discussion, *see* Hendel, *ibid.*
[206] Donoghue v. Stevenson, *supra* note 204.
[207] For discussion, *see* Hendel, *supra* note 196, at 232-33.
[208] *Ibid.*, at 233. For cases in which obligation is imposed in English law due to omission, *see* HALSBURY'S LAWS OF ENGLAND, vol. 33, para. 610 (Butterworths, 4th ed., 1997).
[209] However, a person will be held liable in torts for omission in three situations, the common denominator of which is some degree of liability vis-à-vis another. This liability removes a person from the category of stranger. *See* Hendel, *supra* note 196, at 236.
[210] DANIEL FRIEDMANN, UNJUST ENRICHMENT vol. 1, 141 (2nd ed., 1998) (Heb.).

due to the underlying conception in English law whereby a rescuer is merely a volunteer or a meddler, and obligations should not automatically devolve upon one who did not ask the rescuer to rescue him.[211] This also finds expression in the approach of English law to the question of the right of the rescuer to sue the person who was rescued for damage suffered by the rescuer. The initial approach of English law was that the rescued person has no obligation vis-à-vis the rescuer, because the latter volunteered for the mission; he thereby also volunteered to take upon himself the risk that he would be harmed, and thus in fact endangered himself voluntarily.[212]

The situation changed against the backdrop of the decision of Justice Cardozo of the US Supreme Court in the matter of Wagner, whereby "[t]he emergency begets the man" ("the man" being the rescuer).[213] This American approach influenced the English case-law. Thus, for example, in a case in which a person left his horse unguarded in the street, near children, and one of them threw a stone at the horse which took fright and began galloping away, it was decided that the policemen who was injured while trying to subdue the horse was entitled to sue its owner.[214] It was also ruled that there are types of emergencies in which an ordinary person – who is not a professional such as a policeman or fireman and is not involved such as a parent – will conceivably be permitted to sue the person who created the danger if he took action to rescue and was injured; the rule, however, is that the rescuer may sue only if his act of rescue was reasonable.[215] The resistance of English law to the right of a rescuer to sue is evident in the judgment in which it was ruled that the action of the rescuer would be dismissed, even though the act of rescue was reasonable, if the way in which he was injured was not foreseeable.[216] Further resistance of English law to the right of the rescuer to sue finds expression in another judgment, in which it was mentioned that the rescuer does not enjoy a special status with respect to his right to sue for emotional damage merely due to his being the rescuer, and that the rescuer ought to be treated like any other plaintiff.[217] In short, English law focusses on the rights that it is prepared to grant the rescuer-volunteer

---

[211] Hendel, *supra* note 196, at 234.
[212] *Ibid.*
[213] Wagner v. International Railway Co. 133 N.E. 176, 180 (N.Y. 1921). For discussion, *see* Hendel, *supra* note 196, at 235.
[214] Haynes v. Harwood [1935] 1 K.B. 146. Cited by Hendel, *supra* note 196, at 235.
[215] Chadwick v. British Railways Board 1 W.L.R. 912 [1967]. Cited by Hendel, *supra* note 196, at 235.
[216] Crossley v. Rawlinson [1981] 3 All ER 674, [1982] 1 WLR 369. Cited by Hendel, *supra* note 196, at 235.
[217] White v. Chief Constable of the South Yorkshire Police 1 All ER 1 [1999]. Cited by Hendel, *supra* note 196, at 235. The Court ruled that it would have been possible to arrive at a different conclusion on the basis of a certain interpretation of the Chadwick judgment but instead, it preferred the approach whereby the rescuer has no special status, and he is subject to all the normal criteria of negligence when he sues for compensation for psychological damage. See the judgment *ibid.* at 47.

with respect to his ability and inability to sue for injuries suffered in the course of the rescue. As a rule, the system does not grant the rescuer immunity or quasi-immunity for damage that he caused in the course of the rescue, and in this it is in fact faithful to the common law approach.

Similar to English law, the rule in American law is that a stranger does not have a duty to rescue.[218] In only four states has a real duty to rescue been enacted, the scope in each state being different.[219] But in the other US states, too, the arrangement is different from that found in English law. As opposed to the English system, most US states have adopted laws such as the "Good Samaritan" Law.[220] This Law does not impose a duty to rescue upon a person, but it grants protection – in fact, immunity – to a person who volunteered to save another against being sued for an act that he performed for the purpose of rendering assistance.[221] The Good Samaritan Law was first enacted in the United States in 1959 and by the eighties, it had been passed in one version or another in each of the US states.[222] The intention of the Law is that the rescuer must be treated as a Good Samaritan: he is not obliged to rescue, but he should be encouraged to do so, and he will be protected by the law if he volunteered; moreover, it will not be possible to sue him if he was negligent,[223] as opposed to the original system of the common law according to which it was possible to sue the rescuer if he did not meet the standard of the reasonable man, because he was not asked to help nor did he have a duty to do so.[224] In many US states, immunity under the Good Samaritan Law is granted to any person who performs a life-saving action in an emergency situation; in other states, immunity is offered only to doctors; and in many states, the immunity is not unlimited, for example, it does not apply to a rescuer who acts with gross negligence, malice etc.[225] Over the years, a trend has emerged in the case law to extend the application of immunity, with the aim of

---

[218] Hendel, *supra* note 196, at 236.
[219] Vermont, Minnesota, Wisconsin and Rhode Island. See *ibid.* at 239–44. This obligation may have been enacted in those States due to a series of awful incidents that occurred in those years, including cases of rape in front of people who did not report it. For background to the enactment of those laws following a public outcry, see Hendel, *ibid.* This public outcry contributed to another trend, which is the enactment of the duty to report in various states. This duty does not mandate a rescue operation, i.e., direct contact between the observer and the victim, but rather, a report to the police about what occurred The duty to report relates to a person who is in need to rescue due to the commission of a criminal offence, and not to a person who needs rescuing in a situation that arose naturally, such as a person who is drowning. Hendel explains that it is indeed correct that sometimes, the best way to save a person who is in danger from criminals is by calling the police, but this is not always so. See *ibid.* at 243–44. We will not expand on the duty to report here.
[220] *Ibid.*
[221] *Ibid.*
[222] *Ibid.* at 238; Eric A. Brandt, *Good Samaritan Laws – The Legal Placebo: A Current Analysis*, 17 AKRON L. REV. 303 (1983).
[223] Hendel, *supra* note 196, at 238.
[224] *Ibid.*
[225] *Ibid.* at 239.

encouraging behavior such as that underlying volunteerism.[226] At the same time, the standard has not reached that of a positive obligation, even if the protection has become broader.[227] As such, American case law and legislation have developed the duty to rescue further than was done in the original common law.[228]

Do these two fundamental criteria for distinguishing between a legal obligation and a moral duty – the normative criterion and the efficiency criterion – exist in Jewish law as well?

The duty to save lives and property is established in Jewish law as an obligation according to the normative criterion, for Maimonides included it as law in his *Code* and other authorities followed him.[229] In this, English and American law differ from the binding basis of Jewish law, whereas the laws in European countries are similar to it in principle, although it would appear that the scope of the duty to rescue is broader in Jewish law than in the European systems.

It is noteworthy that in relation to the second criterion of a legal obligation – the power of enforcement and sanction vis-à-vis the violator of the duty to rescue – there is no consensus amongst the halakhic authorities. This question has been discussed in several articles in recent years, and opinions vary.[230] Maimonides' stance in this context, however, is clear and unequivocal: in his opinion, no sanction should be imposed upon a person violating the duty to rescue. He writes:

> Although there is no flogging for these prohibitions, because breach of them involves no action, the offence is most serious, for if one destroys the life of a single Israelite, it is regarded as though he destroyed the whole world, and if one preserves the life of a single Israelite, it is regarded as though he preserved the whole world.[231]

Maimonides' clear position notwithstanding, we agree in principle with Kirschenbaum's argument:

---

[226] *Ibid.* at note 66.
[227] *Ibid.* at 240.
[228] *Ibid.* at 240. In addition to the developments presented above, the case law in the US also expanded the doctrine of "special relationships" which mandates rescuing in certain circumstances, as was mentioned regarding English law. The duty to act where there is a special relationship is not a pure duty to rescue, i.e., a duty to rescue simply because the other requires rescuing. Rather, it stems from the responsibility of the rescuer vis-à-vis the other against the backdrop of existing relations between them, which have been defined by law as a special relationship, including, for example, situations in which one is responsible for the other, such as parent and child, employer and employee, or a person responsible for someone who is dangerous such as a prisoner or a mentally ill person. American case law expanded the category of situations in which such a duty applies, as well as the types of relationships that create a duty *ab initio*, but this expansion of the rule of special relationships is not a substitute for the creation of a duty to rescue. See *ibid.* at 237–38.
[229] See *Tur* and *Shulhan Arukh, Hoshen Mishpat* 426.
[230] For a summary *see* Ben-Shlomo 1996, *supra* note 190, at 5–6, and *see* the articles cited in the notes there.
[231] Laws of Murderers and the Preservation of Life 1:16.

It would be misleading, therefore, to interpret the lack of judicial punishment in Jewish law for the innocent bystander who fails in his duty to come to the rescue of his fellow man in distress as indicating that the duty is merely moral. Rather Jewish law views such failure as nonfeasance, a formal offense of inaction (*delictum mere omissivum*) where action is a duty required by law.[232]

If so, the very fact that no sanction is imposed for breach of the duty to rescue does not necessarily attest to the purely moral nature of this duty. Quite correctly, Ernest Weinrib stated:

> To regard the Talmudic duty as moral rather than legal, however, is to misconceive the Talmudic position. The duty to rescue is not merely a matter of conscience. Despite the absence of a legal sanction, the directive not to "stand idly by the blood of thy neighbor" is legal just as any other norm of Jewish law. Because Jewish law embodies a jurisprudence of obligation, the legal character of the duty to rescue lies in its very existence as a duty, even if its breach is not subject to sanction.[233]

However, according to Maimonides' approach, as we shall prove now, the legal aspects of the duty to rescue are more limited as compared to the opinions of the Jewish law authorities mentioned in Kirschenbaum's and Weinrib's articles.

Not only did Maimonides stress that a person in breach of a duty to save life is not liable to sanction, but he ruled contrary to the position of many authorities, who established a very broad application of the rescuer's right to indemnification, in the framework of which they also ruled that the rescuer must be compensated if he was injured in the course of the rescue, and he must be indemnified for his expenses.[234] Some deduced from these opinions of the authorities that the duty to rescue is a full legal obligation with broad application,[235] apparently as we saw, for example, with respect to four of the US states or many European states. However, we shall see that this conclusion is not correct according to Maimonides. On this point, the approach of English law differs from that of Maimonides, for in English law there is discussion of awarding certain expenses to a rescuer and compensation for his damages, even if only in certain cases. Maimonides, on the other hand, set a fairly limited application of the duty to rescue as compared to other halakhic authorities, and adopted a more complex position, which we shall now discuss.

Some authorities, for example, held that the duty to rescue also applies where it involves some danger to the rescuer.[236] Maimonides' language (Laws of Murderers

---

[232] Kirschenbaum, *supra* note 190, at 207.
[233] Weinrib, *supra* note 190, at 541.
[234] For a detailed review, see NACHUM RACKOVER, UNJUST ENRICHMENT IN JEWISH LAW 94–115 (The Library of Jewish Law: Jerusalem, 1987) (Heb.).
[235] Kirschenbaum, *supra* note 190; Weinrib, *supra* note 233.
[236] See e.g., KESSEF MISHNEH on Laws of Murder 1:14, who mentioned the view according to which a rescuer must put himself in potential danger in order to rescue a person in certain danger, based on the author of HAGAHOT MAIMUNIOT who derived this from the talmudic discussion in the J Trumot (end of chapter 8). The same appears in BEIT YOSEF, Hoshen Mishpat 426:2.

and Preservation of Life 1:14), however, does not imply that the rescuer must endanger himself in order to save another.[237] Moreover, it is noteworthy that although Maimonides in the *code* ruled,[238] following the Talmud,[239] that a person must strive in all ways – including by spending money – to save another, unlike others he did not rule that after the rescue operation the person rescued must indemnify the rescuer;[240] this approach appears to be even broader than that of English law, for example, which is prepared to award costs and compensation for the damages of the rescuer only in certain cases. In the Jewish law sources, the consideration of encouraging the saving of life, and the concern about people refraining from performing acts of rescue led the *Rishonim* and the authorities to lay down *halakhot* on the subject of the rights of the rescuer, *inter alia* the rescuer's rights to indemnification from the rescued person for the expenses incurred in his rescue.[241] However, not only did Maimonides not mention in the *Code* that there is a legal right to indemnification for the rescuer's expenses,[242] but in a *responsum* attributed to Maimonides,[243] the ruling is that the person ransoming the female captive is not entitled to indemnification for his expenses, for the reason that he is performing a religious *mitzvah* of ransoming captives, and therefore he has no legal rights vis-à-vis the captive he ransomed and the ransomer has no right to reclaim his money.[244] Nevertheless, it cannot be deduced from this that according to Maimonides, the duty to rescue has no legal implications, and that the rescuer is considered a volunteer only, as in English law. Indeed, the duty to rescue has legal implications

---

[237] As several authorities inferred from his words. See Resp. Radbaz 6:982, who inferred this from Maimonides' wording in Laws of Murderers 1:14, viz. "Whoever can save …", as opposed to the language of the Talmud in *Sanhedrin* 73a, "is obligated to save him"; according to Radbaz, Maimonides is referring to a situation in which he is able to save him without endangering himself, for example, if he was sleeping under an unstable wall and needed to be woken from his sleep. Similar inferences were drawn from Maimonides' wording by Bayit Hadash, Hoshen Mishpat 426:2; R. Chaim Heller in his Commentary on the Book of Commandments, Negative Commandment 297, note 11. In Sefer Me'irat Einayim, Hoshen Mishpat 426:2, he wrote that the *halakhah* in practice is in accordance with Maimonides.

[238] *Supra* note 179.

[239] *Sanhedrin* 73a.

[240] See, e.g., Piskei ha-Rosh, Sanhedrin 8:2; Tur, Hoshen Mishpat 426; and see Sefer Me'irat Einayim, Hoshen Mishpat 426:2, who noted that Maimonides did not rule in accordance with this view.

[241] For a broad review of the different views on this issue, see Rackover, *supra* note 234, at 173–94.

[242] R. Zalman Nehemiah Goldberg, *On Charitable Obligations*, Yad Re'em in memory of A.M. Lifshitz 97 (Jerusalem, 5735–1975) (Heb.), argued with good reason that Maimonides' view is that the rescued person need not indemnify the rescuer for his expenses, and therefore the Shulhan Arukh did not cite Rosh's ruling, whereby the rescuer has a right to indemnification, since the ruling was in accordance with Maimonides (*ibid.* at 102).

[243] E. Munk, *A New Response to Maimonides z"l*, 1 Perakim 329 (5734) (Heb.).

[244] Maimonides' wording in the responsum is as follows: "The one who performed the *mitzvah* has no claim and has no legal right at all." And see Rackover, *supra* note 234, at 182–83, who rightly wrote, "However, the detailed facts are not known to us from the responsum, and it is therefore difficult to determine the parameters of Maimonides' words."

as well as religious ones according to Maimonides: following the Talmud,[245] Maimonides ruled – unlike English law but similar to American law – that according to the law, the rescuer has immunity from being sued in torts for damage he caused to a third party in the course of the rescue. He said as follows:

> If one chases after the pursuer in order to rescue the pursued, and he breaks objects belonging to the pursuer or to anyone else, he is exempt. This rule is not strict law but is an enactment made in order that one should not refrain from rescuing another or lose time through being so careful when chasing a pursuer.[246]

Nevertheless, it is noteworthy that the rule concerning immunity mentioned by Maimonides is not strict law, as he himself says, but rather, a regulation enacted by the talmudic sages aimed at encouraging a person to render assistance to his fellow.

According to Maimonides, therefore, the commandment to rescue a person who is in danger is primarily a religious obligation. Indeed, Maimonides does not regard it as a moral duty only, for in his view, this is a normative obligation like the other normative obligations mentioned in the *Code*. Maimonides regards the obligation as a "strong" one, for the rescuer must even incur expenses in order to rescue, knowing that he will not necessarily be repaid for them, although he will be immune from being sued if he caused harm. At the same time, the duty to rescue under Maimonides' approach should not be considered a full-blown legal norm according to the modern meaning, whereby a legal norm is accompanied by the possibility of enforcement, or the punishment of one who violates the norm, for as we saw, Maimonides stressed that "there is no flogging from these prohibitions, because breach of them involves no action." Neither was Maimonides of the opinion that there is a legal right to indemnification for the expenses of the rescuer, although he too thought that there is immunity from tort actions for a rescuer who caused injury to a third party while performing the rescue. The situation therefore is that according to Maimonides, the duty to rescue is only a partial (not full) legal obligation; from a religious point of view, however, this is a central, very serious obligation, for as he wrote: "… if one destroys the life of a single Israelite, it is regarded as though he destroyed the whole world, and if one preserves the life of a single Israelite, it is regarded as though he preserved the whole world."[247]

---

[245] *Sanhedrin* 74a.
[246] Laws of Wounding and Damaging 8:14.
[247] This should be compared to the reason cited by Maimonides in the GUIDE (3:40, Pines, 556) for permitting the killing of one who "pursues his fellow man in order to kill him, and … one [who] pursues someone in order to expose the latter's nakedness, for these are acts of wrongdoing that cannot be repaired once they have been accomplished. As for the other transgressions that are punished with death or by order of a court of law, such as idolatry and the profanation of the Sabbath, they do not constitute an act of wrongdoing with regard to someone else, but concern only thoughts; and therefore the transgressor is not killed because of his wish, but only if he commits the transgression."

Have any systems applied the principles of the religious laws within the general-secular law? There were those who argued that the duty to rescue should not be based, for example, on tort law, but rather on an external source, and that the suitable source of inspiration and authority should be the religious law, which successfully bridges between the legal and the moral aspects.[248] Indeed, as far as we know, there has been only one legal system – Israeli law – that has attempted to enact a law mandating rescue, based primarily on the religious-Jewish law, in a bill proposed to the Knesset (the Israeli Parliament) by a religiously observant member of the Knesset.[249] Despite presumptuous attempts by Israeli legislators to replicate the delicate balances achieved by the Sages of Jewish law, including Maimonides with his unique approach, the law that was ultimately passed[250] did not necessarily succeed in achieving this balance, and it is perhaps not surprising that the Law is almost never applied, and borders on the declarative.[251] From Maimonides' perspective, there is a duty to rescue, and it is a serious legal-religious obligation, unconnected to the fact that it carries no sanction. The Israeli law, on the other hand, imposes a sanction in the form of a fine on a person who had a duty to rescue and did not do so, and it does not grant immunity in tort – at least not explicitly – to a person who performed a rescue, although some have sought to deduce immunity in light of the purpose of the statute.[252] Transferring religious norms and translating them into norms of non-religious law is complex. We will return to this example[253] and attempt to incorporate it into the framework of lessons that can be learned, cautiously, from Jewish law in its entirety and from Maimonides' approach in particular to the general, non-religious law.

In concluding this section we will stress that once again we see – similar to what we saw earlier in relation to other laws in the Book of Torts – the extent to which the religious dimension is significant in Maimonides' theory of torts, particularly in his *Code*. Nevertheless, as we have seen, we must not overstate the weight attributed to the religious and prohibitive dimension in the Maimonidean theory of tort.

---

[248] Hendel, *supra* note 196, at 268. Hendel at the present time is a Justice of the Israel Supreme Court.

[249] In 1995, M.K. Hanan Porat proposed the "You Shall Not Stand Idly By Your Brother's Blood" draft law. From the explanatory notes to the bill it emerges that the purpose of the law was to entrench in Israeli legislation the social and moral value which had its source in the Bible (Leviticus 19:16). See Penal Law (Amendment no. 47) (You Shall Not Stand Idly By Your Brother's Blood) Bill, 5755–1995, H.H. 2398.

[250] You Shall Not Stand Idly By Your Brother's Blood Law, 5758–1998, S.H. 245.

[251] Hendel, *supra* note 196, at 269–70.

[252] Hendel contends that in light of the purpose of the legislation, it is inconceivable that a person who attempted to rescue should be in a worse situation than a person who was apathetic. Therefore, he says that the rescuer must enjoy some kind of immunity, albeit not full; this immunity will apply in a case in which there was gross negligence or recklessness, or absence of good faith. Hendel proposes regulating this protection in legislation. See Hendel, *ibid.* at 269–71.

[253] Chapter 8.

5 Visual Trespass

Following what we wrote at the end of the preceding section regarding the relatively light weight that must be attributed to the religious-mystical dimension of Maimonides' tort theory, it is important to note that Maimonides, the arch-rationalist, consistently refrained from ruling in accordance with the talmudic sources relating to a person who causes damage to others by means of unwelcome viewing (*ayin hara*). This concern about unwelcome gazing or viewing has multiple halakhic consequences.[254] Let us examine two examples that involve Maimonides' rulings in his *Code*. The Talmud states that the Sages forbade a person who found a lost garment to spread it out before his guests, and some say that the reason for the prohibition is concern about harm that may be caused by the jealous eye of a guest.[255] Accordingly, Rav ruled in the Talmud that "[i]t is forbidden for a person to stand at his fellow's field during the time it displays a standing crop,"[256] and the reason is so that "one should not cast an evil eye upon it."[257] The second example: the *halakhah* that requires neighbors to erect a barrier between their plots[258] was also explained by saying that only thus is it possible to ensure that "it should not be harmed by an evil eye."[259] However, Maimonides does not appear to have been concerned about an evil eye in reality, for not only is this term not mentioned in his rulings, but in both of the two examples he refrains from citing the talmudic explanations.

On the matter of the prohibition of spreading a garment in front of guests, Maimonides explains that this was prohibited for fear of theft,[260] and he omitted the talmudic reason whereby the prohibition was due to fear of an evil eye. Maimonides presented a rationalist argument, which is not concerned about mystical evil spirits that hover over our world.[261]

---

[254] And *see* ITAMAR WARHAFTIG, THE RIGHT TO PRIVACY IN LIGHT OF JEWISH LAW 105–13 (Mishpetei Eretz: Ofrah 2009) (Heb.).

[255] The Talmud in *Bava Metzia* 30a notes the possibility that this is forbidden "due to the [evil/jealous] eye," and Rashi explains there "that the evil eye of guests will rest on the garment."

[256] *Bava Metzia* 107a.

[257] Rashi, *Bava Metzia* 107a.

[258] *Bava Batra* 2b.

[259] Rashi, *Bava Batra* 2b, s.v. *assur lo*.

[260] Laws of Robbery and Lost Property 13:11.

[261] As explained by RABINOVITCH, YAD PESHUTAH, *supra* note 59, who noted that according to the authors of MASORET HASHAS, ZION YERUSHALAIM, JERUSALEM TALMUD Moed Katan 3:5, s.v. *ve-ein lo sahi meit*: "It was not the way of our Rabbis to cite mystical matters and our Rabbis never mention an evil spirit and in some places these words are omitted." He also mentioned in his Introduction to R. ITZHAK ARIELLI, EINAYIM LA-MISHPAT HA-SHALEM 11 (Jerusalem 5751) (Heb.), who listed seven rules for Maimonides' omissions, and the seventh rule is that Maimonides omits everything that is "supernatural and non-rational." WARHAFTIG, *supra* note 254, at 101 wrote in the same vein, and connected this to the well-known dispute between Maimonides and Nahmanides on the question of the power of sorcery etc. According to Maimonides, all these are prohibited by the Torah as false and spurious (see Maimonides,

With regard to visual trespass (*hezek re'iya*) on a neighboring plot, Maimonides ruled that there is no requirement to build a wall four cubits high (approx. 2 meters) in order to prevent a person from looking into the property of his neighbor, and a low fence of 10 *tefahim* (approx. 1 meter) would suffice. In a *responsum* to the Sages of Lunel who asked him why he did not rule in accordance with the Talmud that it was necessary to build a high barrier due to the evil eye, Maimonides answered that the talmudic statement is not binding in practice; rather, these are words of piety, and in practice a distinction must be made between

> visual trespass, which is definitely a serious harm, since he sees his fellow standing, sitting and attending to his personal needs, and between visual damage as a result of gazing upon his fellow's standing wheat, which is of a metaphysical nature, and therefore prohibited on the basis of pious conduct alone. Now, the Talmud's answer is of a general nature, and does not enter into legal specification. Therefore, the basic rule remains unchanged, i.e., that visual trespass only applies in the context of a communal dwelling place.[262]

The reason that a low fence of 10 *tefahim* is needed, explains Maimonides, is in order to clearly demarcate the boundaries between the neighbors, so that anyone overstepping the boundary will be deemed a trespasser.[263] From that *responsum* Rambam 260 on "visual trespass, which is surely a great harm, that a person sees his fellow when he is standing and sitting and attending to his personal needs," it is possible to deduce the legal parameters of visual trespass according to Maimonides. Visual trespass – observing another's activities inside his private property – is considered a form of trespass on his domain. In certain circumstances, the rabbis considered this trespass to be a form of damage and required that proper steps be taken to prevent it.[264]

It is appropriate at this juncture to summarize the various approaches of the halakhic Sages to the legal parameters of visual trespass, and the difference between their positions and that of Maimonides. Earlier and later commentators and authorities disagreed about the parameters of visual trespass.[265] Some stressed that this was not only a matter of the need to prevent visual trespass, but that there was a prohibition against looking into the domain of another.[266] Others were of the opinion that looking is not harmful in itself, but the very possibility of looking into

---

Laws of Idolatry 11:17), whereas according to Nahmanides (*Nahmanides on the Bible, Deuteronomy* 18:9), they do have substance, but they were prohibited by the Torah.

[262] RESP. RAMBAM 260 (Freiman edition).

[263] In the words of Maimonides' *responsum*, *ibid.*, the need for a barrier of 10 *tefahim* is so that anyone overstepping the boundary "will be deemed a trespasser."

[264] The laws of visual trespass are mentioned in the first chapter of Tractate *Bava Batra*. For a broad overview, see ENCYCLOPEDIA TALMUDIT vol. 8, 659–702; WARHAFTIG, *supra* note 254, at 85–114.

[265] For a summary, see WARHAFTIG, *supra* note 254, at 87–93.

[266] See HIDDUSHEI HA-RAMBAN, Bava Batra 59a, s.v. *detnan*: "Even if the injured party forgave him, it is definitely prohibited for the injurer [to injure him] through looking." This was the

the domain of another inhibits the owner's use of his property, and this constitutes a violation of his property right.[267] According to this explanation, the right of the person suffering the harm creates an obligation on the part of the harm-doer not to look.[268] However, in his discussion of visual trespass, not only does Maimonides not mention the religious prohibition, but his emphasis, as can be seen from his language in the *responsum Rambam* 260, is on the actual harm that a person causes his fellow by looking into his domain. This nicety in Maimonides' formulation is consistent with the words of one of the *Aharonim*, who inferred from the various rulings that on Maimonides' approach, the very act of viewing constitutes harm, irrespective of the user rights of the person being observed.[269] Warhaftig is correct in writing that according to this approach, visual trespass is a type of violation of the right to privacy: "Violation of a person's privacy is a breach of his spiritual protective wall, and this constitutes an extension of the negation of his right to dignity."[270]

C. IMPOSING LIABILITY FOR RISK-CREATING BEHAVIOR: DEONTOLOGICAL AND UTILITARIAN CONSIDERATIONS

Maimonides adopted a far-reaching approach that requires deterrence on the basis of risk-creating behavior even where no actual harm was caused, in accordance with his fundamental ruling in Laws of Property Damages in the *Code*:

> [A]n animal was pasturing and entered fields and vineyards [belonging to others]. Even though it did not cause any damage, a warning should be given to its owner on three occasions. [Afterwards,] if he does not watch his animal and prevent it

---

practical ruling of Rema, *Hoshen Mishpat* 154:7: "But it is forbidden for him to stand at the window and look into the yard of his fellow in order that he not cause harm by looking, thereby transgressing the prohibition." Concerning the boundaries of the prohibition, WARHAFTIG, *ibid.* at 93, wrote that "looking is within the bounds of a negative attribute from which one should distance oneself, and even Balaam praised the Children of Israel who were careful in relation to such looking. It involves not only disturbing the other, but also detriment to the person looking – adoption of a negative attribute of curiosity as to what is happening in the domain of the other."

[267] See SEFER ME'IRAT EINAYIM, *Hoshen Mishpat* 378:4: "Looking *per se* is not trespass, but it causes damage, for example, that his fellow cannot attend to his personal needs in his courtyard due to embarrassment, or that the looking will lead to trespass." For a discussion of whether visual trespass is prohibited due to the breach of the owner's property right of usage, or because it involves the creation of real damage, see EVEN HA-EZEL, *Hilkhot Sh'khenim* 2:16; HAZON YEHEZKEL on T *Bava Batra* 1:5; KEHILLOT YAAKOV, *Bava Batra* 5; WARHAFTIG, *supra* note 254, at 87–92.

[268] WARHAFTIG, *ibid.* at 87.

[269] See EVEN HA-EZEL, *Hilkhot Sh'khenim* 2:16, explaining that the dispute between Maimonides and Ra'avad on several points in relation to visual trespass stems from the fundamental disagreement between them on the nature of visual trespass. Whereas Ra'avad is of the opinion that visual trespass constitutes a violation of the right of usage, Maimonides' approach is that looking *per se* is damaging. And see WARHAFTIG, *ibid.* at 90–91.

[270] *Ibid.*

from pasturing [in other people's fields], the owner of the field has the right to slaughter the animal in a ritually acceptable manner, and tell its owners: "Come and sell your meat." [The rationale is that] it is forbidden for a person to cause damages and then to pay for the damages he caused. Even being an [indirect] cause of damage is forbidden.[271]

Maimonides' ruling is far-reaching in that it allows a person who is liable to be harmed by the animal, "even though it did not cause any damage," to take the law into his own hands, i.e., to slaughter the animal.[272]

It is not surprising that this Maimonidean ruling aroused the opposition of several important halakhic Sages, first and foremost, Ra'avad,[273] who in his critical gloss of Maimonides' ruling wrote that not only "are these things not stated in the Talmud," but they are an innovation on the part of Maimonides, and they are subject to dispute even in principle, for "if a person has a herd of animals, one does not slaughter his whole flock unless it causes damage, [in which case] he will always be required to pay [even] when there was no warning."

We suggest that the root of the disagreement between Maimonides and Ra'avad be seen as a classic disagreement between approaches of corrective justice and those that emphasize the prevention of harm. Ra'avad's approach focuses on repairing the wrong done to the victim by the damager – a type of corrective justice approach,[274] and in any case, as long as no wrong has been done to the potential victim, no judgment should be made against the potential damager, but only "if he damages – he will always pay." Maimonides' approach, on the other hand, aspires to deterrence and focusses on efficient means of "preventing harm," similar to the approaches that are not prepared to view tort law as relying solely on corrective justice, which overly stresses the effect of tort law only in relation to the past and downplays its deterrent effect on future conduct.[275] Indeed, it is possible to view the law of slaughtering the animal as a type of regulation and setting a fine, but discernable here too is a type of "green light" for taking the law into one's own hands for fear of future damage. This ruling of Maimonides contains a type of injunction in the form of the ability to act against the potential damager, particularly by means of preventive action on the part of the potential victim, without

---

[271] Laws of Property Damages 5:1.
[272] Incidentally, in his COMMENTARY TO THE MISHNAH, *Bava Kamma* 4:9, Maimonides ruled in accordance with the view of R. Eliezer "who requires that [every ox] be slaughtered in order that the damages cease."
[273] Lived in Provence (southern region of France) in the eleventh century.
[274] Aristotelian corrective justice approaches require actual damage as a condition for the activation of tort law – unlike Maimonides, who talks about the prohibition against causing harm in cases in which no harm is caused, as we shall see at length later in the chapter. Such Aristotelian corrective justice approaches also require payment from the damager to the victim. See e.g. the principle of correlativity in Weinrib's approach, *infra*, text near note 300.
[275] Israel Gilead, *On the Complementary Approach to the Goals of Tort Law*, IZHAK ENGLARD BOOK 57 (Daphne Barak Erez & Gideon Sapir eds., 2010) (Heb.) [hereinafter: Gilead 2010].

having to involve law-enforcement authorities. For the purpose of the immediacy necessary for prevention, even the potential victim might serve here as a type of long arm of the authorities or agent of the court. If so, this is not a matter of compensation for future harm, but more like prevention and possibly regulation as stated; it is also indicative of Maimonides' approach to the prevention of harm and deterrence, which will be presented in the following chapter. In effect, according to Maimonides' approach, the damager – who in our case is the owner of the animal and also the effective damage avoider – can be prevented from persisting in the activity that is liable to cause damage to another, even if he has not yet actually caused such harm, on condition that it transpires that the owner of the animal is a serially negligent person who has not taken serious measures to guard his animal, despite having been warned three times in prior cases in which he did not watch his animal to ensure that it did not enter private lands.

According to Maimonides, the same preventive outcome is required both from a utilitarian point of view – prevention of future damage and incentive to the damager to reduce the level of his risk-creating activity (here, through concern that potential victims will slaughter his animal),[276] and in relation to shaping a person's qualities; these are deontological considerations, and therefore he also mentions there the prohibition against causing damage, which we dealt with in the previous part. However, here it should be pointed out that introducing Maimonides' deontological consideration (the prohibition against causing damage) as a basis for liability for risk-creating behavior may possibly create an alternative basis for liability; this reflects the understanding of Israel Gilead, whereby a main aspect of tort law is its future effect and not only its effect on the past, and its forward-looking activity also has a moral aspect. According to Gilead

> [i]t is indeed common to connect the concept of 'deterrence' with that of efficiency and to concentrate on optimal deterrence, but this is a mistaken conception. Tortious deterrence originally is also deterrence based on the foundations of justice, deterrence from behavior that is unjust.[277]

Indeed, it would appear that according to Maimonides, the law should deter against risk-creating behavior not only for reasons of efficiency but also out of a deontological consideration – the prohibition against causing damage to one's fellow. At the same time, Maimonides apparently believed that the prohibition against causing damage serves also as a social tool that promotes socially efficient behavior, i.e., that the ramifications of the prohibition against causing damage do

---

[276] As in the famous example of lowering the level of activity of the trains in order to prevent the scorching of agricultural fields from the sparks produced by the friction of the train on the track. *See, e.g.,* Richard A. Posner, *Strict Liability: A Comment*, 2 J. LEG. STUD. 205 (1973); Guido Calabresi & Jon T. Hirschoff, *Toward a Test of Strict Liability in Torts*, 81 YALE L.J. 1055 (1972).

[277] Gilead 2010, *supra* note 275, at 74.

not affect only the religious-deontological dimension but the utilitarian one as well. This emerges clearly from Maimonides' incisive explanation of the difference between Jewish law and Gentile law in relation to obligating a person with respect to damages that his animal caused, which also affects the level of compensation that the owner of a *tam* (innocent) ox that gored must pay. Maimonides explains that the reason that a Gentile owner of an ox that gores always pays full compensation, whether the ox is *tam* or *mu'ad* (forewarned), whereas an Israelite owner of a *tam* ox that gores does not pay full compensation but only half, lies in the difference between Gentile law and Jewish law: "The Gentiles do not hold a person liable for his animal that caused damage" (Maimonides is apparently referring to Islamic law of his day).[278] "Jewish law, on the other hand, not only holds a person liable for the damages caused by his animal, but also prohibits the causing of damage." Maimonides explains the reason for obligating Gentiles to pay full compensation for damages caused by their animals:

> When the ox of a Gentile gores the ox of an Israelite, whether it is *tam* or *mu'ad*, [the owner] pays full compensation. This is a fine for the Gentiles, since they are not careful in their observance of commandments and they do not remove harm, and if we were not to obligate them to pay for the damage done by their animal, they would not watch over it, and would cause people to incur monetary loss.[279]

Thus, according to Maimonides, careful observance of commandments – he is referring primarily to being careful not to cause damage, which is prohibited under the laws of Israel – makes a decisive contribution to the prevention of harm and to the welfare of society and public policy. Therefore, in relation to the Gentile legal systems that do not include a prohibition on causing damage in general and on damages caused by an animal in particular, optimal deterrence must be created vis-à-vis the owner of the animal (full compensation), since "if we were not to obligate them to pay for the damage done by their animal, they would not watch over it, and would cause people to incur monetary loss." It is evident that the prohibitive element in Jewish law is of significance also with respect to the lower level of deterrence in relation to the owner of a *tam* animal that gored – payment of half-damages only – since in a society that observes the biblical commandments, the owners of animals are careful with respect to causing damage, and watch over their animals so that they should not cause damage, and there is thus no need to impose fines on them. Clearly, this is something that could change according to time and place, but that ruling was produced on the basis of a particular reality in which Gentiles did take less care of their animals, and greater deterrence was needed for them.

---

[278] As explained *infra*, text near note 280.
[279] Laws of Property Damages 8:5.

At this point we must note that Maimonides' words (Laws of Property Damages 8:5) are almost certainly based on information that he received about the Islamic law that governed a person's liability for damages caused by his animal.[280] From a draft of Maimonides' manuscript for this ruling it emerges that he amended what he had written in relation to the laws applying to Gentiles, which most likely attests to the fact that he made enquiries about the precise Islamic law pertaining in Egypt, and formulated his ruling accordingly.

Imposing liability for risk-creating behavior is also indicated in the ruling that allows a person to slaughter animals if they cause damage, even if they are being raised by humans. Maimonides rules as follows: "A vicious cat that kills infants may not be kept, and the laws of robbery and of returning lost property do not apply to it, in spite of the fact that its pelt is of some value. If one finds it, he acquires title to it, and when he has killed it the pelt is his."[281]

This far-reaching approach in relation to killing animals that may cause damage emerges from Maimonides' *Commentary to the Mishnah*, in which the different opinions of the Sages concerning the level at which the owner of an ox must watch over his animal to ensure that it does not cause damage are cited. Whereas in the *Code* Maimonides rules in accordance with R. Judah,[282] who requires only a lower level of watching in order to exempt the watchman from liability, in his *Commentary to the Mishnah* he rules that "the law is in accordance with R. Eliezer who requires its slaughter so that the damage ceases."[283]

A similar line of thought is evident in one of Maimonides' *responsa* in which he issues a practical ruling on a question he was asked concerning a very large, tall palm tree that stood in a person's yard and was leaning into the public domain.[284] There was concern that when a strong wind blew in the winter, the palm tree might fall, or its fruits might fall and injure passers-by. Maimonides answers unequivocally that the tree must be uprooted "lest it causes harm." Thus, Maimonides does not wait until the harm is actually caused in order to uproot the tree: he is true to his approach that even the possibility that harm will be caused is sufficient to order the removal of the potentially damaging element.

---

[280] As in R. Rabinovitch's reasonable suggestion in YAD PESHUTAH – LAWS OF PROPERTY DAMAGES 8:5, who in the name of Prof. Moshe Sharon reviewed the accepted position of important streams in Islamic law which exempt the owners of animals for damages caused by the animals. For a summary of the Islamic approaches, see IBN RUSHAD, BIDAYAT AL-MUJTAHID vol. 2 391 (Irman Nyazee & M. A. Rauf trans., Garnet Publishing Ltd., 1996).

[281] Laws of Robbery and Lost Property 15:17.

[282] Laws of Property Damages 7:1: "If one ties up his ox with a halter and shuts it in securely, and it gets out and causes damage, the rule is as follows: If the ox is innocuous, the owner must pay for half of the damage, but if it is forewarned, he is exempt. For Scripture says, *And he has not kept it in* (Exodus 21:29), from which it is inferred that if he does guard it, he is exempt, and this ox was guarded."

[283] COMMENTARY TO MISHNAH *Bava Kamma* 4:9.

[284] RESP. RAMBAM, (Freiman edition) 340.

In sum, in this section we have seen that Maimonides may certainly be characterized as expounding an approach which combines utilitarian considerations of prevention of harm together with deontological-moral considerations which also typify his tort theory.[285]

It will be noted that both in law and economics approaches and other approaches in contemporary theories of tort law, the issue of future harms, i.e., the liability of risk creators who have not yet caused harm but may do so in the future, is still in the gestational period, and the debate is raging. Indeed, some ask: if the purpose of tort law is deterrence, why should this deterrence not be implemented on the basis of risk-creating behavior, rather than on the basis of causing actual damage?[286] The literature contains discussion of several issues concerning future harms, including: the difficulty in locating risk-creating behaviors that have not yet caused damage; the difficulty in assessing the extent of the risk that is created by those behaviors; the problem of imposing liability and awarding damages in the framework of a system in which the calculations are usually based on the outcome (actual harm) and not the risk; and the concern about over-deterrence.[287] The discussion amongst scholars of tort law is now at its liveliest, and some scholars are of the opinion, for various reasons, that pure risk can be regarded as a type of damage, even if only in certain circumstances,[288] but we will not elaborate here.

D. A COMPARATIVE LOOK: BETWEEN MAIMONIDES AND CONTEMPORARY TORT THEORY

1 Theories of Corrective Justice: From Aristotle to Contemporary Scholars

Corrective justice focuses on correcting the wrong done by a particular tortfeasor to a particular victim. According to Aristotle, the examination is limited solely to the relations between the two parties:

---

[285] And *cf.* IZHAK ENGLARD, THE PHILOSOPHY OF TORT LAW 43 (1993) [hereinafter: ENGLARD 1993], according to whom the deterrent capacity of tort law is limited, and the deterrence that stems from societal and penal norms must also be considered. This seems to be consistent with Maimonides' view on observing the commandments as a societal norm that contributes to deterrence.

[286] ISRAEL GILEAD, TORT LAW – THE BOUNDARIES OF LIABILITY, vol. 1, 431 (2012) (Heb.).

[287] *See* references cited by GILEAD, *ibid.*

[288] *See, e.g.*: Christopher H. Schroeder, *Corrective Justice and Liability for Increasing Risks*, 37 UCLA L. REV. 439, 450–55 (1990); John C.P. Goldberg & Benjamin Zipursky, *Unrealized Torts*, 88 VA. L. REV. 1626, 1652 (2002); Claire Finkelstein, *Is Risk a Harm?* 151 U. PA. L. REV. 963, 970–74 (2003); Matthew D. Adler, *Risk, Death and Harm: The Normative Foundations of Risk Regulation*, 87 MINN. L. REV. 1293 (2003); Ariel Porat & Alex Stein, *Liability for Future Harm*, in PERSPECTIVES ON CAUSATION 229 (Hart Publishing, Richard S. Goldberg ed., 2010); Benjamin Shmueli, *I'm Not Half the Man I Used to Be: Exposure to Risk without Bodily Harm in Anglo-American and Israeli Law*, 27 EMORY INT'L L. REV. 987 (2013).

In Aristotle's account of corrective justice, quantitative equality pairs one party with another. Corrective justice treats the defendant's unjust gain as correlative to the plaintiff's unjust loss. The disturbance of the equality connects two, and only two, persons. The injustice that corrective justice corrects is essentially bipolar.[289]

Aristotle based corrective justice on the principle of equality[290] in holding that the wrongful act upsets the equality that exists in people's dealings with each other, even if people are not equal in their means or their morality. Restoring the *status quo ante* repairs the wrong by restoring equality.[291]

From the time of Aristotle until today, various scholars have offered different approaches to corrective justice and have attempted to interpret Aristotle in different ways. Some have agreed with the linking of distributive principles to corrective justice (each with a different view of the relationship between corrective and distributive justice, and the degree of dominance of each of these vis-à-vis the other), and some have advocated total separation. Izhak Englard lists many such approaches in his book.[292] He himself supports the combination of corrective justice with distributive justice, with a preference for the former, by way of a doctrine that he calls "complementarity."[293]

Corrective justice has been perceived since the 1970s as opposed, albeit only sometimes, to law and economics, which is based on optimal deterrence. Initially, it

---

[289] Ernest J. Weinrib, *Corrective Justice*, 77 IOWA L. REV. 403, 410 (1992).
[290] ARISTOTLE, NICOMACHEAN ETHICS, vol. 4. And *see*: ERNEST J. WEINRIB, CORRECTIVE JUSTICE 16 (2012); ERNEST J. WEINRIB, THE IDEA OF PRIVATE LAW 60–61 (1995).
[291] For a discussion on equality in Aristotelian corrective justice, *see* WEINRIB, THE IDEA OF PRIVATE LAW, *ibid*. at 76–80.
[292] For Aquinas's approach and understanding of Aristotle on the said matter, *see* IZHAK ENGLARD, CORRECTIVE AND DISTRIBUTIVE JUSTICE (2009) [hereinafter: ENGLARD 2009], at 12–22. In the Chapter 2 of this work, Englard discusses the approaches of early medieval scholars (from the thirteenth century) that distinguish between the two objectives. In Chapter 3, Englard discusses scholars from a later period (fifteenth century onwards), some of whom continue in the path of Aquinas, whereas some see a possible combination between distributive justice and corrective justice, or the possibility of cases in which the same act is a violation of both distributive and corrective justice. In Chapter 6, Englard discusses the approaches of more modern scholars, from the age of post scholasticism, who also expressed different views on the subject, some criticizing medieval scholars and some even criticizing Aristotle – which was common in the period of the Enlightenment; some emphasizing the division between two types of justice, some seeing a possibility of a combination between them, and some holding that there are additional types of justice. In Chapter 7, he discusses various modern approaches to corrective justice vis-à-vis distributive justice. These approaches include that of Kant, who talks about an additional type of justice – protective justice (*ibid.* at 180). Englard even discusses the approach of Richard Posner, one of the founding fathers of the law and economics school, who regards his view as comporting with that of corrective justice. *See ibid.* at 193–95.
[293] For a discussion of corrective vs. distributive justice, see ENGLARD 2009, *supra* note 292, *passim* (in which corrective justice is understood as "commutative justice"). For elaboration of Englard's complementarian approach, which in fact combines the two objectives, with corrective justice carrying greater weight (ENGLARD 1993, *supra* note 285) see *infra*, Chapter 8. For other approaches, according to which distributive justice is superior or primary, *see* ENGLARD 2009, *ibid*, at 198–99, 201.

was George Fletcher and Richard Epstein who presented their approaches to corrective justice while criticizing the economic, instrumentalist approach conceived at the beginning of its days mainly by Guido Calabresi and Richard Posner, and later Ernest Weinrib, Jules Coleman others.[294] We will discuss these and other approaches in this section, although not necessarily in the chronological order of the advent of the particular approach; we will subsequently examine the compatibility of these approaches with that of Maimonides.

Undoubtedly, the most prominent contemporary theoretician in the area of corrective justice in general, and as a follower of Aristotle in particular, is Ernest J. Weinrib, who asserts that corrective justice is the sole legitimate goal of tort law. Weinrib advocates confining the examination of whether tort liability should be imposed solely to the relations between the two concrete parties – the tortfeasor and the injured party – and disregarding any consideration extraneous to those parties.[295] He insists on the "immediate normative connection between what the defendant has done and what the plaintiff has suffered" in negligence law.[296] Weinrib explains the bipolarity of corrective justice:

> Presenting corrective justice as a quantitative equality captures the basic feature of private law: a particular plaintiff sues a particular defendant. Unjust gain and loss are not mutually independent changes in the parties' holdings; if they were, the loss and the gain could be restored by two independent operations. But because the plaintiff has lost what the defendant has gained, a single liability links the particular person who gained to the particular person who lost. [...] The bipolarity of corrective justice also fashions the remedy, that is, the rectification, that corrective justice accomplishes. The rectification responds to – indeed corresponds to – the injustice that is being rectified. Because the defendant has realized a gain correlative to the plaintiff's loss, the correction entails a loss to the defendant that is simultaneously a correlative gain to the plaintiff. In this way the rectification reverses the unjust act by undoing the excess and the deficiency that constitute the injustice.[297]

Weinrib explains the correlative idea of corrective justice thus:

> Tort liability reflects corrective justice in the following respects. First, to recover in tort, the plaintiff's injury must be to something, such as personal integrity or a

---

[294] For a discussion on these approaches see ENGLARD 2009, *supra* note 292, at 186–208.

[295] WEINRIB, CORRECTIVE JUSTICE, *supra* note 290, at 56; WEINRIB, THE IDEA OF PRIVATE LAW, *supra* note 290, at 56–83; Ernest J. Weinrib, *The Gains and Losses of Corrective Justice*, 44 DUKE L. J. 277 (1995); Weinrib, *Corrective Justice*, *supra* note 289; Ernest J. Weinrib, *Correlativity, Personality, and the Emerging Consensus on Corrective Justice*, 2 THEORETICAL INQ. L. 107 (2001); Ernest J. Weinrib, *Corrective Justice in a Nutshell*, 52 U. OF TORONTO L. J. 349 (2002). And see ENGLARD 2009, *supra* note 292, at 191–93, 196–97 (discussing Weinrib's approach).

[296] Ernest J. Weinrib, *Causation and Wrongdoing*, 63 CHI. KENT L. REV. 407, 409 (1987).

[297] WEINRIB, THE IDEA OF PRIVATE LAW, *supra* note 290, at 63, 65.

proprietary entitlement, that ranks as the embodiment of a right. It is therefore not sufficient that the plaintiff has suffered the merely factual loss of being made worse off or of being deprived of a prospective advantage. Second, the defendant must have committed an act that violates a duty incumbent on the defendant and thus can be regarded as an act of wrongdoing. Accordingly, the modern common law emphasizes the importance of fault, since the defendant is duty-bound not to perform the intentional or negligent acts that constitute faulty conduct. Third, the duty breached by the defendant must be with respect to the embodiment of the right whose infringement is the ground of the plaintiff's cause of action. (…) [references omitted].[298]

And in fact, gain and loss are derivatives of the right of the plaintiff who suffered injury and of the obligation of the defendant not to cause injury, which was violated by the tortious act:

> On the commission of a tort, the plaintiff suffers a normative loss, and the defendant realizes a correlative normative gain. The plaintiff's normative loss consists in the shortfall from what the plaintiff is entitled to under the norm that the defendant's action violated. Conversely, the defendant's normative gain consists in the excess in the defendant's holdings, given the defendant's violation of the norm that the duty signifies. Since the norm underlying both the gain and the loss consists in the defendant's being under a duty not to infringe the plaintiff's right, the normative gain and the normative loss are correlative to each other. Consequently, the defendant's liability to the plaintiff rectifies both the normative gain and the normative loss in a single bipolar operation.[299]

He summarizes the correlative principle of corrective justice thus:

> Correlativity locks the plaintiff and defendant into a reciprocal normative embrace, in which factors such as deterrence and compensation, whose justificatory force applies solely to one of the parties, play no role. The only pertinent justificatory considerations are those that articulate the correlational nature of right and duty. Moreover, correlativity highlights the moral reason for singling out the defendant for liability. Because the actor's breach of duty infringes the sufferer's right, liability reflects the defendant's commission of an injustice. Liability is therefore not the retrospective pricing or licensing or taxing of a permissible act. Nor is the defendant singled out as a convenient conduit to an accessible insurance pool that might spread the overall cost of harm. Conversely, correlativity also indicates why the plaintiff in particular is entitled to recover. The defendant violates a normative bond not with the world at large but specifically with the person to whom the defendant owed the duty. In bringing an action, the plaintiff does not step forward as the

---

[298] *Ibid.* at 134. For correlativity *see also* WEINRIB, CORRECTIVE JUSTICE, *supra* note 290, at 9–37.
[299] WEINRIB, THE IDEA OF PRIVATE LAW, *supra* note 290, at 136. One situation of restoring the defendant's gain (even if he was passive in the causing of the damage) is that "where the enrichment is the consequence of a wrongful act, the right and the duty that define the wrongfulness are the basis of the plaintiff's claim to the defendant's enrichment" (*ibid.* at 141).

representative of the public interest in economic efficiency or in any other condition of general welfare. The plaintiff sues literally in his or her own right as the victim of the defendant's unjust act. Consequently, by linking a particular plaintiff and a particular defendant, the remedy maintains the correlativity of right and duty. Liability transforms the victim's right to be free from wrongful suffering at the actor's hand into an entitlement to reparation that is correlative to the defendant's obligation to provide it. The remedy consists not in two independent operations – one penalizing the defendant and the other benefiting the plaintiff – but in a single operation that joins the parties as obligee and obligor. (...) Thus the various aspects of the damage remedy – that the defendant is obligated to pay, that the plaintiff is entitled to be paid, and that the same amount undoes the injustice perpetrated by the defendant and suffered by the plaintiff – constitute a single whole. (...) The plaintiff's right to be free of wrongful interferences with his or her entitlements is correlative to the defendant's duty to abstain from such interferences. (...) Conceived in this way, private law makes a coherent juridical reality out of the relationship of doer and sufferer.[300]

It seems that Weinrib perceives corrective justice, which relies on culpability and causation, as the sole legitimate goal of tort law. He explains that the law should choose one avenue of justice, because there cannot be integration between corrective and distributive justice: only corrective justice accomplishes the aims of justice.[301]

---

[300] WEINRIB, THE IDEA OF PRIVATE LAW, *supra* note 290, at 142–44.
[301] *See* WEINRIB, CORRECTIVE JUSTICE, *supra* note 290, at 72–75. *See also*: Ernest J. Weinrib, *Correlativity, Personality, and the Emerging Consensus on Corrective Justice*, *supra* note 54, at 108 (2001) (addressing the centrality of corrective justice); WEINRIB, CORRECTIVE JUSTICE, *ibid.* at 61–62 (discussing corrective and distributive justice). According to Weinrib, "[t]he idea of equality allows Aristotle to describe justice in holdings as mathematical operations. Justice functions for holdings as equality functions for mathematical terms. In mathematics, equality relates one term to another through an equal sign. The specific arrangement of the terms on either side of an equal sign, however, depends on the mathematical operation being performed. Just as different mathematical operations link various elements in different ways, so justice in holdings has different ways of ordering the relations among persons. Aristotle calls these different modes of ordering the 'forms' of justice. Justice in holdings assumes two contrasting forms: distributive justice and corrective justice. Each of these forms regulates holdings through a different mathematical operation. Injustice consists in having more or less than the equal allotment due under one or the other of these mathematical operations. In introducing the two forms of justice, Aristotle remarks that distributive justice occurs 'in distributions' and corrective justice occurs 'in transactions.' 'Distributions' and 'transactions' are general terms that refer to all the particular manifestations of the two forms of justice. A transaction is an interaction regulated in conformity to corrective justice. Similarly, a distribution is an arrangement that has the structure of distributive justice. Distributive and corrective justice are 'in' distributions and transactions as the modes of ordering implicit in these arrangements. Distributive justice divides a benefit or burden in accordance with some criterion. An exercise of distributive justice consists of three elements: the benefit or burden being distributed, the persons among whom it is distributed, and the criterion according to which it is distributed. The criterion determines the parties' comparative merit for a particular distribution. The greater a particular party's merit under the criterion of distribution, the larger the party's share in the thing being distributed. Thus distributive justice corresponds to a mathematical operation in which a series of equal ratios align comparative shares with

The principle of correlativity is primary in Weinrib's theory: the tortfeasor alone must pay the whole sum of damages to the injured party only: no less and no more.[302]

According to England, Weinrib's approach builds to a certain extent on George Fletcher's approach of reciprocal and nonreciprocal risks,[303] and on his view that

> comparative merit. [...] Distributive justice, in other words, consists in an equality of ratios. In contrast, corrective justice features an equality of quantities. It focuses on a quantity that represents what rightfully belongs to one party but is now wrongly possessed by another party and therefore must be shifted back to its rightful owner. Corrective justice embraces quantitative equality in two ways. First, because one party has what belongs to the other party, the actor's gain is equal to the victim's loss. Second, what the parties would have held had the wrong not occurred provides the baseline from which the gain and the loss are computed. That baseline, accordingly, functions as the mean of equality for this form of justice. Of course this equality is a notional one. Equality consists in persons' having what belongs to them. The parties do not have the same quantity of holdings, but they are equal as the owners of whatever they do have. This equality is a mean because the parties have neither more nor less than what is theirs. These two aspects of quantitative equality are interconnected. The quantitative equality of gain and loss is the basis for the simultaneous annulment of both in corrective justice. There would be no point, however, in concentrating on this quantitative equality unless the annulment vindicated equality in some sense. For if the initial sets of holdings embodied only an inequality, the subsequent gain by one party at the expense of another, to the extent that it mitigated the initial inequality, would itself be just. Thus attention to the equality of gain and loss in corrective justice presupposes the notional equality of initial holdings, and the annulment of those gains and losses affirms that initial equality. A violation of corrective justice involves one party's gain at the other's expense. As compared with the mean of initial equality, the actor now has too much and the victim too little. Because the actor has gained what the victim has lost, equality is not restored merely by removing the actor's gain (which would still leave the victim with a shortfall) or by restoring the victim's loss (which would still leave the actor with an excess). Rather, corrective justice requires the actor to restore to the victim the amount representing the actor's self-enrichment at the victim's expense.'" *Ibid.* at 61–63 (references omitted).

[302] Weinrib, *Correlativity, Personality, and the Emerging Consensus on Corrective Justice*, supra note 54; WEINRIB, THE IDEA OF PRIVATE LAW, *supra* note 290, at 75, 114–44. See, e.g., ibid. at 116, 119–20 ("The logic of correlativity requires that what is predicated of one element in the pairing be also predicated of the other. Accordingly, the gains and losses must be of the same kind. (...) The correlative gain and loss of corrective justice does not point to a factual loss and a corresponding factual gain. What matters is whether the transaction can be regarded as yielding a normative surplus for the defendant and a normative deficit for the plaintiff. Therefore, liability for a deterioration in the condition of the plaintiff's holdings is predicated not on some parallel improvement in the condition of the defendant's but on the defendant's having unjustly inflicted that loss. Similarly, the plaintiff recovers the defendant's gain not when the plaintiff has suffered merely a factual loss but when the defendant's enrichment represents an injustice to the plaintiff").

[303] George P. Fletcher, *Fairness and Utility in Tort Theory*, 85 HARV. L. REV. 537 (1972). Fletcher states that the use of the tort law system in order to attain social aims creates an inappropriate mixture between corrective justice and distributive justice. Fletcher himself takes corrective justice as a derivative of examining the risk that every party may cause to the other party. In his opinion, in every liability regime (negligence, strict liability, and intentional torts) one should examine the reciprocal risks that the parties create. If the risks are reciprocal or relatively equal, then the defendant should not be held liable if he caused the damage, and each party will bear his/her own harms. But if the wrongdoer put the plaintiff at risk in a nonreciprocal and unilateral way, and the plaintiff was harmed, then the defendant should be held liable. Reciprocal risk exists where from the beginning, the defendant's activity puts the plaintiff at

coexistence between distributive justice and corrective justice is impossible: they are fundamentally separate, particularly in their understanding of the standard of reasonableness in negligence.[304] Indeed, Weinrib objects vehemently to the pluralistic approach that injects distributive considerations into corrective justice, which is based on equality:

> Because corrective and distributive justice are the categorically different and mutually irreducible patterns of justificatory coherence, it follows that a single external relationship cannot coherently partake of both. Aristotle's contrast of corrective and distributive justice does not determine whether the law should treat an incident correctively or distributively. But if the law is to be coherent, any given relationship cannot rest on a combination of corrective and distributive justification. When a corrective justification is mixed with a distributive one, each necessarily undermines the justificatory force of the other, and the relationship cannot manifest either unifying structure [...] The problem with combining corrective and distributive justice within a single relationship is that distributive justice splits asunder what corrective justice joins together. Corrective justice involves the intrinsic unity of the doer and the sufferer of the same harm. A distributive criterion disassembles this unity by selecting a feature morally relevant to only one of the parties to the transaction.[305]

The later approach of Jules Coleman, too, espouses correlativity, but here the requirement of correlativity is relatively broad, and includes, for example, vicarious liability, causation, and the ability to prevent the damage.[306] He proposes a mixed conception of corrective justice according to which the parties have a duty to repay the tortious damages for which they are responsible, as a moral basis for liability and compensation, and in this his later approach is closer to that of Weinrib.[307] In fact, Coleman, in dealing with risks and wrongs, argues that the parties have a duty to repair the harms their torts have created as a moral basis for liability, and hence for compensation.[308] According to Coleman, the heart of corrective justice lies in that

---

risk more than the opposite activity, or when from the beginning the risks are nonreciprocal, but become reciprocal due to the negligence of the defendant.

[304] ENGLARD 1993, *supra* note 285, at 12, 24.

[305] WEINRIB, THE IDEA OF PRIVATE LAW, *supra* note 290, at 73, 75.

[306] Jules Coleman, *The Practice of Corrective Justice*, in PHILOSOPHICAL FOUNDATIONS OF TORT LAW 53 (David G. Owen ed., 1995).

[307] See Gary T. Schwartz, *Mixed Theories of Tort Law: Affirming Both Deterrence and Corrective Justice*, 75 TEX. L. REV. 1801, 1807 (1997). See also Christopher J. Robinette, *Can There Be a Unified Theory of Torts? A Pluralist Suggestion from History and Doctrine*, 43 BRANDEIS L.J. 369, 387–88 (2005).

[308] JULES L. COLEMAN, RISKS AND WRONGS (1992). In the past (he has since changed his approach), Coleman regarded distributive justice and *restitutio ad integrum* as arithmetical concepts of gain versus loss. In other words, in his view the loss caused to the injured party (by negligence, recklessness or intentionally by the action of the injurer) must be equivalent in amount to the gain attained by the injurer, and repairing the harm means negating the loss and the gain. See Jules Coleman, *Corrective Justice and Wrongful Gain*, 11 J. OF LEG. STUDIES 421

"individuals who are responsible for the wrongful losses of others have a duty to repair the losses."[309]

Richard Epstein offers a theory of strict liability which is not based on culpability but on causation.[310] According to this theory, the moral justification for imposing liability on the damager is the very fact that he harmed the victim, even if there is no culpability in his actions. In other words, causation alone is a sufficient basis for liability in torts – the damager harmed the victim even if he was not negligent in his deeds.[311] Epstein's conception of corrective justice in fact is based on the moral element of fairness: "You caused it, you are liable."[312]

(1982); Jules Coleman, *Tort Law and the Demands of Corrective Justice*, 67 IND. L. J. 349 (1992). As stated, Coleman himself abandoned his approach to a certain extent, particularly following Perry's critique: Stephen R. Perry, *Comment on Coleman: Corrective Justice*, 67 IND. L. J. 381 (1992). In other words, the harm which has its source in the tort must be repaired, without causing tortious gains. Accordingly, Coleman does not see that the goal of corrective justice is applied in the context of road accidents (under the US regime of negligence), since the tortfeasor has no gain from the accident, and compensation in this context means only the transfer of wealth from the defendant to the plaintiff. At the same time, it would seem that the Aristotelian corrective justice, upon which Coleman wished to rely, can and must – so it seems – be understood as repairing the situation of the injured party, even if this leads to a change for the worse in the situation of the injurer. But it must be noted that Coleman did not call to refrain from imposing liability in cases in which the gain was not equivalent to the loss. He only suggested in such cases not to base liability (even if only with respect to the difference between the injurer's gain and the injured party's loss) on corrective justice, but rather on distributive justice, in line with the Aristotelian doctrine according to which whenever tortious liability is established, at least one of the two objectives – distributive justice and corrective justice – must be applied. Coleman himself, as we said, changed his position, particularly in light of the fact that his previous explanation did not serve as an incentive for any kind of action to prevent harm. See Jules Coleman, THE MIXED CONCEPTION OF CORRECTIVE JUSTICE, 77 IOWA L. REV. 427, 432 (1992). According to his new approach, since 1992, corrective justice does not necessarily aspire to cover losses, but emphasizes the rights of the individual and the responsibility of individuals to each other, such that the focus is on repairing the wrong. *Ibid.* at 435.

[309] Jules Coleman, *Tort Law and Tort Theory: Preliminary Reflections on Method*, in GERALD J. POSTEMA (ED.), PHILOSOPHY AND THE LAW OF TORTS 183, 184 (2001).

[310] RICHARD A. EPSTEIN, A THEORY OF STRICT LIABILITY (1980); Richard A. Epstein, *Intentional Harms*, 4 J. LEG. STUDIES 391 (1975); Richard A. Epstein, A *Theory of Strict Liability*, 2 J. LEG. STUDIES 151 (1973).

[311] Epstein's causation requirement is different and special. It is not the "but for" criterion, which is the normal factual causation criterion in tort law, but causation that is closer to normal, non-legal language. As such, his approach is based on strict liability combined with "strong" causal connection, And *cf.* Richard W. Wright, *Causation in Tort Law*, 73 CAL. L. REV. 1737, 1827 (1985).

("[T]he concept of corrective justice embodied in the tortious-aspect causation requirement clearly continues to control the decision of actual tort cases. Despite more than a half-century of academic assaults on the causation requirement, the courts almost invariably reach results that are consistent with it. The requirement and the underlying concept of corrective justice exert a very strong normative pull, even when judges do not articulate that pull but rather couch their decisions in the currently fashionable language of loss-spreading and wealth-maximization.")

[312] KENNETH S. ABRAHAM, THE FORMS AND FUNCTIONS OF TORT LAW 166–67 (3rd ed., 2007).

Corrective justice is perceived by Glanville Williams as an expression of a moral principle. In his view on this point, as opposed to Epstein but similar to Weinrib and Coleman who came later, justice in tort law relies on culpability/fault. But he in fact splits justice into two:[313] (a) ethical retribution, which concentrates on the damager and on it being necessary that he – as opposed to anyone else – repair the evil that he caused; (b) ethical compensation, which concentrates on the victim, and on it being necessary that he receive compensation as a benefit. Ethical compensation also attests to the fact that the plaintiff was indeed injured and must be afforded relief. The source of justice lies in fairness and decency/rightness.[314] Weinrib believes that regarding the compensation as being derived from justice constitutes an educational principle both for the damager and for others, and through this means, tort law serves as an instrument for suppressing anti-social elements, thus contributing to the elevation of the common good in society.[315]

Other scholars at various times have examined corrective justice through the eyes of punishment and retribution.[316] On this view, the aim of tort law, too, is to punish in the sense of retribution, for example, by denying the damager some benefit. This of course is different from the rationale of repairing the evil, and the focus is primarily on the damager and not on a correlative conception. We will address this issue of punitive damages, which is of course central in this context, as well as the question of whether their aim is indeed to punish the damager for a deliberate action, in the next chapter. A retributive-punitive approach also led to the formulation of the principle *ex turpi causa non oritor actio*.[317] At the same time, clearly not every punitive approach is also retributive, and sometimes the goal of punishment is revenge or a future change in behavior, in which case it is not a matter of pure retribution.[318] Moreover, not all retribution ultimately compensates, and of course, there is no consensus as to whether the tort mechanism is a suitable one for achieving a retributive goal by way of compensation.[319]

---

[313] Glanville L. Williams, *The Aims of the Law of Tort*, 4 CURRENT LEGAL PROBS. 137, 141–42 (1951).
[314] Williams, *ibid.* at 142. And see ENGLARD 2009, *supra* note 292 (discussing the relations between retribution and corrective justice).
[315] Williams, *supra* note 313, at 143.
[316] See ENGLARD 2009, *supra* note 292, who throughout his book reviews the approaches of scholars from different periods. See also GILEAD, *supra* note 286, at 220–23, and the references there.
[317] GILEAD, *ibid.* at 222; Ronen Perry, *The Role of Retributive Justice in the Common Law of Torts: A Descriptive Theory*, 73 TENN. L. REV. 177, 206–23 (2006).
[318] GILEAD, *ibid.*
[319] For discussion see GILEAD, *ibid.* at 223. For the main features of the different approaches, see JAMES GRIFFIN, WELL-BEING, ITS MEANING, MEASUREMENT AND MORAL IMPORTANCE 275, 282–83 (1986). Amongst the exponents of the retributive approach in torts, see Jeremy Waldron, *Moments of Carelessness and Massive Loss*, in PHILOSOPHICAL FOUNDATIONS OF TORT LAW 387, 389–91 (David G. Owen ed., 1995); GILEAD, *ibid.* at 224; COLEMAN, RISKS AND WRONGS, *supra* note 308, at 220–26.

There are also communitarian approaches, which are even further removed from Aristotelian corrective justice. Scholars explain that the common good is in fact the good of the individuals who comprise the collective, and the conception of society in this context is – unlike corrective justice – instrumentalist: society serves as an instrument for creating the frameworks, the arrangements and the institutions that will increase the welfare of individuals.[320] In this context, communitarian concepts highlight the welfare of the whole and social interests more than Weinribian approaches of corrective justice do.[321] Such communitarian approaches do not take into consideration only the personal choice of a person, but also the fact of his membership in the society in which he lives.[322]

Various examples of this may be found. We will focus on the tortious context, and on society's demand that the individual sometimes waive his personal welfare and personal liberty – albeit only partially – in order to promote the welfare of the whole, even though it is not that individual who is in fact causing damage: this demand entails the various consequences of applying utilitarian approaches, but also liberal/libertine ones. Indeed, according to the communitarian approach, liability in torts may be incurred in situations in which the risk to which the victim was exposed and which actualized was not created by the plaintiff but by a third party. In such situations, the victim may claim, according to the communitarian approach, that although it was not the defendant who created the risk, he ought to have acted to neutralize or prevent it. Owing to the importance of mutual help and solidarity for a robust society, a communitarian approach will be more prone to impose liability for omissions than the liberal and libertine approaches, which would limit insofar as possible duties that arise from omissions, due to their encroachment on freedom of action and the self-realization of the individual.[323]

Another approach, which may be a variation on the communitarian conceptions, is expounded by Kenneth Abraham. Abraham explains that there are those who perceive corrective justice as a derivate of community standards.[324] According to this perspective, one must determine what are the standards of a particular community, whether by tracing its traditional customs or by an ex post determination of the jurors deciding a tort action – who belong to that community – as to whether the act

---

[320] John Rawls, *Social Utility and Primary Goods*, in UTILITARIANISM AND BEYOND 159, 172 (Amartya Sen & Bernard Williams eds., 1982); JOHN FINNIS, NATURAL LAW AND NATURAL RIGHTS 305 (1980). For discussion, *see* GILEAD, *supra* note 286, at 171–72.

[321] For a review of communitarianism, *see* WILL KYMLICKA, CONTEMPORARY POLITICAL PHILOSOPHY 208–72 (2nd ed. 2002).

[322] *See* the discussion in GILEAD, *supra* note 286, at 173. And *see* the following principal sources: MICHAEL SANDEL, LIBERALISM AND THE LIMITS OF JUSTICE 55–59, 152–154 (1982); ALISDAIR MACINTYRE, AFTER VIRTUE: A STUDY IN MORAL THEORY 204–05 (1981); CHARLES TAYLOR, HEGEL AND MODERN SOCIETY 157–59 (1979); WILLIAM SULLIVAN, RECONSTRUCTING THE PUBLIC PHILOSOPHY 173 (1982).

[323] *See* GILEAD, *supra* note 286, at 177.

[324] ABRAHAM, *supra* note 312.

being adjudicated meets those standards.[325] This conception would seem, naturally, to belong more to a civil legal system in which there are juries, even though judicial determination in accordance with community standards is also conceivable – a type of standard of the "reasonable member of the community," without the decision-maker having to actually belong to that typical group. As Abraham says, the purpose of corrective justice must be examined today in juxtaposition to the aim of civil redress. According to this theory, monetary payment to the victim cannot fully compensate him for the harm suffered, and neither can it fully repair the wrong: in fact, the payment does not presume *ab initio* to constitute full compensation or full repair of the wrong.[326] It is merely an expression of social recognition of the tortious act in general, and of the violated rights of the victim in particular. As such, the payment is intended to be *proportional* to the gravity of the harm, *and not necessarily equal to it*. According to Abraham, what is common to the theory of civil redress and corrective justice is the conception of tort law from the moral aspect of the relationship between the damager and the victim. The moral aspect looks at the past and tries to fix it, unlike the other aims which are based on the future effect on potential damagers, or the use of tort law for instrumentalist purposes.

Finally, John Goldberg and Benjamin Zipursky present the civil recourse approach, a type of alternative approach to corrective justice. According to the civil recourse approach, tort law is in fact a reaction to wrongs more than to losses: it offers the victims of wrongdoing a right to the implementation of private law, to recourse against the person responsible for those wrongs.[327] This obviously is not a pure corrective justice approach, in which losses are the most important element.[328]

2 Between Maimonides and Theories of Corrective Justice

Englard points out as follows:

> It is a most noteworthy fact that in the whole classic Jewish (rabbinic) literature one does not find an attempt of defining the notion of justice, neither that of law. Generally, it appears that the rabbis were considerably more interested in concrete solutions than in abstract legal concepts.[329]

---

[325] Catherine Wells, *Tort Law as Corrective Justice: A Pragmatic Justification for Jury Adjudication*, 88 MICH. L. REV. 2348 (1990) (explaining that according to Abraham, absolute liability, too, can be explained in a certain sense according to these types of standards of corrective justice).
[326] Englard, too, contends that often, imposing tortious liability does not really restore the situation to its former state: ENGLARD 2009, *supra* note 292, at 113.
[327] John C.P. Goldberg & Benjamin C. Zipursky, *Tort Law and Moral Luck*, 92 CORNELL. L. REV. 1123 (2007); Benjamin C. Zipursky & John C.P. Goldberg, *Torts as Wrongs*, 88 TEX. L. REV. 917 (2010). *And see* Emily Sherwin, *Interpreting Tort Law*, 39 FLA. ST. U. L. REV. 227 (2011) (discussing their approach).
[328] *See* Sherwin, *ibid.* at 228, and the references in footnote 4, there, to Jules Coleman, Arthur Ripstein, and Stephen Perry.
[329] ENGLARD 2009, *supra* note 292, at 111.

According to Englard, some of the Hebrew translations of Aristotle even translate the term "corrective justice" as *yosher*,[330] which means integrity or possibly, honesty.

In our opinion, Englard's statement is not accurate, and insofar as the *Guide* is concerned, in presenting the "removal of the wrongs" (or "putting an end to acts of injustice") – which is undoubtedly similar to corrective justice – as one of the two meta-aims of tort law, Maimonides was certainly interested in abstract legal concepts. We will now attempt to see how Maimonides approaches the goal that today we call corrective justice and its alternatives, and whether the different approaches presented in the former section (D.1) are more or less compatible with that of Maimonides.

(a) Between Maimonides and Weinrib

First, to the question of whether the Aristotelian-Weinribian approach is compatible with that of Maimonides.[331]

Points of similarity may be found between the doctrines. They both take into consideration both the victim and the damager, and in principle Maimonides' approach does not ignore the benefit to one party which constitutes the loss of the other.

The question is how, according to Weinrib, does the law establish a particular mechanism that has a particular rationale? How do we trace the connection between the rationale and the mechanism? Weinrib answers that indeed, Maimonides' theory is seen as compromising overarching religious categories. But he also has certain mechanisms.

One such mechanism is found in an explicit contrast between *knas* (fine) and *mammon* (monetary obligation).[332] The question is, what is the logic of the distinction between *knas* and *mammon*? The answer is that *mammon* is corrective justice, and *knas* is a legal relationship other than corrective justice.

The same distinction between *mammon* and *knas* also applies to the distinction between the laws of wounding and the laws of damaging in the *Code*. But even within the laws of damaging, *tza'ar* (humiliation, or a type of emotional harm) and *nezek* (damage, physical harm) are *knas*, and *shevet* (loss of employment) and *ripui* (payments for medical treatment) are *mammon*[333] according to Maimonides' legal analysis.

---

[330] ENGLARD 2009, *ibid.* at 113, note 496.
[331] Our thanks to Prof. Ernest Weinrib for his lengthy discussions with us on this topic, following his lecture responding to our lecture: Yuval Sinai & Benjamin Shmueli, *Maimonides' Concept of Corrective Justice*, in a workshop on THEOLOGIANS IN A JURIST'S ROBE: RELATIONS BETWEEN THEOLOGY AND LAW IN THE JUDAEO-ISLAMIC MILIEU, (University of Toronto, March 20, 2017). These discussions helped us in writing about the relationship between Maimonides' theory and that of Weinrib. Quotations from Weinrib in this section for which there is no reference have their source in Weinrib's oral response to the said lecture.
[332] Passage in the Laws of Property Damages 2:7–8.
[333] Laws of Wounding and Damaging 5:7.

Not all the examples in Maimonides are corrective justice; but those passages are liability issues and are rationalized by corrective justice.

However, we think that Maimonides' approach is also different from that of Aristotle, and Weinrib's correlative approach does not seem to comport with that of Maimonides, for even where Maimonides considers both parties to the tort, he does not always look at them both together or at the benefit of the one vis-à-vis the loss of the other. Sometimes, special regard is paid to the education of the damager, as well as his punishment and retribution for his acts, even irrespective of any damage that was caused. The amount of compensation is sometimes not equivalent to the damage due to the application of various principles in addition to corrective justice which affect the final outcome. The effect of distributive principles can be seen within the principle of restoring the situation to its prior state as well as others. The broader the spectrum of a legal phenomenon, we argue, the more pluralistic it is going to be. That applies not only to Maimonides but to Aristotle as well: he was also a pluralist, with several kinds of justice. These conclusions pertain to several issues. Let us now look at some of Maimonides' above-mentioned rulings that support this conclusion.

It is clear that Maimonides' theory is not confined to corrective justice. For example, fine (*knas*) is not corrective justice, the prohibition against cursing the deaf is not based on a conception of corrective justice. Weinrib would probably agree that Maimonides' approach to the prohibition against cursing the deaf discussed earlier (Section A.3, discussing the Book of Commandments, negative commandment 317) is educative. Maimonides' position whereby the immoral conduct of the damager must be considered – irrespective of the situation of the victim, and even if the person who was exposed to the wrongful conduct suffers no harm, such as the deaf person who did not hear the curse and was therefore not humiliated by it – distinguishes his conception of justice from the Aristotelian concept of corrective justice espoused by Weinrib and others. It seems that according to the principle of correlativity formulated by Weinrib, there is no room to prohibit cursing the deaf, for if no suffering was caused to the deaf person by the cursing, then the defendant's action cannot be defined as a tort, and in any case there is no reciprocity: even if the curser derived benefit (by blowing off steam with the curse), the deaf person has not suffered a loss. Maimonides' statement that the Torah "is concerned not only with the one who is being cursed, but with the one who is uttering the curse,"[334] too, would certainly be unacceptable to Weinrib if each side is regarded separately and not from a correlative perspective. He would certainly call to examine the situation of *both* the curser and the cursed *together*, and would allow the action only if it was proved that the defendant in fact harmed the plaintiff; the wrongful action of one of the parties, and the harm that is likely to befall the soul of the perpetrator are insufficient, if the other party is not actually harmed.

---

[334] Book of Commandments, negative commandment 317. And *see* text *supra* near note 26.

Maimonides' ruling whereby it is permitted to slaughter an animal which has entered the field of another even before it causes damage is also incompatible with the Aristotelian-Weinribian approach to corrective justice.[335] As long as no damage was caused, there is no tort which justifies taking action against the property of the owner of the animal, as stated by Ra'avad[336] who disagreed with Maimonides on this point, presenting a position that was closer to that of Aristotle/Weinrib.[337]

Another subject that Maimonides discusses that is incompatible with the Aristotelian-Weinribian approach to corrective justice concerns the level of compensation that is paid – exactly equivalent to the harm or not. Some understood Maimonides to be saying that the aim of the compensation paid for the damages caused by the property of a person is to restore the *status quo ante*.[338] Indeed, from Maimonides' statement in the *Guide* that "he who has caused damage to property shall have inflicted upon him damage to his property up to exactly the same amount,"[339] one infers that the compensation is set to be equivalent to the damage caused to the victim, similar to the Aristotelian-Weinribian approach to corrective justice in which there is equivalence between benefit and loss, and not only, for example, proportionality, as Abraham proposes.[340] Moreover, from several rulings in the Book of Torts in the *Code*, a similar picture emerges. Thus, in one place Maimonides writes:

> This is the operating principle: Whenever a person pays for the damage that he caused, it is considered a monetary obligation (*mammon*). Whenever he pays more or less – e.g., the double payment (for theft) or half the amount of damages – the amount that is greater or less than the principal is considered to be a fine (*knas*).[341]

In other words, the basis for the compensation for monetary damage is that the payment is consistent with the damage caused. However, a deeper look into compensation for monetary damage in Maimonides' rulings reveals that there is no total equivalence between the damage that was caused to the victim and the level of compensation paid by the damager. On the contrary, a careful examination of the rulings concerning the assessment of compensation for damages reveals a conception of law that differs in several details from the Aristotelian and/or Weinribian concept of corrective justice that talks about restoring the *status quo ante*.[342] Indeed, as we saw at the end of the last chapter, Maimonides often combines considerations of distributive justice with other considerations. When determining the level of

---

[335] Laws of Property Damages 5:1. And see text *supra* near note 274.
[336] See text *supra* near note 273.
[337] See text *supra* near note 274.
[338] NOVELLA OF R. HAYM SOLOVEITCHIK ON MAIMONIDES, LAWS PERTAINING TO DISPUTES 5:2 (Heb.).
[339] GUIDE 3:41.
[340] See text *supra* near note 326, discussing the proportionality principle.
[341] Laws of Property Damages 2:8.
[342] See Laws of Property Damages 7:8–13; Laws of Wounding and Damaging 7:15.

compensation, too, Maimonides does take into account considerations of distributive justice, but it is clear that removal of the wrong – corrective justice – definitely takes priority, according to Maimonides' theory as well. Let us recall also that in the *Guide*, the distributive objective was not included in the two meta-aims of tort law that Maimonides mentioned there – removal of wrong and prevention of harm. In this, the approach of those scholars who combined distributive considerations within the consideration of corrective justice is similar to that of Maimonides, and the approaches of Weinrib and Fletcher, who warned against such a combination, differ from his.

Weinrib's approach is also criticized by Ariel Porat, who is of the opinion that the array of cases that present themselves these days does not allow the interests of parties other than the two sides to the tort – the direct damager and victim – to be ignored.[343]

Introducing additional distributive considerations alongside the considerations of repairing the harm in fact answers these criticisms of Weinrib, who believes only in corrective justice.

A manifestation of the introduction of distributive considerations by Maimonides can be seen in relation to the subject of the compensation that a person pays for damages caused by his animal:

> If an animal causes damage to growing crops, the damage is estimated on the basis of a sixty-fold area, and whoever is ordered to pay (compensation), whatever owner or bailee, must pay this amount. Thus, if an animal eats an area sown with a *seah* [an ancient measure of volume equivalent to approx. 0.2 bushels] of seed, and evaluation is made of the previous value of a portion of the same field sixty times this area, and of its present value after an area of one *seah* has been despoiled, and (compensation) must be paid for the difference. Similarly, if an animal eats an area sown with a *kab* [an ancient measure of volume equivalent to approx. 0.035 bushels] or quarter-kab or even a single stalk, it is evaluated as part of sixty times its area.[344]

---

[343] Ariel Porat, *Questioning the Idea of Correlativity in Weinrib's Theory of Corrective Justice*, 2 THEORETICAL INQ. L. 161, 165–72 (2001). Also of interest are Porat's remarks at the Conference in Honor of the Retirement of Prof. Izhak Englard from the Supreme Court held at the Faculty of Law of Bar-Ilan University on 21 December 2005. Porat offers the following example: A swerves his car so as not to hit B, a child, but he hits C. A will be liable under a liability regime of negligence, since he ultimately hit C, and the harm to B that was averted has no significance. Porat suggests that in such cases, there should be some degree of consideration – even if not full – of the harm that A averted from B by turning the wheel, and not only of the harm caused to C. True, in his opinion it should not be decided definitively that A is not negligent due to the benefit that B derived from the fact that the harm was caused to C and not to him; however when A's action is assessed, some consideration should be given to the fact that his action vis-à-vis C prevented harm to B. Porat offers this example in order to explain that the implementation of Weinrib's pure corrective justice approach, based only on consideration of the two parties to the actual tort, is problematic.

[344] Laws of Property Damages 4:13.

What is the reason for this unique assessment of the damage? Some see this as part of the tendency to be lenient with the damager,[345] for "the tendency in this ruling is not to impose the full measure of the law on the damager in paying the damages. Not to be too hard on him."[346] This leniency apparently stems from the fact that he is not necessarily a well-to-do person with "deep pockets," and in Maimonides' days there was certainly no insurance. Therefore, due to considerations of distributive justice, leniency was shown to the damager in respect of the payments he was required to make.

A slightly different reason is suggested by Maimonides in his *Commentary to the Mishnah*:

> This law comes to bridge between the victim and the perpetrator, such that if we were to determine the worth of this *amah* [cubit, approx. 18"] the seed of which [the animal] ate, he would be liable for a large sum, and also if we were to determine the worth of this field with its planting of such and such *se'in* [plural of *seah*], and then we determined how much it was worth after one *amah* of it had been eaten for example, then the difference between the two assessments would be very small.[347]

This passage suggests that the assessment of the damage is intended "to bridge between the victim and the perpetrator"; it is designed to produce a damage assessment that is neither too high vis-à-vis the damager[348] nor too low vis-à-vis the victim. Maimonides' reasoning is similar to the model proposed by Aristotle, whereby the aim of distributive justice is to provide a system that relies on equality of proportions in determining the extent of entitlement of every member of the community to the goods or in determining the burdens that are distributed amongst the members, and in this context, the burden of the tort compensation is divided between the damager and the victim. This approach of distributive justice with respect to the determination of compensation can also be understood in light of the fact that in earlier times there was no insurance or "deep pockets" to provide full compensation; rather, everything was paid by the damager himself, hence the need "to bridge between the victim and the perpetrator" in order that the loss be spread "locally" – even if only partially – between the parties involved, so that the damage should not fall on one party alone. Therefore, distributing and spreading the loss are thrown into the pot of considerations, and the level of compensation is not determined solely in light of the victim's losses.

---

[345] See ARUKH HA-SHULHAN, Hoshen Mishpat 394:5 ("*vezehu kula lamezik*"); PISKEI HA-ROSH, Bava Kamma 8:1.
[346] Zerah Warhaftig, *Assessment of Damages*, 3 MAGAL 7–11 (5740–1980) (Heb.). And see ABRAHAM SHEINFELD, TORTS 295–96 (Heb.).
[347] COMMENTARY TO THE MISHNAH, Bava Kamma 6:2.
[348] Cf. MEIRI, BEIT HA-BEHIRA, Bava Kamma 55b in commenting on the *mishnah*: "And if you should say that the patch is assessed at its full value, and he pays its value, the damager would incur a heavy loss."

In the last example we discerned a certain leniency with respect to the damager. In relation to another aspect of the payment of damages, however, a tendency to severity with respect to the damager emerges, viz., in Maimonides' explanation of the ruling whereby the damager "is obligated to pay the full amount of the damage, from his most choice property, as stated (Exodus 22:4): 'Payment should be exacted from his choice field and his choice vineyard.'"[349] Here, payment of compensation is not in cash, but by the transfer of land from the damager to the victim. The payment amounts to the same, but the question is whether that payment will be executed by transferring a choice field (with a smaller area), or a less choice field (with a larger area). One may ask, why be hard on the damager and obligate him to pay for the damage by means of his best assets? Why should he not be able to pay with his lesser assets, or at least those that are average? Maimonides provides the reason: "For the sake of the repair of the world the victim will collect his damages from the best of what the damager has in order that damage and domination will not increase amongst people."[350] In other words, in order to deter damagers and to prevent an increase in the incidence of causing damage, damagers are obligated to execute the compensation from their best property. According to Maimonides, the function of the compensation is not to make full restitution aimed at restoring the situation to its exact former state (as in the Aristotle's and Weinrib's conception of corrective justice), but to serve also as a punishment imposed on the damager in order to deter him and others from causing damage.[351] As stated, the amount of compensation will be the same, but if for this purpose the damager has to give away his most successful and choice assets, this will be good and effective deterrent. And indeed, we have seen that different scholars over the years have discussed corrective justice in the context of a retributive and punitive or quasi-punitive conception, and their approaches are in fact more compatible with that of Maimonides than is the Aristotelian-Weinribian approach.

In the previous chapter we also mentioned the opinions of those later authorities who inferred from Maimonides' rulings that payments for wounding are not intended to restore the monetary loss.[352] Indeed, we will see now that the assessment of bodily injuries – on the basis of payments for damages, pain, medical treatment, loss of employment and humiliation – is not intended as a restoration of the situation to its previous state in a format similar to that of Aristotelian corrective justice: its aims are different.[353] Thus, for example, payment of compensation for

---

[349] Laws of Property Damages 1:2.
[350] COMMENTARY TO THE MISHNAH, *Gittin* 5:1.
[351] For a similar conception in relation to interpretation of the *mishnah* in *Gittin* 5:1, see Sagit Mor, *The Ethics of Compensation – Corrective Justice in the Talmudic Theories of Tort Law*, 2 RESHIT 25, 33 (2010) (Heb.).
[352] SOLOVEITCHIK, *supra* note 338, s.v. *ela*; GUSTMANN, *supra* note 122, 21b, 194.
[353] For elaboration *see* HARAV SHAGAR, *HALIKHOT OLAM – HALAKHAH* AND HISTORY 33–46 (Alon Shevut, 5776–2016) (Heb.).

pain cannot be seen purely as a monetary payment for physical pain, and the proof is that according to Maimonides, the victim's economic situation, too, must be considered,[354] which means that a wealthy victim will command a higher payment for pain than a poor one. This is different from the Aristotelian-Weinribian approach to corrective justice, which does not distinguish between the wealthy and the poor person but looks at the benefit and the losses incurred by the parties to a specific tortious event. One scholar wrote, with good reason, that Maimonides' approach to compensation for pain was intended to appease and reconcile the parties by means of a monetary payment, hence the difference between a wealthy person and a poor person.[355] With respect to payment for humiliation, too, account is taken of the social status of the damager and of the victim, and the rule was devised that "all is according to the person who humiliates and the one who is humiliated."[356] As Maimonides explains:

> How is humiliation assessed? It depends upon the relative status of the one who causes the humiliation and the one who is humiliated. Humiliation caused by an insignificant person cannot be compared with humiliation caused by a great and eminent person. The humiliation caused by the lesser individual is greater.[357]

Maimonides' opinion that there is a difference in the compensation that must be awarded to different people for humiliation, for example, and that the test must be concrete, looking at the actual person who causes the humiliation and the one who suffers it, apparently contradicts the Aristotelian approach, which is based on equality. Indeed, this approach seems *prima facie* to be opposed to Weinrib's corrective justice, although a rationale may possibly be provided for these rulings whereby they reflect true and full repair of the loss.

Another example: it appears that the compensation that the damager is required to pay for medical treatment does not relate only to a fixed monetary sum. "The obligation with respect to medical treatment is more serious and more comprehensive – to actually restore the victim's health."[358] Here too, one can say that the Weinribian approach to corrective justice would not require more than payment in the amount of the treatment, rather than efforts to actually heal. However, the duty "to actually restore the victim to health," which means, for

---

[354] Laws of Wounding and Damaging 2:9.
[355] HaRav Shagar, *supra* note 353, at 41–42.
[356] *Bava Kamma* 83b.
[357] Laws of Wounding and Damaging 3:1. On the matter of evaluating the humiliation, Maimonides writes in Laws of the Virgin Maiden 2:5: "They evaluate how much a father and the girl's family would give to prevent [these relations] from taking place with this individual. This is the amount [the man] is obligated to pay."
[358] HaRav Shagar, *supra* note 353, at 39, who infers from Maimonides' ruling in Laws of Wounding and Damaging 2:14, 16, that the possibility of exemption from this obligation by an advance payment of the assessed medical costs is an enactment that was designed to help the injurer, but "the fundamental law is that he is actually obligated to heal him," as appears in *Birkhat Avraham*, *Bava Kamma* 83b, s.v. *ripui*.

example, to bring him a doctor who will cure him and not only to pay compensation to the victim,[359] can be seen as a true and full repairing of the loss. The injurer, too, has a particular interest in the victim being cured by a doctor, as Maimonides says: "If the injured says to the offender, 'Fix a definite sum in agreement with me and give it to me and I will see to my own cure,' his request is not granted, for the offender can reply, 'Possibly you will not cure yourself and I shall be looked upon as a wrongdoer.'"[360] The import of this ruling is that the right of the injured person to demand compensation for his treatment is limited. He cannot demand of the injurer to pay him and he will attend to his own cure, for the injurer can say to him that he is concerned that the injured person will not cure himself properly, and then the injurer will bear the great stigma of being called a wrongdoer.[361] The obligation with respect to medical treatment is therefore to provide the actual treatment, i.e., the treatment of the injured person is the responsibility of the injurer.[362]

Even if Weinrib would not agree to regard the last two examples – of pain and humiliation, and of medical treatment – as pure corrective justice according to the Aristotelian approach that he espouses, it is possible that this can be seen as broader and more flexible corrective justice which might ultimately restore the *status quo ante* in the most practical way.

Another subject on which the Maimonidean approach and a Weinribian-Kantian approach appear at first glance to be similar relates to bodily integrity. Upon careful examination, however, differences between the approaches emerge. Weinrib explains Kant's approach to the right to bodily integrity.

> The body houses the free will and is the organ of its purposes. Thus every human being has an immediate – or, as Kant puts it, an "innate"[363] – right to the security of his or her physical constitution against injury and constraint by another, except, as in the case of legal punishment, where such constraint is itself a vindication of right. Correspondingly, everyone is under a duty to abstain from coercing or doing violence to another. A breach of this duty is incompatible with the equality of the interacting parties as free purposive beings. For by such a breach one actor treats another not as a self-determining being but as the instrument of an extrinsic purpose.[364]

On this point there is of course a similarity between Weinrib-Kant and Maimonides, who based his Laws of Wounding on the need to preserve the body. However, there is an important difference between them. According to Weinrib and Kant, a person has a right to his body, and by virtue of that right a duty is imposed on the other not

---

[359] See, e.g., Laws of Wounding and Damaging 2:16–18.
[360] Laws of Wounding and Damaging 2:17.
[361] The source is *Bava Kamma* 84b–85a.
[362] For further discussion, see KOVETZ SHI'URIM KETUBOT 218; HAZON YEHEZKEL 9:1; SHI'UREI RABBI SHMUEL ROZOVKY, Gittin 12:2 (no. 234).
[363] IMMANUEL KANT, THE METAPHYSICS OF MORALS 63 (Mary Gregor, trans., 1991).
[364] WEINRIB, THE IDEA OF PRIVATE LAW, supra note 290, at 128.

to injure that body. According to Maimonides, the conception is religious, and preservation of bodily integrity is a duty imposed on every individual for himself by virtue of being created in the image of God. Therefore, it is forbidden for a person to injure himself or to commit suicide. This conception is completely different from the secular-Kantian approach that is based on the right of a person to his body – a right which of course includes a person's right to injure himself.

Hence, even though it is certainly possibly to attribute a clear deontological dimension to Maimonides' theory, it can hardly be said that this dimension parallels all of the elements of the corrective justice theory of Aristotle and Weinrib. However, approaches to corrective justice other than those reviewed in Section D.1 may be found, which are more similar to that of Maimonides. We shall now examine Maimonides' approach vis-à-vis these other approaches.

(b) Between Maimonides and Other Approaches of Corrective Justice

Glanville Williams' approach[365] is very similar to that of Maimonides in the two elements of justice that he mentions. The first element of Williams' conception of corrective justice, i.e., moral retribution, resembles that of Maimonides. As will be recalled, the latter's focus was on the damager and on his obligation to remove the wrong and thus repair the damage he caused. Williams stresses the educative principle regarding both the damager and others. Focussing also on the victim's need to receive the benefit is of course common to the classic corrective justice approaches too, and it is consistent with correlativity, whereas retribution and education as a basis for the requirement to remove the wrong is less compatible with those approaches, and more so with that of Maimonides. In addition, asking for forgiveness from the victim who has suffered bodily harm, which Maimonides requires,[366] is closer to the second element mentioned by Williams, which focusses on the victim and on ethical compensation.

Richard Epstein's approach regarding causation[367] might also be compared to the rather unique approach of Maimonides to indirect damages (*grama*). Whereas indirect damages are exempt from compensation according to the opinions of many Jewish scholars, Maimonides in the *Code* obligates the damager in cases of *grama* as well, the rationale being that it is prohibited to cause damage;[368] the rationale of causation and the need to impose liability on the person who caused the damage fits in well with Maimonides' approach.

The communitarian approaches discussed[369] also seem to be closer to Maimonides' approach than do the classic corrective justice approaches. As we saw in Section B.4,

---

[365] See text *supra* near note 313.
[366] Laws of Wounding and Damaging 5:9.
[367] See text *supra* near note 310.
[368] Laws of Property Damages 5:1; Laws of Wounding and Damaging 7:7.
[369] See text *supra* near notes 320 until 326.

Maimonides rules that there is a duty to rescue, as well as a duty to prevent harm to another. In fact, the defendant has a duty to try to prevent the harm to his fellow, even though he was not responsible for it. This is a type of "tortious education" – which Williams too emphasized – that must be perceived, according to these approaches, as an act of assistance to another that increases the welfare of the helper, and not as an onerous obligation, on the understanding the helping another is a worthy thing and should be incentivized.[370] As opposed to this, the Weinribian-Kantian system of corrective justice categorically rejects the duty to rescue, for tort liability is based on the element of correlativity. After all, it was not the defendant who created the risk that materialized; he is not the harm-doer, and liability in tort cannot be imposed on him. In fact, an approach such as this distinguishes explicitly between the obligation not to cause harm to another and the absence of an obligation to assist another.[371] Weinrib indeed explains the difference, as he sees it, between the approach of Jewish law and that of the common law as he understands it.[372] He says that in the common law, the victim does not have a general right to be saved, or for time and money to be sacrificed for that purpose in particular. As opposed to this, under classic Jewish law, adopted by Maimonides, the by-stander has a duty to save – even if only in certain circumstances.[373]

The civil recourse approach of Goldberg and Zipursky[374] would also seem to be more similar to Maimonides and to Williams. Goldberg and Zipursky's approach too, like that of Maimonides in the *Guide*, is less concerned with repairing harm and more with removing wrongs.

The approaches which view corrective justice as an expression of punishment[375] share many similar elements to those in Maimonides' approach, which, as will be recalled, stressed the proximity of tort law to criminal law. This is particularly so with respect to laws pertaining to wounding, which Maimonides regards as directed

---

[370] GILEAD, *supra* note 286, at 178.
[371] *See* especially Ernest J. Weinrib, *Law as Kantian Idea of Reason*, 87 COLUM. L. REV. 472, 488–489 (1987). *See also* Weinrib, *Corrective Justice in a Nutshell*, *supra* note 54, at 353–54 ("As participants in a regime of liability, the parties are viewed as purposive beings who are not subject to a duty to act for any particular purpose, no matter how meritorious"). Others argue that when the burden imposed upon the rescuer is not heavy, and when there is a ceiling to the compensation that can be imposed upon a person who rescued, it is possible to impose a duty to rescue. *See* Richard W. Wright, *The Standards of Care in Negligence Law, Justice and Tort Law*, in PHILOSOPHICAL FOUNDATIONS OF TORT LAW 249, 271–74 (David G. Owen ed., 1995). *See also* GILEAD, *supra* note 286, at 178 note 36.
[372] Ernest J. Weinrib, *Rescue and Restitution*, *supra* note 190.
[373] *See* Weinrib, *ibid.* at 59–60, and an analysis of Maimonides' approach at 60. Weinrib devotes the rest of the article mainly to the question of whether a person who performs a rescue must incur expenses for the rescue, and if he is entitled to indemnification for expenses if incurred; Weinrib also analyses Jewish law on this subject.
[374] *See* text *supra* near note 327.
[375] *See* text *supra* between notes 316 and 319.

primarily at achieving punitive objectives. Moreover, in the following chapter we will discuss at length the model that Maimonides presented in explanation of the payment of punitive damages whereby the damager pays double, four-fold and five-fold the damage that he actually caused. Needless to say, this model is not based on considerations of corrective justice but on utilitarian-punitive considerations, which will be elaborated there.

3 Various Considerations Alongside Considerations of Efficiency in Calabresi's Theory as Opposed to Maimonides' Theory

A detailed comparison between Maimonides' theory and that of Guido Calabresi, one of the pioneers of the school of law and economics in the United States, will be undertaken in the next chapter, which is wholly dedicated to the utilitarian aspect of these two theories. In this section we will compare the two theories with respect to the way in which they incorporate deontological considerations alongside those of efficiency. We have seen Maimonides' approach to this subject; let us proceed to examine that of Calabresi.

(a) Deontological Considerations and Rules of Inalienability

Even though Calabresi is one of the founding fathers of the school of law and economics, he did not regard efficiency as the be-all and end-all, and he sought to combine considerations of justice with those of efficiency.

In Calabresi's early writings in particular, justice seems to be no more than the "final stop on the journey": moral considerations must fix a certain "ceiling" to the implementation of an economic approach, even if they are not regarded as an independent and separate objective. In other words, Calabresi in his early writings in fact sets the boundaries of optimal deterrence within considerations of justice.[376] True, only deterrence is an acceptable objective to Calabresi as a monist, but other considerations have a place in two main cases. The first is when the outcome of his approach does not lead to deterrence, and then it must be abandoned in favor of other means or other objectives.[377] The second case is when justice serves that approach as a moral upper limit and a constraint, and not as an objective, in the sense that if a system of economic efficiency leads to a very

---

[376] GUIDO CALABRESI, THE COSTS OF ACCIDENTS 293–300 (1970); Guido Calabresi, *Toward A Unified Theory of Torts*, 1:3 JTL 1, 1–2 (2007); Calabresi & Melamed, *supra* note 126, at 1104–05; Calabresi & Hirschoff, *supra* note 276, at 1180.

[377] CALABRESI, *supra* note 376, at 152, 160; Israel Gilead, *On the Boundaries of Optimal Deterrence in Tort Law*, 22 MISHPATIM – HEBREW U. L. REV. 421, 478–79, 481 (1993) (Heb.) [hereinafter: Gilead 1993]. For a description of cases in which Calabresi suggests, due to problems of information, to limit the application of the efficient deterrence, see Gilead, *ibid.*, at 457–58; CALABRESI, *supra* note 376, at 86–88.

immoral outcome in a particular case, it will not be accepted, even if it is extremely efficient.[378]

Calabresi's well-known article of 1972, co-authored with Melamed, seemingly goes in that direction too, albeit only on the matter of inalienability.[379] As will be recalled, the article deals with the means of protection of legal entitlements, and the authors present three sets of rules for this purpose: property rules, liability rules and rules of inalienability. They say that there are entitlements which under no circumstances may be transferred, not even if the owner of the entitlement agrees to the transfer or sale, and not even if the transfer would be efficient economically.[380] We would never allow a person to sell himself into slavery, or to sell his organs for implantation into another, even if the transaction is a very efficient one, e.g., in the case of the sick wealthy person, who is liable to die or whose health is liable to deteriorate even further if he waits in line for a transplant, and the seller of the kidney who is too poor to feed his children. The latter will not be permitted to make the transaction of his own free will,[381] nor does society allow him to set a price for an act such as this, for this would be licensing an act that is neither moral nor worthy[382] (at most, society will set an *ex post* price if the unlawful act has already taken place and an action in tort was brought in respect of that act[383]). Society will sometimes set limitations and attach conditions to a transfer but not prohibit it completely.[384] This seems to be somewhat paternalistic, for it contradicts the basic economic assumption that a person is the best possible negotiator regarding his own affairs, and in the circumstances, this may be a very good deal for him.[385] Nevertheless, due to the moral aspect, here too Calabresi dismisses the efficient outcome that is not moral, and he does not allow for entitlements to be alienated, even if the two parties are interested in this occurrence. However, one must wonder whether the reason for inalienability here is mainly that of economic efficiency and the many externalities for third parties in addition to a distributive reason, rather than (only) a question of morality. The answer is apparently not

---

[378] CALABRESI, *supra* note 376, at 25–26, 31. For another similar approach, although different with respect to the conception of justice, *see* Schwartz, *supra* note 307, at 1819–20.

[379] Calabresi & Melamed, *supra* note 126, at 1111–14.

[380] *Ibid.* at 1092–93, 1111–14.

[381] *Ibid.* at 1112.

[382] *Ibid.*

[383] Thus, society will not permit the sale of a kidney, but if a person lost a kidney in a car accident, this kidney will have a price. *See ibid.* 1112–13, note 44.

[384] *Ibid.* at 1111–12. For implementation of that partial transfer and partial alienability, *see* Susan Rose-Ackerman, *Inalienability and the Theory of Property Rights*, 85 COLUM. L. REV. 931 (1985).

[385] We will not deal here with the question of legal paternalism, a term that has more than one meaning, and the question of whether it is possible to discuss it in itself in terms of efficiency as opposed to morality. See *ibid.* 1113–14 and the references there; EYAL ZAMIR & BARAK MEDINA, LAW, ECONOMICS, AND MORALITY (2010), Chapter 10.

unequivocal, although there is no doubt that for at least some cases of inalienability, such as selling a kidney, the matter is one of a moral constraint combined with considerations of efficiency.[386]

Calabresi has additional reservations to the implementation of optimal deterrence. He himself admits that some aims are suited to certain types of accidents, whereas others are suited to other kinds of accidents,[387] and that the economic theory cannot really offer solutions to every matter that involves prevention and the costs of accidents.[388] In hard cases, Calabresi indeed recommends abandoning the law and economics approach where it is not effective, and turning to other approaches.[389]

Hence, Calabresi is prepared to limit optimal deterrence by considerations of justice. Justice, from his point of view, is not equivalent to optimal deterrence, for justice is not a "pure" and independent aim. Calabresi does not, therefore, espouse a pluralistic approach in which optimal deterrence is the dominant aim amongst all legitimate aims, but rather, a monistic approach that concentrates totally on optimal deterrence, but may stop short when it encounters a barrier to its implementation, mainly in cases that are particularly immoral. In this way Calabresi introduces a certain balance into his consequentialist theory, and that balance derives from a deontological dimension. Hence, Calabresi does *not* combine deontological considerations into his theory in a true and deep fashion. What he does here is more in the nature of public policy. When an efficient act is extremely immoral, it should not be executed, even according to his approach.

---

[386] "Although these rules of inalienability are substantially different from the property and liability rules, their use can be analyzed in terms of the same efficiency and distributional goals that underlie the use of the other two rules" (Calabresi & Melamed, *supra* note 126, at 1111). Calabresi and Melamed indeed explain that inalienability is based on a situation in which the transaction creates many negative externalities for third parties. They illustrate this with the example of pollution, and conclude that sometimes, the prohibition against selling the possibility of polluting constitutes the most efficient outcome, for it is cheaper to refrain from polluting than to pay for its costs, including to third parties who are harmed by the pollution. On the other hand, in their example of selling a kidney (at 1111–12), they mix in moral considerations – "moralisms" – and conclude that the rules of liability in such a case of selling a kidney are "not appropriate" (at 1114). One might wonder why it is permissible to sell pollution that harms the neighbors, and it is to be prohibited only where it is not economically efficient, but the sale of a kidney and putting a price on it is not "appropriate" and is clearly not to be permitted, as the authors note explicitly there. Should the act not be prevented by moral considerations in both the cases, and instead, should considerations of efficiency be applied in each of the cases, and the transaction permitted if it is worthwhile economically? In any case, Calabresi and Melamed say explicitly that the negative externality of that moralism is not always assessed in a way that will indeed prevent the transaction, and for this purpose they present "softer" examples than that of selling a kidney or pollution. See *ibid.* at note 43. As such, this is a mixture of moral considerations and considerations of efficiency.

[387] CALABRESI, *supra* note 376, at 15.
[388] *Ibid.* at 18.
[389] *Ibid.* at 152, 160.

It is possible to find earlier work, and especially later work of Calabresi in which he is more ready to recognize considerations of justice.[390] Calabresi also explains that there is a lack of clarity surrounding the term "justice", for it can be interpreted in different ways.[391] This, however, would seem to refer mainly to distributive justice[392] and not necessarily corrective justice[393] – the distinction between the

---

[390] In his book, Calabresi acknowledges considerations of soft justice and their effect on the shaping of liability in torts. See CALABRESI, *supra* note 376, at 78–81; Guido Calabresi, *Torts – The Law of the Mixed Society*, 56 TEXAS L. REV. 519, 525 (1978). But Gilead 1993, *supra* note 377, at 428 note 20 believes that according to Calabresi, like Posner, considerations of justice should not be acknowledged as appropriate objectives of tort law. Already in 1970, in his book THE COSTS OF ACCIDENTS, Calabresi regards justice as a constraint that may at most impose a veto on advancing the goal of increasing cumulative welfare (Calabresi, *ibid.* at 25). He says that the discussion on moralist approaches must be conducted from the perspective of costs and benefits (Calabresi, *ibid.* at 23). Izhak Englard, *The System Builders: A Critical Appraisal of Modern American Tort Theory*, 9 J. LEG. STUD. 27, 30, 34–35 (1980)) indeed regards Calabresi as a monist with a radical instrumentalist approach, for who the considerations of justice are even liable to frustrate the purpose of promoting the cumulative welfare.

[391] CALABRESI, *supra* note 376, at 5.

[392] See, e.g., Calabresi & Hirschoff, *supra* note 276, at 1077–84, in a discussion of considerations of distributive justice and spreading the harm with respect to a criterion that primarily weighs the good, as opposed to Hand's formula and as opposed to the approach of George Fletcher; Calabresi & Melamed, *supra* note 126, at 1114–15. But the relatively intensive discussion of the distributive element does not necessarily imply its acceptance and combination with considerations of efficiency. But see Calabresi & Hirschoff, *ibid.* at 1082, esp. note 90, where the authors call upon the courts not to ignore distributive considerations, and at 1083, where they call for distributive considerations to be combined in a real way, not only with the best decision maker criterion, but also with the Hand formula, and not only as second or third fiddle, if (sadly, in their eyes) distributive considerations continues to be the operative criteria. They explain (at 1084) that this will only facilitate the use of the best decision maker test and of the Hand formula. Their point of departure is not distributive considerations, and these cannot explain, in themselves, the best decision maker test, but they can get support and reinforcement from this criterion (ibid, at 1084–85); Guido Calabresi, *The Pointlessness of Pareto: Carrying Coase Further*, 100 YALE L. J. 1211, 1223–26 (1991), who criticizes the separation between considerations of maximization and those of distribution. Calabresi also adds that the disregard for distributive considerations on the part of the economists constitutes a total failure (at 1227), and is sorry that he did not sufficiently emphasize the place of distributive considerations in his early writings (at 1229). According to Gilead 1993, *supra* note 377, at 428 note 20, signs of this approach can already be discerned in Guido Calabresi, *First Party, Third Party, and Product Liability Systems: Can Economic Analysis of Law Tell Us Anything About Them?*, 69 IOWA L. REV. 33 (1984). In this article, Calabresi even criticizes Posner for over-emphasizing considerations of efficiency. In his later writing, Calabresi also comes out against purely monistic approaches. See Guido Calabresi, *The Complexity of Tort – The Case of Punitive Damages*, in EXPLORING TORT LAW 333, 334 (M. Stuart Madden ed., 2005).

[393] It is possible to find rare statements in Calabresi's writing acknowledging that corrective justice exists, although in a relatively weak manner. Actually, Calabresi describes a historical stage at which people began to feel that they deserved compensation as repair of a wrong, and corrective justice became compensation for indirect tortious behaviors as well. See CALABRESI, *supra* note 376, at 32–35, 37–38. This occurred, notwithstanding the following statement (Guido Calabresi, *Towards a Unified Theory of Torts*, at 9): "The corrective justice scholars are quite right to say that we would lose something of value if we were to lose that which corrective justice represents. For at any given moment the justice imperatives that the

two is important. Distributive justice as optimal deterrence does not look at the concrete damager and victim. It is concerned with a conception of tort law as an instrument, i.e., its two aims – optimal deterrence and distributive justice – are instrumental. Calabresi and Hirschoff also explain that in their view, the term "justice" combines distributive considerations with pure efficiency.[394] But despite this mitigation or change of Calabresi's position to a certain extent, it still may not be said that Calabresi is a pluralist, even of the type who clearly prefers one aim over the other but genuinely tries to combine other aims. Considerations of distributive justice figure to a greater extent in Calabresi's later writing, and considerations of corrective justice and morality seem to figure less in that same writing, except as constraints in cases in which invoking economic-utilitarian criteria entail extremely immoral consequences.

(b) Between Maimonides and Calabresi

As we saw, Maimonides too regarded the efficient prevention of harm as just one consideration, albeit extremely central, in the determination of tortious liability, together with many other, varied considerations. Some of the reservations mentioned by Calabresi were also recognized by Maimonides. However, upon inspection of the reasons for these reservations, it will become evident that alongside the similarity between the two approaches, there are also three fundamental differences between Maimonides' view and that of Calabresi.

Firstly, the meta-halakhic/philosophical foundation for Maimonides' tort theory, as presented in this chapter, is significantly different from the line of thought of modern theoreticians of general-secular law in general, and of the economic approach to tort law in particular. Whereas Maimonides regarded "welfare of the body" – education towards good values and religious norms – as central elements of tort theory, the exponents of law and economics spoke mainly of utilitarian considerations, incentives, aggregate welfare, deep pockets etc.

Secondly, like Calabresi, Maimonides also thought that there are cases in which the law acts in paternal fashion *inter alia* due to the moral aspect, and does not

---

corrective justice notions of a given society represent must be served. And that is the reason for the continuing survival and appeal of such scholarship." However, he bases tort law – in this article too – on considerations of efficiency (*ibid.* at 9: "But we would lose something just as essential if we were to abandon general deterrence and liability-rule system-building"). What is the solution according to Calabresi? "Well, one solution would be if we could split off completely the right to recover (limiting that according to our then extant notions of corrective justice), from the charging of those activities that we want to have pay so that they will have incentives to be safer. If we could make people pay according to the incentives that we want them to face, and give recovery only if, and when, pre-existing notions of corrective justice justify recovery, and if we could do both completely separately from each other, the Scott v. Shepherd paradox [a case Calabresi is dealing in his article – the authors] would be avoided." See *ibid* at 8. See also CALABRESI, *supra* note 376, at 302–03.

[394] Calabresi & Hirschoff, *supra* note 276, at 1078.

accept the assumption that a person can take care of his own affairs in the best possible manner. As will be recalled, we reviewed the paternalistic approach of Calabresi and Melamed in relation to the inalienability rule, and the example they present concerning the negation of a person's ability to sell his organs for transplantation into another person by virtue of this rule. A similar approach emerges also from Maimonides' ruling obligating an injurer to pay for the injuries he caused to the victim, even if the victim had given his explicit consent: "If a person tells a fellow: 'Blind my eye' or 'Cut off my arm and you will not be liable,' he is liable for the five effects [i.e., full compensation for the injuries], for it is well known that a person does not genuinely desire this."[395] According to Maimonides, the prohibition against causing bodily injury, particularly injuries leading to permanent disability to the extent of losing an organ, is *ius cogens* – non-negotiable. As such, even if the victim drew up an explicit agreement with the injurer which stated explicitly that the injurer will be exempt from payment for the injury – this provision cannot exempt the injurer from paying compensation in tort, due to the paternalistic assumption that "[i]t is known that a person does not genuinely desire this."[396]

One may assume that the intention is that the person does not *truly* desire to lose an organ,[397] even if *prima facie* it does not appear that there was any particular coercion and he agreed of his own free will. Maimonides adds that all this applies

---

[395] Laws of Wounding and Damaging 5:11.
[396] What Maimonides wrote was understood by SHULHAN ARUKH, Hoshen Mishpat 421:12 as having a broad application, i.e., even if he said explicitly to the victim "in order to be exempt," the injurer must pay (and see MAGGID MISHNEH on Laws of Wounding and Damaging 5:11, emphasizing that according to Maimonides, it is absolutely impossible to negotiate on a matter of injury to an organ that does not heal). This outcome is not consistent with those authorities who hold that if the victim said in unequivocal language that it was his intention to exempt, then he – the injurer – is exempt from paying compensation (see Rema on SHULHAN ARUKH, Hoshen Mishpat 421:12, and SeMA ad loc. 21–22).
[397] This approach is very appropriate for Maimonides in light of his well-known statement in Laws of Divorce 2:20, regarding cases in which the husband is compelled by the court to divorce his wife, and "The court should have him beaten until he says 'I am willing'." Maimonides asks, "Why is this *get* not void, for he is being compelled?" His answer is incisive: "The concept of being compelled against one's will applies only when speaking about a person who is being compelled and forced to do something that the Torah does not obligate him to do, e.g., a person who was beaten until he consented to a sale, or to give a present. If, however, a person's evil inclination presses him to negate [the observance of] a *mitzvah* or to commit a transgression, and he was beaten until he performed the action he was obligated to perform or he dissociated himself from the forbidden action, he is not considered to have been forced against his will. On the contrary, it is he himself who is forcing his own conduct to be debased. Therefore, with regard to a person who refuses to divorce his wife – he wants to be part of the Jewish people, and he wants to perform all the *mitzvot* and eschew all the transgressions; it is only his evil inclination that presses him. Therefore, when he is beaten until his evil inclination has been weakened, and he consents [to the divorce], he is considered to have performed the divorce willfully." In other words, this is not a matter of compulsion but of revealing a person's *true* wish, which is to follow in the path of Torah. The same may be said here too: a person's true wish is not to violate the prohibition against physically injuring another.

only in relation to bodily injury, as opposed to property damage, in relation to which the consent of the victim to exempt the damager from payment is valid.[398]

As such, similar to Calabresi and Melamed, who by virtue of the inalienability rule negated the possibility of selling organs from transplantation even if the sale would seem to be desired by both parties and would take place with their consent, Maimonides too denied the validity of agreements exempting the injurer for payment for amputating limbs. There is, however, a significant difference between Calabresi and Maimonides regarding the reason for invalidating an agreement that would permit the amputation of a person's limb. Calabresi primarily stresses considerations of efficiency as a basis of inalienability, whereas considerations of justice are invoked by him rhetorically and in a secondary role. As opposed to this, Maimonides' paternalistic approach does not stem mainly from considerations of efficiency. According to Maimonides, giving consent to personal injury is ineffective, since a person does not have permission to injure himself, by virtue of the religious prohibition:

> It is forbidden for a person to injure anyone, neither his own self nor another person, Not only a person who causes an injury, but anyone who strikes in strife an upright Jewish person, whether a minor or an adult, whether a man or a woman, violates a negative commandment…[399]

We accept Yair Lorberbaum's supposition that harm caused to a person's body is also harm to the image of God reflected in the injured person.[400] Some explain the reason for the prohibition against striking one's fellow, even if he has given his consent to being struck, by saying that a person is not the master of his body and therefore he is not permitted to injure himself.[401] On this matter, Ilan Sela wrote aptly that the distinction between the consent of the injured person with respect to his body, which does not exempt from payment, and the consent of the person whose property was damaged, in which case the damager is exempt from payment

> lies in the interest protected by each of the following doctrines: the prohibition against injuring was designed to protect against injury to the Divine image in the human being and therefore the injured person cannot allow the injury, whereas the laws of property damages were designed to protect against damage to a person's property, hence the property owner may waive this right.[402]

---

[398] As Maimonides goes on to say in his ruling in Laws of Wounding and Damaging 5:11: "When by contrast, a person tells a fellow, 'Tear my garment…' or 'Break my jug, and you will not be liable,' he is not liable."

[399] Laws of Wounding and Damaging 5:1.

[400] LORBERBAUM, *supra* note 21, at 219.

[401] See PITHEI HOSHEN 2:2:7.

[402] ILAN SELA, PAYMENTS FOR INFLICTING PERSONAL INJURIES IN JEWISH LAW: BETWEEN CRIMINAL LAW AND CIVIL LAW 332 (Doctoral Dissertation, Bar-Ilan University, Ramat Gan, 2008) (Heb.).

According to this distinction, he adds, "The prohibition against injuring and the obligation to pay compensation for breach of this prohibition has a punitive dimension." Indeed, the religious conception whereby a person is not permitted to do anything he wishes with his body and he is not considered the sole owner of his body can be inferred from Maimonides' ruling that a person is forbidden to commit suicide, and if he does so, he has "spilt blood, and he has committed the sin of killing."[403] If so, the religious dimension (and particularly the prohibition against injuring) occupies an important place in Maimonides' tort theory; needless to say, this dimension is totally absent in the general-secular theory of Calabresi.

Thirdly, Maimonides, like Calabresi, is of the opinion that there are rights which by law may not be realized if their realization entails a very immoral outcome, even if that outcome may be efficient from an economic perspective. At the same time, there would seem to be a significant difference between Maimonides and Calabresi with respect to the nature of the moral objective, its weight and its scope in the framework of tort law. Calabresi preserves the superiority of the goal of efficient deterrence and economic efficiency but he is prepared to make concessions when the outcome is very immoral (and of course, it is the social-legal-general secular point of view that determines what is an immoral act). In this, he introduces a certain balance to his utilitarian doctrine, which stems from a deontological dimension. In effect, Calabresi's doctrine is not about a moral *objective*, but rather, a moral *constraint* on the objective of efficiency. Maimonides, on the other hand, regards the religious-moral prohibition not to cause harm as a significant component of his tort theory alongside the utilitarian goal of preventing damage.

E. CONCLUSION

In this chapter we addressed the deontological, philosophical and religious foundations of Maimonides' tort theory. Maimonides regards putting an end to acts of injustice or removing the wrong as an important aim of tort law, alongside other aims, which are directed at the meta-aim of the "welfare of the body." We looked at the similarities and the differences between this aim and the theories of corrective justice. Maimonides emphasizes educational, punitive, religious (prohibition against causing damage) and social aspects that shape this aim of "removing the wrong" in particular, and tort law in general. Therefore, the application of tort law and the conception of corrective justice is wider according to Maimonides' approach than according to narrow conceptions of corrective justice that place the emphasis on the correlative framework of the damager/victim. Tort law, according to Maimonides, is designed not only to restore the *status quo ante*, but to repair the

---

[403] Laws of Murderers and the Preservation of Life 2:2. In the following ruling (2:3), Maimonides understands the verse (Genesis 9:5), "And surely your blood of your lives will I demand an account" to refer to a person who commits suicide.

qualities of the damager, to shape him as a person who contributes to a society which dutifully observes the religious precepts and is careful not to cause damage to the property, and primarily the body, of a person who is created *imago dei*. Moreover, Maimonides incorporates distributive considerations into his theory, particularly on the subject of compensation, and as we will see in the following chapter, there is a certain similarity between the utilitarian considerations of the Maimonidean theory of tort and the economic approach to law.

5

Consequentialist Considerations in the *Guide for the Perplexed*

A. CONSEQUENTIALISM, LAW AND ECONOMICS, AND MAIMONIDES

The present chapter discusses the consequentialist considerations emphasized by Maimonides in the *Guide*, part 3, chapters 40–41. In these chapters, Maimonides undertakes a comprehensive theoretical analysis of the main biblical and talmudic principles of tort law and criminal law. According to Maimonides, these two fields of law are closely related. Some of the consequentialist rationales that Maimonides suggests for the tort and criminal laws are innovative, like many other innovative philosophical insights and rationales included in the *Guide of the Perplexed*.

"Consequentialism" has a variety of meanings, only some of which appear to be reflected in some way in the Maimonidean theory. Consequentialism often refers to a normative theory that asserts that the only factor that ultimately determines the morality of an act or a rule (or anything else) is its consequences.[1]

For Maimonides, the consequentialist element is in no way the only element by virtue of which the morality of an act or a rule must be examined, for we saw in Chapters 3–4 that deontological, educational, corrective justice and religious elements occupy a significant place in his theory, alongside the consequentialist aspect on which this chapter will focus.

Moreover, adoption of a primarily law and economics agenda raises a particular question as to its relevance to Maimonides, who is known for his conceptual-philosophical orientation.[2] Despite looking at torts as a whole, law and economics, as it is commonly understood, reflects the US Legal Realist[3] movement's anti-conceptual

---

[1] *See, e.g.*, EYAL ZAMIR & BARAK MEDINA, LAW, ECONOMICS, AND MORALITY 18 (Oxford: Oxford University Press, 2010).
[2] ISADORE TWERSKY, INTRODUCTION TO THE CODE OF MAIMONIDES (MISHNEH TORAH) 371 (New Haven: Yale University Press, 1980).
[3] On the relations between law and economics and legal realism, *see* Morton J. Horwitz, *Law and Economics: Science or Politics?* 8 HOFSTRA L. REV. (1980) 905 ("Law-and-economics emerges to fill the intellectual vacuum left by Legal Realism"). *See also* Matthew C.

(or legal-formalist) jurisprudential orientation, in according primacy to efficient outcomes. At the same time, we will see that although Maimonides' works do not relate to all the consequentialist aspects as they are defined in contemporary theories, the consequentialist elements that constitute an important – though, as stated, not exclusive – part of his theory cannot be ignored.[4] In his well-known book, Twersky already noted the extent of socially oriented explanations in Maimonides' various works.[5] In the context of those socially oriented explanations, Twersky emphasized the difference between Maimonides' *Code* and the *Guide*, saying that "the Maimonidean Code of Law is not an excessively socially oriented document. Social concern and socially determined modes of abstraction and rationalization are far greater in the *Moreh* [*Guide*]."[6]

Indeed, in the wake of Twersky's work, we will pay utmost attention in this chapter (and in Chapter 6) to the differences between the two books. As is known, the *Guide* speaks in a different idiom from the *Code*. The *Guide* is a philosophical and theoretical composition (part of the Greco-Arab philosophical discourse of that time), and in many ways it does not even attempt to account for talmudic (as opposed to biblical) law – particularly the law of torts, whereas the *Code* is a detailed codex (usually based on the talmudic and post-talmudic sources) which includes halakhic rules to be applied in daily life. For this reason, traditional Jewish law has largely ignored the "policy" statements found in the *Guide*, especially in cases where the argument is not supported by the halakhic positions adopted in either the *Code* or in the Talmud.

In relation to our subject, we will discover that whereas in the *Code*, as we saw in Chapters 2–4, no special tendency to emphasize the societal and consequentialist aspects is evident in Maimonides' discussion of tort law, he did place great emphasis on these aspects in his explanation in the *Guide* of the reasons for tort law and criminal law.

At the beginning of Chapter 3:40 of the *Guide*, Maimonides states his goal as rationalizing the rules included in the Book of Torts. Nonetheless, some rationales of torts and criminal law presented in the *Guide* are not mentioned explicitly in the *Code*, nor in the talmudic and post-talmudic literature preceding it. However, as

---

Stephenson, *Legal Realism for Economists*, 23 J. OF ECONOMIC PERSPECTIVES 191–211 (2009); Gregory Shaffer, *A New Legal Realism: Method in International Economic Law Scholarship*, in Colin B. Picker, Isabella Bunn & Douglas Arner, eds., INTERNATIONAL ECONOMIC LAW – THE STATE & FUTURE OF THE DISCIPLINE 29–42 (Oxford, England and Portland, Oregon: Hart Publishing, 2008).

[4] Several authors have dealt with various economic aspects of Maimonides' theory. *See, e.g.*, Walter E. Block, *Jewish Economics in the Light of Maimonides*, 17 INT. J. SOCIAL ECONOMICS 60 (1990); Joshua D. Angrist & Victor Lavy, *Using Maimonides' Rule to Estimate the Effect of Class Size on Scholastic Achievement*, 114 Q. J. OF ECONOMICS 533–75 (1999). However, as far as we know, Maimonides' overall approach to law and economics in general, and to law and torts in particular, has not been studied.

[5] TWERSKY, *supra* note 2, at 443–47.

[6] *Ibid.* at 445.

shown later,[7] the *Code* does contain some expressions and views which may be viewed in retrospect as an initial preliminary approach to the fully developed consequentialist approach found only in the *Guide*.

The definition of consequentialism excludes, for example, ethical egoism – the view that an act is right if and only if it leads to the best outcomes for the actor.[8] We see that Maimonides too would agree with this exclusion, for he emphasizes that one of the objectives of the Torah in its entirety is not to permit a person "to act according to his will and up to the limits of his power, but [to be] forced to do that which is useful for the whole."[9]

Maimonides does not go into the well-known dispute concerning cognitive rationality,[10] but from what he writes, as quoted below in this section, it may be inferred that people act according to motivational rationality.[11] The assumption of this rationality, as explained by contemporary scholars, is that individuals act to maximize their own well-being; they do not act out of genuine altruism, nor out of a sense of idealism, nor of duty when such duty conflicts with their own self-interest.[12]

Maimonides certainly made no mention of such a comprehensive definition. However, it is evident that Maimonides, who was an avowed rationalist, was indeed aware of a person's motivational rationality in maximizing his well-being, and of the role of law in restraining this motivation and harnessing it to the public welfare. As he says in the *Guide*, the reasons for laws pertaining to property are clear, and their purpose is to serve as an "estimation of the laws of justice with regard to the transactions that of necessity occur between people,"[13] *inter alia* "lest one of them should aim at increasing his share in the whole and at being the gainer in all aspects"[14] so that the gain should not be wholly that of one party, but that the laws will be directed at "mutual help useful for both parties."[15] In addition, the imposition of monetary sanctions is intended to deter people, and it is based on the assumption that they are rational and solicitous of their finances no less than they are solicitous of themselves and their relatives, as Maimonides says in the *Guide* in relation to killing an animal with which a human being has lain carnally:

> so that its owner should watch over and take care of it, just as he takes care of his own family, in order that he should not lose it. For men are as solicitous for their property as for their own selves; some of them even prefer their property to themselves. However in most cases they hold both in equal esteem…[16]

---

[7] *Infra* Chapter 6.
[8] ZAMIR & MEDINA, *supra* note 1, at 18.
[9] GUIDE OF THE PERPLEXED 3:27 (English translation by Pines, 510).
[10] ZAMIR & MEDINA, *supra* note 1, at 11–12 and the references there.
[11] *Ibid.*
[12] *Ibid.* at 11–12.
[13] GUIDE 3:42 (Pines, 568).
[14] *Ibid.*
[15] *Ibid.*
[16] *Ibid.* 3:40 (Pines, 556).

Maimonides bases his reasoning here on the rational behavior of most people who seek to maximize their assets.

Did Maimonides expressly advocate another consequentialist theory, one which is current today? Normative (or welfare) economics may be a candidate. According to this theory, which focuses on incentives for future behavior, the desirability of acts, rules, policies etc. are determined on the basis of their consequences alone. Moreover, it is a welfarist theory in that the effect of an act, rule, policy etc. on an individual's well-being is the sole determinant of its desirability.[17]

Here, too, it is difficult to say that Maimonides examined the desirability of laws solely in light of their consequences, and we have certainly not found in his writing any complete, detailed theory of the welfare which the law must aspire to maximize. Nevertheless, it is clear that in the *Guide*, Maimonides explained the law of tort and criminal law as laws that are tested in light of their abilities to bring about the hoped-for consequences, similar to the consequentialist theories that focus on incentives for future behavior. Thus, for example, according to Maimonides in the *Guide*, a very important purpose of tort law is "the prevention of acts causing damage,"[18] and Maimonides says that in order "[t]o provide great incentive to prevent damage, man is held liable for all damage caused."[19]

In the next chapter of the *Guide*, Maimonides attaches great weight to consequentialist considerations in the sense of creating incentives for future behavior, explaining that the purpose of the penal sanctions and the punitive damages is to deter the tortfeasor.[20] Indeed, this text in the *Guide*, which will be analyzed in Section B.2, appears to express consequentialist theory and the emphasis on preventive measures possibly better than any other Maimonidean text, or any other classical halakhic text in the entire corpus of medieval rabbinic sources. Unlike other cases in which one can point to some basic (as opposed to modern) economic analysis of law in Jewish medieval texts, as we will see in this chapter (Section B.2 and C.2), in relation to the issue of punitive damages it seems that more than 800 years ago, Maimonides indeed presented an original and relatively highly developed economic analysis.

In Maimonides' writings it is also possible to find certain aspects of the welfarist rhetoric, albeit in somewhat limited fashion. As we saw in Chapter 4, Maimonides emphasizes that one of the objectives of the Torah as a whole is welfare of the body.[21]

This is not the place for a detailed comparison between the concept of welfare of body and various contemporary theories of welfare. For our purposes, however, it is clear that Maimonides emphasizes social utility, as Twersky showed, particularly in the *Guide*. This finds expression both in the overall reason he offers for the classes of

---

[17] ZAMIR & MEDINA, *supra* note 1, at 12.
[18] GUIDE 3:40 (Pines, 555).
[19] *Ibid.* Translated by the authors from the Hebrew edition edited by Michael Swartz 2002 [hereinafter: Swartz ed.], 574 (Pines, *ibid.* translated: "In order that great care should be taken to avoid causing damage, man is held responsible for damage deriving from.").
[20] *Ibid.* 3:41.
[21] *Ibid.* 3:27.

laws of the legal parts of the *halakhah* and in the particular reason given for the specific legal rulings. Thus, for example, Maimonides offered a patently social-utilitarian rationalization of "the laws of property concerned with the mutual transactions of people," and as he says in the *Guide*:

> The utility of this class [laws of property] is clear and manifest. For these property associations are necessary for people in every city, and it is indispensable that rules of justice should be given with a view to these transactions and that these transactions be regulated in a useful manner.[22]

Maimonides proposed a clearly social-utilitarian reason for Jewish criminal law as well:

> The utility of this is clear and manifest, for if a criminal is not punished, injurious acts will not be abolished in any way and none of those who design aggression will be deterred. No one is as weak-minded as those who deem that the abolition of punishments would a merciful on men. On the contrary, this would be cruelty itself on them as well as the ruin of the order of the city. Mercy is to be found in His command, may He be exalted: 'Judges and officers shalt thou make thee in all thy gates' (Deuteronomy 16:18).[23]

Indeed, deterrence occupies a central place in Maimonides' criminal theory.[24]

Emphasis of the social-consequentialist dimension is also evident in the reasons for the laws included in the Book of Torts in the *Code*, as explained by Maimonides (3:40), one of the central objectives of which is to prevent the causing of harm. The utility of the commandment to return lost property was explained by Maimonides both on the societal level and the consequentialist level: "While this is an excellent moral quality from the point of view of good relations, it is also of utility because there is reciprocity. For if you do not return a thing lost by somebody else, the thing lost by you will not be returned…".[25] In the *Guide* Maimonides also explained in a consequentialist and pragmatic fashion the laws pertaining to the breaking of the neck of the heifer (*eglah arufah*, Deuteronomy 21), which is a religious ritual of slaughtering a heifer, performed by the elders of the city in which the body of a murdered person was found (whereas the murderer has not been found). According to Maimonides' explanation in the *Guide*, this precept is not considered to be a ritual of atonement – contrary to what Scripture and the *Code* seem to be saying[26] – but a means of finding the murderer. In other words, the commotion surrounding the heifer, the activity and the utterances etc. will rouse the people to search for traces of the criminal.[27] Moreover, the severity of the punishment meted out to a person who strikes his father and mother and curses them was explained by

---

[22] *Ibid.* 3:35 (Pines, 536).
[23] *Ibid.*
[24] Section B.2.
[25] GUIDE 3:40 (Pines, 556).
[26] *See* Laws of Murderers 10:2, where Maimonides speaks of *kapparah*.
[27] GUIDE 3:40 (Pines, 557).

Maimonides as being due, *inter alia*, to "its destroying the good order of the household, which is the first part of the city [i.e., the basic unit of society]."[28] Indeed, the importance of family loyalty and social solidarity is also evident in other places in the *Guide*, where Maimonides mainly emphasizes the consequentialist aspect – and not necessarily the religious one – that underlies the precepts pertaining to preservation of the family unit.[29]

In this chapter, therefore, we will examine the consequentialist elements in Maimonides' tort theory, basing ourselves primarily on what he wrote in the *Guide*. We will discover that even though this is not a comprehensive theory according to all the criteria of contemporary literature for examining such theories, the element of consequentialism in Maimonides's theory is nevertheless solid and basic, even if it is accompanied by other elements that cannot be disregarded. After discussing the consequentialist aspects of Maimonides' tort theory we will conduct a comparative examination of the similarities and differences between this theory and the modern theories of law and economics in tort law, including the theories of some proponents of the economic analysis of law in general and of tort law and punitive damages in particular.

B. THE STARTING POINT: CONSEQUENTIALIST CONSIDERATIONS IN MAIMONIDES' TEXTS

1 *Prevention of Acts Causing Damage and the Effective Ability to Control Test (EAC)*

In the *Guide* Maimonides explains the reasons for the laws of tort – laws that are set out in the Book of Torts in the *Code* – saying that "they are all concerned with

---

[28] GUIDE 3:41 (Pines, 562).
[29] This, for example, emerges from what Maimonides writes in the GUIDE (3:49, Pines, at 601–02), explaining the foundations of family law in consequentialist-societal terms. After quoting Aristotle in his *Nicomachean Ethics* on the value of friendship ("I say then: it is well known that friends are something that is necessary for man throughout his whole life") as well as on the value of family loyalty and social solidarity, Maimonides adds: "The same things [the importance of friendship] may be found to a much greater extent in the relationship with one's children and also in the relationship with one's relatives. For fraternal sentiments and mutual love and mutual help can be found in their perfect form only among those who are related by their ancestry. Accordingly, a single tribe that is united through a common ancestor – even if he is remote – because of this, love one another, help one another, and have pity on one another; and the attainment of these things is the greatest purpose of the Law." On this social basis Maimonides (*ibid.*) explains the prohibition on harlotry, for it will not be known who is the father and the family of a child born of a harlot and therefore he will not have relatives who can help him. Another explanation offered by Maimonides there, *ibid.* at 602, for the prohibition on harlotry relates to its negative consequences: "for if harlots were permitted, a number of men might happen to betake themselves at one and the same time to one woman; they would inevitably quarrel and in most cases they would kill one another or kill the woman, this being – as is well known – a thing that constantly happened." And he concludes: "In order to prevent these great evils and to bring about this common utility – namely, knowledge of the line of ancestry – harlots ... are prohibited."

the removal of wrong (or as translated by Pines: "with putting an end to acts of injustice") and with the prevention of acts causing damage."[30] Note that Maimonides explicitly mentions two objectives: "the removal of wrong" looks backward: once the damage has occurred, it seeks to right the wrong that has been done – a type of corrective justice; whereas the second objective looks forward, and it nature is preventive – "the prevention of acts causing damage"; it is more similar, as we shall see in the following section, to the consequentialist conception that is typical of the proponents of the economic analysis of law. It will be stressed that the preventive objective, on which Maimonides focusses primarily in the *Guide*, constitutes a significant component in the array of considerations of tort liability, to such an extent that in the opening to his explanation of the details of the tort laws, Maimonides accords this objective the attribute "of justice."[31] Today we might define this as "preventive justice," i.e., that the consequentialist objective of finding the effective way of preventing the harm can be considered as no less justified than the corrective objective of compensating for wrongs after they have occurred.[32]

As elucidated in the previous chapter, in the *Guide* Maimonides viewed the prevention of acts causing harm as only one – albeit central – consideration in determining tort liability. Maimonides placed this idea alongside the corrective justice consideration and numerous other considerations (some of them mentioned in the *Code*), especially deontological and religious ones, in addition to some distributive considerations.[33] As we have shown, Maimonides emphasized both the prevention of acts causing harm and the deontological-moral dimension which explains the behavior of the tortfeasor, as part of the overarching objective of "welfare of the body" and shaping the good morals of people living together in society.

In enumerating the goals of tort law in the *Guide*, Maimonides emphasized primarily the consequentialist element of preventing acts causing harm, without detracting from other elements mentioned in the *Guide* and in his other works. We would stress that we are not claiming that all the details of tort law can be explained by consequentialist rationalization, as proposed by Maimonides in the *Guide* for the rules pertaining to tort law. Maimonides' statement in the *Guide* that "[t]he generalities of the commandments necessarily have a cause and have been given because of a certain utility; their details are that they are that in regard to which it was said of the commandments that they were given merely for the sake of commanding

---

[30] GUIDE 3:40 (Pines, 355). We prefer "removal of wrong" as translated by Friedlander, 342.
[31] *Ibid.* "These laws contain considerations of justice to which I will draw attention." A detailed discussion of all Maimonides' considerations of justice (corrective, distributive and preventive) as compared to modern scholars was presented *supra* Chapters 3–4.
[32] *Cf.* Gary T. Schwartz, *Mixed Theories of Tort Law: Affirming Both Deterrence and Corrective Justice*, 75 TEX. L. REV. (1997) 1801, 1832–33 (seeing optimal deterrence in tort law as "more just" than corrective justice, which he calls "protective justice". In his view, deterrence involves not only economic-utilitarian but also ethical and moral principles. We expand on Schwartz's approach *infra* Chapter 8).
[33] *See, e.g.*, GUIDE 3:42 (Pines, 568–69) regarding the issue of liability of trustees.

something,"[34] i.e., the details do not have a rational cause or utility, is well known. Of course, there are other major elements that determine liability in torts which are mentioned in the *Code* but not in the *Guide*. What is emphasized in the *Guide*, however, are the consequentialist elements on the basis of which Maimonides seeks to impose tort liability. These elements will be analyzed in this Chapter.

(a) The General Rule of Liability

In the *Guide*, Maimonides deviated from the line of interpretation accepted by many halakhic scholars who based tort liability on *peshiah* (negligence or fault) on the part of the defendant, and sought to base liability for damages caused by a person's property on a different, unique basis. But many of the later halakhic authorities (*Aharonim*) and some contemporary scholars had difficulty identifying the theoretical rationale on which Maimonides' theory is based.[35] In this section we offer a new interpretation of Maimonides' tort theory as set out in the *Guide*.

In the *Guide*, Maimonides states that the purpose of tort law is "the prevention of acts causing damage," and not necessarily to compensate for past damages, or to repair that which is in need of repair, or to restore the *status quo ante*. According to Maimonides:

> To provide great incentive to prevent damage, a man is held liable for all damage caused by his property or as a result of his actions so that the man will pay attention and guard it lest it causes damage,[36] if only it was possible for him to be cautious and take care not to cause damage. Therefore we are held liable for the damage deriving from our beasts, so that we should keep watch over them; and also for damage from fire and from a pit, for these two belong to the works of man [or according to another translation: "which are the product of human action"[37]], and he can keep watch over them and take precautions with them, so that no harm is occasioned by them.[38]

These words contain several of the fundamentals of the consequentialist (economic) analysis of tort law, but naturally, Maimonides' work does not contain all of the elements appearing in the modern literature. Particularly instructive is his use of the terms "incentives" and "prevention of acts causing damage," which almost appear to be drawn from one of the modern textbooks of the economic analysis of tort law. These ideas are definitely not characteristic of writing in his time. According to Maimonides, the imposition of liability for monetary damages caused by a person or

---

[34] GUIDE 3:26 (Pines, 508).
[35] *See* Chapter 2.
[36] The first sentence is translated by the authors from Swartz ed., 574 (Pines, 555, translated: "In order that great care should be taken to avoid causing damage, man is held responsible for damage deriving from …").
[37] GUIDE 3:40 (Swartz ed., 574, translated by the authors).
[38] GUIDE 3:40 (Pines, 555).

his property is intended to provide an incentive to prevent tortious events. Liability is imposed on those who can most effectively prevent the causing of damage, even if there is no fault attached to their acts, and as Maimonides stresses, "a man is held liable for *all* damage caused by his property or as a result of his actions."[39]

It will be noted that not only is there no mention in the *Guide* of the element of ownership as a basis for liability in tort,[40] but ownership is mentioned only in the context of the damage caused by animals and not in the context of damage caused by fire or a pit or by humans which according to Maimonides are the "product of human action."[41] The basis for liability stems from one of the meta-objectives of tort law – the prevention of acts causing damage – by virtue of which we impose liability on the person who can prevent the damage in the most effective manner.

Imposing liability on the owners of an animal was intended to ensure that the owners would watch over it so that it would not cause damage to others, and as Maimonides writes elsewhere, "Should they not be held liable for damage caused by their animals, they would not take care of them and thus would inflict loss on other people's property."[42]

The same applies to the imposition of liability on a person for a mishap occurring through his own act (such as a pit or a fire) which stems from the fact that they (the pit or the fire) are "the product of human action" and therefore "he can keep watch over them and take precautions with them, so that no harm is occasioned by them," i.e., he is the most effective damage avoider and therefore he must bear the liability.

In other words, we must distinguish between different types of damages, as Maimonides states in the *Guide*, where he distinguishes between damages "caused by the person's property," which are "the damage deriving from our beasts" (tooth, foot, and horn damages), and damages "caused by human action," which are fire and pit and of course, damage caused directly by a person to another's property.[43] Maimonides also distinguishes between damage caused by a person or by his property to another's property, and bodily injury caused by a person, such as wounding and killing, which he includes in the subsequent chapter of the *Guide*[44] as part of penal law.

It will be noted that Maimonides' distinction in the *Guide* between damages caused by a person's property and damages caused as a result of his actions is not identical to the talmudic distinction between "damages caused by property" and "damages inflicted by a person."[45] The difference is this: according to the Talmud,

---

[39] Ibid. (Swartz ed., 574).
[40] We already saw in Chapter 2 that according to the common interpretation of the CODE (the "*yeshivah* reading"), ownership lies at the basis of tort liability in Maimonides' approach ("the theory of ownership").
[41] GUIDE 3:40.
[42] Laws of Property Damages 8:5.
[43] GUIDE 3:40.
[44] Ibid. at 3:41.
[45] See e.g., *Bava Kamma* 4a.

damage caused by fire and a pit are included in "damages caused by property," and only damages caused directly by a person himself are included in the category of damages inflicted by a person. This distinction was actually adopted by Maimonides in the *Code*.[46] In the *Guide*, on the other hand, Maimonides deviated from the talmudic classification that he had adopted in the *Code*, and instead he included fire and pit in the damages that are caused by a person's actions.[47]

Indeed, as discussed in Chapter 3, Section C.3–4, the various types of harms in Maimonides' theory differ significantly: damage caused by a person's property (property damages), damage caused by a person who injures another (wounding), and damage caused by a person who harms another person's property.

In sum: in the *Guide* Maimonides proposes a liability regime whose rationale is effective damage prevention. If the tortfeasor has a connection with the object that caused the damage, he must compensate the victim. The connection may be ownership of an animal, but it can also be some other degree of relationship (pit or fire), as long as the person has the ability to exercise effective control over it (as stressed by Maimonides: "... if only it was possible for him to be cautious and take care not to cause damage"[48]). We call this the **Effective Ability to Control Test (EAC)**, because the object that caused the damage is under his control and he is therefore considered to be the most effective avoider of damages. The person in control must guard himself and his property so that they do not harm others, and for this reason alone, i.e., prevention, he should bear liability.

In light of one of the consequentialist objectives appearing at the beginning of the *Guide* 3:40 ("the prevention of acts causing damage"), Maimonides explains later in that chapter the reasons why an ox that kills a person by goring is subject to stoning[49] and an animal with which a human has lain carnally is killed.[50] With respect to slaughtering an animal that kills a man, Maimonides emphasizes that this "is not to be regarded as a punishment for it [the animal] – an absurd opinion that the heretics impute to us – but as a punishment for its owner."[51] It will be noted that Maimonides deviates here from the accepted interpretation of the Sages according to which this is a legal-halakhic action, based on the principle that "as the owner is put to death, so is the ox put to death".[52] However, according to Maimonides in the *Guide*,

---

[46] In his distinction in the Book of Torts between Laws of Property Damages (which includes damage caused by animals as well as pit and fire damages) and Laws of Wounding and Damaging (which includes damage caused directly by a person himself).
[47] For further discussion *see supra* Chapter 3, Section C.2.
[48] GUIDE 3:40 (Pines, 555).
[49] Exodus 21:28–30.
[50] Leviticus 20:15–16.
[51] GUIDE 3:40 (Pines, 556).
[52] See Sanhedrin 36b. Apparently, as Aharon Kirschenbaum says, this is evidence of the exalted value of human life, to the extent that criminal liability is imposed on the animal that kills, as emerges from the halakhic sources. See AARON KIRSCHENBAUM, JEWISH PENOLOGY 228–29 (Jerusalem: Hebrew University Magnes Press, 2013) (Heb.). Also *see* the sources cited there.

the Bible prescribed that the ox be stoned only in order to incentivize the owner to guard it.[53] In his words:

> For this reason it is forbidden to use its flesh, so that its owner should take great care in watching over it and should know that if it kills a child or an adult, a free man or a slave, he will obligatorily lose its price; and if he has been warned about it, he must pay compensation over and above the loss of its price.[54]

Maimonides thus explains the matter according to his method whereby the purpose of tort law is to prevent damages and to provide incentives for the effective damage avoider, and in this case, the effective damage avoider is the owner of the ox that is stoned. In other words, according to Maimonides the reason is utilitarian.[55] "This is also the reason for killing a beast with which a human being has lain," adds Maimonides, and explains, according to his consequentialist approach, "so that its owner should watch over it and take care of it, just as he takes care of his own family, in order that he should not lose it. For men are as solicitous for their property as for their own selves."[56] The monetary sanction is intended to deter people, and it is based on the assumption that they are rational and that they care about their property.

(b) Exceptions: Cases of Exemption from Liability

There are exceptions to Maimonides' general rule of liability, which means that the owner of the animal is not always considered to be the most effective damage avoider. However, these are in fact not exceptions from the Maimonidean rule; rather, they represent the consistent application of the consequentialist rule of liability proposed by Maimonides in the *Guide*. Here the explanations offered by Maimonides differ from the common talmudic explanations for cases of exemption from tort liability, such as in tooth and horn damages in the public domain and the innocent ox (*tam*) that gored: the talmudic explanations appear to have been based on considerations other than general talmudic tortious ones, and as such they must be seen as aberrant laws that are not necessarily consistent with the normal rules.

---

[53] KIRSCHENBAUM, *ibid.* wrote: "However, it seems that Maimonides does not deal sufficiently with the application of the term punishment to an animal: why are rules derived from this formal analogy, 'As the owner is put to death so shall the ox be put to death'?"

[54] GUIDE 3:40 (Pines, 556).

[55] It is interesting that Jackson explained the biblical law, too, on a utilitarian basis, although slightly different from that of Maimonides, and not on the basis of punishment of the ox, as did other scholars. See BERNARD S. JACKSON, WISDOM-LAWS: A STUDY OF THE MISHPATIM OF EXODUS 21:1–22:16 (Oxford: Oxford University Press, 2006), at 256–66. See esp. 257: "My view remains that the stoning of the goring ox is a purely utilitarian measure designed to ensure that it will not kill (a person) again." It may be that Maimonides' explanation too, which deviates from the common interpretation whereby this constitutes punishment of the ox, relates to the literal reading of the scriptural law that stresses that "the owner of the ox shall be innocent" (Exodus 21:28).

[56] GUIDE 3:40 (Pines, 556).

As is known, there is a real difficulty in identifying the rational jurisprudential considerations underlying the talmudic laws of tort, to the extent that Avishalom Westreich expressed doubts as to the very existence of such considerations, writing that the contents of talmudic law relating to various tort topics (cases of exemption in tort) rely on a reading of the text that creates "a halakhic system that is totally separate from other considerations that are relevant to the rest of tort law. To be blunt, this is not an internal legal theory but a theory the crux of which is neutralization of the jurisprudential dimension of this branch of the *halakhah*."[57] Indeed, as we shall show in this chapter, Maimonides' tort theory, the underlying rationales of which (both in relation to the laws governing liability in tort and to the aberrant laws) were explained clearly in his *Guide*, is perfectly suited to provide a rational explanation of the laws of tort in their entirety (and not only the exceptions) by invoking considerations of economic efficiency and social considerations.

There are cases in which liability is not imposed on the owners, although they are often the effective damage avoiders as they are in a position to control their property. Let us look at some examples.

Halakhah exempts the owner of an animal that caused damage using its teeth or feet while passing through the public domain (i.e., damage caused by eating and gnawing, as well as by trampling whatever it encounters on its way). Maimonides explains the exemption in line with his consequentialist view:

> These laws contain considerations of justice to which I will draw attention. Thus one is free from responsibility [for the damage caused by] a tooth or a foot in the public place. For this is a matter with regard to which it is impossible to take precautions, and they rarely cause damage there.[58] Moreover he who puts a thing in a public space is at fault toward himself and exposes his property to destruction.[59]

Maimonides believes that no liability should be imposed on the owner of a beast that caused damage (by tooth or foot) in the course of its regular passage through the public domain because he is not the most effective damage avoider. This is because on the one hand, the cost of preventing the damage, if it were to be imposed on the owner of the beast, would be very high due to the difficulty involved in preventing damage caused by an animal passing through the public domain. On the other hand, the expected damage is relatively light because "they rarely cause damage there."[60] Maimonides wrote elsewhere: "If the animal causes damage in a normal way by tooth or foot, its owner is exempt because it had the right to walk there [in the

---

[57] Avishalom Westreich, *Tort Law – Between Religion and Law: Interpretative and Legal Processes in Tort Law in the Talmud*, 26 SHENATON HAMISHPAT HA'IVRI 203, 209 (2009) (Heb.).
[58] The phrase "and they rarely cause damage there" is a translation by the authors of the GUIDE 3:40, Swartz ed. 574. It will be noted that Maimonides' statement in the GUIDE to the effect that damages from foot are rare is in direct contradiction to the Talmud *Bava Kamma* 2b, according to which – "foot – its damage is common."
[59] GUIDE 3:40 (Pines, 555).
[60] See, e.g., *Bava Kamma* 3a.

public domain] and it is natural for an animal to walk about and feed normally or to break things as it walks along."[61]

Maimonides also considered the potential victim and his own ability to prevent the damage, adding in the text of the *Guide* (3:40) that whoever left something in the public domain shares the fault for the damage that he incurred. Because he exposes his property to loss it is proper to impose on him liability for the damage and to exempt the owner of the animal from liability. In light of this, it is clear why the owners of animals were not held liable for tooth and foot damage in the public domain: it was the responsibility of the injured party to remove or guard his produce. In this case, the person who will assume the loss is the one who left the object that was damaged, because he was better able to prevent the physical damage to the object than the owner of the animal. In other words, the person who places an object in the public domain is the most effective damage avoider, not the owner of the beast.

Why did the Sages allow animals to be led into the public domain[62] rather than prohibiting it, so that no damage would occur to others?

Maimonides does not address this question in the *Guide*. Nevertheless, R. Nachum Rabinovitch, a contemporary commentator on Maimonides, clarified the economic rationale underlying this exemption according to Maimonides:

> There is a type of damage that can occur, but if a prohibition is imposed on the owners, the limitations on economic activity will be intolerable. For example, in an agricultural society such as the one in ancient times, if it had been prohibited to lead beasts through the public domain except in cages or in chains, it would have imposed a great burden on the raising of cattle and on the cultivation of land, which was carried out using the labor of beasts. The result would have been much greater public damage than the damage that may be caused to private property by beasts that eat or crush the fruit in the public domain. Therefore, not only was the shepherd allowed to lead beasts through the public domain, but under certain circumstances the beasts were allowed to walk by themselves there.[63]

This rationale (as well as the rationale presented by Maimonides) not only addresses the question of who is the most effective damage avoider, but also weighs the damage to the individual who may be harmed by animals walking through the public domain against the damage that would be caused to society if a blanket prohibition were to be issued against owners leading their animals through the public domain. In other words, it is inconceivable to prevent animals from walking in the public domain entirely, because of the

---

[61] Laws of Property Damages 1:8, according to Klein's translation. It is important to give an account of the original terminology, discussed by Bernard S. Jackson, *Maimonides' Definitions of Tam and Mu'ad*, 1 JEWISH L. ANNUAL 168–76 (1978).

[62] The animals in the public domain were usually accompanied, and only under certain circumstances the beasts were allowed to walk by themselves (*cf.* R. Rabinovitch *infra* note 63).

[63] R. Nachum L. Rabinovitch, *Liability for Property that Caused Damage*, in Zvi Haber ed., 25 MA'ALIOT – MAIMONIDES' 800 YEARS COMMEMORATIVE VOLUME (Ma'aleh Adumim, 2005) 71, 73 (Heb.).

damage to aggregate social welfare in general. To do so would reduce the level of desirable social activity, and it would have a chilling effect on such activities because people would be deterred beyond the optimum level. The equivalent today would be choosing not to drive or take school or youth movement trips for fear of liability. Some activities ought not to be prohibited, in order not to harm the aggregate welfare. In the time of Maimonides, this was the case in relation to animals walking in the public domain.

As opposed to the case of tooth and foot damage, the owner of the beast is liable for horn damage (goring, biting, and kicking) according to the *halakhah*, even if the damage occurred in the public domain. Why does the rule here differ from that of tooth and foot damage in the public domain? Maimonides explains that "[The owner of the beast] can prevent horn damage and such, and those walking in the public domain cannot protect themselves against this damage. Therefore, the rule regarding horn is everywhere the same [i.e., it entails liability even in the public domain]."[64] Maimonides clarifies the law by carefully examining who is the most effective damage avoider – the owner of the beast or the injured party. In the case of horn damage, the cost of prevention of the damage by the owners is not high, and it is significantly lower than the costs of preventing tooth and foot damages, for the tooth and foot damage are determined: "where it caused the damage by an activity which it is its way to do always, in accordance with the custom of its species."[65] In other words, it is normal for an animal to trample whatever it walks on and to eat the food it finds along its path, and therefore the cost of preventing these acts in the public domain is high. By contrast, horn damage is defined as a departure from the regular nature of the animals and as an act "which it is not its way to do always."[66] Thus, the cost of preventing such damage, if it is imposed on the owners, is not particularly high, for only on rare occasions does a beast gore. In other words, this is not an inconceivable situation, although it is infrequent, and the owners have the ability to take reasonable cautionary measures that would prevent the animals from goring and kicking.

At the same time, Maimonides adds that people passing through the public domain who are likely to be injured as a result of the exceptional behavior of the animal "cannot protect themselves against this damage" (horn damage), because they have no control over the behavior of the animal.

(c) Splitting the Liability between the Tortfeasor and the Injured Party
(The Case of the Goring Ox)

Jackson wrote that "[t]he goring ox must count as the most celebrated animal in legal history."[67] The Bible imposes full liability on an ox owner only if he had formal

---

[64] GUIDE 3:40, authors' translation of the Swartz ed., 574.
[65] Laws of Property Damages 1:2, according to the translation of Jackson, *Maimonides' Definitions of Tam and Mu'ad*, *supra* note 61, at 168.
[66] Ibid.
[67] JACKSON, *supra* note 55, at 256. And *see* his extensive discussion of the biblical law of the goring ox, *ibid.* at 255–90.

notice that his ox had gored on three previous occasions;[68] the Talmud calls this an ox that is *mu'ad* [an ox that had gored habitually and is declared forewarned – *mu'ad*]. According to the *halakhah*, the owner of an innocent ox (*tam*) is liable only for half the damages, whereas the owner of an ox that is *mu'ad* is liable for full payment for the damages.[69]

Various explanations have been given by modern scholars for the puzzle of the innocent ox, namely, why the owner pays only half damages. David Daube, for example, suggested that in ox injury cases it is difficult, if not impossible, to know who was at fault.[70] Reuven Yaron used Daube's insight to explain that the defendant pays only half the damages in a crude attempt by the law at loss sharing,[71] and Steven Friedell used this rationale to explain why the owner of the innocent ox is held to strict liability.[72] Indeed, this rationale or any other of the suggested explanations provides a reasonable explanation for the biblical[73] or talmudic laws of *tam*.[74]

In the *Guide*, Maimonides suggests a different explanation. From the context of what Maimonides writes there, following the discussion of tooth and foot damages, it would appear that in his opinion, the owner of the *tam* ox pays half damages because he cannot be regarded as the effective damage avoider. Since it is not the way of the ox to gore frequently, his owner does not know what caused the ox to gore that particular time and how to prevent such infrequent behavior in the future. In this case it is preferable to split the liability between the owner of the ox and the victim, for the injured party, too, ought to have taken precautionary measures on his part and been wary of the ox even if it was not considered a *mu'ad* ox, since all oxen can potentially gore. In relation to a *mu'ad* ox, however, the owner is aware of the fact that his ox gores in certain circumstances, and he can therefore effectively prevent the ox from goring in similar situations in the future.

Indeed, talmudic sages disagree as to whether the obligation to pay for half the innocent horn damages is a monetary-tort type of liability or a fine.[75] The opinion that Maimonides endorses in his *Code* as the rule is that half damages

---

[68] Exodus 21:36.
[69] This liability is expressed in Exodus 21:35: "And if one man's ox hurt another's that he die; then they shall sell the live ox, and divide the money of it; and the dead ox also they shall divide."
[70] David Daube, *Direct and Indirect Causation in Biblical Law*, 11 VETUS TESTAMENTUM 246, 259 (1961).
[71] REUVEN YARON, THE LAWS OF ESHNUNNA 193 (1969).
[72] Steven F. Friedell, *Some Observations on Talmudic Law of Torts*, 13–14 DINE ISRAEL 65, 89 (1986–1988).
[73] We are not dealing here with the possible explanations of the biblical law. For a detailed discussion *see* JACKSON, *supra* note 55, at 276–90.
[74] For a summary of the possible explanations of the talmudic texts, *see* AVISHALOM WESTREICH, HERMENEUTICS AND DEVELOPMENTS IN THE TALMUDIC THEORY OF TORTS AS REFLECTED IN EXTRAORDINARY CASES OF EXEMPTION (PhD thesis, Bar-Ilan 2006) (Heb.) [hereinafter: WESTREICH 2006].
[75] *Bava Kamma* 15a.

constitute a fine.[76] In the Talmud this opinion was justified by the assumption that oxen do not gore without a reason and therefore they do not require special guarding. The liability of the owner of an innocent ox that gored does not follow from the essence of the law, because by that standard he should be totally exempt from payment. Nevertheless, the Torah imposed on him payment for half the damage so that he would watch his animal in the future.[77]

This explanation of the law of half damages, as presented in the Talmud, does not appear in express form in the *Guide*, but it is not necessarily inconsistent with it. R. Rabinovitch's explanation of some of the economic considerations of horn damages seems sound. He writes that there are unforeseeable damages that nevertheless cannot be regarded as entirely the result of an unavoidable mishap (*ones gamur*), such as damages caused by the goring of a *tam* ox. Even though animals that graze are normally tame, the Torah sought to require their owners to exercise increased caution to prevent damage from abnormal behavior such as their becoming unruly and striking out. Full payment was not imposed, because the damages are infrequent and unforeseeable; even the half damages is a fine,[78] imposed due to the difficulty of determining which measures could be taken without undue detriment to agricultural activity. In the case of an ox that gores, however, the victim is not able to take preventive measures, and therefore the owner cannot be entirely exempted, as he is in the case of tooth and foot damages in the public domain. Owners do not intend to cause damage; however, they clearly prefer to keep their animals despite the potential for damage rather than protecting themselves from any prospective obligation for damages by ridding themselves of their animals – a solution that would harm society as a whole.[79]

In modern terms, one may say that according to the rationalization presented in the *Guide*, the imposition of liability for horn damage reflects optimal, but not overdeterrence of the effective damage avoider in order that he use effective monitoring and means of prevention without causing a complete disruption of socially and economically desirable agricultural activity.

In one central aspect, however, there still appears to be a difference between the talmudic law and Maimonides' explanation in the *Guide*. Regarding the former, the rule of half damages imposed on the owner of the *tam* ox that gored appears to be an exception that deviates from the normal rules of liability in talmudic tort law,[80] particularly according to the view that the payment is defined as a fine rather than a civil law monetary liability. According to Maimonides' explanation in the *Guide*, however, this is not an exceptional rule, but rather, it derives from the rule of liability

---

[76] Laws of Property Damages 2:7.
[77] Bava Kamma 15a.
[78] See Laws of Property Damages 2:7, where Maimonides states: "All who pay half the damage pay a fine."
[79] Rabinovitch, *supra* note 63, at 73.
[80] See WESTREICH 2006, *supra* note 74.

whereby in each case, one must identify the effective damage avoider. The very imposition of tort liability on the owner of the ox in relation to both tooth and foot damage as well as damages caused by a *tam* ox are intended to serve as a type of deterrent and to create an incentive for preventing the damage, and there is no difference, with respect to this rationale, between payment of full and payment of half damages. Why should the owner of the *tam* ox that gored be liable for only half damages? The reason is that it cannot be said in this case that the owner of the ox, rather than the victim, is the effective damage avoider, for the act of goring is still defined as an aberrant act that does not follow the normal pattern of behavior of the *tam* ox, and therefore the owner pays only half damages.

2 Maimonides' Consequentialist Analysis of Criminal Sanctions and Punitive Damages

(a) Deterrence as the Major Goal of Punitive Damages

In the context of penology, the core of the doctrine of utilitarianism or consequentialism, as formulated by its founder, Jeremy Bentham, is the war on crime in an attempt to prevent or reduce it.[81] The most important objective of utilitarian penology is to prevent crime and to deter people from engaging in crime (general deterrence), as well as to teach the transgressor a lesson that will prevent or deter him from repeating his wrongdoing (specific deterrence). Utilitarian elements may also be found in Jewish law,[82] but they receive particular emphasis in the *Guide* (3:41). As it does with respect to the consequentialist objective of tort law, so too with respect to criminal sanctions and punitive damages in tort does the *Guide* emphasize the preventive-consequentialist objective. It may be said that for Maimonides, of all the goals of punitive damages, deterrence is the major one.

First, it is important to note that in modern law, a certain discomfort is evident with the exclusive division that the traditional theory makes between criminal law and civil law. Various jurisprudential remedies, including the subject of our discussion – punitive damages in tort – are considered to be hybrid sanctions. Many developments in modern Western case law and legislation have led scholars to recognize this intermediate type of middleground jurisprudence, in which civil and criminal characteristic are co-mingled.[83] This intermediate type is an integral part of Jewish law, which from its inception embraced such "hybrid creations," namely, the laws of fines (*dine kenasot*). Fines constitute a third theoretical category in Jewish law, the definition of which is simple: payment that the court imposes on

---

[81] See, e.g., Hugo Adam Bedau, *Bentham's Utilitarian Critique of the Death Penalty*, 74 J. OF CRIM. L. & CRIMINOLOGY 1033 (1983).
[82] KIRSCHENBAUM, *supra* note 52, at 104–07.
[83] See, e.g., Kenneth Mann, *Punitive Civil Sanctions: The Middleground between Criminal and Civil Law*, 101 YALE L.J. 1795 (1992).

the defendant as a punishment for his deeds and not as compensation for the damage caused to the victim.[84]

Thus, when discussing the question of punitive damages in Jewish law we must bear in mind that in that system there is a certain co-mingling of criminal penalties and tort damages,[85] and as such there is no clear distinction between criminal sanctions and punitive damage in torts. The premise is that Jewish law rarely awards punitive damages, but there are definitely some instances in which such damages are awarded.[86]

Note that according to biblical law, the fine is paid to the victim and not to the state, as in modern legal systems (also by virtue of Jewish law being extra-territorial law), which is another manifestation of the co-mingling of criminal and tort sanctions.[87]

Under Jewish law punitive damages are imposed if the acts are especially severe or when it is necessary to rebuke the tortfeasor. In such situations, general economic considerations of deterrence are invoked, such as double payment by the thief in the case of "normal" theft,[88] four- or five-fold payment of the amount of the damage in the special case of theft of an ox or a sheep and its slaughter or sale,[89] and compensation for a woman who was raped,[90] seduced,[91] or whose honor was impugned.[92] What all these cases have in common is the severity of the acts.

Aharon Kirschenbaum's important comment is pertinent here: in view of the complexity of the reasons for criminal behavior, it is not surprising that there is a mixture of justifications for criminal punishment in the *halakhah* and of its objectives.[93] A classical representation of this differential approach is to be found in Maimonides, who presented different, co-existing objectives of punishment.[94] In relation to punishment and imposing punitive damages Maimonides mentioned two objectives in the *Guide*, and thus the doctrine of redress and the utilitarian-consequentialist approach find expression in the one chapter (3:41).

---

[84] KIRSCHENBAUM, *supra* note 52, at 474–77.
[85] The close connection between tort law and criminal law was discussed at length in Chapter 3.
[86] For an extensive discussion of the policy lines in imposing punitive damages, see YUVAL SINAI, APPLICATION OF JEWISH LAW IN THE ISRAELI COURTS (Jerusalem: Israel Bar Press, 2009) 195–209 (Heb.).
[87] And therefore laws of fines, like laws of property, are a function of an action brought by the injured party. If no action is brought by the injured party, there is no legal process. See KIRSCHENBAUM, *supra* note 52, at 476.
[88] Exodus 22:6; Maimonides, Laws of Theft 4:1.
[89] Exodus 21:37; Maimonides, *ibid.* 1:16. We discuss the difference between normal and special theft and robbery according to Maimonides in the next section. For an extensive discussion of these matters in biblical law, see BERNARD S. JACKSON, THEFT IN EARLY JEWISH LAW (Oxford: Oxford University Press, 1972) [hereinafter: JACKSON, THEFT].
[90] Deuteronomy 22:29; CODE, Laws of the Virgin Maiden 1:1–2.
[91] Exodus 22:16; CODE, *ibid.* 1:3.
[92] Deuteronomy 22: 13–21; CODE, Laws of the Virgin Maiden 3.
[93] KIRSCHENBAUM, *supra* note 52, at 714.
[94] *Ibid.* at 714–15.

On the one hand, punishment must be administered in the spirit of "an eye for an eye", open retribution, clear revenge: "If he has injured [the person's] body, he shall be injured in his body, and if he has injured him in his property, he shall be injured in his property."[95] On the other hand, however, in the passage which appears later in the same chapter of the *Guide*, Maimonides emphasizes the element of deterrence, stating that the magnitude of the punishment is determined in accordance with the need for deterrence in relation to the act. In the *Code*, as opposed to this, the emphasis is on rehabilitation and atonement in the context of punishment.[96]

We have already mentioned that Maimonides proposed a clearly societal-utilitarian explanation for the criminal laws in the Bible.[97] Indeed, deterrence occupies center stage in Maimonides' penal theory in the *Guide*. He discusses the optimal level of punishment and presents four parameters or conditions for considering criminal sanctions.[98] Because of the mingling between criminal sanctions and punitive damages in Jewish law, these parameters are especially relevant to the issue of punitive damages, and it seems that in this chapter of the *Guide* Maimonides intends to apply them to tort events as well. Maimonides writes:

> A preliminary remark: whether the punishment is great or small, the pain inflicted intense or less intense, depends on the following four conditions.
>
> 1. *The severity of the crime.* Actions that cause great harm are punished severely, whilst actions that cause little harm are punished less severely.
> 2. *The frequency of the crime.* A crime that is frequently committed must be suppressed by severe punishment; crimes of rare occurrence may be suppressed by a lenient punishment considering that they are rarely committed.
> 3. *The amount of temptation.* Only fear of severe punishment restrains us from actions for which there exists a great temptation, either because we have a strong desire for these actions, or are accustomed to them, or feel unhappy without them.
> 4. *The facility with which the act may be done secretly, and unseen and unnoticed.* From acts performed with such facility we are deterred only by the fear of a severe and terrible punishment.[99]

---

[95] GUIDE 3:41 (Pines, 558). In this context, we should notice the contrast between the literal text of the Bible (Exodus 21:24), which refers to physical punishment – literally "an eye for an eye" – and the normative talmudic law, which prescribes that the tortfeasor will pay monetary compensation to the injured person – "an eye for an eye – money" and not "an actual eye for an eye" – as determined by the majority of *Tannaim* in the discussion in *Bava Kamma* 63b–64a. For a comprehensive, up-to-date summary of the topic of "an eye for an eye" in Judaism, see KIRSCHENBAUM, *supra* note 52, at 901–54.

[96] See e.g., Laws of Wounding and Damaging 5:9; Laws of the Sanhedrin 13:1; *ibid.* 17:7; Laws of Witnesses 12:3–10; and in the background: Laws of Repentance.

[97] GUIDE 3:35 (*see supra* Section B.1).

[98] GUIDE 3:41 (Pines, 560).

[99] GUIDE 3:41 according to the translation of Friedlander (1956), p. 345.

Maimonides suggests that when determining the sanction, we must consider the severity of the acts (retribution and utilitarianism),[100] but even more importantly, the dominant goal of the sanction is deterrence. This can be achieved with reference to three additional key elements: the *frequency* of the act for which we want to impose a penal sanction (general deterrence); the degree of *temptation* that the person who commits the offense is facing (specific deterrence); and the *ease* with which the offense is committed without being noticed or its perpetrator caught by the legal authorities (deterrence – utilitarianism).

In the following two sections, we discuss how Maimonides uses the various components of deterrence to explain the rationale behind those cases in which punitive damages are imposed. Even if we regard the first parameter mentioned in the *Guide* as deontological, the other parameters mentioned there strongly emphasize the consequentialist-societal element.[101]

The great weight that Maimonides attributes to the consequentialist-deterrent aspect is illustrated and emphasized (in the next two sections) in his explanation of the difference between a thief and a robber and between the stealing of sheep and cattle.

(b) A Test Case: Payments of a Thief as Opposed to a Robber

Biblical law establishes a special set of rules dealing with property theft.[102] It distinguishes between the case in which the stolen property [an animal] remains in the hands of the thief, and the case in which the stolen property is no longer under the control of the thief who slaughtered it (to eat the meat) or sold it. In the first case, the thief must pay double compensation to the property owner.[103] If the stolen property is already beyond the thief's control since he sold or slaughtered it, however, the compensation he must pay is significantly higher: four-fold for stealing sheep and five-fold for stealing cattle.[104]

---

[100] According to KIRSCHENBAUM, *supra* note 52, at 780, and he apparently means that the severity of the offence impacts on the severity of punishment either due to the element of retribution, that is, the punishment fitting the crime, or because the magnitude of the loss caused to society requires a severe punishment in order to prevent the occurrence of the damage, i.e., utilitarianism.

[101] Later in the same chapter in the GUIDE, Maimonides invokes both deontological and consequentialist explanations in rationalizing the severity of the punishment for smiting and cursing one's father and mother, which he says is "because of the great impudence of the thing and its destroying the good order of the household, which is the first part of the city" (GUIDE 3:41, 583–584). The deontological aspect relates to the severity of the deed – the impudence – and the consequentialist-societal aspect is the harm to the social order.

[102] For a comprehensive discussion *see* JACKSON, THEFT, *supra* note 89.

[103] Exodus 22:6.

[104] Exodus 21:37; 22:1–3.

Biblical law mentions various offences of theft.[105] The post-biblical-tannaitic sages[106] distinguish clearly between theft (*gneivah*) and robbery (*gezeilah*).[107] This distinction was emphasized by Maimonides as well.[108] Similar to theft, robbery is an act of taking property from a person without his consent. The basic difference between robbery and theft is that the thief acts secretly, while the robber acts overtly;[109] robbery involves the use of force (or the potential for the use of force),[110] whereas theft does not contain an element of violence.[111] There is, of course, a connection between the two elements of robbery – openness and force. By its nature, the use of violence requires the presence of a person at whom the violence is aimed. As such, robbery is carried out in the open rather than secretly. Nevertheless, from a societal perspective, the violence that underlies robbery exacerbates the severity of the deprivation of property, according to Maimonides' first parameter. Thus, if the perspective is strictly a moral one, the compensation for robbery should be at least as high as that for theft. Somewhat surprisingly, however, the Bible imposes payment on the robber only for the value of the property, whereas the thief pays double.

These biblical laws raise a cluster of questions: (a) Why does the Torah impose double payment on the thief but not on the robber? (b) Why is a four-fold payment imposed on a thief who stole a sheep if he benefitted from the theft by slaughtering or selling the animal, rather than a double payment as in the case of regular theft? (c) Why is a five-fold payment imposed on a person who stole cattle, and not a four-fold payment?

These questions are among the most challenging in Jewish law, and many sages throughout the ages, as well as present-day scholars, have searched for the rationale underlying the various rates of compensation imposed in different cases of theft, and underlying the differences between theft and robbery.[112] Various solutions have been proposed, but it is difficult to find a rational and convincing one, especially from the point of view of a contemporary jurist.

Maimonides proposes a unique solution in the *Guide*: all the details of the laws become clear if the primary aim is to achieve deterrence. We would stress that we

---

[105] For a detailed analysis of the biblical offences see JACKSON, THEFT, *supra* note 89, at 41–67.
[106] *Ibid*, at 68–82.
[107] For citations from the talmudic literature that supports this distinction, see JACKSON, *ibid*. at 26.
[108] And therefore Maimonides was careful in the *Code* to distinguish between laws of theft and laws of robbery. See *supra* Chapter 3, Section C.5.
[109] JACKSON, THEFT, *supra* note 89, at 26. And according to Maimonides, Laws of Theft 1:3.
[110] JACKSON, *ibid*. at 28. And also according to Maimonides, *ibid*. and in Laws of Robbery 1:3.
[111] But there is an exception: Exodus 22:1–2, the law allowing the killing of the nocturnal intruder, is clearly part of the theft laws. See further JACKSON, THEFT, *supra* note 89, where different forms of robbery and the terminology applicable to them are also discussed.
[112] For a detailed discussion of the different explanations of these questions given by scholars, see JACKSON, THEFT, *supra* note 89, at 41–48, 130–38. For a detailed discussion of the explanations of the commentators, see NEHAMA LEIBOWITZ, STUDIES IN *SHEMOT* (EXODUS) 361–71 (Jerusalem: Elinar Library, 1981).

are not necessarily arguing that Maimonides' rationale explains the biblical law more satisfactorily than other explanations, and we do not wish to delve into the details of the dispute between the various authorities on these questions, or to determine which is the best explanation. What is important to us here is to describe Maimonides' unique method, which includes consequentialist elements mentioned in modern approaches to economic analysis of the laws of punitive damages, such as the approaches to be presented and discussed later, although there are some important differences, as shall be elaborated.[113]

Modern literature attempts to propose an economic analysis of the payments of the biblical thief (double, four-fold and five-fold).[114] However, the economic-consequentialist underpinnings of the rules appear to be less prominent in the classical sources pre-dating Maimonides. Quite the contrary: other reasons (moral, religious and theological) were given in the talmudic literature and by the commentators.[115] It is important to note that Maimonides was not the first who, in explaining the payments of the thief, adopted an interpretation containing various consequentialist characteristics. Interpretations based on economic considerations may be found in the works of two important Sages[116] – also, like Maimonides, living in Egypt – who were active before Maimonides' time: Philo of Alexandria[117] and R. Sa'adia Gaon.[118] Indeed, the tendency to provide rational-philosophical explanations is common to all three – Maimonides, Philo and R. Sa'adia Gaon – and it is also known that Maimonides held R. Sa'adia in high esteem and was

---

[113] *Infra*, Section C.2.
[114] *See e.g.* Moshe Bar-Niv (Bornovsky), *Economic Aspects of the Law of Double, Four-Fold and Five-Fold Payments*, 17 DINE ISRAEL 211 (2003) (Heb.).
[115] For a summary of the different interpretations and the difficulties involved in each, *see* Bar-Niv, *ibid.* at 212–22. *See also* JACKSON, THEFT, *supra* note 89.
[116] And one could add a third Sage, R. Hananel, whose explanation mentioned *infra* note 141 is based on the economic aspect (benefit derived from the theft), although somewhat less noticeably than that of the two who will be mentioned now.
[117] In explaining why the Torah sought to distinguish between the slaughter and sale of the ox and the slaughter and sale of the sheep, Philo points to the different economic utility to man from cattle and from sheep: "The ox contributes more to man than do sheep. The latter provides man with four benefits: milk, cheese, wool and lambs: the ox [furnishes] five; [three of which are the same as those of the sheep] milk, cheese, and the offspring; an in addition [two are peculiar to itself] ploughing and threshing" (PHILO, THE SPECIAL LAWS, Book 4:3 ("On Theft")). Bar-Niv, *supra* note 114, wisely commented that even though this explanation is not convincing (and *see* LEIBOWITZ's critique of this explanation, *supra* note 112, at 366–67), it demonstrates the great importance of sheep and cattle as a source of wealth in the biblical period.
[118] *See* the statements attributed to R. Sa'adia Gaon that are cited in Ibn Ezra's Commentary to Exodus (*see* LEIBOWITZ, *supra* note 112, at 366) whereby the amount of compensation for the ox is greater "due to the greater harm that will be done to the owner of the ox than the owner of a sheep, because he will plough with it." According to R. Sa'adia's explanation, therefore, we find that the different amount of compensation for the ox and for the sheep represents the different economic contribution of each.

sometimes even influenced by his work.[119] Nevertheless, it must be emphasized that there is a great difference between Maimonides and the other two. Whereas the economic element in the work of Philo and R. Sa'adia Gaon is very partial and undeveloped, and the interpretations they offer do not necessarily deviate from what appears in the Talmudic literature,[120] Maimonides in the *Guide* presents a comprehensive consequentialist theory, relatively well developed for those times, which does not have a basis in the Talmud;[121] rather, it explains the differences in the level of punishment for the different cases on the basis of the principle of deterrence. This is something entirely new, and it does not exist in any way in the halakhic sources that preceded it – neither in the Talmud, nor in the writings of R. Sa'adia Gaon or Philo.

Similar to other subjects in which the societal aspects are far more prominent in the *Guide* than in the *Code* and the talmudic literature, societal aspects relating to the payments of the thief do not receive much emphasis in the *Code*.[122] In the talmudic literature, however, other explanations – which surprisingly receive no mention in the *Guide* – are offered that are totally unconnected to the consequentialist elements so strongly emphasized in the *Guide*.[123] This is another example of the originality of the societal-consequentialist reasoning appearing in the *Guide* in explanation of tort law and criminal law in general, and of the double, four-fold and five-fold payments in particular.

Maimonides' position is special and even very uncommon for his time. He dealt with this issue in light of his fundamental consequentialist approach, whereby criminal sanctions are imposed in view of the ultimate goal, which is to achieve deterrence:

---

[119] See ROBERT BRODY, RAV SA'ADIYAH GAON (Littman Library of Jewish Civilization, 2011).

[120] Thus, for example, it seems that the passage from PHILO cited in note 117 is very similar to what R. Meir says in *Mekhilta* 106 ("He came and saw how precious was labor before the Creator of the Universe. An ox which labors – the payment is five-fold, and a sheep, which does not labor – the payment is four-fold"). And see Bar-Niv, *supra* note 114, at 235–36.

[121] Although it is possible to find several expressions in the Talmud that bring to mind various aspects of Maimonides' interpretation, such as the statements in *Bava Kamma* 67b–68a, "because he became rooted in sin" or "because he has sinned repeatedly," which were uttered in the context of the difference between theft which entails double payment and slaughter and sale, which entail four- and five-fold payments. Indeed, as we shall discuss in Section C, Maimonides used the frequency of the act as a central element of his analysis of these rules, but there is a significant difference between the Talmud and the consequentialist theory of Maimonides.

[122] See Laws of Theft 1:4–7. Nevertheless, in Laws of Theft in the *CODE*, too, we find formulations that are consequentialist in nature relating to certain matters. See, *e.g.*, Laws of Theft 5:1, which explains that the prohibition on buying from stolen goods from the thief is based on the fact that such a purchase motivates the thief to steal. And see *infra*, end of Section B.

[123] See *Mekhilta Mishpatim* 12; *Tosefta Bava Kamma* 7:3; *Bava Kamma* 79b (which cited other reasons for dealing more severely with the person who steals an ox than with one who steals a sheep: R. Meir says, because the ox works in the field, and the thief deprived him of its labor, and R. Yohanan Ben Zakkai explains, because of human dignity – he carries the sheep on his shoulders and is debased, but the ox walks by itself).

A robber with violence is not ordered to pay anything as fine (Lev. v. 24).... The reason of this rule is to be found in the rare occurrence of robbery; theft is committed more frequently than robbery, for theft can be committed everywhere; robbery is not possible in towns, except with difficulty; besides, the thief takes things exposed as well as things hidden away; robbery applies only to things exposed; against robbery we can guard and defend ourselves; we cannot do so against theft; again, the robber is known, can be sought, and forced to return that which he has robbed, whilst the thief is not known. On account of all these circumstances the law fines the thief and not the robber.[124]

Maimonides' explanation of the difference between a robber and a thief is different from the theological explanation of the Talmud,[125] and it is based on a few of the parameters of deterrence.[126]

Maimonides' approach also fits in with the social, tribal structure of the biblical period. As Bar-Niv argues, robbery in a society in which people lived within their protected, domestic circles was probably quite difficult and quite risky. A robber might encounter physical resistance from those guarding the property, or be subject to persecution and revenge on the part of the victims. Even a robber who lived outside of the village or the tribe would be likely to arouse concern or suspicion. In other words, robbery in this social structure was dangerous due to the expectation of injury to the robber and the relatively high probability of getting caught.[127]

Indeed, under these social conditions, the act of robbery involves a relatively high potential cost to the robber, expressed in both the direct cost of executing the robbery and in the risk involved in capture and restitution. A robber would also be aware that precautions may be taken to guard against robbery, which may motivate him to rob less often or only in cases when he expects to encounter less resistance. It is therefore reasonable to assume that the prevalence of acts of robbery in the biblical period, as Maimonides himself writes, was relatively low. Potential robbers who are calculating and manage their risk even at a rudimentary level would choose other, more efficient ways. One of them is theft. Indeed, the arguments about the

---

[124] GUIDE 3:41 (Friedlander, 345).
[125] See Bava Kamma 79b, which offers a religious-faith-based explanation by R. Yohanan Ben Zakkai for the question that was asked by his students: Why was the Torah more severe with the thief than the robber? He answered them, "This one equated the honor of the servant [the person] to the honor of his master [God]." In other words, both the thief and the robber are transgressors of the Law of the Torah, but what the thief does is worse, at least in terms of the relationship between man and God; in terms of contemporary law one could say that the *mens rea* of the thief on the religious plane is at a more serious level than that of the robber. On the difficulties of this explanation see Bar-Niv, *supra* note 114, at 214–16.
[126] See Section A. The parameter of the severity of the act seems less relevant to our discussion, because there is no difference in this regard between robbery and theft: in both cases the result of forfeiture of the object is similar.
[127] Bar-Niv, *supra* note 114, at 221–22.

relative rarity of the act of robbery do not apply to acts of theft. The nature of theft is such that the thief comes in secret and therefore does not expect to be easily identified. In addition, the thief does not usually expect to clash violently with the owner or protector of the property.

Maimonides' consequentialist analysis might indeed receive support from a comparison of the thief to the robber from the point of view of their incentive. In fact, this is a rational rule of cost-benefit[128] according to which the greater the anticipated cost of executing the forbidden act – and for our purposes, the cost involved in committing the theft and its consequences, including the chance that he will get hurt, cost of tools, allocation of time, planning etc. – relative to the anticipated profit, the lower the motivation and inducement to commit the offense. If so, the lower the value that remains in the hands of the thief after deducting the anticipated payment that he will have to make, the less he will tend to commit the act. Hence, the greater the compensation that is awarded, the lower will be the thief's gain and the profitability of the theft.

Maimonides' unique reasoning that "against robbery we can guard and defend ourselves; we cannot do so against theft"[129] warrants attention. The possibility that the robber's potential victims are prepared for him and that they can take precautions against him serves as a partial defense against robbery and as a certain preventive measure. No such prevention is usually possible against theft, which could be another reason for imposing four- or five-fold compensation payments on the thief to cover other instances of theft that he is likely to have committed. Maimonides appears to introduce an important economic element here: imposing a certain degree of obligation on the injured party to take preventive measures against damage. To Maimonides it makes sense to create an incentive for a person to guard more carefully against a robber than against a thief because the cost of protection against a sophisticated and cunning thief is probably higher than the cost of protection against robbery.

(c) Four- and Five-Fold Payments for the Theft of Sheep and Cattle

The thief may be liable for double, four-fold, or five-fold payment, with the multiplier of the compensation depending, as noted, on the object of the theft and on the thief's handling of the stolen property. As mentioned in the previous section, a series of problems arises with respect to the law of four- and five-fold compensation. Why was this special law enacted specifically for sheep and cattle? And why is there a distinction between compensation for sheep and for cattle?

Maimonides offers an explanation based on the prevalence of sheep and cattle stealing during the relevant biblical period:

---

[128] According to Bar-Niv's analysis, *ibid.* at 221–22.
[129] GUIDE 3:41 (Friedlander, 345).

> It is right that the more frequent transgressions and sins are, and the greater the probability of their being committed, the more severe must their punishment be, in order to deter people from committing them; but sins which are of rare occurrence require a less severe punishment. For this reason one who stole a sheep had to pay twice as much as for other goods, i.e., four times the value of the stolen object: but this is only the case when he has disposed of it by sale or slaughter (Exod. xxi. 37). As a rule, the sheep remained always in the fields, and could therefore not be watched as carefully as things kept in town. The thief of a sheep used therefore to sell it quickly before the theft became known, or to slaughter it and thereby change its appearance. As such theft happened frequently, the punishment was severe.[130]

As such, the consequence from the point of view of compensation, and the reason for this consequence is as follows:

> The compensation for a stolen ox is still greater by one-fourth, because the theft is easily carried out. The sheep keep together when they feed, and can be watched by the shepherd, so that theft when it is committed can only take place by night. But oxen when feeding are very widely scattered, as is also mentioned in [the Book of Nabatean] Agriculture, and a shepherd cannot watch them properly; theft of oxen is therefore a more frequent occurrence.[131]

Hence, Maimonides' approach to the matter is essentially deterrent, i.e., because the act (stealing an ox) is relatively common, it is appropriate to treat it with severity, not because it is highly objectionable from a moral point of view but precisely because of its frequency. Maimonides' explanation of the difference between stealing sheep and stealing an ox is different from the explanations in the Talmud.[132]

As noted by Bar-Niv,[133] it appears that according to Maimonides' approach there is no more inherent harm in stealing sheep and cattle than stealing any other chattels. However, because of the higher societal damage resulting from the large number of cases of theft of sheep and cattle, it is necessary to treat these thefts more severely, so that the profitability of stealing sheep and cattle will decline and the extent of this prohibited activity will decrease. Indeed, it seems that the aim is to provide incentives for the potential thieves not to steal. It is not the case that the theft of sheep and cattle is more morally reprehensible than other types of theft. Theft is theft. The difference must be rooted in something else. Maimonides accounts for the high incidence of this type of theft by the fact that cattle and sheep are naturally difficult to guard. In ancient times sheep and cattle fed mainly by grazing. To this end, the sheep and cattle were scattered in the field. Often, depending on the condition of the grazing areas and on the season of the year, it was necessary to travel with the animals to remote areas, making it much easier for the thief to steal.

---

[130] GUIDE 3:41 (Friedlander, 344).
[131] *Ibid.* (Friedlander, 344–45).
[132] *See* the reasons of R. Yohanan Ben Zakkai and R. Meir mentioned in note 211 *supra*.
[133] Bar-Niv, *supra* note 114, at 230.

From what Maimonides writes we see, according to our explanation, that the reason that compensation for the theft of cattle is higher than for the theft of sheep lies in the different costs of guarding cattle and sheep. The Torah dealt more severely with the theft of cattle because it is harder to guard cattle than sheep. The severity of the rule regarding the cattle stems from two factors, which are in fact a cause and its derivative: the difficulty in guarding that leads to high costs of guarding, which stem from the greater frequency of thefts. Therefore the raising of cattle becomes more expensive, and the products of the cattle and the services that they provide increase in price.

In many ways Maimonides adopts what today we would call optimal deterrence. This approach assumes that the perpetrators of the prohibited acts behave rationally. In other words, the decision whether or not to steal is an economic cost-benefit decision and it is a function of the profits expected from the theft. Indeed, following Bar-Niv's explanations,[134] we can demonstrate that Maimonides' reasoning regarding the theft of sheep and cattle is consistent with modern economic concepts of potential tortfeasors managing their risks.

How is it possible to reduce the number of thefts? One way is by increasing the means of guarding, with the result that the cost of committing the theft increases, *inter alia* because the thief must invest more time and resources into commission of the theft when greater security is in place. Accordingly, when the level of security is higher, the level of thefts decreases. On the downside, increasing security measures requires the allocation of resources, and this means directing those resources to guarding instead of to the production of other goods and services. It may, however, be possible to achieve a similar reduction in the level of thefts in another way, which was adopted in biblical law according to Maimonides' explanation, namely, by means of increased deterrence which expresses itself in higher compensation payable by the thief. Increasing the compensation lowers the anticipated profit on the part of the thief, and in all events, it reduces the profitability of the theft. Bar-Niv correctly wrote that the advantage of the biblical approach according to Maimonides' explanation lies in the fact that it aspires to achieve a reduction in the level of theft with a no-cost formula – i.e., by means of greater efficiency.[135]

According to Maimonides, biblical law seeks to preserve the cheaper methods of raising sheep and cattle, and prevent their theft by increasing the cost to the thief through an increase in compensation. Apparently, this interpretation provides a good explanation for increasing the compensation imposed on sheep and cattle thieves as opposed to thieves of other assets. But biblical law imposes such compensation on the thief who slaughtered or sold the stolen property, and not on every thief. Is this interpretation (and its economic aspects) consistent with the basic argument of the prevalence of theft?

---

[134] The analysis in the following paragraph is based on Bar-Niv, *ibid.* at 230–31, 236–37.
[135] *Ibid.* at 237.

The Talmud explains that the law deals severely with a thief who slaughtered and sold the sheep, obligating him to pay four- and five-fold, as opposed to one who merely stole and who pays only double, "because he [the former] became rooted in sin" or "because he has sinned repeatedly."[136] Indeed, Maimonides too invokes the frequency of the act as a central element in his analysis of these laws in the *Guide*, and this element is also mentioned in the *Code*, though in a relatively modest way.[137] The Talmud seems to use the expression "became rooted in sin" as a religious or moral justification for administering severe punishment as retribution for a person who transgressed repeatedly and in increasing measure.[138] Maimonides, however, regards the frequency of the act (of slaughtering and selling) as the element that affects the need for deterrence from the consequentialist aspect (and not retribution), separate from the religious dimension.

Maimonides explains: "The thief of a sheep used therefore to sell it quickly before the theft became known, or to slaughter it and thereby change its appearance."[139] This statement of Maimonides may be explained in two ways. According to the first possibility, the answer to the question of why the punishment is more severe in the case of the thief who slaughters and sells than for one who does not do so lies in the level of deterrence that is required: the thief is afraid of being caught, and it is more common for him to slaughter and sell than to keep the stolen sheep, in order to reduce the chances of the stolen object being found in his possession. He therefore requires deterrence at a higher level (four- or five-fold punitive damages) in order to stop him from slaughtering and selling. According to this explanation, there is no difference between *professional* thieves and those who are committing theft for the first time.

There is, however, another possible explanation of Maimonides' statement, according to which we must distinguish between two types of thieves: those who steal as an occupation and those for whom stealing is an exceptional event. This distinction makes economic sense. As Bar-Niv explains, a *professional* thief deserves to be held liable for punitive damages which are more than double; if he slaughters and sells, this means that this is his *modus operandi* – he is used to doing so, he is a serial criminal, and he takes measures to ensure that no signs of the theft remain in his proximity.[140] This additional parameter obscures the theft and displays regularity in its commission. This may also have been the intention of the Talmud, according to one explanation of the expression "because he became rooted in sin."[141] It may

---

[136] *Bava Kamma* 67b–68a.
[137] And *see*, *e.g.*, Laws of Robbery and Lost Property 3:6 (which is severe in relation to a person who is a serial robber, and imposes a fine on him).
[138] As per the commentaries of most of the commentators who concur with Rashi, *Bava Kamma* 67b, s.v. *shenishtaresh* [because he became rooted], i.e., put down roots, meaning that his sinning grew stronger, for he had already transgressed a first and a second time.
[139] *Guide* 3:41 (Friedlander, 344).
[140] Bar-Niv, *supra* note 114, at 228.
[141] R. Hananel, in his commentary to *Bava Kamma* 67b, explains the word "*nishtaresh*" on the basis of the Aramaic in the sense of gain, meaning that the thief gained and benefitted from the

also be possible to explain Maimonides' statement in the *Guide* in this way, although such an interpretation would be largely speculative, since Maimonides does not distinguish explicitly between the professional and the non-professional thief.

It follows from this second explanation that the purpose of biblical law in imposing punitive damages is to deter professional sheep and cattle thieves, who know immediately what to do with the stolen property, i.e., to conceal it and the evidence. This is perhaps similar to car thieves in our day and age, who immediately send off stolen vehicles to be dismantled, leaving no trace behind. The value of a functioning car may be much greater than that of its parts, but in a situation in which many vehicles are stolen and immediately disassembled, the chances of being caught are small, and therefore the profit may ultimately be greater. In the same way, a live animal is probably worth more than its meat, but if it is slaughtered (or sold) and out of the thief's hands, and if the thief, due to the slight chances of being caught, repeats this process many times, the possibility of preventing additional tortious events is small.

We agree with Kirschenbaum who thinks that the fines of four- and five-fold payments were designed to deter professional cattle and sheep thieves whose intention was to make large profits, for such thefts are ultimately intended for the preparation of meat for consumption, the preparation of animal parts for various industries, or simply for sale on the market. The Torah is interested in punishing the main perpetrator of such wholesale criminal trade, in all its aspects, and to frighten him and deter him from stealing the ox or the sheep.[142]

To sum up this section: the clearly consequentialist aspects of Maimonides' approach in the context of the laws of theft and robbery find expression in three principal ways, the first two of which are mentioned in the *Guide* and the third in the *Code*: 1. Deterrence of thieves and robbers; 2. Incentives for potential victims, too, to prevent theft; 3. A prohibition on buying from thieves or robbers, as mentioned in the *Code*, if it is known that the item is stolen, in order to reduce the chances of theft; his in fact is in order not to support criminals and cause them to continue stealing because they see that they have a market, for this would be reaping the fruits of their wrongdoing.[143] Maimonides thus lends support to one of the meta-objectives of tort law in general – the prevention of acts causing damage – by presenting a normative arrangement that tackles the problem from all angles, and

---

theft, for he sold it to another. Under this explanation the economic element – the profit – is the decisive factor, and the interpretation is similar to the second explanation cited in the text, according to which the professional thief who derives profit should be dealt with severely. If this is indeed how Maimonides should be interpreted, it may well be that he relied on R. Hananel's explanation, as he often does.

[142] Aharon Kirschenbaum, *Studies in Agency for a Criminal Act (Part I)*, 4 DINE ISRAEL 55, 78 (1973) (Heb.).
[143] Laws of Robbery and Lost Property 5:1.

provides an incentive for both the tortfeasor and the injured party to prevent theft and robbery cases, as well as imposing a prohibition against purchasing from the tortfeasor who stole.

C. A COMPARATIVE LOOK: SIMILARITIES AND DIFFERENCES BETWEEN THE *GUIDE* AND CONTEMPORARY LAW AND ECONOMICS SCHOLARSHIP

It is obvious that halakhic sages, including Maimonides, had no knowledge of modern economics and of the method of law and economics. They did not use the categories of this method in their thinking, and they did not formulate their views to fit its principles and details. Nevertheless, it is possible that in certain cases the halakhic authorities adopted intuitively a position for which modern scholarship of law and economics would supply a good explanation. In our opinion, this is particularly evident in the case of Maimonides' tort theory.

Revisiting Maimonides' texts in the *Guide*[144] in light of the contemporary methods can provide us with a new contemporary interpretation of Maimonides' tort theory. This interpretation rationalizes and clarifies Maimonides' various rulings, which are difficult to explain otherwise. Indeed, a careful comparison of Maimonides' explanation in the *Guide* with the writings of some of the prominent contemporary scholars of the economic analysis of tort law reveals a somewhat surprising similarity between them.

Maimonides' tort theory, as we saw in the previous chapter, also contains deontological aspects which bear much similarity to the conceptions of corrective justice, as well as patently religious aspects such as the prohibition on causing damage. Naturally, these aspects are not found in the doctrines of most of the exponents of law and economics. Nevertheless, insofar as the consequentialist aspects are concerned, the analysis in this chapter will point out interesting parallels between Maimonides's theory and those theories, and will identify the similarities and differences between them.

1 *Calabresi, Posner, and Maimonides' Test for Tort Liability*

The consequentialist part of Maimonides' tort theory as emerges from the particular chapter in the *Guide* (3:40) that was analyzed[145] may be compared to several of the basic economic analyses of the founding fathers of law and economics. We compare the Maimonidean theory primarily to that of the fathers of (tort) law and economics since Maimonides did not present a well-developed economic analysis of tort law in the consequentialist parts of his theory, but rather, a basic economic way of thinking

---
[144] As presented in the preceding part.
[145] Section B.1.

lacking many of the modern elements which are found in later, more fully developed theories in this field. As such, one can at most compare Maimonides' theory to the theories of the founding fathers, which, naturally, are relatively basic in comparison to recent economic analyses of law. Although the law and economics approaches presented by the founding fathers are sophisticated when compared to that of Maimonides, they nevertheless seem to be the most suitable comparison with the consequentialist parts of the Maimonidean theory. We are referring primarily to Guido Calabresi's strict liability no-fault doctrines of the cheapest cost avoider and best decision maker, and to elements of Richard Posner's fault-based Hand formula, as well as others.

(a) Calabresi's Cheapest Cost Avoider and the EAC Test

Guido Calabresi is generally credited with several contributions to modern tort law, some of them described briefly in Chapter 1. In this Section we will mention only those contributions that seem to have some parallels in Maimonides' theory.[146]

Calabresi's foremost contribution lies in his repudiation of the approach whereby the central objective of tort law is to compensate for damage caused in the past and to bring about a restoration of the original situation based on a conception of fault.[147] According to Calabresi, the objective of tort law is to avoid the costs resulting from a tort event, or at least to reduce them as much as possible as part of a theory postulating a need to achieve optimal deterrence, based on the understanding that it is neither possible nor desirable to try to prevent all accidents, because the cost would be infinitely high.[148] Calabresi is one of the first theorists to lay out broad considerations of efficiency. Several decades ago he opposed the fault-based method that dominated tort law at the time, whereby liability was imposed for negligence, and argued that this method does not promote deterrence.

Calabresi's approach seems to be quite similar to that of Maimonides. According to Maimonides, as we have seen, the goal of tort liability (together with deontological, corrective justice and religious considerations) is to reduce the costs created as a result of a tortious event – "the prevention of acts causing damage" in the words of Maimonides in the *Guide*.[149] Hence, like Maimonides, Calabresi too criticized traditional well-accepted fault-based tort theories and argued that one of

---

[146] As presented *supra* Section B.1. Some parallels between Calabresi's doctrine and specific Jewish legal sources (but not Maimonides!), in the context of environmental damage, are mentioned by Ruth Sonshine, Jonathan Reiss, Daniel Pollack, Karen R. Cavanaugh, *Liability for Environmental Damage: An American and Jewish Legal Perspective*, 19 TEMPLE ENVIRONMENTAL L. & TECHNOLOGY J. 77 (2000).
[147] *See, e.g.*, Guido Calabresi & Jon T. Hirschoff, *Toward a Test of Strict Liability in Torts*, 81 YALE L.J. 1055, 1056–59 (1972) (rejecting the Hand formula).
[148] GUIDO CALABRESI, THE COSTS OF ACCIDENTS: A LEGAL AND ECONOMIC ANALYSIS 69 (New Haven: Yale, 1970).
[149] GUIDE 3:40 (Pines, 555).

the main objectives of tort law is to avoid the costs resulting from a tort event. There are also other similarities between the tort theories of the two.

Calabresi focused on general deterrence (market deterrence), which assumes that no one knows what is better for the individuals in society than the individuals themselves; therefore, as long as they are aware of alternatives available to them and of their costs, society must allow them to choose between these alternatives. Individuals will act rationally and use the information at their disposal to calculate the efficiency of the various alternatives, to internalize the costs of accidents and of prevention, and to reduce them.[150]

Maimonides too placed great emphasis on general deterrence, as we saw, not only in relation to tort law but also in relation to criminal punishment; to a large extent, actual liability as well as the question of whether punitive damages will be imposed are determined in light of the principle of deterrence. Maimonides' analysis would appear to assume that tortfeasors and potential injured parties are rational and choose between alternatives on the basis of a cost-benefit criterion. On the basis of this assumption, one can understand the entire array of incentives for potential tortfeasors and injured parties which in Maimonides' opinion underlie Jewish tort law.

Let us now examine the similarity between Calabresi and Maimonides in relation to the question of who should bear tort liability.

Maimonides' EAC test from Chapter 3:40 of the *Guide* and Calabresi's theory are very similar, even if Maimonides, obviously, did not use Calabresi's terminology. Needless to say, Maimonides did not develop and justify his test with the special clarity and rationality that characterizes Calabresi's THE COSTS OF ACCIDENTS (1970) and later articles.

According to Calabresi, the different fault-based methods do not achieve optimal deterrence and the prevention of accidents or of their costs. In *The Costs of Accidents*, Calabresi developed the test known as the *cheapest cost avoider*, whose objective is to reach an optimal point of deterrence at which the total costs of the accident and the costs of preventing the accident will be lowest. In this way, tort law will achieve efficiency, i.e., optimal deterrence at the lowest cost, avoid accidents, and increase aggregate welfare.[151] According to this doctrine, strict liability is imposed on the person who can prevent the damage in the cheapest way. It should be emphasized that the cheapest cost avoider liability test is different from the "regular" strict liability regime, whereby the tortfeasor is always the one who is liable, irrespective of his fault and of the question of whether he was the cheapest cost avoider. Under the cheapest cost avoider doctrine, it is not always the tortfeasor who bears strict liability, as the cheapest cost avoider might at times be the injured

---

[150] CALABRESI, *supra* note 148, at 70–71, 95 (also distinguishing between general deterrence – of the market – and specific deterrence, whereby society must consider all the relevant parameters related to the accident and decide what it will approve).
[151] *Ibid.* at 26–31.

party. The objective of tort law according to this approach is to reduce the number of accidents and the costs of those accidents should they occur.

It may or may not come as a surprise to discover that even without having been exposed to Maimonides' approach as expressed more than eight hundred years ago in the *Guide*, Calabresi suggested an approach that is in many ways similar, although not identical, to Maimonides' EAC test of liability, although of course, Maimonides did not use Calabresi's terminology of "the cheapest cost avoider." It should be recalled that according to Maimonides' test, liability is imposed on those who can most effectively prevent the causing of damage, even if no fault attaches to their acts, similar to what Calabresi wrote some eight hundred years later.

However, the tests are not identical. As we saw in Section B.1, Maimonides argued that the imposition of liability depends on the answer to the question of who can avoid the accident more effectively. The most important element of the EAC test is *control*, and the person who has (actual or potential) control over the cause of the accident is considered the most effective avoider of the damage. Note that control is significant in modern law as well.[152] The most effective avoider is usually also the cheapest cost avoider, but not always, as the Maimonidean test depends on *control*, unlike the Calabresian test. According to Maimonides, the fact that the property is in a person's possession and therefore under his control is the reason why he is considered the most effective avoider of damages. As we explained, he must guard himself and his property so as not to harm others, and for this reason alone – i.e., prevention – liability should be imposed on him. Calabresi would probably explain this in a slightly different way from Maimonides: an owner of a living creature is the cheapest cost avoider because the creature is in the possession of the owner, and therefore his costs for avoiding the damage are relatively low compared to others.

We have seen so far that Maimonides discusses deterrence and the prevention of acts causing damage. But what is special about any economic theory – that of Calabresi and of others – is that it also considers the cost of preventing damage to be a social harm. Therefore, proponents of the economic theory of law talk not merely about deterrence, but about *optimal* deterrence, which is aimed at reducing the cost of accidents and the cost of accident prevention. In other words, this is not only an attempt to prevent accidents, but also to reduce, in various ways, the costs of the accidents that do occur, for example by changing the level of activities of the tortfeasor. Are these elements also present in Maimonides' work?

Maimonides does not invoke the modern concepts of optimal deterrence, and does not specify this element explicitly. He does, however, look for deterrence that

---

[152] For example with respect to property damages (*e.g.*, in some countries in the case of damage caused by dogs: *see*, *e.g.*, sec. 41A of the Civil Wrongs Ordinance (New Version), 5728–1968, 10 LSI 266, (1968) [Isr.]), and with respect to employee damages (*e.g.*, vicarious liability, restricted to cases of control and employee compliance with the framework and mission of the job).

takes into account the costs of prevention, and therefore does not impose liability on those whose prevention costs are high relative to the costs of the accident. This may be inferred from the *Guide*, where he writes that the damage avoider is liable only for damages in relation to which "it was possible for him to be cautious and take care not to cause damage."[153] But if a person has no ability to prevent effectively the occurrence of the damage, he is exempt from liability. To illustrate this point, Maimonides offers the example of the animal owner who is exempt by the *halakhah* from damages caused by the animal's feet or teeth as it walked in public domain: "For this is a matter with regard to which it is impossible to take precautions, and they rarely cause damage there."[154] Why is it not possible to prevent damage caused by tooth and foot? After all, the owner can avoid such damage by preventing the animal from walking in the public domain. The explanation appears to be that deterrence of this type is considered to be *over-deterrence* rather than *optimal deterrence*, because denying animals the right of passage in the public domain, especially in the ancient world, involves prevention costs that are too high and detrimental to social welfare, whereas the cost of the damage they prevent is relatively low (tooth and foot damage is relatively rare). Therefore, the owner of the animal is exempt from liability for tooth and foot damage in the public domain, resulting in optimal deterrence.

The cheapest cost avoider doctrine, however, suffers from several drawbacks, some of which Calabresi himself mentioned in a well-known article he wrote with Jon Hirschoff in 1972.[155] Calabresi and Hirschoff improved this test and devised the similar-but-different test of the "best decision maker."[156] According to this doctrine, liability is imposed on the entity belonging to the group that is in the best position to reach

> [A] decision as to which of the parties to the accident is in the best position to make the cost-benefit analysis between accident costs and accident avoidance costs and to act on that decision once it is made. The question for the court reduces to a search for the cheapest cost avoider… The issue becomes not whether avoidance is worth it, but which of the parties is relatively more likely to find out whether avoidance is worth it.[157]

The best decision maker test is different from the fault-based liability test of negligence. It differs also from the economic concept of negligence, to be discussed in the next section, whereby failure to prevent the damage is defined as negligence and results in the imposition of liability. The best decision maker must examine

---

[153] GUIDE 3:40 (Pines, 555).
[154] Ibid.
[155] Calabresi & Hirschoff, *supra* note 147.
[156] Ibid.
[157] Ibid. at 1060–61 (describing the difference between the cheapest cost avoider and the best decision maker).

whether and how much to invest in prevention, knowing that if damage occurs he in any case bears its cost, which is likely to affect his level of activity.

The best decision maker liability test is similar to the cheapest cost avoider test in that they are both different from the "regular" strict liability regime. Under the best decision maker doctrine, as under the cheapest cost avoider doctrine, it is not always the tortfeasor who bears strict liability, as at times the best decision maker happens to be the victim. In other words, strict liability is the foundation of the best decision maker regime, but the liability is not always imposed on the tortfeasor. In these cases the tortfeasor does not bear the cost of the damage, and the loss should lie where it fell.

Unlike Calabresi's "cheapest cost avoider" test, which has some parallels in Maimonides, as we saw, his later "best decision maker" test involves not only the efficient ability to prevent damage but primarily the information available on the expected damage and its associated risks. Can we find a parallel for this in Maimonides? Maimonides makes no mention of a "best decision maker" as distinct from the effective prevention of acts causing damage (more of a "cheapest cost avoider") that was explicitly stressed as the basis for tort liability in the *Guide*. But it appears that the foundations of the best decision maker can serve to elucidate several of Maimonides' rules in his *Code*.[158]

As in the case of Calabresi, the owner of the animal is not always considered to be the most effective damage avoider (the Maimonidean test) or the cheapest cost avoider and the best decision maker (the Calabresian tests). There are cases in which the liability should not be imposed on the owners, even though they are often the effective damage avoiders, the cheapest cost avoiders or the best decision makers. To be precise: according to Calabresi's approach, like that of Maimonides, these are cases in which the cheapest cost avoider or the best decision maker does not belong in the category of tortfeasors, but rather of those who suffer injury. This means that the damage will fall entirely on the shoulders of the injured party, and he will receive no compensation. Indeed, as we have seen, Calabresi does not follow a common standard of strict liability because under a regime of strict liability imposed exclusively on the tortfeasor, there is no incentive for the victim to prevent damages, which is a good reason for developing a standard which, although based on strict liability, is nevertheless different from it.

For example, although the manufacturer is typically the best decision maker as compared to the consumer, and he is held liable if he could have prevented the damage or reduced the cost of the accident by appropriate expenditures, the manufacturer is not liable if the consumer uses the product in a different and unusual way that deviates entirely from its original purpose and endangers him.[159]

---

[158] In Chapter 6 Section C we will see parallels to the best decision maker in the *Code*.

[159] Consider a person who uses a large lawn-mower, designed only to cut grass, for other purposes – albeit important ones – such as riding on it to the hospital carrying a wounded person.

It is within his power to prevent the damage in the best way by refraining from inappropriate use, especially if such use is dangerous.[160] In such a case he could have weighed the balance of cost and benefit better. Strict liability is imposed on the best decision maker whether he happens to be the tortfeasor or the injured party, irrespective of whether the other party did what ought to have been done.

As we said in the previous section, Maimonides has a similar explanation for the *halakhah* holding the owner of an animal liable for horn damage in the public domain although he is exempt from tooth and foot damage there: he explicates the law by carefully examining who the effective damage avoider is – the owner of the animal or the injured party.

Using Calabresi's terms, it is possible to say that Maimonides believes that no liability should be imposed on the owner of an animal that caused tooth and foot damage in the course of its regular passage through the public domain because he is not the cheapest cost avoider or the best decision maker. The reason is that on one hand, the cost of preventing the damage, if it were to be imposed on the owner of the beast, is very high owing to the difficulty of preventing damage caused by a beast passing through the public domain; on the other hand, the expected damage is relatively light because "they rarely cause damage there."[161] In the case of horn damage, however, the cost of prevention of the damage by the owners is not high, and it is significantly lower than the costs of preventing tooth and foot damages. This is because it is normal for an animal to trample whatever it walks through and to eat the food it finds along its path, and the cost of preventing these acts in the public domain is therefore high. By contrast, horn damage is defined as a departure from the regular nature of the animal. Thus, the cost of preventing the damage, if it were to be imposed on the owners, would not be particularly high, for only on rare occasions does an animal gore.

As we saw, Maimonides also took into consideration the potential victim and the degree of his ability to prevent the damage, adding that whoever left something in

---

The lawn-mower may be capable of driving on the road, but when the blade breaks and the owner is injured, he himself is the best decision maker. If the blade broke as a result of cutting the lawn in a rocky area, however, the owner of the lawn-mower is not the best decision maker: rather, the manufacturer, who ought to have striven to design a machine that would avoid damage in such cases, is the best decision maker. Calabresi & Hirschoff, *supra* note 147, at 1064. In the case of riding the lawn-mower on the road, it is true that it is the manufacturer's decision not to take advance measures to prevent damage in cases of rare and unusual use of the product, based on the consideration that even if he were to take such measures he may not succeed in preventing the damage. Calabresi emphasizes that the reason the manufacturer is nevertheless exempt in these cases is not related to the consumer's contributory negligence (which is part of the fault-based regime, rejected by him), but because in these cases, it is the user who is the best decision maker.

[160] Calabresi even compares this situation with the original meaning of the assumption of risk theory, namely that a victim who freely and consciously chooses to expose himself to a known risk is not entitled to compensation. Calabresi & Hirschoff, *supra* note 147, at 1065.

[161] GUIDE 3:40 (Pines, 555).

the public domain "is at fault toward himself." In today's terms, this would be called a type of assumption of risk, or severe and very high contributory negligence – for he exposes his property to loss, and therefore it is proper to impose on him liability for the damage and to exempt the owner of the animal from liability. It is clear, therefore, why the owners of animals were not held liable for tooth and foot damage in the public domain: it is the responsibility of the injured party to remove or guard his produce because "he who puts a thing in a public space is at fault toward himself and exposes his property to destruction."[162] In Calabresi's terminology, the one who places an object in the public domain, not the owner of the beast, is the cheapest cost avoider of the damage and the best decision maker. As with Calabresi, there is no division of responsibility between the parties for contributory negligence on the part of the person leaving the object, but a decision one way or another about full responsibility.

At the same time, as we saw,[163] Maimonides adds that people passing through the public domain who are likely to be injured as a result of the exceptional behavior of the animal cannot protect themselves against this damage (horn damage), because they have no control over the behavior of the animal. Moreover, it is reasonable to assume that simply passing in the street cannot be considered a case of assumption of risk or even contributory negligence, even if at times such passing turns out to be dangerous. Clearly people have no alternative, and it would not be reasonable to impose liability for the simple activity of walking in the public domain.

This point is reminiscent of the imposition of liability on drivers and owners of vehicles as the best decision makers according to Calabresi and Hirschoff, whose explanations involve insurance and regulation, which did not exist in the Middle Ages. According to Calabresi, there are two main considerations for imposing liability in this case. One consideration is distributive – it is more correct to impose liability on drivers than on pedestrians. The second consideration concerns information and the ability of a person to direct behavior through insurance and regulation. In other words, because driving is a regulated activity (as opposed to walking, which is not regulated and cannot be supervised efficiently), it is more effective to insure driving than walking, and to impose liability on the driver rather than on the pedestrian, even if, for example, the latter jumped out in front of a car. Driving is a regulated activity in that the driver receives information from the insurance company. In some places, the insurance premium varies with the level of the risk.[164] By means of the insurance, it is possible to verify the safety measures that each driver purchased, which places the driver in a better position than the pedestrian to weigh the costs of prevention against those of the accident. It is also possible to set standards (e.g., air bags, ABS, etc.), whereas it is not

---

[162] Ibid.
[163] Supra Section B.1.b.
[164] CALABRESI, supra note 148148, at 247–48, 252–53.

possible to determine whether or not a person crosses the road cautiously, because it is difficult to distinguish among various categories of pedestrians based on their potential for accidents. Imposing insurance on pedestrians would result in a problematic uniform insurance, as all pedestrians would be paying the same amount, without regard to the degree of risk. Even if it were possible to test this risk, insurance of this type would still be differential, based on the degree of risk that the pedestrian poses to himself, even if considered as part of a group, so that children, the sick, the disabled, and the elderly would most likely pay more, again resulting in a distributive and social problem. Drivers are therefore better decision makers than pedestrians. Imposing liability on drivers is likely to cause them to change their behavior, whereas pedestrians are not likely to change their behavior in any case, as they are already affected by the risks posed by vehicles, and they are likely to exercise similar care whether or not liability is imposed on them.

Similarly, Maimonides explains that there is no logical reason for imposing liability on whoever walks in the public domain in a normal manner and is injured by a goring or kicking beast. Such a person cannot be regarded as a best decision maker, and in any case his behavior will not be changed if he were recognized as such. All he can do is hope that an animal will not suddenly go wild and cause harm. This is in complete contrast to those leaving their property in the public domain, who expose their property to loss (in the case of common tooth and foot damages), and who must therefore be regarded as the best decision makers. These latter need not pray for good fortune but rather, protect their possessions and not leave them without supervision in the public domain. Unlike pedestrians in the public domain, they have logical alternatives, namely to place their vessels elsewhere and thereby reduce the level of their activity or carry them on their persons.

This is the place to address the similarities and differences between Maimonides' position on the matter of liability for innocent (*tam*) ox damage[165] and Calabresi's best decision maker theory. On the one hand, as we saw in the case of Calabresi, one can suggest that according to Maomonides the rule regarding the *tam* ox also expresses a societal view. According to this, incentives must be provided to the owner of the animal to guide his behavior to take precautions and to think creatively about doing so, even if at the time it may have seemed to him that he did everything possible to prevent the damage. In any case, if it transpires that the owner of the animal does not properly watch over it, and it repeats the goring at least three times,[166] the animal is declared likely to gore (forewarned). Here the owner pays the *full* cost of the damage if he did not guard the animal properly, because he is a serial tortfeasor who is not deterred by payment of half-damages.[167] On the other hand, we

---

[165] *Supra*, Section B.1.c.
[166] Maimonides, Laws of Property Damages 1:4; 6:1.
[167] *See also* the discussion about serial tortfeasors in the next section.

must bear in mind the differences between Maimonides' innocent ox rule and Calabresi's best decision maker theory. The major difference is that the owner of the ox is not liable for the *full* horn damage caused by an innocent ox but pays an amount reduced by *half*. This difference follows from an even more significant difference between Calabresi and Maimonides that is discussed in this chapter, regarding the appropriate type of liability: strict liability for the best decision maker (Calabresi) as opposed to liability that is more than negligence but less than strict (Maimonides).[168]

The example of horn damage by a *tam* ox can serve as a test case in which it is difficult to determine unequivocally who can optimally prevent the cost of the damage caused by goring, because this is a rare and unforeseen damage. As noted by R. Rabinovitch, "It is not possible to define precisely what cautionary measures can help without detriment to the possibility of maintaining the agricultural activity."[169] In cases of this type it may be preferable to divide liability between the tortfeasor and the injured party, thereby establishing an appropriate balance between creating an incentive for the owner of the animal to find ways of preventing the unforeseeable damage and between causing over-deterrence by the disruption of economically and socially desirable agricultural activity. On the other hand, the division of liability provides an incentive also to the potential victim to take reasonable precautionary measures in order to avoid the results of unforeseeable damage.

Of course, not all the differences between Maimonides and Calabresi are differences in fundamental jurisprudential conceptions, and it may well be that they are also connected to the different historical backgrounds and circumstances in which they operate.[170]

(b) Posner's Hand Formula, Contributory Negligence, and Maimonides

Despite the great similarity between what Maimonides writes at the beginning of Chapter 3:40 in the *Guide* introducing the EAC test and the Calabresian test of the cheapest cost avoider, later in the chapter Maimonides did not use Calabresian terminology when explaining the exemption for tooth and foot. The phrase that Maimonides uses, namely, "Whoever leaves something in the public domain is at fault (*posheah*) toward himself and exposes his property to loss," may admittedly be explained as assumption of risk, i.e., a situation in which a person enters into a dangerous situation intentionally and of his own initiative and as such he is the

---

[168] We expand on this in Chapter 7 Section B.
[169] Rabinovitch, *supra* note 63, at 73.
[170] For example, we saw that for Calabresi, the subject of insurance constitutes a major consideration, whereas in Maimonides' time there was no insurance and the tortfeasor would pay for everything himself. We will deal with distinctions such as these in Chapter 7.

cheapest cost avoider and possibly also the best decision maker, according to Calabresi's approach which is based on strict liability. Of course, from the point of view of the rationale, this cannot be discounted, but it is hard to avoid the fact that Maimonides nevertheless used the phrase "is at fault (*posheah*) toward himself," which is associated with elements of *peshiah*-negligence. Therefore, the similarity between Posner's approach and the Hand formula and between Maimonides' theory must also be examined, particularly the component of regarding one who leaves objects in the public domain as being negligent vis-à-vis himself, liable for the entire damages – a type of contributory negligence in the magnitude of 100 percent.

In Chapter 1 we briefly mentioned some of the characteristics of Richard Posner's tort theory; now we will analyze in more detail only those elements that relate to the contributory negligence and comparative negligence doctrines, emphasizing the difference between Calabresi's and Posner's theories.

Even though we use a general term – contributory negligence – there are actually a few terms in use for a situation in which the injured party contributed to the injury inflicted on him. In many countries liability in such situations is governed by what is termed the "comparative negligence rule," i.e., the negligence rule coupled with the defense of contributory negligence.[171] "Pure comparative negligence" is a relative defense which reduces the compensation according to the part of the fault of the injured party.[172] In a minority of countries and U.S. jurisdictions, the older doctrine of contributory negligence (which is different from comparative negligence, in that there is no comparison between the negligence of the two parties in causing the damage) still prevails. According to this doctrine – the source of which presumably lies in the claim of lack of clean hands of the injured party in that he has the nerve to sue when he has even a small part in the damage – the injured party will not receive any part whatsoever of the compensation if he too was negligent, and if he had a part in causing the damage – without comparison to and irrespective of the negligence of the tortfeasor.[173] There are several rationales for this doctrine, some which see it as a punishment for the plaintiff's misconduct, and some of them simply explaining that the policy is of "making the personal interests of each party depend upon his own care and prudence."[174] In a number of common law jurisdictions, however, the critical point is 50 percent, which is called "modified comparative negligence": if the contributory negligence exceeds 50 percent, the injured party will receive no compensation at all, and if it is less than 50 percent, he will receive full compensation.[175] In only two US jurisdictions, Nebraska and South Dakota, we find a different standard, of "slight-gross system," which is, in fact, a

---

[171] PROSSER & KEETON ON TORTS (5th ed., 1984) 468–79.
[172] *Ibid.* at 471–73.
[173] *Ibid.* at 451–62.
[174] *Ibid.* at 452.
[175] *Ibid.* at 473–74.

more extreme incarnation of modified comparative negligence.[176] A similar solution is found in Israel's Liability for Defective Products Law.[177]

If so, the term "contributory negligence" is in fact a type of all-or-nothing calculus. The fault of the injured party here is critical, and if present it means that he will receive no compensation at all. The situation of comparative negligence relates to division of the damage between the tortfeasor and the injured party, in the sense that the proportion of moral fault of the injured party, as assessed by the court, is deducted from the compensation to which he is entitled, so that if his contributory negligence is 40 percent, he will receive compensation amounting to only 60 percent of his damages.

Posner's improvement of the Hand formula was accompanied by an economic calculation of the extent of contributory negligence of the injured party. We will refer here to the relative defense in the sense of Posner's Hand formula in general as "contributory negligence."[178]

Posner based his approach on negligence rather than on strict liability. Hence, his economic approach is different from both corrective justice and strict liability. Posner relied on the Hand formula, which compares the costs of prevention with the expected cost of the harm in order to determine culpability.[179] The formula is based on economic efficiency, with the understanding that society is not interested

---

[176] Under this standard, as PROSSER & KEETON explain, "[T]he plaintiff's negligence is a bar to recovery unless his negligence is 'slight,' and the defendant's negligence by comparison is 'gross.' The plaintiff who meets this threshold criterion still has his damages reduced by the proportion of the total negligence that is attributable to him. Because 'slight' has been held to be merely a term of comparison, which varies according to the conduct of the parties, the present system appears to function more satisfactorily than earlier approaches which attempted to establish absolute standards for determining whether the plaintiff's negligence was 'slight.'" *Ibid.* at 473–74 (references omitted – the authors).

[177] *See, e.g.*, HARRY SHULMAN ET AL., LAW OF TORTS—CASES AND MATERIALS 627–706 (5th ed., 2010) (describing the laws of defective products in the US). In Israel's Liability for Defective Products Law 1991, the orientation of the common law is preserved, for the basic principle of this Law is the absolute liability of the manufacturer; however, one of the few defenses in the Law – which means that the liability thereunder is not entirely absolute, even though it is not negligence either – is that of gross contributory negligence. Indeed, only grioss contributory negligence can reduce the compensation in any way. Section 4.b of the Defective Products (Liability) Law 1980, S.H. 1980, 86 [Isr.]. The section states as follows: "It will not be a defense to an action against a manufacturer that negligence of the injured party contributed to the damage, but if the injured party was grossly negligent, the court may reduce the amount of compensation having regard to the extent of his negligence." A low level of contributory negligence will not entail a reduction of the compensation by a correspondingly low proportion, as is the case with comparative negligence. Indeed, it seems similar to the slight-gross system in common law.

[178] It seems that each of the frameworks (contributory negligence or comparative negligence) can fit the Hand formula. Whether one is applicable will depend on the jurisdiction. For instance, contributory negligence states would bar liability, even if the Hand formula runs true, if a plaintiff is also negligent.

[179] RICHARD A. POSNER, ECONOMIC ANALYSIS OF LAW (Aspen Publishers, 7th ed., 2007).

in preventing accidents at any cost and by investing infinite resources.[180] The tortfeasor is considered negligent when the burden (B, the cost of prevention) is smaller than the expected damage, which is the product of the probability of harm (P) and of the degree of loss (L): $B<PL$. A person is considered negligent if he spends 80 to prevent damage expected to be 100, but not *vice versa*. Unlike the approach adopted by Calabresi, if it was necessary to invest 100 to avoid damage of 80, not only is the person who did so not negligent but neither does he pay the 80; he pays nothing. According to the strict liability approach, however, he will pay 80 because liability is absolute and without fault.[181] The difference is therefore a distributive one: whether or not the injured party will be compensated.

Note also that under a best decision maker regime, even if a manufacturer claims that his product is the safest, liability is imposed on him if his product actually caused damage, as mentioned in the former section (Section C.1.a). In this case, therefore, the liability is imposed on the best decision maker even if he is not the cheapest cost avoider, but we estimate and perhaps hope that he will become the cheapest cost avoider in the future. According to Calabresi and Hirschoff, there is no escape from imposing *strict* liability on him, if the goal is true prevention, even if at the moment it does not seem possible to produce a safer product. Posner believes that it is necessary to apply here a fault-based regime with contributory negligence, which means that the consumers, and not only the manufacturer, have a duty to try to prevent the damage, and their compensation may be reduced if they have not done so.[182] According to Posner, imposing liability (only) on the manufacturer in this case, purely in order to incentivize him to develop the product in the future even though at present it is considered safe, as suggested by Calabresi, is not effective, because this eliminates the incentive of the consumer-operator to take steps to reduce the harm. Posner argued that "[a] strict liability standard without a contributory negligence defense is, in principle, less efficient than the negligence-contributory negligence standard."[183]

Maimonides' rationalization of the exemption for tooth and foot damages and the difference between these and horn damages can apparently be explained by either of the two economic methods of Calabresi and Posner. We saw how Maimonides' approach could be explained by Calabresi. Nonetheless, Maimonides' approach may well be closer to that of Posner. Maimonides wrote: "These laws contain considerations of justice to which I will draw attention."[184] It is conceivable that Maimonides is referring here to economic efficiency-enhancing justice, and not, for example, to corrective justice, "For this [tooth and foot in the public

---

[180] WILLIAM M. LANDES & RICHARD A. POSNER, THE ECONOMIC STRUCTURE OF TORT LAW 85–88, 96–107 (Cambridge, MA: Harvard University Press, 1987).
[181] Richard A. Posner, *Strict Liability: A Comment*, 2 J. LEG. STUD. 205, 208 (1973).
[182] In the lawn-mower example, he should move the stones. See Posner, *ibid.* at 213–14.
[183] *Ibid.* at 221.
[184] GUIDE 3:40 (Pines, 555).

domain is exempt] is a matter with regard to which it is impossible to take precautions."[185] In other words, using Posner's Hand formula, the cost of preventing these actions in the public domain (B) is high when animals commonly pass through it. The possibility of reducing the level of this activity was not a real one given that animals were the exclusive means of transportation and transfer of cargo. On the other hand, Maimonides also asserts that tooth and foot "rarely cause damage there,"[186] meaning that the probability of harm (PL) by tooth and foot in the public domain is relatively low compared to the cost of prevention (B). Maimonides, like Posner, does not merely consider the prevention costs of the tortfeasor vis-à-vis the expected damage, but examines the fault of the injured party as well, even though he does not split the damages between the parties, as he writes in the *Guide*: "He who puts a thing in a public space is at fault toward himself and exposes his property to destruction."[187] His fault lies in leaving his property in the public domain without protection, resulting in it being damaged. He could have not left it there (thus lowering the level of his activity, even if it is convenient for him to place his property there) or taken it with him. As noted, this may be regarded as assumption of the risk according to the approach of the best decision maker, although the words "is at fault (*posheah*)[188] toward himself" appear to indicate a notion of fault. Either way, the approach appears to be economic, as it seems to relate to the objective of preventing damages (and not corrective justice) mentioned by Maimonides earlier in the same chapter (3:40). If so, the rationale is similar to that of Posner and the Hand formula, but the outcome is different, since there is no splitting of damages between the parties.

It would also be possible to follow Posner's approach in analyzing Maimonides' rationalization of the liability of the owner of the animal for horn damages, even if they occurred in the public domain. Because kicking and goring are less common actions of animals than are eating or trampling in the process of walking, it is possible to prevent accidents involving prevention costs that are not particularly high relative to the cost of tooth and foot damage, for example, by restraining the animal. Let us assume that the cost of prevention is 10. On the other hand, the damage caused by kicking and goring may be particularly high, say 500. Therefore, even if the probability that such accidents will happen is not high, let us say 5 percent of cases, the expected damages may be considerable. An economically minded person will invest 10 to prevent an expected damage of 25 (5 percent of 500), and if he did not do so, he is considered to be negligent. But if the probability of such an accident is extremely low, say 1 percent, the opposite result from that mentioned by Maimonides will ensue, because an economically minded person would not invest

---

[185] *Ibid.*
[186] *Ibid.*
[187] *Ibid.*
[188] *Ibid.* (authors' translation from Swartz ed., 574).

10 in order to prevent expected damage of only 5 (1 percent of 500), whereas according to Calabresi, liability will always be imposed on him as a tortfeasor.

Indeed, as we saw, one can say that Maimonides imposes liability on the owner of the animal for horn damages that occurred even in the public domain because he is – in Calabresi's terms – the best decision maker under the circumstances. Maimonides justifies not imposing liability on the owner of the animal for tooth and foot damages for exactly the same reason. His considerations are consistent with the central rationale of the best decision maker in general, particularly with regard to not imposing liability on pedestrians because they are not considered to be the best decision makers. Similar to Calabresi, Maimonides does not assess the concrete situation but explains the meaning of the Talmud based on a group test, involving the group of the owners of animals versus the group of the people who walk in the public domain and the group of people who leave their vessels and their fruit in the public domain, in various situations. When the animal eats or tramples in the public domain, which are regular and common acts, the best decision maker is the owner of the fruit that was eaten or trampled, because he should have prevented the results of a likely and foreseeable act. By contrast, in cases in which the animal gores and kicks, it is for the owner of the animal to be careful, because he is the best decision maker and such actions of the animal are less frequent, and in any case, pedestrians walking normally in the public domain have no practical way of avoiding such occurrences. In both cases we see that it is possible to examine the situation using the Hand formula of economic negligence. Maimonides' rhetoric is closer to the Hand formula in cases of tooth and foot damage than in cases of horn damage.

It would seem that in their explanations of the talmudic rule, different scholars have different understandings regarding contributory negligence, and it is not possible to formulate a uniform approach to the Jewish law on this subject. What is clear, however, is that negligence on the part of the injured party does not create an automatic presumption of exemption from payment – in whole or in part – on the part of the tortfeasor in every case,[189] as it does in the case of traditional contributory negligence in the common law.[190] With respect to Maimonides' approach, however, as expressed in the *Guide*, the situation appears to be clearer. When Maimonides discusses the matter of a person who "is at fault (*posheah*) toward himself" in the *Guide*, he presents a rationale that is clearer and more general than that which is presented only in specific contexts in the *Code*[191] and in the talmudic sources.[192] Maimonides regards this as a central element in determining who will bear the liability – the tortfeasor or the injured party. It is clear why Maimonides' outcome is not compatible with contributory negligence, since it is

---

[189] Friedell, *supra* note 72, at 97–98, 108. For Friedell's comprehensive discussion of the topic *see ibid.* at 97–110.
[190] PROSSER & KEETON, *supra* note 171, at 451–62.
[191] *See* Laws of Wounding and Damaging 1:11.
[192] *J Bava Kamma* 2:8.

clearly a matter of all or nothing. The rationale is similar, but not the outcome. This approach seems very similar to that if the modified comparative negligence in common law, as we explained in the beginning of this section. Why is it not pure comparative negligence? Since in his analysis in the *Guide* Maimonides seems to be comparing the defendant and the paintiff, asking who is more at fault, and from his words it seems not to be a matter of precise division by percentage according to the fault of the injured party, but of imposing liability on the defendant only if his negligence was greater than that of the plaintiff.[193] In this approach, a mid-point – 50 percent – is determined. Whoever was negligent beyond this mid-point of 50 percent will bear liability for the entire amount of the damages. Accordingly, contributory negligence in a lesser proportion will not entail any reduction of compensation, and if it exceeds 50 percent there will be no compensation at all. As such, Maimonides' approach may be closer to what the common law today calls modified comparative negligence, although his words are very general and we are not absolutely sure what version of contributory negligence Maimonides would have actually adopted.

Thus we see that the modified comparative negligence approach is closer to that of Maimonides, although contemporary law gives the court discretion to decide in each case if the case is one of gross contributory negligence, whereas Maimonides is more formalistic and sets the point at 50 percent. In practice, the approaches are almost identical, for it may be assumed that according to Maimonides' approach too, this 50 percent is only an estimation and there is no possibility of actual measurement in each case.[194]

---

[193] Friedell, *supra* note 72, at 97–98, 108. Friedell presented this view with respect to talmudic sources, and in this he disagreed with the approach of Albeck, who held that if both parties were negligent, the compensation is divided between them. *See ibid.* at 101–06. Friedell says that Albeck has a problem understanding the *Tosafot*, which was the basis of his approach. According to Friedell, the talmudic view that he himself is presenting emerges primarily from the approach of the *Tosafot*, which must be understood correctly, even though it is not entirely clear that this is indeed the approach in the Talmud, due to the scant talmudic discussion of contributory negligence. *See ibid.* at 100; Albeck, who understood the matter differently, did not fully support the approach of *Tosafot*. *See ibid.* at 105–07. For Albeck's response, *see*: Shalom Albeck, *Response*, 13–14 DINE ISRAEL 231, 232–33 (1986–1988) (Heb.). Friedell indeed held that most probably, the talmudic approach is that the defendant is liable only if he was more negligent than the plaintiff, as part of the general proclivity of the Talmud to limit tort liability. *See ibid.* at 109. In Friedell's view, even in cases of greater negligence on the part of the plaintiff – more than 50 percent – sometimes defendants were nevertheless held liable, because compromises are preferable to litigation in Jewish law, and it was preferable to make a partial payment to the plaintiff. *See ibid.* at 110. In our view, when Friedell wrote this he was not aware of Maimonides' formulation in the GUIDE; one would imagine that had he had that text available to him, it would probably have supported his conclusion. In our view, however, this conclusion is at most correct only with respect to characterization of Maimonides' method, for as we have said, characterization of the talmudic approach on this question is not unequivocal, and could be taken in several directions.

[194] Even though according to Posner's approach, it is possible to insert into the formula not only the negligence but also the contributory negligence and to obtain an accurate result with respect to the amount of reduction.

The payment of only half damages in the case of the innocent ox (*tam*), too, may be explained by Posner's contributory negligence doctrine, although the wording of Maimonides' rationalization of the half damage payment in his *Guide*[195] does not necessarily reflect Posner's theory; it speaks rather in terms of EAC, regarding both the tortfeasor and the injured party as effective damage avoiders in a similar way.[196] In Posner's terms, therefore, it may be said that in relation to the *tam* ox, the degree of negligence of the injured party is similar to that of the tortfeasor, and there is always a contributory negligence of sorts of 50 percent.

If so, the rationale underlying Posner's contributory negligence may be suited – to some extent or another – both to the cases in which the tortfeasor is exempt from liability and as an explanation of the rule of the *tam* ox. In any event, there seems to be a difference here: according to Posner both negligence and contributory negligence are examined in each and every case, whereas in the *tam* ox ruling it is always, in each and every case, half damages for each party, which makes it closer to Calabresi in the sense that he also does not examine each case on the merits.

Admittedly, it is important to recall that the standard of care required of the owner of a *tam* ox according to most opinions in the talmudic literature is that of strict liability,[197] and not negligence, as in other property damages.[198] Under this standard, if the *tam* ox gores, then even if the owner guarded it in an appropriate manner he will bear strict liability and pay half damages. This is as opposed to the *mu'ad* ox, for which the required standard of care is at a lower level than the *tam* ox, according to some views in the Talmud.[199] According to the Talmud, the maximum payment for a *tam* ox that gored will always be at the rate of half the damage and no more; in other words, it is not a matter of all or nothing, but rather, it is the "all" that is payable. According to the talmudic view that is accepted as law, the owner of the *tam* ox must make this payment of half damages in every case and irrespective of his negligence. This rule whereby the *mu'ad* ox requires guarding at a level that is inferior whereas the *tam* ox is subject to strict liability seems very surprising to the commentators on the Talmud and to modern eyes as well. According to the common talmudic interpretation it seems that the special law of payment for the damages of a *tam* ox stems from the definition of payment of half damages of the *tam* ox as a fine, i.e., although most *tam* oxen are tame and do not usually gore, nevertheless the Torah fined the owner for half damages if the *tam* ox did in fact

---

[195] GUIDE 3:40, (Pines, 575).
[196] Maimonides' approach was presented in Section B.1.c.
[197] See, e.g., the opinions of the sages mentioned in the Mishnah and in the talmudic discussion in *Bava Kamma* 45b–46a.
[198] See, e.g., M *Bava Kamma* 6:1 (which exempts the owner of sheep who put his sheep into an enclosure and locked the gate properly: if they nevertheless escape and cause damage, he is exempt).
[199] Mainly according to the opinion of R. Judah in M *Bava Kamma* 4:8. Various reasons were given in *Bava Kamma* 45b–46a for the difference in the standard of care for a *tam* ox and a *mu'ad* ox.

gore, in order to encourage owners to guard their oxen better. On this conception it may be possible to understand why half damages are paid wherever damage is caused, i.e., strict liability, irrespective of the negligence of the owners. It is important to create a permanent and uniform deterrent at the level of half damages so that the owner will invest, at least, in creating reasonable safeguards in order to reduce the chances that the *tam* ox will gore.[200]

In the *Guide*, however, there is no reference to the required standard of care in relation to different sorts of property damage and other kinds of damages (damages caused by a person to property, and injuries that a person causes to another person). This is because the discussion in the *Guide* is general and does not go into the details of the laws. In the *Code*, as we shall see in the following two chapters, Maimonides does indeed elaborate on the details of the required standard of care for each type of damage, and even rules in the same way as those talmudic sages who held that there is a different standard of care for the owner of a *tam* ox as opposed to the owner of a *mu'ad* ox.[201]

In the Appendix, which deals with the general rule of liability, namely, on whom to impose tort liability and with the specific topic of contributory negligence, we summarize similarities and differences between Maimonides' tort theory as reflected in the *Guide* 3:40,[202] and between the theories of Calabresi and Posner.

2 The Multiplier Approach, The Societal Redress Extra-Compensatory Damages Approach, and Maimonides' Test for Punitive Damages

Some of Maimonides' arguments in his *Guide* regarding punitive damages and criminal sanctions that have been presented[203] have surprising parallels in the studies of contemporary scholars. Particularly instructive is the comparison between Maimonides' statments and the modern law and economics literature, which contains several economic justifications of criminal sanctions and punitive damages. In this section we examine the similarities and differences between these contemporary approaches and the Maimonidean model, and the innovations in Maimonides' model compared to the contemporary legal views.

---

[200] Understanding the law governing the *tam* ox is a complicated matter, which has been attempted by many scholars and commentators, and this is not the place to discuss the various explanations that have been offered. A full understanding would require extensive discussion, which would deviate from the objective of this endeavor, which is to understand Maimonides' tort theory. And as we have said, Maimonides in the GUIDE did not discuss the level of the standard of care that is imposed on the owner of an ox that gores. Neither did he explain, in the CODE, the reason for imposing strict liability for damages caused by the *tam* ox. Therefore we will not enter into this discussion beyond what we have said in the chapter.

[201] Laws of Property Damages 7:1.

[202] Without going into the differences in the required standard of care in relation to different types of damage, as we will show in Chapter 7, which are specified in the CODE only and not in the GUIDE.

[203] *Supra* Section B.2.

(a) Maimonides and Possible Parallels in Contemporary Criminal Law

The four sentencing considerations presented by Maimonides in the *Guide*[204] have parallels in contemporary attitudes of increased stringency in criminal law (concerning sentencing as well as grounds for denial of bail, etc.), and possibly in civil law, in cases of serial torts.

In general, Maimonides' approach resembles those of Cesare Bonesana Beccaria,[205] Gary Becker,[206] and Jeremy Bentham.[207] The cost-benefit analysis whereby for a punishment to produce the effect required, it is sufficient that the evil it occasions should exceed the good expected from the crime, including the calculation of the certainty of the punishment, is found in Beccaria's writings.[208] Bentham explains that "as there are always some chances of escape, it is necessary to increase the value of the punishment, to counterbalance these chances of impunity."[209]

As to the imposition of criminal sanctions and punitive damages, consequentialist-deterrent approaches are interested in the question of optimal deterrence of the offender or tortfeasor, i.e., to make him pay an amount commensurate with the damage – not less, as was the case before the imposition of punitive damages, but not more either. Relying on the *ease* with which the offense is committed, without being noticed or caught by the legal authorities (Maimonides' parameter 4) and on the frequency of the act (parameter 2) as considerations for payment beyond the amount of the damage, certainly indicates an economic approach that is similar to the contemporary economic approach of punitive damages. Such an approach helps prevent tortious events by broadcasting the message that it does not pay to perpetrate the tortious act if eventually the payment for it is significantly higher than the amount of the damage. Payment of the damage only (recovery) in a situation in which there is an incentive to repeat the tortious act serially makes the perpetration profitable. For example, a person who knows that the inspector visits the same place only once a week randomly will calculate the cost of the offense against the gain from it. If parking the car for an entire week on the street costs more than the fine for one day, she will do so repeatedly (assuming that she is not concerned with being labeled a criminal). If she has to pay four or five fines every week, she will think twice.

In criminal law, one such parallel to Maimonides may be found in the writings of William Paley.[210] Paley emphasized what appear to be the same principles stressed by Maimonides, and enumerated the following factors to be considered in

---

[204] GUIDE 3:41, cited *supra* Section B.2.
[205] CESARE BONESANA BECCARIA, AN ESSAY ON CRIMES AND PUNISHMENTS (2nd ed., 1812).
[206] Gary S. Becker, *Crime and Punishment: An Economic Analysis*, 76 J. POL. ECON. (1968) 169.
[207] Jeremy Bentham, *Principles of Penal Law*, in THE WORKS OF JEREMY BENTHAM vol. 1, 365 (John Bowring ed., 1962).
[208] BECCARIA, *supra* note 205, at 94.
[209] Bentham, *supra* note 207, at 402.
[210] WILLIAM PALEY, PRINCIPLES OF MORAL AND POLITICAL PHILOSOPHY (1785); *see* LEON RADZINOWICZ, A HISTORY OF ENGLISH CRIMINAL LAW vol. 1, 251 (London, 1948); Ya'akov Bazak,

determining the severity of the punishment for any given crime: (a) the facility with which the act can be committed; (b) the difficulty in detecting the act; (c) the danger the act presents to the community. Based on these parameters, Paley unreservedly supported capital punishment for stealing sheep and horses, not because these thefts are by nature more heinous than many simple felonies that are punishable only by imprisonment or transportation (banishment), but because sheep and horses were property more vulnerable to theft. Based on this consequentialist approach, the terror of capital punishment is needed to protect against this felony.[211]

There are also two English verdicts that adopt a similar line of reasoning to that of Maimonides in explaining the law of four- and five-fold compensation.[212] In 1964, an English farmer was sentenced to three years imprisonment for stealing a sheep. The court reasoned that such an offence disturbs the relationship of trust that is vital between neighboring farmers in the valleys where sheep graze together in the open fields.[213] In 1975, a man "of good character" was sentenced to six months imprisonment for filing three false tax returns, resulting in a loss of £176 to the Revenue Department. The court reasoned that this type of offense was prevalent and therefore it required a deterrent penalty because it was not easily detectable.[214]

Thus, parallels were found in the Common Kaw literature both to some of the four parameters proposed by Maimonides for deciding on punishment, and to punitive damages at the four- and five-fold level. In the next section we will mention more significant similarities between Maimonides' analysis of the difference between payments of the thief and the robber on the one hand, and on the other hand, the modern approaches in the American literature to punitive damages.

(b) Maimonides' Approach to the Difference between a Thief and a Robber: Between the Multiplier and the Societal Redress Extra-Compensatory Approaches

We argue here that Maimonides' approach to the difference between a thief and a robber[215] is found on the scale between two modern approaches to punitive damages – the multiplier and the societal redress extra-compensatory approaches.

Under certain circumstances, as we have seen, courts have recognized the right to include a punitive element in civil tort law, i.e., awarding damages that do more than compensate the individual victim, often in order to express repugnance towards particularly serious, intentional and heinous acts. In other words, in certain

---

Maimonides' Views on Crime and Punishment, in JEWISH LAW AND CURRENT LEGAL PROBLEMS 121, 122–23 (Nahum Rakover, ed., Jerusalem: The Library of Jewish Law, 1984).
[211] PALEY, *ibid.*
[212] Mentioned in DAVID A. THOMAS, PRINCIPLES OF SENTENCING 14, note 1 (London, 1970); Bazak, *supra* note 210, at 124–25.
[213] Thomas, *ibid.*
[214] *Ibid.*
[215] *Supra* Section B.2.

circumstances, courts have the power to award damages the objectives of which are punishment, education and deterrence in civil law.[216]

However, there are different approaches to the rationale of punitive damages in contemporary scholarship and case law. Some traditional approaches indicate that punitive damages are most likely to be awarded in cases where *the harm or potential harm is very serious or the tortfeasor's behavior is reprehensible*.[217] Since according to many traditional views, punitive damages should be uncommon and should be awarded only for *malicious, intentional torts*, it follows that such damages should be awarded only in those cases in which both deterrence and punishment are particularly important.[218] At the same time, recognition of punitive damages according to the traditional approaches has been the subject of significant criticism, the argument being that the civil context is not suitable as a forum for awarding punitive damages, and that the mingling of criminal principles with the civil is wrong.[219] Other scholars have recently focused on *revenge and the dignity of the victim, as part of victims' rights*.[220] Such an approach, unlike the instrumental, economic and societal approaches which will now be addressed, does not and cannot take into consideration other injured parties, but only the plaintiff-victim, for this is a matter of personal revenge for personal suffering experienced by the plaintiff.

In the last two decades, scholars have also presented several approaches that regard punitive damages as a way to provide *redress* for the victim and/or as *a societal compensation goal*. According to some of these approaches, punitive damages are in fact extra-compensatory damages for the plaintiff; however, from the defendant's standpoint these damages are what he must pay in the eyes of society, which wants to suppress this behavior but not through criminal (or quasi-criminal) sanctions. Let us examine a few major approaches that advocate this line of thought.

---

[216] For an historical overview of the case law on punitive damages, *see* Steve P. Calandrillo, *Penalizing Punitive Damages: Why the Supreme Court Needs a Lesson in Law and Economics*, 78 GEO. WASH. L. REV. 774, 780–93 (2010); Dorsey D. Ellis, *Fairness and Efficiency in the Law of Punitive Damages*, 56 S. CAL. L. REV. 1, 12–20 (1982).

[217] Neil Vidmar & Matthew Wolfe, *Punitive Damages*, 5 ANN. REV. L. & SOC. SCI. 179, 192 (2009). *See also* David Partlett, *Punitive Damages: Legal Hot Zones*, 56 LA L. REV. 781 (1996).

[218] For example, Thomas B. Colby, *Clearing the Smoke from Philip Morris v. Williams: The Past, Present, and Future of Punitive Damages*, 118 YALE L.J. 392, 421–67 (2007), suggested that punitive damages are properly conceived of as a form of punishment for private wrongs. *See also* Thomas B. Colby, *Beyond the Multiple Punishment Problem: Punitive Damages as Punishment for Individual, Private Wrongs*, 87 MINN. L. REV. 583, 602 (2003) [hereinafter: Colby 2003].

[219] *See, e.g.,* Anthony Sebok, *Punitive Damages in the United States*, in: Helmut Koziol & Vanessa Wilcox (eds.), PUNITIVE DAMAGES: COMMON LAW AND CIVIL LAW PERSPECTIVES (TORT AND INSURANCE LAW) 155, 174–75 (Vienna/New York, 2009); Colby 2003, *ibid.* at 602; Matthew Parker, *Changing Tides: The Introduction of Punitive Damages into the French Legal System*, 41 GA. J. INT'L & COMP. L. 389, 413–14 (2013); David G. Owen, *A Punitive Damages Overview: Functions, Problems, and Reform*, 39 VILL. L. REV. 363, 382–83 (1994).

[220] Dan Markel, *How Should Punitive Damages Work?*, 157 U. PA. L. REV. 1383, 1394–95 (2009); Mark Geistfeld, *Punitive Damages, Retribution, and Due Process*, 81 S. CAL. L. REV. 263, 269–74 (2008); Benjamin C. Zipursky, *A Theory of Punitive Damages*, 84 TEX. L. REV. 105, 106 (2005); Colby 2003, *supra* note 218, at 602.

Margaret Jane Radin may have been the first to focus on redress.[221] She argued that redress provides a more useful framework for understanding punitive damages, forcing the wrongdoer to recognize that what he did was wrong.[222] She suggested that redress seeks to "symbolize public respect for the existence of certain rights and public recognition of the transgressor's fault in disrespecting those rights."[223] Matthew Parker explained that Radin's argument was that redress is not necessarily about monetary restitution, but rather it acts to affirm public recognition of certain rights and wrongs, and therefore there is a certain incommensurability between the harm caused by a tort and the corresponding damage award.[224]

Catherine Sharkey argued that "[p]unitive damages have been used to pursue not only the goals of retribution and deterrence, but also to accomplish, however crudely, a societal compensation goal: the redress of harms caused by defendants who injure persons beyond the individual plaintiffs in a particular case."[225] She therefore suggests that in cases of intentional torts, *societal damages* should be awarded.[226] These are actually extra-compensatory damages awarded to the plaintiff, but from the defendant's standpoint this is merely what he must pay because society is interested in reducing this type of behavior, but not through criminal sanctions.

One might think that punitive damages would lead to over-deterrence. However, the *multiplier approach* – the common economic analysis of law for punitive damages – suggests otherwise.[227] Since many injured parties, for a variety of reasons, do not actually sue,[228] and many tortfeasors end up not

---

[221] Margaret Jane Radin, *Compensation and Commensurability*, 43 DUKE L.J. 56 (1993).
[222] *Ibid.* at 56, 61, 85.
[223] *Ibid.* at 61.
[224] Parker, *supra* note 219, at 404.
[225] Catherine Sharkey, *Punitive Damages as Societal Damages*, 113 YALE L.J. 347, 351–52 (2003).
[226] *Ibid.* See also Thomas C. Galligan Jr., *Disaggregating More-Than-Whole Damages in Personal Injury Law: Deterrence and Punishment*, 71 TENN. L. REV. 117 (2003).
[227] Here we will examine the basic multiplier model of Shavell and Polinsky. Over the years, certain reservations to the model were expressed, but they concentrated mainly on the methods of calculating the effective multiplier in various tortious situations, and they do not affect the essence of the model. *See, e.g.*, Keith N. Hylton & Thomas J. Miceli, *Should Tort Damages Be Multiplied?* 21 J.L. ECON & ORG. 388, 410 (2005); Richard Craswell, *Damage Multipliers in Market Relationships*, 25 J. LEGAL STUD. 463 (1996); Lucian A. Bebchuk & Louis Kaplow, *Optimal Sanctions when Individuals are Imperfectly Informed about the Probability of Apprehension*, 21 J. LEGAL STUD. 365 (1992); Dilip Mookherjee and I. P. L. Png, *Marginal Deterrence in Enforcement of Law*, 102 J. POL. ECON. 1039 (1994).
[228] Victims do not sue, *inter alia* because of their own disinclination to do so, their assessment of the cost of filing and conducting a suit relative to the compensation they might expect, the unwillingness of their attorney to manage the claim due to issues of cost-effectiveness, evidentiary problems and uncertainty, and even because of various errors made in the enforcement process. And cf. IZHAK ENGLARD, THE PHILOSOPHY OF TORT LAW 145–46 (1993); A. Mitchell Polinsky & Steven Shavell, *Punitive Damages: An Economic Analysis*, 111 HARV. L. REV. 869, 888 (1998); Ellis, *supra* note 216, at 25–26; In re Zyprexa Products Liability Litig., 489 F. Supp. 2d 230, 247 (E.D.N.Y. 2007) ("Despite this effective civil prosecution network, there are usually a substantial number of potential harmed plaintiffs who never press their claims").

paying,[229] merely requiring tortfeasors to pay for the damage they cause would result in under-deterrence.[230]

For example, a tortfeasor causes with sufficient certainty a harm of ten dollars to each of six persons, but due to some insubstantial reasons only two of them are expected to bring actions against him. This tortfeasor is expected to internalize a cost of twenty dollars only, even though the cost of the negative externalities of his acts is sixty dollars (ten dollars for six persons). Consequently, Polinsky and Shavell explain that enforcement of punitive damages increases the level of deterrence afforded to potential (mostly serial and mass) tortfeasors, ultimately resulting in optimal deterrence – provided the correct amount of punitive damages is awarded.[231] In other words, if in those cases in which tortfeasors already pay damages they are subjected to punitive damages by reason of having acted in a deliberate and reprehensible manner, then even though this represents a certain overpayment *locally, in total* these tortfeasors will be paying at most for the aggravated wrong they caused, which would create optimal deterrence (or something approaching optimal deterrence) and not over-deterrence.

As Polinsky & Shavell explain, if tortfeasors take this possibility into account in advance, it will lead to greater efficiency in their actions and consequently to increased aggregate welfare. In the example provided in the last paragraph, if the tortfeasor would be found liable with a two-in-six (which is one-in-three) chance, damages should be $60. The harm is $20 (10x2), and it is multiplied by 3 (1/0.333). The total damages should be $60. $20 represents compensatory damages and the remainder, $40, is the optimal amount of punitive damages.[232]

Similar approaches were invoked in federal courts fairly recently by two judges who are among the founding fathers of the school of tort law and economics, and whose economic approaches to tort law were presented in Section C.1. In *Ciraolo v. City of New York*, Judge Guido Calabresi used the same substantive approach as the multiplier, calling it "socially compensatory damages."[233] In *Mathias v. Accor Economy Lodging Inc.*, Judge Richard Posner also applied the multiplier approach in practice.[234] These judgments were delivered prior to recent developments in the Supreme Court where the multiplier approach was dismissed in practice.[235]

---

[229] See, e.g., Richard J. Pierce, Jr., *Encouraging Safety: The Limits of Tort Law and Government Regulation*, 33 VAND. L. REV. 1281, 1295–97 (1980).
[230] ENGLARD, *supra* note 228, at 145–46.
[231] Polinsky & Shavell, *supra* note 228, at 873–74, 888–90.
[232] The formula for calculating punitive damages according to optimal deterrence examines the expectancy that the court will impose liability on the tortfeasor vis-à-vis the scope of the damage. See Polinsky & Shavell, *supra* note 228, at 888–90.
[233] *Ciraolo v. City of New York*, 216 F.3d 236, 243 (2d Cir. 2000). See also Guido Calabresi, *The Complexity of Torts – The Case of Punitive Damages*, in EXPLORING TORT LAW 333 (M. Stuart Madden ed., 2005).
[234] *Mathias v. Accor Economy Lodging Inc.*, 347 F.3d 672 (7th Cir. 2003).
[235] See Calandrillo, *supra* note 216 (presenting an overview of the denial of the multiplier approach in US Supreme Court judgments).

Under the multiplier approach, the basis for punitive damages is the desire to reach optimal deterrence and not under-deterrence or under-enforcement; punitive damages are not (necessarily) based on the fact that the act is malicious and reprehensible, contrary to the accepted rhetoric and traditional approaches to this matter.

After having examined the major approaches of the scholars concerning punitive damages, it remains to examine where Maimonides' approach, as it manifests itself in relation to the difference between a thief and a robber, could be placed. In our opinion, its place is between the *multiplier* and the *societal redress extra-compensatory* approaches.

Note that in the *Guide*, Maimonides does not focus on the non-economic, deontological explanations that are common today when imposing punitive damages, which consider the maliciousness of the action. Maimonides focuses on results and on deterrence. For example, the ease of performing the act (parameter 4 in the *Guide*) refers to the many cases in which the perpetrator does not pay for his actions because he is not caught. This serves as a disincentive to engaging in the negative behavior. This is usually also related to the frequency of the act (parameter 2), because the attractiveness of performing a prohibited act when it is easy to do so is great and its frequency is likely to increase.

As mentioned, the primary reasons for non-payment lie in the difficulties of identifying the tortfeasor, suing him, and enforcing judgment against him. The higher the probability that the tortfeasor will avoid payment, the greater the need to increase the rate of payment when it is exacted – when a thief is caught and is sued in torts – in order to maintain optimal deterrence. The texts analyzed in Section B.2 show clearly that Maimonides was aware of the aforementioned economic justification, which emphasizes the issue of enforcement, as he writes at the end of this statement: "The robber is known, can be sought, and forced to return that which he has robbed, whilst the thief is not known."[236] Maimonides' statements, however, indicate that deterrence does not depend only on enforcement capability but on other factors as well. It is possible that Maimonides provides a broader answer to the question of when to impose on the thief payment for more than the value of the theft. Indeed, in practice the incidence of the act of theft may be higher than that of robbery, and the temptation (parameter 3) greater to come under cover of darkness and steal, without confrontation, especially in circumstances in which the perpetrator would be subjected to severe community punishments, such the ban and banishment, if he was caught. Moreover, it is logical that the thief continues to steal until he is caught, which may take a long time, given that acts of theft are carried out in secret; the robber, on the other hand, is likely to be caught sooner due to the overt nature of his actions, and is therefore able to carry out fewer acts of robbery. In this situation the thief has a greater incentive to steal because his act pays

---

[236] GUIDE 3:41 (Friedlander, 345).

more. Furthermore, it is reasonable to assume that until the thief is caught he will have caused damage several times, so that in view of the profit realized from theft until capture, and due to the factor of deterrence against him and other existing or potential thieves, the amounts of payments imposed on him are significantly higher than the amount of the damage. If he was required to return only what he had stolen, it would pay for the thief to steal several times until caught. If he knows in advance that he will have to return more,[237] theft becomes less profitable, and the optimal deterrence may be a way to prevent the tortious event.

This Maimonidean approach recalls the *multiplier* approach, as we argue now but it nevertheless does not ignore the *societal redress* underlying the *extra-compensatory* damages. The multiplier may be relevant according to certain parameters of efficiency. Thus, for example, because the chances of apprehension of the thief are smaller than those of the robber in Maimonides' view, the burden of compensation should be increased in the case of the thief, and this brings to mind the multiplier approach. In fact, a higher multiplier is required for the thief than the robber, just as the serial or mass wrongdoer will pay more than one who is not a serial or mass wrongdoer. In order to deter the thief, therefore, a higher fine must be imposed on him; the robber who does not come under the cover of darkness, on the other hand, is easier to discover; as such he is naturally subject to greater deterrence even without juridical intervention, and therefore a smaller fine will suffice in his case.

Indeed, the *multiplier* approach of Shavell and Polinsky seems very similar to Maimonides' approach in that they both regard the chances of actual apprehension as an element of effective deterrence. There are, however, some differences between the two.

The first difference is that Maimonides' approach focousses more on the punitive aspect, and the term "punitive damages" is better suited to it, whereas there is no real punitive element in the multiplier approach but rather, optimal economic deterrence.

The second difference lies in the focus. Whereas Shavell and Polinsky focus closely upon previous acts in which the wrongdoer was not apprehended, Maimonides focusses on effective deterrence in the specific case at hand, where the chances that the thief-wrongdoer will be apprehended are examined. In all events Maimonides was not exposed – so it seems to us – to the criticism of the US Supreme Court according to which, as will be recalled, there is a problem with recognizing the multiplier approach because the defendant is in fact being tried for incidents that were not actually adjudicated in court, and he has not had the opportunity to defend himself in relation to these incidents, contrary to due process. Shavell and Polinsky are able to present a fairly exact calculation of the sum that the wrongdoer must pay, in order to compensate exactly for the wrong he did – no more (over-deterrence) and no less (under-deterrence) – as part of optimal deterrence, in order not to repeat the

---

[237] And possibly this doubling of the amount is based on the assumption that he is probably caught about half of the time he steals, and/or that he can conceal about half the stolen property.

wrongful act. It seems to us, however, that the ground for awarding the extra, so-called "punitive" compensation, is different. Whereas according to the multiplier approach, the wrongdoer is sued not only for the present wrong but also for previous wrongs, and as such, the criticism of the Supreme Court regarding non-compliance with due process is correct, the ground for awarding the additional damages according to Maimonides focusses on the concrete case being adjudicated, and the compensation is paid for that case only. It is true that according to Maimonides, too, the compensation is increased in order to deter the wrongdoer from repeating that concrete act, but he is not punished for previous acts; rather, he is more a candidate for deterrence in this case, due to the fact that he has succeeded many times and not been caught. For this reason he is also very tempted to continue to commit the same wrong, thinking that this time, too, he will be successful.

There is no doubt, however, that deterrence and the multiplier approach are not the only interests informing Maimonides' theory of punitive damages. Maimonides, as will be recalled, also discusses the parameter of the severity of the offence, which affects societal welfare, reminiscent of the *societal redress* approach underlying *extra-compensatory* damages. This parameter defines punitive damages as compensation for harm to society and not only for the injury to the specific victim. This idea of harm to society emerges, e.g., from the reason given by Maimonides in the *Guide* for the severity of the biblical punishment for a person who strikes and curses his father and mother: "because this thing is destroying the good order of the household, which is the first part of the city [the basic unit of society]."[238] Indeed, as we saw,[239] the importance of family loyalty and social solidarity is also evinced in other places in the *Guide* in which Maimonides emphasizes mainly the societal-consequentialist – rather than the religious – aspect underlying the rules relating to preservation of the family unit. We therefore find that according to Maimonides, imposition of punitive damages is not based solely on deterrence but also on the principle of societal redress.

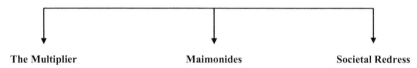

FIGURE 5.1 Placing Maimonides' approach to the difference between a thief and a robber between the modern approaches

However, there is also another component of Maimonides' approach to punitive damages, one which is special and possibly even unique as compared to modern approaches; Maimonides' approach cannot be described fully without relating to this component, as we shall now see.

[238] GUIDE 3:41 (Pines, 562).
[239] Section A.

(c) The Uniqueness of Maimonides' Approach in Incentivizing the Injured
Party to Take Precautions as a Precondition For High Punitive Damages

Maimonides' approach differs from the modern approaches in another component. The *multiplier* approach concentrates strongly on providing incentives for the tortfeasor not to commit a wrong, or else he will be required to compensate the injured party who sues him also for cases in which he was not caught. The *societal redress* approach, too, deals with social harm, and provides incentives for the wrongdoer to refrain from doing wrong, or else he will be required to pay more than the damage he caused to the plaintiff, due to the overall societal harm he has caused. Maimonides' approach, however, also stresses the provision of incentives for the victim. This is evident in Maimonides' explanation of the difference in the level of punitive damages for robbery – where the robber pays only for what he stole – and for theft, where the thief pays double compensation. The reason for this, according to Maimonides, is that when the victim of robbery does not take sufficient action to prevent the damage, he receives lower punitive damages. Maimonides thus tries to incentivize the victim as well, and unlike the focus of the modern approaches, does not provide incentives only for the tortfeasor or the criminal to refrain from their despicable acts.

The statement that a type of *fine* or tax is imposed on the victim who himself did not do enough to prevent the harm is very important, and it belongs on the consequentialist-economic plane.

It may be possible to equate this to the case in which the injured party actually sought out the harm, in the sense of an eager victim, if he assessed that he would receive several times the value of the damage, i.e., a case which in the modern literature is referred to as moral hazard,[240] even though this is not discussed in the context of punitive damages as far as we know. Such a case could be very relevant as a basis of moral hazard, particularly in a system that awards high punitive damages, in which case the victim at times really does prefer to suffer harm and to sue for punitive damages.[241] The compensatory damages here are not withheld from the victim. He will receive them, but he will not receive punitive damages, as opposed to a victim who was capable of preventing the damage and tried to do so.

Hence, in modern approaches there is at most a positive incentive for injured parties to sue after the event. They will receive compensation, but they have no incentive to invest effort in preventing the damage in advance, even where they can do so. They may even have a certain incentive not to prevent the damage if, in view of the type of activity and the fact that many victims do not sue, they might be awarded

---

[240] *See*, generally, Tom Baker, *On the Genealogy of Moral Hazard*, 75 TEXAS L. REV. 237 (1996); Jacob Loshin, *Insurance Law's Hapless Busybody: A Case Against the Insurable Interest Requirement*, 117 YALE L.J. 474 (2007).

[241] In cases of serious bodily injury he might not do so, due to concern about physical harm, but in other cases it is possible that he will.

more than the value of the damage they have suffered. Maimonides provides an incentive for the *victim*, as well, to prevent the damage. He will still receive compensation, but less as compared to an injured party who was not in a position to prevent the damage, and who will also be entitled to double, punitive damages.

Maimonides' approach may resemble the determination that the injured party is the best decision maker according to Calabresi and Hirschoff, or that there is contributory negligence on his part according to other economic approaches such as the Hand formula. Let us now elucidate these two matters.

A good way to deal with incentives for the victim, particularly if he can be classified as an eager victim, is by means of doctrines of liability, such as *contributory negligence*. This matter has hardly been discussed in the context of punitive damages, even though Robert Cooter does deal with it briefly.[242] Can this incentive for the injured party indeed be translated into a kind of contributory negligence, in the sense of the Hand formula? True, there is no reduction of compensation from the capital, as in the Hand formula, following the division of liability, but compensation is deducted from the component of punitive damages (which may be reduced to zero) and this can be similar in principle.

If the kernel of Maimonides' approach is adopted, then, based on the modern rationale of the *multiplier* approach or that of *societal redress*, there is nothing to prevent reducing the compensation due to *contributory negligence*, while at the same time awarding punitive damages.[243] In such a case, the contributory negligence is deducted from the actual, real (non-punitive) damages awarded to the injured party, because he has a part in the harm caused. This is not necessarily inconsistent with him being awarded, concurrently, punitive damages as an economic deterrent for the tortfeasor according to the multiplier approach, or in order to make the tortfeasor put right the societal wrong, which he must do in any case,

---

[242] Robert D. Cooter, *Economic Analysis of Punitive Damages*, 56 S. CAL. L. REV. 79, 96–97 (1982) (dealing with the propriety of allowing liability insurance to cover punitive damages, arguing that "when punitive damages are awarded in addition to compensatory damages, victims are usually overcompensated. Thus, even if critics are correct and such insurance leads to an increase in injuries, victims who receive compensatory plus punitive damages may be better off than if they never suffered the accident at all. If both parties are better off as a result of insurance, it should not be prohibited." *Ibid.* at 96. Cooter also deals with the problem of the eager victim: "Generally, a defense such as contributory negligence will prevent inadequate precaution by victims." *Ibid.* at 97. However, he does not relate to the problem beyond this, i.e. beyond the ramifications of punitive damages as absolute liability on the part of the person who is in breach of contract, which if imposed together with compensatory damages, are liable to create excessive protection against breach, *ibid*. Of course, in order to prevent a situation of an eager victim, the punitive damages could be placed in a special state fund for the benefit of victims, but we are not dealing with this at present).

[243] Unless, for example, it is a matter of a deliberate act on the part of the tortfeasor, in which case the court may consider not ruling that there was contributory negligence, thus also giving expression to the traditional approaches to the heinousness of the act and the intention of the tortfeasor.

irrespective of any possible fault of the injured party, according to the societal redress approach. Thus there is no contradiction between a reduction of the real compensation alongside the award of punitive damages. The objectives are different and can *exist* separately. Recall that according to Maimonides' approach, both the actual addition of the punitive damages and the deduction due to contributory damages from that addition, are affected in relation to the component of punitive damages. The implication of the modern approaches, on the other hand, would seem to be that the deduction for contributory negligence here – as in every case of contributory negligence – would be from the real damages, together with a concurrent award of punitive damages. On the level of principle, it presumably makes no material difference from which component – real damages or punitive damages – the deduction is made, for in both cases the compensation to the injured party is reduced, and the difference may be purely theoretical.[244]

It is therefore possible that the logic of the economic approach to contributory negligence is similar to the economic logic that guided Maimonides.

Finally, we will examine the possibility of equating Maimonides' approach – which provides incentives for the *victim* as well – not only to the economic rationale of contributory negligence, but also to the rationale underlying Calabresi and Hirschoff's best decision maker, which imposes liability on the tortfeasor and rejects the notion of contributory negligence. It may be that providing incentives for the injured party by denying punitive damages in the event that he did not take precautionary measures is a type of application of Calabresi and Hirschoff's doctrine, whereby the injured party is the best decision maker due to his ability to adopt precautionary measures, albeit in a manner differing in two parameters from that presented by Calabresi and Hirschoff. The first parameter is that compensation in general is not denied altogether as a result of the best decision of the injured party, but only the punitive component; nevertheless, the entire punitive component is deducted, and not only a part thereof, as in the case of pure comparative negligence. The second parameter deals with the identity of the groups that are examined. Whereas the best decision maker doctrine traditionally examines groups of tortfeasors vis-à-vis groups of injured parties, Maimonides here in fact examines different groups of injured parties as to their ability to adopt preventive measures. Maimonides compares different groups of victims: the victim of a robbery is a better decision

---

[244] One may question this conclusion of negative incentive for the victim by way of reducing the compensation or a kind of contributory negligence and ask whether, when there is an intentional act on the part of the tortfeasor, which is not directly aimed at a particular victim, it is possible talk about deterrence of the victim. Precautionary measures that will be taken by a victim in such situations will only divert the criminal to commit the crime elsewhere, and therefore such measures are a social waste. This would seem to be the economic justification for not recognizing contributory negligence in criminal law, and there is a certain logic to this. However, it would appear that if every potential victim (for example, a homeowner whose apartment can be broken into) would take care and would adopt precautionary measures, there would be no other place to which to divert the crime.

maker than the victim of a theft,[245] and therefore, if he did not adopt preventive measures he is still awarded compensation but not punitive damages from the tortfeasor – unlike the case of the victim of the theft – in order to incentive others in the same situation to take precautionary measures. Thus we find that there is a certain degree of logical similarity to the doctrine of the best decision maker, even though the application is different from that of Calabresi and Hirschoff.

D. CONCLUSION

In this Chapter we discussed the major consequentialist elements in Maimonides' tort theory, based primarily on what he wrote in the *Guide*. We saw that even though this is not a consequentialist, comprehensive theory conforming to all the extant criteria, the element of consequentialism in Maimonides' theory is solid and fundamental, notwithstanding the concurrent existence of other elements that cannot be ignored. In the matter of punitive damages and criminal sanctions, this element is strongly emphasized – more so than in other cases. We also saw that Maimonides' general approach to the objectives of tort law, mainly as emerges from the *Guide*, reveals an extremely important consequentialist objective – prevention of acts causing damage and deterrence – that runs like a common thread through the tort law in his corpus.

Reading Maimonides' texts in the *Guide* analyzed in this chapter in light of contemporary methods can provide us with a new contemporary interpretation of Maimonides' tort theory. A careful comparison of Maimonides' explanation in the *Guide* to the writings of some of the prominent scholars of contemporary scholarship of economic analysis of tort law reveals a somewhat surprising similarity between them.

In this chapter, therefore, many aspects common to Maimonides' tort doctrine and modern theories were examined, both with respect to tort liability in general and with respect to its proximity to criminal law and the subject of punitive damages. Over and above the comparison to the doctrines of the fathers of law and economics in torts – Calabresi and Posner – with respect to tort liability, we also saw a certain proximity between the consequentialist approach of Maimonides and the modern approaches to punitive damages. We saw a certain similarity between his approach and the economic multiplier approach, but in our view, there is also similarity to the moral idea of societal redress in extra-compensatory damages. Maimonides also examines the role of the injured party and not just that of the tortfeasor in the damage, and not only in the regular case of tort liability but also in the case in which punitive damages are awarded and it must be decided whether to reduce this component due to the contribution of the injured party himself to the damage.

---

[245] Even if he is not a better decision maker than the perpetrator himself, who is not exempt from paying the compensation himself.

Maimonides' tort theory as expressed in the *Guide* is constructed, in our view, on three different levels. On the first level are the two objectives of tort law. The more predictable objective is the deontological aim of *removing wrong* (a type of corrective justice, discussed in Chapter 4), and the second, which is surprising in view of the period in which it was first conceived, is the social-consequentialist objective of *preventing damages*, which was analyzed in this chapter. These objectives, presented by Maimonides in the *Guide* (3:40), constitute the foundation-stone of his tort theory.

At the second level stands the Maimonidean test of liability, a test that is substantively different from all the tests that have been suggested to date in the common interpretation of Maimonides and the Talmud. This test is based on a reading from the *Guide*. In the *Guide*, Maimonides departed from the line of interpretation accepted by many halakhic scholars who based tort liability on *peshiah* (negligence or fault) on the part of the defendant; he sought, instead, to base liability for property damages on a different, unique basis, which we call *the effective ability to control test* – the EAC test. According to this test, we argue, liability is imposed on the *effective damage avoider*. This level has been also discussed at length in this chapter.

At the third level is what we call the Maimonidean *differential model*, which will be discussed in the Chapter 7. But before this, and after fully understanding the *Guide*'s EAC test and how the rules of liability are rationalized by the consequentialist view of the *Guide* – with the assistance of contemporary law and economics methods – in the following chapter we revisit the earlier problematic texts of the *Code*.

APPENDIX

The Rules of Liability and Contributory Negligence according to Maimonides in the Guide *3:40 Compared with Calabresi and Posner*

Maimonides' Approach	Calabresi: Cheapest Cost Avoider and Best Decision Maker	Posner: Negligence from the Economic Aspect and the Hand formula
1. The basis for liability of the tortfeasor: EAC Test – effective damage avoider test.	Maimonides' approach is similar to Calabresi's doctrines, particularly to the cheapest cost avoider.	Maimonides' approach is less compatible with Posner, although in certain matters, as we shall see in Chapter 7, Maimonides imposes on the effective damage avoider a standard of care of negligence or close to negligence (in the framework of his differential approach that will be presented there).
2. Tooth and foot damages in the public domain (the owner is exempt) – analysis of the talmudic issues according to Maimonides' approach ("is at fault toward himself")	Calabresi's doctrines – strict liability imposed on the tortfeasor or on the victim according to the question of who is the cheapest cost avoider or the best decision maker – are compatible with Maimonides' explanation. From the consequence of liability for all or nothing – strict liability either of the tortfeasor or the victim is less suitable from the point of view of the rhetoric of *peshiah* (used by Maimonides).	The doctrine of contributory negligence of Posner and the Hand formula – division of liability between the tortfeasor and the victim and reduction of compensation for the victim at the rate of his contribution to the injury caused to him – is compatible with Maimonides' explanation more in terms of the rationale of "is at fault toward himself" which is more suited to negligence, as well as mention of the elements of a rate of damage that is not high

(continued)

(continued)

Maimonides' Approach	Calabresi: Cheapest Cost Avoider and Best Decision Maker	Posner: Negligence from the Economic Aspect and the Hand formula
		and the fact that it is not frequent (Hand formula). However, from the point of view of the result of dividing liability, his approach is less compatible with Posner's doctrine. It seems that the closest approach to that of Maimonides is the modified comparative negligence approach.
3. A *mu'ad* ox that gored in the public domain – the owner must pay full damages. Maimonides asks, who is the effective damage avoider – the owner of the ox or the passers-by ("regarding which precautions can be taken in all places and … those who walk in public places cannot take care". I.e. the emphasis is on effective control, rather than on the question of who was negligent).	Maimonides' approach is very similar to Calabresi's, both in its result and in its rationale (particularly the cheapest cost avoider, but possibly also the best decision maker, as in the example of drivers and pedestrians, due to the element of control).	There is a wide disparity between the rationale of effective control in Maimonides' theory and negligence in Posner's theory.
4. The rule of the *tam* ox that gores and whose owner is liable for half damages – Maimonides' explanation.	Calabresi's all or nothing doctrines are not compatible with the rule of the *tam* ox with respect to the result of half damages. With respect to the rationale, it is possible to provide, according to Maimonides, an intermediate explanation whereby there is a type of strict liability for half the damages only.	Posner's doctrine is compatible with the rule of the *tam* ox in the rationale of division of liability between the tortfeasor and the injured party. It is partially compatible from the point of view of the result, for according to Maimonides, the division of liability is fixed – 50 percent for each party, and according to Posner, contributory negligence reduces the compensation to the victim at a varying rate, depending on the level of his contribution to the damage.

6

Revisiting the Problematic Texts of the *Code* in Light of the *Guide* and Contemporary Scholarship

A. USING A CONSEQUENTIALIST RATIONALIZATION IN VARIOUS PLACES IN THE *CODE*

Once we have understood the *Guide*'s "effective ability to control test" (EAC test) and how the rules of liability, including the splitting of liability and the exceptions, are rationalized by the consequentialist view of the *Guide*, we can return to the earlier texts of the *Code*. Many of the problematic texts in the *Code* mentioned in Chapter 2 of this book are revisited in this chapter, and are reinterpreted and explained in light of the consequentialist view of the *Guide*'s EAC test, Calabresi's cheapest cost avoider doctrine, and Posner's Hand formula.

Many scholars and commentators have addressed the contradictions between the *Guide* and the *Code*. We should note that the *Guide* speaks in a different idiom from the *Code*. Some scholars have even spoken of "two different Maimonides":[1] the traditional halakhist of the *Code*, and the controversial and innovative philosopher of the *Guide*.[2] In relation to torts, too, we note the difference between the two works. The focus in the *Guide* is on a general overview of the consequentialist and policy considerations and the formulation of the EAC test; all of this is absent in the *Code*.

It is certainly not our intention here to decide profound questions such as the extent to which a halakhic/legal approach is reflected in the *Guide*, and whether it is possible to use the *Guide* in order to explain Maimonides' legal theory in a particular area. We note that the classical *yeshivah* curriculum, reflected in the writings of Lithuanian scholars in the last 150 years (whose interpretation of

---

[1] *See, e.g.,* JACOB S. LEVINGER, MAIMONIDES AS PHILOSOPHER AND CODIFIER (Jerusalem: Bialik Institute, 1989) (Heb.). *See also supra* Chapter 1, Section E.
[2] E.g., in the case of offerings – *korbanot*: GUIDE 3:32.

Maimonides' *Code* was discussed previously),[3] does not usually refer to the *Guide* as a source that can enlighten the perplexed in the ways of the *Code*. Nevertheless, many scholars were in fact able to find a link between the *Guide* and the *Code* in various areas, and we intend to follow this path, with due caution. We are convinced that it is not possible to present the complete tort theory of Maimonides based on the *Code* alone, without the statements about the incentives for preventing harm and the EAC test that appear in the *Guide*. These statements in the *Guide* represent a crystallized, clear, and more mature overview of the foundations of tort liability, probably fully developed at a later stage of Maimonides' life. Indeed, we argue that at least regarding tort law, the two works are in many ways complementary. One may therefore revisit the earlier texts of the *Code* and find that many of the views expressed there may be rationalized in the best, most comprehensive way in light of the later *Guide*'s overview.

Of course, there are significant differences between Maimonides' formulations with respect to the reasons for the tort laws in the *Guide*, in which the emphasis is primarily on the consequentialist-social aspects, and his formulations in the Book of Torts in the *Code*, where he places greater emphasis, as we demonstrated at length in Chapters 3–4, on the deontological and religious aspects, and where many of his formulations – such as the concept of *peshiah*[4] – are closer to the talmudic, and sometimes even biblical, sources. Nevertheless, we should stress that despite the said differences, it is certainly possible to find formulations in the *Code* that are similar in spirit to the consequentialist-economic orientation of the *Guide*. In this section, we will confine ourselves to presenting two rulings in the *Code* in which Maimonides openly invokes consequentialist-economic rationalizations.

A consequentialist rationalization emerges from Maimonides' instructive explanation of the difference between Jewish and non-Jewish law regarding the liability imposed on a person for the damages caused by his animal, which also affects the amount of compensation paid by the owner of an innocent ox (*tam*) that gored.[5] Maimonides explains that the reason that damage caused by the ox of a Gentile owner must always be compensated in full, whether the ox was innocent (*tam*) or forewarned (*mu'ad*), whereas a Jewish owner does not make full payment for damage caused by his innocent ox, lies in the differences between Jewish and Gentile/Islamic law: the Gentiles do not impose liability on a person for damages caused by his animal (referring apparently to Islamic law in force at that time).[6] In Jewish law, by contrast, not only is liability imposed on a person for damages caused by his animals, but the causing of damage is also prohibited *per se*. Maimonides

---

[3] In Chapter 2 of this book.
[4] See Chapter 2, Section C.2.
[5] Laws of Property Damages 8:5.
[6] See Chapter 4, Section C, presenting the basis for Maimonides' assumption regarding Islamic law, and a survey of commonly accepted positions about important streams in Islamic law that exempt owners of animals from damage caused by their animals.

explains the reason for imposing liability on Gentiles for full compensation of the damage caused by their animals:

> This is a fine imposed on the Gentiles because, being heedless of the scriptural commandments [not observing carefully the biblical commandments prohibiting causing damage] they do not remove sources of damage. Accordingly, they would not take care of them and thus would inflict loss on other people's property.[7]

It appears from Maimonides' statement that careful observance of the commandments (he refers primarily to exercising care not to cause damage – the causing of damage being prohibited by Jewish law)[8] makes a decisive contribution to damage prevention and to the welfare of society. Therefore, in non-Jewish legal systems, such as an Islamic system, if there are no accepted norms that prohibit causing damage in general, and damage by animals in particular, it is necessary to create an appropriate deterrent for owners of animals. This is because if they are not charged full payment for the damages caused by their animals, "they do not take care of them and thus would inflict loss on other people's property."

The consequentialist justification offered in the *Code* is an innovation on Maimonides' part, and to the best of our knowledge it does not exist in earlier sources. The said explanation is not based on the Talmud, in which completely different reasons were given for the differences in the rules applying to Jews and Gentiles with respect to the amount of compensation paid for damages caused by an ox.[9] The explanation in the *Code* is indeed intended to relate only to a particular rule, but the tone of Maimonides' words indicates that in his opinion, the full payment that is imposed on the non-Jewish owner of the ox is intended to create a real incentive to increase the means of oversight of the ox and thus to prevent the damage and to internalize costs rather than transferring the costs to others. This is a clearly consequentialist explanation, and it is very similar to the consequentialist approach that is evident in the *Guide*.[10] It is possible that Maimonides' formulation in the *Code* constitutes an early, undeveloped stage of the approach that was later presented in a fuller and more consolidated form in the *Guide*.

Another point which must be noted in Maimonides' unique rationalization of the liability borne by the non-Jewish owner of an ox relates to the nature of the prohibition against causing damage. This prohibition was emphasized more strongly in the

---

[7] Laws of Property Damages 8:5.
[8] Laws of Property Damages 5:1.
[9] See Bava Kamma 38a; T Bava Kamma 4:2 (For a discussion, see Bernard Jackson, *Liability for Animals in Roman Law: An Historical Sketch*, 37 CAMBRIDGE L.J. 122, 139–42 (1978). In his COMMENTARY TO THE MISHNAH, *Bava Kamma* 4:3, Maimonides offers a completely different explanation to that offered in the *Code*.
[10] *Guide* 3:40, as analyzed *supra* Chapter 5.

Code, as part of the religious dimension of tort law, which is more prominent in the *Code* than in the *Guide*.

As discussed in Chapter 4, in his *Code* Maimonides regards the religious-moral prohibition against causing damage as a very important component of his tort theory, alongside other objectives. We already noted the emphasis that Maimonides places on the fact that "one is forbidden to cause damage with the intention of paying for the damage he causes. Even to bring about damage indirectly with this intention is forbidden."[11] Maimonides rules with regard to a long list of tort events that the tortfeasor is "exempt by human law [from liability for the cost of the damage], but is liable by Divine law."[12] This is applied in the Talmud and by Maimonides to cases of indirect causation.[13]

Note, however, that the prohibition against causing damage is not a purely religious one: sometimes it has real legal consequences. It is by virtue of this prohibition that Maimonides permits the owner of the field to slaughter an animal that has strayed onto his property several times, despite the fact that it has not yet caused damage.[14] This is a preventive-deterrent measure against the owner of the animal, because he did not guard it adequately. Similarly, from the prohibition against causing damage Maimonides derives the general ban that the Sages issued against the raising of small domestic animals and small beasts in the Land of Israel in regions that contain fields and vineyards, since it is the nature of the animals to enter fields and vineyards and cause damage. Furthermore, because it is prohibited to cause damage even if one intends to pay for it, the raising of small animals was allowed only in places where they could cause no damage, i.e., in forests and deserts.[15] Note further that from the text quoted earlier in the chapter (regarding the liability of the Gentiles for damages caused by their animals), it seems that Maimonides believes that the prohibition against causing damage also serves as a social tool that promotes socially-efficient behavior. The prohibition also contributes to social solidarity, the forging of civic responsibility, and concern for the other. Moreover, it promotes community spirit, which is a characteristic of Jewish law in general and of Maimonides' philosophical theory in particular.

Now, as argued in Chapter 4, although the prohibition against causing damage constitutes a significant element in Maimonides' writings, the importance of the prohibitive-religious element in his tort theory should nevertheless not be overstated.

---

[11] Laws of Property Damages 5:1. *See, e.g.*, CODE, Laws of Property Damages 13:3, 13:15.
[12] *See* Laws of Property Damages 4:2, 14:14; Laws of Witnesses 17:7.
[13] However, there may well be biblical bases for the choice of the particular cases. *See* Bernard Jackson, *The Fence-Breaker and the Action* de pastu pectoris *in Early Jewish Law*, 25 J. OF JEWISH STUDIES 123–36 (1974).
[14] Laws of Property Damages 5:1.
[15] *Ibid.* 5:2.

At no time does Maimonides or the talmudic sources give any indication of a conception whereby every payment for property damage must be regarded as a punishment based on the prohibition against causing damage; rather, these payments should be considered civil compensation.

It appears, therefore, that according to Maimonides' conception, the prohibition against causing property damage is not necessarily the most important one (as other halakhic authorities assumed).[16] It co-exists alongside other elements that are no less important, such as the prevention of acts causing damage, deterrence, emphasis on the moral conduct of the tortfeasor, and more.

Furthermore, from Maimonides' rulings in the *Code* it appears that it is sometimes permitted to create potential damage in order to achieve important objectives, although the tortfeasor must nevertheless pay for the damage.[17] This is reminiscent of Calabresi and Melamed's Rule 2, i.e., the liability rule in favor of the injured party – the victim – according to which the tortfeasor is permitted to cause damage if his acts are efficient, but he must pay for the harm he causes.[18] Indeed, the activity as a whole may be economically desirable, but if harm ensues, that person must pay because he is the main beneficiary of the activity. This also illustrates the importance of economic considerations in the *Code* as well as in the *Guide*.

Let us now consider a second example of a formulation in the *Code* that is based on consequentialist-economic reasoning, namely, the slave example mentioned in Chapter 2.

According to Maimonides, considerations of efficiency justify exempting the master from paying for damage caused by his slaves: "[s]hould he [the slave] be annoyed at his master, a slave might go and set a fire to a wheat stack worth [in order to make his master liable] a thousand dinar or do similar damage."[19]

Thus, it is certainly possible to find certain expressions of consequentialist-economic thinking in various rulings in the *Code*. Indeed, we believe that in the *Guide*, Maimonidean theory reached its peak of sophistication and clarity, but it does not necessarily contradict what appeared earlier in the *Code*: on the contrary, various rulings from the *Code* are easily understood in light of what Maimonides wrote in the *Guide*.

Finally, we turn to contemporary writings. As noted, in our opinion there is room for a conversation between Maimonides and contemporary theories. First, we showed (in Chapter 2) that it is difficult to understand the basis for tort liability in Maimonides' work, especially in the *Code*, and that the common interpretation (provided by scholars and rabbis) failed to address this difficulty adequately. Next, we

---

[16] See, e.g., Tur, *Dinei Nezikin, Hoshen Mishpat* 378.
[17] See, e.g., Laws of Property Damages 13:3, 13:15.
[18] Guido Calabresi & A. Douglas Melamed, *Property Rules, Liability Rules, and Inalienability: One View of the Cathedral*, 85 Harv. L. Rev. 1089, 1116, 1119 (1972).
[19] Laws of Theft 1:9.

showed (in Chapter 5) that Maimonides stressed various consequentialist considerations and displayed initial and basic signs of economic analysis in the *Guide*. Nevertheless, we noted that it is difficult to find in Maimonides' work, even considering what he wrote in the *Guide*, a coherent, modern law and economics theory, embracing all its principles and details. However, by drawing an analogy with some law and economics theories, we are able to provide a logical explanation of the basis for tort liability according to Maimonides. We think this is exactly the point: the new literature of contemporary law and economics sheds new light on the medieval sources.

B. THE EAC TEST AS THE BASIS FOR TORT LIABILITY

In Chapter 2 we saw how difficult it was for scholars and rabbis of recent generations to explain in a satisfactory manner the basis for tort liability according to Maimonides. It seems to us that there is no need to seek forced justifications for what Maimonides writes,[20] because his theory in the *Code* is made perfectly plain in light of the clear explanations he provides in the *Guide*. As we saw in Chapter 2,[21] the inference derived by Warhaftig and the *yeshivah* reading from the beginning of the Book of Torts is incorrect, and Maimonides does not seem to have considered *ownership* as the most important element of tort liability. Furthermore, Warhaftig and the *yeshivah* reading ignored the fact that at the beginning of the Book of Torts, Maimonides explicitly mentioned two elements (and not just one, as they wrote) for imposing liability for damage caused by a living being. One element is *control*, as Maimonides writes in the *Code*: "If any living creature under human control causes damage the owner must pay compensation." The other element is a property connection: "for it is their property that caused the damage."[22] The combination of these two elements explains many laws in the *Code*.[23] This is particularly the case if the *Code* is interpreted in light of the consequentialist rationale in the *Guide*. As we saw in Chapter 5, from what Maimonides writes in the *Guide* it emerges that the basis of liability for property damages does not necessarily lie in ownership; rather, a principal meta-objective is to prevent acts causing damage. This is determined by the EAC test, according to which liability should be imposed on the most *effective damage avoider*, who is not necessarily the *owner*: it is the person who *controls* the object causing the damage or the defect that

---

[20] We discussed the difficulty of finding a satisfactory rationale for the ownership theory in Chapter 2, Section C.4.
[21] Chapter 2, Section E.
[22] Laws of Property Damage, 1:1.
[23] See R. NACHUM L. RABINOVITCH, Yad Peshutah Lesefer Nezikin, Laws of Property Damage 1:1, 22 (Jerusalem 2006) (Heb.).

has been created by him (i.e., the object which caused the accident). According to Maimonides in the *Guide*, as stated, tort liability should be imposed on the person who has effective control of the "property" (damage caused by animals) or of that which he brings about (fire, pit and causing injury himself), for this incentivizes the person who can effectively prevent the damage.[24] The rationale of the EAC is consequentialist; its purpose is to prevent acts causing damage effectively and efficiently, similarly to the economic rationale underlying Calabresi's cheapest cost avoider doctrine.

From this explanation it follows that the requirement of ownership in the *Code* for the imposition of liability does not refer specifically to the formal owner of the damaging property, because at times even a person who has some form of property connection (and not necessarily one that amounts to actual ownership) is liable under a broad understanding of ownership.[25] It also follows that the element of ownership is required only for damage caused by a living being, and not necessarily for every type of tort liability, such as pit and fire, as many commentators incorrectly believed.[26] Moreover, the rationale offered by Maimonides in the *Code* for the slave example, which those advocating the common interpretation (the ownership theory[27]) had trouble explaining, becomes very understandable according to Maimonides' explanation in the *Guide*. It is clear from the *Code*[28] that the nature of the exemption of the master from liability for his slave is consequentialist: even though the slave is his property, the master cannot control all his actions and therefore he cannot be considered as the effective damage preventer. Quite the contrary: as Maimonides writes, the slave has a clear incentive to cause damage in order to harm his master; therefore, it is more effective to hold the slave liable, and thus reduce the chances that he will commit a tort.

We are not arguing that all the details of tort law can be explained on the basis of the EAC test in the *Guide*. Obviously, there are other major factors that determine tort liability and that are mentioned in the *Code* but not in the *Guide*.[29] All this

---

[24] GUIDE 3:40.
[25] According to R. RABINOVITCH, *supra* note 23, who inferred this from Maimonides' rulings holding liable also those who have some monetary legal connection, such as a watchman (Laws of Property Damages 4:10), a court-appointed guardian (*ibid.* 6:3); even a robber has a certain monetary connection to the robbery he commits, for the stolen object "thus remains in the possession of the robber and is his responsibility until he hands it back" (*ibid.* Laws of Robbery and Lost Property 1:7).
[26] Our method solves the problem facing those who accept the common interpretation of Maimonides (the ownership theory): see Chapter 2, Section C.3.
[27] See ibid.
[28] Laws of Theft 1:9.
[29] Good examples of this are causation, which is mentioned extensively in the *Code* but not in the *Guide*, as well as the deontological and religious aspects that are emphasized in the *Code*. In addition, the standard of care that is required from different categories of tortfeasors is discussed in various rulings in the *Code*, as elucidated *infra* Chapter 7, and this discussion is absent from the *Guide*.

notwithstanding, it definitely appears to us that certain rulings in the *Code* are satisfactorily explained by the EAC test in the *Guide*.

C. BEST DECISION MAKER IN MAIMONIDEAN TEXTS

Maimonides believes that liability should be imposed on the most *effective damage avoider*, a doctrine that seems very close to Calabresi's *cheapest cost avoider*. But as we have seen, in his later writings (and especially in his joint article with Hirschoff), Calabresi improved the test, imposing tort liability on the best *decision maker*, i.e., the party that is in the best position to weigh the costs of the damage and of its prevention. Can we find a parallel for this in Maimonides?

Now, Maimonides makes no mention of a best decision maker, and of course, we are not claiming that he adopted this doctrine in all its particulars. Nevertheless, it would appear that the basic elements of the best decision maker can serve to elucidate several of Maimonides' rulings, indicating that he also attributes decisive importance to the question of who has the *information* to best weigh the costs of the damage and of its prevention.

With regard to the imposition of liability for damage caused by a pit owned by partners, Maimonides wrote that a partner who finds that the pit is uncovered has exclusive liability for the damage as long as his partner is not aware of the fact that the pit is uncovered.[30] The innovation of this ruling is that although the first partner is also liable for the maintenance of the pit, if in the meantime "the second [partner] finds it uncovered and does not cover it, the second is liable." But the question remains: why absolve the first partner, even if he did not know that the pit was uncovered? According to the best decision maker rationale, the answer is evident: liability should be imposed only on the party who is in the best position to weigh the costs of the damage and of its prevention, and in this case it is clear that the best decision maker is the second partner, who discovered that the pit was uncovered. The first partner lacked the *information* about the pit being uncovered; therefore it is not right to hold him liable until he learns about the fact of the pit being uncovered and nevertheless does not take the necessary measures to cover the pit within the amount of time reasonably required to rectify the situation. Thus, imposing liability for damage depends on the information about the damage as well as on the ability to effectively prevent it.

Clearly, the ruling here is not consistent with the *ownership* theory, for from a formal point of view, both partners are owners, and as such, both ought to have been either liable or exempt. It is therefore clear from the ruling that ownership is not a sufficient condition for liability; rather, the dominant element is *information*. Neither is this a *fault-based* liability regime, for if the tort lies in the existence of the open pit, there should be no difference between the liability of the first partner and of the second partner, as a person may be liable for omissions on his territory

---

[30] Laws of Property Damages 12:7.

without his concrete knowledge. It is sufficient, for example, for a hole to be found in the fence of a building site and for a child go through it and be injured in order to render the contractor liable for his omission, even if he did not know about it. Fault-based liability is based on foreseeability on the part of the defendant. This means that the liability of the contractor is based on the fact that he should and could have known about the omission, even if he had no actual knowledge of it. In our case, actual knowledge (based on information) is what distinguishes between the two partners, and it can be attributed to a regime of best decision maker and not one of fault and negligence.[31]

The importance that Maimonides attributes to the element of information as the basis for liability is also apparent in other rulings in the Book of Torts.[32] It should be emphasized, however, that Maimonides did not adopt all the elements of Calabresi's best decision maker rule, as far as the regime of liability imposed on the best decision maker is concerned. As noted, in Calabresi's approach the *best decision maker* always bears *strict liability*, whereas Maimonides, as we will see in the next chapter, imposes *differential* liability, which is not always strict but at times is less than that, i.e., closer to negligence.

D. IMPOSING LIABILITY ON THE INJURED PARTY

In Chapter 2,[33] the reasons for exceptional cases in which the tortfeasors were exempt from liability were discussed. In that context, the following questions were asked *inter alia*: Why are the owners of animals that caused damage in the public domain by eating or trampling exempt, and why are they liable for damage caused by their animals by means of goring even when such damage occurred in the public domain? And why is the owner of a dog held liable when the dog was incited by a second person against a third person and that third person suffered injury, whereas the owner is exempt if the inciter himself was the victim of his own incitement?

Different answers have been offered for these questions by scholars and commentators, some more and some less convincing. To us, the answer to them all seems patently clear in light of Maimonides' EAC test explained in the *Guide*, which examines who is the most effective damage avoider: is it the owner of the ox as in damages by goring, or rather, the victim, as in regular tooth and foot damage, in

---

[31] One may see this example as similar to the "the last-clear-chance" doctrine, which is employed in contributory negligence jurisdictions and has been replaced in some of them with comparative negligence. This doctrine means that: (a) a negligent plaintiff can argue that the defendant had the last clear chance, and thus mitigate his own contributory negligence; and (b) a negligent defendant can argue that the plaintiff had the last clear chance to avoid the accident, and thus he (the defendant) should not be held liable. See Restatement (Second) of Torts, §§ 479–80. It seems that the Third Restatement rejects the "the last-clear-chance" doctrine in cases of comparative negligence. See Restatement (Third) of Torts (Apport.), §3, Cmt. b.
[32] See, e.g., Laws of Theft 4:12.
[33] Chapter 2, Section D.2.

which the injured person is considered as one who "is at fault toward himself"?[34] This is a question that depends on various consequentialist considerations, similar to those of Posner and Calabresi. According to this explanation, as will be recalled, this is not a matter of an exception to a rule of liability, but rather, of the consistent application of the consequentialist rule of liability of the *effective cost avoider*, whereby it is sometimes the *victim*, rather than the perpetrator, who is the effective cost avoider. The relevant rulings in the *Code* can be explained in this way as well, alongside a possible explanation of some of the issues according to the theory of economic negligence of Posner and the Hand formula.

Here it should be emphasized that according to some of the explanations of Maimonides' approach, such as the "ownership and strict liability theory" (proposed by Warhaftig following the *yeshivah* reading presented in Chapter 2), the major element by virtue of which liability is imposed is ownership. These explanations made scant reference to Maimonides' use of terms related to *peshiah* in certain rulings in the *Code*. However, as we saw in Chapter 5, there is certainly room for the element of *peshiah* in what Maimonides writes in the *Guide*, albeit in a very specific context – the contribution of the victim to the damage ("is at fault toward himself"). This can be explained, as we saw, both in a manner similar to contributory negligence and to Calabresi's best decision maker.

In accordance with Maimonides' method in the *Code*, in most cases no explanation or rationalization is given for the rulings (as it is in the *Guide*), and consequently, it is difficult to ascertain his reason for each ruling. Therefore, the consequentialist explanations whose rationale is similar to that of Calabresi or Posner are not necessarily the only correct ones, and other explanations of those rulings, including deontological explanations relating to corrective justice and to the moral fault of the tortfeasors and the victim, are certainly possible.

We will examine several rulings from the *Code*. In relation to each, two possible explanations will be proposed, one according to the EAC test of the *Guide* and the rationales of Calabresi or Posner, and the other according to the rationale of the *peshiah* theory.

We will begin with the dog case in the *Code*.[35] The ruling there seemed difficult to understand, but it can be easily explained in light of the EAC test in the *Guide*, and in fact, in light of Calabresi's best decision maker as well. As will be recalled, the question arises as to the basis for the difference between the case in which one person incites the dog of another (the owner) against a third person, in which case the owner is liable, and the case in which that same person incited the dog against himself (the dog bit the inciter), in which case the owner is exempt.[36]

---

[34] GUIDE 3:40 (Pines, 555).
[35] Laws of Property Damages 2:19. *See* Chapter 2, Section D.1.
[36] This discrepancy raises difficulties, as will be recalled, according to both the theory of ownership and that of *peshiah*.

Indeed, Maimonides' ruling could be easily explained using a rationale similar to that mentioned by Calabresi regarding the exceptional and non-standard use of a product (the example of the lawn mower).[37] Calabresi identifies the user as the best decision maker and exempts the manufacturer from liability due to the impossibility of taking into account a type of exceptional activity such as riding on the lawn mower on the road, even in order to bring a wounded person to the hospital. In the case of the dog, Maimonides bases his ruling on the talmudic rule that "anyone who performs an unusual act and another causes him injury, he [the other] is exempt."[38] This means that the injured person is viewed as someone who brought the damage upon himself by his abnormal behavior, and therefore the *halakhah* exempts the injurer from liability.[39] In this case, given the fact that the injured person deviated from standard behavior and behaved abnormally by inciting the dog, the owner of the dog is not liable for the harm subsequently caused by the dog.

It should be noted that in the ruling in the *Code*, Maimonides emphasizes that the liability of the owner of the dog is related to *information* and *knowledge*, and therefore, it makes sense to explain the basis for the ruling in its entirety in terms of the best decision maker. As such, when a person incites a dog against another person, the owner of the dog is liable, because he is the best decision maker, and in Maimonides' words, "since he *knows* that his dog bites when incited, he ought not to have left it loose."[40] As opposed to this, when that same person incites the dog against himself, he is liable for the damage because he himself is the best decision maker.[41]

It is noteworthy that some modern legal systems adopt an approach of strict or almost strict liability in relation to damage caused by dogs, as an exception to the fault-based regime.[42] Indeed, the ruling relating to the inciter can also be explained according to the assumption of risk defense, which in modern law entails the imposition of liability for all the damage in its entirety on the shoulders of the

---

[37] Chapter 5, Section C.1.a.
[38] *Bava Kamma* 24b and 20a.
[39] See Hazon Ish, *Bava Kamma* 8:7. See also Birkat Shmuel, *Bava Kamma* 16.
[40] Laws of Property Damages 2:19.
[41] In Calabresi's words) in a conversation with the authors on May 28, 2014, New Haven, Connecticut): "because he is better able to take care of himself, since he made an unexpected use, and therefore has better *knowledge* than the owner, just like in the lawn mower example".
[42] For example, in part D1 of the Civil Wrongs Ordinance (New Version), 5728–1968, 2 LSI 12, (1968) (Isr.), the legislator stipulated that the owner of the dog or whoever is in charge of it has strict liability for damage caused by the dog regardless of fault (§41a). There are three exceptions to this rule, whereby the injured party cannot use this section and should sue on the basis of regular negligence, which is more difficult to prove and also exposes him to contributory negligence. The exceptions are: (a) incitement of the dog by the injured party (§41b(1)); (b) assault by the injured party on the owner or on his relative of first degree (§41b(2)); (c) trespassing by the injured party on the owner's property (§41b(3)). It appears that this special statutory arrangement relies on the same foundations and rationale as the theories of Calabresi and Maimonides.

victim. According to this defense, the victim knowingly put himself in that situation, which is very appropriate for the case of a person who incited the dog of another against himself.

Another type of case in which the victim remains liable for the damage and the owner of the animal is not considered the effective damage avoider can be seen in Maimonides' ruling in the matter of one who entrusts his animal to a watchman, and the animal causes damage. In the *Code*, Maimonides rules that "a person who entrusts his animal to an unpaid watchman, a paid watchman, a renter or a borrower, these individuals assume the owner's responsibilities. If [the animal] causes damages, the watchman is held liable."[43] Even though they are not the formal owners of the animal, they "assume the owner's responsibilities," for they are the effective damage avoiders due to the fact that they have the ability – as well as the obligation – to guard the animal effectively.[44] However, later in the ruling (according to Maimonides' corrected text quoted in Chapter 2), Maimonides distinguishes between various cases in which the animal caused damage: (1) If the owner entrusted his animal to a watchman who "guarded the animal in an excellent manner, as he should, and it got loose and caused damage, the watchman is not liable," and the owner, too, is not liable in this case for the damage caused by his animal; (2) If the owner entrusted the animal to an unpaid watchman, who guarded it in an inferior manner, the owner is held liable. In Chapter 2[45] we asked, what is the difference between the two cases, and what is the basis for tort liability which can explain the said ruling? As we said there, it is not possible to explain this ruling according to the theory of *ownership and strict liability*, but it is also difficult to explain it according to the theory of *peshiah*. In both cases the owner entrusted the animal to a watchman, and it was the latter who guarded it at a particular level; from the point of view of the *owner*, however, it is difficult to point to different conduct in the two cases which could lead to the first case being considered as one of unavoidable mishap (*ones*), thus exempting him from payment, whereas in the second case he will be considered to be at fault and held liable for payment.

In light of Maimonides' consequentialist approach and the EAC test in the *Guide*, and in light of Calabresi's best decision maker criterion, it is now possible to revisit this problematic ruling and to answer the question. An examination of other rulings relating to watchmen disperses the fog and proves that the deciding criterion in Maimonides' method is the *effective damage avoider*. In the present case, the effective damage avoider may be the *owner* or the *watchman*, depending on the circumstances pertaining to the conditions of guarding: to whom did the owner entrust his animal to be guarded, and what was the level of guarding that was required from the watchman. If the owner indeed entrusted the animal to a

---

[43] Laws of Property Damages 4:4 (authors' translation).
[44] As Maimonides writes, Laws of Property Damages 4:10.
[45] Chapter 2, Section D.1.

watchman, the watchman "assumes the owner's responsibilities" in that he is the effective damage avoider; therefore he is required to guard the animal and his liability sometimes replaces that of the owner of the animal, who is totally exempt. Sometimes the outcome is the opposite. The question of the liability of the watchman or the owner for the damage depends on the level of guarding required of the watchman, as emerges from what Maimonides writes elsewhere, as there is a difference in the level of guarding required from the four types of watchmen: the paid watchman (and the renter and borrower) is required to guard "in an excellent manner,"[46] whereas the unpaid watchman need only guard "in an inferior manner."[47] What is the difference between "an excellent manner" and "an inferior manner" of guarding? Guarding in an excellent manner requires constant physical presence and attention on the part of the watchman, i.e., active guarding, as opposed to inferior guarding on the part of the unpaid watchman, who need only to create secure conditions, such as putting up a fence, but he himself is not obliged, for example, to stand guard actively and constantly.[48] Indeed, Maimonides rules that if the watchman "guarded it [the animal] in an excellent manner as he should and it got loose and caused damage – the watchman is not liable," and the owner, too, is exempt from payment, for he entrusted the animal to the watchman at the level of "excellent guarding" that can serve as the effective preventer of damage, and "they ensured that there would be excellent guarding as there should be, and what else could they have done?"[49] As opposed to this, if the owner entrusted his animal to an unpaid watchman, the outcome is otherwise, for this watchman is not required to guard in an excellent manner, and only if he was at fault in his guarding will he be liable to pay. Accordingly, in such a case the unpaid watchman does not "assume the responsibilities of the owner," for he is not the effective damage avoider – rather, that role is filled by the owner. Therefore, Maimonides ruled that if he guarded in an inferior manner, "if he is an unpaid watchman – he is not held liable, and the owner is liable." Imposition of liability on the owner in the said case will create a disincentive for the owners from the outset to entrust the animal to an unpaid watchman: this is desirable from the point of view of efficiency, which prefers encouraging owners to entrust their animals to watchmen who are held to a high standard, and who are able to prevent potential damage more effectively. This is also the reason for the exemption from liability of the owner who entrusted the animal to

---

[46] See Laws of Leasing 3:9.
[47] This is logical, for he has no benefit from guarding, as opposed to the other three types of watchmen.
[48] Rabinovitch, *supra* note 23, at 122.
[49] According to Rabinovitch, *ibid.*, at 123. The basis for this becomes clear in light of the discussion in the following chapter of regimes of liability. If an owner entrusted an animal to a watchman in order that he guard it an excellent manner, and the watchman did indeed guard it excellently, even if not in a water-tight manner, the owner has acted appropriately, for he weighed his decision well, whereas the watchman prevented damage as efficiently as he could, even if it was not perfect – but we do not require perfection. Consequently, both are exempt.

a paid watchman or to a renter or a borrower who is held to a higher standard of guarding, even if in practice these watchmen guarded in an inferior manner. The watchmen themselves will be liable, because they did not meet the required standard of guarding.

In fact, this is very reminiscent of Calabresi's best decision maker who, by means of the information available to him, identifies the cheapest cost avoider. In fact, if we explain Maimonides by using Calabresi's terminology, the owner of the animal, by entrusting the animal to a paid watchman who guards it in an excellent manner, he has in fact identified the cheapest cost avoider. Accordingly, the paid watchman is the cheapest cost avoider, and the owner of the animal is the best decision maker. The latter can "induce" the former, by paying for his guarding, to guard in an excellent manner.

Alternatively, it may also be possible to explain the matter in terms of *negligence and fault*: the owner who entrusts his animal to a watchman who guards in an excellent manner is not negligent, as opposed to a person who entrusts the animal to a watchman who from the outset has no great interest in guarding in an excellent manner. The latter owner will be required to bear the cost of the damage and cannot claim it from that watchman. The very choice of that unpaid watchman may constitute a type of negligence and fault, and the owner in such a situation has no one to blame but himself. Nevertheless, it should be noted that although deeming the owner to be at fault due to the very choice of an inferior watchmen is logical according to the modern common law doctrine of negligence, it would be quite difficult to accept this argument in the context of the talmudic theory of *peshiah*, at least according to the approach of some halakhic authorities.[50]

The imposition of tort liability on the owner or on the watchman, depending on who is the effective damage avoider, appears in other rulings of Maimonides as well. Maimonides rules that the owner must pay for the damage caused by his animal, even if he entrusted an ox which was tied up to a deaf-mute, a mentally incompetent person or a minor, and the watchman ultimately guarded it in an excellent manner.[51] Ra'abad disputed this ruling, saying: "I have not found a source for this," for the owner handed over a bound ox; he did not rely on the guarding of the deaf-mute, the mentally incompetent person or the minor, and there is no reason to impose strict liability on the owner. In this case too, it would appear that the basis of the matter is that entrusting an animal to a deaf-mute, a mentally incompetent person or a minor cannot be considered as entrusting the animal to watchmen who "assumed the responsibilities of the owners" as in the previous ruling, for these are

---

[50] See, e.g., TOSAFOT *Bava Metzia* 93a, s.v. *i hakhi* (that the decision of the owner of the animal to entrust it to an unpaid watchman instead of a paid watchman should not be viewed as *peshiah* on the part of the owner, because ultimately he entrusted it to a "sane person" (*ben da'at*), and any sane watchman, even if he is unpaid, normally watches at a high standard, even beyond what is required of him by law).

[51] Laws of Property Damages 4:6.

individuals "who do not have reason"[52] and their guarding cannot be relied upon, since the knot is liable to loosen and one cannot rely on those watchmen to know how to fix the problem. Maimonides clarified this by saying "even if the animal was guarded in an excellent manner." R. Rabinovitch, explains that according to Maimonides, in keeping with his previously mentioned method, guarding in an excellent manner means constant guarding.[53] Consequently, liability is imposed on the owner, who is a more effective damage avoider than those watchmen. Moreover, imposing liability on the person who entrusted the animal to such watchmen will incentivize that person not to entrust his property to watchmen who are not sane, but to those who are possessed of reason, and who therefore, in Calabresi's terms, are the best decision makers; as such it is a desirable thing in itself, from the point of view of avoiding damage.

Alternatively, and similar to the example of entrusting an animal to an unpaid watchman, here too it appears that opting for a deaf-mute, a mentally incompetent person or a minor to guard the ox, even if it is tied, may very well involve negligence on the part of the owner, and it may therefore be possible to explain this ruling on the basis of negligence and fault.

The examples that were discussed at the beginning of this section (liability for tooth, foot and horn damages in the public domain) are based on Maimonides' specific words in the *Guide*, which explain the exemption from liability for damage caused by animals by means of the EAC test. It seems feasible to explain several other exemptions for damages of *pit* and *fire* – exemptions which various commentators and scholars struggled to understand – on the same basis. We will confine ourselves to an analysis of two cases in which an exemption from liability was given to the tortfeasors in cases of fire. The Mishnah and the Talmud mention a major exception to a person's liability for the damage caused by a fire that he lit,[54] namely, an exemption from payment for articles that were buried in a grain heap and were damaged in a fire. Many struggled with the reason for this exemption.[55] Here is not the place to elaborate on the laws of fire damage to buried property,[56] but we will offer one possible – although neither necessary nor exclusive – explanation for Maimonides' ruling on this matter.[57]

---

[52] According to Maimonides in the parallel ruling, *ibid.*, 12:8
[53] Rabinovitch, *supra* note 23, at 126.
[54] M Bava Kamma 6:7, and gemara ad loc., 61b.
[55] One of the great early authorities even stated with certitude that this rule is irrational and therefore "it is scriptural decree that the Bible exempted in the case of fire damage to [utensils that were] buried." PISKEI HAROSH, Bava Kamma 6:13. For a similar approach in interpreting what is written as the basis for an exemption according to some of the *Amoraim*, *see*: Avishalom Westreich, *Tort Law – Between Religion and Law: Exegetical and Legal Processes in Talmudic Tort Law*, 26 SHENATON HAMISHPAT HA'IVRI 203, 212 (2009–2011) (Heb.).
[56] *See* ENCYCLOPAEDIA TALMUDIT vol. 2, 235–36.
[57] Laws of Property Damages 14:9.

The liability of a person who lights a fire in a grain heap in which items were hidden is limited to payment only for "articles that it is likely for farmers to hide in their grain heaps such as a thresher or sower" as Maimonides writes in his commentary to the Mishnah, "but other than for these types of articles he is not liable."[58] It seems only logical that agricultural implements are hidden in the field at the end of a day of work in the field, and in this case the kindler of the fire will be liable and not exempt, but it is less likely that a person hides other utensils and valuable objects in the field, and in this case he will be exempt. True, Maimonides does not explain the reason for the difference between the two rules regarding hidden objects.[59] However, according to the *Guide* and in light of the Calabresian best decision maker test, a reasonable explanation can be proposed, whereby imposition of tort liability on the person lighting the fire depends on the question of whether he, rather than the victim, is in the best position to consider the costs of the anticipated damage and of its prevention. As will be recalled, Maimonides wrote in the *Guide* that the owner of an ox is not liable to compensate a person "who puts a thing in a public space" for tooth and foot damages, for the victim "exposed his property to destruction,"[60] and therefore the victim should be deemed to be in the best position to weigh the costs of the damage and its avoidance, for he knowingly endangers himself by exposing his property to the foreseeable risks. If so, this may also be the rationale for the rule relating to the person who buries articles in a grain heap when such utensils are generally not buried in such places. The person who buries the articles in this unusual place – and not the tortfeasor who lit the fire – is in the best position to weigh the costs of the damage that is likely to be caused, for he is aware of the aberrant act of burying and the risks it entails.[61]

In this example, too, it may be possible to explain the law alternatively, according to the test of negligence and foreseeability or the theory of *peshiah*.[62] Such explanations are not problem-free, however, because the test of foreseeability may not distinguish between the person who buries agricultural implements and one who buries other articles. It is possible that in both cases, it is not to be expected that objects will be buried there, but it is also possible that in both cases this is foreseeable, or that in all events, one can expect to find agricultural implements buried in the field although not other objects that are unconnected to working the land.

---

[58] COMMENTARY TO THE MISHNAH, *Bava Kamma* 6:7.
[59] Laws of Property Damages 14:9.
[60] GUIDE 3:40 (Pines, 555).
[61] The tortfeasor should be held liable for the damage caused by the fire only to the extent that such damage is not abnormal and it was not caused by abnormal behavior on the part of the injured party. Therefore, Maimonides ruled as follows in Laws of Property Damages 14:12: "If one sets fire to another's building, he must pay for everything in it, since it is customary for people to keep all their utensils (articles) and all their goods in their houses."
[62] *See* SHALOM ALBECK, GENERAL PRINCIPLES OF THE LAW OF TORT IN THE TALMUD 75–77, 163–67 (2nd ed., Tel Aviv: Dvir, 1990) (Heb.) (explaining the exemption for the case of the buried implements according to the method of *peshiah*).

It may be that it all depends on the usage of the particular time and place, so that here too, matters are less unequivocal according to the test of foreseeability than according to Calabresi's doctrine.

We wish to propose a similar explanation for another of Maimonides' rulings in the *Code*, which exempts the person who lights a fire from the damage caused by the fire: "[When] a camel that is loaded with flax passes through the public domain, and the flax that enters the shop is ignited by the lamp belonging to the shopkeeper and then sets fire to the entire building – the owner of the camel is liable, because he overloaded [his camel]."[63]

Here too it is possible, using the EAC test from the *Guide*, to explain that the owner of the camel will be liable because he is the *effective damage avoider*. In fact, in his conscious, aberrant action of overloading the beast, the owner of the camel created the risk, and he is therefore liable for the damage, more so than the shopkeeper whose candle was alight in the shop. Alternatively, on the *negligence* test, it is possible that the shopkeeper's *contributory negligence* would entail some level of deduction, but he would nevertheless be entitled to some compensation at least, unless the damage was totally unforeseeable; in that case, even according to the negligence test, the owner of the camel would be liable for the entire damage.

In the last ruling from the *Code* that we shall discuss, Maimonides actually cites the reason for the ruling, and that reason is amazingly similar to the reason that he cited for a similar case in the *Guide*. In the *Code* Maimonides exempts a person who is sleeping from liability for damage that was caused in a situation in which another person came and lay down beside him or laid articles beside him.[64] The explicit rationale suggested by Maimonides in the *Code* in relation to the sleeping person is that "if one places an article alongside a person who is asleep and the latter breaks it, he is exempt, seeing that the one who put it down is deemed forewarned (*mu'ad*) and commits an act of an negligence (*hamu'ad shepashah*)."[65] However, this need not necessarily be understood in terms of moral fault, for this reasoning in the *Code* is very similar to the rationalization cited in the *Guide* whereby the owner of an animal that caused damage in the public domain is exempt for damages of the type of tooth and foot, since he who leaves a thing in a public place "is at fault toward himself and exposes his property to destruction."[66] We have already seen that this reasoning sits very well with contributory negligence and with the Hand formula of economic negligence. Indeed, the ruling of the sleeping person, too, can be explained according to Posner as well, for if the negligence of the tortfeasor is compared to that of the injured party, one can say that the negligence of the injured party is gross.

---

[63] Laws of Property Damages 14:13 (authors' translation).
[64] Laws of Wounding and Damaging 1:11.
[65] *Ibid.*
[66] GUIDE 3:40 (Pines, 555).

Even though Maimonides' reasoning appears to be different from that of Calabresi in that it invokes terms of *peshiah*, the result whereby liability is imposed only on the injured party can be explained satisfactorily according to Calabresi's method as well: a person who lies down next to a sleeping person or places an object beside him acts in an abnormal fashion and he – and not the sleeping direct tortfeasor – must bear liability for the damage he incurs. It is he who knowingly entered that situation and therefore, if we use Calabresi's *best decision maker* terminology, he is better situated than the sleeping person to weigh up the costs of the damage, and it is easier for him to prevent the occurrence of the accident. Liability therefore passes over to him, in effect similar to the cases of the person who buries articles that are damaged by fire or the person who leaves articles in the public domain.

We showed here that the consequentialist analysis proposed (in this Chapter until now) for the rulings in the *Code* is not the only possible one, but our main purpose in this revisiting of the rulings in the *Code* was to show how the rulings can be explained well *also* by virtue of the consequentialist conception of the *Guide* and by recourse to modern tort doctrines, and that this rationale may be suited no less, and maybe more, than others in explaining some of the difficulties in the rulings.

E. SPLITTING THE LIABILITY BETWEEN THE PARTIES (THE *TAM* OX)

When we examine the *Code* through the prism of what Maimonides wrote in the *Guide* concerning the *tam* ox,[67] as discussed in Chapter 5,[68] we discover several fundamental differences in the law of the *tam* ox as elucidated and explained in each of the two works. The first difference relates to the reason and the legal basis for the payment, and the second difference relates to the specifics of the laws concerning payment of half damages in the case of a *tam* ox and full damages for a *mu'ad* ox.

As we saw in Chapter 5, even though the rule is the same – payment of half damages in relation to the *tam* ox – the explanation for the talmudic rule[69] differs from that of Maimonides' ruling in the *Guide*. Whereas it appears that the talmudic rule imposing partial compensation by the owner for damage caused by the innocent ox that gored is an exceptional law that deviates from the standard rules of liability in talmudic tort law – in particular according to the opinion defining the payment as a fine (*kenas*) and not as a (civil law) monetary payment – according to Maimonides' explanation in the *Guide*, this is not an exceptional law, but rather a rule stemming from the need to identify the effective damage avoider in every case. Moreover, the very fact of imposing tort liability on the owner of the ox both for tooth and foot and for damage caused by an innocent ox is designed, in

---

[67] GUIDE 3:40 (Pines, 555).
[68] Section B.1.c.
[69] Based on a biblical rule: Exodus 21:35.

Maimonides' opinion, to serve as a type of deterrent and an incentive to prevent the damage, and for the purposes of this rationale, there is no difference between payment of *full* or payment of *half* damages. However, it is possible that in the *Code*, too, one can discern the first buds of the Maimonidean conception which does not differentiate in principle between the liability of the owner of the goring ox for half damages (when the ox was innocent – *tam*) and his liability for full damages (when the ox owner was forewarned – *mu'ad*). This conception emerges from a very specific context in the *Code* explaining why Gentiles must pay full compensation for damage caused by an innocent ox that gored, as opposed to a Jew, who must pay only half damages. In the first section of this chapter, we discussed Maimonides' consequentialist explanation of this ruling: "Should we not hold them liable for the damage caused by their animals, they would not take care of them and thus would inflict loss on other people's property."[70]

According to this explanation in the *Code*, which is very similar in its consequentialist tone to that in the *Guide*, payment of the damage that was caused by the goring of the *tam* ox is designed to create an incentive for the owner of the *tam* ox to guard his ox and to prevent damage. According to Maimonides, the difference in the level of payment by the Jew and the Gentile does not stem from the fact that the basis for payment of full damages is entirely different from the basis for payment of half damages, as could be explained according to the Talmud (i.e. that half damages is a fine and full compensation is a civil law monetary payment), but from the fact that the level of deterrence that is required for the Gentile, who is not bound by the religious prohibition against causing damage, is greater than that required in relation to the Jew, who is assumed to heed the prohibition against causing damage.

Nevertheless, and despite the similarity between the Maimonidean reasoning in this specific ruling in the *Code* and the general, principled conception in the *Guide*, it is difficult to ignore the fact that many of the details of the laws in the *Code*, which distinguish between the liability for half damages in the case of a *tam* ox and liability for full compensation in the case of a *mu'ad* ox,[71] are difficult to explain according to Maimonides' method in the *Guide*. Thus, for example, Maimonides ruled in the *Code*, similar to the talmudic law which imposes strict liability in the case of a *tam* ox that gored, that the owner must pay even in the case where "an ox breaks loose and causes damage after its owner had tied it with a rope and locked it [in a corral] in an acceptable manner. If it is a *tam*, he is required to pay only half the damages."[72] However, Maimonides rules that if the ox was *mu'ad*, the owner is exempt.[73] In other words, in relation to a *mu'ad* ox and payment of full damages, the owner does not bear strict liability, whereas in relation to a *tam* ox, strict liability is

---

[70] Laws of Property Damages 8:5.
[71] *See* details of the laws in Laws of Property Damages 7.
[72] Laws of Property Damages 7:1.
[73] *Ibid*. According to *Bava Kamma* 45b.

imposed and the owner pays for half the damage that was caused, even if he guarded the ox appropriately. This differs from contemporary law, in which strict liability means liability on the part of the tortfeasor for all the damage, and not half or any other proportion thereof. This difference in the standard of care between a *tam* ox and a *mu'ad* ox, which is emphasized only in the *Code*, may be explained with relative ease if we accept the assumption that the basis for liability for the damage caused by the *tam* ox is fundamentally different from that in the case of the *mu'ad* ox, i.e., that payment of half damages in the former case is imposed irrespective of the level of guarding on the part of the owner, whereas the payment in the latter case is a payment in tort that is connected to the level of guarding required of the owner. Needless to say, this distinction relating to the required level of guarding on the part of the owner of each type of ox receives no mention at all in the *Guide*, and indeed,[74] it would appear that in the *Guide* Maimonides was not seeking to explain all the details of tort law. It is therefore difficult to say that the puzzle of the *tam* ox was fully resolved in the *Guide* and that the text in the *Guide* was successful in this case in illuminating the ruling in the *Code*. On the contrary, this ruling highlights the difference between the two works.

Another possible connection between Maimonides' rationalization in the *Guide* and the details of the rulings in the *Code* relates to his fundamental distinction between *tam* and *mu'ad* at the beginning of the Book of Torts in the *Code*. In Chapter 3 we saw, following Jackson, the importance attributed by Maimonides in the *Code* to his basic and innovative distinction between *tam* and *mu'ad* (which is different from what appears in the Talmud), upon which Maimonides placed great emphasis.[75] As will be recalled, Maimonides distinguished between animals acting in two different ways. The first was "the one which did an act which it is its way to do always, in accordance with the custom of its species – that is the one (traditionally) called *mu'ad*"; and the second related to an animal "which changes and does an act which it is not the way of all its kind to do always, for example, the ox which gores or bites – that is the one (traditionally) called *tam*."[76] One scholar explained that what Maimonides' meant by saying that the owner of an animal is liable for "an act which it is its way to do always," is that "it is standard for it to cause damage."[77] However, this does not appear to be the correct explanation of what Maimonides wrote in the *Code*, in light of the fact that in the *Guide* he wrote explicitly that tooth and foot damages in the public domain are *not* standard.[78] Even though tooth and foot damages are not necessarily standard, as Maimonides wrote in the *Guide*, he defined them in the

---

[74] Chapter 5, Section B.1.
[75] In the first chapter of the Book of Torts.
[76] Laws of Property Damages 1:4, according to Jackson's translation.
[77] Albeck, *supra* note 62, at 107.
[78] GUIDE 3:40 (Pines, 555).

Code as acts that "it is the way" of the animal to do.[79] Assuming that there is no contradiction between the sources, this would mean that these damages are defined as "the way" of the animal to do, even though they are not necessarily standard, i.e., the animal may indeed cause damage of this type, but this is less standard than other potential damage that it is liable to cause in the public domain. It would therefore appear, as Jackson says, that according to Maimonides, "[t]he distinction between *tam* and *mu'ad* thus no longer relates to the attestation of the same type of activity on previous occasions; *tam* and *mu'ad* now denote different types of activity."[80]

What is Maimonides' rationale for the distinction between these two types of acts? It may be that the explanation for this fundamental distinction is related to the existence of the element of *knowledge* on the part of the owner of the ox, which defines him as the *best decision maker* in Calabresi's terms. In other words, full liability should be imposed on the owner of the animal only in those cases in which the damage was caused as a result of behavior which is normal and habitual. Who, if not the owner, knows the normal patterns of behavior of his animal – did the animal, in practice, and unlike other animals, gore three times with its left horn, thereby becoming forewarned (*mu'ad*)?[81] Therefore, the owner's ability to weigh the anticipated damage before it occurs is better than that of the injured party, who is not necessarily aware of that unusual behavior of the animal. This is not the situation regarding behavior that is unexpected, in relation to which the element of the owner's knowledge is weaker and therefore he is not to be made to bear the full damage.[82] A similar distinction was drawn by Calabresi (following common law precedents) in the context of the best decision maker when he spoke of a cow that trespassed and a cow that bit a neighbor, or a tiger that mangled somebody and a tiger that is simply chewing grass rather than tearing at meat.[83] These animals are capable of causing damage in different ways, but some ways are more normal and some are less so.

Here, too, it may be possible to explain the law in accordance with the principles of negligence and the theory of *peshiah*, for if the owner knows his animal and knows how it acts, even if it acts in an unusual manner, this should possibly be regarded as a type of foreseeability of the damage that the animal is liable to cause, which could serve as a basis for holding the owner liable for full damages.

---

[79] Laws of Property Damages 1:8.
[80] Bernard S. Jackson, *Maimonides' Definitions of* Tam *and* Mu'ad, 1 JEWISH L. ANNUAL 168, 173 (1978).
[81] Laws of Property Damages 7:2.
[82] He pays only half damages, unlike in Calabresi's method. *See* Chapter 4, Section C.1.a.
[83] Guido Calabresi & Jon T. Hirschoff, *Toward a Test of Strict Liability in Torts*, 81 YALE L.J. 1055, 1066 (1972).

F. INCENTIVE FOR PREVENTING DAMAGES: IMPOSING LIABILITY
FOR RISK-CAUSING BEHAVIOR

A good illustration of Maimonides' fundamental attitude toward prevention of damage (emphasized in the *Guide*) is shown in his rulings in the *Code*. Maimonides suggests a far-reaching approach that mandates deterrence of risk-causing behavior even if it did not cause actual damage. He writes:

> A beast that was grazing and broke away and entered fields and vineyards, even if it did not yet cause damage, its owners are warned three times. If he did not guard his beast and prevent it from grazing, the owner of the field has the right to slaughter the beast ritually and say to its owner: "come and sell your meat." For one is forbidden to cause damage willfully, with the intention of paying for the damage he causes. Even to bring about damage indirectly with this intention is forbidden.[84]

Maimonides' ruling is far-reaching in that it entitles the person who *may* sustain damage on the part of the beast, "even if it did not yet cause damage," to seek relief on his own and slaughter the beast. We have already dealt with this ruling and the opposition to it on the part of some of the great halakhic sages.[85]

This ruling has extensive ramifications from various aspects, both tortious and non-tortious (including deontological, religious, property-related and criminal aspects), such as: self-help on the part of the victim under the aegis of the law, with the victim serving as a type of long arm of the law, e.g., in cases of forcing the trespasser off the property, or preventive regulation of risk-creating behaviors even though they have not caused damage, such as behavioral rather than consequentialist offences and others. We dealt with such possible ramifications in Chapter 4. Of course, it is possible to examine the matter in accordance with the laws of injunctions that are designed to pre-empt risk-creating behavior that is likely to develop into actual risk. However, we are not dealing here with the reality of formal submission to the court prior to the act in order to obtain such an injunction to prevent future damage, but with the ability of a potential victim, even without the enforcement authorities, to avoid the obstacle and even to eliminate it. We will deal here only with with the consequentialist aspects of this ruling.

Revisiting this ruling in the *Code* in light of the *Guide* suggests that Maimonides' approach that proposes deterrence and focuses on efficient means of "the prevention of acts causing damage"[86] is not prepared to embrace the view that tort law relies exclusively on corrective justice, a view which brings into relief the operation of tort law in relation to the past only, minimizing the significance of its deterrent effect with respect to the future.

---

[84] Laws of Property Damages 5:1.
[85] *See* Chapter 2, Section D.4.
[86] GUIDE 3:40 (Pines, 555).

It is possible to regard the Maimonidean ruling in this case as the imposition of a fine. However, we can also perceive it as a type of preventive order that allows for harming the potential tortfeasor precisely by means of a preventive act on the part of the potential victim, without involving the authorities (inspectors or police officers). Due to the need for immediate action – for in some cases it is not reasonable to wait for judicial intervention, and the passage of time is a critical factor – the potential victim even serves here in some way as the long arm of the authorities, an agent of the court. As such, this is not a case of compensation for future damage, but more of prevention and perhaps regulation, which also sheds light on Maimonides' approach to the prevention of damage and deterrence. According to Maimonides, it is possible to prevent the injurer, who in this case is the owner of an animal and the most effective damage avoider (we assume of course that the neighbors erected a fence), from continuing the activity that can cause damage to another. This is to be done even if the animal has not yet caused such damage in practice, if it transpires that the owner of the animal is a serial tortfeasor who did not take serious supervisory measures and precautions with regard to his animal despite having been warned three times, and did not prevent his animal from entering private lands. This may be compared to revoking the operating license of a business that does not meet safety regulations mandated by law.

As part of the discussion of Maimonides' ruling that it is permissible to slaughter an animal that entered a field more than three times even if it did not cause damage, we must emphasize that this is dictated both by consequentialist considerations, and by ethical (deontological) considerations, which is why he mentions the prohibition against causing damage in that ruling.

Maimonides believes that the prohibition against causing damage also serves as a social tool that promotes efficient social behavior. This can be seen in another of Maimonides' rulings[87] which suggests that caution in observing the commandments plays a decisive role in preventing damage and in contributing to the welfare of society. It is possible to characterize Maimonides as having adopted an economic approach to damage prevention, primarily on the basis of the effective damage avoider. These considerations coexist with deontological-moral ones, which also characterize Maimonides' tort theory and complement the economic considerations.

Having reached the said understanding, we can revisit Albeck's question discussed in Chapter 2[88] concerning the apparent contradiction between Maimonides' said ruling on the manner of slaughtering an animal that strays into the field of another, and the ruling that follows it. (The Sages forbade the rearing of small animals in the Land of Israel.)[89]

---

[87] Laws of Property Damages 8:5.
[88] *See* Chapter 2, Section D.4.
[89] Laws of Property Damages 5:2.

One must understand why Maimonides offered different legal solutions in these two rulings, which are not positioned one after the other by accident: in the first ruling, he fined only the person who was at fault in his guarding of the animal, and in the second ruling he totally forbade the rearing of the animals for all. It should be noted that not only are these consecutive rulings; Maimonides connected these two rulings to each other (saying at the beginning of the second ruling, "because of this"), hinting that the jurisprudential policy is the same for both. What is this policy, and on what is it based? Moreover, elsewhere Maimonides ruled that every person is permitted to take his compost and manure out into the public domain during the set hours for this activity and to amass them there for thirty days in order that it be trodden upon by people and animals. And nevertheless, he ruled that if these substances cause damage, the owner is liable.[90] Here too one must ask why Maimonides allowed the owner of the waste products to cause damage to many, and still ruled that if he causes damage he must pay. Why did Maimonides not rule, similar to his fundamental ruling mentioned at the beginning of this section, that "one is forbidden to cause damage willfully, with the intention of paying for the damage he causes"?[91] In other words, one ruling contains a prohibition against causing damage, and if a person was not careful not to transgress this prohibition, in that he allowed his goat to trespass in the neighbor's yard – even if the goat had not yet caused damage – the goat is slaughtered. In the following ruling, there is a blanket prohibition on raising small domestic animals for fear that they will cause damage. In the third ruling we see that it is in fact permitted to cause damage by depositing waste in the public domain, but the damage must be paid for.

It would appear that the basis for the differences in Maimonides' rulings lies in economic-consequentialist considerations, but within the framework of earlier, normative sources which Maimonides cannot avoid. In this context, we accept Rabinovitch's assertion[92] that on the one hand, some things were prohibited by the Sages, such as raising small domestic animals or small beasts within the settled area, even though this is detrimental to the livelihood of the farmers. The reason for this is that the damage that is likely to occur from raising the livestock is great and very common. On the other hand, however, although some things may be permitted, anyone "owning" the defect must pay for the damage, e.g., depositing waste in the public domain. This applies, in our opinion, to an animal that grazed and strayed onto the property of others, whose owners were fined in the form of the slaughter of the animal only if it strayed three times. Clearly, the welfare of the pubic was weighed up against the damage to the individual, and in any event the case was

---

[90] Ibid. 13:15.
[91] Ibid. 5:1.
[92] Nachum Rabinovitch, *Liability for Property that Caused Damage*, in Zvi Haber ed., 25 MA'ALIOT – MAIMONIDES' 800 YEARS COMMEMORATIVE VOLUME 71, 86 (Ma'aleh Adumim: Ma'aliot, 2005).

discussed on its merits and regulations were enacted in order to promote the economy without causing loss to the injured party. In view of the fact that the person taking out his waste products was held liable for the damages this caused, even though the act itself was not forbidden, there is no doubt that someone who does not really need to do so will refrain from taking the waste out into the public domain, for he will not wish to put himself needlessly at risk of having to pay for the damage from that waste. In any case the number of those taking out the waste in the community will decrease, and for this reason too, the damage will be reduced. The same holds true, in our opinion, in relation to the goat that grazes in the fields of others: it will not be worthwhile, from the aspect of economic welfare, to totally prohibit the goat's grazing activities, due to their importance to the ancient agricultural economy, despite the concern that from time to time goats will enter the fields of others. We have therefore not found a rule forbidding the goat to graze in those fields altogether, just as there was no prohibition on the goat remaining in the public domain even though it was liable to cause tooth or foot damage there; just as we would not expect today to outlaw driving completely in places in which driving is likely to do more damage than in other places, even though the driver will be liable for damage caused in that area. On the other hand, a fine was imposed on the owner if he did not guard the goat and it trespassed on the property of another three times, in order to encourage him to prevent future damage. In other words, from the point of view of probabilities, what we have here is a certain degree of prevention of private damage, alongside the utility to the agricultural economy as a whole. This explanation is in keeping with Maimonides' line of thinking, as expressed in the *Guide*, and it is likely to elucidate the relevant rulings in the *Code* as well.

G. CONCLUSION

In this chapter we revisited some of the problematic texts in the *Code* and attempted to cast light on them in view of the consequentialist objective of tort law elucidated in the *Guide*. In this way we tried to resolve some of the difficulties that were raised in Chapter 2. At the same time, we clearly saw that the *Guide* and the *Code* do not always speak with one voice. Sometimes, a general rationalization offered in the *Guide* in relation to a particular ruling, such as that relating to the *tam* ox, cannot be reconciled with the details of the ruling as specified in the *Code*.

Maimonides' tort theory is constructed, according to what we have demonstrated in Chapters 3–5, on three different levels. The first two (the two meta-goals of torts and the EAC test) have been already discussed. They are based primarily on texts from the *Guide*, but as we saw, they have different parallels in rulings in the *Code*, and it is even possible by means of these texts, as well as with the insights of modern scholars of tort law, to elucidate some of the rulings that are difficult to understand on the *yeshivah* reading of the Book of Torts in the *Code*, mentioned in Chapter 2. At the third level of Maimonides' tort theory, which derives from the *Code*, we present the *standard of care* (or liability regime) that is required from the effective damage avoider in order to hold him liable. This third level will be discussed in the following chapter.

7

Maimonides' Standard of Care:

A *Differential Liability Model*

A. PRESENTING MAIMONIDES' DIFFERENTIAL LIABILITY REGIME

This chapter suggests that Maimonides adopted a differential liability model. As we noted earlier,[1] Maimonides did not advocate the common fault-based regime and *peshiah* as the sole basis for tort liability. On the other hand, we disagreed with Warhaftig and Haut's sweeping suggestion that Maimonides imposed absolute/strict liability on all types of tort cases.[2] We argue that Maimonides accepted a more complex liability regime, which we call a *differential model*.

A careful examination of Maimonides' writings reveals that he favored different liability regimes for different categories of damage. This differentiation means that he did not consistently apply one liability regime to all types of tort cases.

Maimonides' tort theory, we argue, is based upon a fundamental distinction between two questions: (a) upon whom should tort liability be imposed; and (b) what is the standard of care that should be imposed in each case, on the scale between negligence and strict liability. Attention to the distinction between these two questions may help us solve some of the difficulties mentioned in Chapter 2,[3] which derive from incorrect, although common, interpretations.

Maimonides answers the first question in the context of monetary damages caused by a person or his property (but not in cases of murder, wounding, theft or robbery) by applying the EAC test, i.e., his test for determining liability; this question

---

[1] *See* Chapter 2.
[2] Irwin H. Haut, *Some Aspects of Absolute Liability under Jewish Law and Particularly, Under the View of Maimonides*, 15 DINE ISRAEL 7 (1989–90); Zerah Warhaftig, *The Basis for Liability for Damages in Jewish Law*, STUDIES IN JEWISH LAW 211, 218–21, 224–27 (1985) (Heb.). And *see* Chapter 2.
[3] *See* esp. Chapter 2, Sections C.1 (presenting the fact that Maimonides did not impose strict liability on the tortfeasor in a comprehensive fashion) and D.3 (asking whether the standard of care in damages caused by a person to the property of another is that of strict liability or negligence).

does not necessarily depend only on *peshiah* (negligence),[4] as noted in the previous chapters, but on whoever is the *effective damage avoider*, and this is determined by the element of *control*. Determination of the *identity* of the effective damage avoider, however, does not necessarily mean that the answer to the second question is that *strict liability* is borne by the avoider, as Warhaftig and Haut, and perhaps some contemporary law and economics scholars,[5] argued. This is because according to Maimonides, the standard of care is *topic-dependent*. Often liability gravitates toward an optimal level that is higher than negligence but lower than absolute or strict liability. In other words, the question of the standard of care, which precedes determination of the identity of the avoider, might already depend on *peshiah*, due to economic-consequentialist or deontological considerations, with a separate rationale for every category of cases.

The distinction between these two questions may clarify why Maimonides includes in his regime both the component of *peshiah* and that of effective control (the EAC test). As we saw in Chapter 2, these two components – particularly according to the *yeshivah* reading[6] – appear to contradict each other. Even if there is no contradiction, it is difficult to explain the role of each component and how each operates in the normative tort-halakhic framework in general, and in Maimonides' theory in particular.[7] In this chapter, we will see that in fact, these are two components that combine to form one complete theory of torts. The solution lies in the fact that each component relates to a different question. The EAC test determines who will bear the tort liability for monetary damages caused by a person or his property, whereas the component of *peshiah* (negligence) is one of the standards of care (alongside other standards) that should be applied to the effective damage avoider, i.e. the person who has control.

Maimonides conducts an innovative weighting of these two questions for different types of cases: this appears in the Book of Torts (*Sefer Nezikin*) in the *Code*,[8] in which he discusses the different standards of care that he imposes for different types of damage.

In this chapter we attempt to define precisely the standard of care adopted by Maimonides in his *Code* regarding four types of damage: (a) damage caused by a

---

[4] Even though, as we saw in the earlier chapters, the element of *peshiah* is liable to have an effect in the sense of contributory negligence ("… is at fault (*posheah*) toward himself" as Maimonides says in the GUIDE 3:40), which is similar, as we saw in Chapter 5, to Posner's contributory negligence. Nevertheless, the element of *peshiah* appears to be of secondary importance vis-à-vis the EAC test which, as stated, is the central test for determining tort liability according to Maimonides.

[5] See, e.g., Guido Calabresi & Jon T. Hirschoff, *Toward a Test of Strict Liability in Torts*, 81 YALE L.J. 1055 (1972). And see Chapters 1 & 5.

[6] Which is framed in terms of *peshiah* vs. ownership.

[7] Chapter 2, Section C.2.

[8] Admittedly, as we saw in Chapter 5, Maimonides' analysis in the GUIDE is short and general, and he does not discuss the specifics of the rulings in the various categories of tortious incidents.

person to the property of another; (b) injury caused by a person to another; (c) damage caused by property; and (d) death in the form of murder. In each of the first three categories, Maimonides proposes that the person who has *control* in each of these categories, i.e., the *effective damage avoider*,[9] and all four categories will be subjected to a standard of care that is on the scale between negligence and strict liability. In Section B of this chapter we describe the hierarchy of liability regimes and standards of care, from the highest level (closest to strict liability) to the lowest (negligence or fault). We present a scheme that illustrates Maimonides' *differential model* and explains its rationale for the hierarchy amongst the standards of care used in different cases. Finally, we describe the historical background, circumstances, and nature of the tortfeasors in Maimonides' time and in the present era.

1 Damage Caused by a Person to the Property of Another: Strict Liability and Exemption Only in Cases of Force Majeure

Regarding a person who causes damage to the property of another, we learn from the *Mishnah* that a person is liable for all accidents he caused,[10] and the Talmud comments that the tortfeasor must pay, whether the damage occurred unintentionally, through unavoidable mishap (*ones*), or intentionally.[11] Commentators were divided about the degree of lack of intention or *ones* that the tortfeasor must demonstrate. Some maintained that he was liable if the *ones* was not total, but in the case of total *ones*, e.g., if a man fell off the roof in an uncommon wind and caused damage,[12] he was exempt.[13] However, many interpreted Maimonides' view to mean that a man who injures must be held liable even in a case of total *ones*;[14] in other words, Maimonides' ruling regarding the tortfeasor was based on a standard of strict liability. In his words in the *Code*:

> If one damages another's property, he must pay full compensation; for whether one acts inadvertently (*shogeg*) or accidentally in an unavoidable mishap (*anus*), he is regarded as one who acted deliberately. Thus, if one falls from a roof and breaks

---

[9] In the fourth category of the crime of murder as we shall see below in Section A.4, Maimonides adopted a different criterion of liability, that of "an act of causing death."
[10] M Bava Kamma 2:6.
[11] Sanhedrin 72b.
[12] As in the ruling in Tur, Hoshen Mishpat 378, 1–2 (exempting from liability a person who fell in an uncommon wind and harmed another person's body or property).
[13] See, e.g., Tosafot, Bava Kamma 27b, s.v. *veshmuel* (distinguishing between compulsion that is a type of theft, in which case liability is imposed, and compulsion that is a type of loss, in which case liability is not imposed); Rosh, Bava Kamma 3:1; Rema, Hoshen Mishpat 378, 1 (1911–13).
[14] See, e.g., Maggid Mishneh on Maimonides' Laws of Wounding and Damaging 6:1; Siftei Cohen, Hoshen Mishpat 378, 1 (explaining that in the opinion of Maimonides and of Shulkhan Arukh he is also liable in a case of total compulsion). Nahmanides also rules according to this opinion in his commentary to Bava Metzia 82b, s.v. *ve'ata*.

articles, or if one stumbles while walking and falls on an article and breaks it, he must pay full compensation.[15]

According to this source it would appear that Maimonides adopts a *strict liability* standard for the *effective damage avoider*, at least as far as damage caused by a person to the property of another is concerned. However, there appears to be an exception in a case of *force majeure*. Maimonides believes that a person who causes damage to another's property is exempt from payment in cases that he defines as a "strike from Heaven" (*makah biydei shamayim*), as he ruled in the case of the liability of the person who climbed a ladder (the ladder case, mentioned in Chapter 2).[16]

Commentators struggled to explain this rule. As we saw in Chapter 2, Ra'abad[17] questioned the definition of the breaking of a rung, or whether the fact that the rung was eaten by worms was an act of Heaven. He conceded that it could be considered an unavoidable mishap (*ones*); however, at the beginning of the same earlier-cited chapter of the *Code*, Maimonides had already ruled that even though there is an unavoidable mishap the tortfeasor is liable – for example, if he accidently falls off the roof. Here is a case of a person causing damage in an unavoidable mishap, and nevertheless he is liable. We have mentioned the difficulty in understanding the difference between such a tortfeasor under *ones* and one who climbs a ladder and a rung breaks under him.[18]

It is clear that Maimonides draws a careful distinction between *ones* and "a strike from Heaven," and that according to him, if a man climbs a ladder and a rung breaks under him when the ladder was tight and strong, this is not compulsion but a "strike from Heaven." But how do we define a "strike from Heaven," and how does it differ from regular compulsion? Halakhic authorities have offered various definitions for exemptions on account of a strike from Heaven.[19] Some have defined this as the highest possible level of total compulsion "where it was clear that the damage was from Heaven,"[20] or in the more modern formulation of a contemporary rabbinical judge, "… which was an entirely uncommon act, and one could not

---

[15] Laws of Wounding and Damaging 6:1.
[16] Ibid. at 6:4. *See also* Laws of Property Damages 14:2 (providing an additional example of a strike from Heaven).
[17] Laws of Wounding and Damaging 6:4. And *see* Chapter 2, Section D.3.
[18] KESSEF MISHNEH, Laws of Wounding and Damaging 6:1 (Frenkel ed., 1975), who, because of the difficulty (regarding the ruling of the person climbing a ladder) wrote that according to Maimonides, in cases of absolute necessity the tortfeasor should be exempt. But the interpretation of KESSEF MISHNEH does not seem consistent with the simple language of Maimonides' first rule, which holds the tortfeasor liable even when he was under *ones* (and Maimonides did not distinguish between different types of *ones*, as inferred by Maggid Mishneh, ibid.).
[19] *See, e.g.*, RESP. RADBAZ, ibid; EVEN HA'EZEL, Hilkhot Hovel Umezik 6:1 (1962); OR GADOL, Bava Kamma, Section A: 21B s.v. *vehinei* (Shraga Faibel Gerber ed., 1961).
[20] See ARUKH HASHULHAN, Hoshen Mishpat 378:3 (explaining Maimonides' opinion).

imagine such a thing in any way."[21] He may actually mean foreseeability, to use modern terms. R. Nachum Rabinovitch offers a clear definition of a strike from Heaven, which matches Maimonides' use of the term on several occasions:

> [t]he definition of "strike from Heaven" includes two components. On the one hand it is a very rare phenomenon, an unnatural event that occurs very rarely. On the other hand there is the possibility of another force involved in the occurrence, which one cannot foresee how and when it operates.[22]

In light of all this, Rabinovitch seeks to settle Ra'abad's question and explain the difference between the cases of *ones* when one falls off the roof and when the rung breaks on a ladder. According to this explanation, Maimonides imposes liability only in the case of *ones* where had the tortfeasor acted with proper caution, the damage would have been prevented. But:

> [O]ur case is different because "it was strong and tight," he looked and checked the ladder and saw that the rungs were tightly held and there was no sign of weakness of the rungs and that they were strong, *so what else could he have done*? It is not he who removed the rung, and this is nothing but a strike from Heaven.[23]

According to this explanation, although Maimonides believes that the tortfeasor should be held liable for unforeseeable damage as well, this is only in cases in which he could have prevented the occurrence by taking proper precautionary measures.[24] This means that Maimonides imposed a standard of care of almost strict liability; it is not a complete strict or *absolute* liability, however, because the tortfeasor who caused unforeseeable damage but took all required precautions would not be liable, as in this case the damage is a strike from Heaven. This approach of Maimonides is different from a completely strict liability standard of care, which would impose liability on the tortfeasor even in a case in which the injured person climbed the ladder, and a rung which had been strong and tight fell out. The latter standard of care is imposed according to Calabresi's doctrine of best decision maker, which is a strict liability standard,[25] higher than the standard of care used by Maimonides; we can therefore assume that Calabresi would impose liability even in this case. In his opinion, strict liability means that the best decision maker must bear the liability if any damage occurs, even if the damage is unforeseeable and even if he had no opportunity in the actual circumstances to prevent the damage, and his only option was to invest in measures to prevent future damage. Maimonides differs on this

---

[21] AVRAHAM SHEINFELD, TORTS 251, note 5 (1992) (Heb.).
[22] R. NACHUM L. RABINOVITCH, YAD PESHUTAH LESEFER NEZIKIN, Laws of Wounding and Damaging 6:4, 143 (Ma'ale Adumim: Ma'aliot 2007) (Heb.).
[23] *Ibid.*, at 142–43. Emphasis supplied by the authors.
[24] *See also* HAZON ISH, *Bava Kamma* 11, 100:21.
[25] *See* Chapter 5 Section C.1.

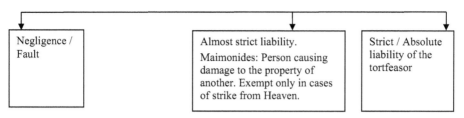

FIGURE 7.1 A person causing damage to the property of another: almost strict liability

point; he proposes a type of liability that falls within the range between negligence and strict liability, closer to strict liability. This type of liability exempts the tortfeasor who did everything he could do in order to effectively prevent the damage but the damage occurred nevertheless, in which case it must be defined as a strike from Heaven.

The nature of the standard of care that entails liability proposed by Maimonides can be elucidated further by comparing the strike from Heaven exemption according to Maimonides with the *force majeure* exemption granted by some modern tort laws to damage caused by an uncommon natural event. Izhak Englard offers two possible definitions of the term *"force majeure."* The first is a natural occurrence that a reasonable person could not have foreseen and that could not be avoided.[26] This is a strict concept, far-removed from simple negligence, and the test is not the degree of reasonableness of the behavior but a person's physical capabilities. The other is a natural occurrence that a reasonable person does not take into consideration because the likelihood of it happening is small, and it cannot be prevented by taking regular precautionary measures.[27] This latter concept of *force majeure* is very close to the absence of negligence, because the test is based on the behavior of a reasonable person regarding natural occurrences. It appears that the first approach is closer to Maimonides' standard of care in this category,[28] which is certainly of a higher level than negligence, and the test is the person's effective physical ability to prevent the damage (the EAC test). But even according to the first approach this does not amount to strict liability of the tortfeasor, because he is exempt from liability for damage he could not have foreseen and which cannot be prevented.

In short, with regard to a person who causes damage to the property of another, Maimonides adopts a regime of *almost strict liability* of the effective damage avoider, with one exception, namely, in the case of *force majeure* (see Figure 7.1).

---

[26] Izhak Englard, Tort Law 196–99 (Gad Tedeschi ed., 2nd ed., 1976) (Heb.).
[27] Ibid.
[28] Some argue that this is not necessarily consistent with the approach of other decisors. See Sheinfeld, *supra* note 21, at 251 (referring to the relations between the above two approaches mentioned by Englard and the position of Jewish law).

2 Injury Caused by a Person to the Body of Another: Three Different Standards of Care

Regarding a person who causes bodily injury to another, Maimonides again proposes what at first seems to be a standard of strict liability: "A person is always deemed forewarned whether he acts inadvertently or deliberately, whether he is awake, asleep, or intoxicated, and if he wounds another person ... he must pay compensation from the best of his own property."[29] Note, however, that unlike in the previous ruling concerning the person who caused damage to another's property, Maimonides does not include an unavoidable mishap (*ones*) in the ruling concerning the person who causes bodily injury to another. Why was it omitted?

Several contemporary scholars explained that this is not an indication of a difference between Maimonides' position regarding the two categories – *hovel* (wounding by a person) and *mazik* (damaging property by a person) – as both are subject to the same standard of care.[30] Others inferred that there is a difference in principle between these two categories:[31] The standard of care of the person who causes bodily injury is lower than that of the person who causes damage to property. The former is not liable in situations of an unavoidable mishap (*ones*), whereas the latter is liable in cases of *ones* as well.

We do not agree with these two cited views. In our opinion, the reason that Maimonides does not impose liability for bodily injury in the case of *ones* as well stems from the fact that there is no uniform standard of care for all five effects for which payment is made as compensation for bodily injury.[32] Maimonides ruled, following the Talmud,[33] that there are three levels of standard of care in relation to payment for five effects of injury. As he writes:

> If one is blown from a roof by an ordinary wind and causes damage, he must pay for four effects but is exempt from paying humiliation (*boshet*). If, however, he is blown off by an unusual wind, he is liable for damage (*nezek*) only and is exempt from payment for the others. If he turns over to break his fall, he is liable for all five effects, including humiliation, because if one has intention to do damage, he is deemed liable for humiliation (*boshet*) caused even though he does not intend to humiliate.[34]

The three standards of care for the five types of payment for injury according to Maimonides, presented from highest to lowest, are as follows:

---

[29] Laws of Wounding and Damaging 1:11.
[30] See, e.g., RABINOVITCH, *supra* note 22, 1:11, s.v. *ben shogeg*; Asher Gulak, *Legal Constraints in Maimonides' Code of Jewish Law*, 6 TARBIZ 383 (1935) (Heb.); Haut, *supra* note 2, at 32; Warhaftig, *supra* note 2, at 224.
[31] See LEVUSH MORDECHAI, Bava Kamma 43.
[32] M Bava Kamma 8:1.
[33] Bava Kamma 27a
[34] Laws of Wounding and Damaging 1:12.

(1) Payment only for the component of *nezek* – liability is imposed in cases of *ones* as well, such as an unusual wind;[35] in other words, a regime of strict or *close to strict liability*. Similar to the existing regime for a person who damages the property of another (discussed in the preceding section).

(2) Payment for the three components of pain (*tzaar*), loss of employment (*shevet*) and medical treatment (*ripuiy*) – liability for an average wind but not for *ones*, i.e., a liability regime of more than regular negligence - gross negligence ("inadvertence close to intentional" – "*shogeg karov LeMezeed*").[36]

(3) Payment for the component of humiliation (*boshet*) – requires a *mens rea* of *intention to harm*, even if not to humiliate.

What is the logic behind the element of creating three different standards of care for the different components of payments for injury? It would appear to be closely connected to the nature of the *bodily injuries*, as we saw in Chapter 3, as a unique field which combines the *penal* with the *civil*.

One could suggest that there is strict liability for the component of *nezek*, for this is the basic component of payment for injury, and its main purpose is to provide reasonable compensation for the injured person – even if it is not necessarily identical to the harm caused.[37] The component of *nezek* for payments for injury is

---

[35] According to several of the commentators on Maimonides, in Maimonides' opinion there is an exemption in the case of total *ones*. See, e.g., *Maggid Mishneh* on Maimonides' Laws of Wounding and Damaging 1:12. However, this view is problematic, in view of the fact that Maimonides ruled that there is an obligation to pay for the component of *nezek* in the following case, which appears to be one of total *ones*, as he says in Laws of Wounding and Damaging 1:12: "If one has a stone in his lap – no matter whether he was never aware of it or whether he once knew of it but subsequently forgot – and when he gets up it falls and causes damage, he is held liable for the damage (*nezek*) alone but is exempt from the remaining four effects."

[36] Similar to Rashi, *Bava Kamma* 27a, s.v. *hayav* ("for example, if he fell as a result of an average wind, it will be close to intentional"). This also appears to be Maimonides' approach as suggested – in our view, correctly – by RABINOVITCH, *supra* note 22, at 1:12, p. 27, who wrote: "Since an average wind is as it sounds – frequent and foreseeable, a person who climbed on the roof and stood in a place from which he is liable to fall – this is gross negligence; in the terminology of the Laws of Murderers, it is appropriate to call this 'inadvertent close to intentional.' Therefore, he is liable for the four effects."

[37] In Laws of Wounding and Damaging 5:6, Maimonides did indeed define the component of *nezek* as a fine, and as we saw in Chapters 3–4, there are penal elements in the five effects payments for injuries that differentiate between them and between payments for property damages, which are intended primarily for the purpose of *restitutio ad integrum*. In Chapter 4, we also discussed the fact that payment for *nezek* in cases of bodily injury is not calculated in such a way as to be identical to the injury caused to the victim. At the same time, it is clear that of the five effects of injury, the type of payment that is called *nezek* is the most basic and primary, and the other four effects are added to this one. This also emerges from the portrayal of matters in the first chapter of Laws of Wounding and Damaging nos. 7–9, in which Maimonides resorts to mentioning scriptural sources for imposing liability in each of the kinds of

therefore very similar to the payment made by a person for the damage he causes to property, in relation to which – as we said in the last section – the standard of care is also at a high level approaching strict liability (exempt only in a case of *force majeure*. It would appear that in relation to other injuries too, there will be an exemption in a case of *force majeure*). The other types of payments made by the person causing injury are considered an *addition* to the *basic component* of payment of *nezek*, and therefore, in order for there to be an obligation to pay, it must be proven that the injurer was at *fault* at some level: *gross negligence* at the very least, in order to be obligated for pain, medical treatment and loss of employment; and intention to cause harm to be obligated for humiliation.

The differences in the liability regimes relating to the five effects payments for injury in Jewish law could be likened to the difference in modern law between regular tortious compensation and *punitive damages*. As we saw in Chapter 5, there are those who distinguish between the basic compensation payments in tort, which are usually intended to provide compensation to the injured person and to restore the former situation, and between punitive damages in which the injured party receives more than the actual harm he suffered. According to some views, regular negligence is not sufficient in order for punitive damages to be awarded; rather, a willful, *intentional* act is required.[38]

Why does Maimonides propose a standard of strict liability for the effective damage avoider in the case of the person who damages another's property, and a lower standard of care (gross negligence) for the payments of pain, medical treatment and loss of employment of a person who causes bodily injury to another? It would appear that Maimonides regards causing bodily injury to another as a wrong of the punishable tort type, and considers the compensation paid by the person causing bodily injury (or at least some components of it) to be a type of *punitive* fine. Therefore, Maimonides requires minimal *mens rea* to impose liability on someone who causes bodily injury, as is required for the imposition of criminal liability, and exempts those who were under *ones*, where no such mental element exists.[39] In any case, the liability of the person who causes bodily injury to another is

---

payment over and above *nezek*. This indicates that the obligation *per se* constitutes an innovation which necessitates finding a scriptural source; this is not the case with respect to the basic effect of *nezek*.

[38] Chapter 5 discussed additional rationales for punitive damages, some economic and some social. We therefore refer here only to the classic rationale of punitive damages in cases in which the tortfeasor acted willfully and intentionally, but this does not negate – even if only with respect to this matter – the other rationales. For elaboration of various rationales for punitive compensation, *see* also *infra*, Chapter 9, in Calabresi's insights on this subject.

[39] According to Maimonides, an example of someone who is exempt from payment (or at least from a portion of the payment) is one who falls off the roof in an uncommon wind, such as a storm that broke out suddenly, or someone who had a stone in his pocket and the stone caused damage, and the man did not know it was there or knew but forgot. In these cases, the tortfeasors are exempt from payments of a criminal nature because this was an unavoidable

not strict, even though this is a grave matter of bodily injury, because the fault implicated is typical of a punitive type of liability.

We have already discussed the connection of parts of tort law to criminal law in Maimonides' approach.[40] The connection is particularly evident in the Laws of Wounding and Damaging in the Book of Torts, which constitute an intermediate area between tort law and criminal law, with patently penal characteristics such as the requirement of criminal intent (*mens rea*). As stated earlier, the component of *mens rea* is a necessary element in penal law but not in a tort that results in damage to property only.[41]

There is, therefore, a rationale for distinguishing between different standards of care for *nezek* and the other four effects, but the question then arises: what is the rationale for creating different standards of care within those four effects, and for creating a standard of *gross negligence* for the purpose of awarding payments for pain, loss of employment and medical treatment, as opposed to a standard of *intention* that is attached to the payment for humiliation? What makes payment for humiliation special? What is the nature of the *intention* that is required for the purpose of payment for *humiliation*?

There is disagreement amongst the authorities on the definition of the intention that is required for obligating payment for humiliation, and its substance.[42] Some authorities are satisfied with *intention to carry out the act* that caused the damage, even if there was no harmful intention.[43] There are those who believe that the required intention must relate to damage and there must be an *intention to harm* in order to engender an obligation for payments for humiliation, even if the intention was not necessarily to humiliate.[44] According to a third view, payment for humiliation is conditional upon the *specific intention to humiliate*, and on this view, general intention to harm is not sufficient.[45] Maimonides' view comports with the second opinion, i.e., that the intention to do damage is sufficient, as we see from the ruling cited in Laws of Wounding and Damaging 1:12: "...if one has intention to do damage, he is deemed liable for humiliation (*boshet*) caused even though he does not intend to humiliate."[46]

---

mishap, but they owe the damage component (*nezek*). For details, see Laws of Wounding and Damaging 1:12, 15.

[40] Chapter 3.
[41] This point will be discussed further in Part B below.
[42] See ENCYCLOPEDIA TALMUDIT 3, s.v. *boshet*, at 42. For a review of the various approaches, see R. ISRAEL ZEV GUSTMANN, KUNTRAS SHI'URIM, BAVA KAMMA 14:3 (Jerusalem 5760–1990).
[43] See Bava Kamma 27a, Rashi ad loc. s.v. *ve-im nit'hapekh* ("and if he flipped in mid-air in order to cushion his fall by falling on someone else") and s.v. *hayav al boshet*; TUR, Hoshen Mishpat 42:13.
[44] See Rabbenu Hananel on Bava Kamma 27a; SHITTAH MEKUBETZET on Bava Kamma 27a (citing Ra'abad).
[45] R. SHLOMO LURIA, YAM SHEL SHLOMO, BAVA KAMMA 2:39.
[46] Laws of Wounding and Damaging 1:12, and RABINOVITCH, *supra* note 22.

What is special about *humiliation* as opposed to other four effects of damages, due to which intention is required in order to obligate payment? Yaacov Habba suggests – correctly, in our opinion – that intention to humiliate is a component of the act (*actus reus*) of humiliation.[47] The harm caused to the victim in cases in which humiliation is involved is not physical injury, but *emotional* and psychological harm. The impact of the harm is closely connected to the intention of the person causing the humiliation. When that person had no intention to humiliate the person who is humiliated, and the humiliation was a chance happening, the impact of the emotional harm and the humiliation caused to the victim, if any, is weak. Habba suggests that this is due to the subjective feeling of the victim, who understands that there was no intention to hurt him, and he is therefore not insulted; it is also due to the reaction of others, who relate to the matter as unintentional, and therefore do not regard the conduct of the person causing the humiliation as constituting degradation of the victim.[48] Indeed, from what Maimonides writes it can be inferred that the audience to the humiliating act is significant, for he rules that humiliation that is not carried out in the presence of other people does not constitute humiliation.[49] Without an intention to humiliate, or at least to do damage, the act of the perpetrator is not defined as an act of humiliation, at least not to the extent that it entails an obligation to pay for humiliation.[50] Therefore, the logic in the requirement of the element of intention with respect to payment for humiliation is that in the absence of intention, the act done by the harm-doer cannot be defined as an act that humiliated the injured party, and in any case there is no justification for the latter to receive additional payment for the component of *humiliation*, over and above the payment for the four effects of *nezek*, pain, loss of employment and medical treatment. According to the said explanation, there is a significant difference in the function fulfilled by intention with respect to humiliation as opposed to the other payments. With respect to humiliation, intention is

---

[47] Yaacov Habba, *Intention as Part of the Creation of the Actus Reus*, 20 MEHKEREI MISHPAT 177, 192–93 (2003) (Heb.).
[48] Habba, *ibid.* at 192.
[49] Laws of Wounding and Damaging 5:7.
[50] Habba, *supra* note 47, at 192. He wrote, *ibid.* at 193 that this conception of intention in humiliation as a condition for the act being humiliating and as an integral part of the humiliation caused by the person who was insulted, is not a matter of consensus (*see, e.g.,* GUSTMANN, *supra* note 42, 2–3). Some assign to intention in humiliation a role similar to that in offences of homicide i.e., intention as an expression of the degree of guilt of the offender. Habba suggests that the difference in the conception might signify that the intention in humiliation stems from the disagreement regarding the type of intention that is required and its nature, as mentioned near note 34. And according to his explanation, if the required intention is intention to cause harm – and as we saw, this is Maimonides' view – there is room for both the said views. Even if intention to do damage suffices, it is still possible that intention is part of causing the humiliation. The intention to harm, *per se*, holds the intention to humiliate the victim, or at least awareness of the humiliation that will be caused to him, for the intention to harm, *per se*, and certainly causing actual harm, is in fact a form of humiliating the victim.

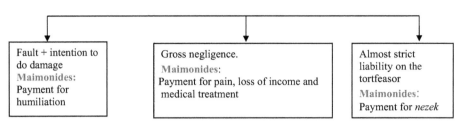

FIGURE 7.2 Injury caused by a person to the body of another: three different standards of care

part of the definition of the act (*actus reus*) itself, and it is not a mental element (or *mens rea*) of a regime of liability. This is not the case with respect to the other four effects, in which there are two regimes of liability: with respect to *nezek*, the standard of care is *almost strict liability*, and with respect to pain, medical treatment and loss of employment, the standard of care is that of *gross negligence* (see Figure 7.2).

3 Property Damage: Negligence

Regarding damages caused by a person's property, such as his animal, Maimonides does not appear to adopt a standard of absolute or strict liability[51] to be imposed on the effective damage avoider. Rather, he imposes at most a standard of care at the level of *negligence*.[52]

According to Maimonides, the owner of an animal has a duty to guard his animal carefully,[53] and if the owner does everything that is required of a good watchman, and damage nevertheless occurs, he is exempt from payment.[54]

It would seem that the exemption granted by Maimonides to a person who guarded his beast carefully,[55] i.e., guarding that requires the constant presence and attention of the watchman,[56] is not because his behavior is not at fault in the simple sense of the term, but because it is not at fault within the meaning of the Hand formula of economic negligence, which in our view is compatible with

---

[51] As Warhaftig argued. See *supra* note 2.
[52] Based only on Maimonides' statement in the GUIDE (3:40) "[t]o provide great incentive to avoid damages a man is held liable for all damage caused by his property," it might appear that Maimonides proposes a standard of *absolute liability* for damage caused by property. But careful examination of the detailed rulings in the *Code* shows clearly that Maimonides does not propose comprehensive absolute or strict liability in cases of damage caused by one's property.
[53] Laws of Property Damages 4:4.
[54] Ibid. at 4:1; Ibid., at 7:1. If, in fact, Maimonides indeed invokes here the standard of a good watchman, this would be interesting for a different reason: applying a contractual standard in a non-contractual situation.
[55] Laws of Property Damages 7:1.
[56] According to the definition of RABINOVITCH, *supra* note 22, 4:4.

Maimonides' approach.[57] According to Maimonides, the basis of liability in the case of property damage is not the fault or inappropriate behavior of the owner of the property; rather, as we saw in the *Guide*, the objective of tort law is to prevent damage being caused, and therefore the owners of damaging property or those by whose action damage was caused are held liable only if the owner "can keep watch over them and take precautions with them, so that no harm is occasioned by them."[58] If the person guarded his animal properly and it nevertheless caused damage, there is no reason to hold him liable for any damage so caused, because he did everything in his power to prevent it. In other words, imposing strict liability on the owners of animals for all damage their animals caused, including damage that would not have been prevented by careful guarding, does not necessarily prevent the occurrence of damage. Furthermore, it is possible that it will constitute over-deterrence in practice, which will result in the owners of animals incurring costs in respect of damage that they have no effective way of preventing, whereas tort laws commonly seek to promote *optimal* deterrence, at a level that does not impose excessively high damage and prevention expenses, rather than over-deterrence.[59] Therefore, there is ample logical-consequential reason for the exemption that Maimonides grants to those whose animals, although guarded carefully, nevertheless caused damage.

If so, this is not strict liability. For example, the result according to Calabresi's best decision maker criterion[60] will presumably be different, and the owner of the beast will pay in any case because there is no limit to improvement of preventive measures. Imposing liability on the owner as the best decision maker will at least provide an incentive for him to consider better ways of prevention in the future, even if he believes that at present it is not possible to guard in a better way and to prevent the damage. By contrast, one may argue that imposing liability on the person causing the damage for unexpected damage promotes over-deterrence; therefore is it is not advisable and should be avoided, which would leave the victim to bear the damage. This claim may support Maimonides' approach.[61]

The question that arises is whether Maimonides' exemption of owners from damage caused by their property is necessarily grounded in a fault-based liability regime. In our opinion there is a plausible explanation of Maimonides' theory. In the *Code* he uses the term *peshiah* quite often,[62] and it therefore seems that he has adopted a standard of care of negligence for the effective damage avoider. But rereading the *Code* in light of the consequentialist approach of the *Guide* (as

---

[57] See Chapters 3 and 5.
[58] GUIDE 3:40 (Pines, 555).
[59] GUIDO CALABRESI, THE COSTS OF ACCIDENTS: A LEGAL AND ECONOMIC ANALYSIS 26–31 (1970).
[60] Chapter 5.
[61] Unless Calabresi also agreed that the injured party is the cheaper cost avoider whenever the damage or he himself (the injured party) is unpredictable.
[62] See Chapter 2, Section C.2.

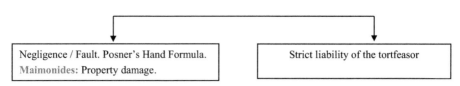

FIGURE 7.3 Property damage: negligence

suggested in the previous chapter), we may consider the possibility of interpreting Maimonides' negligence standard for property damages as similar to Posner's Hand formula. Indeed, as argued,[63] there appears to be a great similarity between the approach of Maimonides in the *Guide* and Posner's Hand formula. Posner's approach, in effect like that of Maimonides, provides incentives to the tortfeasor to take precautions when the cost of such measures is lower than that of the damage caused by the behavior of the tortfeasor. In our case, whoever tied his animal properly took the necessary precautions to prevent damage. If damage nevertheless occurred, it was a rare occurrence because only rarely will an animal succeed in breaking free; therefore, even if the loss is high, the probability of its occurrence is low. In this case, it is sufficient to have tied the animal properly in order to prove a presumption of no negligence. This is compatible with the Hand formula (see Figure 7.3).

4 Murder: Fault

Maimonides' Book of Torts lays out a detailed scheme for the regime of liability for the crimes of murder and homicide. This is part of Maimonides' tendency in the Book of Torts[64] to include laws taken from classic tort law (property damages and bodily injury) together with laws such as those pertaining to murder or to theft, which in modern law are usually classified as part of the criminal law. The present book is far more concerned with the rulings in the Book of Torts which have parallels in modern tort theory than with rulings that today are considered to be part of the criminal law.[65] Therefore we will not elaborate here on the elements of the criminal liability for the crime of murder and homicide; rather, we will deal only with the fundamentals for the sake of completing the picture of the liability regimes that appear in Maimonides' Book of Torts.

---

[63] In Chapter 5, Section C.1.b.
[64] Chapter 3.
[65] Various books have been authored by scholars who dealt with Jewish criminal law. *See, e.g.*, AHARON ENKER, FUNDAMENTALS OF JEWISH CRIMINAL LAW (Bar-Ilan: Ramat Gan, 5767) (Heb.); AARON KIRSCHENBAUM, JEWISH PENOLOGY: THE THEORY AND DEVELOPMENT OF CRIMINAL PUNISHMENT AMONG THE JEWS THROUGHOUT THE AGES (Magnes: Jerusalem 2013) (Heb.).

The punishment for the crime of premeditated murder according to scriptural law is death,[66] and one who kills another inadvertently is exiled to a city of refuge.[67] In order to convict for the crime of murder or homicide, there must be a factual basis – an *actus reus* – which is determined according to a criterion of liability that is unique to the crime of murder, an "act of killing,"[68] as well as a *mens rea* which contains the element of fault – willfulness or inadvertent act in a manner that approximates willfulness. But in cases in which there is no *mens rea* of fault, the killer is exempt from punishment. The talmudic law states the degree of inadvertency of various cases of unintentional homicide, i.e., when the killer does not intend to kill the other, and is not even aware that his behavior is endangering human life, according to the facts of each case, in casuistic fashion. However, Maimonides, as is his way, refashions the various cases and presents them in Laws of Murderers according to general conceptions of degrees of inadvertency.[69] In this context, we are familiar with Maimonides' summary of the distinction between the five different degrees of *mens rea*: the intentional killer, who is liable to the death penalty, three types of inadvertent killers, and a person who kills under *ones* (compulsion) and is exempt from all punishment.[70] Maimonides expresses himself in relation to the three types of inadvertent killers as follows:

There are three types of slayers without intent:

(a) One slays inadvertently (בשגגה) and in complete unawareness… the rule regarding him is that he must be exiled to (one of) the cities of refuge and rescued, as we have explained.

(b) Another slays inadvertently in a manner that is almost an accident (שגגה קרובה לאונס), such as when the death is the result of some unusual circumstance uncommon amid the greater part of human events. The rule regarding him is that he is exempt from exile, and if the avenger of blood kills him, the avenger must be put to death on his account.

(c) Still another slays inadvertently but in a manner that approximates willfulness (שגגה קרובה לזדון) because there is present a circumstance tantamount to negligence, or because he should have been careful but was not. The rule regarding him is that he is not exiled, for exile cannot atone for him since his crime is a serious one… Consequently, if the avenger of blood finds him and kills him, no matter where, he is exempt.[71]

---

[66] Exodus 21:12–14; Numbers 35:15–21, 29–34.
[67] Numbers 35:11–34; Deuteronomy 19:1–10.
[68] Regarding this criterion, *see* Yaacov Habba, *The Requirement of the Act in the Crime of Murder in Jewish Law* 20–21 DINE ISRAEL 475 (2000–2001) (Heb.).
[69] *See*, primarily, Laws of Murderers 6:6–15.
[70] Laws of Murderers 6:1–4.
[71] Laws of Murderers 6:1–4.

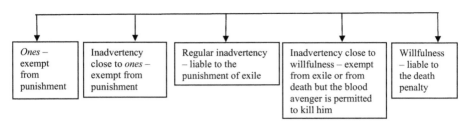

FIGURE 7.4 Offense of murder: degrees according to Maimonides

From this distinction emerges between the three types of offenders who have not acted intentionally, since their act did not reach that level of severity, but neither are they deemed to have committed their act and caused the outcome of the killing of the victim in circumstances of *ones*. In all these three categories there are offenders whose level of criminal liability falls within that same range between willfulness and *ones*, including the intermediate degree of the regular inadvertent killer who must go into exile, and one who killed inadvertently, but in graver circumstances than the regular inadvertent killer (in which case the blood avenger is permitted to kill him), or in less grave circumstances than the regular inadvertent killer (in which case he is exempt from punishment). The distinctions drawn by Maimonides, following the Talmud, between the five degrees of *mens rea* appear to be based on the clear fact that different degrees of fault may be attributed to a killer in different circumstances. The division into inadvertent killing, intentional killing and *ones* is too general, so argues Habba, "and did not respond to the need to distinguish between different degrees of mental state that accompanied the commission of the crime, and between different levels of punishment that should be derived therefrom."[72] Therefore, two other intermediate levels were developed and added – inadvertency close to willfulness, and inadvertency close to *ones* (see Figure 7.4). Enker wrote correctly that Maimonides' approach "is similar to the evaluations of modern law when it examines whether certain behavior is negligent, and distinguishes between levels of negligence – regular or gross – *inter alia* according to the degree of risk it poses to the life of the victim."[73]

Criminal liability for the offence of murder is therefore imposed for intentional murder (the murderer is liable to the death penalty), and for cases of homicide with a *mens rea* of inadvertency close to willfulness (the blood avenger is permitted to kill the killer) and regular inadvertency (the killer must go into exile). The logic in imposing liability in the first two cases is evident, for a person who kills intentionally or close to intentionally bears a high level of fault. But where is the logic in imposing liability on a person who killed totally *inadvertently*? This question clearly concerns

---

[72] Yaacov Habba, *Criteria for Determining the Level of Fault in the Offence of Murder in Jewish Law* 2 KIRYAT HAMISHPAT 265, 269 (2002) (Heb.).
[73] ENKER, *supra* note 65, at 211.

the much broader question, which has been discussed often in contemporary scholarship, about the liability of the *inadvertent transgressor*. In this context, particular noteworthy is the comprehensive research of Arye Edrei dealing with different approaches in the Bible and in the rabbinic literature concerning the reason for which liability is imposed on the inadvertent transgressor;[74] these include approaches that refer to the liability of an inadvertent blameless transgressor simply due to the real harm done by the act, or due to the effect of the inadvertent transgressor on the transgressor himself, who may become accustomed to transgressing. Edrei also discusses several approaches of the Tannaim who, on the other hand, view the inadvertent transgressor as responsible for the act in that he was not as careful as was expected of him. Maimonides apparently adopted this last approach, according to which *fault* attaches to the act of the inadvertent transgressor, and he is therefore held liable for his act, as he says in various places in his writings.

In the *Guide*, Maimonides writes: "As for the *inadvertent transgressor*, he sins, for if he had made efforts to be firm and cautious there would have been no *inadvertence* on his part. But he is not punished in any way, though he *needs atonement* and hence must bring *a sacrifice*."[75] A similar line is adopted in the *Code*: "… the transgressor … should have checked and been careful. Had he examined the matter thoroughly and been careful in asking questions, he would not have transgressed. Since he did not take the trouble to examine and research the matter before acting, he requires atonement."[76] Thus, according to Maimonides one cannot say that the inadvertent transgressor is liable without fault; on the contrary, he is at fault in that he was not sufficiently careful. He therefore bears criminal responsibility, and in the context of the crime of murder, he is liable to the punishment of exile. There is a good deal of similarity between Maimonides' rationale for the liability of the inadvertent killer and between the accepted explanation in modern law for the criminal conviction of a person who commits an offence through *negligence*.[77] In exceptional cases in which modern criminal law permits conviction when the *mens rea* is negligence, i.e., even in the absence of awareness, the rationale is that even though the accused was unaware, he *ought* to have been aware. According to accepted modern approaches, the negligent person is the one who was not aware of the danger he created when it was possible for him to have been aware, had he made a greater effort. The moral basis of this approach, as emerges from what Hart and Fletcher write, lies in the fact that it is consistent with the principle of fault or

---

[74] Arye Edrei, *And a Person who Transgressors Inadvertently – Liability Without Fault? On the Liability of an Inadvertent Transgressor in the Bible and in Rabbinic Literature*, 24 JEWISH LAW ANNUAL 1–62 (5766–5767) (Heb.).
[75] GUIDE 3:41 (Pines, 563–4).
[76] Book of Sacrifices, Laws of Inadvertent Transgressions 5:6.
[77] The similarity between the concept of negligence in modern criminal law and that of inadvertent transgression was pointed out by Edrei, *supra* note 74, at 31–35.

culpability.[78] Criminal law requires of a person to realize his potential for awareness, and this person is responsible, to a certain extent, for the result that ensues when he has not fulfilled this duty.

A similar approach is evident in the words of Maimonides in relation to the liability of the inadvertent transgressor. Nevertheless, we agree with Enker that one must be cautious in drawing a full comparison between the concept of *negligence* in modern criminal law and that of the *inadvertent transgressor* in Jewish law.[79] There are differences between the two.[80] The criterion for fault and for liability in Jewish law seems to be stricter and more meticulous than that of modern law. According to Enker, in Jewish law there is no concept equivalent to the "reasonable man" or the "common man," and he adds:

> In modern law, the competing interests are weighed up against each other. but in jewish law, the matter is one of observing the divine precepts, the ramifications of which are likely to extend beyond a person's normal conceptions, and this affects the balancing process. also, as we have said, the goal of the sanction in jewish law is atonement for the sin, rather than the goals of deterrence and compensation of modern secular law. this difference too may be a factor in determining the required level of care.[81]

Support for Enker's contention can be found in Maimonides' definitions of the three levels of inadvertency in relation to the crime of murder discussed earlier in the chapter. Enker correctly wrote that Maimonides' definition "leaves the impression that the standard of care is higher than 'reasonableness,' but there may be a surplus of strictness in relation to the crime of murder due to the principle of the sanctity of life."[82]

Indeed, the rhetoric and the context in which Maimonides wrote concerning fault in the act of the inadvertent transgressor are more *religious* than the rhetoric and the context of Hart and Fletcher's words. As such, it may be that Maimonides' approach regards awareness as a religious duty, and its absence as entailing the imposition of liability (in the context of the inadvertent killer, the punishment of exile), as Edrei says:

> The most basic requirement from a religious person is to be aware, he is required to direct his attention to his obligation towards the Lord. Lack of awareness as a result

---

[78] H.L.A. Hart, Punishment and Responsibility 136–57 (Oxford, 1968); George P. Fletcher, *The Fault of Not Knowing*, 3 Theoretical Inquiries in Law 265 (2002).

[79] See Enker's hesitation about fully comparing the two concepts: *supra* note 65, at 205 n. 17.

[80] See also Habba, *supra* note 68, at 291, who in discussing the considerations by means of which the fault of the killer is determined in Jewish law, emphasizes that the question of the danger and awareness of it is not the exclusive deciding factor; there are other factors that are likely to come into play on this matter, particularly those that concern the nature of the act, the degree of justification or the lack thereof in causing the danger, and consequently whether and to what extent the fault should be more severe in these cases in order to prevent their occurrence.

[81] Enker, *supra* note 65.

[82] Ibid.

of which a crime is committed is, in itself an offence, it in itself is a violation of the basic duty imposed upon a person, and for this he must bring a sin-offering for his atonement.[83]

B. DIFFERENTIAL LIABILITY: SCHEME, RATIONALE, AND HISTORICAL BACKGROUND

1 Scheme

In Section A we presented Maimonides' differential liability approach. According to Maimonides' method, liability in the context of monetary damages caused by a person or his property (but not in relation to murder, wounding, theft, or robbery) is imposed on the most effective damage avoider. Sometimes, however, this standard of care is close to strict; at other times, it is negligence; at yet other times it is an intermediate level of liability. It all depends on the type of case at hand.

We tried to define the standard of care adopted by Maimonides, based on his interpretation of the talmudic texts, regarding four categories of damage: (a) damage caused by a person to the property of another; (b) harm caused by a person who injures another; (c) damage caused by property (d) and murder. In each of these categories, Maimonides proposed to impose on the defendant liability on the scale between fault, negligence and strict liability.

We described the hierarchy of the standards of care step by step, from the highest one, closest to strict liability (category (a), and the *nezek* payment of category (b)), which Maimonides espouses in cases in which a person caused damage to another's property, to the intermediate standards of care, negligence (category (c)) and gross negligence (three of the five effects payments of category (b)), and to the lowest standard of care – with fault or even with intention (unlawful killing of another human – category (d)). We also presented a range of three standards of care for the different payments for damages caused by person who injures another (category b): (1) Almost strict liability for *nezek* payment. (2) Gross negligence for *pain, medical treatment and loss of employment*. (3) Intention to cause harm for payment of humiliation (see Figure 7.5).

2 Rationale

The rationale of the hierarchy is clear, especially in light of the EAC test and the emphasis on control in the *Guide*. Imposing a higher standard of care for harm caused by a person than for damage caused by his property can be rationalized both deontologically and economically. A person's effective ability to control his own body and prevent his body from causing harm is usually much greater than his

---

[83] Edrei, *supra* note 74, at 62.

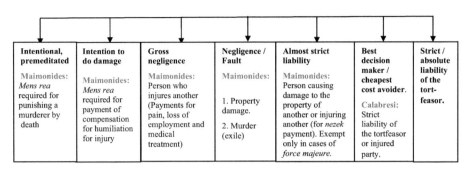

FIGURE 7.5 The complete scheme of differential liability

ability to control his property. Therefore, the standard of care is a function of the actual effective ability to control the actions and prevent the harm. It is easier, and probably less costly from an economic point of view, for a person to control his own actions than to control the actions of others, including animals, slaves,[84] fire, or a pit. Obviously, the costs of oversight of workers and slaves, and of property that may cause damage such as fire or a pit, are generally likely to greatly exceed the costs incurred by a person who is careful not to cause injury himself. True, a person might not pay attention, or he may be drunk or he may cause damage while he is asleep, but in most cases, when he is awake and alert, it would be more difficult for him to watch over the actions of others in order to prevent them from causing harm than not to cause harm himself. The point here is not only economic, but of course, deontological as well. There is also greater logic, from a moral perspective, to imposing a higher standard of care on a person who himself causes injury to another than on a person whose property caused damage, even if the conclusion is that he should and could have watched and supervised better in order to prevent the damage caused by his property, since greater moral fault attaches to a person who is able to prevent injury to others easily than to one for whom it is more difficult. Thus, the basic rationale behind differentiation between property that causes damage and harm caused by a person, whether with his body or with his property, may be justified from various aspects.

Another, no less important, consequentialist rationale for imposing the lower standard of care of negligence for damage caused by property lies in considerations of optimal deterrence. We voiced concerns about over-deterrence in cases of strict liability that could lead to a decline in desirable activities.[85] It is reasonable to assume that this standard of care will cause serious harm to the related industries. There may be a difference between guarding an animal, especially at a time when animals were of great importance for their owners and were used as beasts of burden as well as for their work, meat, and milk, and the case of a manufacturing process or

---

[84] As to the ruling regarding a slave vis-à-vis the element of control, see Chapter 5.
[85] Supra Section A.3.

driving a car. In the case of manufacturing that may be dangerous and cause damage, such as the manufacture of modern electronic and mechanical devices, reality has proven over the years that it is possible to achieve even greater safety, even if at any given time it may appear that the product has reached a maximal safety level. Nevertheless, there may be good reasons here to impose liability on the manufacturer. Even if he can prove that at the moment there is no possibility of reaching a higher level of safety, imposing strict liability – at least according to Calabresi – would induce him to employ experts whose function is to further improve the safety of the product and to develop an even safer product in the future. By contrast, it is possible that the owner of the animal who guarded it in the best possible way could not, at a given time or in the future, guard it any better, and for that reason imposing strict liability would not be efficient. Similarly, investment for the purpose of developing technological improvements in order to prevent future harm is efficient for the reason that in general, those manufacturers have the economic wherewithal and the financial means to do so. The private person who owns an animal, on the other hand, is less likely to be in an economic position to invest in such development, even if such development were possible. Consequently, imposing liability will not cause him to make improvements and become more efficient. On the contrary, it could discourage him from engaging in socially-desirable activities related to animals.

Up to this point we have explained the rationale underlying the difference between damage that is caused by a person's property and the entire range of harms caused by a person. However, as we saw, there is a difference in the standard of care between different types of harm caused by a person. In relation to damage caused by a person to the property of another (laws relating to a person who causes damage), the standard is close to strict liability, whereas in relation to injuries caused by a person to the body of another (laws of wounding) there are three different standards of care for each of the five payments. In Section A, we explained why Maimonides ruled as he did with respect to each of the categories. However, in light of the thread connecting these two categories (wounding and damaging), it is still surprising that Maimonides did not set an identical standard for them both.

The proximity of Jewish tort law to criminal law, especially with regard to bodily injuries caused by people, was discussed in Chapter 3. The deontological orientation of tort law is clearly expressed in the classification of the laws of physical injury (*hilkhot hovel*) as laws which also have typical criminal characteristics (as well as some tort characteristics), because a person's body cannot be measured by economic values alone. A person's body is not his own property but that of his Creator. Injury to the human body is perceived as an injury to "God's image." This conception is important in itself from a value-based perspective, and it is meaningful not only because of its practical effect on the attitude of society toward injury to the human body. Although the law of the tortfeasor is not exactly "an eye for an eye," as Maimonides points out, this does not alter the essence of the tortfeasor's act, "which is deserving of him losing an limb or being injured when he did it, and thus paying for his damage,"[86] because "all eternity, and all the money in the world cannot heal the wound of the injury we caused to man," as noted by the well-known philosopher, Emmanuel Levinas.[87] Therefore, as demonstrated in Chapter 3, Maimonides' tort theory consists of various objectives and considerations that operate in concert. Different objectives predominate in different types of harm.

It is therefore important to pay attention to the legal classification used by Maimonides in the Book of Torts in the *Code*, which, as we saw in Chapter 3, is a detailed and sophisticated classification that has far-reaching consequences with regard to the various objectives of tort law.

The civil-criminal divide is manifest in the distinction that Maimonides makes between various types of harm. In cases of *bodily injury*, the *punitive* aspect of compensation acquires prominence and fulfills the role of ransom. By contrast, in cases where the damage occurs to a *person's property*, the compensation is of a clear and purely *civil* nature, especially when the damage is caused by a person's property and not by the person himself.

In view of the analysis presented in this section, one can understand why Maimonides assigned to a person who injured the body of another a standard of care of gross negligence for the extra payments (pain, medical treatment and loss of employment), whereas for damages to property caused by a person Maimonides assigned a standard of strict liability. A person who injures another is substantively different from those who commit other civil wrongs, including a person who damages the property of another and one whose property causes damage. The person who causes bodily injury to another is executing an act that contains some element of a criminal offence. Consequently, for most of the payments for wounding (except the *nezek* payment), a *mens rea* of criminal intent is required,[88] for according to the *halakhah*, only an offence that was committed unintentionally (regular negligence) is not punishable.[89] The requirement of intention is not unrelated to the compensation made by the tortfeasor to the injured party, for this compensation contains punitive elements as well as tortious ones.[90]

---

[86] Laws of Wounding and Damaging 1:3.
[87] EMMANUEL LEVINAS, WORKS OF EMMANUEL: FOUR ARTICLES FROM "DIFFICULT FREEDOM" (Eliahu Rahamim Zeini trans. & ed., 2002) (Heb.).
[88] See, e.g., Laws of Wounding and Damaging 1:16 (which requires that the element of premeditation be present in order to incur liability for all the payments of the tortfeasor); *ibid.* 5:1 (that the person who injures another violates a biblical prohibition; also mentioned there is a type of special, specific intention – that the injury is inflicted against a background of hostility).
[89] See, e.g., Laws of Murderers 1:1 (which requires criminal intention in order that the killer be liable for punishment); *ibid.* 6:1–4 (which exempts from punishment those who did not kill intentionally but with different degrees of inadvertence).
[90] And see Maimonides, in Laws of Wounding and Damaging 1:3, who says that a person who injures another ought to be wounded, in the sense of "an eye for an eye", but this is not done; rather, payment is made for the injury, which is a type of ransom payment that acts as atonement instead of the corporal punishment. (In this vein, *see* the *Guide*, 3:41.) And see

The special requirement of *intention*, when *criminal* offences are involved, is also evident in Maimonides' responsum in the matter of the brigands,[91] discussed in Chapter 2.[92] Admittedly, emphasis on the element of intention raises a problem if our context is tort law (which deals primarily with unintentional torts). However, by virtue of our present discussion, Maimonides' responsum can be understood easily, for he requires special intention precisely of the person who intends to commit the *criminal offence of theft*, but not of the person who only causes damage to property (in relation to whom the intention is less relevant).

Finally, there is obviously solid logic in the fact that liability for an act of *murder*, in Maimonides' view, requires fault of some kind, at the level of inadvertency at least in order to impose exile, and at the level of willfulness in order to impose a death penalty. The crime of murder clearly belongs in the penal area, and modern law, as we know, requires an element of fault as the *mens rea* for the purpose of a criminal conviction, as opposed to tortious liability that may sometimes be imposed, according to the approaches both of Maimonides and various modern systems, even on a person in whose acts no fault lies, but to whom absolute liability applies.

In sum, within the reality in which Maimonides operated, the fact of a person exercising *control* over the damage had great significance. Because Maimonides' aim was to prevent acts causing damage, he was prepared to impose a higher standard of care on the effective damage avoider to the extent to which he was capable of exercising control over his actions. Therefore, Maimonides chose to regard a person who himself caused damage to another's property as the effective damage avoider and impose on him almost strict liability. The only exemption is the case of *force majeure* ("a strike from Heaven"), where a person truly has no control. When he has control over his actions a strict and absolute liability is to be imposed on him, without examining his fault in each case. In other cases, however, lower standards of care are imposed for reasons mentioned in Section A – each category of cases and its rationale. In the category of bodily injury caused to another there are three different standards of care for the five payments. In most of the payments (excluding the *nezek* payment) an element of quasi-punishment is added, which is characteristic of Maimonides' theory and Jewish tort law in general on this point, in its intermingling with criminal law. In this case Maimonides requires a specific *mens rea* – gross negligence for the payments for pain loss of employment and medical treatment, and the intention to do damage in relation to payment for humiliation – an absolute requirement in criminal law that is hardly ever present in tort law (except in intentional torts

---

Laws of Wounding and Damaging 5:9–11 (which distinguishes between a person who causes injury to a person's body and one who damages his property, and emphasizes the clearly criminal elements attaching to a person who causes bodily injury, such as the requirement of requesting the pardon of the victim).

[91] *Resp. Rambam*, Freiman ed., no. 339.
[92] Chapter 2, Section D.1.

in the common law and very few torts in other legal systems[93]). In the category of damage caused by a person's property, Maimonides' approach cannot support the imposition of strict liability on the owner of the property: he needs to be treated more leniently, i.e., liability is imposed under a fault-liability regime in both the deontological and economical sense (which resembles the Hand formula). Any other standard in that reality, such as strict liability or almost strict liability, may cause over-deterrence. Imposing the lower standard of negligence enables the effective damage avoider who caused damage to defend himself if the required prevention costs were higher than the expected damage, as in the cases of the binding of the animal and the uncommon wind.

Thus, the aim is to prevent harm, but there is a difference in the rulings pertaining to a person causing harm and damage caused by property, due to the element of *control*. On principle, control creates categorization that differentiates between negligence and strict liability. If there is control – in the case of a person who causes harm – strict liability will be imposed; if there is no control – in the case of an animal that caused damage – liability will be imposed only in the case of negligence. However, within the category of a person who causes harm, there is a further distinction. When damage is caused by a person to property, the liability is almost strict, whereas when injury is caused by a person to the body of another person, it involves an element of criminality and therefore the level of liability for most payments (except the *nezek* payment) descends in the direction of a standard of care of at least gross negligence.

3 Historical Background, Circumstances, and Nature of the Tortfeasors: Between Maimonides' Time and the Modern Era

A description of the historical background to Maimonides' activity and of the circumstances in which the rulings that constitute the differential model were devised are also essential to an understanding of the Maimonidean model. Moshe Halbertal has shown that what Maimonides wrote must be viewed through the prism of "Maimonides of his Generation."[94] As we will see in the following chapter, similarities may be found between Maimonides' differential model and various contemporary theories, but there are also quite a number of differences. This is not surprising in view of the difference between the period in which Maimonides flourished and the present time. This difference finds expression on several planes. We will begin with contemporary reality.

Firstly, contemporary tort law operates in an *industrial environment*, with its employers and employees, producers and consumers, drivers and pedestrians, physicians, surgeries, and hospitals. In classic contemporary tort cases, it is easy to find

---

[93] See, e.g., sec. 23 of the Civil Wrongs Ordinance [New Version] [Isr.].
[94] MOSHE HALBERTAL, MAIMONIDES: LIFE AND THOUGHT 7 (Princeton, NJ: Princeton University Press, 2014).

mass tortfeasors with deep pockets, risk managers and entities calculating damages and the economic viability of their businesses. It is also common to manage risk by using data in order to calculate expected costs versus benefits, probabilities, precautions and risks. In such circumstances, it is easier, for example, to impose strict liability – according to the supporters of this standard of care – on those who can prevent the damage in a cheaper and more effective way. Even if occasionally, complete and full liability without a dimension of fault and negligence is imposed on large entities that employ economic calculations and risk managers, this imposition is not likely to bring about the cessation of their activity or reduce their viability. At most it would result in better risk management and a more serious effort to prevent causing harm, which is useful to society as a whole. This is especially true in cases of mass torts (such as mass exposure to pollution or radiation) and serial torts (such as medical malpractice recurring in the same hospital), which were practically non-existent in Maimonides' time.

Secondly, contemporary torts operate in the age of *insurance*, perhaps the most significant loss distributer in society, alongside employers. Most of the activities at the basis of tort claims today are insured activities, and most contemporary scholars not only take this into account but see insurance as an important factor in tort law theory. Insurance directs behavior and provides information, and it is compatible with optimal deterrence, loss distribution, deep pockets, and sometimes also with distributive justice. In this reality it is sometimes much easier to impose strict liability. In most cases, the direct tortfeasor does not pay anyway: the insurance does. The tortfeasor's participation takes the form of premium payments, deductibles, cancellation of no-claim discounts, criminal liability if the tort has criminal aspects to it, risk of being fired or denied promotion in the case of employees, and so on.

Thirdly, and in regard to the former point, contemporary torts operate in a reality of *vicarious liability*, that is, liability imposed on employers for their employees' acts which harmed others or even themselves. At times the state obligates employers to purchase insurance to distribute losses and protect the rights of workers. Contemporary torts also operate within a reality of *state regulation*. At times the legislator regulates the field, for example by introducing a requirement to purchase a certain safety device to help prevent vehicular harm, even if it is not economical for the driver. The legislator enforces the regulation through insurance (insurance is not underwritten until it has been proven that the insured purchased the device in question) or through state mechanisms (such as denying a vehicle test without proof of a required device having been installed). This reality helps prevent damages, and thus is used widely in today's world.

Maimonides experienced a completely different reality, one which still exists today, albeit in only a relatively small percentage of cases. Maimonides issued his rulings in the context of the types of harm mentioned in the Talmud, which were caused mainly by individuals to other individuals: an ox belonging to one person gored another, ate the produce, or trampled on it; a person fell on another or on his property; a person injured another in his sleep – which apparently happened not infrequently in a reality in which several people would sleep in the one bed, surrounded by many objects; a person's animal roamed freely on another's premises; a person was not careful enough and water or a fire from his field passed into the neighboring field; and similar damage between immediate neighbors. Following the Talmud, Maimonides in his *Code* hardly addressed a reality of mass and serial torts, of large and powerful entities causing massive or serial harm to numerous private individuals. He spoke of masters and slaves rather than employers and employees. It is important to note that today, many claims are against employers, based on vicarious liability.[95] In some countries employers carry mandatory insurance, so that each claim against an employer necessarily means a claim against an insurance company. Maimonides does not deal with the reality of *insurance* and torts caused by mass production and modern industry, which is only natural, as Maimonides' time precedes by centuries that of the industrial and consumer revolutions; neither did the practice of insurance exist in the twelfth century.[96] Maimonides' examples, mostly from the Talmud, relate to a *traditional agrarian society*. The issues concern mainly the harm caused directly by a single person or his beast to another single person. In this situation compensation is paid directly from the tortfeasor's pocket to the pocket of the injured party, with no considerations of insurance, sophisticated risk management, etc. In the world of Maimonides, the harm fell in its entirety on the injured person or on the tortfeasor; therefore, careful thinking was required in each case about what kind of liability should be imposed on the effective damage avoider. Neither was there regulation. It should be borne in mind that during most periods, Jewish law developed clearly as a *non-state* or extraterritorial law; as such it contains almost no regulation to help prevent causing harm.

In Maimonides' days, the cost of strict liability in cases of damage caused by one's property was occasionally too heavy. In a world in which a domestic animal was the equivalent of a private car, truck, or motorcycle of today, the imposition of strict liability on the owner of an animal that caused damage, in every case and under all circumstances, without it being possible for the owner of the animal to distribute the loss over other members of the community (as does the driver with respect to other drivers through the loss-distribution mechanism of insurance), could be a real disincentive to owning an animal. It is difficult to control an animal, at times more so than a car. In the reality of those days, for people who had a vital need for

---

[95] This difference between Maimonides' times and our own helps to explain why Maimonides did not adopt the model of vicarious liability in relation to the liability of a master for the damage caused by his slaves. See Laws of Theft 1:9.

[96] Indeed, the halakhic decisors of recent generations had to expand on the questions involved in the application of modern tort law in a context of a modern reality in which the tortfeasor and/ or the injured party are insured. See, *e.g.*, SHEINFELD, *supra* note 21, at 332–35.

transportation, milk, and meat products, etc., not owning an animal could deliver a death blow to all economic activity. Full payment as an expression of strict liability of the owner, repeatedly for every instance of harm caused by the animal, would reduce the level of activity and leave ownership of animals only to the rich, which is undesirable both from the economic and the social-distributive point of view. We called this situation over-deterrence.[97]

The differences in historical background and circumstances are not minor. These significantly different realities result in differences in the rulings that emerge. It is therefore reasonable to assume that if contemporary tort scholars were operating within the reality of Maimonides' time, and vice versa, their approaches would have been more similar.

We have discussed the differences that will affect the harm caused by property – an animal – because of its importance to its owner. One may ask whether the historical differences will also affect the rulings relating to the categories of a person who damages property and a person who injures the body of another person. They may do so: if in fact there is insurance for harm caused by a person, such as medical insurance, there is definitely room for increasing the standard of care. We should bear in mind, however, that insurance played no part in Maimonides' thought, and to try to imagine how he would have ruled in light of this important parameter is pure speculation.

C. CONCLUSION

Maimonides' model of *differential liability* solves many of the problems raised in Chapter 2, in which we dealt with the exegetical and conceptual difficulties of the common interpretation of Maimonides' tort theory. According to the alternative explanation we suggest in this book, and especially in light of the differential model presented in this chapter, we are able to provide most of the answers. It was not possible to provide appropriate responses to these problems in the form of a unitary standard of care of negligence or of strict liability that would be applicable to all tortious events. Opting for differential liability, according to which there is a different standard for each group of cases as appropriate, constitutes a fitting compromise between the selection of either negligence or strict liability as a single, comprehensive, fixed standard that is not always appropriate for the case at hand.

In the context of monetary damages caused by a person or his property, Maimonides attributes importance to effectiveness, and examines, at the first stage, who is the effective damage avoider – the tortfeasor or the victim. At the second stage, however, Maimonides chooses to examine, independently, the standard of care, and he does not rush to assert that the liability of the effective damage avoider will always be absolute, as does Calabresi, or that negligence will be looked at *per se*, in accordance

---

[97] *See supra*, Section A.3.

with the degree of moral fault and the principles of corrective and distributive justice, or according to an examination of the costs of precautions as against the probability of damage, as in Posner's Hand formula. The differential model makes it possible to impose liability on the effective damage avoider at the standard of negligence in some categories; in some others, at a standard closer to strict; and in yet other cases, liability that is situated somewhere on the scale between these two extremes. Understanding the rationales for imposing a different standard in each category of cases constituted the key to presenting a scheme of a differential model of tort liability according to Maimonides.

In our days, too, states sometimes adopt different standards of care in accordance with the category of cases. However, the historical background and the different circumstances in which Maimonides operated are of importance in the context of the differential model that we are presenting as reflecting in effect Maimonides' approach. Thus, for example, attaching strict liability to property damage could have involved over-deterrence in the context of an agrarian society in which the animal that caused damage sometimes represented the sole source of family income, constituting a disincentive to engage in the major occupation of that period. The reality in our day is different. Nevertheless, as we shall see in the following chapter, even if the cow or the ox of Maimonides' times are no longer at center stage, but rather a motor vehicle, the defective product or the polluted air, and despite the changes in the historical background, it is possible to conduct a conversation at a certain level between the old, Maimonidean theory and the modern tort theories, and even to achieve certain results – some of them surprising.

8

Maimonides as a Pluralistic-Differential Scholar and Contemporary Tort Law Theories:

A Dialogue and Lessons

In this chapter we will explore several different directions for creating a conversation between religious law in general and Maimonides' tort theory in particular, and between modern theories, the chapter will in fact take an overview of the process that we have undergone in the framework of the previous chapters

A. FROM CONTEMPORARY TORT LAW TO MAIMONIDES: CHARACTERIZING MAIMONIDES AS A PLURALISTIC-DIFFERENTIAL SCHOLAR

This chapter draws some cautious lessons from a contemporary analysis of torts for Maimonides' theory of torts and vice versa.

The chapter begins with a characterization of Maimonides as a pluralistic-differential scholar. First, the *pluralistic* component: Maimonides' approach may be characterized by invoking the modern tools of monism versus pluralism.

Monistic theories focus solely on the relations between the two parties while disregarding every other consideration. Proponents of pluralistic theories, who throw more than one goal into the mix and attempt to combine them and to deal with cases of contradictions and clashes resulting from the pursuit of the different goals, consider monistic theories as unbalanced and incapable of reflecting the full tortious and societal picture.[1]

The modern distinction between focusing on one goal of tort law – monism – and on a substantive combination of the goals – pluralism – helped us in our characterization of Maimonides' approach and in gaining a deep understanding of it. Indeed,

---

[1] W.V.H. ROGERS, WINFIELD & JOLOWICZ ON TORTS 2 (London, 16th ed., 2002); *Cf.* Steven J. Burton, *Normative Legal Theories: The Case for Pluralism and Balancing*, 98 IOWA L. REV. 535 (2013), passim (distinguishing between monism and pluralism and describing monists as focused on only one value, where pluralists balance all relevant values).

analyses of Maimonides' approach by various scholars in different periods, as discussed at length in the early chapters of this book, were lacking and non-comprehensive, because they did not look at Maimonides as a pluralist. From the comparisons that we have drawn throughout the book (and especially in Chapters 3–5) between the goals of modern law and those presented by Maimonides, it becomes clear that Maimonides is not a monist, i.e., there is not only one single goal upon which his tort theory is based, but several, and therefore, his is a certain type of pluralist theory, one in which there are different goals for different categories of damages. This is one step towards learning lessons from current theories for Maimonides' theory and situating the latter on a pluralist, non-monist scale.

Now to the *differential* component. We saw in Chapter 7 that not only is Maimonides a pluralist, but he is also a differentialist, in that he assigns a different standard of care to each group of cases, and by doing so he adapts the scope of legal liability to the situation and to additional principles.

The *pluralistic-differential approach* is innovative, certainly vis-à-vis ancient legal systems, which to the best of our knowledge did not adopt a similar path, and usually tended towards a more monistic approach. Even as compared to modern approaches, however, Maimonides' approach differs significantly from current pluralist theories of tort law, although there may be a certain similarity to the positive law in some countries, where we find different standards of care in different laws and situations such as negligence, automobile accidents, defective products and more. Indeed, a comparison to current sources may be of benefit. They of course cannot change anything substantive in Maimonides' approach but they certainly can shed light on that approach and present it in a full, comprehensive manner.

However, the comparison must be made with precision, within the bounds that we shall now draw, and it must not be taken too far. Awareness of the differences in thinking between the modern era and the Middle Ages is important for anyone who wishes to examine what Maimonides writes through the prism of modern legal theory. In our context, there is a fundamental difference between the contemporary and the Maimonidean approaches: today, the intellectual proclivity is to craft tort law according to one or more principles, i.e., a normative approach, whereas in the Middle Ages, effort was invested in explaining the existing law. The result is that in Maimonides' eyes, there is nothing wrong with explaining a particular law according to different principles, provided that they are rational. Maimonides has no difficulty in basing a particular law on several reasons. On the contrary: the more rational reasons there are, the better.

We are also aware of the substantive differences between the tendency of the contemporary approach – which is *normative* – and that of Maimonides, which is primarily *explanatory*, seeking to base the existing law on a rational conceptual foundation in accordance with a philosophical-religious conception. Against this background, monism and pluralism, as these are used in relation to Maimonides, have a meaning that is not absolutely identical to the meaning attributed to these terms by some scholars in our generation. Nevertheless, in certain cases,

Maimonides appears to be a *pluralist* in a sense that is closer to the modern sense, in that he did not stop at merely explaining an existing law, but also attempted to set up a type of normative and conceptual jurisprudential model by which to formulate the leading principles of the relevant legal field.

Therefore, even though Maimonides did not present a clear pluralistic approach in terms of the modern pluralism of our times which explains exactly which objective will predominate in each category of cases, his approach clearly expresses a basic pluralistic conception, alongside clear, pronounced differentialism that is absent from many contemporary theories.

Indeed, throughout this book we have seen that Maimonides' approach embraces several goals. In the *Guide*, Maimonides emphasizes the goal of removing wrongs, which parallels the goal of corrective justice. However, alongside this goal, Maimonides also emphasizes consequentialist considerations, and in so doing he concretizes and illustrates the second goal presented in the *Guide*, which is that of preventing the causing of damage, which parallels today's optimal deterrence and cheapest cost avoider. Alongside these goals, we saw that in Maimonides's *Code*, deontological-moral and religious considerations may also be found, which of course converse less with the modern theories, as well as clear signs of distributive justice. We have seen and analyzed all these in earlier chapters. This is indeed a pluralistic, and definitely not monistic, approach. The comparison with the different stanards of care found in modern law also helped us in demonstrating that Maimonides is a *differentialist*. Maimonides, for reasons that he explains, and some of which are utilitarian but others of which are moral-deontological and religious, applied a different standard of care to each group of tortious cases and to each risk-creating activity. In this way Maimonides, with his differentialist approach, arrived at imposing stricter or lighter liability on different categories of damage, as relevant, for example, in accordance with the question of whether the harm was caused to a person's body or his property.

Awareness of the modern theoretical analysis of the goals of tort law and the standard of care was extremely important for understanding Maimonides' theory and defining Maimonidean theory as both pluralist, i.e. based on more than one goal, and differential.

B. DIALOGUE BETWEEN MAIMONIDES AND CURRENT PLURALISTIC APPROACHES

1 Introduction

In the preceding chapters, we presented modern monistic approaches to tort law in order to help us characterize Maimonides as a pluralist and not a monist, and in the earlier section of this chapter we explained that without the recourse to modern law to explain Maimonides' approach on this point, it is doubtful whether it would have been possible to characterize his tort approach fully and accurately. In this section, as we have said, the recourse will operate in the opposite direction: not only will this allow us to learn something from the modern approach in order to present the older reality more correctly, but it will also provide lessons about pluralism from the Maimonidean reality for our day, and at least a certain conversation between pluralistic approaches from different periods.

We will first present the major contemporary pluralistic approaches in tort law theory. We will then proceed to an analysis of Maimonides' approach as compared to those contemporary approaches. We will see that Maimonides' approach was unique – both *pluralist* and *differential* at the same time.

2 Current Mixed-Pluralistic Approaches: An Overview

Ernest Weinrib argued that private law is a "congeries of unharmonized and competing purposes."[2] John Goldberg has stated that in many cases, different tort theories lead to contradictory interpretations.[3] Obviously, creating harmony between different goals would be preferable.

Goldberg opposes pluralistic approaches, claiming that pluralism actually leaves us "puzzle[d] over how exactly the accommodation among tort's multiple purposes is to take place."[4] He asks: "If tort law is a device for deterring undesirable conduct, spreading losses, and restoring the disturbed equilibrium, which of these should it do, and on what occasions?"[5] Goldberg explains that the answer "cannot be 'all three all the time' because the pursuit of one interferes with the achievement of others."[6] He further explains:

> Deterrence might require us to award damages even where no losses are in need of spreading. Concern to spread losses may likewise justify ordering payment where there is no deterrence to be had. If payment is really going to count as corrective justice, we will need a genuine victim with a claim. Yet giving only genuine victims claims cuts against the goal of deterrence. And so on.[7]

On the other hand, the proponents of pluralistic approaches will claim that if some goals clash or are incompatible, courts must weigh their respective values in the case at hand and in accordance with society's current values.

What is special about a coherent pluralistic approach is not only its consideration of multiple goals rather than emphasizing only one goal. It is its quest for a way to combine

---

[2] ERNEST J. WEINRIB, THE IDEA OF PRIVATE LAW 5, 56–83 (1995); *see also* Bruce Chapman, *Pluralism in Tort and Accident Law*, PHILOSOPHY AND THE LAW OF TORTS 250, 277 (Gerald J. Postema ed., 2001) (criticizing Weinrib's approach).
[3] *See* John C. P. Goldberg, *Twentieth Century Tort Theory*, 91 GEO. L. J. 513, 580 (2003).
[4] John C. P. Goldberg, *Ten Half-Truths about Tort Law*, 42 VAL. U.L. REV. 1221, 1249 (2008).
[5] Ibid.
[6] Ibid.
[7] Ibid. (also arguing that "[t]aken on their own terms, pluralist theories are profoundly *immodest* in their conception of the place of tort law in our legal and political system" (*Ibid.* at 1254–55.) (Emphasis in original.)

these goals in particular cases or groups of cases, and primarily to resolve clashes between contradictory goals. In other words, in order to characterize an approach as truly pluralistic, it is not enough to simply discount it as monistic. The approach must be shown to combine different goals or prioritize them in a logical fashion.

This section presents the primary mixed-pluralistic approaches.[8] Scholars in the analytical field of torts have produced differing mixed-pluralistic theories over the years in an attempt to strike a balance. This section now turns to an examination of a number of noteworthy pluralistic approaches to tort law.[9]

The following pluralistic approaches analyzed in this section face the challenge of properly balancing goals and demonstrating a solid pluralistic thesis.

(a) Izhak Englard: "Complementarity" – An Attempt to Reach Harmony between Corrective and Distributive Justice

In 1993, Izhak Englard advanced the concept of "complementarity,"[10] which deals primarily with the clash between corrective justice and distributive justice, and seeks to harmonize these goals. Englard views compensation, or retribution, as a component of corrective justice, and deterrence and loss distribution as components of distributive justice.[11] He believes that other theories have failed to capture the moral dimensions of distributive justice.[12] Indeed, an examination of the parties' wealth prior to the tortious event is probably not compatible with Englard's view of corrective justice, as this factor is unrelated to the tortious event itself. According to Englard, it is always necessary to consider the application of all the goals in every tortious event.[13] Distributive justice need not always contradict corrective justice. Thus, for example, the idea that a wealthy person will be more generous toward a poor person – the concept underlying the theory of distributive justice – is based on a moral notion that underlies the theory of corrective justice. Likewise, the existence

---

[8] Note that not all the approaches try to balance all four goals. Some of them present fewer than four. *Cf.* Burton, *supra* note 1, at 544 ("Feeble theories consider more than one but fewer than all relevant values").

[9] For the purpose of the summary, and in view of the constraints of space, this section covers approaches that are manifestly different from each other. In addition, it is problematic to fully compare the approaches since not all of them deal with and consider all four goals separately and independently. However, each approach tries to strike a balance between goals which are located on different sides of the divide.

[10] IZHAK ENGLARD, THE PHILOSOPHY OF TORT LAW 85–92 (1993); Izhak Englard, *The Idea of Complementarity as a Philosophical Basis for Pluralism in Tort Law*, PHILOSOPHICAL FOUNDATIONS OF TORT LAW 183 (David G. Owen ed., 1995); Izhak Englard, *The Cost of Accidents: A Retrospect View from the Cathedral*, 64 MD. L. REV. 355, 361 (2005) [hereinafter: Englard 2005].

[11] ENGLARD, *supra* note 10, at 145 ("[T]he non-instrumentalist idea of retribution, falling under the concept of corrective justice, confronts the instrumentalist goals of specific and general deterrence, which are associated with distributive justice."); Englard 2005, *supra* note 10, at 360–61.

[12] ENGLARD, *supra* note 10, at 15.

[13] *Ibid.* at 56.

of tortious elements, including causation, is not always sufficient to impose liability – hence the need for a moral basis.[14] Accordingly, in cases in which a wealthy defendant causes injury but is not at fault, the imposition of liability can be regarded as an integration of the two goals.[15] In England's opinion, deterrence falls within the framework of distributive justice, which is possibly consistent with corrective justice because the imposition of liability not only rights the wrong but also deters potential tortfeasors.[16]

While England prefers not to discuss the contradiction between these goals and focuses instead on achieving harmony between them, he does refer to the fact that corrective justice ultimately must be given superior weight. According to England, no tort law can exist without corrective justice at its core, and he therefore explicitly prefers corrective justice to distributive justice.[17] He believes that tortious liability loses the moral component found in fault when deterrence, economic efficiency, and loss distribution are added to the mix.[18]

Some have criticized England's view on the grounds that it simply prioritizes one goal over another rather than achieving real harmony between goals.[19] It seems that a more practical method of reconciling different goals is to strike a balance between them, rather than harmonizing them.[20]

(b) Gary Schwartz: Optimal Deterrence as the Dominant Goal and Its Constraint by Corrective Justice Considerations

In 1997, Gary Schwartz identified three primary goals of tort law: corrective justice, distributive justice, and deterrence.[21] According to Schwartz, the contemporary tortious method does not give what law and economics would regard as adequate consideration to deterrence. In many cases it also fails to restore the *status quo ante* in accordance with principles of corrective justice.[22] Schwartz attacks the notion of

---

[14] Ibid. at 15–16, 54–55.
[15] Ibid. at 16, 54.
[16] Ibid. at 145.
[17] See ibid. at 228; England 2005, *supra* note 10, at 360. See also IZHAK ENGLARD, CORRECTIVE AND DISTRIBUTIVE JUSTICE: FROM ARISTOTLE TO MODERN TIMES (2009) (presenting the intricate history of the distinction between corrective and distributive justice, which is elaborated in the 5th book of Aristotle's NICOMACHEAN ETHICS). This was his way also in his judgment as an Israeli Supreme Court Justice. See, e.g., CA 2825/97 Abu Zeid v. Meckel, 53(1) IsrSC 402, 413 [1999]; CA 3668/98 Best Buy Ltd. v. Fidias Maintenance Ltd., 53(3) IsrSC 180, 191 [1999].
[18] ENGLARD, *supra* note 10, at 111.
[19] See Avner Levin, *Quantum Physics in Private Law*, 14 CAN. J. L. & JURIS. 249, 255 (2001).
[20] But see ENGLARD, *supra* note 10, at 88–89 (emphasizing that complementarity means more than balancing; it means real harmony and integration of contrary and competing interests).
[21] Gary T. Schwartz, *Mixed Theories of Tort Law: Affirming Both Deterrence and Corrective Justice*, 75 TEX. L. REV. 1801, 1804 (1997) (rejecting distributive justice). See especially *ibid.* at 1818, n. 128. See also Jeffrey O'Connell & Christopher Robinette, *The Role of Compensation in Personal Injury Tort Law: A Response to the Opposite Concerns of Gary Schwartz and Patrick Atiyah*, 32 CONN. L. REV. 137, 146 n. 58 (1999) (protesting Schwartz's decision).
[22] Schwartz, *supra* note 21, at 1815–19.

corrective justice as the sole objective of tort law that Weinrib and Coleman supported. He argues that it is difficult for corrective justice to exist alongside deterrence, as deterrence takes into account factors apart from the two direct parties to the tort – the tortfeasor and the injured party.[23] According to Schwartz, deterrence examines the principle of creating risks, whereas corrective justice examines the damage that actually occurred.[24] Pursuant to corrective justice, liability is imposed on the tortfeasor and not necessarily on the best possible avoider of the damage. According to the theory of pure corrective justice, there is no room for distributive considerations, which also take into account other factors.[25] Accordingly, Schwartz wonders whether loss comes from every direction, since hefty costs may ensue if each goal is taken into account separately.[26] He states that the advantages of integrating the two goals exceed the structural costs of doing so.[27] Schwartz discusses cases in which it is possible *ab initio* to achieve a compromise between the goals; however, he ultimately argues for the centrality of optimal deterrence, except in cases where considerations of corrective justice prevent this.[28]

Unlike Engalnd, Schwartz does not purport to attain harmony between goals in every case. Rather, he presents a theory of balances, whereby it is possible to integrate goals without necessarily regarding them as competing. Goals do not clash in practice – they are simply different. Corrective justice begins where the rationale of deterrence ends. In other words, the injured party can demand that the tortfeasor correct the wrong he has committed in cases where deterrence has failed. Schwartz adds that deterrence gives rise to justice of another type. In his opinion, focusing on the goal of deterrence can lead to prevention of the accident *ab initio*, and this is more than just the provision of reparation in retrospect.[29] This is a justice that is "more just" than corrective justice, which he calls "protective justice."[30] Thus, in his view, deterrence involves not only economic-utilitarian, but also ethical and moral principles. Accordingly, corrective justice follows optimal deterrence, which is actually based on protective justice. Schwartz believes corrective justice is secondary

---

[23] *Ibid.* at 1809.
[24] *Ibid.* at 1816.
[25] *Ibid.*
[26] *Ibid.* at 1826 (demonstrating from systems costs in cases of applying corrective justice alone or deterrence alone).
[27] *Ibid.* at 1826–27.
[28] *Ibid.* at 1824 (comparing his pluralistic theory in torts to that of Hart in criminal law).
[29] *Ibid.* at 1831–32 ("It is common to say that 'justice' or 'rights' approaches to tort liability necessarily see tort liability in 'noninstrumentalist' terms. Yet the deterrence that negligence law provides can itself be understood not just as a maximizer of utility but also as a device for achieving justice (or at least as a device for reducing the amount of injustice" [references omitted]).
[30] *Ibid.* at 1832.

and enters the picture in retrospect only when optimal deterrence and protective justice do not succeed.

Schwartz criticizes Englard's theory as an arbitrary attempt to reconcile two irreconcilable goals.[31] Schwartz asserts that balancing goals and not necessarily searching for harmony, which is sometimes impractical, is a more realistic mixed-pluralistic approach.[32] Schwartz admits that realistically, his theory cannot explain and include all cases of tortious liability.[33]

Schwartz's contribution in elucidating practical possibilities for an integrated analysis of differing goals provides strong support for a pluralistic theory of tort law. However, he also manifestly prefers a single specific goal, using another only as a qualifier in relatively rare cases of immorality. Is Schwartz in fact a monist disguised as a pluralist? His approach is close to that of Guido Calabresi, who also takes into account moral considerations only to set a certain "ceiling" when he applies law and economics theory.[34] For example, Calabresi contends that if a system of accident precaution (prevention costs) leads to a very immoral outcome in a particular case, the court should not adopt that system even if it is highly efficient.[35] Thus, in Calabresi's view, justice is certainly not equal in value to optimal deterrence.

Therefore, Schwartz's approach would not seem to be a pluralistic one, asserting the dominance of optimal deterrence, but rather a unified-monistic approach that focuses on deterrence as being constrained and inapplicable only in particularly immoral cases. Schwartz is perhaps slightly more moderate in his rhetoric than Calabresi, offering a number of possible compromises between different goals.

Indeed, characterizing this approach as pluralistic is very problematic. In our opinion, to contend that deterrence must be preferred in each and every case is problematic. Sometimes, compensation and corrective justice should override

---

[31] *Ibid.* at 1819 n.132, 1828 n.187.
[32] *Ibid.* at 1828 ("Working out the sequence of deterrence and corrective justice certainly improves the coherence of this mixed theory. Still, the theory remains apparently mixed in that it includes two objectives that are seemingly quite distinctive").
[33] *Ibid.* at 1834 ("Mixed theories of tort law hold promise. Admittedly, efforts to develop a mixed theory applicable to all of tort law do not immediately pay off").
[34] For an extensive analysis of Calabresi's approach, *see supra* Chapter 5. *See also* his approach, as he presented it recently, mixing in certain considerations of justice, even though he does not frame them in deontological terms, *infra*, Chapter 9. *See also* the following note.
[35] Over the years, Calabresi has made more room for considerations of justice – mostly distributive – in his writings, withdrawing somewhat from the totality of one goal only. *See, e.g.,* Guido Calabresi, "We Imagine the Past to Remember the Future" – *Between Law, Economics, and Justice in Our Era and according to Maimonides*, 26 YALE J. L. & HUMAN. 135, 139–41 (2014) (responding to Yuval Sinai & Benjamin Shmueli, *Calabresi's and Maimonides's Tort Law Theories – A Comparative Analysis and A Preliminary Sketch of a Modern Model of Differential Pluralistic Tort Liability based on the Two Theories*, 26 YALE J. L. & HUMAN. 59 (2014). *See also infra* Chapter 9. Calabresi explains there that although optimal deterrence takes first place in this work since his early writings, he always leaves room for justice and moral considerations, although he does not use the terms deontological considerations).

deterrence in the overall balancing process. An *a priori* determination that one goal prevails in every case, and that any other goal or goals only occasionally constrains it, may shackle tort law to a preference that is not always appropriate.

As opposed to Schwarz, some pluralistic analyses achieved a better balance between the consequentialist and the moral dimensions; however, these analyses did not relate to tort law but to other legal fields.[36]

(c) Mark Geistfeld: Out of a Number of Possible Efficient Outcomes, the Most Moral Will Be Chosen

In 2001 Mark Geistfeld proposed that the most moral and just resolution should be selected from a series of several efficient outcomes,[37] an approach which is the product of the "social welfare function."[38] Geistfeld's theory is a version of economic analysis of law, which is interested in aggregate social utility, social welfare, individual welfare, and distributing the welfare in a more appropriate manner.[39]

According to Geistfeld, the theory of law and economics is incomplete without a moral analysis. He argues that the pure aggregate social welfare is dependent on the welfare of the individual and is connected to notions of equality, personal safety, and justice, which must take precedence over the interest in the tortfeasor's freedom.[40] Economic analysis of law must therefore be limited to examining which rule of liability will best deter immoral conduct at a minimum of costs of accident: it is necessary to choose the moral theory which influences individual welfare justly when there are a number of ways to maximize society's wealth.[41]

This theory may solve numerous tortious situations. However, we think that like complementarity, it does not seem to provide an answer to situations in which corrective justice and efficiency clash, i.e., where one cannot identify a moral outcome among different efficient approaches. In particular, it does not provide an answer when two outcomes are possible: one more efficient but less just, and the other more just yet less efficient.

Geistfeld, like England and Schwartz, does not follow the path of categorization and does not distinguish between tortious events. Rather, he speaks of a single solution which will be compatible with all tortious events.

---

[36] EYAL ZAMIR & BARAK MEDINA, LAW, ECONOMICS, AND MORALITY (Oxford: Oxford University Press, 2010). Their approach will be discussed in the next section.
[37] See Mark Geistfeld, *Economics, Moral Philosophy, and the Positive Analysis of Tort Law*, in PHILOSOPHY AND THE LAW OF TORTS 250, 268 (Gerald J. Postema ed., 2001).
[38] Ibid. See also Matthew D. Adler, *Risk Equity: A New Proposal*, 32 HARV. ENV'L L. REV. 1, 25–28 (2008) (discussing the social welfare approach to distributive issues within the framework of various theoretical policies and regulations).
[39] Ibid.
[40] Geistfeld, *supra* note 37, at 251–53, 265–68.
[41] See ibid. at 265–68.

Sometimes it is impossible to identify and choose, in a non-arbitrary manner, an efficient outcome that is also just (or the most just) or vice versa. In cases in which goals from both categories clash, Geistfeld's theory may not apply in practice.

(d) Fleming James Jr. and Christopher J. Robinette: A Casuistic Approach

The final approach to be presented is not fixated on the dominance of a single goal in relation to every tortious event. Rather, it discusses sorting torts into groups with similar characteristics in accordance with the goals underlying tort law, thereby finding the right, dominant goal for each case on its merits.

Fleming James Jr.'s work as a whole appears to suggest he is a monist devoted to compensation; however, in 1959 he argued that tort law cannot be confined to a single goal because the theoretical analysis of both negligence and strict liability is multifaceted.[42] He attacked the integrated-monistic perspective acerbically, describing it as useless.[43] He suggested that those discussing it were wasting their valuable time, as no unified-monistic theory could provide a complete analysis, and that it was pointless to try and unite something as naturally heterogeneous as the theories underlying tort law.[44] Note, this was written prior to the appearance of law and economics. James called for an empirical analysis of the system by classifying torts with similar characteristics in accordance with the goals relevant to the issues underlying tort law.[45] He suggested that identifying the problem underlying each issue and studying the potential solutions to that problem would accomplish that aim.[46] This interesting approach has somehow been neglected to date.

In a 2005 article, Christopher J. Robinette devalued the unification project in favor of tort theory disaggregation.[47] In his opinion, monistic theories are doomed to failure, both doctrinally and historically, since tort law developed on a case-by-case basis in the common law, rather on a single clear rationale.[48] In order to explain his theory, Robinette analyzed two areas of tort doctrine – automobile accidents and medical malpractice – both of them based on a rule of negligence and both of them cases of unintentional torts.[49] Robinette argued that if it is not possible to give a full, theoretical, unified-monistic explanation of the appropriate solution regarding these two common types of torts, a unified-monistic theory is of no avail in explaining

---

[42] Fleming James Jr., *Tort Law in Midstream: its Challenge to the Judicial Process*, 8 BUFF. L. REV. 315 (1959). This paper was based on the James McCormick Mitchell Lectures, delivered at the University of Buffalo School of Law, April 3–4, 1959.
[43] See Robinette, *supra* note 21, at 378–82 (discussing James Jr.'s approach).
[44] James Jr., *supra* note 42, at 315, 320, 325.
[45] *Ibid.* at 320.
[46] *Ibid.*
[47] Robinette, *supra* note 21, at 413.
[48] Robinette, *supra* note 21, at 371, 412–13.
[49] Robinette, *supra* note 21, at 399–412.

tort law.[50] According to him, deterrence operates differently in each of these two situations, as he questions the deterrent value of tort law in the context of automobile accidents but not in the context of medical malpractice.[51] By contrast, causation is relatively simpler in cases of automobile accidents than in cases of medical malpractice, because it is easy to distinguish and identify the injury caused by the accident.[52] Causation is more complex in medical malpractice cases because of the quasi-contractual nature of the relationship between the patient and the medical system.[53] Additionally, the patient is already sick or injured, which is the initial reason for commencing medical procedures. In such cases, it is difficult to distinguish between the original injury and the injury added by the negligent act. The very nature of medical science complicates the determination of a causal connection between a breach of the duty of care and damage in such cases,[54] and plaintiffs therefore need to engage the services of expensive medical experts. Many medical malpractice cases never become legal suits at all.[55] Those that do are generally concluded with compensation that is less than the real loss incurred.[56] Robinette cites a survey which indicates that only eight percent of medical malpractice victims achieve any compensation in the United States – in other words, only forty percent of the twenty percent who decide to sue.[57] This situation is problematic with regard to the goals of compensation and corrective justice, and it is also contrary to deterrence to a certain extent.[58]

Robinette suggests breaking down the system of tort law into its different components and applying different theories to different situations in order to decide which theory fits.[59] In his opinion, it is not right, from a historical and doctrinal point of view, to engage in an all-embracing discussion of all goals in all situations.[60]

---

[50] Cf. Robinette, *supra* note 21, at 412 ("In comparing just two areas of tort doctrine ... [a] unified theory of torts ... does not appear possible").

[51] Robinette, *supra* note 21, at 402–05.

[52] *Ibid.* at 805 ("Causation in automobile accidents tends to be relatively simple to establish").

[53] *Ibid.* ("Causation in a medical malpractice action tends to be complex and very difficult to establish").

[54] DAVID M. HARNEY, MEDICAL MALPRACTICE 419–27 (2nd ed. 1987) (arguing that this is why the quantum of proof should be less in malpractice suits than in personal injury lawsuits); Robinette, *supra* note 21, at 408 (noting the fact that medicine is a profession that governs itself and sets its own standards).

[55] Robinette, *supra* note 21, at 406.

[56] *Ibid.* at 406–07.

[57] *Ibid.* at 406 (citing DON DEWEES, ET AL., EXPLORING THE DOMAIN OF ACCIDENT LAW 425 (1996)).

[58] *Ibid.* at 405–09. *See also* TOM BAKER, THE MEDICAL MALPRACTICE MYTH 63 (2005) (demonstrating the low aggregated cost of medical malpractice insurance relative to the higher aggregated cost of automobile accident insurance, despite the high rate of medical malpractice deaths relative to automobile accident deaths).

[59] Cf. Robinette, *supra* note 21, at 399 ("The comparison leads me to conclude that various areas in tort law will be understandable only in terms of different rationales").

[60] Robinette, *supra* note 21, at 371, 409, 413.

However, it seems that Robinette's approach differs from that of James Jr. Robinette clarifies that his intention was not to apply the rationales to each case on its own merits, but rather, to advocate a process of grouping cases by doctrine.[61] In other words, the expression "case-by-case" is applicable to torts doctrine, as in the automobile accidents and medical malpractice examples, and goals need to be determined at the level of each tort, for the purposes of tort theory, and not at the level of all torts (like monists would do) or on a literal case-by-case basis.[62]

James Jr.'s approach is fundamentally correct, but it may go too far. Indeed, becoming fixated on a single goal of tort law, as do unified-monistic theories, is even more problematic than his pluralistic approach, since those theories accord preference to a particular goal in every clash, irrespective of the type of tortious event. At the same time, examining every case on its merits without general guidelines regarding which goals are more relevant, as James Jr. suggests, is undesirable and involves substantial administrative costs. A preference for certain goals of tort law can be expressed even *ex ante*. In certain cases, a particular goal is possibly less relevant. A superior vantage point, achieved by examining groups of cases in accordance with their nature, and not in relation to each and every case on its merits, is the preferable way to view the tort system and develop a vantage point.

It is not always clear which goals are irrelevant and fall "outside the game" in relation to a particular issue. Without a clear categorization of goals and cases, it is impossible to apply the theory as a matter of practice, since that would introduce enormous uncertainty regarding the decision of actual cases. The absence of any guiding hand would lead to chaos and even the breakdown of the tort system. Additionally, this approach does not clearly determine the outcome when goals clash, and it simply allows for an unrealistically cumbersome, casuistic, case-by-case examination.

Robinette's approach seems more applicable and balanced at its core, but it needs to be expanded and to identify when to accord dominance to certain goals and when to others, and why.

3 Placing Maimonides on the Pluralistic Approaches Scale

In this section we will attempt to place Maimonides' pluralistic approach on the scale of the modern pluralistic approaches presented in the preceding section.

Englard and Schwartz both attempted to present a pluralistic theory with a similar rationale, according to which the examination of all the tortious issues as a single body, despite the multiplicity of situations illustrated in Section B.2.a and B.2.b, was

---

[61] Christopher J. Robinette, *Torts Rationales, Pluralism, and Isaiah Berlin*, 14 GEO. MASON L. REV. 360 n.179 (2007) (describing the pluralist scholar's task as one of grouping torts at the doctrinal level, *e.g.*, medical malpractice. Robinette agrees that a "case-by-case" approach is not practical. *Ibid.*).

[62] *Ibid.*

based on a fixed analysis of the goals in all the tortious events, which granted dominance to a particular goal. However, this is best categorized as a unified-monistic path, not a pluralistic one. Englard calls for harmony and complementarity between goals, with a preference for corrective justice.[63] A tension exists between attempting to achieve harmony between goals and prioritizing one goal. By contrast, Schwartz also attempts to balance goals, with a qualifying deference to corrective justice.[64] His theory does not strike a real balance between goals, but clearly prefers, *ex ante*, optimal deterrence and accords justice a secondary role only.

Englard's theory prioritizing corrective justice and Schwartz's prioritizing of optimal deterrence are overly broad. A more flexible and less fixed way of thinking is needed, particularly in a world in which tortious situations are so diverse. James Jr. is positioned at the other end of the spectrum. He discusses each and every goal case by case. However, that approach is problematic for legal stability and certainty, and involves excessive specificity, which may lead to a situation in which no theory will find a place.

The analysis of extant pluralistic theories that has been presented in Section B.2 shows that there is room for presenting a solid and intermediate mixed-pluralist theory of contemporary tort law which is neither excessively general nor excessively specific, and takes into account the development of modern tort law. This approach will not advocate decision making on a case-by-case basis, as that process would not resolve cases involving a real clash between goals. It will be different from those of Englard and Schwartz. Geistfeld's approach is also insufficient, as it does not provide a comprehensive answer to the question of a clash between efficient and just outcomes. Accordingly, a certain adjustment of James Jr.'s theory to modern tort law can promote implementation of a proper mixed-pluralist theory. It thus arrives at a specific rationale for each type or group of cases.

In fact, Maimonides' rationale could constitute the basis for a new, genuinely pluralistic approach, rather than a pseudo-pluralistic one. This new approach could adopt the advantages in Section B.2 of the existing pluralistic approaches, abandon their disadvantages, and could be adapted to the current reality. As a basis of that new approach, let us again explore the essence of Maimonides' pluralistic approach. It will be recalled that we argue that his theory is in many ways *pluralistic* and *differential*, meaning that it is in fact an integration of different goals, granting priority to any particular goal in accordance with the different categories of damage. Indeed, we saw that Maimonides' theory embraces several goals: the goal of removing wrongs, which is parallel to corrective justice, and the consequentialist goal of preventing the causing of harm, which parallels optimal deterrence, alongside penal considerations, moral-deontological considerations, religious considerations and

---

[63] See *supra* text accompanying note 10.
[64] See *supra* text accompanying note 28.

considerations of distributive justice. This is undoubtedly a pluralistic approach. The analysis of the existing pluralistic approaches that has been presented in Section B.2 demonstrates that permanently prioritizing one goal over another is not worthwhile, and neither is proceeding case by case; rather, for each category of cases, a particular goal should be designated as dominant. Indeed, in Maimonides' approach too, all the goals find expression, and there is no fixed preference for a particular goal. For every type of harm, Maimonides presents one dominant goal. Thus, for example, in Laws of Property Damages, as Maimonides writes in the *Guide*, the utilitarian goal (prevention of damage) dominates[65] although there is also room for the goal of removing the wrong (corrective justice),[66] and the *Code* also mentions deontological and religious considerations (the prohibition against causing damage),[67] even though these last two are less dominant. Maimonides also discusses the question of prioritizing consequentialist considerations vis-à-vis distributive considerations, in his statement in the *Guide* that although increasing aggregate welfare is important, this should be limited due to distributive considerations – no one should benefit more than anyone else.[68] This last consideration is more dominant in the Book of Acquisition,[69] for as he wrote there,[70] the dominant goal, i.e., the distributive goal, places a constraint on the utilitarian goal (of increasing the profits of the parties) and sets a limit to the ability of one party to profit at the expense of the other party. In Laws of Theft, as opposed to this, the goal of penal sanction and payment of punitive damages is primarily utilitarian (optimal deterrence), even though the moral gravity of the offense is also expressed.[71] The criminal dimension is central not only in Laws of Murderers, but also in the laws applying to a person who injures the body of another,[72] in which the deontological and religious considerations are dominant (prohibition against self-harm, the inalienability prohibition, the duty to

---

[65] See Chapter 5.
[66] See Chapter 4.
[67] Ibid.
[68] GUIDE 3:42. For elaboration, *see* Chapter 3.
[69] As we showed in Chapter 3, this is particularly relevant to the laws concerning harm caused to neighbors and the laws of watchmen.
[70] GUIDE 3:42. For elaboration, *see* Chapter 3.
[71] GUIDE 3:41. For elaboration *see* Chapter 5. There we saw that in relation to punitive damages and penal sanctions, Maimonides in the GUIDE (3:41) set four parameters, including the severity of the act and deterrent considerations. We saw that even in cases in which the act is equally grave from a moral point of view, such as theft and robbery, Maimonides gives greater prominence to the parameters of optimal deterrence, which constitute three of the four parameters, as opposed to the parameter of the severity of the act (parameter 1), which is less dominant in his analysis in the *Guide*, where he concludes that more deterrence is needed for theft than for robbery.
[72] *See* Chapter 3. This is not to say that no civil considerations are included – it is a fact that the injurer pays compensation to the victim, but the compensation that he pays does not include an element of corrective justice. He pays a fine, and there is no correspondence between the harm that was caused and the actual payment.

request forgiveness),[73] whereas in the laws governing a person who damages the property of another, the monetary-utilitarian dimension dominates.[74]

The *differential* element is interwoven with the *pluralist* element. How? Various liability regimes and standards of care are determined based on different catagories of damage, as shown in detail in the previous chapter. Mamonides presented a scale of different catagories of damage: damage caused by a person to the property of another (strict liability); damage cause by a person who injures the body of another (three standards of care, on the scale between fault and strict liability); property damage (negligence) and murder (fault based). We also explained why Maimonides chose to designate each one of these types in a different manner – strict/almost strict vs. fault-based liability, penal vs. civil, deontological vs. consequentialist.

We regard Maimonides' theory as sophisticated, in view of the time in which it was devised – more than 800 years ago – integrating more than one goal into the mix, and presenting a well-organized model. Although Maimonides himself did not, of course, define his theory in the modern terms we use, he definitely presented different goals of torts which in his view coexist.

Unlike some of the modern pluralistic approaches, this view does not permanently prioritize one goal over another, but takes into account several goals in each category of cases. In some categories, removal of the wrong (corrective justice) is preferred, and in some others, the preferred goal is prevention of harm (optimal deterrence). In certain cases, the distributive aspects are important, and in others, religious aspects have a place. However, this intersects with different types of standards of care. In certain categories of cases, liability is based on negligence, and in others, on absolute or strict liability.

Maimonides' approach, which represents more than one objective of tort law and proposes a model of differential liability, could engage in a cautious dialogue with various modern tort theories.

The dialogue is, of course, possible with monistic theories too, for every pluralistic theory is comprised of a balance between different goals, each of which is the center of a monistic approach. Thus, for example, the great innovation of Maimonides' differential theory as opposed to that of Calabresi, who is regarded as a monist whose theory is based on optimal deterrence, lies in the possibility of implementing the EAC test as a super-test for tortious liability, even in liability regimes that are not based on absolute or strict liability, but rather, on fault to some degree or another.[75]

The kernel of Maimonides' pluralistic-differential approach may therefore constitute the basis for a pluralistic approach which on the one hand does not permanently prefer one goal in all categories of cases, and on the other hand does not leave the decision concerning the standard of care for each case to be made on an

---

[73] *See* Chapter 4.
[74] *See* Chapter 3.
[75] *See* Chapter 7.

individual basis. This is a lesson that the modern legal system may learn. Modern law will apparently not generally consider whether the person is himself causing the harm as opposed to causing harm through his property, or whether the person is harming another person physically or economically. Sometimes, it would be appropriate for these distinctions to be considered; in modern law, too, there may be room for dealing more severely with physical harm than with damage to property, and it may not be appropriate to assess both types of harm on the same scale.

Maimonides' approach also incorporates a *religious* dimension, but at the same time it converses with other pluralistic approaches, for its weighting of the different dimensions renders it capable of conducting a dialogue with contemporary theories. Naturally, in modern secular law, religious considerations will have no place; there are also additional differences which prevent a direct adoption of Maimonides' approach in our times. In some cases, the difference is due to the era, as we have seen, for Maimonides' reality was not one of insurance and mass torts: it was primarily agrarian. Nevertheless, the Maimonidean approach is capable of conducting a conversation with the modern approaches, and even of improving them in various aspects, which will be discussed in the next section.

C. FROM MAIMONIDES TO CONTEMPORARY LAW

1 *Possible Lessons for Contemporary Tort Law Theories*

(a) Creating a Pluralistic-Differential Framework in Modern Tort Law

Is it possible to create a pluralistic-differential framework in modern tort law? As we have said, the intention is not to reproduce Maimonides' approach today. Nevertheless, the contribution of Maimonides' approach to the modern conversation might be in its presentation of an approach that is not only pluralist but also differentialist, i.e., an attempt to allocate to each set of cases the standard of care that befits it according to the relevant goal. This is a serious, separate challenge, which awaits detailed treatment in another work. However, we will not desist from mentioning several fundamental lessons – some more comprehensive and general, and some more specific although still important – that may be derived from the Maimonides pluralistic-differential doctrine for modern tort theory discourse.

In the previous chapter, we praised the advantages of differentiation and we also explained the differences between Maimonides' approach and other modern approaches against the background of the times. We explained that Maimonides' approach cannot be detached from the agrarian background of his period and from the nature of the tort claims of individuals against other individuals. Today, however, we live in the industrial world and in a reality of mass tort claims against large bodies, loss distributors and deep pockets, insurers and employers, and we explained the practical differences, including the difficulty encountered by the law in preventing and shutting down production activity altogether, even if it causes damage. We also explained that it is easier to impose strict liability in a reality in which insurance is prevalent and the damager himself does not usually pay for the harm he causes. This was far less appropriate in Maimonides' time, when imposing strict liability for damage caused by a private, uninsured person as a result of his occupation, which provided his livelihood, could well have been catastrophic. We also explained that the reality in which tort law operates today is a common reality of vicarious liability and state regulation; again, these did not exist in Maimonides' time.

Owing to the fact that in today's world, individuals still cause uninsured harms to other individuals, the categories of these harms must be examined today, too, through the standard of care of negligence or close to negligence; absolute or strict liability should be invoked less, and should be left for cases in which insured large bodies are the defendants, and even then, only if appropriate. Accordingly, even today, adaptation of the standard of care to the relevant category of cases must take into consideration, *inter alia*, the question of whether the dispute is between individuals where the outcome of imposing liability will be payment to the victim not by a harmdoer himself, but by his employer or by an insurer. If that were the case, the imposition of strict liability would be problematic.

Therefore, if we accept the Maimonidean theory and seek to derive from it a cautious lesson for our times, it will be hard to agree with the imposition of strict liability if the claim is, for example, that a neighbor's dog broke the plaintiff's vessel, or that there was a breach of privacy between individuals in the framework of a particular action which is of value, and the disturbance was not intentional but only incidental. It would be more correct, as is the case in the positive laws of some legal systems, to define the tort properly, to base it on fault and to establish causation between the breach of duty specified in the law and the damage; and in any case to take into account that there is usually no insurance in such cases, no loss distribution but rather, the damage is attributed wholly to the tortfeasor, who does not always have deep pockets. This does not mean that with regard to all commercial and manufacturing activity, absolute or strict liability will be imposed irrespective of fault, but there will be a greater willingness to impose a standard of care that is further from negligence and closer to absolute liability, for example, on manufacturers in cases of defective products, for the reasons specified in the beginning of this Section C.1.a: the fact that they are insured, risk-managing, carefully strategized loss distributers with deep pockets.

(b) Possible Dissociation between the Element of Control and Strict Liability

In the previous chapters, we discussed the EAC test – the Maimonidean test based on the element of *control*, which is relevant for Maimonides with respect to property damage and damage caused by a person to the property of another. We have already mentioned that this test is similar to Calabresi's doctrine of the cheapest cost avoider, particularly in his placement of the element of control at its center. However, it also differs from Calabresi's doctrine, in that it allows for a dissociation between control and the standard of strict liability, and for different standards of care – negligence, strict liability and also intermediate standards – in the different categories of the tortious events. We believe that this dissociation, which Maimonides in fact identifies, can be relevant today as well. Indeed, it is possible to take the kernel of Calabresi's cheapest cost avoider approach – which clearly is very organized and rational, presenting an approach based on optimal deterrence and prevention of harm – and attach it to standards of care that are not necessarily strict liability, according to the level of control. In this context, it is not necessary to copy into modern law all the minutiae of Maimonides' approach and his differentiations between different standards of care in the different categories of tortious events; what is more, Maimonides' approach is missing reference to those categories that characterize modern law in the post-industrial revolution period, such as mass torts etc. In other words, despite Calabresi's clear rationale and his linking of the element of deterrence to strict liability, such an element (control) can be acknowledged as central to at least some of the categories of tortious events in our day as well, although the practical outcome will not be imposition of strict liability in almost every case, but rather, an assumption that liability is imposed in such cases according to standards of care that may sometimes fall below strict liability.

In Section 2.C we will further fortify this approach for an additional reason, i.e., that it connects and provides a bridge between approaches that appear to be contradictory: Calabresi's approach as opposed to that of Posner and the Hand formula.

(c) Distinction Between Harms Caused by a Person and Harms Caused by Property

Several lessons may be learnt from the Maimonidean tort theory that distinguishes between harms caused by a person himself (Laws of Wounding and Damaging) and those caused by a person's property (Laws of Property Damages), and from the additional secondary distinction that Maimonides makes within the harms caused by a person between bodily injury caused by a person to another (Laws of Wounding) and property damage caused by a person to the property of another (Laws of Damaging).

The first possible lesson concerns the major distinction drawn by Maimonides between property damages caused by a person and damage caused by his property (such as his animals). It might be warranted to adopt such a distinction in modern law as well, at least with respect to the standard of care, which according to Maimonides is at the level of almost absolute liability regarding a person who causes damage, as opposed to negligence if it is the person's property, such as his animal, that caused the damage. Even if one is uncertain about that, it is possible, for example, to determine that from the point of view of the standard of care, nuisances caused by animals will not be equal to other harms that were caused by human carelessness, as opposed to the prevalent conception today that does not necessarily make this distinction. Thus, for example, the standard of care for a person who replaces pipes for the municipality, or cables for the telephone company, who was negligent and did not place warning signals in order to alert pedestrians to the hazard, should possibly be higher than in the case in which some person's animal caused a breach in the fence, which he did not notice, and as a result the animals escaped from the enclosure and caused damage to the neigbors' field. Even if both these cases involve human carelessness, it is possible that the standard of care should be stricter in the first case, when it was the person himself who caused the harm, as opposed to the standard of care in the second case, where the person did not pay attention to the damage done by some other element (animal), even though in both cases the person was at fault (and in both cases there was an omission).

A second possible lesson concerns Maimonides' secondary distinction between injury caused by a person to another person's body and damage caused to a person's property. This distinction has various ramifications, both with respect to the scope of payments for the damage and to the standard of care. In relation to property damage, payment is only for the damage caused, whereas if a person injured the body of another, he pays for additional elements of damage as well (the five effects of damage).[76] In effect, Maimonides attributes harms from wounding mainly to the criminal law, as a fine (including also the requirement of appeasement of the victim as part of the legal duty towards him, and not only as part of the precept of repentence, as a type of restorative justice), and less to the area of private-monatery laws (although in wounding there is also a civil-monatery element, of course). He also rules that a person who causes physical injury to another, when the causation is uncertain, is treated more strictly regarding the imposition of liability, despite the uncertainty than, for example, the owner of an ox that gored a cow.[77] One can therefore dovetail this division between the injurer – in modern terms, a person carrying out an assault – and a person whose property damaged the property of another, with the division that we proposed in Section (a) between damages caused by uninsured individuals and those caused by large, insured bodies. As a result of implementation of Maimonides' approach, it will be possible to say that in a case of physically injuring a person, even intentionally – such as a tort of assault – even if greater compensation will not necessarily be paid or more effects of damage invoked, there should be a greater willingness to raise the standard of care than in relation to damage caused by a person's animal to the property of another. This greater willingness should also extend to the imposition of a liability regime that is

---

[76] See Chapter 3C.
[77] Ibid.

similar to payments of the injurer, whose basic liability for the effect of *nezek* is that of almost absolute liability (as opposed to liability for property damages, which is at the level of negligence). This should apply even when the parties are individuals, and the injurer-defendant is not insured, he does not distribute the loss, and nor does he have deep pockets. Assault is also not normally perpetrated as a productive act that benefits society – quite the contrary: this separates it from examples of damage between individuals in which the activity that is harmful to the victim is sometimes advantageous for the perpetrator and for society, for example, if nuisance was caused to a neighbor by the perpetrator giving singing lessons for his livelihood. In practice, this may mean the introduction of a requirement of a certain *mens rea* into the standard of care – which is done in a very moderate, measured fasion today in tort law (for example, the existence of intentional torts in the common law, or the requirement of *intention* in the tort of assault in Israel), as opposed for example, to the criminal law, in which there is an inherent requirement of *mens rea* alongside the *actus reus*. Indeed, in tort law, a large number of the torts are based on negligence and do not require proof of intention, malice or knowledge at any particular level. In the previous chapter we also showed that this element existed in Maimonides' approach, in his attribution of a relatively high standard of care to a person who wounds another: almost absolute liability with respect to the basic component of *nezek* payments; gross negligence in order to impose additional compensation (pain, medical treatment, loss of employment); and the requirement of intention to harm for the purpose of compensation for humiliation, as opposed to a standard of care of negligence only if it was his property that damaged the property of another. Earlier we explained that Maimonides' view with respect to wounding is that a person is in breach of the prohibition on wounding if the blow was struck in the course of a quarrel. We said that could mean two things: first, that there was a requirement (for some of the payments) that the injurer have *mens rea* to hurt another physically; the second explanation, however, required that the wound be inflicted with the aim of destroying and disfiguring the body of another, as part of the factual element – the *actus reus* – of the offense, and only then would the penal aspect of the payment of a fine come into play.[78]

A third lesson that concerns laws of wounding is the possible increased level of the standard of care in cases of medical malpractice. As we have seen, in Jewish law the standard is stricter for a person – including a physician[79] – who caused bodily injury

---

[78] See Chapter 3.
[79] There have been many views on the subject of a physician's liability in tort in Jewish law. For elaboration and analysis, see AVRAHAM STEINBERG, ENCYCLOPAEDIA OF MEDICAL *HALAKHAH* vol. 7 (Jerusalem, 5766–2006), s.v. *rashlanut refu'it*, 245 (Heb.).; Avaraham Steinberg, *Medical Malpractice – Medical, Public and Halakhic Aspects*, Introduction to ALON GELLERT AND GIDI FREISHTIK, MEDICAL MALPRACTICE IN THE CASE LAW 6 (Ramat Gan, 5760–2000) (Heb.). *See also* R. Zalman N. Goldberg, *Medical Malpractice*, 19 TEHUMIN 317 (5759–1999) (Heb.); David Lau, *Liability of the Physician for Harm Caused by His Treatment*, 16 TEHUMIN 187 (5756–1996)

or property damage to another than for damage caused by a person's property, as part of the differentiation presented by Maimonides in Laws of Wounding, in which the basic payment for *nezek* is made in the framework of a liability regime of almost absolute liability.[80] Because the accepted standard of care in modern law in cases of medical malpractice is usually that of negligence, and other, stricter standards are rarer and relate to specific cases, the courts must sometimes try to achieve the desired result in a convoluted, non-analytical way whose reasoning is hard to justify, even if the outcome appears to be correct. For example, the Israeli Supreme Court heard the appeal in the tragic case of a person who underwent an operation on his leg; after the operation, his leg was put in a plaster cast, but he developed gangrene and the leg had to be amputated below the knee.[81] In retrospect it emerged that the appellant had a defect from birth which could not have been discovered through the routine tests that the doctors performed prior to the operation. It was this defect that led to the development of the gangrene, which was therefore not foreseeable. The original claim was rejected by the District Court, which ruled explicitly that there was no negligence in the doctors' actions, and at most there had been a mistake in discretion, which does not entail liability for negligence.[82] The Supreme Court determined, without invoking the instrument of *res ipsa loquitur*, or making hard and fast pronouncements about the application of this rule in the particular case,[83] that the doctors were negligent, for they should have ascertained prior to the operation the possible existence of a defect that the Court itself said is extremely rare.[84] The decision may be analyzed from different perspectives, and we will not expand on them here. *Prima facie*, however, it would appear that the Court had to engage in real acrobatics to determine that a defect that was very rare and therefore not foreseeable by the doctors was the basis for their negligence, given that foreseeability underlies the duty of care in the tort of negligence; it is difficult to understand how not looking for an extremely rare defect which was in fact not foreseeable could be considered negligence. Is it possible that the judges wished to achieve the result of awarding damages to the unfortunate plaintiff, who entered the hospital with a complete leg and left with his leg amputated below the knee? Were distributive considerations that were not mentioned in the judgment involved here? Were the

---

(Heb.); ELEZER Y. WALDENBERG, RESP. TZITZ ELIEZER 4:13, 5:23; AVRAHAM A. SOFER, NISHMAT AVRAHAM, Yoreh De'ah 336; Ya'acov Porush, *On the Negligence of an Advisor or "The Best of the Physicians are Destined for Purgatory"*, 12 DINE ISRAEL 119 (5744–5745 – 1984–85) (Heb.); AVRAHAM SHERMAN, SUING A PHYSICIAN AND A HOSPITAL IN TORT FOR MEDICAL MALPRACTICE, ASSUTA 205 (Jerusalem, 5766–2006) (Heb.); Hershel Shachter, *Medical Malpractice* in NAHUM RAKOVER ED., JEWISH LAW AND CURRENT LEGAL PROBLEMS 217 (1984); Michael J. Broyde, *On the Assesment of Damages in Jewish Tort Law and its Application to Medical Malpractice*, 5 NAT. JEW. L. REV. 93 (1990–92).

[80] See Chapter 7.
[81] CA 612/78 Pe'er v. Cooper 35(1) IsrSC 720 [1980] (Isr.).
[82] For an account of the judgment of the District Court, see *ibid.* at 722–23.
[83] *Ibid.* at 725–26.
[84] *Ibid.* at 727–28.

fact that the doctors were insured, and that there were deep pockets, as well as loss distribution, involved in this outcome? In such cases one might have cause to consider applying a more rigid and strict standard of care than negligence in some such cases, to be determined after thoughtful deliberation (even though we are not claiming that medical malpractice should necessarily always fall into the category of a standard of care of strict liability), and thus achieve a similar result in an analytical, direct way, which will create greater certainty and prevent possible confusion in applying the standard of care of negligence and the meaning of the term "foreseeability."

Another possible lesson from the Laws of Wounding touches precisely upon the point that was raised in the previous section. The EAC test, at the center of which is the element of control, is relevant for Maimonides with respect to liability for property damage and the laws applying to a person who causes only property damage to another. His differentialism is manifest in the fact that in other categories of harms, he has different criteria of liability. In Laws of Wounding, for example, the *mens rea*, or the existence of a *mens rea* within the *actus reus* of "in the course of a quarrel" (as we explained) is dominant, and not necessarily the element of control; in Laws of Murderers the criterion is the existence of the *actus reus* of an "act of killing." As stated, even if we do not adopt the entire Maimonidean doctrine as is, it is possible to learn from it about not imposing on all of tort law one single criterion for determining liability, and examining each category of tortious events in accordance with the criterion suited to it. This is a less rigid, more dynamic approach than those of England and Schwartz, broader and more comprehensive than that of Geistfeld and still not overly particularistic and casuistic like that of Fleming James Jr., and therefore more balanced.

Notwithstanding all the analysis done until this point, the truth must still be told. Maimonides' approach is sometimes too complex, and not suited to today's law. Thus, for example, we saw in the previous chapter that within the compensation paid by a person who wounds another, there are no less than three different standards of care: almost absolute liability for the basic payment (the component of *nezek*), gross negligence for the three accompanying payments (pain, medical costs and loss of employment), and the requirement of intention to harm in order to impose payment for humiliation. It would be difficult for modern law to split the laws applying to the tort of assault into three different standards of care, and it would not be justified to do so – apparently not even with respect distinguishing between an attacker who causes injury and one who causes a person's death. Therefore, this component of the Maimonidean theory is less suited to adoption by modern law.

(d) Possible Distinction between the Tort of Robbery and the Tort of Theft

The question of whether there ought to be a distinction between the laws applying to robbery and to theft in modern law shall be left for future investigation. We saw that according to Maimonides, not only is there a difference between the laws applying to each, but they are to be found in separate codes, in separate halakhic frameworks – Laws of Theft, and Laws of Robbery and Lost Property. Maimonides bundles the laws of lost property together with robbery due to the element of the remedy; the requirement to return both property obtained through robbery and lost property, even though conceptually, robbery and the return of lost property are otherwise hardly related. The thief, on the other hand, is not obligated to return what he has stolen; his primary obligation is to pay the victim for what he has taken.[85] This is a distinction from which there is apparently nothing to be learnt for the purpose of modern tort theory, and the distinction between the remedies would not seem to be grounds for a total separation between the laws applying to the robber and the thief. Moreover, even if there would be room for such a distinction between the sets of laws in modern law too, it is conceivable that the exact opposite outcome from that obtained by Maimonides could be justified. As will be recalled, according to Maimonides' economic-utilitarian approach the thief requires more deterrence than the robber, manifesting itself in double and four- and five-fold payments that apply only to the thief and not to the robber.[86] This distinction is interesting per se, and there is a rationale to it, but it, too, may be problematic in terms of modern application, in light of the feeling that the law should actually be stricter in relation to the robber, who steals by day fearlessly, uses a weapon and is violent and therefore a danger to human life, as opposed to the thief who comes by night under cover of darkness and flees without having been seen. Hence, if there is already to be a distinction between the laws, and different torts are created with different elements, there is logic in the result that is opposite to overstrictness with the robber vis-à-vis the thief, for example, in the amount of damages or the punitive damages, or at least in equalizing and not differentiating between the two, including them in the framework of one tort and not two, as modern positive law usually does.

(e) Caution when Learning Lessons from Religious Law for Modern Secular Law

The last lesson cautions – in accordance with the discussion in this work – against deriving a problematic lesson from religious law for modern law that is not religious. In the previous section we indeed recommended that Maimonides' distinction between the thief and the robber not be adopted. However, under discussion there was an analytical-substantive difficulty, and not one of principle. In this section, on the other hand, we are discussing a fundamental difficulty involved in deriving lessons from religious law – law which is religious in nature and in its reasoning – for modern, secular law which does not have those characteristics. We will demonstrate

---

[85] *See* Chapter 3.
[86] *Ibid.*

this through the example of the duty to rescue. We dealt with the duty to rescue earlier.[87] We saw that according to Maimonides, there is indeed a duty to rescue, but no sanction is imposed upon a person who is in breach of the duty to save lives. We also saw that Maimonides, too, regarded the duty to rescue as a legal duty and not only a moral one, but for him it was primarily a religious obligation; he limited its scope relative to other Jewish law authorities, and he emphasized the religious dimension as a central one.

As we mentioned, amongst the modern legal systems, only Israeli law, to the best of our knowledge, has attempted to enact a law that mandates rescue, based mainly on Jewish religious law. We shall now elaborate on this, in order to learn that lesson about the caution with which religious law should be adopted in modern Western law.

In 1995, Hanan Porat, a Member of Knesset from one of the Israeli religious parties, submitted the "You Shall Not Stand Idly by Your Neighbor's Blood" Bill to the Knesset. From the explanatory notes to the Bill it may be inferred that the purpose of the Law was to entrench in Israeli statute a moral and social value with its source in the Bible (Leviticus 19:16).[88] In 1998, the "You Shall Not Stand Idly by Your Neighbor's Blood" Law was passed. Amongst the considerations for recognizing the duty to rescue were the communitarian conception that insists that each individual is part of the group, and as a member of the group he bears a duty to rescue; and economic theory according to which the creation of a duty to rescue, particularly in the case of a simple rescue, is justified economically. The investment of the rescuer is minimal, as opposed to the harm that is liable to be caused.[89] Prior to the passage of this Law, Israeli law did not recognize a general duty to rescue such as that subsequently imposed on the "pure" rescuer (a person who has no prior relationship with the person who requires rescuing) both by statute and by case law.[90] The Law does not belong in the field of torts: the Israeli system was influenced by the common law system, and rejected the imposition of a duty in tort due to pure omission,[91] recognizing only pockets of duties

---

[87] See Chapter 4 Section B.4.
[88] Penal Law (Amendment no. 47) ("Do Not Stand Idly by Your Neighbor's Blood") Bill, 5755–1995, HH 2398.
[89] Neal Hendel, *The "You Shall Not Stand Idly by Your Neighbor's Blood" Law: Inspiration and Reality*, 16 MEHKEREI MISHPAT 229, 264–66 (2000) (Heb.).
[90] Ibid, at 258; Uri Yadin, *On the Laws of Saving Life*, 2 MISHPATIM 252 (5731–1971) (Heb.); Miriam Ben Porat, *Helping Others*, 7 IYUNEI MISHPAT 269 (5739–1979) (Heb.). Until that time, there had been a defined obligation for a defined population group: parents vis-à-vis children, firemen in the event of bodily injury and property damage, and the driver and the victim of an automobile accident. See: Eliezer ben Shlomo, *The Duty to Save Lives*, 39 HAPRAKLIT 414, 429–30 (1990) (Heb.).
[91] ISRAEL GILEAD, TORT LAW – BOUNDARIES OF LIABILITY vol. 1, 344 (2012) (Heb.); CA 6649/96 Hadassah Medical Center v. Gilad 53(3) IsrSC 529, 546 (1999), in which Englard J. explains that the traditional law in Israel is that tortious liability is not to be imposed for "pure" omission, unless there is a prior relationship by virtue of which the person has a duty to act. Imposing a duty to act for the sake of another is certainly a violation of the person's liberty.

of rescue.[92] In cases in which the connection between the defendant and between the creation of the risk and the plaintiff is remote, the social reason for imposing liability due to omission gains strength; this reason is the desire to enhance social solidarity, with all that this implies, by requiring the individual to forgo his freedom of action and freedom of choice in order to help another.[93]

Section 1 of the "You Shall Not Stand Idly by Your Neighbor's Blood" Law imposes a duty on a person to offer help to another person in the event that the latter has been harmed due to a sudden occurrence that puts his life, body or health in danger.[94] Thus, a general obligation to rescue is imposed on the "pure" rescuer.[95] The Law does not provide immunity from a tort claim for a person who attempts to rescue.[96] With respect to indemnification, section 2 of the Law states that the court is authorized to award indemnification for reasonable costs and payments, but there is no duty of indemnification, and the provisions of section 5(a) of the Unjust Enrichment Law, whereby

> a person who, in good faith and within reason, acted to protected the life, physical integrity, health, dignity or property of another, and where such person was under no obligation to do so, and incurred, or undertook to incur expenses in connection therewith, the beneficiary shall indemnify him for his reasonable expenses, including any obligations to a third party, and where the benefactor suffered any property damages due to such act, the Court may order the payment of damages to the benefactor, where such order is seen as just in light of the circumstances.

As such, it is evident that in practice, the application is wider than under Jewish law, which does not, as will be recalled, impose a sanction upon a person who did not rescue his fellow.

There are those who argue that Israeli case law accords significant weight to the autonomy of the individual, and it therefore has not recognized a general duty to rescue, even after passage of the Law, i.e., the Law does not constitute an expression of a general duty to rescue, but of a relatively limited and specific arrangement.[97] Thus, for example, Justice Eliezer Rivlin (who later became Deputy President) of the Supreme Court of Israel, noted:

---

[92] CrA 119/93 Lawrence v. State of Israel 48(4) IsrSC 1 (1994).
[93] Gilead, *supra* note 91, at 343.
[94] "You Shall Not Stand Idly by Your Neighbor's Blood" Law, 5758–1998, SH 245.
[95] Hendel, *supra* note 89, at 254; GILEAD, *supra* note 91, at 343; ARIEL PORAT, TORTS vol. 1, 185 (2013) (Heb.).
[96] Hendel contends that in light of the purpose of the legislation, the person who attempted to rescue cannot be in a worse situation vis-à-vis a person who was apathetic. He therefore argues that the rescuer must enjoy a type of immunity, although immunity which is not total. It will not apply, he suggests, in the case in which there was gross negligence, or recklessness or in a case of absence of good faith. Hendel proposes regulating this protection in legislation. *See* Hendel, *supra* note 89, at 270–71.
[97] GILEAD, *supra* note 91, at 344.

We do not recognize a general duty applying to every person, to act to prevent the realization of risks that are liable to harm others, due to the fact that imposition of such a duty is liable to be a serious breach of a person's liberty and autonomy. Therefore, tortious liability for a pure omission will be imposed only when the defendant had a duty to act.[98]

Is this law enforced? A person was convicted by an Israeli court and fined NIS 2000 (about $650) in a case in which he fled the scene, even though he witnessed an assault of another person perpetrated by his friends, leaving the victim lying unconscious and bleeding on the ground.[99] Another example is provided by the case in which a person was a witness to a stabbing incident. The victim, in the course of the incident, called out to this person for help, who stood beside the stabber and ignored the victim. He subsequently left the victim's apartment, skipping over the victim who lay prone on the floor in a pool of blood, with his guts spilling out. The person was convicted under the "You Shall Not Stand Idly by Your Neighbor's Blood" Law.[100] However, these examples are not representative: the Law is hardly ever invoked, to the extent that Supreme Court Justice Neal Hendel in his article says that the Law today is in fact declarative,[101] and other Justices have agreed with him and so stated in their judgments.[102] In Israeli law one can also find the aspect of restitution and compensation for damages for a person who performed a rescue, but this is through other routes, and not necessarily through this Law.[103]

---

[98] CA 2625/02 Nahum v. Doronbaum 58(3) IsrSC 385, 419 (2004). For discussion, see GILEAD, *supra* note 91, at 344. The Court did not acccept the position of Justice Rivlin concerning the appropriate scope of the liability of a lawyer to prevent harm befalling a person who is not his client (GILEAD, *ibid.* at note 232).

[99] CrF (Tel Aviv) 1550/01 State of Israel v. Kogan (published in Nevo database, 07.07.2003).

[100] CrF (Tel Aviv) 40142/06 State of Israel v. Partouche (published in Nevo database, 10.08.2007).

[101] Hendel, *supra* note 89, at 269–70.

[102] See, e.g., CA (Haifa) 1404/05 Bronkash v. Marco Keren, para. 10 of the judgment of Wasserkrug J. (published in Nevo database, 09.05.2006): "The duty to rescue under this law is indeed an independent statutory obligation. In the criminal field, which is the field that could render the substance of the said duty meaningful, the penal sanction imposed according to its provisions upon the person who is in breach of this duty is a fine only. The obvious conclusion is that the Law is primarily of a declarative nature. In the field of torts, which belongs in the civil domain, there may be room to argue that despite the abovesaid, it will be possible to file a claim for damages – in that breach of the said **criminal duty** may constitute the basis for the tort of a breach of a statutory duty; however, it is also doubtful whether this possibility can be pursued, in light of the formulation of the provision. In any case, the conclusion with respect to the said duty being primarily declarative still pertains" (see Neal Hendel, *The "You Shall Not Stand Idly by Your Neighbor's Blood" Law: Inspiration and Reality*, 16 MEHKEREI MISHPAT 229 (2000) (Heb.)).

[103] This refers to cases involving an act of rescue in which a person acted as a Good Samaritan and incurred expenses as a result thereof. Section 5(a) of the Unjust Enrichment Law 5739–1979 grants a volunteer the right to claim his costs from the other person. There is also a possibility of suing the state for the damages of a volunteer under sec. 298 of the National Insurance Law [Consolidated Version] 1995. There seems to be a willingness on the part of judges to define instances of rescue in which the rescuer was injured as accidents that are covered by the Road Accident Victims Compensation Law 5735–1975 in order to provide compensation for the

Enforcement of the "You Shall Not Stand Idly by Your Neighbor's Blood" Law constitutes part of the general discourse on the enforcement of moral and religious norms. In this context, Justice Haim Cohn wrote as follows:

> if the moral commandments of the Bible were to become legal norms: in non-religious systems of law the moral norms cannot be legal norms, because the mechanisms of the law are not capable of – and therefore not interested in – reaching what is in a person's heart and what is going on inside him. This is not the case with Divine law: it adds to the moral precept the warning, "Thou shalt fear thy Lord" (Leviticus 19:14 etc.), because God "[who] is cognizant of thy secret thoughts; similarly in all actions where it is given only to the heart of him who does it [to know the motive], and other people have no insight into it" (Rashi, *ad loc.*) will exact retribution.[104]

Justice Cohn's words make us aware of the complexity of translating religious norms into secular law. This also appies to the argument between Prof. Statman and Justice Hendel in their articles on a full duty to rescue in tort law: Statman contends that the distinction between acts and omission is liable to change in light of our conception of the value of the sanctity of life. Because an active trend of the Supreme Court to anyway extend liability in tort law is evident in many cases, the next stage, from our perspective, will therefore be to recognize pure omission as a basis of obligation in cases of non-performance of a simple rescue.[105] Justice Hendel, on the other hand, argues that it is difficult to justify the imposition of full liability on a person who was in breach of a duty to rescue in tort law, and he therefore proposes another model – the creation of a duty to rescue as an independent duty, with its own rules.[106] As a source for this he proposes religious law, which could constitute a bridge between law and morality:

rescuers. *See, e.g.,* CA (Haifa District) 407/93 Dahan v. Ararat Insurance Co. Ltd. (unpublished); CA 1404/05, *supra* note 102. According to one opinion, the tort of breach of statutory duty can also serve as a basis for recognizing such claims, the statutory duty being the "You Shall Not Stand Idly by Your Neighbor's Blood" Law (para. 19 of the opinion of Justice Cheshin, CrA 2417/99 Har Shefi v. State of Israel 55(2) IsrSC 735 (2001)). For an opposing view, see Judge Yitzhak Cohen in CA 1404/05, *ibid.*

[104] H. COHN, THE LAW 95 (2nd ed., 1997) (Heb). These words were also quoted by Justice J. Tirkel in the framework of his discussion of not preventing the commission of a felony with respect to the distinction between a moral obligation and a statutory duty, and the difficulty of enforcing moral norms. In his opinion, the section regarding non-prevention of a felony must be interpreted narrowly, without detracting from its moral validity, and the "You Shall Not Stand Idly by Your Neighbor's Blood" Law ought to be enforced (CrA 2417/99, *supra* note 104).

[105] Daniel Statman, *"Do Not Stand Idly by Your Neighbor's Blood" – From a Duty of Care to a "Good Samaritan" Duty*, 15 MEHKEREI MISHPAT 89, 101–07 (1999) (Heb.).

[106] Hendel, *supra* note 89. Hendel explains that the Civil Wrongs Ordinance does not contain a particular tort of not acting. Hence, if the court wishes to impose liability, it must do so in the framework of an extension of the tort of negligence. The starting point for determining liability in tort is that a person had an obligation to act in a certain way, and the emphasis is on the conduct of the defendant and the basis for the obligation that binds him, whereas in cases of non-rescue, the focus is on the distress of the person being rescued, and his need. The focus

In order to create a duty to rescue, the law requires an external source, a source with inspiration, status and recognition, which has the ability to create an independent duty to rescue, not within the framework of tort law. What is required is a specific statutory provision; the legal policy of the courts will not suffice. The source of the duty must be one that enjoys wide social consensus. The religious law is an excellent source for fulfilling these requirements. It has a status that allows it to act as a kind of bridge between law and morality, between the real and the ideal. It is also in a sufficiently strong position to overcome the opposition of the system, due to its legal heritage, to the adoption of a duty to rescue. There may be other sources which can serve as the basis for a duty to rescue and enable its acceptance by a legal system that denied it in the past, but this is not what actually happened. An independent formulation of the duty to rescue, albeit only in name, which points to a religious source such as the Good Samaritan Law in the United States and the "You Shall Not Stand Idly by your Neighbor's Blood" Law in Israel, will add moral and historical legitimacy to the adoption of a duty to rescue in the legal system.[107]

Has the Israeli Law of 1998, which was indeed intended to be based on Jewish religious law, succeeded in its task? The legislator attempted to reflect the delicate balances achieved by the Jewish rabbinic authorities, including Maimonides, but the Law that was finally passed did not necessarily succeed in creating a successful balance; it may therefore not be surprising that the Law is almost never applied in Israeli secular civil courts, and that it is borderline declarative law. The Law stipulates a sanction and allows for indemnity, unlike Jewish law but like the European systems of law; it does, however, appear to extend the scope of the Law further than Maimonides, who provided for immunity on the one hand, but did not set a sanction on the other. As stated, Maimonides emphasizes that there is indeed a duty to rescue, and that this is a serious religious-legal duty irrespective of the fact that it does not bear a sanction; its application is fairly limited, however, from the non-religious legal perspective. Hence it is not certain that Israeli law absorbed the complexity of the religious law as reflected in Maimonides' approach, in the attempt of the former to base itself in fact on the Jewish religious law. Thus, despite aspirations of the modern legislators to reflect the rationales of the Jewish law sages, we are not sure that they actually succeeded in doing so. It is tempting to say,

---

moves from the conduct of the defendant to the need of the person being rescued. Moreover, even theories that justify imposing a duty to rescue (the communitarian, economic, and feminist theories) struggle to justify the imposition of liability in tort when there is no connection between the rescuer and the person being rescued (*ibid.* at 264–66). Therefore, according to Hendel J., there is a problem with justifying a duty to rescue as part of tort law. He concludes that a duty to rescue of another type must be created (*ibid.* at 266). He brings an example of a baby who falls into a pool and begins to drown, while a stranger who is standing by the pool does nothing, even though he could rescue the baby without endangering himself. According to Hendel, that person could be held liable under a law which is different from tort law. The solution, in his opinion, is to create a duty to rescue as an independent duty, with its own rules. This is a less broad and less strict obligation than under tort law (*ibid.* at 267).

[107] *Ibid.* at 268.

therefore, that the Israeli Law was not at all successful, and did not succeed in integrating religious law in particular. Obviously a full discussion of this question must include, *inter alia*, the question of the gap between declaration and enforcement, given that there are cases in which legislation sets down laws which are not centered on enforcement, such that the success is measured not necessarily by enforcement but rather by dissemination of the new norm to the entire population and the ability of the population to change its conduct even without massive enforcement. All these issues are clearly beyond the scope of this work, and we have come to no firm conclusions on these questions. It may possibly be assumed – no more than that – that only minimal enforcement in the case of the "You Shall Not Stand Idly by your Neighbor's Blood" Law was not the original intention or goal, and that the law was not intended merely for declarative purposes. Therefore, according to this parameter at least, the attempt to draw upon norms from religious law has not been particularly successful, but we will leave the question open, with room for other opinions.

In any case, what can be inferred from this attempt on the part of the Israeli legislator is that apparently, there is a lesson to be learnt in the opposite direction – a lesson according to which it is not always worthwhile to learn from Jewish law and from Maimonides' approach for the purpose of modern law; alternatively this should be done with utmost caution, which may not have been exercised in this case.

How will we know when to draw lessons from religious Jewish law for modern secular law and when not to do so? The lessons must always be cautious; in this case, however, it is possible that the writing was on the wall, at least for those who study Jewish law in general, and Maimonides' approach in particular, with a careful eye. The duty to rescue, as we have said, is a legal duty according to Maimonides, but an extremely limited one, and *inter alia* it does not include the imposition of a fine or compensation. Unlike other categories, the religious dimension of the duty to rescue is very central and particularly serious. The attempt to transcribe this duty into a law that is not religious, to place sanction at its center, and of course, to enact a law without a religious dimension – which is the heart and center of religious law – is extremely problematic; it is probably not surprising that at least with respect to practical implementation of the Law, it may really not have succeeded. An important lesson derives from this: if there is at all room to transfer norms from religious law to a law that is not religious, this must be done with extreme caution, and such transfer should be avoided if the central consideration on which the religious norm is founded is in fact a religious consideration rather than one that could form the center of a secular law, such as the goals of tort law that have often been mentioned in this work, including deterrence and prevention, corrective justice and removal of wrongs, or distributive justice. All these have played a secondary role in the religious duty to rescue in general, and the duty according to Maimonides in particular, as finds expression in its limited legal application.

2 Bridging between Seemingly Dissimilar Approaches

Our basic assumption is that it is a positive thing to attempt to bridge between approaches that appear to be dissimilar and even contradictory, not with brute force but in a rational way, and that it is necessary to establish in each case whether the outcome of that bridging is good and appropriate. In our opinion, Maimonides' approach to tort law succeeds in presenting several interesting bridges between contemporary approaches that seem remote from each other – some of them major approaches that are connected to the theory of tort law and of law in general, and some of them more particularistic. This is an additional contribution – an extremely important one in our opinion – of the Maimonidean tort theory to the modern conversation in general, and of the cautious but rational possibility of learning something from a religious, ancient law for modern, up-to-date law.

(a) Between Economics and Morality

In previous chapters we examined Maimonides' approach, which in pluralistic fashion combines various monistic goals of tort law, and primarily, the removal of wrong and the prevention of harm, i.e., a combination of the moral consideration of corrective justice and the deterrent-economic-consequentialist-preventative consideration; his approach includes distributive and religious considerations as well. Neither is his conception of justice devoid of consequentialist considerations. Indeed, Maimonides regards justice as one of the elements of the consequentialist way of thinking.[108] In doing so, he does take into account consequentialist considerations, but clearly subjugates himself to deontological constraints. This method may provide unexpected support for contemporary law and economics scholars who argue that being efficient does not necessarily mean being immoral. Such a linkage between economics and morality takes the traditional deontological (corrective justice) approach with the consequentialist approach and sorts each into the suitable category of damages. In this way, the pluralistic-differential discourse may teach us a different way of thinking, i.e., bridging contradictory monistic approaches by emphasizing the advantages of each of them, acknowledging the importance and the uniqueness of each of them, and redesigning each of them by implementing the rationales of different monistic approaches in different types of (not only tort) events. Thus, we also think that both the monistic and the pluralistic discourse may be enriched from this dialogue.

Recently, such a pluralistic discourse, which attempts broadly to create a bridge between the deontological and the consequentialist theories, has been initiated by

---

[108] *See* what Maimonides writes in the GUIDE 3:40 on the fact that justice figures in his consequentialist explanations there, and in his words, "These laws contain considerations of justice to which I will draw attention."

Eyal Zamir and Barak Medina.[109] They posit the combination of economic methodology and deontological morality through the explicit and direct introduction of moral constraints into economic models. They also argue that it is possible to rectify the normative flaws of economic analysis without abandoning its methodological advantages. Zamir and Medina provide examples of the implementation of their proposed approach in several legal fields, including contract law, freedom of speech, antidiscrimination law, the fight against terrorism, and legal paternalism. Their illustrations do not include an analysis of tort law, although such an analysis may be valuable in this discourse, especially given the fact that Coase, Calabresi, and Posner – the founding fathers of the economic analysis of law – and Weinrib, the leading scholar in the field of corrective justice in private law, all focus on the analysis of tort law.

Although we saw that there are essays that deal with the pluralistic approach to tort law, they do not provide a bridge in the same broad manner as Zamir and Medina. The present book analyzed this combination in tort law as well, and suggested that the Maimonidean method of incorporation of moral considerations into consequentialist-social models, which is undertaken in the present book, can be valuable in this discourse. It would indeed appear that Maimonides' pluralistic-differential approach, although basic and less developed than the contemporary approaches (albeit extremely developed for the period in which it was written), and which conducts a conversation with jurisprudential doctrines both contemporary and pre-modern, can open such a discourse with respect to tort law as well, in a slightly different way from the existing modern pluralistic theories which are either less broad or which do not attempt nor presume to constitute a bridge between consequentialist and deontological approaches.

(b) Blurring the Distinction between Civil and Criminal

In ancient legal systems such as Jewish law, criminal law and tort law were interwoven, as we saw, for example, in Maimonides' Book of Torts in the *Code*, which begins with more classical tort rulings in today's terms, proceeds to become more criminal in modern terms, finally ending with Laws of Murderers and Preservation of Life. Penal and tort sanctions are often mixed together. In modern law, the process of separation of the two has apparently been a gradual one. We can still find quite a few remnants of criminal law within tort law, such as with respect to deterrence in general (not necessarily in the economic context, but more in the traditional context); with respect to punitive damages, albeit according to the traditional reasoning that they are awarded in cases of malicious and intentional acts;[110] in laws of evidence, which in various jurisdictions allow for the use, in some

---
[109] ZAMIR & MEDINA, *supra* note 36.
[110] See *supra* Chapter 4, and a discussion of the various functions of punitive damages and the various reasons for this institution, *infra* Chapter 9, in Calabresi's insights.

form or another, of evidence that was obtained in a criminal process, to save having to present this evidence again in the subsequent civil-tort process due to the difference in the burden of proof (beyond reasonable doubt in the criminal process as opposed to the balance of probability in the civil process)[111] etc. Maimonides' approach presents a mixture of the two, as we have seen throughout this work and mentioned in several places, including in this chapter (for example, with respect to intention and in the course of a quarrel in the Laws of Wounding, or compensation as opposed to fine etc.).

We do not intend to argue that this combination is suited in its original form to modern law. It is very possible that it is not suited, as some may think, or that it is suited only partially, as a type of intermediate area underlying which are civil-penal sanctions, as we saw, for example, in the discussion of the approach of Kenneth Mann, who mentions the implementation of these intermediate sanctions either by the state, with respect to civil fines, or by the individual, with respect to punitive damages.[112] Also of interest here is the approach of Guido Calabresi in his new book, in which he mentions recourse to tort law as an alternative to criminal law in cases in which society very much wishes to deter but has good reasons for not invoking criminal law. As he explains later in Chapter 9 of this book in this context, it is sometimes possible to do certain things in the civil arena which would not be possible if the matter were to be classified as criminal. Punitive damages can sometimes be used that way.[113]

The bridge between criminal law and torts that manifests itself in Maimonides' approach can and should stimulate thoughts about such a combination in our day as well. Contemporary positive law sometimes presents such combinations as already extant, and the literature at times presents them as ideal. As for the actual impact on tort law, we have seen several proposals in Section C.1.c, such as the introduction of *mens rea* – even if only partially – to the tort of assault on a person and more. But our goal, as stated, is not necessarily to identify specific rulings that should be adopted unchanged by modern law, but rather, to broaden the framework of the discourse and the thinking with respect to the possible blurring of the boundaries between the criminal and the civil-tort systems. As in every case of blurring between fields, this has both advantages and disadvantages, but we must not shrink from the discourse, and we must not ignore the possible future developments that may result from this thinking.

---

[111] Which is an invocation of an *a fortiori* argument that circumvents the principle that the judge can only consider what is before him, and therefore must consider the evidence himself in the trial court in making his decision, and not rely on another court that heard or saw the evidence. See, e.g., sec. 42A(a) of the Evidence Ordinance [New Version] (Isr.).

[112] Kenneth Mann, *Punitive Civil Sanctions: The Middleground Between Criminal and Civil Law*. 101 YALE L.J. 1795 (1992). *See* discussion in Chapter 3.

[113] *See* discussion *infra* Chapter 9, as part of the discussion of punitive damages and their purpose in general, and of the approach to use of tort law in light of a reality of refusal to grant a bill of divorce in the Jewish sector: GUIDO CALABRESI, THE FUTURE OF LAW AND ECONOMICS: ESSAYS IN REFORM AND RECOLLECTION 120, 129 (2016).

(c) Possible Bridge between Economic Approaches Based on Fault and Economic Approaches Based on Strict Liability

We have compared Maimonides' approach (in Chapter 5), for example with respect to the EAC test, to Calabresi's cheapest cost avoider that is based on strict liability, and we have discerned no small measure of similarity between the two, even if only with respect to property damages. In the same vein, we have seen that the logic of negligence in its economic sense and in general is relevant to Maimonides in some of the categories of damages and with respect to contributory negligence, where the similarity to the approach of Posner and the Hand formula stood out. Now, these two modern approaches of two of the founding fathers of the economic approach to law in general, and to tort law within law and economics in particular, are completely different, but we saw that Maimonides' approach, which from an overall perspective is both pluralistic and differential, enables one to look at tort law from an interesting vantage point which links the two seemingly contradictory economic approaches in a certain way, but also does not ignore distributive and religious principles. Even in the categories of damages in which Maimonides' approach seems close to that of Calabresi, his ability to separate between the question of *control* (which according to him serves as a test for tort liability) and that of the *standard of care* to be imposed upon the person causing harm, and the application of a standard of negligence (which is similar to that presented by Posner) or an intermediate standard between negligence and strict liability in some of the categories (and not always strict liability like that of Calabresi), opens the way for thinking about *pluralistic differential* approaches today. Such modern law approaches – the creation of which must, in our opinion, be thought about, in order to enrich the pluralistic pool of approaches in tort law beyond those existing today, even if Maimonides' approach is not transcribed unchanged into modern law with its more industrial backdrop and which differs in several aspects from Maimonides' agragian environment in which there was no insurance – are not only more balanced at base, but they also connect rationales which seem diametrically opposed. Thus, a middleground approach such as that of Maimonides proves that the approaches such as those of Calabresi and Posner – who obviously were not aware of the existence of such an approach 800 years before they presented their own – are not as contradictory as they appear to be at first glance, and that it is possible to formulate an approach that forms a bridge between them.

Even if Calabresi and Posner and their supporters would not agree to such a middleground approach, pointing out its drawbacks in general and for our days in particular, and they were to contend that a middleground approach destroys the firm foundation of any radical approach, we are of the opinion that opening up the mind to the creation of pluralistic approaches that achieve a balance between the radical monistic approaches is one of the significant benefits of a full understanding of Maimonides' approach after reading the modern sources, even if that approach is not implemented as it stands.

(d) Bridging Between an Economic Approach and a Social Approach with Respect to Punitive Damages

With respect to the issue of punitive damages too, we have seen an interesting, pluralistic bridging between consequentialist considerations that converse with the economic approach to punitive damages today, i.e., the multiplier approach of Shavell and Polinsky, and other approaches which emphasize more the social consideration, such as the extra-compensatory societal redress approach of Catherine Sharkey.[114] At first glance, the connection between the economic approach to punitive damages that contends that this is compensation that in fact expresses optimal deterrence and not payment over and above the damage, and the social approaches that presume that there is overcompensation for the damage but that it has societal importance, seems remote. Maimonides indicated an approach to what could today be called punitive damages, in respect of double, four-fold and five-fold (theft) payments, and the difference with respect to a thief who in certain matters must make these payments. His approach appears to bridge the different thinking behind these two modern approaches, in that it takes into account, in pluralistic fashion, both economic-consequentialist considerations and societal considerations. Indeed, he created a list of four parameters for imposing criminal sanctions and punitive damages, some of which are more consequentialist-economic and deal with optimal deterrence (such as the risk of being caught or the chances that this is not the first act perpetrated by the offender-injurer, although we have also mentioned differences between these considerations and the multiplier approach) and some of which are more moral-societal (such as the severity of the act).

Beyond the need for balanced, mediational thinking here as well, such an intermediate approach could possibly participate actively in the present discourse in the United States on the role of punitive damages, following the acceptance in recent years by the federal courts of the economic rationale in the rulings of Judges Calabresi and Posner – amongst the founding fathers of the economic approach to law – as opposed to its rejection in a string of rulings of the Supreme Court.[115]

D. CONCLUSION

In this chapter, we in fact completed a journey in two directions that was undertaken throughout the entire book:

(a) *From modern law to Maimonides' approach*: we turned to the existing modern monistic approaches in order to understand that Maimonides is not a monist; we turned to the existing modern pluralistic approaches

---

[114] *See* Chapter 5.
[115] *Ibid*. And *see also* the discussion of Calabresi's insights *infra*, Chapter 9, regarding punitive damages.

in order to understand the essence of Maimonides' pluralistic-differentialist approach, which does not accord permanent priority to a particular goal and for each group of cases, but neither does it determine the goal in each case on an individual basis.

(b) *From Maimonides' approach to modern law*: we turned to Maimonides' approach in order to raise the possibility of creating a pluralistic-differential approach, which differs from the existing pluralistic approaches. We also discussed the possible lessons that modern law may derive from various elements of Maimonides' tort theory, even if this theory should not be transcribed unchanged as a basis for modern law, due to the differences in time, place, and way of thinking. A pluralistic-differential theory such as that presented by Maimonides is not only balanced at base, but it can also serve as a source of inspiration, *mutatis mutandis* and with the appropriate caution, as to how to bridge between approaches that seem fundamentally remote from each other, as was demonstrated on various planes.

Indeed, as the title of this book indicates, the Maimonidean theory is capable of conducting a dialogue with both monistic and pluralistic contemporary tort theories, bringing the different dimensions into the mix: law, religion, economics, and morality.

This dialogue between Maimonides and contemporary tort theories provides an opening – wide, according to some, but others say narrow – for contemporary scholars to consider other ways to enrich the current tort theory theories. However, this proposed further research begins at the precise point at which our book ends; perhaps it will be conducted by others.

9

Reflections on Maimonides' Tort Theory

Guido Calabresi

A. "WE IMAGINE THE PAST TO REMEMBER THE FUTURE" – BETWEEN LAW, ECONOMICS, AND JUSTICE IN OUR ERA AND ACCORDING TO MAIMONIDES

1 *Preface*

My first point is a caveat: There is always a danger of reading ancient texts and ancient scholars in modern ways; we can't help it. The authors show in this book that Maimonides was a precursor of law and economics. If you look at what the authors say people said of Maimonides in the nineteenth century, you see that they tried to make him a fault scholar,[1] because the nineteenth century was so concerned with fault. So today, there is nothing strange about reading Maimonides to be a precursor of law and economics, because so much of what is going on in this area

---

Senior Judge, United States Court of Appeals for the Second Circuit; Sterling Professor Emeritus of Law and Professorial Lecturer in Law, Yale Law School. I thank Matteo Godi, my law clerk during the 2018–19 term, for his edits and comments. The first part of this chapter is based on: Guido Calabresi "We Imagine the Past to Remember the Future" – Between Law, Economics, and Justice in Our Era and according to Maimonides, 26 YALE J. L. & HUMANITIES 135 (2014), a response to Yuval Sinai & Benjamin Shmueli, *Calabresi's and Maimonides's Tort Law Theories – A comparative Analysis and A Preliminary Sketch of a Modern Model of Differential Pluralistic Tort Liability based on the Two Theories*, 26 YALE J.L. & HUMAN. 59 (2014), following a lecture at a panel on "Tort Law in a Comparative Context," the 17th International Conference of the Jewish Law Association, Yale Law School, August 1, 2012. The second part of this chapter is based on a response to Benjamin Shmueli & Yuval Sinai, *A Contemporary View on the Maimonidean Tort Theory: A Consequentialist Analysis of Punitive Damages as a Test Case,* following a lecture at a panel on "A Contemporary View of the Maimonidean Tort Theory – Law, Religion, Economics and Morality," Wolff Lecture 2016, Institute on Religion, Law & Lawyer's Work, Fordham Law, 1.26.16. The authors have attempted to convert Judge Calabresi's spoken response into written form. As a result, not all of the language is Judge Calabresi's.

[1] *Supra* Chapter 2.

of law is that way. Is it right or is it not? Alex Bickel often said (quoting Namier[2]): "we imagine the past to remember the future."[3] And there is something of that in what is going on in this book. But that only helps us to understand things which were there. How known they were to the people who lived there, in their own time, is less clear.

Despite this caveat, there clearly is a lot in what Maimonides was doing which can be viewed as profoundly modern. To the extent that the authors say, I think correctly, that some of the things that I said (seemingly first in the United States) in the last half of the last century were presaged and said first by Maimonides,[4] I have got to say that that gives me much more pleasure than my dear friend's Izhak England finding that some of the things were said by some German scholar in the nineteenth century. For any number of reasons, I am much more pleased to be presaged by Maimonides.

2 Empirical Differences in Time and Their Implications

It is very important, as the authors have said, to distinguish between particular results in particular situations that Maimonides described and his approach, because particular results may differ depending on the empirical situation of the time.[5] There is nothing strange with people in the nineteenth century using "assumption of risk" to conclude that the workers, in situations in which they are believed to be better able to avoid the harm, should be the bearers of the loss. Conversely, in the twentieth century, we moved to the opposite view. For a judge that is a problem because a judge has to deal with all the old precedents. That is why Fleming James, my teacher, wanted to get rid of assumption of risk as a doctrine, and substitute for it the same thing under another name – so that the precedents would not be there and we could use the new empirical viewpoint.

And so when one describes Maimonides's treatment of the ladder accident as an act of God[6] or discusses the question of whether *respondeat superior* should apply as to slave and master,[7] one must realize that all of those things may well have been

---

[2] LEWIS B. NAMIER, CONFLICTS: STUDIES IN CONTEMPORARY HISTORY 69–70 (1942) ("When discoursing or writing about history, [people] imagine it in terms of their own experience, and when trying to gauge the future they cite supposed analogies from the past: till, by double process of repetition, they imagine the past and remember the future").
[3] ALEXANDER M. BICKEL, THE SUPREME COURT AND THE IDEA OF PROGRESS 13 (1970) (quoting Namier's discussion of history with approval in an analysis of judicial lawmaking).
[4] See supra Chapter 5, Section C.1 and Chapter 7, Section A.
[5] See supra Chapter 7, Section B.3.
[6] See Code, Laws of Wounding and Damaging 6:4 (if one is climbing a ladder and a rung slips from under him and it falls and causes damage). For a detailed discussion supra Chapter 7, Section A.1.
[7] See CODE, Laws of Theft 1:9 (the exemption of the master from damage caused by his slave). For a detailed discussion *supra* Chapter 2, Section C.3, and Chapter 6, Section A.

due to empirical differences between that time and now. As such, they are much less important than whether one is asking the same kind of question or not.

Distributional consequences can also be very different in different times. The authors have pointed this out, both in terms of the availability of insurance and of other things,[8] and have correctly explained that these differences might well lead one to conclude that Calabresi would do what Maimonides argued for had Calabresi been there then.[9]

3 Are there Differences between the Differential Liability and the Cheapest Cost Avoider/Best Decision Maker Doctrines?

I would rather focus on the differences that the authors have pointed out between Maimonides's point of view and mine – because I think in fact they are less great than they might appear.

First, regarding Maimonides's "differential liability approach", according to which for each group of cases there is a different standard (negligence, strict liability, or some intermediate standard) as appropriate.[10] There are different ways of looking at that. One is that there were some areas in which Maimonides seemed to rely on fault more than on strict liability, while the authors say I relied on strict liability (whether on injurer or on victim) throughout.[11] However, one may characterize this differently. I had thought from the beginning that there were some areas where strict liability did not work. Medical malpractice was one of them.[12]

The question of whether those areas are big or small is an empirical one, not a difference in approach. More importantly, does Maimonides's partial liability approach allow splitting between parties?[13] Can we split between one party and another and use fault to some extent and non-fault to some extent as well (such as in the *tam* ox issue)? One must consider that when I started writing, I was writing in a context, specifically in an Anglo-American and American context, which was very peculiar. Tort law in the United States at that time was one of "all or nothing." One put the loss on one party or on the other. One did not split. That was a very deep common law tradition – it is hard to say what was the reasoning behind it, but it was always there – and it was under those circumstances that I was writing.

Later on, I wrote a little article[14] in which I said that things were happening in American Tort law that were as important a change as the coming of insurance had

---

[8] See *supra* Chapter 7, Section B.3.
[9] Ibid.
[10] See *supra* Chapter 7.
[11] See *supra* Chapters 5 and 6.
[12] See Guido Calabresi, *The Problem of Malpractice: Trying to Round Out the Circle*, 27 U. TORONTO L.J. 131 (1977).
[13] See *supra* Chapters 5, Section B.1.c, and 6, Section E.
[14] Guido Calabresi & Jeffrey O. Cooper, *New Directions in Tort Law*, 859 VAL. U. L. REV. 30 (1996).

been at the beginning of the twentieth century. This was the coming of splitting. Tort law, now and in the future, had to be analyzed in view of the fact that it no longer required an "all or nothing" placing of the loss on one side or on the other.

This was partly due to the coming of so-called comparative negligence.[15] But it also followed from any number of other things, statistical cause being one of them. Indeed, I have been saying in my teaching – I haven't written it – that we may even get to a kind of science fiction of partial proximate cause. In time we may no longer say "you are the proximate cause" or "you are not." There may come to be situations in which we will say, "you are more of a proximate cause" or "less," and therefore split to some degree. One finds some presages of this idea in Maimonides.

However, more importantly, we must ask: "what does comparative negligence compare"? We call it comparative negligence, but it isn't. In the United States, what is called comparative negligence is also comparative responsibility. And this has been said by court after court.[16] Sometimes it is even comparative non-fault. Indeed, the law of New York has expressly said that one may split according to comparative non-fault.[17]

When one does that, there is also the possibility of employing a comparative responsibility in which one takes into account whether one party is, because of its negligence, the cheapest decider, the least cost avoider, the best decision maker. And the moment one does that, one has a system which is extraordinarily like Maimonides's – one in which, because somebody is at fault, he becomes (to some extent) the best decision maker, and so damages are split. It means that according to him, indeed, applying the cheapest cost avoider or the best decision maker approach does not necessarily mean imposing strict liability on the avoider or decision maker; damages can be split. For that reason, in my recent teaching, I say that when people say "comparative negligence has won over non-fault, and non-fault-splitting," they are too simplistic. Rather, comparative negligence may represent a more sophisticated splitting in which non-fault combines with fault to form the basis for determining who is the better decision maker. It may well be that it is this approach that has been winning out in the United States. And this approach is also extraordinarily like Maimonides.

Nonetheless, one should be careful, because to the extent that too much splitting, or even too much consideration of the possibility of splitting, becomes extremely expensive in an administrative sense we may choose not to do it. Thus, Judith Kaye, the great Chief Judge of New York, said in a decision applying statistical cause that

---

[15] See supra Chapter 5.
[16] See, e.g., Miller v. Am. President Lines, Ltd., 989 F.2d. 1450, 1459 (6th Cir. 1993); Moffat v. Caroll, 640 A.2d 169, 175 (Del. 1994). See also, RESTATEMENT OF TORTS (THIRD): APPOINTMENT OF LIABILITY § 8 (2000).
[17] See Laws of 1975, Ch. 69 (1975), codified in N.Y. C.P.L.R. 1411–13. The Report of the Judicial Conference explained that in the new statute the phrase "culpable conduct" was "used instead of 'negligent conduct' because this article will apply to cases where the conduct of one or more of the parties will be found to be not negligent, but will nonetheless be a factor in determining the amount of damages." 21 ADMIN. BD. of the Judicial Conference ANN. REP. 240 (1976).

there are some things we won't let the defendant prove, because it is just too costly do it.[18] So the question of whether, when one is dealing with only two people, as Maimonides did, it was cheap enough to do it but in other circumstances it may not be, is again an empirical question, not one of "approach."

4 On Justice and Deontological Considerations

The authors show that Maimonides integrates into his tort theory both deontological and economic-consequentialist considerations.[19] Well, I do not talk deontologically, but that does not mean that much of what I have written does not have elements in it that are very similar to deontological analysis. For instance, I have written in "Toward a Unified Theory of Torts"[20] that at any given moment there will be expectations that arise from systems that were established because of their economic consequences. These expectations lead people to believe that they have a right to recover. As a result of this, we think they should recover, even though in that situation their recovery isn't economically justified.[21] I have analyzed in these terms the great opinion of the eighteenth Century, *Scott v. Shepherd*,[22] the flying squib case, and suggested that this is why the case had to come out as it did.

I might ask, did such "expectations" arise in this way, or did they arise not from economic reasons but directly for deontological reasons? Who knows. Consider the old debate: is the reason for kosher that certain meats were dangerous, as Maimonides himself wrote in *The Guide for the Perplexed*,[23] and it was efficient to prohibit them, or were they prohibited for independent reasons? Today it doesn't matter: such rules come to have a life of their own. For a long time, Catholics didn't eat meat on Friday. The original reason for this pretty clearly was to give a subsidy in a certain century to the fishing industry in Portugal. But this didn't matter after a while, because the rule got a life of its own. Thus, one can talk of such things deontologically or one can talk of them using other words, but it isn't really that different.

More importantly is the fact that often, if we are to do truly sophisticated economic analysis, we must take into account not just the effect on the parties to a deal but also on people outside the deal. People sometimes say that, "even if someone is willing to sell his or her body or take a risk, such behavior cannot be permitted." They give paternalistic reasons or say it is against God's will. I don't much think that's what going on. I think these are other ways of saying that there are many people who are offended, who are hurt morally, if someone sells

---

[18] Hymonovitz v. Eli Lily & Co., 73 N.Y.2d 487 (1989).
[19] See *supra* Chapters 3–5.
[20] Guido Calabresi, *Toward a Unified Theory of Torts*, 1:3 JOURNAL OF TORT LAW, Article 1 (2007).
[21] *Ibid.* at 6.
[22] 3 Wils. 403, Common Pleas (1773) 96 Eng. Rep. 525 (K.B.).
[23] MAIMONIDES, THE GUIDE FOR THE PERPLEXED 3:48 [hereinafter: GUIDE].

himself or herself into slavery.[24] And to ignore these costs, which traditionally economists have not taken into account, is a mistake. It is a pure mistake in economics. That's what I am writing about now, because these are as much costs as any direct harm to me. It is as much part of my utility function that I am offended by the fact that you have sold yourself, as it would be if I sold myself. And that cost must be taken into account if one is to seek a truly complete efficiency system.

The reason why we will not let certain things be sold in the market is because others are offended by such sales.[25] Now one can call it "God's will," which is one very powerful way of speaking (and, to the extent one is religious, one may well talk of it that way). Or one can use economic language – that something that is happening creates a moral cost that must be taken into account (which is a very secular and utilitarian way of speaking). In fact, we can almost always speak either way to describe what is going on. And the choice of language depends on what describes it best for us, what resonates most to the audience to whom we are speaking.

I tend to write, because I am in an American context, in the more economic way, and yet the result, the analysis, is not that different from Maimonides. This is because Maimonides always seems to ask: "Does it cost too much? Is taking my offense into account too harmful in terms of the result? Or is it not?" And when he does that, we see that the analysis is very much the same as mine.

In fact, Maimonides himself wrote that "Whether the punishment is great or small, the pain inflicted intense or less intense, depends on the following four conditions."[26] Of these, the first condition, "[t]he greatness of the sin," is directly relevant.[27] "Actions that cause great harm are punished severely, whilst actions that cause little harm are punished less severely."[28] It seems that this statement (taking into account the cost and the harm caused by the offense)[29] reflects considerations quite similar to my analysis.[30]

To put it another way, the object of law, as Maimonides said very clearly, is justice.[31] But justice, as Maimonides clearly saw, also includes these economic

---

[24] On the rule of inalienability see generally, e.g.: Guido Calabresi & A. Douglas Melamed, *Property Rules, Liability Rules, and Inalienability: One View of the Cathedral*, 85 HARV. L. REV. 1089 (1972); Susan Rose-Ackerman, *Inalienability and the Theory of Property Rights*, 85 COLUM. L. REV. 931 (1985).
[25] GUIDO CALABRESI, THE FUTURE OF LAW AND ECONOMICS: ESSAYS IN REFORM AND RECOLLECTION (2016) [hereinafter CALABRESI, THE FUTURE OF LAW AND ECONOMICS].
[26] GUIDE 3:41.
[27] Ibid. For a detailed discussion see supra Chapter 5, Section B.2.
[28] Ibid.
[29] See supra Chapter 5, Section C.2 (comparing Maimonides' concept of harm to societal redress extra-compensatory approaches).
[30] For a detailed analysis, see infra Section B of the present Chapter.
[31] See supra Chapters 3–4 (expanding on corrective and distributive justice) and Chapter 5, Sections A and B (expanding on consequentialist and preventative justice).

factors.[32] Justice is not only what in my book *The Costs of Accidents* I call "other Justice."[33] I never meant "other Justice" to be justice as a whole. What I meant by "other Justice" was that we may not be able to explain everything – that there are still issues that go beyond our explanations. But true justice is the whole thing. Justice includes straight traditional economic efficiency, as Maimonides said.[34] It also includes that which one can say is "God's will," or as I might say it, that which results from taking into account what "other people are offended by." And it includes distributional considerations as well.[35]

But, the object of the whole thing, as Maimonides clearly understood, was and remains to make this system of law, like every other, approach justice as much as humans possibly can.

B. A COMBINATION OF GOALS IN PUNITIVE DAMAGES: MAIMONIDES, THE COMMON LAW, AND THE U.S. SUPREME AND STATE COURT RULINGS

1 *Maimonides' Emphasis on Consequentialist Considerations*

It would seem that in the case of criminal sanctions and punitive damages, Maimonides places great emphasis on deterrence and efficiency in the last three of the four parameters he presents: (1) The severity of the crime; (2) the frequency of the crime; (3) the amount of temptation; and (4) the facility with which the act may be done secretly, unseen and unnoticed.[36] While parameters 2 and 4 obviously concern deterrence and efficiency, attention should also be paid to parameter 3. The parameter of temptation is one of simple cost-benefit. Temptation means that a person wants to do something and derives benefit from it; to prevent him from doing that thing, one has to raise the cost of it. If instead of temptation you say: "I would gain $1000 if I did this," then the penalty has to be greater to deter you than if you would only gain $50. Temptation has the same role. Temptation may be money, but it may also be other things. Thus, the Learned Hand cost-benefit test[37] refers to costs but not just in terms of money; in other words, these may very well be temptation in

---

[32] *Supra* Chapter 5.
[33] GUIDO CALABRESI, THE COSTS OF ACCIDENTS: A LEGAL AND ECONOMIC ANALYSIS 78, 81 (1970).
[34] *See supra* Chapter 5 Section A.
[35] For distributional considerations *see*, *e.g.*, Guido Calabresi, *The Complexity of Tort – The Case of Punitive Damages*, in EXPLORING TORT LAW 333, 334 (M. Stuart Madden ed., 2005); Guido Calabresi & Jon T. Hirschoff, *Toward a Test of Strict Liability in Torts*, 81 YALE L.J. 1055, 1077–85 (1972); Calabresi & Melamed, *supra* note 24, at 1114–15 (1972); Guido Calabresi, *The Pointlessness of Pareto: Carrying Coase Further*, 100 YALE L.J. 1211, 1223–29 (1991). *See also supra* Chapter 3 (expanding on distributive justice).
[36] *Guide* 3:41, 580. For a detailed discussion *see supra* Chapter 5.
[37] *See*: Conway v. O'Brien, 111 F.2d 611, 612 (2nd Cir. 1940); United States v. Carroll Towing Co., Inc., 159 F.2d 169, 173 (2nd Cir. 1947); RICHARD A. POSNER, ECONOMIC ANALYSIS OF LAW

Maimonides's sense, rather than money, on one side of the balance. For example, if I enjoy driving, the benefit to me is not that I get money for driving fast, but my pleasure from it! This is exactly what Maimonides said in the parameter of temptation:

> *The amount of temptation.* Only fear of severe punishment restrains us from actions for which there exists a great temptation, either because we have a strong desire for these actions, or are accustomed to them, or feel unhappy without them.[38]

In fact, in terms of a true cost-benefit analysis, it cannot matter whether the costs are monetizable or not because – to the economist – joy, temptation, or feeling bad when deprived of something are all the same thing. They are all part of utility.

The authors also demonstrate the Maimonidean emphasis on the consequentialist dimension when they discuss the laws pertaining to the breaking of the heifer's neck – the religious ritual of slaughtering a heifer, performed by the elders of a city in the vicinity of which the body of a murdered person was found and the murderer has not been found.[39] According to Maimonides, the commotion surrounding the heifer, the activity, and the utterances will rouse the people to search for traces of the criminal.[40] Interestingly, this appears to be a form of group or collective liability – not because the townspeople did anything wrong, but in order to induce them to find the guilty person. Liability is imposed not on the person who can best avoid the accident, but on those who can most readily lead you to the one who can avoid it. This is akin to what I call the best informant, best briber liability.[41]

It is also interesting that a similar logic can be found in ancient English laws that based liability on grounds other than fault. For example, a statute from 1285 provided as follows:

> Cap. I: Forasmuch as from Day to Day, Robberies, Murthers, Burnings, and Theft, be more often used than they have been heretofore, and Felons cannot be attained by the Oath of Jurors, which had rather suffer Strangers to be robbed, and pass without Pain, than to indite the Offenders, of whom great Part be People of the same Country, or at the least, if the Offenders be of another Country, the Receivers be of Places near [...].
>
> Cap. II: And if the Country will not answer for the Bodies of such manner of Offenders, the pain shall be such, that every Country, that is to wit, the People dwelling in the Country, shall be answerable for the Robberies done, and also the Damages; so that the whole Hundred where the Roberry shall be done * * * shall be answerable for the Robberies done. * * * And after that the Felony or Robbery is

---

167–71 (7th Ed., 2007); ROBERT COOTER & THOMAS ULEN, LAW & ECONOMICS 349–53 (6th ed. 2012).
[38] GUIDE 3:41, 580.
[39] *Supra* Chapter 5, Section B.2, referring to Deut. 21 and to the GUIDE 3:40.
[40] GUIDE 3:40, 577.
[41] It is very close to the best decision maker test for liability. *See* Calabresi & Hirschoff, *supra* note 35.

done, the country shall have no longer Space than forty days, within which * * * it shall behove them to agree for the Robbery or Offence, or else that they will answer for the Bodies of the Offenders.[42]

This statute was amended 300 years later, to read:

> [T]hat the Inhabitant and Resiants of every or any such Hundred * * * wherein negligence, fault or defect of pursuit and fresh suit, after hue and cry made, shall happen to be, * * * shall answer and satisfy the one moitey or Half of * * * such sum and sums of money, and damages, and shall [by virtue of 13 Edw. Ist. 2] be recovered or had against * * * the said hundred * * * in which any robbery or felony shall at any time hereafter be committed or done * * *.[43]

A similar provision was contained in the Code of Hammurabi.[44] See also *Clark v. Inhabitants of the Hundred of Blything*, a judgment from 1823.[45] Indeed, this happens all across the law. Why, for example, do we limit the liability of the debtor in bankruptcy and put some liability on creditors like banks? One of the reasons is to let the debtor start again. But another is to cause the banks to close the debtor down before things go too far. The banks are in a good position to stop the debtor.

We are always doing this sort of thing, sometimes imposing the loss on the injurer and sometimes on the person who can give us the information and who has the greater knowledge. In other words, the incentive is directed toward the person who can avoid the damage, and so the objective of deterrence is served. The bank, because it knows it is liable, will say: "I am going to close you down." And the debtor will be more careful, because he knows that he may be closed down. Thus, the reason is not only to find out how risky the situation is, but also to put the loss where it can best have a preventative effect. That is a fundamental part of the law.

Maimonides employed consequentialist methodology in explaining the biblical laws by means of the three different parameters of punishment that constitute optimal deterrence and that lie at the base of criminal sanctions and of punitive damages. He did this in explaining the difference between robbery and theft, and

---

[42] 13 Edw. I Statute 2 (1285). And see HARRY SHULMAN, FLEMING JAMES ET AL., CASES AND MATERIALS ON THE LAW OF TORTS 54 (4th ed., 2003).

[43] 27 Eliz. C. 13 (1585). And see SHULMAN & JAMES, *supra* note 42, at 55.

[44] Sections 22–24, circa 2250 bc. Shulman and James explain that this statute was "requiring compensation of loss by the city and governor in whose jurisdiction a crime was committed, if the brigand was not captured." See SHULMAN & JAMES, *supra* note 42, at 55.

[45] King's Bench, 1823, 3 Dowling & R. 489. As Shulman and James explain, this was an "[a]ction for civil damages under the Riot Acts (9 Geo. 1, c. 22). * * * The intention of the legislature in passing this & the other statutes of the same nature, was twofold: to render the inhabitants of hundreds vigilant for their own sake as well as that of the public, by making them interested in the prevention of offences; and where that is impossible, in the apprehension and conviction of offenders. This particular statute contains provisions which are applicable to both those objects, for section 7 renders the hundred liable to make satisfaction for the injury sustained, & section 9 provides that they shall not be so liable if the offender is apprehended & convicted within six months after commission of the offence." See SHULMAN & JAMES, *supra* note 42, at 55–56.

between double, four-fold, and five-fold compensation in relation to sheep and cattle.[46] This is not the only way one can explain these laws, of course. But what is interesting is that Maimonides chose to explain them by using components of optimal deterrence and consequentialism, and not in any other way.

As the authors point out,[47] it would appear that according to Maimonides, because of the higher societal damage resulting from the large number of cases of sheep and cattle theft, it is necessary to treat these thefts more severely than others. This is in order to lessen the profitability of stealing sheep and cattle and therefore to diminish these prohibited activities. Moreover, the aim in distinguishing between the punitive damages awarded for stealing sheep and those awarded for stealing cattle is directly to provide the correct level of incentives on potential thieves of each. Thus, the authors argue that compensation for the theft of cattle is higher than for the theft of sheep because of the different costs of guarding cattle and sheep.[48]

Now, regardless of whether or not this is empirically correct, it is certainly consequential. That is, we might argue about whether Maimonides had it right as to whether it was worth doing this or not. Today, one might ask whether the outcome would be the same as to sheep and cattle. It may be that Maimonides was empirically wrong. It may be that in the same situation today we might come out the opposite way because the circumstances are now different. For example, in the nineteenth century, people thought of workers as being the best decision makers whereas in the twentieth century they did not think that way, and so workers' compensation was introduced. Therefore, there was nothing wrong *theoretically* when people said: "The law should concentrate on the worker, because the worker can choose whether to work or not." We say today that that was empirically wrong. However, if we were to go back nearer to the time, to the beginning of the nineteenth century, when free workers were genuinely free, it may even conceivably be the case that the nineteenth century decisions were empirically right in their time.

But in the end that is irrelevant, for although in terms of immediate results today it may be empirically correct to say "That's why we do this and that", when we are talking about matters that are centuries old we cannot possibly know the underlying factual context. We adopt an approach, and an explanation for that approach, which is correct in view of the person's statement of what the facts were at that time. He may have been right or he may have been wrong; we cannot possibly say one way or the other. Some historians might say he was right whereas others would say not. Some might say that he made up those facts because he wanted that particular result

---

[46] For a detailed discussion *see supra* Chapter 5.
[47] *Supra* Chapter 5, Section B.2.
[48] *Ibid.* (explaining that it is harder to guard cattle than sheep, and that leads to high costs of guarding, which stem from the greater frequency of thefts. Therefore the raising of cattle becomes more expensive, and the products of the cattle and the services that they provide increase in price. Increasing the compensation lowers the anticipated profit on the part of the thief, and in any case, it reduces the profitability of the theft and increases efficiency).

to benefit his family who were sheep owners. All that may or may not be, but it is irrelevant in this discussion. What matters here is that the approach is the correct one from a theoretical point of view. One of the errors that critics make in looking at the work of ancient and not-so-ancient nineteenth century scholars is that, because the critics believe these scholars to have been empirically wrong on the basis of what we know today, the critics fail to recognize that the model that these scholars applied was a perfectly correct one.

So, apart from whether we think Maimonides was correct in his time, or whether we think he is correct in our time, the key thing is that his model is clearly consequential. What matters here is the methodology. And I therefore agree with the authors that Maimonides was actually formulating a conceptual model which could be used to explain things other than sheep and cattle.

2 Maimonides as Pluralist

Maimonides was, however, also concerned with the fact that victims care about compensation not only in terms of restitution being made for their damages, but also in terms of their relationship to their injurers – that they somehow have a right for restitution to be made by those who have injured them. Now, that is no part of the classic law and economics view of torts. It is very much a part of what I call the "Goldpursky" or "Zipgold" view – a combination of the views of John Goldberg and Ben Zipursky, who have focused on that aspect of tort law.[49] And just as one cannot ignore the fact that tort law serves the public goal of deciding how many accidents we can tolerate – when is an accident worth its costs and who should pay for accidents to deter those accidents that are not worth having – so I think that realistically tort law also serves a more private role. If one looks at the world as it is, one must realize that one of the things that tort law does is to deal with the feeling that injured people have, whether we like it or not, that they have a right to be compensated by the person who has injured them. I think this corrective justice feeling is also part of what society wants.

I believe that Maimonides saw both of those aspects and made them both part of his theory. One aspect might be called religious or deontological, and the other consequentialist. But what is important, rather than what they are called, is that they are both present in his theory.

In a wonderful way, then, Maimonides was not a reductionist in the manner of Richard Posner, nor a reductionist in the sense that Ben Zipursky is sometimes accused of being. But one must also realize something else: that these two relationships, these two Maimonidean goals, the public and the private one – what

---

[49] See, e.g.: John C. Goldberg & Benjamin Zipursky, *Torts as Wrongs*, 88 TEXAS L. REV. 917 (2010); John C. Goldberg, & Benjamin Zipursky, *Civil Recourse Revisited*, 39 FLA. ST. UNIV. L. REV. 342 (2011).

Maimonides called the removal of wrong and the prevention of damages – affect each other.[50] Each affects the other, as we will see in the following Parts.

3 Action in Trespass and Action in Case: Two Approaches Pushing Each Other in the Common Law

A classic case of these two approaches affecting each other at common law was the early English case of *Scott v. Shepherd*,[51] in which a person threw a lighted firecracker into a marketplace. To protect themselves, two people tossed the dangerous thing away, and it finally exploded injuring another person. The law of England at that time seems very strange to us today. There were two ways of being awarded tort compensation. One was an action in trespass, whereby a person recovered if they were injured by another person directly. It was immaterial if the injurer was at fault. Deterrence was not the goal. The idea was that a person who had been injured directly had a right to recover from the other whether the other was at fault or not. Straight Aristotle, straight Zipursky. The injury had to be direct because it was necessary to stop somewhere: one could not be responsible for injuring distant victims. That was the meaning of compensatory justice at the time.

There was another tort-like action in the law at that time, and that was the action on the case. The action on the case dealt with injuries, direct or indirect, at fault or not at fault (although often negligent), where the objective and the effect of the law was to put incentives on people to be more careful. This was very similar to Maimonides's consequentialism. You charge a person who is an innkeeper a certain amount in order to make him look after the people who are staying at the inn. Deterrence was crucial to it.

The interesting thing about this was that the action on the case did not grant recovery to a person who was injured by somebody who was intentionally wrongful. Why not? Deterrence would seem to be called for here. The reason that it was not necessary to impose tort damages on such a person was because a person who intentionally wronged another was hanged!

The law of trespass was concerned with the relationship between two people and somebody's right to recover. The action on the case was not especially concerned with compensation, but with deterrence. Financial deterrence by imposing damages was not needed for intentionally wrongful acts because you "deterred" the wrongdoer by hanging him.

The situation in *Scott v. Shepherd* was that a person injured another intentionally, by throwing a fire cracker into a market place, and the injured person was not entitled to recovery in trespass because the injury was indirect – the fire cracker was passed on by various people. Neither was the victim entitled to recovery in case, because the act

---

[50] GUIDE 3:40.
[51] See *supra* note 22.

was intentional. That was extremely problematic, because people had come to expect recovery when they were injured indirectly by somebody who was negligent, or not at fault, and it seemed absurd not to be compensated when somebody had injured them indirectly but intentionally.[52] Not surprisingly the Court in *Scott* v. *Shepherd* found a way of giving compensation, even though the individual judges disagreed on how.

In other words, the two approaches – the public (how much deterrence is wanted) and the private (when does a victim have a right to be made whole by her injurer) – pushed each other, each shaping what the other would do. Maimonides understood this.

4 Tort Law as a Middle Ground between Civil and Criminal Law

One may ask why it is appropriate to call much of Maimonides's discussion of robbery and theft "tort law", as the authors do,[53] when it would appear that it very much falls into the category of what we would call today criminal law, even insofar as it concerns punitive damages. Why is it at all warranted to understand Maimonides theory as being about tort law?[54]

Maimonides was largely dealing with areas in which the penalty that was imposed on the injurer-criminal was a financial one. As such, it was more like what we think of as torts, including intentional torts, than as criminal law, where the penalty may be a fine, but generally also involves jail, stigma, and other things, like capital punishment. We must, however, realize that jails are something quite new. The penitentiary was a Quaker invention, in the eighteenth and early nineteenth centuries. Prior to that there was capital punishment, whipping, deportation, *and* what today looks like torts. Maimonides was dealing with wrongdoing from that financial aspect, which is why it is relevant, although not identical to modern tort law.

There are, moreover, actually two reasons that enable us to regard what Maimonides was talking about as torts. One is that the penalty was in money terms, and the second that the penalty went to the victim, rather than to the state. So that what you have in his approach are both elements of tort law. First, that the deterrence operates through the medium of money, i.e., the aspect of law and economics. Second, that the penalty is paid to the victim, for both compensatory reasons and Zipurskian reasons. It is this combination of reasons that allows the authors to include this part of Maimonides in the category of torts.

As to punitive damages: in my view, one of the functions of punitive damages is to constitute a bridge between civil and criminal law. Punitive damages are a way of

---

[52] For a similar rule in Jewish Law *see* CODE, Laws of Wounding and Damaging 4:5–7.
[53] *Supra* Chapter 3, Section B.
[54] Based on a question asked by Prof. Benjamin Zipursky, the moderator of a panel on "A Contemporary View of the Maimonidean Tort Theory – Law, Religion, Economics and Morality," Wolff Lecture 2016, Institute on Religion, Law & Lawyer's Work, Fordham Law, 1.26.16.

using the liability rule to address behavior that in some sense is viewed as criminal, but as to which we are reluctant to impose all of the consequences associated with criminal acts. Because it is civil, we can do certain things which we cannot do when the matter is criminal.

In criminal law, damages are not normally paid to the victim. The act is forbidden, period. One cannot buy the right to do a crime by paying damages to the victim. Interestingly, in many civil law countries, one finds the criminal and the civil together in the same system: the victim can bring an action for damages in the framework of the criminal procedure. And, in a way, punitive damages are the American way of doing what is done in some circumstances in Europe, which is having the civil and criminal cases tried together. But, in fact, punitive damages in America do far more than approaching, in a civil way, what is close to criminal.

5 Punitive Damages: The Economic Multiplier Approach vs. the Punitive Approach, Supreme and State Court Rulings

Extra-compensatory damages are being awarded under our law today for a wide variety of different reasons. In this section, I will discuss two polar opposite reasons: the Multiplier and the Right to Punish, and the tension between Supreme Court holdings and state courts as to these two reasons. In the next section, I will list an additional group of reasons.

The Multiplier applies when a repeat wrongdoer does not get caught often enough and therefore would not be made to pay enough without a multiplier when caught.[55] If we want people in that situation to bear a cost that provides them with correct incentives, we charge them many times more than for the single injury. Gary Becker won the Nobel Prize for that relatively trivial insight in criminal law: do not impose on the crook a penalty which is equal to the value of the watch that was stolen, because this will not deter all the crooks who are not caught. The penalty must be much steeper.

This is even more important and obvious in tort law where, for example, General Motors might take into consideration that they will only be made to pay one time in ten if they injure a certain number of people. If they are to make socially appropriate decisions as to how much safety is worthwhile, it will be necessary to charge them approximately ten times as much for each case in which they are held liable. One cannot know exactly how much should be charged at each time for the sake of maximum economic efficiency. But one can know that there are situations in which the cost will not be high enough unless it exceeds that which is warranted by the individual occurrence.

---

[55] See A. Mitchell Polinsky & Steven Shavell, *Punitive Damages: An Economic Analysis*, 111 HARV. L. REV. 869 (1998).

This has nothing to do with whether the person or the company is at fault in its action. The liability may be strict product liability. It is simply a matter of achieving a proper cost-benefit analysis and endeavoring to ensure that this analysis leads to the desired result. Fault is not part of extra-compensatory or punitive damages in that context, and they are often imposed without fault.

At the other extreme is the position taken by the Supreme Court in *Philip Morris USA v. Williams*,[56] which is consistent with the history of punitive damages in the United States, as described by both Tom Colby[57] and Cathy Sharkey.[58] Colby describes the situation in which somebody has done something terribly wrong, as a result of which the person who is injured has a right to feel more than normally injured and has a right to be compensated for more than the norm – the classic punitive damage situation, which is what the Supreme Court was concerned with: Goldberg-Zipursky writ large.

The existence of both the multiplier reason for extra-compensatory damages and the classic punitive reason for them is a source of problems. In some situations, punitive damages require extra fault that causes greater injury, whereas in other situations extra-compensatory damages may be paid out with no fault at all. We are back to the tension between the private and the public role of torts that I talked about earlier when I discussed the case of the thrown firecracker. Any number of us who are injured might say: "Why don't I have a right to the extra compensation?" Of course, if the multiplier were not paid to the victim but were paid elsewhere, then that would not happen.

In the present situation there will be a tension between these two approaches, both of which exist and which are recognized by Maimonides.

The U.S. Supreme Court decides, as it does, in the cases that come before it, and then it is ignored by the state courts. Indeed, the state courts have not stopped doing something very different from what the U.S. Supreme Court has said: they simply call what they do by a slightly different name. Judges are good at that. We are all good at that.

---

[56] 549 U.S. 346 (2007).

[57] Thomas B. Colby, *Beyond the Multiple Punishment Problem: Punitive Damages as Punishment for Individual, Private Wrongs*, 87 MINN. L. REV. 583 (2003). See also Thomas B. Colby, *Clearing the Smoke from* Philip Morris v. Williams: *The Past, Present, and Future of Punitive Damages*, 118 YALE L.J. 392 (2007).

[58] Catherine Sharkey, *Punitive Damages as Societal Damages*, 113 YALE L.J. 347 (2003). See also: Catherine Sharkey, *Crossing the Punitive-Compensatory Divide, in* CIVIL JURIES AND CIVIL JUSTICE: PSYCHOLOGICAL AND LEGAL PERSPECTIVES 79 (Brian H. Bornstein, Richard L. Wiener, Robert Schopp & Steven L. Willborn, eds., 2008); Catherine Sharkey, *Federal Incursions and State Defiance: Punitive Damages in the Wake of* Philip Morris v. Williams, 46 WILLAMETTE L. REV. 449 (2010); Catherine Sharkey, *The Exxon Valdez Litigation Marathon: A Window on Punitive Damages*, 7 U. ST. THOMAS L.J. 25 (2010); Catherine Sharkey, *Future of Classwide Punitive Damages*, 46 U. MICH. J.L. REFORM 1127 (2013).

The authors say that some federal judgments of mine[59] and of Judge Richard Posner[60] acknowledging the multiplier in practice were handed down prior to the developments in the Supreme Court, where the multiplier approach was seemingly forbidden.[61] To be precise, the Supreme Court has not totally denied the multiplier. As Colby and Sharkey both say, damages that factor in the multiplier are acceptable if they are called by another name. If they are called "punitive damages," then the Supreme Court's ruling barring them holds. If, however, the damages are called "extra-compensatory" – that is, damages which are given for reasons, such as the multiplier, that are not punitive – then, according to Colby and Sharkey, nothing in the Supreme Court's decision would bar the states from awarding such damages. It is only if they are called "punitive," if language implying a criminal element is involved, that they are prohibited. But where there is little or no fault, as in products liability, how can the punitive damages be "criminal" in the sense that the Supreme Court is referring? As a result, since the Supreme Court's decision, there have been some state court decisions which have said that "We do multiply and talk about multiplier," and that "We are not really doing anything punitive." So I don't think one can say that the Supreme Court has forbidden the multiplier approach. It simply has barred it in a particular, punitive, context.

6 The Combination of Goals in Relation to the Issue of Punitive Damages

As I said earlier, one of the functions of punitive damages is to constitute a bridge between civil and criminal law. But there are in fact many reasons for awarding extra-compensatory damages. Some of the reasons are punitive, while the objective of others is merely to raise the cost to the injurer. Some of them are purely to award enough in those cases in which the injurer actually pays to cover the cases in which he does not do so – the multiplier. As described earlier, the multiplier can be applied where there is no fault, and we do award punitive / extra-compensatory damages for that reason. Conversely, punitive damages may be awarded because the victim incurred extra harm by the actions of the injurer – where the injury in Maimonidean terms is more severe. There may also be situations in which a victim is contributorily negligent, and then you may want to reduce the punitive damages,[62] as I show in the next part, where I discuss putting incentives on the victim. But you would not want to do this in the multiplier situation.

The reasons for extra-compensatory damages, however, go well beyond the punitive and multiplier contexts. And the question that must be asked is: what are the reasons for awarding these extra damages, and what are the consequences of these reasons?

---

[59] Ciraolo v. City of New York, 216 F.3d 236, 243 (2d Cir. 2000).
[60] Mathias v. Accor Economy Lodging Inc., 347 F.3d 672 (7th Cir. 2003).
[61] *Supra* Chapter 5, Section C.2.b.
[62] *Supra* Chapter 5, Section C.2.c.

The different reasons for punitive damages have many very different consequences in terms of: (a) whether the wrongdoer is permitted to be insured against the wrongdoing; (b) how much fault is required – and whether extra great fault is required; (c) how much of the damages does the victim actually get – ought the plaintiff get the damages, or should they go to a fund; (d) whether the defendant's wealth is relevant; (e) whether the victim needs to show compensatory damages before non-compensatory ones can be awarded; (f) how relevant are damages to other parties injured in the accident; (g) whether we want to provide an incentive that is greater than the market incentive – an incentive that comes close to prohibition, although it is not quite prohibition; (h) whether because one party has won, another party can't bring a suit for the same cause of action; and (i) what alternatives to imposing such damages would serve to achieve the same goals. In an earlier article of mine I presented a few different reasons for awarding damages that are extra-compensatory.[63] I now offer some additional ones.

One of the reasons is the multiplier. As mentioned, Sharkey and Colby actually suggest calling this type of punitive damages by another name, something other than punitive damages – extra-compensatory damages.

Another reason for extra-compensatory damages is when we want the sanctioned conduct to approach criminality. In such situations we ask whether the extra-compensatory damages are sufficiently close to criminal sanctions to warrant requiring criminal law safeguards against double jeopardy, as to demand extra evidence before assigning liability – i.e. standards applied before finding someone guilty of a crime.

In my most recent book, THE FUTURE OF LAW AND ECONOMICS,[64] I cite Benjamin Shmueli, because he refers to this sort of punitive damages in relation to a situation in which an orthodox Jewish man cannot be ordered to give his wife a *get* (bill of divorce) and the religious court cannot order that he be put in jail until he does so (at least in certain cases); it might, however, be possible to impose extra damages in order to induce him to comply.[65] Such a turning to the civil arena may allow you to do certain things that you cannot do through the use of criminal law. There are times when punitive damages can be used that way.

A third reason for punitive damages is that we may want to provide an incentive for a private party to act like a civil attorney general and to bring a suit to control

---

[63] Guido Calabresi, *The Complexity of Torts – The Case of Punitive Damages*, in EXPLORING TORT LAW 333 (M. Stuart Madden ed., 2005).
[64] CALABRESI, THE FUTURE OF LAW AND ECONOMICS, *supra* note 25, at 120, 129 (2016).
[65] Benjamin Shmueli, *What have Calabresi & Melamed got to do with Family Affairs? Women Using Tort Law in order to Defeat Jewish and Shari'a Law*, 25 BERKELEY J. GENDER L. & JUSTICE 125 (2010); Benjamin Shmueli, *Tort Actions for Acts that are Valid according to Religious Family Law but Harm Women's Rights: Legal Pluralism in Cases of Collision between Two Sets of Law*, 46 VAND.T J. TRANSNAT'L L. 823 (2013); Benjamin Shmueli, *Post Judgment Bargaining*, 50 WAKE FOREST L. REV. 1181 (2015).

behavior. The point here is not to rely on the attorney general to go after such wrongdoers. This may explain treble damages in antitrust cases.

In England, punitive damages were a way of awarding damages – actually, compensatory damages – to people who did not have a right to such damages under existing tort law. For instance, a woman could not be compensated adequately because she did not earn enough money, and monetary compensation could not be awarded for certain kinds of emotional damage. Where it was thought that such monetary compensation was due, the damages were called "punitive" and awarded. This is a fourth, and completely different reason.

Possibly the most interesting reason for punitive damages is what I call the tragic choice reason. This occurs in a situation where, nominally, fault as defined by the Learned Hand test governs, but where we do not want the injurer to raise the defense that he was not negligent under that test. If he makes such a defense, we impose punitive damages. One such example is the Ford Pinto case,[66] in which the gas tank was situated in a particular place in the car to save money. In certain accidents such cars burst into flames. It did not happen often. Because it was cheaper to put the gas tank in that particular place, Ford did not change it, even after some accidents has occurred. In effect, Ford said: "There was nothing wrong, it wasn't negligent to put the gas tank where we did, because it costs more to put the gas tanks someplace else than to burn a few babies." But that is an argument that one is not allowed to make, so the plaintiff was awarded massive punitive damages.

In effect, what we are saying is that there are circumstances where liability is strict, and not based on negligence. We cannot adequately define these circumstances ex ante. But the person who acts in such situations knows perfectly well that he cannot defend himself by saying, "I was O.K. on the basis of a cost-benefit analysis." The person causing an injury may well have conducted a cost-benefit analysis that led him to injure rather than face the costs of safety. But he absolutely may not raise a defense based on that analysis! If he tries to avoid paying up, he will be hit with punitive damages. This is the tragic choice element. It says: "Just don't come and tell us something we don't want to hear – like burning babies is O.K. Shut up and pay up."

The same applies to driving through a poor section of the city. A person cannot claim that it was cheaper to drive fast and injure people there under the Learned Hand formula: he should just "shut up and pay up".

The point is that while negligence is the normal standard, there are contexts in which defendants will not be permitted to make the defense that they were not negligent. Actually a strict liability standard is applied here, because the cost resulting from knowing about the underlying cost-benefit analysis is too great. Don't tell us the outcome of the cost-benefit analysis, because we do not want to

---

[66] Grimshaw v. Ford Motor Co., 119 Cal.App.3d 757, 174 Cal. Rptr. 348 (1981).

hear it. Obviously, that's a completely different reason for punitive damages from the others.

The reason for extra-compensatory damages that the U.S. Supreme Court has focused on is that of victims' rights. This is not surprising, because the type of cases the Supreme Court deals with are not torts cases, but cases of individual rights, in which our Constitution says: "It is my right; you don't have a right to infringe that." And that sounds like: "You have done me harm, I have a right to compensation, not just for my damages, but for the emotional, theoretical fact that you have trodden on me." Indeed, the people who landed here – the nonconformist first settlers – were extraordinarily conscious of their rights: "Don't tread on me, these are my rights. I have these rights which you cannot infringe, so keep out. Such a concept of my right also gives me the right to retribution, to take vengeance, to get at you." It is a mistake not to recognize that this is part of American tradition too.

This is in fact the only explanation for another set of cases, the death penalty cases, which do not deter and which are not just. If they can be justified at all – and I don't think they can – it is only by virtue of the fact that the family of a person who is killed says: "You have done me wrong; I have a right against you." This is one view – I call it "the Colby view" – of the punitive damages which the Supreme Court discussed. According to Colby, this view helps to explain why there are punitive damages in the United States and not in Europe. Some version exists in the United Kingdom, but unlike anything in the United States.

It should come as no surprise that the U.S. Supreme Court sees punitive damages only in this light, given that its docket consists, in huge part, of constitutional rights and death penalty cases. This reasoning is not all there is to tort law, but it plays some part in it. It links torts to this same constitutional tradition. And it is not surprising that the Supreme Court should extrapolate from the cases it hears to another area like torts that it knows very little about, and say: "That is about the same thing." And then other people will say: "No, no, there's a lot more than that to punitive damages," even though they are all called by the same name, and come under the same umbrella. Indeed, this is what Maimonides is talking about.

In view of this wide set of reasons, there are different decisions as to whether the risks can be insured, whether fault is needed, and so on and so on, and what kind of semi-criminal protections are given.

But to each of these bases for extra-compensatory damages there are also alternatives, other ways of achieving the same goal. For example, the alternative to the multiplier is the class action: one person brings the suit and collects for all of the victims. However, this alternative has some problems. The Supreme Court has been very restrictive of class actions. From a deterrence point of view they do work, but the problem is that the lawyers get most of the money. It is interesting that Europe, which does not have punitive damages, is now trying to establish class actions and also beginning to award punitive damages. And the alternative to punitive damages in the English system is to expand liability. The alternative to truly punitive extra-compensatory damages is expansion of criminal sanctions, perhaps with the victims taking part in the criminal trial.

The interesting thing is that according to the way in which the authors describe Maimonides,[67] all of these different reasons, which have not fully been sorted out in American law, are present in his work. It seems that Maimonides considered all of these different factors in discussing criminal sanctions and punitive damages, and that he invoked different types of extra-compensatory damages in different situations. Think of it this way: the Supreme Court's decision in *Philip Morris USA v. Williams*[68] pushes state courts to say: "I want extra-compensatory damages for this reason," or "I want them for a different reason." Traditionally, state courts did not make such distinctions. Rather, they awarded them differently in a variety of contexts, which is what Maimonides also said. But, let me say it again, the fact that they used the same term does not mean that state courts did not use them differently in different contexts.

State courts preferred to have an all-encompassing definition that allowed them to do different things at different times. The authors suggest that that is what Maimonides was also doing. I believe this is what courts in the United States have traditionally done. But they are now struggling with this approach, because of the Supreme Court's taking one meaning and saying, "This is the meaning we attribute to it." The Court seems to be viewing punitive damages only from the point of view of punishment of the wrongdoer, which Colby says is the traditional American reason for them. But after the Supreme Court came out with its decisions, Colby and Sharkey said: "If you want to give extra-compensatory damages for other reasons, just call them something else. Don't call them punitive damages; call them extra-compensatory, or whatever, because all the reasons listed for extra-compensatory damages remain there." And I would add that they all seem to be there, in Maimonides as well.

I want to move on to a very different, but in fact closely related example of the need to pay more than the market value. Sometimes we do not forbid or bar something and make it criminal, but we are close to doing so, and we therefore award damages that might be as much as three times the market value. This might be what we want to do in some cases of takings by eminent domain. In the *Kelo* case,[69] the owners of houses in New London that were taken were given market value. Everybody was furious because they said that market value is not the appropriate compensation when somebody who is a private person takes private property, even if she is doing so for the public good.[70] In such circumstances, we may not

---

[67] *Supra* Chapter 5.
[68] *Supra* note 56.
[69] Kelo v. City of New London, 545 U.S. 469 (2005).
[70] *Cf.* Guido Calabresi, A Broader View of the Cathedral: The Significance of the Liability Rule, Correcting a Misapprehension, 77 L. & CONTEMP. PROBS. 1 (2014) (discussing countries that allow takings by eminent domain while compensating only value in use, not market value. And

necessarily want to prohibit the taking, but may still wish to discourage it, by assessing damages/payments at a level that is greater than market value. And as Justice Kennedy, of all people, said during the oral argument: "Wouldn't we all feel better in this situation if instead of giving only market compensation, we gave two or three times market compensation?"[71] That is then still an economics-related way of doing it. It doesn't even begin to get to what Zipursky would say is also involved, that there are some harms to individuals for which people have a right to get more than market-value compensation, not for market reasons, but for others. Why should we think of punitive damages only in terms of the multiplier? We often simply want the price to be more than market price, because we are not tied to the market.

To sum up, there are many different reasons for punitive damages. Maimonides recognized this combination of goals, the fact that you do different things in this area of law, that you do them together, rather than as separate things – here you have this and here you have that – and it is this recognition of the combination that made him uniquely a non-reductionist scholar.

7 Putting Incentives on the Victim to Take Precautions and the Possibility of Reducing Punitive Damages

The authors say that, according to Maimonides, there is no contradiction between a reduction of the real compensation and awarding punitive damages.[72] I agree. Negative incentives to victims also work.

The authors show that Maimonides said that since the victim is able to take more preventative measures in the case of the sheep than in the case of the cattle, it is important to charge the injurer more in the case of the cattle.[73] Now, we do not know whether that was true then. As I mentioned earlier, one of the problems of trying to go from the present to the past is that we do not really know what went on back then and we tend to read the past in terms of what happens today. But it

---

see ibid. at 10, demonstrating from cases of takings for public purposes in Italy and referring to Giuseppe Franco Ferrari, *Fundamental Rights and Freedoms, in* INTRODUCTION TO ITALIAN PUBLIC LAW 271–72 (Giuseppe Franco Ferrari ed., 2008), who discusses the divergence between market value and compensation paid in Italian cases of expropriation). And *see* Calabresi, *ibid.* at 10–11 (explaining that in the *Kelo* case there was a private developer who was given eminent domain to take individual properties in eastern Connecticut for redevelopment purposes. The public purpose was the commercial improvement and upgrading of the area for the benefit of the city. But the immediate beneficiaries of the right to take the property by eminent domain were private developers).

[71] Transcript of Oral Argument at 22–23, Kelo v. City of New London, No. 04–108 (U.S. argued Feb. 22, 2005) ("Are there any writings ... that indicate[] that when you have property being taken from one private person ultimately to go to another private person, that what we ought to do is to adjust the measure of compensation, so that the owner ... can receive some sort of a premium for the development?").

[72] *Supra* Chapter 5, Section C.2.c.

[73] Ibid.

certainly suggests that Maimonides was saying that this was an appropriate way of giving some incentive to the victim as well as to the injurer, and that is what justified the four-five compensation in the case of stealing sheep and cattle.

In any case, awarding punitive damages may create the equivalent of a moral hazard if they go to the victim, in that the victim may do less than what a victim would normally do. There is therefore a reason not to give punitive damages or to reduce them, in order to cause the victim to do exactly what he would have done without them. There are reasons why the injurer must pay punitive damages. For instance, because of the multiplier. But if such extra damages are given to a particular victim, he may say: "I'm playing a lottery, and I want to take chances, and perhaps get the punitive damages." That may become an argument for not giving *all* of such damages. You want to give enough, so that the victim goes after the injurer, there has to be an incentive to bring the suit. And so it may be desirable to award some extra-compensatory damages, in order to reduce the chances that other people are injured (which is what Sharkey talked about). But how the punitive damages are allocated and how much they are given to the individual victim turns on this issue.

Interestingly, the authors say that over-compensation in one case covers under-compensation in other cases.[74] Sharkey, instead, has written that in many of these instances punitive damages should be charged to the defendant but should not go to the plaintiff. That is, enough should go to the injured person to provide him with an incentive to bring the suit, but *not all of the damages* should go to him. And the excess should go – for instance, if the damage is due to shoddy building of a road – to build a better road, so that other people could enjoy it, and so that other people who suffered the same injury but did not sue and did not receive similar compensation could also have some benefit.

Thus, focusing also on victim incentives, as Maimonides did, is important and very interesting. You may definitely want to place a greater incentive on the victim when it is the victim who can prevent the damage more easily. But the victim should also avoid over-spending on safety. Split strict liability is relevant here. This is a situation in which the loss should be partly but not completely on the victim. That is really the theme of Calabresi and Hirschoff,[75] and of what I call "Calabresian cheapest cost avoider." Once you allow splitting you go beyond Calabresi and Hirschoff's best decision maker, but it is not inconsistent with what we said there. In an article I wrote with Jeff Cooper,[76] I say that the recent changes in tort law that allow splitting are as important a change in allocation of losses as was the advent of insurance policies. The coming of insurance redid all of tort law in the twentieth

---

[74] *Ibid.*
[75] Calabresi & Hirschoff, *supra* note 35.
[76] *See* Guido Calabresi & Jeffrey O. Cooper, *New Directions in Tort Law*, 30 VALPARAISO U. L. REV. 859 (1996).

century and splitting is going to redo it all in the twenty-first century. And again it is interesting that Maimonides discussed this.[77] This is not absolute liability on the injurer, it is strict liability in part on both sides, for you have to have incentives on both the victims and the injurers.

C. CONCLUSION

Reading the ancient sages, like reading the canonic works of literature – be they *The Divine Comedy* or *King Lear* – is essential to understanding modern law. Such writings give powerful insights into how analogous problems were viewed in different times. Sometimes, after allowing for empirical differences, the approach of the sages – and Maimonides certainly among them – seems strikingly similar to modern approaches. At first, one must wonder whether one is reading the modern into the past, or whether it truly is there. But when one nevertheless concludes that the similarities are indeed present, one is doubly rewarded. For then one is led to a fuller and deeper understanding of both the past and the present.

It was with skepticism that I initially came to the authors' work. After further reading and much thought, I became convinced that they are right and that there is a great deal in Maimonides that presages both my work and sophisticated modern law and economics generally. This is a reason to rejoice. Not only can we now better understand that great man – Maimonides – and the breadth of his thinking, but we also have a clearer picture of the strengths and weaknesses of modern scholarship.[78] This is precisely what law and humanities – law and history, law and literature – can lead to. I am grateful to the authors for making me, as well as my writings, part of their project.

In closing, I note my full agreement with the authors that one can characterize Maimonides's approach to criminal sanctions and punitive damages as a mixture between the equivalents of multiplier and of social redress extra-compensatory damages approaches. But I think that Maimonides presents a mixture between much more than just these two different goals and reasons for punitive damages. And this is yet another reason why Maimonides was so remarkable.

---

[77] *Supra* Chapter 5, Section B.1.c.
[78] And, indeed, a mutual contribution may be discerned when comparing the ancient sources with the modern ones. See *supra* Chapter 8.

Index

Abraham, Kenneth, 201–2
Aharonim, 161, 169–70, 187, 229
Albeck, Shalom, 42, 65, 67
   General Principles of Law of Tort in the Talmud, 42
   laws of damages to neighbors, 125–26
   Peshiah, 41, 63, 65, 71, 306
Al-Farabi, 139
animals
   killing an animal with which a human being has lain carnally, 224, 231–32
   killing animals if they cause damage, 191, 205, 287, 305–7
   rearing of small cattle in the Land of Israel, 71, 306–7
   tam and *muʿad*, 101–2, 304
Aristotle, 30, 384
   corrective justice, 15, 36, 134, 192, 194, 198, 201, 203–4, 208–11
   distributive justice, 15, 36, 134, 198, 207
   equality, 209
   and Jewish rabbis, 36, 134, 202
   and Maimonides, 36, 134, 203–4, 207–9, 211
   Nicomachean Ethics, 36, 134
assumption of risk, 258, 260, 294, 374
atonement fine (*kofer*), 96
Aumann, Robert, 36
Austin, John, 163
Avraham, Michael, 59–60

Bar-Niv, Moshe, 245, 247–49
Beccaria, Cesare Bonesana, 269
Becker, Gary, 269, 386
Bentham, Jeremy, 238, 269
best decision maker

Calabresi, 25, 252, 255–61, 263, 265, 278–79, 291–95, 297–301, 304, 314, 322, 375–76, 382, 394
   and cheapest cost avoider test, 255–58
   and Maimonides, 256–61, 265, 278–79, 291–95, 297–301, 304, 314, 322, 375, 382
   and strict liability, 256–57, 260–61, 263
Bible, 31, 34, 97, 120–23, 169–70, 173–74, 181, 361, 364
   an eye for an eye, 112, 152–53, 330
   exempts the elder from loading or unloading, 155–56
   exempts the finder of lost property from returning the item to its owner, 156
   fine, 239
   innocent ox (*tam*), 236
   payments of a thief as opposed to a robber, 242, 245
   prevalence of sheep and cattle stealing, 246, 248, 250
   prohibition against causing damage, 165–66, 168–69, 171, 190
   property theft, 241, 243
   sanctity of human life, 142
   stealing from a Gentile, 148–49
   stoning the ox that killed a person, 232
   system of organization, 98
   various categories of damages, 97
Bickel, Alex, 374
bodily integrity
   Maimonidean approach, 210
   Weinribian-Kantian approach, 210
Book of Acquisition (*Sefer Kinyan*), 81, 84, 86–87, 97
   in the *Code*, 9, 74, 123
   distributive justice, 131, 134, 136, 351

397

Book of Acquisition (*Sefer Kinyan*) (cont.)
  Laws of Neighbors, 83, 124–26, 128, 135
  rationale, 131, 134
Book of Civil Law (*Sefer Mishpatim*), 81, 84, 86–87
  in the *Code*, 74
  damage caused by watchman, 83
Book of Commandments
  compensation for wounding, 112
  prohibition against cursing another person, 143–45
  prohibition against stealing, 145
Book of Judges (*Sefer Shoftim*)
  damages caused by plotting witnesses, 83
Book of Torts (*Sefer Nezikin*), 143
  and the Bible, 82, 94, 97, 103, 105, 285
  classical laws of torts, 81, 97
  classification, 9, 16, 29, 32, 81–84, 87, 94, 96, 142, 331
  compensation, 127
  conceptualizations, 15
  corrective justice, 12, 205
  criminal law, 81, 323
  difficulties, 62
  Genizah, 74
  and the *Guide*, 33, 285–86
  law of the pursuer, 174, 183
  and Laws of Damages to Neighbors, 124, 126
  laws of murderer and preservation of life, 142, 323
  laws of property damages, 98, 142
  laws of robbery, 142
  laws of theft, 142, 323, 360, 385
  laws of wounding, 142
  mass and serial torts, 335
  masters and slaves, 335, 374
  and the *Mishnah*, 83, 123
  objectives of tort laws, 132
  opening of the book, 39, 43, 49, 54, 61, 72, 75–76, 78, 101, 103, 289, 303, 308
  peshiah and ownership, 62, 64
  and private civil law, 84
  process of formation, 74
  prohibitions, 163–65
  psychological damage, 130
  and rationale of prevention of damage, 141
  and regulation, 335
  relate to a traditional agrarian society, 335, 337, 353
  religious component, 159, 163–64, 184, 285, 287
  religious-prohibitive dimension, 171
  sanctity of human life, 143
  social-consequentialist dimension, 226, 285–89, 306
  standard of care for each type of damage, 268
  system of organization, 98
  and the Talmud, 62, 66, 82–83, 94, 285–86, 316, 325, 328, 334–35
  theology of sin and atonement, 171
  topics included, 29, 81, 83–86, 93, 171, 323
  and Twersky's book, 32
  unique characteristics, 16
Book of Women (*Sefer Nashim*)
  damages caused by rape, seduction, and slander, 83
Brand, Itzhak, 98
burden of proof
  balance of probability, 90, 369
  in criminal law, 90, 369
  preponderance of the evidence, 90, 369
  in tort law, 90, 369
Burton, Steven, 20, 31

Calabresi, Guido, 3, 24–25, 35, 38, 194, 368
  American context, 375, 378
  best briber liability, 380
  best decision maker, 25, 252, 255–61, 263, 265, 278–79, 291–95, 297–301, 304, 314, 322, 375–76, 382, 394
  cheapest cost avoider, 25, 252–58, 260, 263, 284, 290–91, 297, 340, 344, 355, 370, 375–76, 394
  collective liability, 380
  considerations of efficiency, 213–15, 217, 219–20, 252–53, 378–79, 386
  considerations of justice, 213, 215–17, 219, 377, 379
  and contemporary tort law and economics, 31, 252, 254
  contract law and tort law, 89
  corrective justice, 216–17
  Costs of Accidents, The (1970), 253, 379
  criminal law and tort law, 89
  deontological considerations, 213–15, 217, 377–78, 383
  distributive considerations, 214, 216–17, 258–59
  empirical differences in time, 374–75, 377, 382, 393, 395
  federal judgment, 388
  Future of Law and Economics, The, 389
  general deterrence, 253
  and Hand formula, 355, 370
  information, 258, 291, 297, 381
  insurance, 258–59, 375, 394
  liability of the debtor in bankruptcy, 381
  and Maimonides, 31, 89, 213, 217, 219–20, 251–54, 256–60, 263, 265, 267–68, 293, 301, 314, 352, 370, 374–76, 378, 380, 395
  and Maimonides' test for tort liability, 251–54, 260

as monist, 213, 215, 345
optimal deterrence, 213, 215, 217, 252–54, 345, 352, 355
and Posner, 261, 263, 355, 370–71
punitive damages, 31
beyond reasonable doubt, 90, 369
reducing the costs of accidents, 215, 252–55
reflections on Maimonides' tort theory, 373–75, 378, 380, 382–83, 385, 387, 391–95
regulation, 258
socially compensatory damages, 273
splitting the liability, 235–36, 260, 267, 284, 301, 375–76, 394
strict liability theory, 25, 27, 252–53, 260–61, 263, 292, 314, 330, 336, 370, 375
tort law as an alternative to criminal law, 369
Toward a Unified Theory of Torts, 377
Calabresi, Guido and Melamed, Douglas
inalienability, 129, 213–14, 218–19
and Maimonides, 162
property rules, liability rules, and inalienability, 126, 128–29, 162, 214, 288
Rule 2, 288
categories in tort, 2, 7–8, 27, 81
damage caused by animals, 102
damage caused by the person himself, 9, 29, 45, 76, 81, 96–97, 103, 107, 111, 229–30, 290, 310–11, 328, 333, 353
damages caused by a person's actions, 29, 102–3
damages caused by property, 2, 7, 9, 12, 29–30, 73, 76, 81, 102–4, 107, 230–31, 291, 310–11, 328, 333, 335–36, 353–54
damages that are not discernible, 94–95
emotional damage, 390–91
murder, 30
nuisance and damage caused by neighbors, 9, 29, 81, 97
objectives of tort in different categories, 9, 29, 80–81, 96
a person damaging the property of another, 2, 7, 9, 29–30, 68–69, 81, 84, 93–94, 231, 328, 336, 352, 354, 359
a person injuring his fellow, 2, 7, 9, 29–30, 81, 94, 111, 231, 328–30, 336, 352–53
and standard of care, 27
standard tort law, 9, 29, 81
visual trespass, 185–86
causation, 21
between the breach of duty and the damage, 354
and corrective justice, 196, 199, 211, 343
indirect damages (*grama*), 211, 287
method of causation of the damage, 44
prohibition against causing damage, 211, 287

statistical cause, 376
uncertain causation, 97, 110, 356
cheapest cost avoider
Calabresi, 25, 252–58, 260, 263, 284, 290–91, 297, 340, 344, 355, 370, 375–76, 394
Maimonides, 252–54, 256–58, 260, 290–91, 297, 340, 355, 370, 375
Coase, Ronald H., 24, 38, 368
Code of Hammurabi, 381
Cohn, Haim, 364
Israeli Supreme Court Justice, 364
Colby, Tom, 387–89, 391–92
Coleman, Jules, 194, 198
corrective justice, 198, 200, 344
ethical compensation, 200
ethical retribution, 200
commandment to restore lost property
source for the prohibition against causing harm, 169–70
Commentary to the Mishnah, 29, 76, 80, 140, 149, 151, 157, 191, 207, 299
corrections, 74
common law, 41
action in case, 384–85
action in trespass, 384–85
all or nothing, 375
contributory negligence, 265
four- and five-fold payments, 270
intentional torts, 271–72, 333, 357, 368, 384–85
and Maimonides, 270, 297, 384–85
modified comparative negligence, 261, 266
negligence, 41, 56
punishment, 89
strict liability, 44
tort law, 87
US jurisdictions, 261
communitarian approaches, 201
and Maimonides, 211, 287
society, 201
comparative negligence, 261–62
comparative responsibility, 376
and contributory negligence, 261–62, 376
modified comparative negligence, 261, 266
pure comparative negligence, 261, 266, 279
splitting according to comparative nonfault, 376
compensation, 85
assessment of the damage, 207
awards for medical malpractice, 115, 347
from the best of the tortfeasor's property, 140
from their best property, 208
between fire and animal or pit, 107

compensation (cont.)
  bodily injury, 27, 94, 108–9, 111–14, 116–18, 208, 210, 316–18, 330–32, 356, 359
  and corrective justice, 20, 22, 205, 342, 345, 348
  common law, 384
  and criminal law, 89, 111–13, 385
  for damages caused by animals, 206
  damages not discernible, 95
  damaging, 111
  deep pocket, 22, 89, 207
  distributive considerations, 221
  ethical compensation, 200
  fire, 106–7, 127
  as form of religious atonement, 160
  full damages, 67–68, 101, 109, 190, 205, 208, 218, 236–38, 259–60, 285–86, 301–2, 304, 312
  half damages, 66–67, 101–2, 190, 205, 236–37, 259, 267, 301–2
  humiliation, 209–10, 316–20, 328, 332, 357, 359
  indirect damages (grama), 211
  medical treatment, 209–10
  partial compensation in situations of uncertain causation, 110, 356
  payments of a thief as opposed to a robber, 241–42, 245
  pit, 106
  and the prohibitive dimension, 161, 167–68
  property damages, 108–9, 111, 172, 205, 331, 356
  as a punishment or a fine, 6, 8, 80, 94–95, 112, 123, 204–5, 208, 318, 356–57, 369, 385
  punitive aspects, 93, 331
  ransom, 85, 142, 331
  and the rationale of prevention of damage, 140
  as restitution for the damage caused, 6, 22, 93, 109, 160, 172–73, 288, 331
  retribution, 200
  right the wrong, 11
  scope, 104
  standard laws of tort, 126
  the civil basis, 165
  for a victim of crime, 28, 88
  for a woman who was raped, 239
  for a woman who was seduced, 239
consequentialist approach, 2, 13–14, 38, 123
consequentialist offences, 305
  considerations, 28
  and contemporary tort law and economics, 35, 222–23, 227
  deterrence, 269, 274–76, 278, 280, 286, 288, 302, 305, 341
  ethical system, 34
  incentives for future behavior, 225, 229, 232, 238
  and Maimonides, 30, 222–25, 227, 232–33, 238–39, 241, 243–44, 246, 249–52, 280–81,
  284–86, 288–90, 293, 295, 301–2, 306–8, 311, 322–23, 329, 340, 350–52, 367–68, 377
  meaning, 222, 224
  and morality, 367–68
  normative (or welfare) economics, 225
  Paley, 270
  prevention of damages, 132, 136, 138, 188, 192, 217, 220, 225, 228–29, 231
  and the prohibition against causing harm, 164
contemporary tort theories, 2, 31
  bridging between contemporary approaches, 355, 367, 370–71
  business risk theory, 58
  civil recourse approach, 202, 212
  cognitive rationality, 224
  and Common law, 40
  communitarian approaches, 201, 211
  compensation, 22
  corrective justice, 21, 31, 192, 194, 200
  between criminal law and civil law, 238
  distributive justice, 22
  goals of tort law, 19–20
  insurance, 334–35, 375
  law and economics, 15, 24, 26, 28, 30–31, 192, 251, 311
  between laws applying to robbery and to theft, 118–23, 359–60
  laws of intellectual property, 76
  lessons from Maimonides tort theory, 19, 30–31, 111, 184, 338, 341, 353–57, 359–60, 366, 370, 372
  liability of risk creators, 192
  liberal approaches, 201
  and Maimonides, 18, 30, 32, 35, 37, 78, 114–15, 131, 136, 138, 145, 192, 194, 223, 229, 251, 268, 277–78, 280, 288, 301, 309, 332–34, 336–40, 352–54, 359–60, 367, 369, 371–73, 385, 387, 391–93, 395
  and Maimonides' differential model, 333
  mass torts, 334, 353, 355
  monism and pluralism, 136, 338–39
  monistic approaches, 131, 338, 340
  normative approach, 37, 339–40
  operate in an industrial environment, 333, 335, 353, 355
  operate within a reality of state regulation, 334–35, 354
  optimal deterrence, 24, 189
  and the ownership theory, 56
  partial compensation in cases of uncertain causation, 111, 356
  pluralistic approaches, 26, 338–41, 350
  restorative justice programs, 114
  and Roman law, 40

secular law, 217, 220, 353, 360
serial torts, 334
strict liability, 294
  and talmudic tort law, 65
  theories of welfare, 225
  between torts, criminal law and contract law, 87, 89, 91–93
  utilitarian approaches, 201
  vicarious liability, 334–35, 354
contract law
  compensation, 90
  enforcement, 90
  negotiation, 90
  strict liability, 90
contract law and tort law, 87, 89–92
  in Maimonides, 92
contributory negligence, 45, 258, 260–62
  common law, 265
  comparative negligence, 261–62, 376
  different understandings, 265
  and Jewish law, 265
  and Maimonides, 265–68, 278–79, 300, 370
  modified comparative negligence, 261, 266
  punitive damages, 388
Cooper, Jeff, 394
Cooter, Robert, 278
corrective justice, 15, 20, 71, 192
  Aristotelian-Weinribian approach, 203–5, 208–10
  and the civil recourse approach, 202, 212
  and civil redress, 202
  and communitarian approaches, 201, 211
  correlativity, 21, 193–98, 200, 204, 211, 220
  culpability, 196
  and deterrence, 344, 348
  different theories, 21, 192, 194, 200, 203–4, 208, 211, 220
  distinction between wounding and damaging, 12
  and distributive justice, 36, 134, 193, 196, 198, 204–6, 217, 342–45
  and economic analysis of law, 25
  England, 36
  equality, 193–94, 198, 209
  fairness, 199
  harmony with distributive justice, 342–45, 350
  between *knas* (fine) and *mammon* (monetary obligation), 203–5
  level of compensation, 205
  and Maimonides, 194, 202–4, 206, 208, 211, 228, 251–52, 263–64, 293, 305, 337, 340, 350–52
  and negligence, 21, 199
  and Posner, 262

property damages, 132
proportionality, 205
punishment and retribution, 200, 204, 208, 211–12, 342
  and risk causing behavior, 188
  Weinrib, 3, 21, 30, 38, 368
  Weinribian-Kantian approach, 211–12
criminal law
  actus reus, 357
  burden of proof, 90, 369
  the consent of the individual to the injury, 116, 218
  criminal sanctions, 90, 238, 240
  deterrence, 226
  forgiveness, 114
  general deterrence, 238
  laws of murderers, 93
  laws of theft and robbery, 93
  laws of wounding, 93–94, 110, 132, 173
  liability of an inadvertent blameless transgressor, 326–27
  and Maimonides, 269, 305
  mens rea, 90, 95, 117, 123, 318–19, 331–32, 357
  penology, 238
  person who commits an offence through negligence, 326
  policy of penal considerations, 93
  restorative justice, 114, 356
  social-utilitarian reason, 226
  specific deterrence, 238
criminal law and tort law, 2, 8, 18, 20, 28–30, 80, 82, 84, 86–87, 89, 91–93, 98, 123, 171, 212, 330, 369
  burden of proof, 90, 369
  contemporary tort law, 369, 385
  deterrence, 89
  in Maimonides, 92–94, 319, 332, 368–69, 385
  procedural differences, 90
  prohibitive dimension, 163
  standard of care, 90
criminal sanctions, 13, 30, 88, 90, 123, 225
  act may be done secretly, 240, 379
  amount of temptation, 240–41, 379–80
  civil-criminal sanctions, 92, 369
  deterrence, 241, 244, 253
  frequency of the crime, 240–41, 379
  four parameters of Maimonides, 240–41, 268, 371, 378–79, 381, 392, 395
  policy, 93
  and punitive damages, 272, 280, 351
  severity of the crime, 240, 242, 371, 379, 388
cursing another person
  prohibition against, 144–45, 204

damage that involves a criminal law element
　murder, 323, 351
　robbery, 9, 81, 385
　theft, 9, 81, 173, 323, 351, 385
　wounding, 9, 81, 93–94, 173, 213, 323, 330–33, 351, 356
damages caused by foot, 66–67
damages caused by horn, 66
damages caused by a person
　strict liability, 45
damages caused by tooth, 66–67
Daube, David, 236
deep pocket, 23, 89, 217, 359
　insurance, 334, 353–54, 357
　mass tortfeasors, 334
deontological, 8
　Calabresi, 213–15, 217
　constraints, 28
　corrective justice, 11
　elements of Maimonides' tort theory, 138, 213, 222, 228, 241, 243, 251–52, 285, 288, 293, 305–6, 311, 328, 330, 340, 350–51, 367, 377, 383
deterrence, 13–14, 123, 213
　on basis of risk creating behavior, 192
　compensation, 89, 195, 208
　criminal law and tort law, 89, 385
　general deterrence, 238, 253
　as major goal of punitive damages, 238, 241–42, 245, 247–50, 253
　punishment, 89
　of risk causing behavior, 70, 187–88
　specific deterrence, 238
　take care of animals, 190
differential model, 14–15, 27, 29–30, 96–97, 281, 292, 310–11, 317, 336, 339
　and the Bible, 97
　and the cheapest cost avoider/best decision-maker doctrines, 375
　historical background, 328, 333, 336
　between Maimonides and contemporary theories, 340, 375
　rationale, 328
　scheme, 328–29, 337
differential-pluralistic model, 2, 27–28, 30
　a different standard of care for each category, 27
　of Maimonides, 136, 338–41, 350, 352–53
　in modern tort law, 353, 367–68, 370, 372
distributive justice, 15
　Book of Acquisition, 134, 136, 351
　deterrence, 342–43
　in different times, 375
　harmony with corrective justice, 342–45, 350
　and human rights approaches, 26
　insurance, 334
　level of activity, 336
　loss distribution, 342–43
　Maimonides, 31, 220, 228, 337, 340, 351–52
　nuisance, 131–32
　optimal deterrence, 24, 217
Dobbs, Dan B., 90
duty to rescue, 85, 173–74, 181, 361, 364
　American law, 178–81, 183, 365
　application where it involves some danger to the rescuer, 181
　common law, 176–77, 179–80, 212, 361
　and corrective justice, 212
　duty of the doctor, 174
　enforcement criterion, 176–77, 180–81, 183–84, 361–66
　English law, 177–82
　European legal systems, 176, 180–81, 365
　France, 176
　Germany, 176
　and Good Samaritan Law, 177, 179, 365
　hiring others to rescue him, 174
　Israeli law, 184, 361–65
　between Jewish law and common law, 175, 180, 212
　and law of the pursuer, 174, 183
　legal obligation or a moral duty, 173, 175, 180–84, 361, 364–65
　modern legal systems, 176
　normative criterion, 175, 180–84, 361, 364–66
　person's property, 174
　religious implications, 183–84, 361, 364–66
　rescuer's immunity, 179, 183–84, 362
　rescuer's right to indemnification, 181–83, 362, 365
　Russian Criminal Code, 176
　spending money, 182–83
　scope, 173–75, 180–82, 212, 361–62, 365–66
　suing the rescuer, 179
　Talmud, 175, 181–83
　Weinribian-Kantian approach, 212

economic analysis of law, 3, 11–12, 217
　aggregate welfare, 22, 24, 135, 217, 235, 253, 273, 351
　Calabresi, 3, 24, 31, 35, 38, 213, 215, 252, 254, 263, 280, 293, 345, 368, 370–71, 377
　Coase, 24, 38, 368
　consequentialist approach, 11, 13, 222–23, 227–29
　cost vs. benefit, 11
　cumulative welfare, 11
　deep pockets, 11, 217, 334
　do not incorporate religious norms, 12
　instrumental approach, 11
　leaders, 24, 38, 213, 251, 273, 280, 368, 370–71

Learned Hand formula, 25, 27, 252, 260–62, 264–65, 278, 284, 293, 300, 321, 323, 333, 337, 370, 379, 390
liability of risk creators, 192
and Maimonides, 12, 59, 132, 138, 221–22, 225, 227, 229, 233, 251, 254, 263–64, 268–69, 280–81, 288–89, 306, 322, 328, 367, 370, 372–73, 377, 379, 383, 395
multiplier approach, 31, 268, 270, 272–73, 275–78, 371, 386–88, 395
optimal deterrence, 24, 213, 215, 217, 237, 248, 252–54, 269, 322, 329, 334, 340, 343, 345, 352, 355, 371, 381–82
Posner, 24, 35, 38, 252, 263, 280, 293, 368, 370–71
prevention of damages, 229
punitive damages, 243
recent approaches, 252
risk management, 58, 334–35
economics, 2, 6–7, 11, 17–18, 23–24, 30–31, 33–34, 38, 59, 88, 90, 101, 113, 132, 162, 194, 196, 209, 213–15, 217, 220, 223, 227–28, 234, 237, 239, 243, 246, 248–50, 262, 269, 272, 274, 279, 285, 288–90, 311, 318, 329–30, 334, 336, 343–44, 360–61, 365, 368, 371, 377–78, 386
and morality, 367–68, 372
Edrei, Arye, 326–27
Englard, Izhak, 31, 37, 197, 202, 315
and Calabresi, 374
complementarity, 193
CORRECTIVE AND DISTRIBUTIVE JUSTICE: FROM ARISTOTLE TO MODERN TIMES, 36–37, 134, 193
criticism on the *peshiah* theory, 42
Enker, Aharon, 325, 327
Epstein, Richard, 194, 211
corrective justice, 199
strict liability theory, 199

feminism, 26
fire
articles that were buried in a grain heap, 298–99, 301
and the Bible, 105–6
camel that is loaded with flax passes through the public domain, 300
essential characteristics, 105–6
his arrows, 105
his property, 105
scope of the payments, 107
in Talmud, 104–5
five effects [heads] of injury, 108–9, 112, 172
damages (*nezek*), 108, 112, 203, 208, 316–20, 328, 331–33, 357–59

humiliation, 108–9, 113, 117, 203, 208–10, 316–20, 328, 332, 357, 359
intention, 117
knas (fine) and *mammon* (monetary obligation), 203
loss of employment, 108–9, 113, 203, 208, 317–20, 328, 331–32, 357, 359
medical treatment, 108–9, 113, 203, 208–10, 317–20, 328, 331–32, 357, 359
pain, 108, 112, 203, 208, 210, 317–20, 328, 331–32, 357, 359
standard of care, 316–20, 330, 332–33, 340, 352, 357, 359
as type of atonement fine, 152–53
Fletcher, George, 194, 206, 326–27
reciprocal and nonreciprocal risks, 197
forgiveness
and atonement, 113, 160, 172–73
and compensation, 114, 116
in criminal process, 114
in Laws of Wounding, 113, 115, 172–73, 352
in medical malpractice, 114
in modern law, 114–15, 173
in property damages, 172–73
and restorative justice, 114
in tortious actions, 114, 173
and Williams, 211
foundations of the Maimonidean theory
conceptualization of distinct categories of damage, 96
connection to criminal law, 29, 80, 82, 86, 93–94, 220, 319, 332
consequentialist elements, 222–23, 227, 229, 232, 238, 240–41, 243–44, 250–52
corrective justice, 220, 222, 228, 251
deontological elements, 138, 220, 222, 228, 241, 251
deterrence, 226
different goals for different categories of damage, 29, 96, 131, 339, 352–53
differential standard of care, 308, 310–11, 317, 328, 333, 336, 339–40, 352–53, 355, 359, 375
educational elements, 143, 220, 222
laws of damages to neighbors and standard laws of torts, 124
laws of property damages and laws of wounding and damaging, 108, 323, 329–30, 355
laws of wounding and laws of damaging, 111, 113, 115, 331
Maimonides as a Pluralistic-Differential Scholar, 136, 338–41, 350, 352, 367–68, 370, 372
prohibition against causing harm, 161–65, 168
rationality, 185, 224, 228, 293
reading all his works, 29, 80
religious elements, 159, 161, 184, 220

foundations of the Maimonidean theory (cont.)
  some objectives are more dominant, 29, 80, 132, 331, 340, 351–52
  philosophical elements, 220
  religious elements, 138, 171, 220, 222, 228, 251, 287
  scope of tort law, 29, 80
  various objectives work together, 29, 80, 132, 331, 383
four heads of damage
  and damage to neighbors, 125–26
Friedell, Steven, 236
  criticism on the *peshiah* theory, 42, 67, 69

Geistfeld, Mark, 31
  the most moral resolution should be selected from several efficient outcomes, 346, 350
Geonic, 1
Gilead, Israel, 189
Goldberg, John, 31, 202, 212, 341, 383, 387
Greco-Arab, 15, 30, 139, 223
Guide of the Perplexed, The, 2, 31, 138–41, 143, 152
  Aristotle, 134
  Bible, 98, 103–4, 222–23
  cases of exemption from liability, 233–34
  the *Code*, 10, 30, 33–34, 102–3, 223, 244, 284–86, 288–90, 293, 300–5, 308, 322
  consequentialist considerations, 13, 30, 131–32, 136, 138, 140, 143, 162, 165, 222–23, 225–27, 229, 231–33, 238–39, 243–44, 246, 249–52, 280–81, 284–86, 288–90, 293, 295, 301–2, 306–8, 311, 323, 340, 380–84
  corrective justice, 37, 134
  criminal law and tort law, 93, 223, 225
  criminal sanctions and punitive damages, 13, 93
  damages caused by a person's property and damages caused as a result of his actions, 230, 290, 310, 328–30, 333, 353
  damages caused to property and bodily injury, 230, 331
  deterrence, 240–41, 244, 248–50, 253–55
  distributive justice, 9, 37, 81, 131, 134–35, 206
  explanatory approach, 37, 87, 339
  an eye for an eye, 112
  goals of the Book of Acquisition, 9, 81
  innocent ox (*tam*), 236–37
  jurisprudence of the Torah, 86
  mitzvah of returning lost property, 154
  model of punishment, 38
  objectives of punishment, 240
  ownership, 230
  parameters for criminal sanctions and punitive damages, 240–42
  policy of penal considerations, 93
  preservation of the family unit, 227
  prevention of damages, 13, 102–3, 131–33, 136, 140, 143, 162, 165, 206, 217, 225–29, 231–33, 235, 237–38, 246, 250, 252, 254–57, 264, 278, 280–81, 285, 289, 302, 305–6, 322, 340, 350–52, 384
  punishment for a person who strikes and curses his father and mother, 276
  rationale of laws of property, 134
  rationale of laws of watchmen, 135
  rationale of limitations of profits, 135
  rationale of the laws pertaining to the breaking of the neck of the heifer, 226, 380
  rationality, 37, 61, 339
  reasons for commandments, 133
  reasons for laws pertaining to property, 224, 226
  reasons for tort law, 60, 223, 225–28
  religious component, 159
  removal of wrong, 9, 13, 81, 131–32, 134, 136, 140, 143, 203, 206, 211, 220, 228, 340, 350–52, 384
  socially oriented explanations, 225–27, 240, 244, 276, 285
  between the stealing of sheep and cattle, 241, 246–48, 382
  stoning the ox that killed a person, 60, 96, 231–32
  and the Talmud, 244
  theft (*genevah*) and robbery (*gezelah*), 123, 245–46, 270, 274–75, 277, 280, 360, 381, 385
  tort law objectives, 2, 9–10, 13–14, 30, 81, 131–32, 134, 140, 143, 206, 250, 280–81, 308, 340, 350, 352
  yeshiva world, 10, 34, 223, 284
Gulak, Asher, 41, 163

Habba, Yaacov, 320, 325
Halbertal, Moshe, 5
  Code and Philosophy, The, 33
  Code and The Talmud, The, 33
  Jurisprudence, 33
  Maimonides, *Life and Thought*, 32–33, 133, 333
Hand, Learned, 25, 27, 252
  and Maimonides, 260–61
Hart, H.L.A., 326–27
Haut, Irwin H., 15, 44–45
heads of damage, 83
  and the Bible, 82, 97–98, 103
  the common denominator, 99–100
  damages that are caused by animals, 76, 98–101
  extent of liability, 100
  fire, 82, 98–99, 102, 105–6, 127, 299–300
  foot, 66–67, 98, 100, 102, 230, 233–35, 237–38, 255, 257, 259–60, 263–65, 292, 298–301, 303
  horn, 66, 100, 102, 230, 232, 235, 237, 257–58, 264–65, 298
  in the public domain, 100
  ox, 82, 98–100, 102, 104–5, 286, 292, 297–99, 304, 334

Index

ox, pit, and fire, 12
pit, 82, 98–99, 102, 104–5, 291
pit and fire, 29, 55, 76, 102–5, 230–31, 290, 298, 329
psychological damage, 130
tooth, 66–67, 82, 98, 100, 102, 230, 232–35, 237–38, 255, 257, 259–60, 263–65, 292, 298–301, 303
Hendel, Neal
   Israeli Supreme Court Justice, 363–64
Hirschoff, Jon, 217, 255, 258, 263, 278–80, 291, 394

Ibn Rushd, 139
inalienability, 213–14, 218–19, 351
   bodily harm, 129
instrumentalist, 20, 23–25
insurance, 89
   contemporary torts, 334–35, 375
   and deep pockets, 334, 353–54, 357
   differential, 259
   and distributive justice, 334
   employers carry mandatory insurance, 335
   and loss distribution, 334
   and Maimonides, 335–36, 353–54, 370, 375
   medical insurance, 336
   and optimal deterrence, 334
   and regulation, 258–59, 334
Islamic law
   blood money, 143
   and Jewish law, 285–86
   liability for damages caused by animals, 190–91, 285–86
Israeli law, 361–66
   duty to rescue, 184, 361–65
   and Jewish religious law, 184, 361, 364–66
   Justice Eliezer Rivlin, 362
   Justice Haim Cohn, 364
   Justice Neal Hendel, 363–64
   Liability for Defective Products Law, 262
   requirement of, 357, 369
   Unjust Enrichment Law, 362

Jackson, S. Bernard, 103
   Mishpatim portion of Exodus, 97
   tam and *mu'ad*, 66, 101, 303–4
James, Fleming Jr., 31, 347, 349–50, 359, 374
Jewish law of torts
   and criminal law, 28
   and the doctrine of *peshiah*, 41, 50
   fault-based theory, 44
   general, 6
   laws of fines (*dine kenasot*), 238
   and Maimonides, 253
   and modern intellectual property law, 57
   modern theories, 29, 40–41, 50, 93, 175, 180

   part of civil law, 6, 8, 93
   prohibitive dimension, 161, 163–64, 171
   promotion of communality, 164
   religious dimension, 159–60, 171, 184
Judaism and economics
   general, 34
   Levine, Aaron, 34–35
   Liebermann, Yehoshua, 34
Judeo-Islamic world, 15

Kant, Immanuel, 210–11
Karo, Yosef, 156
Kaye, Judith
   Chief Judge of New York, 376
Kelsen, Hans, 163–64
Kirschenbaum, Aaron, 180–81, 239, 250

Law and History, 395
Law and Humanities, 395
Law and Literature, 395
Laws of Damages to Neighbors, 124–26
   and the Book of Torts, 124
   distributive considerations, 135
   injunctions, 126–27, 130
   and modern tort law, 124
   the nature, 124–25
   payments, 126, 130
   psychological damage, 130
   rationale, 131
   remedies, 126–27
   right to cause damage, 128–29
   and standard laws of torts, 124–30
   in the Talmud, 124–25
Laws of Damaging, 84, 94, 330
   civil in nature, 116
   damages that are not discernible, 94–95
   and laws of neighbors, 129
   and laws of wounding, 111, 116
   mens rea, 95
   payments, 116
   punitive aspects, 94–95
   right to cause damage, 129
Laws of Lost Property
   acquisition of moral qualities, 140, 154–55, 157
   commandments relevant to the return of lost property, 171, 226
   doing that which is upright and good and return the object, 154–57
   the obligation to prevent financial loss, 170
   social-consequentialist explanation, 226
Laws of Murder and Preservation of Life, 73, 83–85, 87, 93
   accepting ransom from a murderer, 141

Laws of Murder and Preservation of Life (cont.)
control over feelings of hatred and anger, 150
exempts the elder from loading or
  unloading, 155
helping another person load up his animal or
  unload it, 149–50
factual basis (*actus reus*), 324, 359
five different degrees of *mens rea*, 324–25
general conceptions of degrees of inadvertency,
  324–25
intentional killer, 324–25, 328
mens rea of fault, 324, 332, 352
obligation to build a rail around the roof, 85
person's obligation to preserve his own life, 85
prohibition against eating food that is dangerous
  to one's health, 85
prohibition against murder, 163, 171
prohibition against suicide, 220
punishment, 324
sanctity of human life, 141–43
scheme of liability regimes, 323–25
shedding of blood, 142–43
slays inadvertently, 324–26
three types of inadvertent killers, 320, 324–26
Laws of Property Damages (*nizkei mamon*), 73–77,
  79, 81, 83–84, 87, 96–97, 108
animals and pit and fire, 97, 102–4, 290
atonement, 172
cases in which it is permissible causing
  damage, 162
common denominator, 99–100
connection to civil-private law, 109
corrective justice, 132
criterion for liability in tort, 167–68
Genizah, 76–77
Gentile whose oxen gored the ox of an Israelite,
  141, 190, 285–87, 302
innovation, 165
internal distinctions, 98, 100, 102
and laws of neighbors, 125, 128, 130
nature of commandments, 166
order, 102–3
payment for half the innocent horn damages
  constitute a fine, 237
pit and fire, 105
prohibition against animals wondering in the
  fields, 141, 164, 188
prohibition against causing damage, 161–62,
  164–66, 168–72, 188, 190, 286–87, 306–7, 351
prohibition against raising domestic animals in
  the Land of Israel, 164, 168–69, 287, 307
psychological damage, 130
punitive aspects, 95
and R. Shimon Shkop, 167–68

self-help, 305
and the Talmud, 98, 100
Laws of Property Damages and Laws of Wounding
  and Damaging, 108–9, 111, 173, 323, 329–31,
  333, 355–56
awarding damages in cases of uncertain
  causation, 110–11, 356
in the Bible, 108
payments, 356
in the Talmud, 108
Laws of Repentance
atonement, 113, 172
forgiveness, 172
robber should repent and return the stolen
  property, 157–58
Laws of Restoration of Lost Property, 83, 93
Laws of Robbery (*gezelah*), 73, 83–84, 93, 97, 191,
  360, 385
acquisition of good qualities, 146, 148
coveting and desiring, 147–48
one does not accept the object from the
  robbers, 158
payments, 160
prohibition against encouraging robbery, 146
prohibition against robbery, 161, 163, 171
rehabilitation of the robber, 158
repent and return the stolen property,
  157–58
robbing a Gentile, 148–49
Laws of Robbery (*gezelah*) and the Return of Lost
  Property, 87
and the Bible, 121, 124
intention, 122
and laws of theft, 118–21
main characteristic of the robber, 120–21,
  124
robbery and return of lost property, 119,
  123–24
Laws of Theft (*genevah*), 73, 83–84, 86–87, 93, 97
and the Bible, 120–23
buying from a thief, 146
double-fold payments, 122, 213, 239, 241–44, 249,
  277–78, 360, 371, 382
five-fold payments, 119, 213, 239, 241–44, 246–47,
  249–50, 270, 360, 371, 382, 394
four-fold payments, 122, 213, 239, 241–44, 246,
  249–50, 270, 360, 371, 382, 394
intention, 122, 332, 360
and laws of robbery, 118–23
main characteristic of the thief, 120–22
payments (fines), 121–23, 160
prohibition against theft, 161, 163
societal aspects relating to the payments of the
  thief, 244

two-fold payments, 205
weights and measures, 151
Laws of Wounding, 84, 93, 330
  atonement, 113, 172
  bodily integrity, 210
  and criminal law, 89, 93–94, 108
  education of the injurer, 152–53, 157
  an eye for an eye, 152, 330
  forgiveness, 113–16, 154, 172–73, 352, 356
  intention, 117–18, 317–20, 328, 331–32, 357, 359, 369
  between *knas* (fine) and *mammon* (monetary obligation), 203
  and laws of damaging, 111, 115–16
  mens rea, 117, 317–19, 321, 331, 357, 359
  payments, 93, 111–14, 116–18, 160, 172, 208, 316–18, 330–32, 356, 359
  payments as a type of atonement fine, 153
  payments for injuries caused with the consent of the victim, 115–16, 218–19
  prohibition against causing injury, 116–17, 161, 163, 171–72, 218–20, 357
  punitive dimension, 112–13, 116–18, 172, 220, 317, 319, 330–33, 350–51, 356
Laws of Wounding and Damaging (*hovel umazik*), 73–76, 79, 81, 83–84, 87, 95–96, 108
  in the Bible, 94
  an eye for an eye, 112
  five effects of injury, 112
  and laws of neighbors, 125, 128–29
  payments for damages caused with the consent of the victim, 115–16, 219
  psychological damage, 130
  right to cause damage, 128–29
  in the Talmud, 94
  victim allows the damager to cause him damage or injury, 97
  between wounding and damaging, 73, 84, 94, 97, 111, 113, 115–16, 172, 316, 355
Learned Hand formula
  and contributory negligence, 262, 279, 300, 370
  and Maimonides, 260–61, 264–65, 278, 293, 300, 321, 323, 333, 337, 370, 379
  Posner's improvement, 25, 27, 252, 260–62, 264–65, 278, 284, 293, 300, 321, 323, 333, 337, 370
Levinas, Emmanuel, 153, 331
Levine, Aaron
  Economic, Morality, and Jewish Law, 34
  Judaism and economics, 34–35
  THE OXFORD HANDBOOK OF JUDAISM AND ECONOMICS, 34
Levinger, Yaacov, 75
liability of a person for damages he caused, 68

basis for the obligation, 165, 167–68
civil, 165, 168
and corrective justice, 165
obligation of the debtor to repay his loan, 165, 168
obligation to pay for property damages, 165
Lieberman, Yehoshua
  Judaism and economics, 34
Lorberbaum, Yair, 219
Loss distribution
  as a form of self-insurance, 23
  meaning, 23

Maimonides' response, 29, 47–48, 63–64, 80, 122, 182, 186–87, 191, 332
Mann, Kenneth, 92, 369
medicine, 1
  Maimonides, 133
  preventive medicine, 133
Medina, Barak, 38, 368
mens rea
  robber, 122
  thief, 122
  wounding, 117, 317–19, 321, 331, 357, 359
Method of the Book, The 31
  between the *Code* and the *Guide*, 33, 223, 284, 308
  comparative law, 31
  comparing Maimonides times to the modern period, 35
  economic analysis of law, 31, 35
  economics and Jewish Law, 35
  interdisciplinary character, 31, 35
  Judaic studies, 31
  law and religion, 31, 35
  legal history, 31
  legal theory, 31
midreshei hamekhiltot, 99
Mill, John Stuart
  ON LIBERTY, 145
Mishnah
  Bava Kamma, 82, 99, 101–2, 125
  four heads of damage (*avot*), 82–83, 99–100, 102, 125
  person who causes damage to the property of another, 312
Mishneh Torah: Code of Maimonides, 31
  and the Bible, 34, 97
  Book of Acquisition (*Sefer Kinyan*), 74
  Book of Civil Law (*Sefer Mishpatim*), 74
  Briskers commentary, 52
  classical commentaries, 53, 72
  classification, 32, 72–73, 93

Mishneh Torah: Code of Maimonides (cont.)
  consequentialist considerations, 224
  and contemporary tort theory, 284, 288
  corrections, 74
  general, 5, 16
  Genizah, 73
  and the *Guide*, 10, 29–30, 32–33, 80, 140, 223–24, 284–86, 288–90, 293, 300–5, 308, 322
  jurisprudence, 32
  manuscripts, 48, 191
  method of codification, 16
  opening rulings of the Books, 75
  religious aspects, 131, 184
  structure, method, and classification, 32
  and the Talmud, 16–17, 33–34, 65, 185–86, 223, 302–3
  theology of sin and atonement, 171, 173
  titles of the books, 75
  Twersky's book, 32
  unique characteristics, 16
  using a consequentialist rationalization, 284–86, 288–89, 293, 301–2, 305–8, 311, 322–23, 329, 340, 352
  yeshivah world, 10
monistic approaches, 26, 31, 37, 53, 131
  ancient legal systems, 339
  Calabresi, 213, 215, 345
  contemporary tort theories, 131, 338, 340
  corrective justice, 25
  Fleming, James, Jr., 347
  and Maimonides, 28, 131, 136, 338, 340, 352
  optimal deterrence, 25
  and social-economic considerations, 26
  unified-monistic theory, 25, 345, 347, 349–50
morality, 2
  deontological, 2, 11, 13, 21, 34–35, 38, 64, 89, 113, 115, 132, 136, 138–40, 144–45, 149, 151–52, 154, 156, 159, 161–65, 181, 183–84, 189, 192, 195, 198–99, 202, 211, 213–15, 217, 220, 226, 228, 242, 247, 249, 262, 280, 287, 306, 326, 329–30, 337, 340, 342–46, 351, 361, 364–65, 367–68, 371
  and economics, 367–68
Muslim (*shari'a*), 15

negligence
  and culpability, 27
  economic approach, 27
nuisance, 97
  distributive justice, 131–32, 135
  laws of damages to neighbors, 124
  who must desist from causing a nuisance, 25, 125

objectives of punishment
  atonement, 240
  deter people from engaging in crime, 238
  deterrence, 240–41, 244, 253–54
  Maimonides, 239
  rehabilitation, 240
  retribution, 240–41, 249
  utilitarian penology, 238, 241
objectives of tort law, 19, 73, 79
  Book of Acquisition, 131
  Book of Torts, 132
  Code, 133
  compensation, 22
  consequentialist, 9, 26, 30, 81
  corrective justice, 2–3, 7, 9, 13, 19–20, 26, 81, 131–32, 136, 138, 192, 194, 196, 281, 340–43, 350–52, 366–67, 383
  a criminal rationale, 131
  damage caused by a person, 131
  deontological, 9, 30, 136, 138
  deterrence, 20, 26, 213, 343, 366–67, 379, 381, 384
  and distributing loss, 23
  distributive justice, 9, 13, 19–20, 22, 81, 131, 134, 136, 207, 343, 366–67, 370, 379
  in the *Guide*, 131–32, 134, 140, 143, 250, 280–81, 308, 340, 350, 352
  instrumental, 23
  loss distribution, 23
  Maimonides' various books, 131
  monistic approach, 19, 131, 136, 338
  murder, 131
  nuisance, 132
  optimal deterrence, 19, 24, 88, 131, 189, 192–93
  pluralistic approach, 19, 131, 136, 338, 352
  preventing damages, 2, 9, 13, 71, 81, 131–33, 136, 138, 140, 143, 162, 165, 188–90, 217, 226–29, 231–32, 238, 246, 250, 252, 254–55, 263–64, 277–78, 280–81, 286, 288, 302, 305–6, 308, 314, 322–23, 329, 332–34, 340, 350–52, 355, 366–67, 384
  property damages, 131–32
  religious, 136, 138
  removal of wrong, 2, 13, 131–32, 134, 136, 138, 140, 143, 281, 340, 350, 366–67, 384
  restoring the status quo ante, 22
  retribution, 200
  robbery, 131
  social, 11, 20, 23
  some objectives are more dominant, 9, 29, 80–81, 331, 340, 351–52
  various objectives work together, 9, 29, 80–81, 331
  wounding, 131–32
optimal deterrence,
  Calabresi, 213, 215, 217, 252–54, 345, 352, 355
  consequentialist-deterrent approaches, 31, 269
  and corrective justice, 343–44

as a instrumental goal, 24
and insurance, 334
law and economics, 193
and Maimonides, 38, 165, 237, 248, 254, 322, 329, 340, 352, 382
as a primary monistic goal, 25
punitive damages, 273–75, 351, 371, 381
ownership and strict liability theory, 48–49, 51, 53–56, 61, 63–65, 291, 293
business risk theory, 58–59
and the *Code*, 53
difficulties, 40, 42, 53–54, 56, 58, 67, 69–70, 78, 289, 295
versus fault-based theory (*peshiah*), 42
new creation or invention, 55, 57
rationale, 56, 58
ox
and Calabresi's best decision maker, 260
mu'ad, 66, 101–2, 190, 236, 259, 267–68, 285, 300–4

Paley, William, 269
parameters for criminal sanctions and punitive damages, 268–69, 371, 379, 381, 389, 395
Parker, Matthew, 272
pedagogical elements of Maimonides' tort theory, 138, 143
acquisition of moral qualities, 140–41, 143–46, 148–52, 154, 288, 293
control over feelings of hatred and anger, 150
education of the injurer, 152–53, 157–58, 204, 211, 217
prohibition against cursing another person, 144–45
prohibition against stealing from a Gentile, 149
social-educational, 140, 143, 152, 204, 220, 223
penal laws, 14
peshiah (negligence/fault) theory, 45, 47, 49, 53, 56, 61, 63–65, 71–72, 75, 258, 260–61, 264–65, 285, 293, 300
in the *Code*, 293, 297, 300–1, 311, 322, 373, 375
difficulties, 40, 42–43, 67, 69–70, 295
elements of negligence and foreseeability, 42
foreseeability, 65, 67, 69–70, 292, 299–300, 304, 314, 358–59
as a uniform principle of tort liability, 40, 42–43, 45, 61, 78, 229, 281, 310–11, 336
in the Talmud, 43
versus the theory of ownership, 42
Philo of Alexandria, 243–44
philosophical elements of Maimonides' tort theory, 138–41, 143, 152, 157, 217, 220, 222, 225, 228, 339
in the *Guide*, 222–23

the promotion of communality, 164
rationale for punitive damages, 243
sanctity of human life, 141–43
philosophy, 1
pit
and the Bible, 104–6
essential characteristics, 104–5
owned by partners, 291
owner, 105–6, 291
in the Talmud, 104
pluralistic approaches, 26–27, 31, 37
Aristotle, 204
balance between the consequentialist and the moral dimensions, 346
Burton, Steven, 31
Calabresi, Guido, 215, 217
casuistic approach, 347–50
combine different goals in particular cases, 342
current mixed pluralistic theories, 341–42, 345, 350, 368, 370–71, 383
current theories, 339–41
Englard, Izhak, 31, 342–46, 349–50, 359
Geistfeld, Mark, 31, 346, 350, 359
Goldberg, John, 31
James, Fleming Jr., 31, 347, 349–50, 359
and Maimonides, 28, 131, 136, 204, 338–41, 349–50, 352, 359, 367, 383
nature, 136
Robinette, Christopher, 31, 347–49
Schwartz, Gary, 31, 343–46, 349–50, 359
Williams, Glanville, 31
Zipursky, Benjamin, 31
Polinsky and Shavell, 273, 275, 371
Porat, Ariel, 206
Porat, Hanan, 361
Posner, Richard A., 24, 35, 38, 194, 251, 260, 368
contributory negligence, 263, 267–68, 278–79, 300, 370
economic approach to negligence, 27, 252, 255, 262–63, 265, 267, 293, 300, 321, 333, 370
fault-based regime, 263
and Learned Hand formula, 25, 27, 252, 260–62, 264
and Maimonides, 251, 260, 263–64, 267–68, 293, 323, 333, 383
products liability, 27
property damages, 14
damage caused by animals, 54–55, 66–67, 100–1, 104, 190–91, 230
different types, 54
removal of the potentially damaging element, 191
strict liability, 45

property rule and liability rule, 214
  in Maimonides, 128–29
punishment
  common law, 89
  level of punishment, 38
  for negligence, 89
  for theft, 89, 122–23
  for torts, 89
punitive damages, 28, 86, 88, 93, 200, 213
  act may be done secretly, 269, 274
  amount of temptation, 274
  circumstances for recognition, 270
  combination of goals and reasons, 388–89, 391–93
  contemporary theories, 227, 243, 270–71, 277, 279–80, 318, 360, 368–69, 371
  and corrective justice, 213
  between criminal law and civil law, 238, 385–86, 388
  and criminal sanctions, 240, 268–69
  deontological explanations, 274
  deterrence, 225, 238, 241–42, 245, 247–50, 253
  economic approaches, 271–73, 278, 371
  enforcement, 274
  England, 390–91
  Europe, 386, 391
  four parameters of Maimonides, 240–42, 268–70, 274, 276, 371, 378–79, 381, 387–88, 391–95
  frequency of the act, 247–49, 269, 274
  hybrid sanctions, 238
  incentivizing the injured party to take precautions, 277–80, 393–94
  Jewish law, 239
  Maimonides consequentialist analysis, 238–39, 241, 243–44, 246, 249–50, 268–69, 274–80, 371, 379, 381–83
  modern approaches in the American literature, 270, 379, 386–87, 391–92
  multiplier approach, 31, 246, 268, 270, 272–73, 275–78, 371, 386–89, 391, 393–95
  objectives, 271
  optimal deterrence, 273–75, 351, 371, 381
  possibility of reducing punitive damages, 393–94
  punitive approach, 386–88
  redress, 272
  religious reasons, 243, 249
  revenge and the dignity of the victim, 271
  severity of the crime, 276
  societal approaches, 271–72, 371
  Societal Redress Extra-Compensatory Damages, 268, 270–72, 274–78, 280, 371, 388–89, 391–92, 394–95
  theft payments, 93, 160
  theological reasons, 243, 245
  traditional approaches, 271

US Federal courts, 273, 371
US Supreme Court, 273, 275, 371

Ra'abad, 188, 205
  in his criticism of Maimonides' ruling, 70, 297, 313–14
Rabinovitch, Nachum, 42, 165, 169, 234, 237, 260, 298, 307, 314
Radin, Margaret Jane, 272
Rashi, 174–75
religious, 26
  atonement, 173
  awareness as a religious duty, 327
  duties and prohibitions, 159
  elements of Maimonides' tort theory, 138, 184, 217, 220, 222, 228, 251–52, 276, 285, 287, 305, 338–40, 350–53, 367, 370, 372, 383
  injury to the human body is perceived as an injury to, 330
  moral, 220
  mystical, 184
  nature of religious obligation, 163, 181
  obligation to preserve the body and life, 160, 163
  obligation to preserve the property, 160, 163
  payments as a form of religious atonement, 160
  prohibition against causing damage, 9, 82, 131, 160, 166–68, 189–90, 220, 251, 286–87, 302
  prohibition against causing damage to life, 160
  prohibition against causing injury, 2, 7, 116–17, 160, 218–20, 357
  prohibition against looking into the domain of another, 186–87
  prohibition against purchasing from the tortfeasor who stole, 251
  prohibition against self-harm, 11, 160–65, 169, 171–72, 351
  prohibition against stealing from a Gentile, 149
  ransoming captives, 182
  and secular law, 162, 184, 353, 360, 364–67
  sins against one's fellow man vis-à-vis sins against God, 151
  theological aspects, 171–73
Rishonim, 161, 169, 182
risk-causing behavior
  and corrective justice, 188
  deontological and utilitarian considerations, 187, 189
  not causing actual damage, 70, 187, 305–7
  and prevention of harm, 188–89
Rivlin, Eliezer
  Deputy President of the Israeli Supreme Court, 362
robbery
  characteristics, 242, 245, 360

Robinette, Christopher, 31, 92, 347–49
Roman law, 41
  culpability (culpa), 41

Sa'adia Gaon, 243–44
  and Maimonides, 243
Sages of Lunel (Provence), 47–48
Saladin the Great, 133
sanction
  a central element in the definition of law, 163
  and legal obligation, 164, 181
  the role of the sanction, 163
  violation of prohibition, 163
Schereschewsky, Benzion
  criticism on the *peshiah* theory, 42
Schwartz, Gary, 31
  optimal deterrence as the dominant goal, 343–46, 350
  protective justice, 344
scope of tort law
  between civil law and criminal law, 8, 29, 80, 82, 84, 86–87, 89, 93, 171, 323, 331, 352, 368–69, 385
  between contract law and criminal law, 87, 89
secular, 2
  application of religious laws in secular law, 184, 353, 360, 364–67
  Calabresi, 220
  modern theoreticians of secular law, 217
Sefer Hahinukh, 144
Sela, Ilan, 94, 113, 118, 219
serial negligent, 71
Sharkey, Catherine, 272, 371, 387–89, 392, 394
Shkop, Shimon, 55–57, 166
  commandments, prohibitions and obligations, 166–68
  private monetary norms, 166–68
Shmueli, Benjamin, 389
Shulhan Arukh, 16, 18
Silberg, Moshe, 159
slave, 77, 288, 290
social, 2
  economic, 38
  prohibition against causing damage, 189
  promotion of communality, 164
  solidarity, 164
standard of care, 2, 26, 28
  absolute liability, 27–28, 44, 68–69, 110, 131, 263, 311, 314, 321, 332, 336, 352, 354–55, 357–59, 395
  almost strict liability, 321, 328, 330, 332–33, 352
  automobile accidents, 339
  close to negligence, 354
  damages caused by a person to property, 110
  damages caused by a person to the property of another, 68–69, 268, 316–17, 332–33, 336, 355–56
  damages caused by property, 45, 312, 321–22, 328–29, 356–57
  between damages caused by property and damages caused by a person, 231, 355–56
  damages to neighbors, 131
  different categories of damage, 15, 30, 310–11, 317–19, 323, 328, 330, 332, 336–37, 339–40, 352–55, 359, 375
  differential liability regime, 15, 97, 310
  each category, 27
  effective damage avoider, 14
  fault, 27, 30, 109, 323, 328–29, 334, 337, 352
  fault-based liability theory, 39, 252–53, 255, 263, 291, 294, 310, 322, 352
  gross negligence, 318, 321, 328, 331–33, 357, 359
  Guide, 268
  hierarchy of liability regimes, 312, 328
  humiliation, 319–20, 328, 332, 357, 359
  inadvertently (*shogeg*), 312
  intentionally, 68, 312
  intermediate standards, 27
  between laws of damages to neighbors and standard laws of torts, 130
  medical malpractice, 357, 359, 375
  minimal *mens rea*, 110
  more than negligence, 117, 260
  mu'ad ox, 267–68, 300
  murder, 312, 323, 328, 332, 352
  negligence, 2, 7, 11, 15, 27–28, 30, 41, 68–69, 90, 109, 117, 131, 255, 267–68, 292, 300, 310–12, 315, 317, 319, 321–22, 328–29, 331, 333–34, 336, 339, 352, 354–55, 357–59, 370, 375, 385, 390
  ownership and strict liability theory, 39, 42
  person who has caused damage to the property of another, 312–13, 315–16, 318–19, 328, 330–32
  peshiah, 7, 29, 45, 69
  property damages, 117, 131, 267–68, 323, 336, 340
  between property damages and wounding and damaging, 109, 355–58
  robber, 122
  scale, 27
  strict liability, 2, 14–15, 27–28, 30, 44–46, 68, 199, 236, 252–53, 256–57, 260–63, 267–68, 292, 294, 302, 310, 312–19, 321–22, 328–29, 331, 333–37, 340, 352, 354–55, 357, 359, 370, 375–76, 387, 390, 394
  strict liability and exemption in cases of *force majeure*, 312–15, 318, 332
  between a *tam* ox and a *mu'ad* ox, 303
  tam ox, 267–68
  theft, 122, 332

standard of care (cont.)
  unavoidable mishap (*ones*), 60, 68–69, 237, 295, 312–14, 316–18
  wounding, 117, 268, 312, 316–18, 320, 328–33, 340, 352, 357, 359
  between wounding and damaging, 316–17
Statman, Daniel, 364
stoning the ox that killed a person, 96, 231–32
strict liability, 28
  in the Talmud, 49
strict liability theory, 72
  applies to all types of tortfeasors, 45–46
  Calabresi, Guido, 25, 252–53, 260–61, 263, 292
  and Posner, 262–63

Talmud, 31
  casuistic, 13
  degree of inadvertency of various cases of unintentional homicide, 324
  exceptional cases, 65
  exempts the finder of lost property from returning the item to its owner, 154
  helping another person load up his animal or unload it, 149
  law of pursuer, 174
  liability of animals, 59
  obligation to prevent financial loss, 170
  one does not accept the object from the robbers, 158
  repent and return the stolen property, 157–58
  sanctity of human life, 142
  second chapter of *Bava Batra*, 124–25
  stealing from a Gentile, 148
  stoning the ox that killed a person, 60
  tort liability on animals, 60
talmudic laws of tort, 17, 65
  Bava Kamma, 82
  and the Bible, 66, 103
  cases of exemption from liability, 232
  categories of damage, 66, 76
  compensation in situations of uncertain causation, 110, 356
  between damages caused by property and damages caused by a person, 103, 230
  an eye for an eye, 112
  four heads of damage, 100
  harm caused by individuals to other individuals, 334–35
  innocent ox (*tam*), 236–37
  liability of person for damages he caused, 68
  limited scope of liability, 65
  list of damagers, 82–83
  meta principle for obligations in tort, 99

  payment for half the innocent horn damages constitute a fine, 237, 267, 301–2
  person who causes damage to others by means of unwelcome viewing (*ayin hara*), 185–86
  person who causes damage to the property of another, 312
  prohibition against causing harm, 165, 288
  standard of care of the *tam* ox, 267–68
  system of organization, 98
  between theft (*genevah*) and robbery (*gezelah*), 119–20, 123, 242–45, 247
theft
  of cattle, 241–42, 246–48, 250, 382–83, 393
  characteristics, 242, 245–46, 360
  five-fold payments, 93, 119
  four-fold payments, 93, 119
  payments, 93
  professional thief, 249–50
  of sheep, 239, 241–42, 246–50, 382–83, 393
  two-fold payments, 93, 119
tort liability
  animal that kills a person, 96
  animals, 59
  assumption of risk, 258, 260, 294, 374
  bodily injury, 318
  brigands breached the fence, 62, 122, 332
  burden of proof, 90, 369
  cases of exemption from liability, 232–34, 237, 255, 258, 260, 263, 265, 267, 284, 292–94, 298–300, 313, 321–22
  in the *Code*, 39
  comparative negligence, 261–62, 376
  contributory negligence, 45, 258, 260–62
  control, 311, 328, 332–33, 354–55, 359, 370
  correlativity, 212
  damage caused by animals, 54–55, 62, 66, 73, 78, 84, 101, 103, 122, 230, 285, 290, 292, 295–98, 300, 302, 304, 322, 329, 333, 336–37, 355–56
  damage caused by the person himself, 45, 50, 73, 77, 82, 84, 104
  damages that a worker caused to others, 58
  definition of the act (*actus reus*), 320–21
  effective ability to control test, 2, 14, 167–68, 227, 230–31, 233, 235, 252–54, 260, 267, 281, 284, 289–90, 292–93, 295, 298, 300, 308, 310–11, 315, 328, 352, 354, 359, 370
  effective avoider of damage, 2, 14, 167, 231–37, 254–57, 267, 281, 289–90, 292, 295–98, 300–1, 306, 309, 311, 313, 315, 318, 321–22, 328, 332–33, 335–36
  English law, 380–81
  in exceptional cases, 65–67
  fault, 11, 51–52, 57, 90, 322

fault-based liability theory, 39, 44, 78, 252–53, 255, 263, 291, 294, 310, 322, 352, 373, 376
fire, 55–56, 78
general rule of liability, 229, 268
in the *Guide*, 14, 251, 254–56, 260, 266
on the injured party, 292–95, 300, 322
imposition of, 15
incentive to prevent tortious events, 230
inciting another's dog, 64–65, 292–94
information, 291–92, 294, 297, 381
limited scope of liability, 65
litigation, 90
master, 54
modified comparative negligence, 261, 266
negligence, 51
of the owner of an innocent ox, 237
ownership, 14, 44, 46–47, 49, 53, 59, 64
ownership and strict liability, 29, 45
ox, 55, 59
person's intention to cause damage, 62–63, 122
person's intention to steal, 63, 123
peshiah, 7, 11–12, 14, 29, 40, 43, 45, 47, 49, 51–53, 56–57, 64
between *peshiah* and ownership, 76, 78
pit, 55–56, 78, 106, 291
prohibition against causing damage, 165
prohibition against causing injury, 8
property damages, 44–46, 60–61, 104, 106, 230, 322, 329, 359
psychological damage, 130
pure comparative negligence, 261, 266, 279
risk causing behavior, 70, 187, 189, 191, 305
robbery, 310
slave, 54, 288, 290
splitting the liability, 235–36, 260, 267, 284, 301, 375–76, 394
strict liability, 45–46, 49, 253, 256–57, 260–63
strike from heaven, 69, 313–15, 332, 374
in the Talmud, 13, 16–17
theft, 310, 328
visual trespass, 185–86
watchman, 46–49, 92, 295–98, 321
wounding, 310
yeshiva reading, 52
Tosafists, 175
Tur, 18, 160
Twersky, Isadore, 10
classification of the *Code*, 75
between the *Code of Maimonides* and the *Guide*, 33, 223
INTRODUCTION TO THE CODE OF MAIMONIDES, 32

socially oriented explanations in Maimonides' works, 223, 225
the study of Maimonides, 39

visual trespass, 185
legal parameters, 186
on a neighboring plot, 186
prohibition against looking into the domain of another, 186–87
violation of property rights, 187

Warhaftig, Itamar, 187
Warhaftig, Zerah, 15
business risk theory, 58–59
criticism on the *peshiah* theory, 42
ownership and strict liability theory, 14, 42, 44–51, 53, 58–59, 61, 289, 293, 310–11
peshiah vs. ownership, 44–45, 47, 51, 68
and the *yeshiva* reading, 45
Weinberg, Yehiel Yaakov, 42, 58–59
Weinrib, Ernest, 3, 181, 194
compensation, 200
corrective justice, 194–96, 198, 200–1, 203–4, 206, 208–11, 344, 368
duty to rescue, 212
and Kant, 210, 212
and Maimonides, 203–4, 209–11
private law, 341
welfare economics, 34
Westreich, Avishalom, 233
Williams, Glanville, 31
corrective justice, 200, 211–12
and Maimonides, 211–12
wounding, 111, 230
actus reus, 117–18, 357, 359
and the Bible, 117
in the course of a quarrel (*derekh nitzaion*), 117–18, 357, 359, 369
and damaging, 111, 113, 115
payments, 109
request for forgiveness, 97, 154
Wozner, Shai
R. Shimon Shkop, 166–67

Ya'akov, ben Asher
Arba'a Turim, 160
Yaron, Reuven, 236
yeshiva reading, 53
abstract, analytical, and conceptual thinking, 73
Brisker/Soloveitchik school, 52–53
common interpretation, 39, 43, 46, 73, 288, 290, 310, 336

yeshiva reading (cont.)
  difficulties, 29, 39, 46, 51, 57, 288, 310, 336
  hakira, 53, 57
  ownership and strict liability theory, 10, 14, 29, 43–44, 48–49, 53, 68, 73, 289, 293, 308
  peshiah and ownership, 43, 46, 51, 53, 57, 72, 311

R. Shimon Shkop, 55–57
rationale, 59–60

Zamir, Eyal, 38, 368
Zipursky, Benjamin, 31, 202, 212, 383–85, 387, 393
Zuri, Yaakov Shmuel, 41

For EU product safety concerns, contact us at Calle de José Abascal, 56–1°,
28003 Madrid, Spain or eugpsr@cambridge.org.

www.ingramcontent.com/pod-product-compliance
Ingram Content Group UK Ltd.
Pitfield, Milton Keynes, MK11 3LW, UK
UKHW020204060825
461487UK00018B/1548